Lord, you have made so many things!
There is the ocean, large and wide,
Where countless creatures live,
Large and small alike.
Psalm 104 Verses 24-25

The Living Shores of Southern Africa

George & Margo Branch
Photography by Anthony Bannister

Drawings by Margo Branch

C. Struik Publishers, Cape Town

Photographic credits:

All photographs were taken by Anthony Bannister, with the exception of the following:
The Argus: Fig. 133
Bruce Barnetson: Plates 136 & 149, Fig. 174
William Blankley: Fig. 346
George Branch: **Plates** 6 9 11 13 14 16 35 36 42 45 46 48-50 52 56 58 62 68 76-79 82 91 93-95 98-102 105 107-109 127 129-131 134 137 140 141 144 155 158 164. **Figs.** 19 23 29 31 37 42 45 52 56 57 58 63B 71 87 88 95 102 103 105 106 115 116 118 120 122 123 125A 129 142 147 173 177 178 182 185 188 191 192 193A 196 199 202-214 219 220 225 233 235 238 239 248 253 258 261 262 267 268B 269D 270 276 277 286A 286F 287A 287B 287E 297 298 304A 305 308 311 312 313 318 322 323 335 342 343 354 355 357 361 365 367 368 375 377 388

Margo Branch: Fig. 331
Prof. G.J. Broekhuysen and Dr Barbara Silberbauer: Fig. 242
David Cram and the Sea Fisheries Institute: Fig. 156
Pierre de Baissac: Fig. 363
Roy Cruikshank: Figs. 154 & 164
Michael Cherry: Fig. 108B
Rick de Decker: Fig. 131
Alex Fricke: Figs. 78 & 222
Joe Henschel: Fig. 168
Allan Heydorn: Figs. 99 & 132
Phil Hockey: Fig. 46B
Podge Joska: Electron micrographs in Figs. 283 & 306
Sydney Kannemeyer, S.A. Museum: X-rays in Fig. 296

Anne Linley: Electron micrographs in Figs. 92 & 110
Steve Lipschitz: Pneumograph traces in Figs. 173B, C
Johan Lutjeharms, National Research Institute of Oceanology, Dr O.G. Malan & N.M. Walters, National Physical Research Laboratory: satellite photograph in Fig. 3
Eugene Moll: Figs. 134 & 135
National Parks Board: Fig. 10
Natal Mercury: Fig. 2
Steve Pheiffer, Kelp Products Pty Ltd: Fig. 167
Dave Pollock: Plate 3, Figs. 161 & 176
Martina Roeleveld, S.A. Museum: Fig. 326
Robin Stobbs: X-ray in Fig. 334
Frank Swingler: Fig. 108A
Ben Tromp: Echogram in Fig. 145
Chris van Niekerk: Fig. 136

C. Struik (Pty) Ltd,
Struik House, Oswald Pirow Street, Foreshore, Cape Town

First Edition 1981
Second Impression 1983
Third Impression 1985

Designed by Wim Reinders, Cape Town
Lithographic reproductions by Unifoto (Pty) Ltd, Cape Town
Photoset by McManus Bros (Pty) Ltd, Cape Town
Printed and bound by Tien Wah Press (Pte) Ltd, Singapore

ISBN 0 86977 115 9

Front cover: The hermit crab *Dardanus arrosor* in a helmet-shell, *Phalium labiatum zeylanicum* (George Branch)
Back cover: Living coral with gracefully expanded polyps, *Dendrophyllia* sp. (Anthony Bannister)

Mrs Lynett Joy Moore
Mrs V. T. Mills
H. M. Nagel
Pierce & Jean Newton-King
D. F. Niven
Carel A. Nolte
Orbit Motors
Dr & Mrs I. M. Patz
Mr & Mrs T. M. Pellatt
M. J. & M. L. Penrith
Pick 'n Pay Wholesalers (Pty) Ltd
Mr & Mrs Frank Pienaar
Johannes Arnoldus Vosloo Pienaar
Plascon Parthenon Paint Company
Port Elizabeth Museum
Sydney Press
G. H. L. (Curly) Read
Richards Bay Coal Terminal Co. Ltd
Richards Bay Coal Terminal Co. Ltd
G. A. Rissik
Sirion & Sally Ann Robertson
T. R. Robson
Mrs M. K. Rowan
Dr J. P. Rourke
Shealagh Savage

Professor & Mrs S. C. Seagrief
Professor Margaret M. Smith
South African Association for Marine Biological Research
South African Museum
Jan & Ann Stekhoven
Sandy Stretton
N. B. & M. E. Swart
E. E. H. Testi
Erik & Diana Todd
University of Port Elizabeth Library
Dr S. T. van der Horst
Mrs E. D. van Eck
Dr & Mrs P. Vorster
Elisabeth S. Vrba
Mr & Mrs P. J. Wakefield
A. V. Ward
Johannes Arnoldus Vosloo Webb
Dr Ion Williams
Derric H. Wilson
B. C. Winkler
Peter Witney
James Yeowart
A generous donation was received from the Zoological Society of Southern Africa.

PREFACE

For both of us, marine biology is not just a way of earning a living; it is a way of life. Indeed, this book would never have been written if it had not been for the great pleasure we have had from the sea and for a desire to communicate this experience.

The book is really two books in one. Part 1 deals with the ecology of different coastal environments: how the animals and plants interact with one another and how they adapt to the challenges that each habitat presents them. In addition there is a chapter concerned with the interaction between man and the sea. Each of these chapters is a unit and can be read independently.

Part 2 has quite a different flavour and we visualise that it will be used as a reference to identify animals and plants and to learn something of their biology and the groups to which they belong. As an introduction, the visual key on pages 8 & 9 illustrates the main groups of animals and plants and directs the reader to the colour plates and text that are relevant for each group.

Two indices appear at the back of the book: a scientific index that gives only the scientific names, and a general index giving both subject material and common names. The scientific index is expanded to show the geographic range of each species.

Over the last 20 years we have become increasingly aware of the marine heritage in southern Africa, and of how fragile some of its components are. At the same time there has been a change in attitude from one of plundering to one of preservation, and much of this arises from our increased knowledge and understanding of how easy it is to decimate fish stocks, to hunt whales to the point of extinction, to destroy coral reefs by blasting and to degrade estuaries by siltation – and how difficult it is to restore them afterwards. If we are to enjoy the greatest benefit from our oceans in the future, we will need to conserve the sea and its life, and to manage our own activities accordingly. We have a magnificent coastline richly endowed with marine life. Let's keep it that way.

M. & G.B.

VISUAL GUIDE TO MARINE LIFE

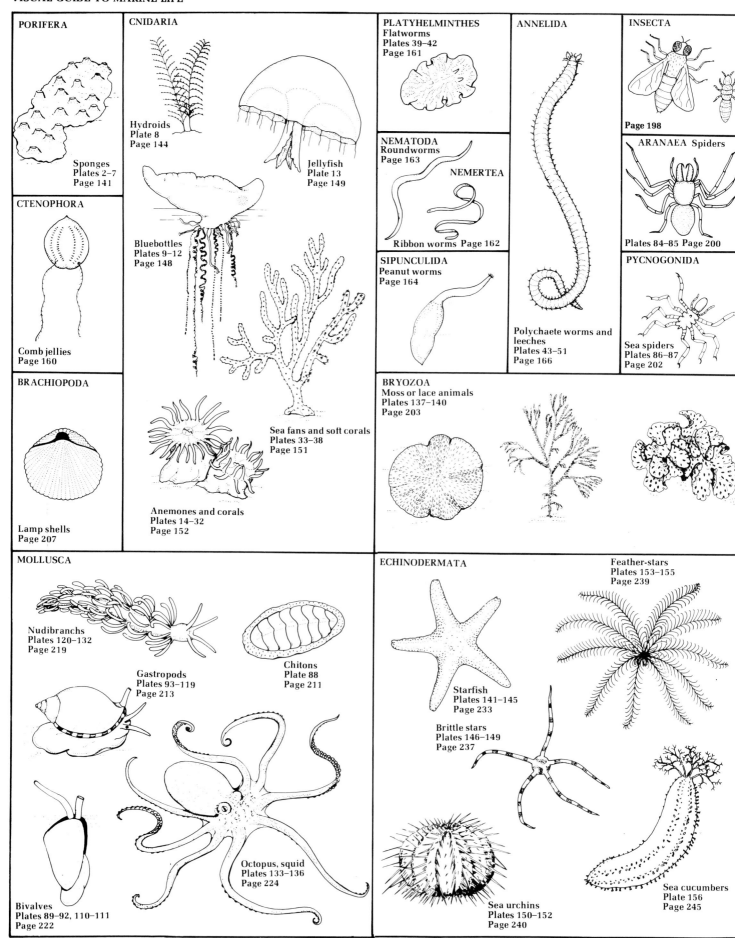

PORIFERA

Sponges
Plates 2–7
Page 141

CTENOPHORA

Comb jellies
Page 160

BRACHIOPODA

Lamp shells
Page 207

CNIDARIA

Hydroids
Plate 8
Page 144

Jellyfish
Plate 13
Page 149

Bluebottles
Plates 9–12
Page 148

Sea fans and soft corals
Plates 33–38
Page 151

Anemones and corals
Plates 14–32
Page 152

PLATYHELMINTHES
Flatworms
Plates 39–42
Page 161

NEMATODA
Roundworms
Page 163

NEMERTEA

Ribbon worms Page 162

SIPUNCULIDA
Peanut worms
Page 164

BRYOZOA
Moss or lace animals
Plates 137–140
Page 203

ANNELIDA

Polychaete worms and
leeches
Plates 43–51
Page 166

INSECTA

Page 198

ARANAEA Spiders

Plates 84–85 Page 200

PYCNOGONIDA

Sea spiders
Plates 86–87
Page 202

MOLLUSCA

Nudibranchs
Plates 120–132
Page 219

Gastropods
Plates 93–119
Page 213

Chitons
Plate 88
Page 211

Octopus, squid
Plates 133–136
Page 224

Bivalves
Plates 89–92, 110–111
Page 222

ECHINODERMATA

Feather-stars
Plates 153–155
Page 239

Starfish
Plates 141–145
Page 233

Brittle stars
Plates 146–149
Page 237

Sea urchins
Plates 150–152
Page 240

Sea cucumbers
Plate 156
Page 245

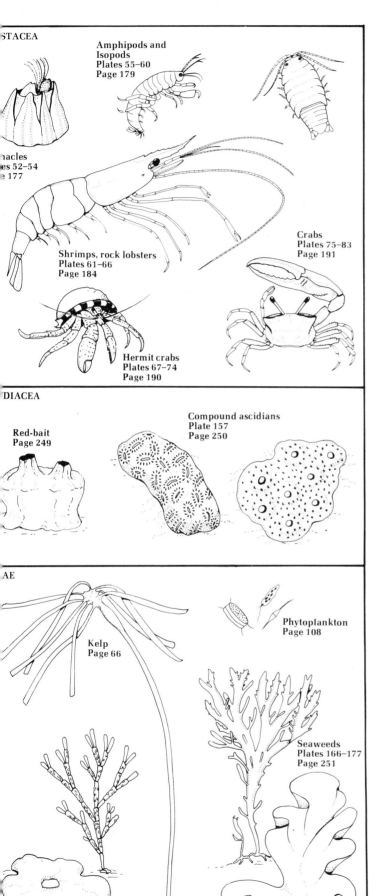

STACEA

Amphipods and
Isopods
Plates 55–60
Page 179

nacles
es 52–54
e 177

Shrimps, rock lobsters
Plates 61–66
Page 184

Crabs
Plates 75–83
Page 191

Hermit crabs
Plates 67–74
Page 190

DIACEA

Red-bait
Page 249

Compound ascidians
Plate 157
Page 250

AE

Kelp
Page 66

Phytoplankton
Page 108

Seaweeds
Plates 166–177
Page 251

CONTENTS

ACKNOWLEDGEMENTS

Many people have contributed to the making of this book. We have often felt like McFadyan's definition of ecologists – 'chartered libertines roaming over the established disciplines and plundering at will'. It is for this reason that a great debt is owed to many scientists who have so willingly contributed their findings, often in an unpublished form, and to those whose work has been the source of this book. We have not always been able to acknowledge them in the text or to cite their work, but we would like to single out the following: Dr Anton McLachlan of the University of Port Elizabeth; Peter Shelton, Steve Lipschitz, Nigel Jarman and Dr Peter Best, all of the Sea Fisheries Institute; Norman Pammenter, Natal University; George Begg, Oceanographic Research Institute, Durban; Professors Gideon Louw and Alec Brown, Drs Peter Greenwood and Chris McQuaid, Kim Damstra, Podge Joska, Bruce Bennett, Dave Muir, John Cooper and Muffy Seiderer, all of the Zoology Department, University of Cape Town; and particularly Professor John Field and Drs Charles and Robbie Griffiths whose work has been extensively referred to and who have helped in many other ways.

Specific thanks are due to several people who criticised the drafts of various sections of the book: Professor John Day, Professor Alec Brown, Dr Naomi Millard, Professor John Field, Dr Allan Heydorn, Frank Shillington, Dr Peter Best, Dr Dave Pollock, Peter Shelton, Richard Simons and Andy Payne.

A number of people helped collect animals for photography and we would like to thank Dr Alan Hodgson for pleasurable hours spent under water; Reg Willan who collected the handsome beast that adorns the cover of the book; Lyn Kapp who let me into the secret of where to collect *Marginella*; and Deirdre Richards and Mrs Connolly. Special mention must be made of Mr and Mrs Giles who loaned us many of their precious shells from their personal collection, and to Billy Liltved whose beautiful collection of cowries was raided to make up one of the plates.

Various experts helped with the identification of animals and plants, and in particular we are grateful to Dick Kilburn who checked and updated the names of all molluscs; Dr Terry Gosliner who checked the nudibranch photographs and allowed access to his own splendid collection of nudibranch photographs; Dr A. J. Prins for identification of insects and Richard Simons who identified many of the algae and whose critical examination did much to ensure the accuracy of the seaweed paintings.

We would like to thank Anthony Bannister, not only for his superb photographic contribution to the book, but also for the very happy collaboration we enjoyed and for the great deal he so willingly passed on about the art of photography. Many other people contributed photographs to the book and they are separately acknowledged in the list of photographic credits, but we would like to repeat here our warm thanks to them all. All our own photographic equipment and processing were attended to by Developprint, whose helpful co-operation was much appreciated.

The Trustees of the Trust Fund have done a magnificent job in helping to raise the necessary funds to keep the price of this book down. All of them are gratefully thanked but we are sure none of them will be offended if we single out Angus Burns, Dr Naomi Millard, Margie Wakefield and Podge Joska for the enormous amount of time and effort they put into this task. Although they were not Trustees, many others helped with the Trust Fund and the distribution of brochures, including Sue Harvey, Trevor Mare, Beryl Britten, our parents, and Penny Moxham, the editor of *Fathoms*. At the same time we must express our appreciation to the many private individuals and business companies who contributed to the Trust Fund. It has been especially heart-warming to see how many of our friends have dug into their pockets to support us. Without your help, we could not have produced this book.

We were both appreciative and filled with admiration at the flair shown by the Wanderer and Hilary Mauve in helping to promote the Trust Fund through the pages of *The Argus* and the *Constantiaberg Bulletin* respectively.

We are grateful to Anne Field and Dave Muir who spent many hours beautifully inscribing the special editions.

Several people have helped with the typing of the manuscript, including Beryl Wallace and Podge Joska and more particularly Sandy Tolosana, but the brunt of this task has been cheerfully borne by Leonora Freeland who also merged many a split infinitive and smoothed the grammar with her usual efficiency.

Many of our friends have helped in less tangible but equally important ways. Sakkie and Rona le Roux conserved our familial harmony by entertaining our children on many occasions; Mick Cooper provided legal advice; Judy Mare passed on many practical tips that have helped Margo with the artwork; and the staff of the Tsitsikama Coastal National Park, where many of the photographs were taken, are thanked for their warm hospitality.

We have appreciated the professional yet friendly atmosphere that our publishers have created and in particular would like to thank Pieter Struik, René Gordon and Walther Votteler for the polish that they have brought to this book.

This book has been a mammoth task, shared by our

children, Bryony and Trevor, who have tolerated exclusion, shared our discoveries and been remarkably adaptable in fitting in with our needs.

Our final thank you is the most important – and one that should have been said before. To our parents we owe everything, for without their love and nurturing, not only would this book never have been undertaken, but it could never have given us the pleasure that it has.

Acknowledgements for second impression

Several people kindly drew to our attention errors in the first impression, and particular thanks are due to Drs Eckart Schumann, Berg Flemming, Johan Lutjeharms and Dick Kilburn.

Beady-eyed conchologists soon spotted that the shell on the cover had been reversed and had a left-handed spiral: but here at least we are in good company – even Rembrandt reversed his etching of *Conus marmoratus*.

As the famous ichthyologist J. L. B. Smith remarked, there is only one sure-fire way to avoid errors – don't publish!

We have tried to rectify the errors that have come to our attention, but in the interests of keeping down the price of this second impression, corrections have been kept to a minimum.

M. & G. B.

Photographer's acknowledgements

I would like to thank the many people and organisations for assistance so kindly given me whilst taking photographs for this book. Their help was always offered in a most willing and friendly way, in spite of inconveniences suffered, and for this I am especially grateful. Those that particularly come to mind are:

The Directors and staff of the National Parks Board of South Africa, the Natal Parks Board, and the SWA/Namibia Directorate of Nature Conservation; Rod and Moira Borland; Dennis and Susan Bower; Mike and Carolynn Bruton; Joan Lawrenson and Lyn Wood. To my wife Barbara I owe special thanks, as well as to my children Andrew, Sue and David, and to Maudanne, without whose support and patience, my work would have been quite impossible. Special thanks also to George and Margo Branch, and to Robbie and Joh Robinson, for their warm hospitality on so many occasions, and to Bruce Barnetson for the use of his superb pictures and camera housing. To the Nikon division of Frank & Hirsch go my thanks for their efficient maintenance of my equipment, keeping it working perfectly at the edge of the sea and beyond.
Finally my thanks go to Sir Peter Scott, through whose encouragement I first began to take the sea and its amazing animals seriously as photographic subjects.

A.B. 1981

1. THE RESTLESS SEAS

One of South Africa's leading marine biologists recently began his presidential address to the Royal Society of South Africa by describing all he would desire in a woman. She should be 'profound, playful, enigmatic and wayward ... unpredictable ... with unfathomable depths ... and mysterious'. And he has found all of these attributes in the sea. The sea has always fascinated people; not only the scientists who probe her secrets, but the fishermen, sailors and divers who know the sea from first-hand experience, and the holiday-makers and the men on the street who relax on her shores.

Southern Africa has one of the most exciting coastlines for anyone with an interest in the sea and its life. Part of this fascination lies in the movement of the sea, which has a strong influence on the plant and animal life, and forms the focus of this chapter. Different currents bathe the east and west coasts. At the tip of South Africa's Cape Peninsula the cold current of the west coast meets that of the warmer south-east coast, and there can be few places in the world where such a narrow strip of land separates seas which are so different in temperature and the life they support.

The properties of sea-water

The very nature of sea-water has a strong influence on marine life. Water buoys the body, so that submerged animals and plants need to expend less energy supporting their own body masses against gravity in comparison with land-dwellers. They thus need less supportive tissue. For example, this means that marine algae can afford to increase their chlorophyll-bearing tissue because they need less support: they are therefore soft and floppy when compared with woody land plants, but are capable of growing faster because they are able to photosynthesise more efficiently.

Temperature fluctuations are much smaller in the sea than on land, partly because water absorbs or loses a great deal of heat without much change in temperature. While terrestrial organisms have the continual problem of losing water to the air, freshwater inhabitants have to avoid gaining too much water from the dilute medium in which they live. The salt content of sea-water, however, is similar to the body fluids of most animals, which consequently have no problems of water-loss or gain if they live in the sea. In these ways sea-water is a comfortable medium to live in.

On the other hand, oxygen is less readily available in sea-water than on land. This is because oxygen diffuses through water comparatively slowly, and is thus not rapidly replaced after being used up by animals respiring or by bacterial decomposition of waste material. As a result many marine animals have large external gills and some

means of circulating water over the gills; and species that lack these adaptations are often sluggish and slow-moving.

A more important limitation is that water filters out light, so that sufficient light for plants to photosynthesise is only present in the upper (euphotic) layers of the sea. As all animal life ultimately depends on the ability of plants to use energy from sunlight to produce a food source, this limitation is an important one, for only the top 50 to 100 m of the ocean can support plant life. All the animals in deeper waters thus depend on food sinking down from the upper skin of the ocean. The only exception to this is a unique and recently discovered community of organisms living around deep-sea vents in the ocean's crust. Here bacteria use a chemical source of energy instead of light – the sulphurous chemicals released due to volcanic action. A whole community of animals revolves around these bacteria, using them as a food source.

Increase in depth also results in an increase of pressure. Every increase of 10 m depth is roughly equivalent to adding one atmosphere of pressure. Even for animals living at great depths under tonnes of pressure, this is not actually a problem, for the pressure inside their bodies is the same as that of the surrounding water, so there is no question of their bodies collapsing. However animals that change depth must balance the internal and external pressures. Even this is only a problem to animals that have gas spaces in their bodies, for gas expands and contracts as pressure changes, while the rest of the body, being essentially fluid, is incompressible. Fish brought up too rapidly by fishermen often die as the gas in their swim bladders expands. Air-breathing mammals and birds are limited in how deep they can dive because their lungs collapse. Despite this, man has recently succeeded in diving to 100 m without any artificial breathing aids: though he is still put to shame by the whales which descend over 1 500 m, as we know to our cost when they become entangled in cables on the ocean floor. Whales, seals and other diving mammals are not troubled by the 'bends' that human divers fear. The reason is that they do not breathe under water as do scuba divers. Under increased pressure, some of the nitrogen in the air that divers breathe becomes dissolved in the blood. If the diver surfaces too quickly, the decrease in pressure causes the nitrogen in the bloodstream to form bubbles of gas which then expand with painful, sometimes lethal, results. This is why divers have to allow time to ascend slowly, giving the nitrogen a chance to escape from the bloodstream. Because other mammals do not attempt to breathe under water, nitrogen never dissolves in the bloodstream to the extent that it causes problems.

Superimposed on these properties of sea-water, the

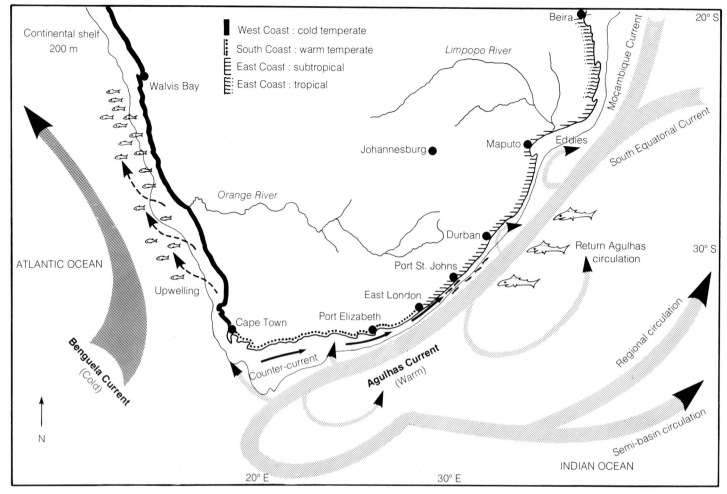

Fig. 1 **Map of southern Africa showing the major currents and the four coastal regions, each of which sustains distinctive marine animals and plants.**

movement of water profoundly influences the nature of southern Africa's coastline and life in her seas. In particular, currents, waves and tides each have different but equally important effects.

Currents

Two major current systems sweep our coasts: the Agulhas flowing down the east coast, and the Benguela up the west coast. The Indian Ocean has a huge gyre of water circulating anticlockwise, driven by the winds. This equatorial water mass splits when it reaches Madagascar, part moving around the island and down the coast of Moçambique, where it is called the Moçambique Current, while a second stream passes around the eastern side of Madagascar. The two currents may follow a tortuous route but usually they unite again as they flow along the coast of Natal, forming an input into the Agulhas Current. This is the mightiest current bathing the South African coast, and brings warm water from the tropics to the east coast. As the Agulhas moves southwards its central core follows the edge of the continental shelf, where the relatively shallow coastal waters abruptly become deeper. Conventionally we take this margin to be at a depth of 200 m (about 100 fathoms), although part of the reason for this is that navigational

charts were originally marked only in terms of 10, 100 or 1 000 fathoms, and there was not much choice in selecting a depth contour that coincided with the continental shelf! The edge of the continental shelf swings away from the shore from Transkei southwards, deflecting the Agulhas Current away from the coast (Fig. 1). As a result, the south coast, from about Port St Johns to Cape Point, has cooler coastal waters and a different set of animals and plants from the Natal and Moçambique coasts.

Close inshore, cooler pockets of water often flow parallel to the coast, but in a direction opposite to the Agulhas Current. On the south coast this counter-current is more frequent, but off the Natal coast it is squeezed close to the shore and is often overpowered by the Agulhas, so that it is less predictable. Its importance in the life-cycles of several species is gradually coming into focus. For instance it seems probable that the famous 'sardine run' on the Natal coast is due to sardines *(Sardinops ocellata)* following this inshore counter-current northwards, until they are forced inshore by the narrowing and patchiness of this current and are often stranded on the beaches in huge numbers (Fig. 2). These sardines are usually immature animals. Their disappearance from Natal waters after the sardine run is still something of an enigma, but it has been suggested that they then move

Fig. 2 The frenzy of the sardine run off Durban.

offshore and into the Agulhas which sweeps them back to their spawning grounds in the south-western Cape. Several other fish also move north with this current in winter, including the elf or shad (Pomatomus saltator) which feeds on sardines. After arriving in Natal waters, the elf mature sexually and the ripe and running females move offshore into the Agulhas which drives the young elf larvae southwards to the cooler waters where they develop for about two years before joining the northward migration again.

The Agulhas is a swift and massive current, up to 160 km wide and flowing at a speed of up to 5 knots (2,6 m per second), transporting 80 million tonnes of water per second, so it is not surprising that it also has a strong influence on the sediments. Inshore, where the current is weak, the sediments are fine or even muddy like the mud banks that form the rich sole grounds off the south-western Cape and are formed mainly from particles swept down rivers or from the coastline. Directly beneath the main body of the Agulhas Current the sea bed is scoured and consists mainly of coarse shell fragments. The speed of the current is sufficient to form underwater sand dunes – great 8 m 'ripples' – that are driven southwards by the current. The effect of the Agulhas on the sediment has important ecological consequences, for animals are particular about the sort of sediment in which they live, and coarse sediments are unstable and contain so little organic material that they hold little attraction for most species.

Sweeping southwards, the might of the Agulhas is sometimes pitted against strong south-westerly winds which drive before them massive waves in a direction opposite to the Agulhas. This has the effect of shortening the distance between the waves and accentuating their height. At times two or more waves become superimposed, creating a single wave of frightening proportions, reaching up to 20 m in height – as tall as a five-storey building! Such freak or killer waves are periodically responsible for massive damage to ships, the bows of the ship dipping down into the trough that precedes the wave and then being crushed as the oncoming mountainous wave breaks down onto the deck. There has been speculation that the mysterious disappearance of the Waratah was due to such a freak wave.

Towards the south the Agulhas swings eastwards as the Return Agulhas Current. Part of the water then joins the large gyre circulating around the basin of the Indian Ocean (the basin circulation), but three other circuits exist, like a series of concentric rings, each smaller than the preceding one (Fig. 4). These are referred to as the 'semi-basin circulation', the 'regional circulation' and the 'Return Agulhas

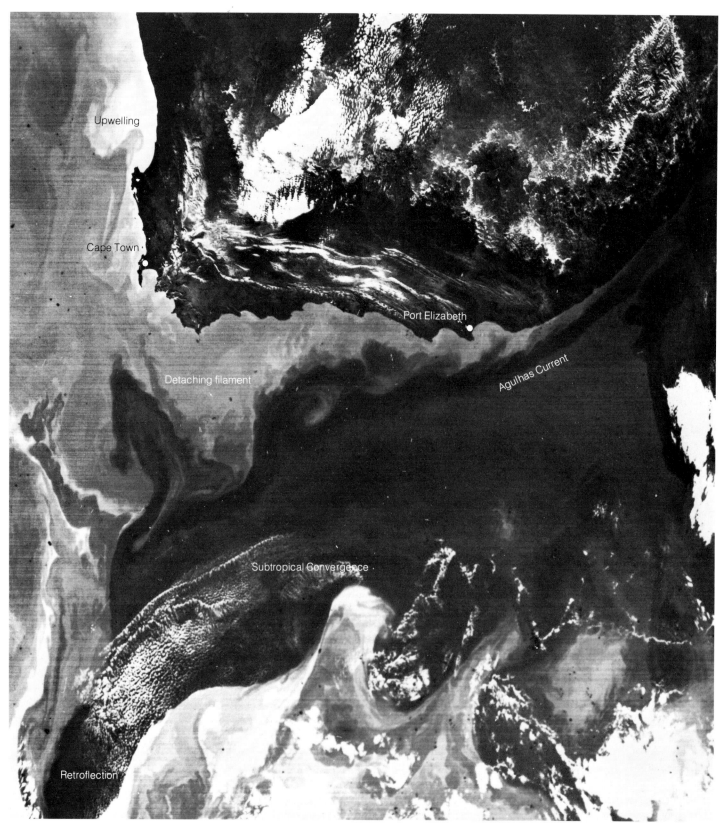

Fig. 3 Satellite photographs are being increasingly used to plot the ocean's currents. This remarkable photograph of the currents around southern Africa was obtained by using an infra-red sensor on board the NIMBUS-7 satellite on 16 June 1979. Warm currents appear dark, cold currents appear pale. The very pale patches are cloud cover. The warm Agulhas Current, seen coursing down the east coast, has local eddies inshore. South of Port Elizabeth the current moves away from the coast, following the continental shelf. Filaments detach and may swirl around Cape Point. Further south the Agulhas Current veers eastwards (retroflection) and flows alongside the cold waters of the west wind drift (convergence). Huge waves may mix the two water masses. Cold water inshore on the west coast is due to upwelling. (With acknowledgement to Dr J.R.E. Lutjeharms.)

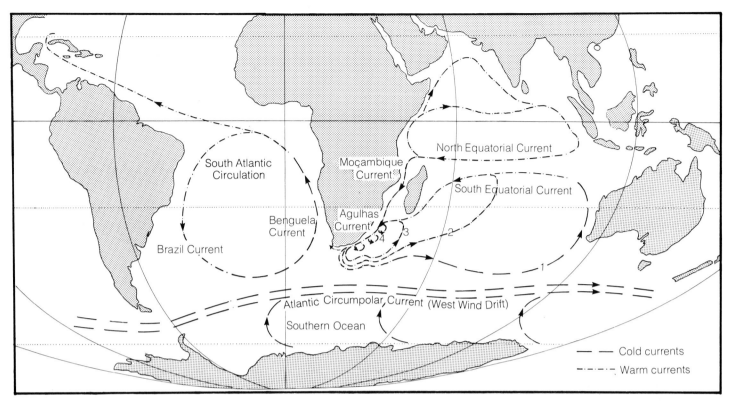

Fig. 4 The major sea currents in the southern hemisphere. The cold Benguela Current sweeps up the west coast of southern Africa while the warm Agulhas Current travels down the east coast and then follows four circulation routes: 1. Basin circulation around the Indian Ocean; 2. Semi-basin circulation cutting across the Indian Ocean; 3. Regional circulation running below Madagascar; 4. Return Agulhas circulation very close to the coast.

circulation'. The smallest of these circuits is almost a series of large eddies lying just outside the main Agulhas Current, and this water will take only a few weeks to re-enter the Agulhas. On the other hand the basin circulation will take almost a year to return water to the coast of South Africa. These four circulation paths have great importance for animals and plants. It comes as no surprise that several of our Natal species are common on Madagascar, for instance. Many animals have larvae that are planktonic, floating or drifting in the current until returned to the coast where they can settle onto the bottom and change into the adult stage. Some species such as the spiny lobster (*Panuliris homarus*) have a long-lived larva that is able to survive four to six months of planktonic life, and is probably transported in the semi-basin circulation. Most invertebrate larvae live only a few weeks, and for these short-lived larvae it would be fatal to be caught up in such a lengthy circulation, and the shorter circuits, or inshore eddies and counter-currents, are therefore important to them.

Sharks and turtles may also make use of these circulation patterns. Sharks are often segregated by size, animals of different sizes occurring in different areas. Several tropical species such as *Carcharhinus obscurus* (the brown shark) have nursery areas close inshore in Natal where pregnant females drop their young. The young sharks make their way down the Agulhas to the shallows off the Eastern Cape and, after growing, they move out into deeper waters and then northwards, using one of the shorter circuits

described above. The benefit of this circular route is not only that it makes use of currents, thus minimising energy spent on swimming, but it also ensures that by the time the juveniles return to their birthplace they are large enough to avoid being cannibalised by the larger sharks.

Loggerhead turtles, *Caretta caretta* (Figs. 5-7), breed on the sandy beaches of northern Zululand, females clumsily crawling ashore to dig holes in which batches of eggs are deposited. The nesting season is linked with a warming of the Agulhas Current in October or November and is postponed if water temperatures are lower than normal. The result is that hatchlings (Fig. 7) always emerge when sea temperatures are at their highest, in February and March, and when the Agulhas Current is closest inshore.

In comparison with the rest of the Indian Ocean the Agulhas is unusually rich in floating organisms such as the Portuguese man-o'-war, *Physalia*, and its relatives *Vellela* and *Porpita* (Plates 9-12), as well as the floating purple-shelled *Janthina* (Plate 105) which form the main diet of young turtles. For almost three years the young loggerheads probably remain in the recirculation routes of the Agulhas, mainly in the semi-basin and regional circulations, enjoying the warm current and rich food that speed their development. Only after this are they mature enough to return to the coast where their diet changes from floating organisms to shallow-water organisms that are attached to the bottom; and at an age of about four they are able to begin breeding.

The west coast of South Africa receives an entirely dif-

Fig. 5 A loggerhead turtle lumbers up the beach to lay eggs.

Fig. 6 A remarkable picture of the eggs being laid.

Fig. 7 Four months later the hatchlings emerge and head for the sea.

ferent system of currents. Travelling in the subantartic Southern Ocean from west to east is a large cold current, the Antarctic Circumpolar Current (or West Wind Drift). North of this circles the South Atlantic Circulation which brings cool water from the south to our west coast, forming the Benguela Current. Naturally this is a cold current, so while bathers rejoice in the warm waters of the east coast, the west coast is bitingly cold. Here the coldness of the current has a profound influence on the climate, for air passing from the cold sea to the hot land will not yield its moisture, so that the land along the west coast of southern Africa is arid and desert-like, although coastal fogs are frequent.

As this current moves slowly up the west coast, so deep cold water is pushed upwards into the shallower areas. This process primes the water mass for the local and dramatically important action of seasonal south-east winds that blow across the Cape Peninsula and up the west coast.

To understand the effects of the South-Easter we must digress briefly. Any wind tends to move the upper layers of the sea in the same direction as the wind. However, due to the rotation of the earth, a moving body in the southern hemisphere will be deflected to the left of its path. In the northern hemisphere it would be deflected to the right. This deflection is due to Coriolis forces. We can understand the reason for this if we realise that as the earth spins, there is a local vertical component of rotation around which objects will tend to spin clockwise in the southern hemisphere and anticlockwise in the northern hemisphere. Thus a moving body tends to get "left behind" if it is approaching the equator. In the southern hemisphere, water being blown north toward the equator will be deflected left and travel north-west.

This effect is of overriding importance on the west coast of southern Africa where the surface layers of the Benguela Current are driven almost parallel to the coast by the southerlies and south-easterlies, but because of Coriolis forces the surface waters are deflected away from the coast (Fig. 8), and deep cold water must rise up to replace it: a process called upwelling.

These deep waters are rich in the nutrients needed for plant growth, having lain beneath the euphotic zone where the absence of light has prevented plant life from using the nutrients that accumulate. When this water upwells into the light, tiny floating plant life – phytoplankton – capitalises on the nutrients, and dense 'blooms' of phytoplankton then develop, transforming the colour of the water with their abundance. Planktonic animals – zooplankton – feed on the phytoplankton, and both may be eaten by filter-feeding fish such as the anchovy or sardine: so it is not surprising that the west coast is one of the richest fishing grounds in the world, and as a result supports large colonies of sea birds and seals. Small wonder that the Namibian Topnaar, descendants of the Hottentots, culminate a praise-poem to the sea with the words 'flow you fleshrich waters'!

Upwelling occurs in other parts of the world, such as the west coasts of Peru, California and West Africa; all situations where currents run parallel to west coasts and towards the equator. However, in South Africa the south-easterly winds reinforce the process so that we find some of the most clearly defined and intense upwelling in the world. The intensity of this upwelling is a function of how hard and how long the winds blow and, as the South-Easter prevails in summer, so upwelling is greatest then. This brings about a curious situation on the west coast: water temperatures are often lower in summer than in winter, and also fluctuate greatly from day to day. On one occasion a change from 17 °C to 8 °C was recorded over a seven-hour period! Such rapid changes can stun animals, and mass mortalities of fish sometimes result.

Northward moving long-shore currents continually sort and shift sands along the coast. The Orange River, with its huge catchment, pours sediments into the sea in times of flood and some of these sediments are added to the coastline north of the river mouth. The coastline is thus growing, as evidenced by the shipwrecks on the Skeleton Coast that are now hundreds of metres inland. Bays such as Sandwich Harbour which, within living memory provided deep-water shelter for ships, are slowly being engulfed and are now shallow lagoons or, like Conception Bay, have practically disappeared.

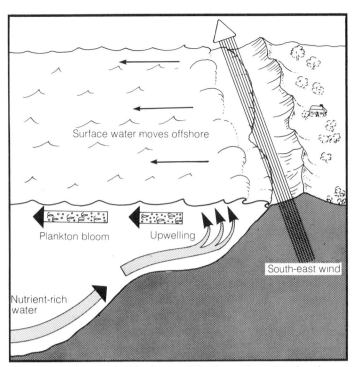

Fig. 8 The south-east wind blowing parallel to the west coast pushes the surface waters before it. Because of Coriolis forces, the water is deflected to the left of the wind, thus moving offshore. Deeper waters then well up, bringing nutrients to the surface, allowing planktonic plant life to thrive.

On the northerly parts of the west coast there is an additional and completely different water movement. Beneath the Benguela a deep slow-moving tongue of water may drift southwards. This water mass characteristically has very low levels of oxygen and is thus unsuitable for most animals. The factors causing low oxygen levels are not fully understood, but off Walvis Bay is a well-known 'azoic' (a-=without, -zoic=animals) area of mud, largely lacking in animal life, where gases can be smelt at times and the hydrogen sulphide may even combine with fresh water to form dilute sulphuric acid that can corrode metals. This area may be the centre from which the oxygen-deficient waters move southwards. In addition, this deep water mass accumulates wastes and dead organisms. These are decomposed by bacteria, using what little oxygen remains in the water, and the water becomes even more stagnant. Sometimes this water is driven inshore where it can cause mortality of fishes and other sea life. Its most spectacular effect is to drive crayfish before it, and in an attempt to avoid the low oxygen levels the crayfish may migrate into the shallows and be stranded. Mass strandings of millions of crayfish have periodically been recorded, the most recent being at Eland's Bay, where the crayfish were piled over a metre high in places.

The contrast between the Benguela and the Agulhas manifests itself in the different species found on the two coasts. Professor T.A. Stephenson was one of the first biologists to determine how species change as one moves around the coast, and he recognised three major faunal 'provinces' on the east, south and west coasts, shown in Fig. 1. The east coast from southern Moçambique to Port St Johns in Transkei is referred to as the subtropical province for while it has many tropical organisms such as corals, tropical fish and a multitude of crabs, there are also many species which do not extend into the tropics. As the Agulhas swings away from the coast in the south, a second region – the warm temperate south coast province – can be recognised, stretching from Port St Johns to about Cape Point. Few tropical species occur here, while there are many species unique to the area. The cold temperate province of the west coast, from Cape Point to about Walvis Bay, is characterised by its colder waters, and a number of species are either limited to this area or reach their maximum abundance here: for example, the perlemoen (*Haliotis midae*), the commercially important crayfish (*Jasus lalandii*) and the vast beds of kelp that thrive in the nutrient-rich upwelled water. The west coast has fewer species than the south or east coasts, but a higher total biomass of animal and plant life.

Waves and the nature of the coastline

The coastline of Africa, and particularly South Africa, is somewhat different from that of most other countries, being very sheer and having few sheltered bays. One of the reasons for this is rooted in the long-past geological history of the continent. Africa was originally part of a much larger continent, Gondwanaland, which included South America, India, Madagascar and Antarctica (Fig. 9). If we shuffle these land masses like a jigsaw it is astonishing how closely their coastlines still fit one another. About 160 million years ago the continents began rifting apart and moving away from one another – a process that continues

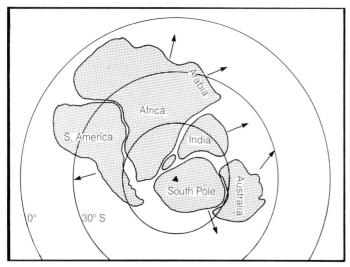

Fig. 9 Africa, South America, India, Australia and Antarctica were once united in a single continent, Gondwanaland, which has been rifted apart, leaving Africa with a sheer coastline and few sheltered bays.

even today, at a rate of about 8 to 16 cm a year. The force thrusting the continents apart is the volcanic eruption in certain regions of the sea floor. For example, there is a ridge in the centre of the Atlantic continually erupting and creating 'new' sea floor while the 'old' sea floor is pushed away on either side. The rifting apart of the continents left Africa with a sheer coastline and a comparatively narrow continental shelf. Other countries have since had their coastlines radically modified, but for various reasons Africa has been left comparatively unchanged.

A second factor that has more recently affected the southern African coast has been the rise and fall of the sea level. Over the past 300 000 years there have been four glacial periods. The most recent, only 20 000 years ago, locked up sufficient sea-water in the form of ice to lower sea levels by about 120 m. Effectively this would have extended the coastline between 50 and 150 km out to sea. On the other hand there were interglacial periods when the earth was warmer than at present and the melting of ice elevated the sea up to 50 m above present levels: the Cape Peninsula would then have been an island, and most of South Africa's coastal towns and cities are built on land that was at one time under water. Several raised beaches around the coast testify to this fact, including shell deposits at Langebaan and fossil oysters attached to rocks at Reunion (near Durban) that are poised 20 m above sea level. One of the concerns of environmental scientists is that the excessive use of coal, wood and fossil fuels may increase the amount of carbon dioxide in the air, which could in turn alter the amount of heat retained by the earth's atmosphere and trigger melting of the ice caps. However there seems to have been little change in sea level over the last 5 000 years and the modern rate is a 10 cm rise per century.

South Africa has never been covered by extensive ice fields, unlike much of northern Europe, North America and the southerly parts of New Zealand and South America. In these areas glacial action carved deep U-shaped valleys which have subsequently been drowned by the rising seas to form lochs and fiords. The relatively low and seasonal rainfall over South Africa has meant that the country has relatively few large estuaries. Thus the sheer coast created at the time of the rifting of Gondwanaland is still preserved, with very few sheltered bays.

The pounding of strong waves is a major factor eroding and shaping the coastline. Waves around the world generate a collective force equivalent to a 50 megaton nuclear blast each day. Wind blowing over the sea is the cause of waves. Contrary to popular belief, waves do not drive water forwards: rather the water moves in vertical circles, remaining more or less in the same spot as the waves advance (Fig. 11A). By analogy one can think of a whip being waved from side to side: ripples pass down the whip like waves, but the whip itself does not move forward with the ripples. When waves approach shallow areas, the sea bottom provides friction and slows the waves so that they bunch up and become higher. A point is reached where the circular motion of the water is interrupted and the wave

Fig. 10 A freak storm drives monstrous waves ashore, contemptuously crushing cottages in the Tsitsikama Coastal Park.

crest topples forward, breaking on the shore (Fig. 11B). As they break, waves scour the shore, shifting sand and eroding rock. The more violent the waves, the greater the effect, so on rough beaches only coarse sand is left behind, while in sheltered bays or lagoons the sediment is fine and more stable.

Waves often reach the shore at an angle and induce longshore currents that run parallel to the coast (Fig. 12A). These may continually shift sediment along the beach: but as fast as the sediment is scoured away and moved up the

coast so it may be replaced from further down. While the actual coastline may be slowly cut back, the beach sand is being replenished continually. Much of Natal has long unconsolidated sandy beaches and the coastline is almost straight. However on the south coast the shore is a mosaic of different rock types interspaced with sandy stretches. Where hard rock formations, such as Table Mountain Sandstone, project from the coast, they resist erosion and deflect the currents and diffract the waves. A common feature of this coast is the series of 'half-heart' bays that are

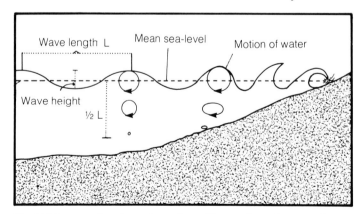

Fig. 11A As waves travel over the surface of the sea the water moves in a series of circles but does not move in the direction of the waves. A bluebottle floating on the surface thus bobs up and down but is not driven forwards as the waves pass. Fig.11B The circular movement of water caused by waves becomes less marked in deeper water and the effect ceases at a depth that is half the wavelength (L). In shallow areas the circular motion of the water is interrupted by the sea floor, causing the wave to topple over and eventually break on the shore.

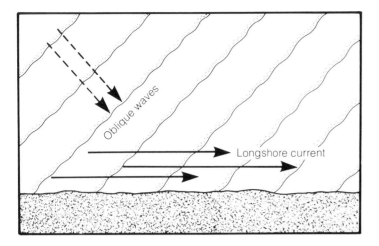

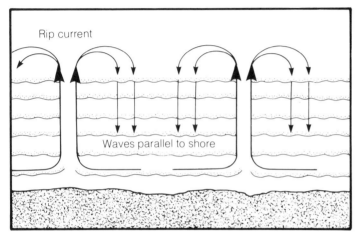

Fig. 12A Waves that travel obliquely to the shore drive a longshore current.
Fig. 12B When parallel to the shore, waves cause powerful rip currents that run at right angles to the shore and can be dangerous to bathers.

special interest when industrial or sewage effluent is to be deposited into the area, for they can too easily redeposit these wastes in the most inappropriate places. A special study has been made of water movements at Koeberg on the west coast where South Africa's first nuclear power station is being developed. Nuclear stations require large quantities of cooling water and the station at Koeberg will use roughly 8 million cubic metres of sea-water a day for this purpose. This water will be returned to the sea uncontaminated but about 10 °C hotter, and studies have been made to anticipate the biological consequences. Over an area of about 2 km² the sea will be heated by 6 °C, creating a pocket of water not unlike that of False Bay in terms of temperature, and perhaps south coast warm-water species will establish themselves there: a situation that is being monitored with interest by biologists.

Waves that arrive with their crests parallel to the shore create quite different currents. Such waves cause water to rush up the shore as they break, but there must be a return flow again in the face of other oncoming waves. They do so by forming jets of water, or rip currents, that rush outwards at right angles to the shore, often at great speed and for up to 2 km offshore under the most severe wave conditions. This water then rejoins the incoming waves and is recirculated. Thus cells of water may be formed, continually circulating in the surf (Fig. 12B). This can have important consequences as it establishes a semipermanent body of water associated with a particular stretch of beach. Rip currents are dangerous to bathers, and anyone caught in one should not attempt to fight against it to reach the shore but rather swim parallel to the shore until they are free of the rip and able to return to the beach more easily.

Waves entering a bay are spread out around the bay and their energy reduced as a result. It is possible to calculate how the shape of the bay matches the energy of the waves .and hence predict which parts of the shoreline will be

protected by rocky promontories and face away from the prevailing wave direction. Algoa Bay at Port Elizabeth is a familiar example (Fig. 13). Waves are refracted around rocky Cape Recife and have scoured out the half-heart bay in which the harbour shelters.

There is obviously an important balance between the rate at which sand can be scoured away by the waves and the rate at which it is replaced. Reclamation of sandy areas by stabilisation of moving sand dunes on Cape Recife has, for example, reduced the input of sand into the bay, so that no longer can there be any replacement of sand that is eroded away. The erection of the breakwater for Port Elizabeth Harbour has worsened this effect.

Similarly the breakwaters and piers across Durban beach refract the waves but also prevent the input of sediment so that some areas have been built up while in others, whole beaches have been eroded away.

Since the prevailing waves move north-easterly, they create half-heart bays facing north on the west coast and east on the south coast (Fig. 3). However local conditions such as wind direction, the shape of the coastline and the prescence of rocky headlands or estuary mouths can modify these nearshore currents.

The direction and strength of longshore currents are of

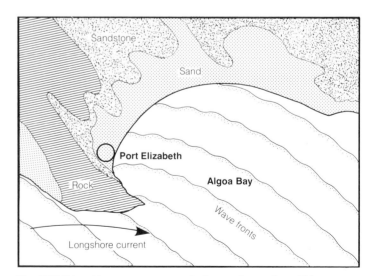

Fig. 13 Half-heart bays are a common feature on the southern African coast, and are formed where a rocky headland deflects the longshore currents. Algoa Bay is a typical example. Breakwaters projecting into the sea can have the same effect, so that the beach piles up on one side of the breakwater and is eroded away on the other.

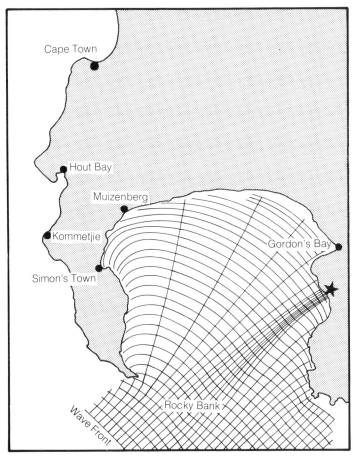

Fig. 14 **The prevailing waves drive into False Bay from the south west, and their force is dissipated around the bay which is thus fairly sheltered. However, some of the waves entering the bay are slowed down by Rocky Bank and then converge near the mouth of Steenbras River (starred in the figure) where they overlap to form 'killer waves'.**

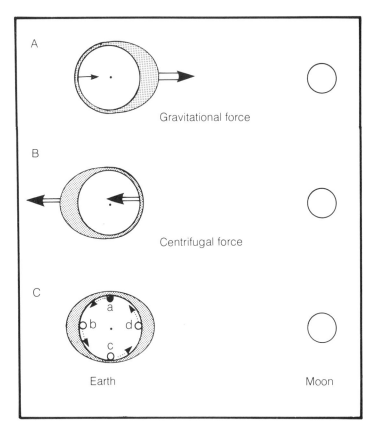

Fig. 15A The moon's gravitational attraction 'bulges' the sea outwards to cause a high tide on the near-side of the earth. Fig. 15B Since the earth and moon spin around each other (see Fig. 16), the centrifugal force throws the sea outwards to create a second high tide on the far side of the earth.
Fig 15C Thus there are two high tides at opposite sides of the earth at the same time. Because Earth rotates, any place (a) will move through points b, c and d, experiencing two low tides each day at a and c, and two high tides at b and d.

eroded in the future, and which are stable. False Bay at the Cape is particularly interesting in this respect, for the rocky east and west shores resist erosion while much of the northern sandy beach is being scoured. The way in which the waves are spread out in the bay is, however, complicated by Rocky Bank, an underwater platform of rock that rises up at the mouth of the bay. Waves are retarded by Rocky Bank and then converge, focusing on a point somewhere between Cape Hangklip and Steenbras River mouth (Fig. 14). Thus while parts of False Bay are sheltered because the waves are spread out, other parts experience heavy waves and the focusing of waves can lead to the notorious freak waves that have killed many an angler. The array of crosses mounted on this coast is mute testimony to this phenomenon.

The cause of tides
One of the most intriguing aspects of the shore is that twice a day the tide rises and floods it and then ebbs again to leave it exposed. Tidal action is mainly due to the gravitational force of the moon which pulls the waters of the earth towards the moon, so that the seas of the earth 'bulge out' on the side facing the moon (Fig. 15A). Thus it is easy to understand why there is a high tide at that point of the

earth that faces the moon. However there is also a high tide on the opposite side of the earth at the same time. This is due to quite a different effect. The gravitational pull of the earth and moon on each other means that they spin around each other as a unit. The earth is so much larger that the moon does most of the spinning but even so the imaginary axis of rotation is about 4 800 km from the centre of the earth (Fig. 16). This sets up a centrifugal force which overcomes the gravitational pull of the moon on the far side of the earth, throwing out a bulge of water on the side of the earth facing away from the moon (Fig. 15B). Thus there are two equal high tides on opposite sides of the earth: one caused by the moon's gravity and the other due to water being centrifugally thrown outwards. Because the earth also rotates on its own axis, any point on the earth's surface experiences two high tides every day. Just as high tides occur where the water 'bulges' outwards, so this water must be drawn away from other areas, which therefore have a low tide (Fig. 15C).

It must be remembered that the moon orbits around the earth once every 28 days, thus moving one twenty-eighth further around the earth each day. Because of this, high tides occur slightly later each day, being delayed about 25 minutes each tide or 50 minutes a day.

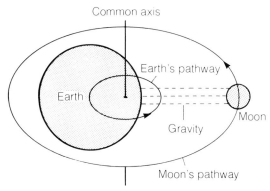

Fig. 16 The earth and moon are held together by gravitational attraction and act as a single unit spinning on a common axis. This axis lies within the radius of the earth because Earth is 100 times the mass of the moon. The spinning action causes a centrifugal force that makes the sea bulge out on the outer face of the earth, giving rise to a high tide.

Another complication is that the sun also exerts a pull on the sea, although, despite the sun's greater size, its effect is much less than that of the moon because it is so much farther from earth. However, during the new and full moons, the sun, earth and moon lie more or less in a straight line (Fig. 17) and the pull of the sun then reinforces the action of the moon and extra-high tides occur, with of course extra-low tides elsewhere. These are the spring tides which expose more of the shore than at other times, making the extreme, low-shore life accessible to collectors. On the other hand, during the first and third quarters of the moon, sun and moon act at right angles to each other and the tides are therefore less marked: during these neap tides waters do not rise as high or drop as low. Spring tides occur once a fortnight, the tidal range gradually reducing after each spring tide to the neap a week later (Fig. 17).

Places to live

Five major habitats exist in the sea, distinguished by the nature of their substrata and the amount of water movement. Rocky intertidal shores provide a firm substratum for the attachment of plants and animals, but are exposed twice a day by the tides and are often lashed by strong wave action. Sandy beaches, in contrast, have an unstable substratum that is continually modified by waves and currents. On the west coast the giant kelps form a calmer underwater forest-like habitat. In estuaries the water is calmer still and the sediment muddier and more stable, but organisms have to contend with river-water diluting the sea-water. Finally in the open sea there is no firm substratum and organisms must either drift or be able to swim.

The ecology of these very different habitats is explored in the following chapters.

Fig. 17 During the full moon, the gravitational forces of sun and moon are on opposite sides of Earth and reinforce the high tides so that the tidal range is great during this period (spring tides). During the third quarter, sun and moon act at right angles and tend to cancel each others gravitational pull so that tidal range is reduced (neap tides). At the new moon, moon and sun are again aligned to produce large spring tides, while the first quarter moon brings smaller neap tides.

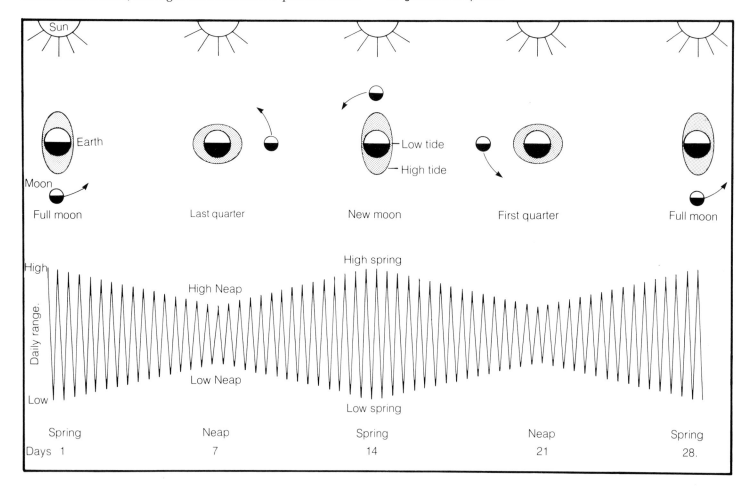

REFERENCES
Popular articles and books

Baird, D. 1970. The Natal 'sardine run'. *S. Afr. Shipping News and Fishing Industry Review*, Vol. 25: 70-71.

Ballard, R. D. & Grassle, J. F. 1979. Incredible world of the deep-sea rifts. *National Geographic*, Vol. 156 (5): 680-705.

Brown, A. C. 1980. Challenge of the sea. *Transactions of the Royal Society of S. Afr.*, Vol. 44 (2): 133-143.

Condon, T. 1972. Beneath Southern Seas – The Story of Skindivers' Exploration of Southern Seas. *Fin-diver Magazine*, Durban.

Day, J. H. 1977. Marine biology in South Africa. Chapter 4 in *"A History of Scientific Endeavour in South Africa"*, (Edited by A. C. Brown). Royal Society of South Africa, Cape Town. pp. 86-108.

Lutjeharms, J. R. E. 1978. Studying the ocean by satellite. *S. Afr. Shipping News and Fishing Industry Review*, Vol. 33 (10): 28-31.

Schumann, E. H. 1980. Giant wave. *Oceans*, Vol. 13 (4): 27-30.

Siegfried, W. R. 1980. The Benguela ecosystem. *Oceans*, Vol. 13 (4): 20-26.

Scientific references

Brown, A. C. & Jarman, N. 1978. Coastal marine habitats. Chapter 8 in *"Biogeography and Ecology of Southern Africa"*, (Edited by M. J. A. Weiner). W. Junk, The Hague. pp. 1239-1277.

Cook, P. A. 1978. A prediction of some possible effects of thermal pollution on marine organisms on the west coast of South Africa, with special reference to the rock lobster, *Jasus lalandii*. *Transactions of the Royal Society of S. Afr.*, Vol. 43: 107-118.

Heydorn, A. E. F. *et al.* 1978. Ecology of the Agulhas current region: an assessment of biological responses to environmental parameters in the Southwest Indian Ocean. *Transactions of the Royal Society of S. Afr.*, Vol. 43: 151-190.

Newman, G. G. & Pollock, D. E. 1974. A mass stranding of rock lobsters, *Jasus lalandii* (H. Milne Edwards, 1837) at Elands Bay, South Africa (Decapoda: Palinuridea). *Crustaceana*, Vol. 26: 1-4.

Stephenson, T. A. & Stephenson, A. 1972. *Life Between Tidemarks on Rocky Shores*. W. H. Freeman, San Francisco. pp. 25-35.

2. ROCKY SHORES

Fig. 18 Three species of *Littorina* are practically the only inhabitants of the high-shore on the east coast.

Fig. 19 The mid-shore is dominated by barnacles.

The intertidal rocky shore must be one of the most stressful habitats for animals and plants. Put yourself in the position of an animal living there. Imagine being submerged twice a day for six hours when the tide rises, experiencing cold water and wave action; and then being exposed to the air during low tides, being subjected to the blazing sun with temperatures of up to 40 °C and losing as much as 70 percent of your body water to the air. All the vital functions of life such as respiration, excretion and reproduction must be adapted to function in two completely different environments: marine at high-tide and essentially terrestrial at low-tide. This then is part of the fascination of rocky shores: the ways and means animals have of surviving the variable and often harsh physical conditions.

We can recognise a gradient in the physical stresses intertidal organisms experience. Low on the shore the period of exposure at low-tide will be brief. Moving up the shore conditions become more and more harsh and the period of exposure increases. Not surprisingly, fewer and fewer plants and animals manage to live in the higher regions of the shore. Particular species are adapted to particular conditions, so species that cannot tolerate exposure occur near the bottom of the shore while hardier species live near the high-tide mark. Thus animals and plants are regularly zoned in bands on the shore. The causes of this zonation have long intrigued biologists, and have led to a study of the ways in which physical and biological processes may control where particular species can live.

ZONATION PATTERNS

On most rocky shores we are able to recognise four distinct zones. At the low-tide level algal beds form an obvious band called the infratidal zone. Above this there is usually a second algal-dominated zone, supporting different species of algae, and called the lower Balanoid zone. Only higher on the shore in the upper Balanoid zone do animals predominate, limpets and barnacles (*Balanus* spp = barnacles, hence Balanoid) being the most characteristic. Even higher on the shore only a few species of plant and animal life are found but the tiny gastropod *Littorina* is very abundant and gives its name to this uppermost zone: the Littorina zone. These four basic zones are modified on the east, south and west coasts, and are occupied by different species as summarised in Figs. 20, 21 & 24.

The East Coast

Highest on the shore in the Littorina zone, few species are hardy enough to tolerate the harsh conditions and three snails, *Littorina africana*, *L. kraussi* and *Nodilittorina*

EAST COAST ZONATION

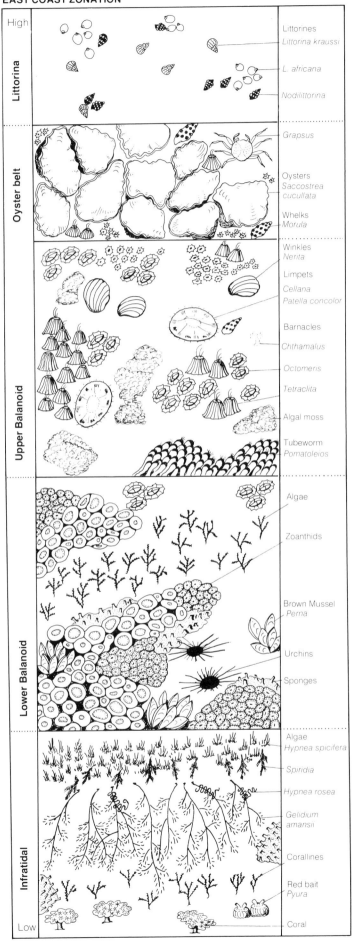

natalensis (Fig. 18) and tufts of the alga *Bostrichia* are practically the sole inhabitants.

Immediately below, at the top of the Balanoid zone, occurs a dense band of the Natal rock oyster, *Saccostrea cuccullata*. This gives way to a mixed community of brown mussels *(Perna perna)*, barnacles such as *Tetraclita* and *Octomeris* (Fig. 19) and limpets such as *Cellana capensis* and *Patella concolor*. Below this several species of zoanthids shroud the rocks of the lower Balanoid zone and are among the most characteristic of east coast organisms (Plate 27).

Still lower down the shore dense algal beds include species such as *Hypnea spicifera*, *Spiridea* and *Callithamnion*. Right at the bottom of the shore wave action is at its most fierce, and a different suit of algae predominates, including the hardy corallines and *Gelidium amansii*. Very few animals inhabit this infratidal zone although urchins and octopus hide in holes and, where the algae are sparse or there are sheltered pools, heads of coral may occur.

The South Coast

The same four zones described above for the east coast occur on the south coast, but support quite different species. Highest on the shore the Littorina zone is characterised by the same tiny snails that appear in their thousands and give their name to the zone, but on the south coast, there is only a single species, *Littorina africana*. A single alga is also common, the flat-bladed *Porphyra* (Plate 172b). Sheltering under the rocks on the high-shore is the common shore crab, *Cyclograpsus punctatus* (Plate 83).

It is in the upper Balanoid zone that animals predominate. Particularly common are limpets such as *Patella granularis* and *P. oculus*, the barnacles *Octomeris angulosa*, *Tetraclita serrata* (Fig. 20), and higher up the shore, *Chthamalus dentatus*. The winkle *Oxystele variegata* is one of the obvious inhabitants. Few algae occur in the upper Balanoid zone although the sea lettuce *Ulva* (Plate 166f) and the knobbly *Iyangaria* (Plate 167l) are typical.

The lower Balanoid zone here supports thick beds of algae, particularly *Gigartina radula*, *G. stiriata* (Plate 171) and *Gelidium pristoides* (Plate 176b). Interspersed between the algae are small numbers of animals including the limpet *Patella longicosta* and winkles such as *Oxystele sinensis* and *O. tigrina*. In pools, whelks (*Burnupena* species) are common and scavenge for dead or damaged animals, and anemones abound.

On the south coast there is an additional and particularly interesting zone that is lacking on the east coast. This is the Cochlear zone, named after the limpet *Patella cochlear* that forms a dense band at the low-tide mark, sandwiched between the infratidal and lower Balanoid zones. These limpets reach an astonishing density of up to 2 600 per m²: a higher density than is achieved by any other limpet of this size anywhere else in the world. How they manage to live at such densities is a fascinating story, described later

Fig. 20 East coast zonation

SOUTH COAST ZONATION

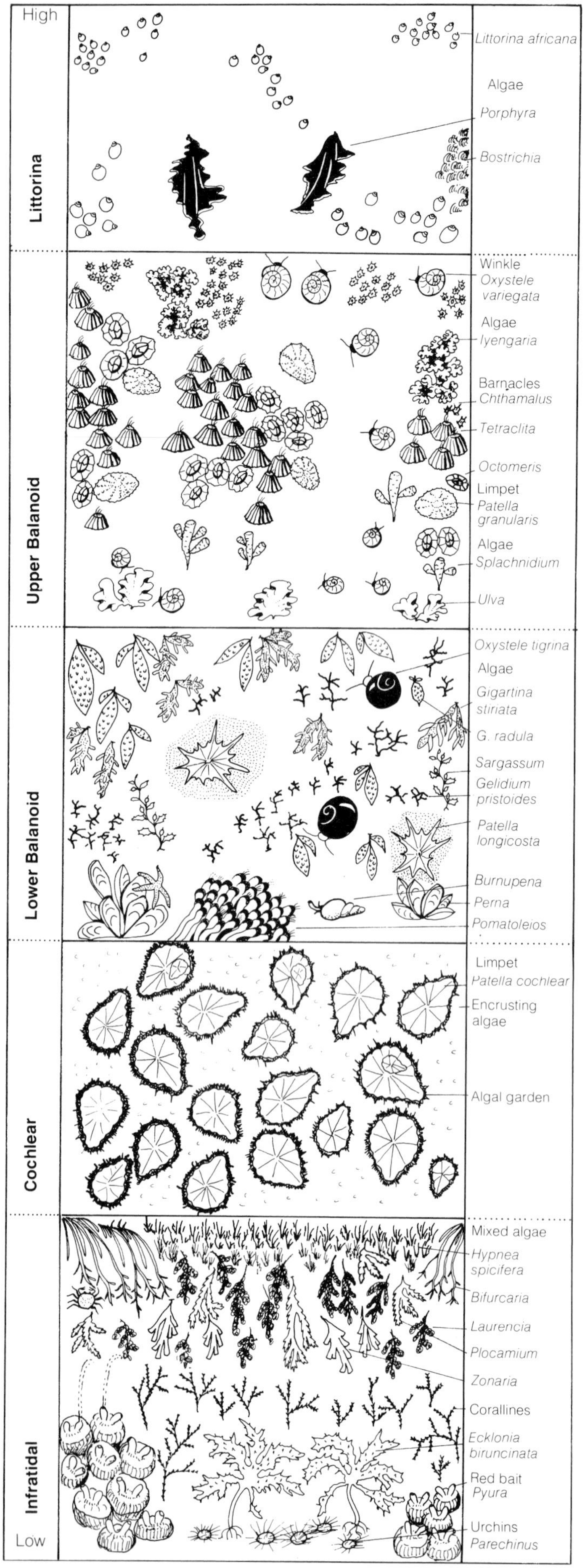
High
Littorina
Upper Balanoid
Lower Balanoid
Cochlear
Infratidal
Low
Littorina africana
Algae
Porphyra
Bostrichia
Winkle
Oxystele variegata
Algae
Iyengaria
Barnacles
Chthamalus
Tetraclita
Octomeris
Limpet
Patella granularis
Algae
Splachnidium
Ulva
Oxystele tigrina
Algae
Gigartina striata
G. radula
Sargassum
Gelidium pristoides
Patella longicosta
Burnupena
Perna
Pomatoleios
Limpet
Patella cochlear
Encrusting algae
Algal garden
Mixed algae
Hypnea spicifera
Bifurcaria
Laurencia
Plocamium
Zonaria
Corallines
Ecklonia biruncinata
Red bait
Pyura
Urchins
Parechinus

Fig. 21 South coast zonation

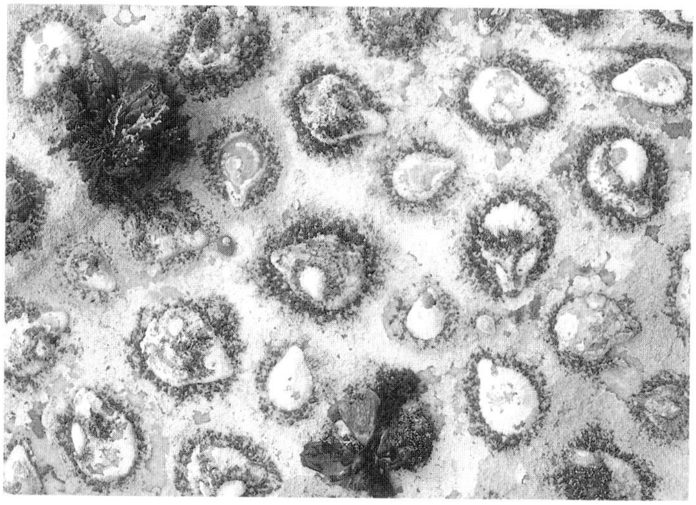

Fig. 22 Low on the shore the limpet *Patella cochlear* dominates. Note the regular spacing of the animals, the fringes of algal 'garden' around each limpet and the juveniles living on the shells of larger limpets.

Fig. 23 In the infratidal zone grow dense beds of red-bait, *Pyura*.

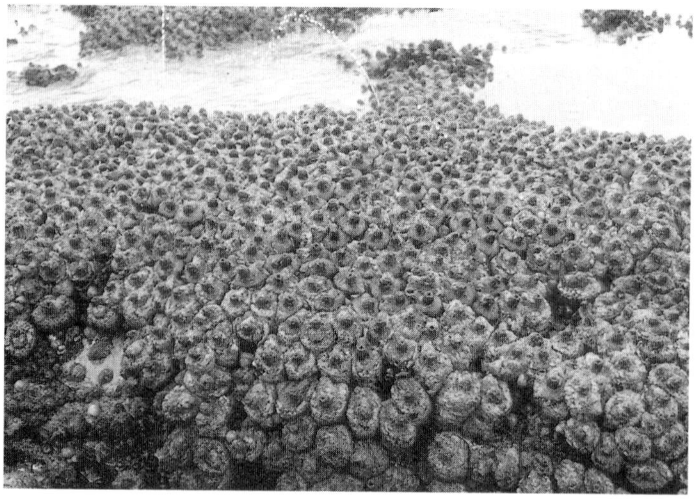

in this chapter. They are so densely packed that juveniles are mostly found living on the backs of adults, perhaps because this is the only 'safe' space where larvae can settle and not be eaten by the adults: not surprisingly these dense assemblages of limpets largely prevent algae from settling, and the zone appears barren compared with the lush growth above and below (Fig. 22, Plate 163).

Below the Cochlear zone, the infratidal zone supports dense colonies of red-bait, *Pyura stolonifera* (Fig. 23) in addition to thick stands of several algae such as the corallines, *Hypnea spicifera*, species of *Plocamium* and *Laurencia*, the wave-loving *Bifurcaria brassicaeformis* and the prickly-bladed kelp, *Ecklonia biruncinata*. Where shelter from the waves is available, large numbers of urchins, *Parechinus angulosus* (Plate 152), cover the rocks and can have a devastating effect on the algae, leaving only the resistant paint-like encrusting *Lithothamnion*. Starfish are also common in this zone, including *Henricia*, *Patiria* and the predatory *Marthasterias* (Plates 143-144).

The West Coast

Zonation on the west coast is similar to that of the south coast, but the most spectacular change is the addition of vast subtidal kelp beds which are discussed in a later chapter. The Littorina zone supports the same species as on the south coast. The upper Balanoid is again dominated by animals, having large numbers of limpets, particularly *Patella granatina* and *P. granularis,* but supports far fewer barnacles.

The lower Balanoid zone supports its usual cover of algae: mostly flat-bladed red algae such as *Aeodes* and *Iridea* (Plate 172) and the spongy dead-man's fingers *Splachnidium* (Plate 167j); and there are often massive sandy colonies of the tubeworm *Gunnarea capensis* (Fig. 42).

The Cochlear zone remains a feature of the west coast, but in the northern regions a second limpet, the tall domed *Patella argenvillei,* also abounds in this zone, which is thus called the Cochlear/Argenvillei zone. The intertidal zone resembles that of the south coast with beds of red-bait and algal mats of species such as *Champia lumbricalis* and *Bifurcaria brassicaeformis.*

LIFE-CYCLES AND THE ESTABLISHMENT OF ZONATION

Many intertidal organisms have in their life-cycle some stage during which they are dispersed in the water, allowing wide distribution of the species. As an example, mussels produce tiny top-shaped trochophore larvae which have bands of cilia propelling them through the water. These give rise to a second larval stage, the veliger, with a bivalve shell and two lobed projections covered by hair-like cilia. Like the trochophore, the veliger is able to swim, although it is so tiny that it is very much at the mercy of the currents and waves. The two larval stages last about a week and the tiny animal then settles and attaches on to rocks, metamorphosing into a miniature version of the adult. Many other groups of animals such as winkles, limpets, worms and barnacles have corresponding larval stages that float in the water and are dispersed in this way to new areas. Algae have spores that fulfil the same function and the details of these life-cycles are described in later chapters where the major groups of animals and plants are dealt with.

The advantage of a larval stage is that it allows dispersion away from the area already occupied by adults and in this way prevents the population from becoming over-crowded. It also allows escape from competition with other species, or from areas where predators have built up in number. For species living in an unstable habitat dispersion is vital, for the larvae allow the species to colonize new areas as the old habitats occupied by adults are eliminated. This is a common occurrence in the sea; for example, rocky shores are often smothered by sand and must

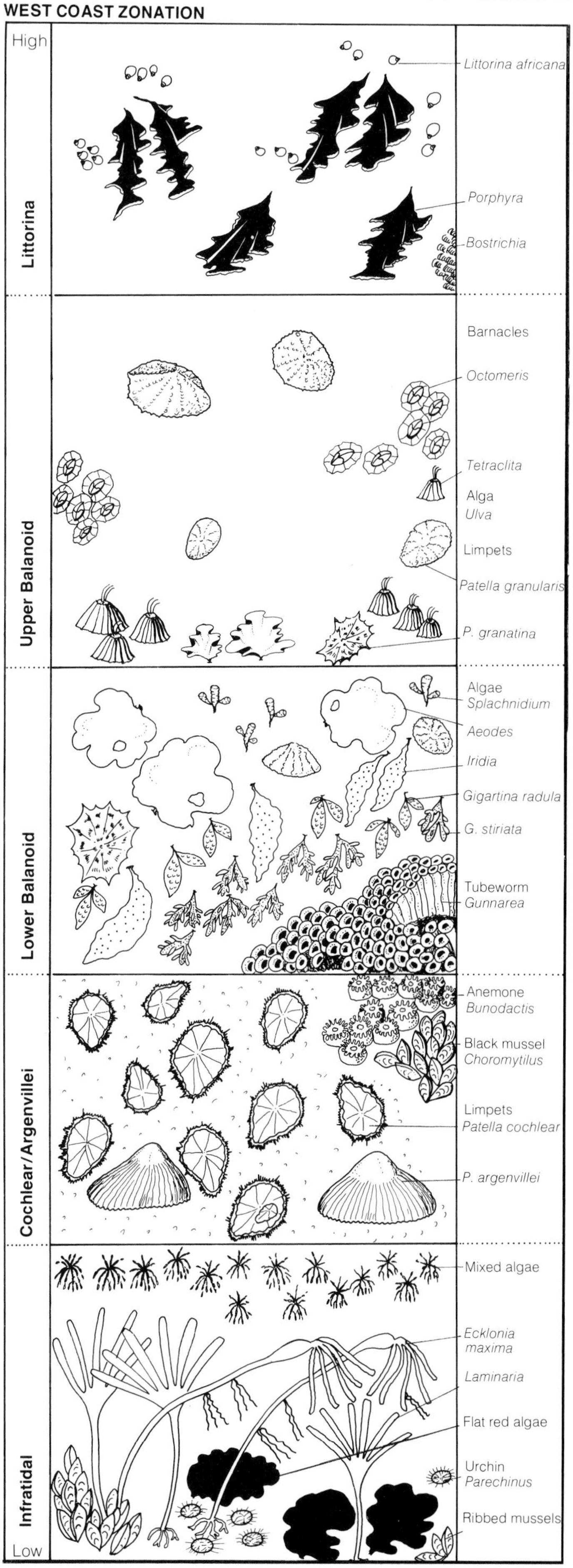

Fig. 24 **West coast zonation**

WEST COAST ZONATION

High

Littorina — *Littorina africana*, *Porphyra*, *Bostrichia*

Upper Balanoid — Barnacles, *Octomeris*, *Tetraclita*, Alga *Ulva*, Limpets, *Patella granularis*, *P. granatina*

Lower Balanoid — Algae *Splachnidium*, *Aeodes*, *Iridia*, *Gigartina radula*, *G. stiriata*, Tubeworm *Gunnarea*

Cochlear/Argenvillei — Anemone *Bunodactis*, Black mussel *Choromytilus*, Limpets *Patella cochlear*, *P. argenvillei*

Infratidal — Mixed algae, *Ecklonia maxima*, *Laminaria*, Flat red algae, Urchin *Parechinus*, Ribbed mussels

Low

then be recolonized by organisms when they are uncovered once more.

On the other hand, having a dispersive stage like a spore or a larva can be a risky proposition. Heavy losses of larvae always occur. They are eaten by predators in the plankton and they must find a suitable area in which to settle before their brief life ends. As an example, during its life-span a limpet will produce about six million eggs, of which an average of only two will survive to the point where the offspring themselves successfully reproduce.

Another problem is that dispersive spores or larvae are small and vulnerable to the elements. Not surprisingly, some species have reduced this stage in their life-cycles. For instance, the alga *Bifurcaria brassicaeformis* lives in areas of wild wave action where the chance of spores settling is remote. Its spores are anchored to the adult by gelatinous stalks and begin to grow there, only later growing on to the rocks. The benefits of dispersion are thus lost to this alga, but the risks are also diminished. Several animals similarly lack a larval stage. Whelks such as *Nucella dubia* and *Burnupena* species have elaborate egg

capsules which they cement onto the rock (Plate 93). Their larval stage is either shortened or eliminated altogether. A more striking case is the high-shore plum-coloured anemone, *Actinia equina* (Plate 16). Most anemones have a swimming larva, but the high-shore is too harsh for such a vulnerable stage and *Actinia* broods its young inside its gastric cavity, juveniles eventually being 'born' through the mouth of the adult. If the anemone is gently squeezed this 'birth' may be induced prematurely and it is astonishing to see how many juveniles pop out of the mouth.

Species with a larva or with spores rely on these stages to locate new habitats. In many cases this seems a random process, settling occurring practically anywhere on the shore. Those larvae or spores deposited too high on the shore will die of desiccation; those settling within reach of competitors, grazers or carnivores may similarly die. Only the few that happen to settle in a suitable zone will survive. On the other hand, some larvae are very fussy about the area and type of substratum on which they choose to settle. As an example, barnacle larvae have a preference for certain light intensities, specific amounts of water movement and suitable pits or crevices in which they wedge themselves. Above all they prefer to settle where there are already adults of their own species, for the success of adults is in itself a recommendation that the site is suitable.

Species that live attached to particular plants depend on their larvae to select the right plant. The limpet *Patella compressa*, for example, is found practically only on the kelp *Ecklonia maxima* which is chosen by the limpet's swimming larvae. Many of the larvae of the lace-like bryozoans (Plates 137-140) not only choose a particular plant but are able to select the youngest part of the plant. This remarkable adaptation ensures that they are not lost as the older parts of the plant break up, and that they settle on a part of the plant that is least likely to have other organisms already attached to it.

Larvae that are particular about where they settle can control the zonation of the adults. This is specially true if the adult is sessile – permanently fixed to the substratum.

Species with mobile adults are able to alter their position as they age. Two particularly interesting examples are the winkles *Oystele variegata* and *Littorina africana*. In both cases there is a size gradient in the population : juvenile *Oystele* occur near the bottom of the shore, while increasingly larger animals are found higher up, which suggests that as the animals age they migrate up the shore. Experiments have been done on these winkles, taking high-shore specimens, marking them with paint and then releasing them low down on the shore. Similarly, small specimens from the low-shore were marked and moved up-shore. In both cases the animals wasted no time in returning to the zones from which they were originally taken (Fig. 25), covering up to 30 m a day to do so – a formidable performance for such a tiny animal. We still do not understand how the winkles manage to orientate in the right direction to find their way back to their preferred zones, however, the underlying reasons for this migration are discussed later in this chapter.

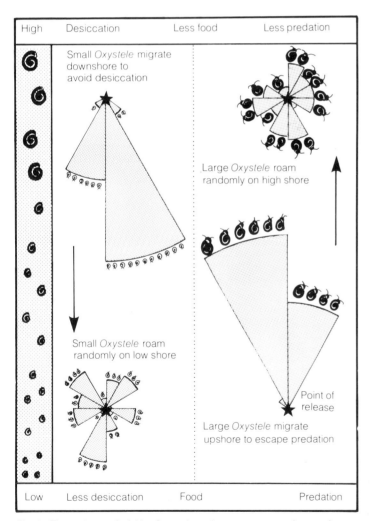

Fig. 25 The variegated winkle, *Oystele variegata,* moves upshore as it ages. Small animals will move back down the shore if experimentally released in the high-shore, since desiccation is too stressful there. Larger animals migrate upshore when released low on the shore, thus escaping intense predation but in doing so, moving to a zone where food is scarcer.

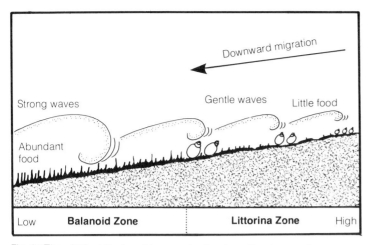

Fig. 26 The winkle, *Littorina africana,* migrates down the shore as it grows larger and is able to tolerate heavier wave action, and is then able to make use of a richer food source.

In the case of *Littorina* the reverse zonation pattern exists. Very small animals tend to occur highest on the shore and larger animals lower down. Wave action decreases up the shore and it seems that the small animals, which cannot cling tightly, survive only right at the top of the shore; while the larger individuals are able to resist the waves better and migrate down the shore. Why should they choose to do so? It would appear that this is directly connected to the fact that lower on the shore there is greater algal growth on which the littorines can feed. In experiments, larger animals were attached to slender nylon lines and then tethered to the rock face, either on the high-shore or in the zone below, where they normally occur. This tethering left the animals free to move around and feed but unable to migrate away. Adults tethered lower on the shore grew faster, proving that the food source there was more adequate. On the other hand, juveniles did not fare at all well if tethered lower on the shore, in spite of the richer food supply there, because they were buffeted about by the waves. Thus *Littorina africana* starts its life high on the shore to escape waves and then moves downwards to richer feeding grounds when it is large enough to withstand the waves (Fig. 26).

ADAPTATIONS TO PHYSICAL STRESSES

Organisms living between the tide marks have had to evolve special adaptations to survive the physical stresses of the habitat, which include water-loss, temperature extremes, a range of light intensities, changes in salt concentration and the problems of pounding waves.

Desiccation

Some plants and animals avoid the issue of water-loss by sheltering in pools or moist crevices, or by living in or under seaweeds. Common examples are the starfish, *Patiriella exigua* (Plate 141), several species of worm and the tiny shrimp-like amphipods. The seaweed *Porphyra* (Plate 172b) avoids water-loss by growing high on the shore

in winter when the dangers of water-loss are reduced, but enters a microscopic phase of its life-cycle (the conchocelis) and in this form bores into shells and remains buried during summer.

In the 1940s Professor G. J. Broekhuysen, who later became well-known for his research on birds, undertook a study of several gastropod snails common in False Bay. He showed that high-shore species such as *Littorina africana* are remarkably tolerant of water-loss. This tiny snail can be kept dry in a matchbox for literally weeks, remaining dormant until it is reintroduced to water, when it crawls out of its shell and resumes activity, seemingly unharmed by this treatment. On the other hand species found near the low-tide mark die after losing relatively little water and cannot survive high on the shore. Thus the zonation of animals reflects how tolerant they are to physical conditions such as desiccation.

Body design also plays a rôle in determining how long an animal is able to survive desiccating conditions. Water-loss occurs only from the surface of an organism. As a body becomes larger its surface area does not increase as much as its volume: roughly, we can say that as the volume is cubed the surface area is squared. Thus larger organisms have a greater volume (and hence a greater store of water) but a relatively smaller surface area from which to lose it. A perfect example of the importance of this is the distribution of the winkle *Oxystele variegata* mentioned above. Small animals are confined to the low shore because they lose water too fast to colonise higher regions but, as the winkles

WATER LOSS

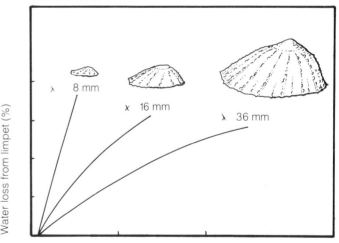

Fig. 27 Large limpets lose water much more slowly than small ones, but the shape of the limpet shell provides poor resistance to water-loss, having a large mouth and containing relatively little water compared with a globular, small-mouthed *Nerita* shell.

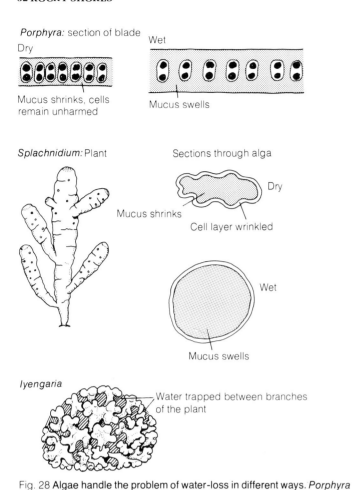

Porphyra: section of blade

Dry

Mucus shrinks, cells remain unharmed

Wet

Mucus swells

Splachnidium: Plant

Sections through alga

Mucus shrinks

Dry

Cell layer wrinkled

Wet

Mucus swells

Iyengaria

Water trapped between branches of the plant

Fig. 28 Algae handle the problem of water-loss in different ways. *Porphyra* surrounds its cells with mucus; *Splachnidium* is like a bag of mucus; and *Lyengaria* has a reservoir of water between its knobbly branches.

grow larger and thus lose water more slowly, they migrate upwards.

Shell shape can influence the rate at which an animal loses water. Limpets are singularly poorly-adapted in this sense, for their cap-shaped shells have a wide mouth from which water-loss takes place. Possibly this is one of the

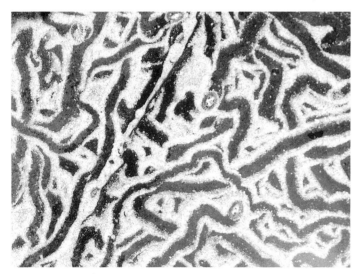

Fig. 29 The limpet *Siphonaria capensis* ploughing through sand that covers the rock face, leaving trails to and from the limpets' home scars.

reasons why the number of limpet species declines on South Africa's east coast and even more in tropical Moçambique, where the sun's heat increases desiccation. In these hotter regions they are replaced by several *Nerita* species (Plate 115), *Nerita albicilla* being particularly common. The shells of nerites are also cap-shaped but are much more domed than those of limpets and have a relatively small mouth, presumably making them better-adapted to a sub-tropical or tropical climate.

Among the South African limpets, some such as *Patella granularis* and *P. granatina* migrate up the shore as they age, much as *Oxystele variegata* does. To help overcome the problem of increased desiccation in the high-shore, shell shape changes in these species as they age, becoming more and more domed. This allows the animals to increase body volume without a proportional increase in the circumference in the mouth of the shell, and this again reduces water-loss (Fig. 27). Significantly, those species that do not migrate upshore remain a constant shape as they grow; a tall, domed shape is unnecessary.

Many marine snails have evolved an operculum: a horny or calcareous structure, attached to the foot, which blocks off the shell mouth when the snail retreats into its shell. Undoubtedly this 'door' deters some predators, but it also reduces water-loss from the animal.

Some seaweeds also have special adaptations to help them tolerate water-loss. *Porphyra* occurs higher on the shore than most algae, and its flat blades contain large quantities of a mucus-like material which surrounds the cells. It is this mucus that loses water as the plant dries, while the cells remain unaffected and are not distorted or damaged. *Porphyra* can lose an enormous amount of water without damage, shrinking to as little as one-tenth of its original size in the process, but when the plant is resubmerged the mucus rapidly takes up water again, restoring the plant to its former size. By shrinking during low-tide *Porphyra* also decreases the surface area from which water-loss can occur. Another alga, the 'dead-man's fingers', *Splachnidium*, is similarly laden with mucus that helps the alga survive water-loss (Fig. 28).

Other seaweeds reduce water-loss in a different way: the knobbly cushion-shape of *Iyengaria*, the filamentous mat of *Cladophora contexta* and the berry-like expansions on *Caulerpa racemosa* all hold water, thus providing an external source of water during periods of desiccation.

The above adaptations all involve body structure, but the behaviour of animals can also be important in reducing water-loss. For instance, limpets are well known for their ability to return to a fixed position on the rock after feeding, where their shells have grown to fit the contours precisely, forming an almost watertight seal. The limpets must therefore have a means of orientating and of 'knowing' the locality of home sites. The simplest way is for the limpets to retrace their paths following a mucous trail, but they do not always do this. Even this apparently simple method is quite complex, for each limpet must be able to recognise its own trail from that of other limpets. Limpets recognise from which direction a trail is laid down and will always backtrack on a trail to locate the home site. In some species this homing behaviour is very rigid and the rock becomes etched by the mucus of the limpet's foot, leaving readily recognisable scars on the rock (Fig. 29). Limpets recognise their own scars and will always orientate themselves precisely in the same way on the home scar. Even if they are removed from their home scar and placed a few centimetres away they nevertheless find their way home. Most likely they are following old trails, but even this is not

Fig. 31 Three *Littorina africana* hang one from the other, attached to the rock by a mucous thread to reduce contact with the hot rock. (x7)

HEAT GAIN AND LOSS

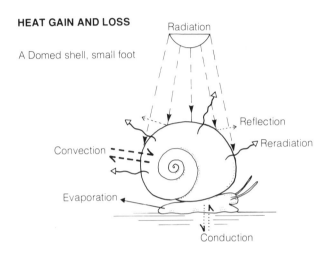

A Domed shell, small foot

Radiation

Reflection

Reradiation

Convection

Evaporation

Conduction

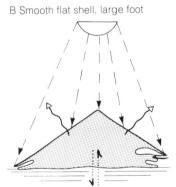

B Smooth flat shell, large foot

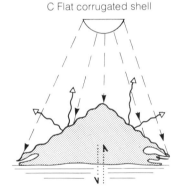

C Flat corrugated shell

Increased conduction
Increased radiation
Reduced reradiation
   compared with A

Reduced reradiation compared with A
Increased reradiation compared with B

D Shell shapes

High shore on bare rock
Ridged high shell
Helcion pectunculus

Low shore in pools
Smooth low shell
H. pruinosus

Temperate shores
Littorina africana knysnaensis

Tropical shores
Nodilittorina natalensis

Fig. 30A An animal such as a winkle gains and loses heat through various avenues. Fig. 30B Limpets have a flat shell and large foot, increasing both gain of heat by radiation and conduction of heat from the rock.
Fig. 30C If they have a corrugated shell, this increases the heat they lose by reradiation.
Fig. 30D This is why high-shore or tropical species often have tall, ridged or pimpled shells.

certain, for they still locate their homes if the rock is scrubbed to remove the trails. Thus we are still not certain how they manage to find their home sites with such precision.

Temperature

During low tide, organisms may be exposed to the blazing sun and to temperatures as high as 47 °C. As we might expect, high-shore species are able to tolerate higher temperatures than low-shore species, but a more interesting question is whether the body may be adapted to reduce the intake of heat. Heat gain and loss take place through various avenues (Fig. 30): radiation from the sun is the most important source of heat, but heat can also be gained by convection from the air and conduction from the rock face. If the body becomes hotter than the air or rock, it can of course, in turn, lose heat to them. Heat from the sun can be reflected, and the body can also cool down by evaporating some of its water-supply and by re-radiating heat back into space.

The shape, colour and texture of the body can be adapted to reduce heat uptake and to increase heat loss, thus keeping the animal as cool as possible. In this respect some animals have evolved better body designs than others. If we compare a limpet with a winkle, we soon realise that the limpet has a singularly bad design in terms of heat gain and loss: the flat shell exposes a large surface area to the sun's radiation and the large foot, so admirably suited for clinging onto the rocks, allows a rapid gain of heat from the rock.

Winkles have much taller, round shells and a comparatively small foot, thus reducing these avenues of heat uptake. Perhaps this is one of the reasons why there are relatively few limpet species in the tropics and along South Africa's east coast, in comparison with the cooler south coast. Species of *Littorina* that live so high on the shore have an unusual method of reducing heat even further: they attach their shells to the rock by mucus and then pull the body back into the shell, thus reducing contact with the rock (Fig. 31).

While organisms can theoretically cool down by evaporation, this is obviously a doubtful proposition in the intertidal zone where loss of body water may in itself be dangerous. Here re-radiation is a more feasible way of losing heat. This too is affected by the shape of the body, for an increase in the surface area allows greater re-radiation. Ridges, ripples or even tiny projections achieve an increase in surface area, and it is particularly interesting that these features are often best developed in high-shore animals such as *Nodilittorina natalensis* (Fig. 30D) and the limpet *Helcion pectunculus* (Fig. 30D), and are most obvious in the tropics. This effect is made even more fascinating by the fact that it was discovered by a zoologist who is blind. In fact this probably led him to consider shell shapes and textures in such an original way.

Light

For plants, light intensity is a vital issue. Obviously they need light to photosynthesise, and the shape of the plant influences the amount of light it receives. Broad, flat plants such as *Ulva*, *Porphyra* and *Aeodes* (Plate 172) have large surface areas and are able to absorb much light, photosynthesising and growing faster than cylindrical forms such as *Bifurcaria* and *Splachnidium* (Plates 167 & 169). A flat blade also ensures that the photosynthetic pigments occur near the surface of the plant.

Part of the problem faced by intertidal plants is that photosynthesis cannot occur when the plant is dry, for the carbon dioxide must be dissolved in water. Because the high-shore is covered less often by the tides, the time available for photosynthesis is limited, and not surprisingly high-shore species are often flattened to allow rapid photosynthesis during the brief period of submergence.

Contrary to what one might expect, many algae in the intertidal zone suffer from too much light since the chlorophyll that absorbs light is destroyed if the light is too bright. When plants photosynthesise they take up carbon dioxide. We are able to follow this process by using radioactive carbon C^{14} which allows us to determine the rate of photosynthesis by measuring the speed by which the plant takes up radioactive carbon dioxide. For several intertidal algae tested in this way (*Gigartina radula*, *Ulva* and *Gelidium pristoides*), we found, much to our surprise, that they photosynthesise fastest at a depth of 1 m and not on the surface of the water where they receive the greatest amount of light. This prompted experiments to see if algae could live higher on the shore than they do, if provided with shade. Small screens were built to shade the rock face

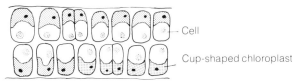

Ulva : Section through blade

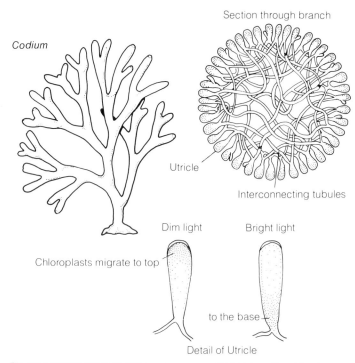

Fig. 32 Intertidal algae must tolerate a range of light intensities. *Ulva* has cup-shaped chloroplasts that can migrate toward the inner part of the cell if light is too bright. *Codium* has a stem made up of interconnecting tubules with surface utricles. Within these, the chloroplasts are free to migrate up or down depending on light intensity.

high on the shore, and sure enough, various species such as the sea lettuce *Ulva* and *Enteromorpha* began to grow under the screens, well above their normal zones. This is an important result for it shows that sunlight can limit how high on the shore algae normally grow.

Plants have evolved means of handling excess sunlight. For example, the vivid colours of lichens that occur at the highest levels of the shore (Plate 159) screen out much of the light and in this way protect the vulnerable chlorophyll. In *Ulva* the chlorophyll is concentrated in cup-shaped bodies (chloroplasts) which can migrate within the cells, coming to the cell surface when the light is low but retreating if the intensity becomes too great. *Codium* has a similar but more spectacular mechanism; the whole plant is made up of a series of interconnecting tubes that emerge at the surface of the plant as bulbs called utricles. These house the chloroplasts which can migrate to the surface of the utricles or down into the centre of the plant depending on conditions. Thus plants have a variety of adaptations all allowing them to make the best use of prevailing light conditions (Fig. 32).

Salinity

Sea-water has a salt content of about 35 parts per thousand but high on the shore pools may become diluted by rain or concentrated by evaporation. As a result we find few species living in these pools. One species, the stringy green alga *Enteromorpha* is astonishingly tolerant of changes in the salinity and flourishes in high-shore pools where there are no other algae to compete with it and few animals to make a meal of it.

Oxygen levels also fluctuate in these high-shore pools: by day the algae photosynthesise and the water becomes super-saturated with oxygen while at night algae use up the oxygen and the water may become deficient in oxygen.

Wave Action

Waves are a feature of most rocky shores, but create problems for plants and animals, although several species seem particularly well-adapted to strong wave action. The limpet *Patella cochlear,* red-bait *Pyura stolonifera* and the algae *Gelidium amansii* and *Hypnea spicifera* are characteristic of rough areas.

Animals that feed by filtering particles out of the water often use wave action to their advantage, for waves continually replace the water from which they draw their food supply. *Pyura* (Fig. 23) thrives in strong currents which aid the flow of water through its filtering apparatus, as discussed in Chapter 21. Therefore, *Pyura* grows larger where the surge of water is strongest, and is less successful in calmer and deeper waters.

Barnacles feed by using the mesh of hairs on their legs to sieve particles from the water (see Chapter 13). Some, such as *Octomeris* (Fig. 47A), abound on wave-beaten rocks and experiments show that they will only feed when water movement is strong, and by simply holding their legs out into the waves they filter out particles as the water rushes between the legs. Other species, such as *Tetraclita* (Fig. 19) and the goose barnacle *Lepas* (Plate 53), have more fragile legs and prefer calmer waters, feeding only when the water movement is moderate. This means that they must expend energy beating their legs through the water to obtain enough food. If the water is stationary or too slow-moving, the barnacles stop feeding, presumably because they would then have to spend more energy sweeping the water with their legs than they would obtain from the food they would be able to collect.

Some organisms avoid waves by sheltering in crevices or under larger species, but of greater interest are those organisms which have adapted their body forms to allow them to occupy wave-beaten areas.

Many species have evolved methods of improving and strengthening the way in which they attach themselves to the rock face. Algae such as the kelps *Ecklonia* and *Laminaria* and the wiry *Bifurcaria* send out root-like haptera that fix firmly to the substratum. Mussels attach themselves by a golden beard-like byssus produced by the foot as sticky threads that harden into a tough anchor on contact with sea-water. Oysters and barnacles cement their shells permanently to the rock face.

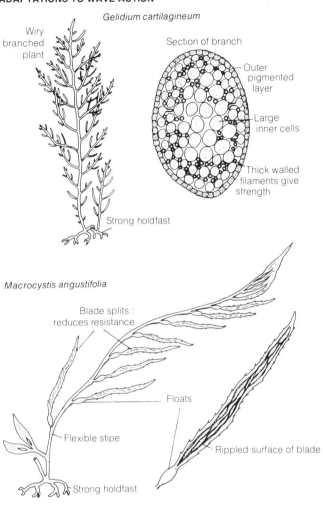
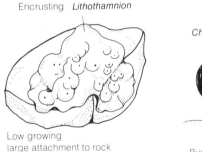
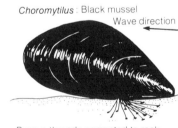

Fig. 33 Wave action is a problem for both algae and animals. Some plants have developed tough, wiry branches and strong holdfasts; others have flexible rippled blades; while yet others are low-growing and firmly attached. The mussel develops a beard of tough threads to cement itself to rock.

Limpets are renowned for the power with which they cling to rocks and a special study has been made of them. Contrary to popular belief, limpets do not cling by suction. If they did, the maximum force they could exert would be equivalent to one atmosphere of pressure, but in fact their force of attachment exceeds this by a factor of five. A force of over 100 kg is needed to dislodge a large limpet! The mechanism of attachment is actually adhesion – caused by the release of mucus between the foot and the substratum. We all know how difficult it is to separate two sheets of glass when they have a film of water between them, and limpets operate on a similar basis.

Interestingly, different species of limpet differ in their powers of adhesion. Those that occur in wave-beaten areas, such as *Patella cochlear*, cling tenaciously. They achieve this partially by producing a very thin film of mucus (which improves adhesion) and partly by having a very rigid foot which does not readily flex away from the rock. The ability to cling tightly has, however, cost the animals something: they are no longer as mobile as they might be. Other limpets are more mobile because they have a flexible foot and produce abundant mucus. They can move faster, escape predators more readily, and feed over a wider range but can only attach relatively weakly to rocks. Thus for some species the ability to cling on to the rock face may be critical, while for others, mobility is essential.

Adaptations of body shape and structure can also reduce the effect of wave action. For instance the algae *Gelidium amansii* and *G. cartilagineum* (Fig. 33) have fibrous tissues that strengthen them and, as in many algae that are wave beaten, they also have rounded branching blades that not only offer little resistance to the waves but are flexible so that they sway with the current. Other algae form encrusting sheets (Plate 170) over which waves pass unimpeded (Fig. 33).

While streamlining of the body reduces resistance to waves, for most organisms it is not a practical solution, because waves do not come predictably from one direction – they rush up the shore and then surge back in the opposite direction as they retreat. There are only a few species that can rely on a consistent direction of water movement. One of them is the limpet *Patella compressa* which lives exclusively on kelp plants and can depend on the kelp swaying with the waves, so that the current always flows from the base towards the tip of the plant. *Patella compressa* not only wraps its shell around the cylindrical stripe or stem to fit the alga as closely as possible but has a beautifully streamlined shell. Furthermore it sits head downwards on the kelp, facing into the current.

The texture of the body also influences how much resistance it offers to the waves. Contrary to what we might expect, a completely smooth body is not always the best design. A slight roughening of the body can reduce the amount of turbulence behind the body, which will in turn minimise the drag of water on the animal (Fig. 34). If this seems odd to us at first, we need only ask why golf balls have a dimpled surface instead of being completely smooth. For this reason many algae have a rippled surface – *Macrocystis* (Fig. 33 & Plate 94) and *Stypopodium* to name just two. Experiments have proved that limpet shells with slightly raised ridges or a granular surface (Fig. 34) present less resistance to strong currents than completely smooth-surfaced, limpet-shaped cones. This phenomenon is also found amongst those giants of the ocean, the whales. Thereby hangs a tale: we are able to calculate in theoretical terms how fast the whale should be able to swim if we

STREAMLINING

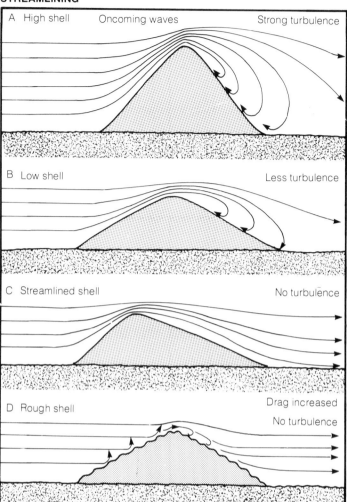

Fig. 34 The shape of a body such as a limpet shell influences how much it resists water movement.

know its size, the force its muscles exert and the density of the water – yet for years whales have made fools of scientists, for they swim much faster than the speed of which they are theoretically capable. This has long been known as 'Gray's paradox', after the famous zoologist, Sir James Gray, who first described the problem. The whale's secret lies in the design of its body, for not only is it streamlined, but much of its body is covered in shallow furrows running along the body. These allow the water to flow smoothly over the whale so that it is possible for it to swim faster than predicted (Fig. 35).

A totally different problem is encountered where waves

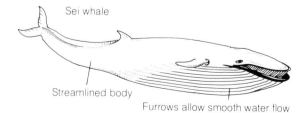

Fig. 35 Because of their body-shape and contoured underbelly, whales are more efficient swimmers than we would expect.

drive sand over rocks, scouring and even burying them for long periods. This condition is familiar to people living on the east coast, where tons of sand may be dumped overnight, covering rocks and sometimes even burying tidal swimming pools. Some species are able to tolerate periodic burial, while others simply die. Oysters, mussels, chitons and certain anemones survive the treatment provided they are not buried for too long and some algae, such as the tough fibrous *Udotea*, *Halimeda* and *Caulerpa filiformis* (Plates 166 & 167) seem to thrive in such sandy areas.

All of these physical stresses – water-loss, temperature, salinity and wave action – are only aspects of the ecology of rocky shores, for organisms must also be able to get along with their neighbours – and these biological interactions are perhaps even more fascinating and often demand the most extraordinary adaptations.

BIOLOGICAL INTERACTIONS

The food web: Who eats who?

On rocky shores the seaweeds that cover much of the lower shores are the central characters in the food web, for they are able to utilise the sun's energy for photosynthesis and thus convert simple inorganic compounds (carbon dioxide and water) into complex organic compounds. All plants, including the seaweeds, are therefore referred to as primary producers. Animals in turn eat these plants and use the energy trapped in their organic compounds to power their own growth, and they are thus termed primary consumers. Phytoplankton also photosynthesises, but we know from work in False Bay that phytoplankton is of relatively little importance to the rocky shore animals, in comparison to the dense growth of seaweeds.

A host of animals eat the seaweeds, including chitons, winkles, limpets, and some crabs, as well as the tiny shrimp-like amphipods and isopods. Curiously, relatively few of these attack mature seaweeds, preferring to scrape the seemingly bare rocks to remove algal sporelings and diatoms. Algae that manage to escape this grazing may then grow fast enough and large enough to be relatively immune to herbivores. Nevertheless, grazers have a dramatic effect on the distribution of seaweeds, for they forage so efficiently over the rocks that scarcely any sporelings survive. This is most obvious in the middle and upper portions of the shore where the harsher physical conditions slow the growth of algal sporelings and increase the chance of their being eaten. This has been dramatically proven by experiments in which all the grazers (or even just the limpets) have been removed from the shore. In most cases this results in a luxuriant growth of algae, even in areas high on the shore where algae were previously non-existent. This clearly demonstrates the potency of grazers in determining algal density and distribution.

On the low-shore, seaweeds have a better chance of escaping being eaten, and so thick algal beds usually dominate this zone. What might surprise us is that if grazers such as limpets are transplanted from the mid-shore and experimentally kept amongst the algae on the low-

shore, some of them actually starve to death despite this seeming abundance of food. The reason is that they depend on small algal spores and diatoms that they can scrape from the rock face and they cannot handle the large seaweeds. Of course, not all grazers suffer this way, but the finding is still important, for it helps explain why the low-shore is dominated by algae while the mid and upper shores are inhabited largely by animals. One animal that clearly breaks this pattern is the limpet *Patella cochlear* which forms such dense populations low on the shore. The effect of colonies of this limpet is so great that where it occurs there is an abrupt change from the dense algal growth in the intertidal zone to the bare, limpet-dominated Cochlear zone (Fig. 22, Plate 163). Once again it is solely the grazing activities of this limpet that prevent algae from growing here and simple experimental removal of limpets proves the point for, in the absence of limpets, algae soon become established. The effect of grazers on algal distribution is easy to understand, but the fact that filter-feeders can modify the zonation of algae is not so immediately apparent. Mussels may filter the water so efficiently that algal sporelings never have a chance to settle and grow where mussels

Fig. 36 These four growths of alga owe their existence to the fact that they settled on limpet shells where they were not grazed: the surrounding rock is eaten bare by the limpets.

carpet the shore. As a result the mussel zone on the east and south coasts has virtually no algae. Very recent experiments have shown that if mussels are cleared away dense algal mats form within days (Fig. 37).

Fig. 37 The filtering action of mussels normally prevents algae from settling on mussel beds. But when this patch was cleared in the middle of a dense mussel bed, a lush growth of algae soon developed.

Fig. 38 A summary of energy-flow through the food web on a rocky shore.

Thus it seems that grazers and filter-feeders control algae mainly by eating their sporelings and in this manner preventing them from becoming established, but in general they do not attack the adult plants. This seems peculiar, for, with our land-based view of life, we are used to thinking of herbivores consuming plants. If algae are not eaten, what happens to them? Most intertidal seaweeds have marked seasonal patterns of growth, many growing fastest in the cooler winter and spring months. The summer is too fierce for them and it is a common sight during this time of the year to see sun-bleached dead algae, particularly after spring low-tides when the beach is exposed for a longer period than usual. Waves and sandscour also take their toll, particularly of plants which have been weakened by grazers nibbling at their stalks. In these ways large quantities of dead or weakened plants are torn free and tossed around by the waves. Some of this debris is washed ashore where it is often trapped under rocks on beaches littered with boulders. Here the flat cockroach-like isopod *Ligia* (Plate 55.) gathers in vast numbers to feed on the material. Subtidally the sea urchins such as *Parechinus* (Plate 152) catch the debris and feed on it. For some unknown reason these urchins seem very sensitive to sunlight and are most active at night, during the day often holding shells or other rubble over themselves, rather like sunshades.

Most of the detached seaweed is broken into fine parti-

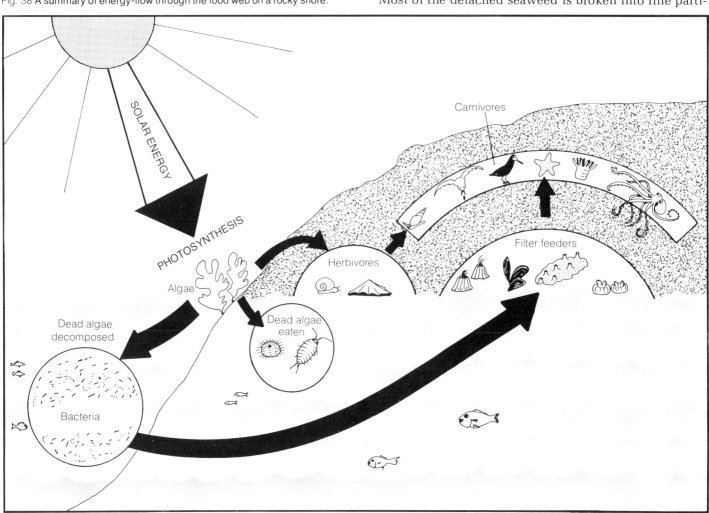

Fig. 39 The anemone, *Pseudactinia,* feasts on a shrimp.

cles by the abrasive action of the waves. Far from being lost to the rocky shore, this particulate matter seems to form the main food source for many organisms. The tiny particles are colonised by bacteria which have the potential to grow very rapidly by using the organic material as an energy source, decomposing it in the process and breaking the particles into tinier fragments. Particles and their bacteria can then be filtered out of the water and consumed by animals such as sponges, barnacles, mussels, red-bait, oysters and tubeworms. The details of how these animals achieve this and how their body structures are modified to allow filtration are described in later chapters dealing with each of these groups, but in general terms each has some device such as a net-like structure or a mucous web through which water can be strained to filter out the particles. It is because much of the algal growth only becomes available as a food source once it is in this form that filter-feeders dominate most shores, usually making up more than half the flesh-weight of animals on rocky shores. Filter-feeders also become more important on wave-beaten shores where the turbulent water normally contains more organic particles and where water movement continually brings in fresh food.

All of the primary consumers (grazers and filter-feeders) are eaten by other animals – the secondary consumers. Fig. 38 summarises the food chain on rocky shores and emphasises that the seaweeds are the most important primary producers, and that although they are eaten by grazers, most end up being killed by heat or torn off the rocks by waves and enter the detritus food chain. In this event they are broken down and colonised by bacteria which are then eaten by filter-feeders, which in terms of numbers and biomass are usually much more important than the grazers.

Adaptations of predators

Three feeding methods have been developed by predators on rocky shores. Some sit and wait for their prey; others are active hunters, searching out their prey; and a third group mainly scavenge on dead or weakened animals. The clearest example of this latter group is supplied by the *Burnupena* snails which are the marine equivalent of jackals and hyenas. Although they are capable of hunting, they have the most extraordinary ability to detect and locate wounded and dead animals, becoming excited by the merest trace of a dead animal in the water. Once roused they locate their prey by simply moving against the water currents, and thus in the direction from which the scent must have come. It is easy enough to demonstrate this by dropping a crushed periwinkle into a pool containing *Burnupena*: before long they cluster around the prey pushing one another aside to get close enough to feed.

Sea anemones are among the predators which have adopted the sit-and-wait approach. They trap unwary prey in their tentacles and then engulf the food by folding their tentacles inwards directly into the mouth (Fig. 39). For anemones this method of feeding appears to be a little precarious for the chance of catching any sizable prey seems remote. It is therefore not surprising that many anemones supplement their diet by trapping plankton or catching waste matter and dead organisms. Even the tiny caprellid amphipods that cling to seaweeds (Plate 56) feed in a similar manner, waiting for prey to swim past and then snapping out with their jaw-like pair of first legs (see Chapter 13 for details of their structure). Caprellids are amazingly aggressive little animals, often reaching out to attack animals such as nudibranchs far larger than themselves, and normally succeeding in repelling these animals.

Animals which hunt actively often need special adaptations to aid in prey capture. For instance the spiders (see Chapter 15) have poison fangs. The well-known cone shells (Plate 119) so popular with shell collectors have a specially modified radula that no longer acts as a rasping ribbon as in most snails but consists of arrow-like barbs that can inject poison into the prey. Some cones have particularly potent toxins such as the tropical *Conus geographicus* which has been known to be lethal to man. Most South African cones are not this potent but they should still be handled with caution.

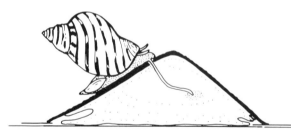

Fig. 40 The whelk, *Nucella dubia*, drills a hole through the shell of its limpet prey and then thrusts its proboscis down into the soft tissues to feed.

Fig. 41 A neatly-bevelled hole drilled by a whelk in a bivalve.

Fig. 42 The whelk, *Argobuccinum*, (6 cm) feeding on the reef-worm *Gunnarea*.

Fig. 43 The starfish *Marthasterias* (25 cm) humped in a feeding posture over a red-bait, *Pyura*.

Fig. 44 The commonest rock-pool fish; klipvis, *Clinus superciliosus* (15 cm).

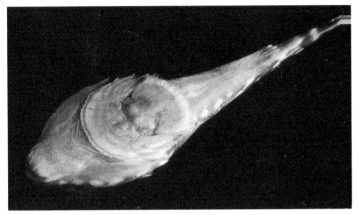

Fig. 45 Dorsal and ventral views of the suckerfish *Chorisochismus*, which feeds on limpets.

A

B

Fig. 46 Gulls are principally scavengers (A), but the black oyster catcher (B) feeds mainly on mussels and limpets. This oyster catcher has been banded (on the left leg) by ornithologists. Here it encourages its chick to climb a rock ledge.

Many predatory snails such as the *Nucella* species and *Morula granulata* are able to bore through the shells of their prey, using a combination of their rasping radula and a corrosive chemical that dissolves the shell. This drilling leaves a neat, easily-identified bevelled hole in the shell (Figs. 40 & 41), through which the predator thrusts its proboscis to feed.

Much more remarkable has been the finding that the whelk *Argobuccinum pustulosum* (Plate 117, Fig. 42) has evolved special glands which produce concentrated sulphuric acid. At first it was thought that this was an aid to drilling through shells, but *Argobuccinum* could never be induced to drill shells or feed on molluscs. In fact it actually feeds almost exclusively on the worm *Gunnarea* that forms banks of sandy tubes (Fig. 42). *Argobuccinum* thrusts its proboscis down the tube, pours in sulphuric acid and then has only to wait for the tube and the worm to dissolve before it sucks up the almost predigested meal.

The starfish, *Marthasterias glacialis* (Plate 143), is also an important predator. Mussels are its favourite diet and it hunches over its prey, attaching to it by its multitude of tube feet with which it pulls the valves of the mussels apart. Of course the mussel clamps its shell tightly closed but the starfish has a second line of attack: it turns its stomach inside out over the mussel and pours digestive juices over it, including a muscle relaxant that eventually causes the mussel to relax and open up. *Marthasterias* also feeds on unlikely prey such as red-bait (*Pyura*). To do so, it sits astride the red-bait and inverts its stomach through the nipple opening of the red-bait and down into the soft interior — the victim's tough external coat is no defence against this method of feeding (Fig. 43).

Octopus are voracious predators particularly of crabs, and one quite often sees crabs scuttling out of the water as an octopus approaches. The most common southern African octopus (*Octopus granulatus*) is large enough to rip its prey apart with its long tentacles, although it does have a vicious parrot-like beak as well. Curiously it seldom seems to bite when handled by humans, and even when it does, its bite is not dangerous. In contrast, the tiny Australian blue-ringed octopus has one of the most potent venoms of any animal and can kill a man in seconds.

Many fish are predators including the abundant gobies and klipvis (Fig. 44). Interestingly the common goby (*Coryphopterus caffer*) starts life as a predator, feeding first on tiny copepods, then later on amphipods, but as it ages its diet changes and it mainly eats the sea lettuce (*Ulva*) that grows in high-shore pools. A much more specialised predator is the cling-fish, *Chorisochismus dentex* (Fig. 45), which has a modified pectoral fin that forms a powerful sucker enabling it to cling to wave-beaten rocks. It has two sharp 'canine' teeth that it uses to rip unwary limpets off the rocks, selecting limpets that are moving around and hence less tightly attached. The limpet is swallowed whole, shell and all and we once found a 90 mm shell inside a cling-fish 192 mm long. After the limpet is digested the shell is coated with mucus to ease its passage through the gut, or the shell may be regurgitated.

On tropical reefs some predatory fish have evolved a much more devious way of hunting; they can change colour to mimic harmless fish and thus sneak up on the unsuspecting prey, hiding in the midst of a shoal of the fish they mimic.

Birds also prey on rocky shore animals. Gulls (Fig. 46A) will scavenge almost anything, but have learnt the trick of dropping mussels from a height on to rocks to break the shells. Far more refined is the oystercatcher (Fig. 46B) which sneaks up on limpets and then stabs them off the rocks, or alternatively scissors open mussels by inserting its beak and cutting the muscle that holds the two valves of the shell together. Try and open a live mussel yourself, even using a knife, and you will be filled with admiration for the dexterity of the oystercatcher.

Adaptations to avoid being eaten

Just as predators are adapted to prey capture so the prey have corresponding adaptations to counter the predators and some are so fascinating and bizarre that they belong in the realms of science fiction.

The first line of defence is to avoid detection. For example, the starfish *Patiriella exigua* (Plate 141) usually has a startling variety of colour patterns which, although vivid when we look closely, have the effect of breaking up the outline of the animal and blending it into the confusion of colours on the rock face (Plate 88). Interestingly this wide range of colours disappears in areas where the rock is a uniform colour; on dull black shale, *Patiriella* is a dark green colour, so that it merges into the background. We still do not know how different populations of the starfish, living on different types of rock, manage to develop a colour pattern which matches the colour of the rocks so exactly in each case.

Another animal that develops different colours under different circumstances is the limpet *Patella granularis* which is normally plain brown with speckles of white, but has a dark black-brown form that lives among mussels, and a form with a broken, striped pattern that occurs amongst barnacles (Fig. 47). Again we are ignorant of how these patterns become established; they may be genetically inherited but they could just as well result from different diets in different habitats. One of the beauties of working on the southern African coast is that there are so many challenging questions like this that can be answered by anyone with the curiosity – and the patience – to perform relatively simple experiments.

Many of the cowries hide by enveloping their shell in a fleshy mantle which resembles a piece of seaweed (Plate 106). This accounts for the cowries having such attractively shiny shells that are never weathered. However, if a cowrie is detected by a predator, it still has the option of withdrawing and sheltering in its shell.

Octopus achieve camouflage in a different way by changing their colour to match the background. Other animals such as crabs have somewhat distinctive outlines and to counter this the seaweed crab (*Dehaanius*) has developed special hooked hairs which it uses to attach

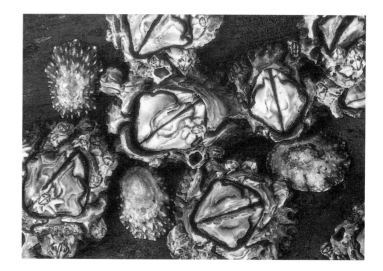

Fig. 47 The limpet, *Patella granularis,* has two forms: (A) a speckled variety that is camouflaged amongst barnacles (*Octomeris*) and, (B), a smooth dark-brown variety found concealed amongst mussels (*Perna*).

pieces of seaweed to its body to break its outline (Fig. 48). These bits of seaweed may actually grow onto the animal and effectively hide it.

Very recently a completely different form of camouflage has been discovered in an American limpet, *Acmaea paleacea*. This limpet always lives on eel grass (*Zostera*) and has developed a method of extracting some of the chemicals from its food plant and incorporating them in its shell. Because of this, predatory starfish seem unable to distinguish the limpet from the plant even when they walk right over it! Probably this chemical camouflage will be found more widely now we have become aware of it. It is, after all, a sensible adaptation, for many marine predators rely on scent to detect their prey.

Some organisms deter predators by being unpalatable or poisonous. The stinging cells of sea anemones, spicules in sponges, the release of an unpleasant purple fluid by the sea slug *Notarchus*, the poisonous nature of many nudibranchs and the seaweed *Caulerpa*, and the production of sulphuric acid by the alga *Desmarestia* are all examples of defensive structures. Some anemones such as *Anthothoe stimpsoni* (Plate 20) have long threads (acontia) laden with stinging cells, which can be shot out of the mouth or even directly through the body wall. The limpet *Cellana* defends itself by sliding its mantle right over its shell when in contact with a predator. This unusual reaction is doubly effective for the mantle is laden with mucous cells that pour out a noxious mucus clearly repellent to whelks and starfish, and at the same time the slippery mantle prevents predators from getting a grip on the shell (Fig. 49). The false limpets *Siphonaria* exude a milky mucus highly repellent to predators.

An alternative measure is to have a body that is so unattractive as a food source that it is ignored by predators. For instance, the encrusting algae *Hildenbrandia* and *Ralfsia* (Plate 170) have a very low energy content and all the coralline algae (Plate 170) have tissues loaded with calcium carbonate.

Many poisonous organisms are brightly coloured and have striking patterns. Vivid examples are the sponges, (Plates 2-6), sea anemones (Plates 14-21) and nudibranchs (Plates 120-132). These aposematic colours serve as a warning: they allow predators to learn very quickly that a particular colour or colour combination is associated with unpleasant consequences.

Some animals are perfectly palatable in themselves but may acquire an offensiveness second-hand. Several species of nudibranch sea slugs eat hydrozoans or anemones and are able to extract the stinging cells of their prey, transmit them through their bodies and then store them for later use against predators. The beautiful blue *Glaucus atlanticus* (Plate 131) is a case in point, for it feeds on the Portuguese man-o'-war *Physalia* (Plate 11) which has unpleasant stinging tentacles that are well known to bathers.

The domiid crabs acquire unpleasantness by carrying a cloak of sponge (or some other noxious organism). The crab's last pair of legs is specially modified for this purpose being bent up over its back to grip the sponge (Plate 7). As the sponge grows it may envelop the crab completely so that the crab has to cut itself out when it moults. In a similar way some hermit crabs detach anemones from the rocks and place them on their shells where they grow (Plate 67). Perhaps the most fascinating case is the boxer crab, which wanders around clutching a pair of anemones – one in each nipper – and, like a sparring boxer, threateningly pokes the anemones at other animals (Fig. 48).

Palatable organisms must avoid predation in other ways. Many limpets and gastropods have well-developed escape responses, triggered by scent or contact with predators, and flee in the opposite direction. The winkles (*Oxystele* species) have an especially well-developed response, spinning around and 'running' from the predator (Fig. 50). Many limpets do the same, often 'mushrooming' upwards first to avoid any further contact with the predator. These animals are able to recognise predatory species from non-predatory ones and do not waste time or energy reacting to the latter. More intriguing is the way in which some limpets (*Patella oculus* and *P. granatina*) change their reactions to predators as they age; small individuals flee for

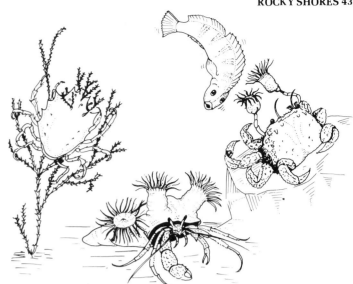

Fig. 48 Three forms of defence: while the crab *Dehaanius* camouflages itself by sticking bits of algae to its body, the hermit crab *Eupagurus* grows anemones on its shell, and the boxer crab *Lybia plumosa* holds two tiny anemones in its nippers and fends off predators with them.

Fig. 49 The limpet, *Cellana capensis,* rolls its mantle over its shell to fend off a predatory whelk (held between an experimenter's fingers).

Fig. 50 The limpet, *Patella oculus,* and the winkle, *Oxystele tigrina,* flee from a predatory starfish, *Marthasterias.*

their lives, but large animals become aggressive, lifting up their shells and smashing them down on to predators such as whelks or starfish, often damaging the predator in the process. Their reactions are specific to particular predators; while moderate-sized limpets will attack the whelks, this would be folly with the larger starfish and only very large limpets attempt retaliation against them. This shows that even simple invertebrates are capable of unexpectedly refined responses to their predators.

The escape response of *Oxystele variegata* has a sequel. Early in this chapter we discussed the size gradients of this winkle; small animals lose water fast and so are confined to the low-shore, while larger specimens migrate up the shore. The question left unanswered was what benefit this migration is to the larger winkles. Experiments were undertaken in which large animals were caged on the high-shore and low-shore, and the results revealed that the winkles gained mass more rapidly if caged low on the shore, so it would seem that there is more food there and, in

Fig. 51 Various shells, showing devices such as spines, shortened spires, thick lips or narrow mouths, evolved to resist attack from predators. One shell (top centre) lacks all these features.

this sense, upward migration is a disadvantage. On the other hand, when these winkles were tethered to the rock with light nylon lines (allowing them to move around and feed but confining them to a particular zone), many more of the large animals were eaten by predators on the low-shore than on the high-shore. These winkles therefore seem to be trading off the disadvantages of food shortage in the high-shore against the benefits of lower predation and it seems that once they are large enough to tolerate the physical conditions in the harsher high-shore, it pays them to migrate upwards to avoid predation.

As a final line of defence against predators, animals may develop protective structures such as the hard, spiny, exoskeleton of rock lobsters and the spines of sea urchins. The shells of molluscs have a similar function. These defensive features cost the animal something in terms of the materials and energy put into this structure, and it must also expend some energy carrying the heavy shell around. Consequently, the shell must be strong enough to fulfil its function while involving the smallest amount of material possible. The structure of shells can influence their effectiveness in resisting predators. Two common mollusc predators are fish that crush the shells, and crabs that either crush the spire or cut their way into the shell from the mouth using their pincers. If the shell is tightly coiled, each coil reinforces the previous one and the vulnerable spire is shortened in the process. The cone shells have done just this, and the cowries carry this adaptation to extremes, sinking the spire right into the middle of the shell.

Shell shape often makes it difficult for a predator to get a grip. Try picking up a smooth-shelled cowrie with a pair of narrow pincers! The top-shaped *Calliostoma* shell (Plate 115n) is difficult to grip as well. Spines and knobs increase the size of the shell and strengthen it without the addition of a great deal of material. One gastropod, *Xenophora,* achieves this same effect by gathering shells of dead snails and cementing them on to its own shell as projecting 'spines'. The specimen shown in Fig. 52 was collected off Durban and had even incorporated clinker coke into its shell; testimony to what lies on the sea bed off Durban!

Because crabs often start cutting their way into the shells at the mouth, the lip is frequently strengthened with a ridge or the mouth is narrowed to a slit and often armed with projecting teeth. Many molluscs in addition block off the open mouth of the shell with a hard door-like operculum.

Predation seems to be much more intense in the tropics and it is significant that the incidence of all these antipredator adaptations of shell shape similarly increases in the tropics. Typical tropical examples are the cones, cowries, *Murex,* and the spider shells (Fig. 51). Thus where the need is greatest, adaptations are most frequently found. In Britain, one particular whelk, *Nucella,* has a thick heavily ridged shell in calm waters where attack from crabs is a problem but a thin, smooth shell in areas where waves exclude crabs. On our own shores *Nucella cingulata* reveals a similar range of shell structure (Plate 116), possibly for similar reasons, although no investigation has yet been made of this species. *Murex tribulus,* a Red Sea species, is well known for its formidable array of sharp spines which must surely deter many predators. With the cutting of the Suez Canal this species invaded the area which now forms the Bitter Lakes. Here it has no predators and it is of great interest that its spines are accordingly much reduced. With the lifting of the evolutionary cause for the spines, the animal no longer needed to waste energy on constructing an elaborate defensive shell.

Sheer size may deter predators as well. For instance, *Natica* drills holes through the shells of the black mussel *Choromytilus* and other bivalves in order to feed on them. The larger the mussel, the greater the reward for the predator, but the longer it must take to drill through the shell. It is almost as if the *Natica* do their own cost-benefit analysis, for when they are small they confine their activities to small mussels, not wasting time on large ones which have shells too thick for them to drill through. Large *Natica,* on the other hand, tend to ignore the small mussels and attack larger animals that give a greater return of food for the time invested in drilling.

Symbiosis: Back-scratching

As a complete contrast to the predator-prey relationships, some species are mutually beneficial, sharing a symbiotic relationship. For example cleaner shrimps (Plate 64) perform a useful service to other animals, including fish, cleaning their surfaces, removing dead scales and parasites, and obtaining food for themselves in the process. Cleaner fish have a similar function, even swimming inside the gaping mouths of other fish for this purpose. Cleaner shrimps and fish are usually vividly coloured, making it easier for other fish to recognise them, and because of their useful function they are not preyed upon by their clients.

A more intimate relationship exists between corals and unicellular algae (Zooxanthellae) which occur within the coral's tissues. The algae use the nitrogenous waste-products of the coral and provide the coral with a waste removal service as well as aiding in the formation of the coral's calcium carbonate skeleton by removing and using the carbon dioxide produced by the coral. Details of the process are described in Chapter 9. The zoanthids so common on the east coast also contain Zooxanthellae. The giant clam *Tridacna* (Plate 89) concentrates Zooxanthellae in the folds of its mantle which projects from between the lips of the shell, and this is one of the reasons why this mantle is often so vividly coloured. If it were not for the photosynthesis of these algae and the food they yield to the clam, it would be impossible for these clams to reach their enormous size.

Some nudibranchs have taken this process a step further; they feed on seaweeds but are capable of keeping the algal chloroplasts (the bodies responsible for photosynthesis) intact and storing them in their own bodies where they carry on photosynthesising to the benefit of the nudibranch.

Fig. 52 The gastropod, *Xenophora,* cements other shells onto its own shell.

The fight for food and space

Both food and space are often in short supply on rocky shores and plants and animals will frequently compete for these needs. This competition sometimes occurs between members of the same species (intraspecific competition) if their numbers increase beyond the point where the needs of all the individuals can be met. This point is usually defined as the carrying capacity of the environment. Such competition is very clearly shown in the limpet *Patella cochlear,* in which an increase in density results in a decrease in the average size of individuals, a decrease in growth and an increase in the death rate and, perhaps most importantly, a reduction in the number of eggs females produce (Fig. 53). All of these effects result from a shortage of food.

For barnacles and other sessile organisms, space is often in short supply, for there is a limited amount of rock to which they can attach. As a result barnacles often crowd one another, overgrow each other or pile one on top of another in an attempt to attach to a hard substratum. Experiments have shown that when crowded, barnacles divert more of their energy into growth and less into egg production, so that they are able to grow taller and reach above their companions when extending their filtering appendages into the water to feed. When they are isolated, the barnacles use most of their energy in reproduction, thus leaving more offspring and, in the absence of competition, having no particular need to grow tall. In a similar way mussels are often densely packed (Fig. 54) and with each year's settlement of juveniles, the young individuals may insinuate themselves between the adults to attach to the rocks, often loosening the adults in the process so that they are swept away by wave action.

Competition between plants often centres around the need to obtain sufficient light for photosynthesis, and sporelings are sometimes prevented from growing if they settle under adult plants where they are shaded.

Thus in various ways competition has adverse effects – decreasing growth, survival and reproductive ability – and

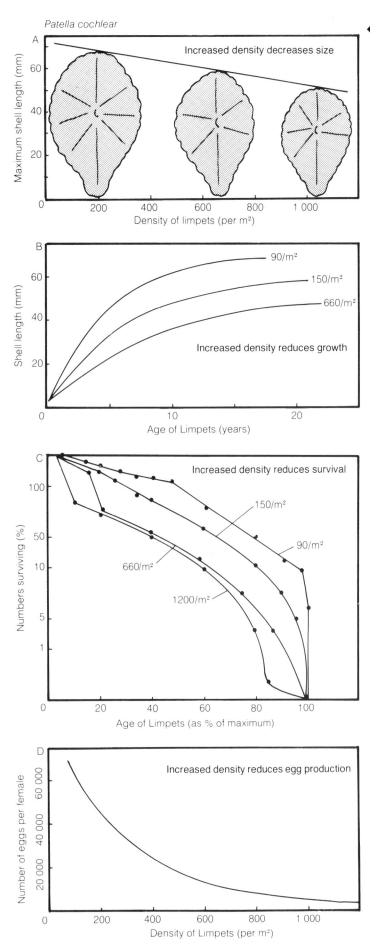

Patella cochlear

A — Increased density decreases size

Maximum shell length (mm) / Density of limpets (per m²)

B — Increased density reduces growth

90/m²
150/m²
660/m²

Shell length (mm) / Age of Limpets (years)

C — Increased density reduces survival

150/m²
90/m²
660/m²
1200/m²

Numbers surviving (%) / Age of Limpets (as % of maximum)

D — Increased density reduces egg production

Number of eggs per female / Density of Limpets (per m²)

Fig. 53 The limpet, *Patella cochlear,* often lives at a very high density: the higher the density, the greater the competition for food. These graphs show that increased density reduces the size of the limpet, its growth rate, survival, and the average number of eggs produced by each female.

it would obviously be beneficial if organisms could evolve ways of reducing competition between members of their own species.

One solution is for the adults and juveniles to live in different areas. An example is *Littorina africana,* discussed earlier in this chapter, in which juveniles occur higher on the shore (where wave action is least violent) but adults move down the shore to seek richer feeding-grounds and consequently avoid competing with the juveniles. Another possible case is the limpet *Patella granularis;* juveniles are limited to the lower portions of the shore because they are unable to tolerate the harsh conditions of the high shore but, as they age and toughen, they move steadily up the shore, separating adult and juvenile populations in the process.

Not all animals can simply keep moving to avoid competition. For instance once barnacle larvae have settled down and cemented themselves to the rockface their position is fixed for life. It is therefore important that the larvae do not choose to settle so close to one another that there is no room for subsequent growth. To this end, barnacle larvae perform a circular jig before finally attaching themselves, and only if they fail to encounter another barnacle or larvae during this jig will they cement themselves to the rock and metamorphose into the adult stage (Fig. 55). This ensures they have enough elbow room in which to grow. In the same way the limpet *Patella cochlear* spaces itself out forming a regular pattern on the rocks and keeping the maximum possible distance between neighbours (Fig. 22), thus ensuring enough room around each animal for it to feed. This same species has taken things a stage further by developing a unique 'multi-storey' arrangement with juveniles living on the shells of adults (Fig. 22) where they can feed on the algae that grow on the shell. In this way

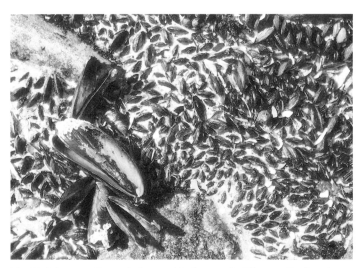

Fig. 54 A dense settlement of young black mussels *(Choromytilus)* ousts adults from the rock face.

animal upon animal can be stacked up – in one instance no less than 35 individuals were found living on top of one another! This reduces the problem of competition for space and food. The spatial arrangement and multi-storey stacking succeed only because *Patella cochlear* has a fixed home scar on the rock (or shell) to which it faithfully returns after feeding, so that the limpets do not wander randomly over the rocks but occupy a fixed spot. Juveniles living on shells also return to their own host's shell after each feeding excursion. When the juveniles become too large to live on a shell, they descend to the rock face and form their own scars there; but do not do so unless there is enough space available. If adults are removed from the rock experimentally, it takes a single high tide for the shell-dwelling juveniles to locate the vacated scars on the rock face and to occupy them. This shows that the juveniles do descend from their shells at high tide to explore the rock and to feed there, yet it is a mystery how they manage to arrange themselves in precisely the same sequence of stacking each time they return to their host shell.

In these ways careful spatial arrangement can minimise the competition between individuals. However, for *Patella cochlear* this is not sufficient, for it occurs at higher densities than any other limpet of its size anywhere in the world, reaching up to 2 600 individuals per square metre. This seemingly-intolerable high density is made possible by the unique relationship *P. cochlear* enjoys with a few species of tiny red algae, which form a narrow fringe around each limpet (Plate 98). *Patella cochlear* grazes away almost all other algae that settle in this zone, leaving only the tough white coralline *Lithophyllum* and the fringes of its 'gardens'. This explains why the Cochlear zone is so bare in comparison with the lush algal growth above and below it (Plate 163). If these limpets are removed, their gardens at first flourish because they are no longer being grazed, but after about six to eight weeks they disappear because they are outcompeted by other algae or grazed away by other animals. The gardens thus depend on *Patella cochlear* for their maintenance and in return supply it with its main food source. Rather like a mowed lawn, these algae actually grow faster when continually grazed by the limpets than when left ungrazed, and the feeding activity of the limpets in fact stimulates growth of the food plant. So high is the turnover of these tiny algae that they can produce as much food per square metre as the giant kelps. This is the secret that allows *Patella cochlear* to live so densely packed and still obtain enough food. We have never been able to solve the question of how *Patella cochlear* manages to remove all other algae from its zone while 'restraining' itself from eliminating the garden on which it feeds.

Another limpet, the long-spined *Patella longicosta* has an even more unorthodox and remarkable lifestyle. It too has gardens of a particular alga, *Ralfsia expansa* (Fig. 56), that supplies its main food. It tends these gardens by removing other algae that settle on them and by preventing larger algae from overshadowing them. *Patella longicosta* does not graze the *Ralfsia* indiscriminately but cuts regu-

Settling of barnacle larva

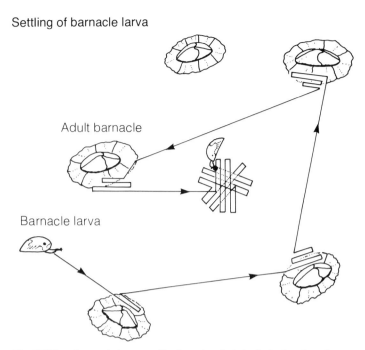

Adult barnacle

Barnacle larva

Fig. 55 When barnacle larvae settle, they do a jig to test whether there is enough space around them before cementing themselves to the rock.

lar paths across it (Fig. 56). Because *Ralfsia* grows from its edge, the paths create a series of growing edges, thus increasing the growth rate of the plant. Even more astonishing is the fact that *P. longicosta* actively defends its *Ralfsia* patch against other limpets and herbivores such as the small perlemoen (*Haliotis spadicea*). It has a home-scar situated on the *Ralfsia* and seldom ventures beyond the patch; but if an intruder tries to feed there, the *Patella longicosta* digs its long spines under the other limpet's shell and pushes violently until the intruder retreats (Plates 100-102). We are used to territoriality in higher animals, but to discover it in the lowly limpet is exciting. Since this discovery other limpets have been found to be territorial. The giant *Patella tabularis* (which reaches a length of 160 mm) displays a very similar territoriality, and the kelp-dwelling *P. compressa* defends the kelp stipe it lives on against others of the same species.

In the case of *Patella longicosta*, territorial responses ensure that the territory owner has enough food. They also result in an unusual life-cycle in the case of this limpet. Juveniles are found almost exclusively living on other shells, eating the *Ralfsia* that grows on them, and are commonly attached to *Oxystele* (Fig. 56). When the juveniles grow too large, they move from these shells to establish scars on the rock face. At first they have no garden and live by eating the hard, encrusting coralline *Lithophyllum* (Fig. 56) which has a low food value. During this period the limpets lose mass and are unable to reproduce. Only later, once they possess 'gardens' of their own, do they grow faster and reproduce. The manner in which they attain gardens is not known but if a territory owner is experimentally removed, its territory is very rapidly occupied by one of the smaller individuals which lacks a

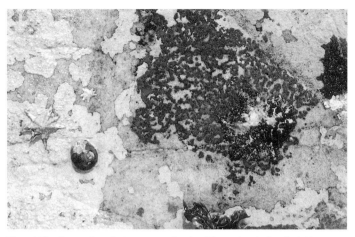

Fig. 56 The limpet *Patella longicosta* begins life on the shells of winkles (lower left), then moves onto a white encrusting alga as it grows larger (extreme left), and finally establishes a territorial 'garden' of the alga *Ralfsia*, through which it grazes irregular paths (right).

garden, so perhaps gardens are acquired literally by stepping into dead limpets' footprints.

All these adaptations – migration, spatial arrangement, differences between adult and juvenile needs, and territoriality – help reduce intra-specific competition.

Competition between species

Competition for food and space occurs between different species as well and is quite clearly illustrated in some interactions between seaweeds. For example, *Porphyra* and *Ulva* are usually found in the high-shore and mid-shore respectively, yet if dense low-shore algal mats are experimentally cleared away, both species colonise these cleared sites. It therefore follows that they are not normally found low on the shore simply because they are out-competed by other species. Encrusting forms, being flat and low-growing, have a particular problem in that other organisms tend to grow on or over them. In answer to this, *Ralfsia* produces antibiotics that deter most organisms from settling on it.

Different barnacle species often compete for space. The larger, faster growing species usually smother or bulldoze their smaller counterparts off the rocks. This may limit some species to certain zones on the shore.

For instance *Chthamalus* species, almost worldwide, occupy the highest parts of the shore, and at least in certain areas this is because there are more efficient competitors lower down.

We should not think that competition is confined to similar kinds of animals: mussels sometimes prevent barnacles from attaching on the rock face, although one common barnacle *Balanus algicola* retaliates by settling densely on the mussel shells and may even have an adverse effect on their growth (Plate 27). Whilst grazing, limpets inadvertently eat newly settled barnacles and hence keep down barnacle densities, but the adult barnacles in turn make it difficult for limpets to feed, and slow their growth.

Most limpets, winkles and other grazers compete for food on a first come, first served basis that has been descriptively called 'scrabble competition'. This sort of competition is rather inefficient for if there is not enough food to go around, much may be wasted on animals which will eventually perish from starvation. A more efficient method is 'interference' competition. An example of this is territoriality in limpets, where the food source is not simply eaten as soon as possible, but the territory holder denies other grazers access to the food by interfering with them. Thus food is not wasted. Another case of interference occurs between two completely different types of animals: the limpet *Cellana* and the small starfish *Patiriella exigua*. Both feed on diatoms and algal sporelings and compete for food but, in addition, *Cellana* will roll out its mantle and release a mucus whenever it touches a starfish and the starfish responds by moving quickly away. At times the starfish even appears partly paralysed after the contact (Fig. 57).

When closely related species live together, competition for food is likely. In some cases the species seem to have solved this problem by evolving more specialised diets and thus avoiding a clash of dietary interests.

The cone shells are a famous example of this. In areas where many different species co-exist some feed on particular types of worms, some on gastropods and yet others feed only on fish.

A similar situation occurs among South African limpets. More species of limpet seems to be packed into the southern tip of Africa than almost anywhere else in the world: one marine biologist described the southern African coast as the cradle of limpet evolution. Again, the existence of all these closely related species is associated with specialised diets in some of the limpets, including the territorial species which defend particular algae, and *Patella compressa* which lives only on kelp plants. One species, the tall-domed *Patella argenvillei*, has developed a most unusual way of feeding: it holds its shell away from the rock face and slams it down on to any large algal fragments washed beneath the shell. This limpet futhermore has a tooth-like edge to its shell to help it grip debris. This method of feeding allows *P. argenvillei* to eat material that is not accessible to any other limpets, and is probably the reason why this limpet can live in the same zone as *Patella cochlear* on the west coast.

If specialisation of diet is a solution to competition, we might expect species to be more specialised when there are more closely-related species living together. The southern African coast provides an ideal testing ground for this idea, for although there are 11 *Patella* species at Cape Point, this number declines to two in Angola and only one in Moçambique. We do indeed find that as the number of *Patella* species increases towards Cape Point, more and more of the species become extremely specialised in their diets.

CONTROLLING FACTORS: ZONATION REVISITED

At the beginning of this chapter zonation was described as a striking feature of rocky shores, but we are still left with a question as to what actually controls the zonation of animals and plants. For years biologists accepted that the increase in physical stress as one moves up the shore sets limits on how high particular organisms can live on the shore. High-shore species are more tolerant of stress and this was accepted as the reason they were able to live higher up the shore. In some cases this is certainly true. For example, water-loss, heat and even light intensity may prevent some algae from living higher on the shore. However, if physical conditions prevent organisms from spreading higher up the shore, we would expect these organisms to be killed periodically by physical stress. In reality this happens but occasionally, and nearly always such deaths are confined to the high-shore. Most species seem to live well within the range of conditions they can tolerate. This has led an American marine biologist, Walcott, to suggest that stress only limits the high-shore fauna and flora. His reasoning is that high-shore animals have no competitors higher up on the shore, so that they border on an unexploited source of food. It will thus pay them to extend as high up the shore as possible to use this food source even if they risk death from physical stress. Lower on the shore, conditions are different. Here each species will have competitors higher up the shore, already using the food there and also better adapted to the harsher conditions. There is thus no advantage for these species to take risks in trying to occupy higher zones already being used by other species, and instead they occupy a narrow band on the shore well within their tolerances to physical conditions.

For these mid and low-shore species, biological interactions seem to be more important in determining where they are able to live. Several examples have been given in this chapter: some algae are prevented from living in certain parts of the shore by superior competitors; barnacles can similarly be limited by competition with other barnacles; grazing limpets and winkles may prevent growth of algae; filter-feeding animals can similarly stop algal spores from settling; and predators such as starfish can determine where mussels are able to live. Thus we realise that for most species it is the presence or absence of other organisms that actually determines what can live where, and not the ability of particular species to tolerate physical stress.

This is an important fact, for it means that when we interfere with one species, we often affect others. It leads on to another vital question: why does no one species take over the environment completely? One school of thought is that certain predators are 'key-stone species' which, by eating organisms that could dominate the habitat, prevent them from ever monopolising the area. This has been proved in America and in New Zealand where Robert Paine, in an experiment, removed large starfish from stretches of the shore and observed that mussels subsequently extended their zonation and lived further down the shore than normal, and more importantly, that they then dominated the shore to such an extent that few other organisms could live there. Very likely our own starfish, *Marthasterias glacialis*, similarly controls mussel popula-

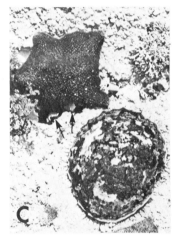

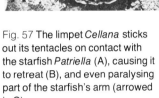

Fig. 57 The limpet *Cellana* sticks out its tentacles on contact with the starfish *Patriella* (A), causing it to retreat (B), and even paralysing part of the starfish's arm (arrowed in C).

tions and the crayfish *Jasus lalandii* has a strong effect on mussels as well (see Chapter 4). The small gastropod *Nucella dubia* which drills holes into its prey also sets limits on how low on the shore the barnacle *Chthamalus* can safely live.

Thus it is certainly true in some cases that predators prevent one species from monopolising a habitat; and red-bait (*Pyura*), some algae, mussels and barnacles have all been shown to be controlled in this sort of way by predators. On the other hand there is also evidence that limpets and winkles compete and influence where other species live. Filter-feeders are able to dictate where algae develop, and grazers are known to influence algal settling and growth. There are other biological interactions of this sort that cast doubt on whether predators are always so important in preventing one species from excluding others.

The answer to this doubt may lie in examining the nature of the species influencing one another. All those that are known to be regulated by predators are sessile species such as barnacles, mussels, red-bait and algae, which are fixed permanently to the rock face and compete for space in which to live; those not limited by predators are all mobile animals such as limpets, winkles and starfish that compete for food and not space.

These two groups therefore compete for different things:

in the first case for space and in the second for food. Once space is occupied it is not available to other organisms until the occupant is removed; but food on the other hand is renewable. Furthermore the sessile space-occupiers cannot escape from predators and if eaten they can only be replaced by a new settling of larvae, while mobile species can escape and can easily re-invade an area even if they are temporarily eliminated by a predator. Thus sessile species are much more likely to monopolise the space for which they compete and are also more vulnerable to predators, so we can understand why predators may be essential in keeping down their numbers. Mobile species, competing for food, pose less of a threat to other competitors since the food they use is renewable, and predators play a smaller rôle in regulating their numbers.

This chapter has focused on the ways in which animals and plants survive the harsh physical conditions of rocky intertidal shores, and their adaptations to one another. As we have seen, biological interactions are usually much more important than physical conditions in determining where each species can live, and have resulted in some most remarkable adaptations.

REFERENCES
Popular articles and books
Branch, G. M. 1981. On the rocks. *African Wildlife.* Vol. 35 (2): 24-27.

Carefoot, T. 1977. *Pacific Seashores: A Guide to Intertidal Ecology.* J. J. Douglas, Vancouver. 208 pp.

Tietz, R. M. & Robinson, G. A. 1974. *Tsitsikama Shore: Tsitsikamakus.* National Parks Board, Pretoria. 115 pp.

Scientific references
Branch, G. M. 1975. Intraspecific competition in *Patella cochlear* Born, *Journal of Animal Ecology,* Vol. 44: 263-282.

Branch, G. M. 1975. Mechanisms reducing competition in limpets: migration, differentiation and territorial behaviour. *Journal of Animal Ecology,* Vol. 44: 575-600.

Branch, G. M. 1975. Ecology of *Patella* species from the Cape Peninsula, South Africa: IV. Desiccation. *Marine Biology,* Vol. 32: 179-188.

Branch, G. M. 1975. The ecology of *Patella* from the Cape Peninsula, South Africa: V. Commensalism. *Zoologica Africana,* Vol. 10 (2): 133-162.

Branch, G. M. 1976. Interspecific competition experienced by South African *Patella* species. Journal of Animal Ecology, Vol. 45: 507-529.

Branch, G. M. 1979. Aggression by limpets against invertebrate predators. *Animal Behaviour,* Vol. 27: 408-410.

Branch, G. M. 1981. The biology of limpets: physical factors, energy flow and ecological interactions. *Annual Review of Oceanography and Marine Biology,* Vol. 19: 235-380.

Branch, G. M. & Branch, M. L. 1980. Competition between *Cellana tramoserica* (Sowerby) (Gastropoda) and *Patiriella exigua* (Lamarck) (Asteroidea) and their influence on algal standing stocks. *Journal of experimental marine Biology and Ecology,* Vol. 48: 35-49.

Branch, G. M. & Marsh, A. C. 1978. Tenacity and shell shape in six *Patella* species; adaptive features. *Journal of experimental marine Biology and Ecology,* Vol. 34: 111-130.

Broekhuysen, G. J. 1940. A preliminary investigation of the importance of desiccation, temperature and salinity as factors controlling the vertical distribution of certain intertidal marine gastropods in False Bay, South Africa. *Transactions of the Royal Society of S. Afr.,* Vol. 28: 245-292.

Day, J. A. 1969. Feeding of the cymatiid gastropod *Argobuccinum argus,* in relation to the structure of the proboscis and secretions of the proboscis gland. *American Zoologist,* Vol. 9: 909-916.

Griffiths, R. J. 1981. Predation on the bivalve *Choromytilus meridionalis* by the gastropod *Natica (Tectonatica) tecta* Anton. *Journal of Molluscan studies,* (in press).

McQuaid, C. D. 1981. Population dynamics of *Littorina africana knysnaensis* (Phillipi) on an exposed rocky shore. *Journal of experimental marine Biology and Ecology,* Vol. 54: (in press).

McQuaid, C. D. 1981. The establishment and maintenance of vertical size gradients in populations of *Littorina africana knysnaensis* (Phillipi) on an exposed rocky shore. *Journal of experimental marine Biology and Ecology,* Vol. 54: (in press).

Newell, R. C. 1979. *Biology of Intertidal Animals.* Marine Ecological Surveys, Kent. 781 pp.

Stephenson, T. A. & Stephenson, A. 1972. *Life Between Tidemarks on Rocky Shores.* W. H. Freeman & Co., San Francisco. pp. 97-162.

Wolcott, T. G. 1973. Physiological ecology and intertidal zonation in limpets *(Acmaea):* a critical look at "limiting factors". *Biological Bulletin, Woods Hole,* Vol. 145: 389-422.

3.SANDY BEACHES

The first impression of sandy beaches is that they are barren and support little life. It is true that relatively few species occur here, but the main reason for this impression is that most of the animals are buried in the sand, only becoming active at night or when the sand is covered by water. Though few in number, the species are of great interest for they have unique adaptations that allow them to occupy what is essentially a harsh environment.

Sandy beaches are a complete contrast to rocky shores in two important respects: firstly, they have no hard substratum onto which animals and plants can attach, so that there are no plants growing between the tide marks. The result is that all plant material must be imported into this system to maintain the food web. Secondly, sandy beaches are unstable; strong waves may scour whole beaches away in a few hours, while at other times gentler waves deposit and build up the beach. The sand is thus continually being worked by the waves, lifted and deposited, shifted away and replaced.

PHYSICAL CONDITIONS

Wave action is the key factor influencing sandy beaches. Strong waves tend to erode away the sand, leaving a narrow beach with a steep face (Fig. 58). Often seasonal storms will cut away the beach while calmer conditions allow sand to be deposited again, forming a wider, more gently-sloping beach. Waves have more subtle effects as well. Strong wave action drives fine particles to the top of the shore leaving a coarse sand at the lower levels on exposed beaches, while on calmer beaches the sand grains are much finer. This has further repercussions. Coarse sand cannot hold water, which drains rapidly through it. In addition, the large spaces between coarse sand grains prevent water from being sucked upwards from the underlying water table because the sand has only a weak capillary action. In contrast, fine sands prevent drainage and also draw water upwards by capillary action so that they are usually water-laden while coarse sands dry out quickly during low tide. The result is that animals living in coarse sands risk desiccation. On the other hand coarse sand is well-drained and the water in it never becomes stagnant, since there is plenty of air between the grains and water flushes swiftly through the sand, bringing oxygen to the animals living there. As oxygen is used up by animals and bacteria, fine sands can easily suffer from stagnation and it is quite common to find a black, smelly sediment underneath the surface layers. Often this smells of hydrogen sulphide because bacteria in these lower, oxygen-deprived layers use sulphur as a substitute, and hydrogen sulphide (H_2S) is produced as an end product of metabolic reactions.

Thus we can see the ripple of effects that wave action has, from its gross effect on the size and shape of the beach, through its effects on the size of sand grains, to its influence on the water and oxygen content of the sand (Fig. 59). If a beach is steep and has coarse sand, it is usually unstable and wave beaten (and often dangerous for bathing), so it is not surprising that on steeper, coarser beaches, fewer species can tolerate the conditions and both the number of species and the number of individuals are reduced.

To visualise the stresses of living on a sandy beach in human terms, imagine yourself scaled down to the size of a 2 cm snail; the waves would then appear to be the size of Table Mountain, each wave tumbling and churning the top 5 m of sand, hurling sand grains the size of boulders and capable of obliterating a width of 5 km of coastline in one storm.

Sandy beaches do, however, have one important compensation: unlike rocky shores, animals can burrow into the sand and move up and down through the sand layers, thus escaping many of the problems associated with this

Fig. 58 Strong wave action cuts steep beaches in Natal.

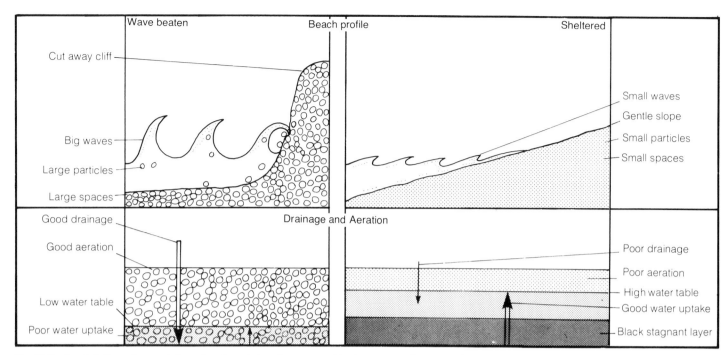

Fig. 59 **Contrasts in the nature and character of sandy beaches exposed to strong or gentle wave action.**

Fig. 60 **Sandy beaches act like giant filters as waves percolate through the sand.**

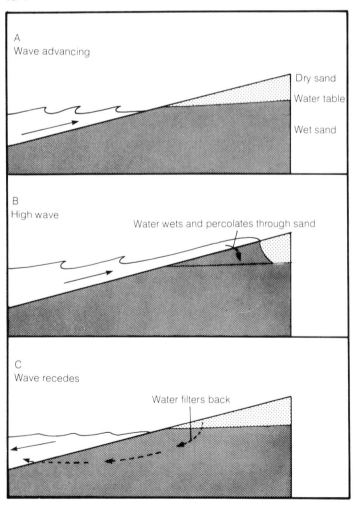

Fig. 61 **Richly-organic spume lies glistening in the sun.**

habitat. If the sand is too dry, it is possible to dig down to the water-table. If the surface is too hot, the animals can escape to cooler, deeper sand. If oxygen levels fall too low, an upward migration is possible. Thus sandy beaches have a third dimension that is largely lacking on rocky shores, and animals are able to choose at what depth in the sand they should live.

FOOD SOURCES

Because no attached plants grow intertidally on sandy beaches, and because even microscopic plants such as diatoms occur only in small numbers, there are no grazing herbivores on sandy beaches. All the animals must depend on plant material and other food being brought into the shore. Some is blown in from the land, but most of it is introduced by the sea. Sometimes vast quantities of algae

SANDY SHORE ANIMALS

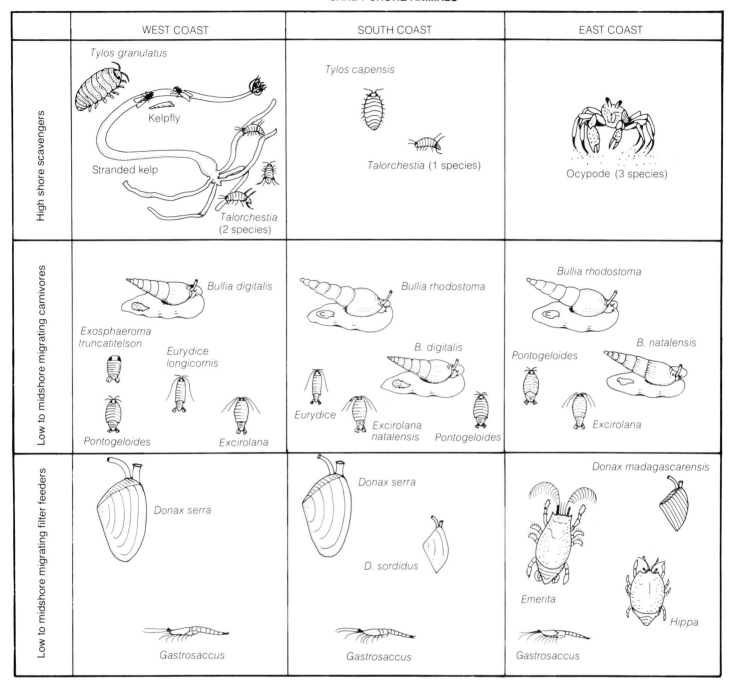

Fig. 62 Common sandy-shore animals of the west, south and east coasts.

and animals are washed up after storms (Fig. 88), and this debris is the major food source for scavengers. The supply of such food is unpredictable and there may be long periods of starvation between times of glut.

A more reliable source of food is the mass of small organic particles suspended in the water. As waves rush up the shore and then recede, the water is filtered through the sand (Fig. 60), leaving behind a scum of particles. At times the surface of the water is whipped up into a froth of organic matter, rich in bacteria, and this spume is left stranded as a thick layer on the beach where it forms an important source of food. As the water percolates down through the sand, so bacteria attack the organic particles,

using them as a food source and in the process breaking them down to simpler compounds. Among these products are nutrients such as nitrates and phosphates which are then returned to the sea as the water seeps out of the beach, and can then be used by plants and phytoplankton. The process of bacterial decomposition is aided by the continual flow of water through the sand, which not only delivers organic material but also keeps the oxygen levels high. The bacteria thus function aerobically (using oxygen), making the decomposition process faster and more efficient.

In this way, sandy beaches filter and purify large volumes of water, and they have been referred to as 'great

Fig. 63(A) *Bullia natalensis* emerging from the sand, siphon erect. (B) *Bullia digitalis* surfs ashore, foot extended like a sail. (C) *Bullia* crawls upshore to feast on a stranded sea-snake.

digestive and incubating systems'. The process is so efficient that one flush through the sand is enough to break down about 95 percent of the organic matter present. Partly as a result of this, sandy beaches contain in themselves very low levels of organic matter – about 0,05 percent – which is far too little to make it worthwhile for animals to try and eat the sand to extract any food, as they may do in other habitats where the organic content is higher.

The filtering and purifying action of beaches is essentially the same process used in sewage treatment. In terms of the ecology of sandy beaches it is important in a number of ways. Firstly, animals may make use of the organic particles, either by filtering them from the water or by scooping them off the surface of the sand before they filter down and are decomposed. The white mussel *Donax serra* and the sea louse *Emerita* are two such particle feeders. Secondly, bacterial populations develop in the sands; they, too, form a food source for animals. Finally, the nutrients that are released can increase the growth of phytoplankton in the surf zone. Usually phytoplankton is not as important as the particulate organic matter. However, where rip-currents set up pockets of water that recirculate in the surf zone (see Chapter 1 and Fig. 12B), phytoplankton may 'bloom', becoming dense enough to discolour this zone. These are the conditions under which the white mussel thrives, filtering the phytoplankton out of the water and consuming it.

ADAPTATIONS OF SANDY BEACH ANIMALS

The problems facing animals on sandy beaches are twofold: the continual beating surge of waves on the shore and the reliance on food that must be introduced to the shore from elsewhere. Animals have overcome the first problem in two ways. Most of the low and mid-shore species can burrow into the sand to reduce the effects of wave action, although some are strong swimmers and emerge into the water column for at least part of the tidal cycle. At the top of the shore lives a different group of animals with a different solution: they have become air-breathing and only emerge from the sand at low tide when there is no danger from the waves. These two groups also tend to feed in different ways. Many of the low-shore species are particle feeders relying on the small organic particles in the water, while all of the high-shore animals are scavengers feeding on cast-up debris.

Aquatic scavengers

One of the most interesting and familiar sandy beach animals is the plough snail *Bullia* (Fig. 63), an animal inextricably linked with Professor Alec Brown, who has done so much research on it. Several species occur around the South African coast, *Bullia digitalis* being commonest on the west coast, *B. rhodostoma* on the south coast and *B. natalensis* on Natal beaches. All three have similar habits. *Bullia* scavenges on dead or dying animals washed up on the beach (Fig. 63C). Rotten red-bait *(Pyura)* is a favourite food but *Bullia* will, with equal impartiality, eat almost

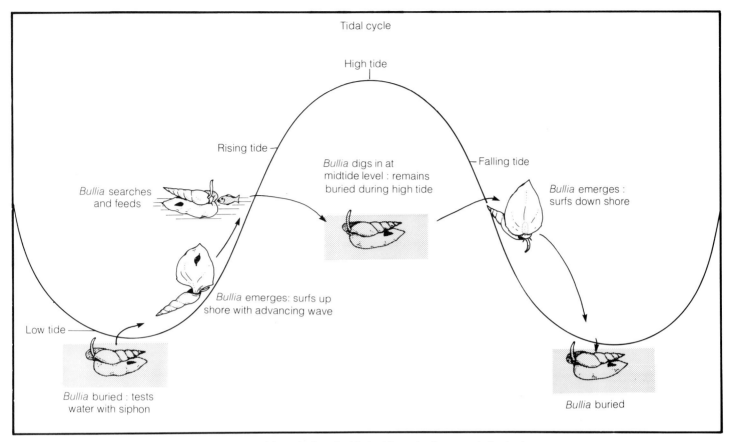

Fig. 64 The plough snail, *Bullia digitalis,* migrates up and down the beach with the tides to feed on stranded animals.

any animal matter, including jellyfish, bluebottles, rotten fish or mussels. This catholic taste in food makes sense when we remember that *Bullia* relies on the chance of something being washed up and cannot afford to be fussy.

Bullia digitalis spends most of its time under the sand, remaining almost completely buried except for the tip of its tubular siphon which it extends to sample the water. As the tide begins to rise, *Bullia* emerges from the sand, particularly if there is any food available, turns on its back and spreads its huge flat foot which acts like an underwater sail. The waves quickly lift the animals so that it surfs up the beach (Fig. 63B). It is no coincidence that the *Bullia* are deposited in the same areas as the waves drop their food. In this way, rather than finding wave action a problem, *Bullia* actually uses the waves as a quick form of transport to its food. Obviously *Bullia* is at the mercy of the waves when it is being washed up or down the shore, and long-shore currents or rip currents could then wash it along the beach or even out to sea. It is thus interesting to find that *Bullia* is absent from beaches where these dangerous currents exist and its presence indicates that swimming is safe.

Once *Bullia* is deposited on the beach it crawls across the sand seeking food. This search is not random: the snails are remarkably sensitive to the presence of food and crawl rapidly and directly towards it, possibly recognising its position from chemicals released by the food. After finding a meal, *Bullia* thrusts out its long proboscis and sucks up any tissue soft enough to be handled. Up to one-third of the snail's mass can be consumed in a single meal. *Bullia* seems immune to the stinging cells of bluebottles and often feeds on the long trailing tentacles of these animals. After feeding, or if no food is located, *Bullia* buries itself again (Fig. 64).

Once the water rises above the mid-tide level, all of the *Bullia* remain inactive and refuse to come out of the sand. How they 'know' that they should not emerge after this point in the tidal cycle is a mystery, but it is clearly a sensible adaptation, for it ensures that the animals are never stranded in the harsh high-shore. When the tide drops again, *Bullia* becomes active and emerges once more, but as the tide is now falling the waves wash the snails down the beach to their original low-tide positions.

The responsiveness of *Bullia* to cast-up prey is astonishing. Dozens of the animals will emerge from the sand and converge on a single dead animal deposited on the beach. This sensitivity prompted research on the response of *Bullia* to various chemicals. One particular chemical, trimethylamine, attracts *Bullia* at concentrations as low as 0,00001 percent. This is particularly interesting, for most fish excrete trimethylamine oxide as a waste product, but once they die, this substance is rapidly broken down by bacteria to form trimethylamine. Thus the amazing sensitivity of *Bullia* to this break-down product allows detection and location of dead fish that are washed up. Equally interesting is the fact that another chemical, buterobetaine, acts as a strong repellent to *Bullia,* causing it to dig deeper into the sand. This too has value, for live sharks and rays contain high levels of betaines, and as these elasmobranchs are major predators of *Bullia*, avoidance of these chemicals is a safety precaution.

A time budget has been drawn up for *Bullia digitalis*, showing how much time it spends on various activities such as burrowing, surfing in the water, crawling or simply remaining buried. The findings reveal that 94 percent of its time is spent passively buried under the sand. The amount of energy the snail must use for each of these activities has also been measured. It 'costs' twice as much energy to surf, crawl or burrow as it does to remain buried. Thus by remaining buried for most of the time, the snails save energy, which effectively makes their food reserves last longer. By sitting quietly and only emerging when it detects food or when it is starving, *Bullia* can make one meal sustain it for about 14 days.

Living in a environment where food is unpredictable, the ability to save energy may be very important, and the lifestyle of *Bullia* is adapted in other ways as well to cope with this problem. The rate at which most animals respire (and use up oxygen in chemical reactions) increases as temperature rises. Now, although respiration is a vital process, it also results in a loss of energy, for heat is lost during the chemical reactions that occur with metabolism. *Bullia* has overcome this problem by not increasing its oxygen consumption as temperature rises. This may be an important way of saving energy, for while the *Bullia* crawl around on the beach they are heated by the sun. *Bullia* also grows very slowly: a large animal may be as much as 20 years old. This too may be an adaptation to unpredictable periods of food shortage.

Bullia has an unusually large foot (Fig. 63B) necessary

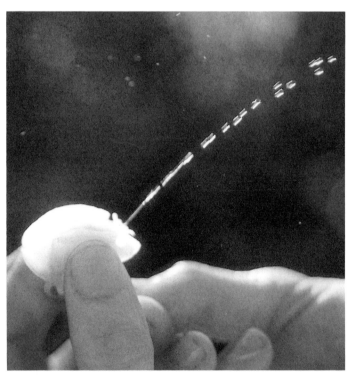

Fig. 65 When picked up, *Bullia* squirts a jet of water from its foot.

for its rapid crawling and its surfing in the waves. The foot seems far too large for the animal ever to withdraw it into the shell, yet it can do so when threatened. The secret lies in the fact that the shell is partly filled with sea-water which is expelled as the foot pulls back. The animal puts this ability to expel the water to good use. When it withdraws into its shell, the foot curls downwards, forming a groove along each side. As the water is squirted from the shell it is directed by these grooves and forms a strong jet that is squirted up to 30 cm (Fig. 65), presumably to scare any predator, including humans who have picked up the snail. Water is also ejected from the shell to 'soften' the sand during burrowing.

An interesting comparison has been made between *Bullia digitalis* and *B. laevissima*. *Bullia digitalis* occurs on wave-beaten beaches and responds to water movement by emerging and surfing up the shore.

It is able to feed out of water on washed-up animals. Its low body-mass (with a specific gravity of only 1,1) allows it to be carried easily by the waves. It is also fairly tolerant of water-loss and high temperatures: conditions it may experience while feeding. *Bullia laevissima* is adapted to a sub-tidal life and occurs in sheltered areas and its response to turbulent water is to dig into the sand. It has a heavy shell (giving the body a specific gravity of 1,8) which tends to prevent waves from washing it around. Since it only feeds under water, it is limited to calm areas where the food is not washed around. As *B. laevissima* rarely emerges from water its tolerances to water-loss and high temperatures are much lower. Thus while *B. digitalis* turns the harsh conditions of wave action to its advantage, capitalising on the water movements, *B. laevissima* avoids water movement and has quite different adaptations and therefore behaves differently.

A similar comparison can be made between two small isopod crustaceans common on many beaches: *Eurydice longicornis* and *Exosphaeroma truncatitelson* (Fig. 251). *Eurydice* (and its relative *Excirolana natalensis*) occurs on beaches exposed to strong wave action and, like *Bullia digitalis*, it becomes active in the presence of currents, emerging from the sand to swim in the water. It too has a rhythm of activity and only swims when the tide is below the mid-tide level. Once the water rises higher than this, swimming ceases and the isopods burrow into the sand, thus avoiding the dangers of being cast up too high on the shore. In other parts of the world *Eurydice* has been extensively studied and shown to have tidal rhythms. It moults regularly once a fortnight about four days before the spring tides occur. Thus while the isopods are soft and helpless after moulting and most likely to be washed ashore, they can rely on the tides becoming higher and higher for the next four days, ensuring that they will never be stranded for very long.

Eurydice will eat any animal matter, fresh or decaying, but it is also an aggressive carnivore and will attack smaller animals. It is not unusual to find it swarming around and attacking cuts on bathers' legs.

Exosphaeroma truncatitelson prefers sheltered beaches

and reacts to currents by burrowing – which reminds us of *Bullia laevissima*. It has no rhythms of activity, simply following the tide level up and down the beach as the water rises and falls. Presumably in calmer areas the dangers of being stranded by waves are not so great. Like *Eurydice*, *Exosphaeroma* is a scavenger and a carnivore, but will eat plant particles as well.

Aquatic particle feeders

Many of the low-shore species on sandy beaches feed on small organic particles. Examples include the sand prawn *Callianassa* (See Chapter 5 for more details), the white mussels *Donax* (Fig. 66), the small shrimp-like *Gastrosaccus psammodytes* (Fig. 70) and, on the east coast, the sea lice *Hippa* and *Emerita*. *Callianassa* builds a tube in the sand in which it lives, circulating water through this passage and capturing organic particles in the process. Most of the remaining species undertake regular migrations up and down the beach each tidal cycle so that they remain in the surf zone. What does it cost these animals to migrate in this way? In three cases (*Bullia*, *Donax* and *Emerita*), it has been possible to measure or calculate the energy spent on migration and, in each case, it is a substantial proportion of the energy taken in as food. Two to three times as much energy is spent on migrating as on remaining buried. So why do they migrate? There are three possible advantages: firstly, the animals are never exposed to air for long and this cuts the risk of desiccation; secondly, there are few predators able to feed successfully in the raging surf; finally, the action of the waves stirs the sediment and keeps organic particles in suspension so that there is not only plenty of food but it is also continually renewed.

The small sand mussel, *Donax sordidus*, moves upshore with the advancing tide and then follows the tide downwards as it falls (Fig. 68). From work on other *Donax* species we know that they respond to the water content of the sand, digging into water-saturated sand in the zone where waves surge up the beach, and extending their long, paired siphons into the water above (Fig. 67). Through one of these siphons water is sucked up, and the suspended organic particles or phytoplankton can then be extracted and eaten. The water is expelled through the other siphon. The inhalent siphon needs to allow the entrance of small organic particles but not sand grains, and it is armed with a neat sieve of fleshy lobes that stretches across the entrance of the siphon and excludes sand (Plate 91). As the tide rises and the sand becomes liquefied, the *Donax* then thrust themselves out of the sand allowing the waves to wash them up the shore. There they very rapidly dig in again, maintaining position and feeding until the tide has risen further, when they repeat the process. As the tide drops, the sand begins to dry out and this is the signal for *Donax* to emerge and allow themselves to be carried downshore again by the waves.

All over the world *Donax* species migrate up and down beaches but the adults of the South African white mussel *Donax serra* seem an exception. Perhaps because they are so much larger than all other species they tend to occupy one fixed position on the shore. Their size may make them too heavy for waves to transport easily. Large *Donax serra* do, however, move to a limited extent, being found higher on the shore at spring tides than at neaps. Juveniles migrate up and down the shore and are commonly found higher on the shore than the adults, perhaps because they are more easily shifted by the waves and are deposited higher up where wave action is reduced.

Another animal that moves up and down the surge zone with the tide is the sea louse or mole crab, *Emerita*, which reacts almost exactly in the same way as *Donax sordidus*,

Fig. 66 The long inhalant and exhalant siphons of a white mussel.

Fig. 67 The white mussel, *Donax serra*, (40 mm) digs into the sand.

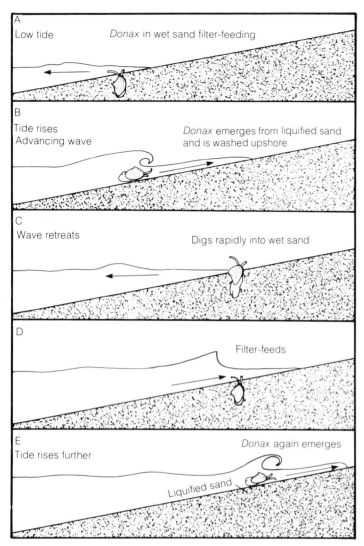

Fig. 68 The white mussel, *Donax,* migrates up the shore with the rising tide. It digs into the sand and filter-feeds (A) until the tide rises enough to liquefy the sand. It then emerges, (B), and is washed up by an advancing wave, digs in rapidly (C), and then resumes filter-feeding (D) until the tide rises high enough to liquefy the sand again (E).

the same time protects the developing eggs held beneath the tail by the female. The eyes are mounted on long thin stalks, allowing complete burial of the body while leaving the eyes free to peep out of the sand.

The most remarkable feature of the mole crab is the modification of the antennae, which are kept safely rolled up under the mouth-parts while the animal rolls up and down the beach, but when they are extended are almost as long as the body. They are equipped with long fringes of hairs, each hair also carrying a smaller fringe of tiny hairs, so that when magnified, the whole structure looks like a net. This of course is precisely its function: to net organic particles as they flow past in the waves (Fig. 69).

Another sea louse, *Hippa* (Fig. 268A), also lives on the east coast, and is easily recognised by its flatter body and short antennae.

There is one additional very common sandy beach ani-

burying itself in the sand until the tide liquefies the sand and then emerging to be washed to a higher level.

The whole structure of *Emerita* is beautifully adapted to the exacting life it leads in the waves (Fig. 69). The barrel-shaped body is ideal for an animal that is rolled up the beach by waves, and it is protected by a tough exoskeleton. The animal digs backwards into the sand, with the last two pairs of limbs excavating a hole and then using the remaining legs 'rows' itself into the hole. All of the legs are highly modified and as a result are totally unsuited to normal walking but, with their spade-like structure, are ideal for digging. The last pair of 'walking' legs is thin and flexible and seemingly useless for locomotion: these legs perform the unusual function of reaching right inside the gill chamber to clear away any sand particles that may slip in. The end of the body forms a long thin telson, bent backwards underneath the body, with a long fringe of hairs that prevents sand grains from entering the gill chamber and at

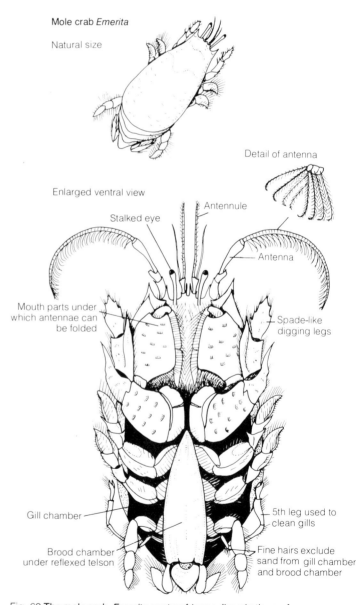

Fig. 69 The mole crab, *Emerita austroafricana,* lives in the surf zone. An enlarged ventral view shows how its body is adapted to allow it to dig quickly. The long feathery antennae are for filtering food from the water.

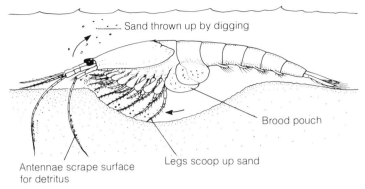

Fig. 70 *Gastrosaccus psammodytes,* a sandy-shore mysid shrimp (25 mm).

Labels on figure: Sand thrown up by digging; Brood pouch; Legs scoop up sand; Antennae scrape surface for detritus

Fig. 71 Stranded kelp is covered by wind-blown sand and is soon eaten by scavenging crustaceans.

mal, the shrimp-like mysid *Gastrosaccus psammodytes* (Fig. 70). Most mysids are planktonic with delicate bodies, and it is quite remarkable that *Gastrosaccus* remains equally frail and has not modified its body structure at all to face the rigours of living on sandy beaches. How it survives is something of a mystery, yet it is very successful. Its saving grace seems to be its versatility, for it can burrow or swim equally well, and always swims facing the current. Its feeding habits are also diverse, for it is able to filter particles out of the water, or swim along just above the sand and scoop up organic matter from the surface of the sand, or it can scavenge for larger, dead animals.

Thus almost all of the low-shore animals on sandy beaches seem to have rhythms of activity, migrating up and down the shore to keep up with the surge as the tide flows and ebbs.

Air-breathing scavengers

On the west coast vast quantities of kelp and other sea-weeds are often thrown up on to the beach (Fig. 71), accumulating near the high-tide mark. This is a rich food source for a number of animals living high on the shore where they have had to become almost terrestrial in their habits, being air-breathing and completing their life-cycles out of the water. By confining their activities to the low-tide period, they avoid the problem of wave action

altogether. However, their life-style increases the risk of death from desiccation and, almost without exception, these species are nocturnal, remaining buried in the sand by day and feeding by night.

The small white 'sand hopper' *Talorchestia capensis* is amongst the most abundant of sandy beach animals, although it takes a night-time visit to the beach to appreciate the vast numbers that crawl out of the sand to feed on kelp: up to 25 000 per m²!

Probably because of the problems of desiccation, juvenile *Talorchestia* are always found lower on the shore where sand is damp, while the adults abound above the high-tide mark (Fig. 72). Sand hoppers emerge from the sand at sunset, but only once the moon rises do they begin their spectacular migration along the beach, spreading down the shore in the process of searching for food. Once they locate a cast-up kelp in suitably decomposed condition they devour it in vast quantities (Plate 60), feeding until dawn when they return up-shore to bury themselves near the high-tide mark.

How the sand hoppers manage to orientate on the beach to locate their normal zone is the most fascinating part of their biology. If they are experimentally moved down-shore during the day they move directly up-shore to the correct zone. If they are shifted up-shore they are somehow aware of being too high on the shore and move directly downwards to their normal zone (Fig. 73A). In these day-time experiments the sand hoppers have been shown to use the position of the sun to orientate. This is not in itself very striking but, what is intriguing, is that the animals have a built-in biological clock which enables them to tell where the sun should be at any particular time of the day. To give an example, if the sun rises to the right of the beach (as one looks out to sea) a *Talorchestia* experimentally transplanted down the shore must 'know' to keep the sun on its left in order to be able to migrate upwards to its correct zone. However, as the day advances, the same animal will have to adjust to the changing position of the sun and in the afternoon, for instance, it will then need to keep the sun on

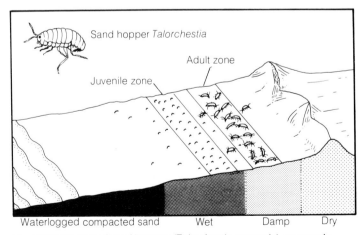

Fig. 72 Distribution of sand hoppers *(Talorchestia capensis)* on a sandy shore. The more vulnerable juveniles occur lower on the shore where the sand is wetter.

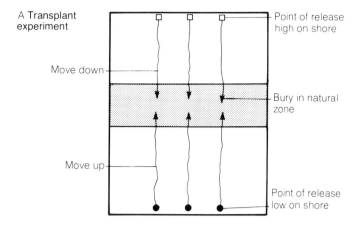

A Transplant experiment

Point of release high on shore

Move down

Bury in natural zone

Move up

Point of release low on shore

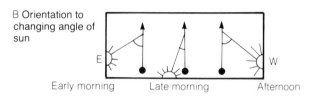

B Orientation to changing angle of sun

E   W

Early morning   Late morning   Afternoon

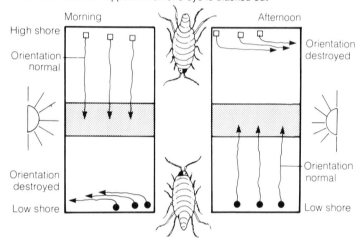

C Orientation of hoppers when one eye is blacked out

Morning   Afternoon

High shore

Orientation normal

Orientation destroyed

Orientation destroyed

Orientation normal

Low shore   Low shore

Fig. 73 The orientation of sand hoppers on a sandy beach. A. Animals transplanted up or down the shore can find their way back to their original zone. B. They do so by orienting to the sun and must thus allow for its changing position during the day. C. If the eye facing the sun is blacked out they are unable to orient normally.

its right to make the same migration back to the correct zone (Fig. 73B).

Its 'clock' must somehow keep pace with the sun's movement, even although the animals are buried for most of the day at a depth where they cannot even see the sun. At night they navigate in exactly the same way except that they use the moon as a reference point instead of the sun. If the hoppers are kept in pitch darkness in a laboratory, they still maintain their rhythm of emergence at night and burial during the day, showing this is a truly endogenous (internal) rhythm and not just a response to sunlight.

It is possible to confuse the poor animals completely by keeping them in darkness during the day and placing them in light at night. They soon adjust to this new rhythm,

emerging during the day instead of the night, but this throws out their internal clocks by 12 hours. If these animals are now taken back to the beach and released low on the shore they orientate in completely the wrong direction, taking the morning sun as an afternoon sun and setting off purposefully towards the sea instead of up-shore.

This shows clearly how the sun or moon are used to orientate, but the animals must also 'decide' whether they should migrate up-shore or down-shore to reach their correct zone. This decision is based on the moisture of the sand: if the sand is wet, the animals move up-shore, if it is too dry, they hop down-shore.

Even more interesting is the finding that on different beaches *Talorchestia* orientates differently to the sun. Animals at Kommetjie, on the west coast of the Cape Peninsula, experience the sun setting over the sea and must orientate accordingly. If they are taken from Kommetjie and released at Fish Hoek on the opposite side of the Peninsula (where the sun rises over the sea) they are disorientated and migrate in the wrong direction, interpreting the rising sun as a sunset and migrating into the sea instead of up-shore (Fig. 74).

Thus each population has a particular internal 'clock' geared to the beach on which the animals live. Even if the eggs are grown in constant conditions of continual darkness, when they hatch out the juveniles orientate in the same way as their parents, suggesting that the orientation may be inherited.

Research has been done on the energy budget of the *Talorchestia capensis* by David Muir of the University of Cape Town. Food that is consumed contains a certain amount of energy and this is used in various ways by the animal. Not all the energy taken in can be used: some is lost

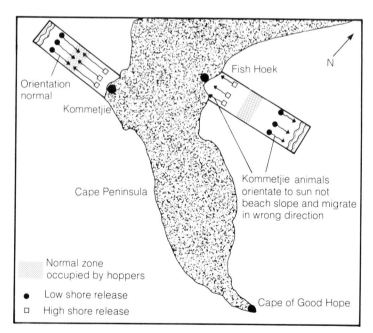

Orientation normal

Fish Hoek

N

Kommetjie

Kommetjie animals orientate to sun not beach slope and migrate in wrong direction

Cape Peninsula

Normal zone occupied by hoppers

● Low shore release

□ High shore release

Cape of Good Hope

Fig. 74 If sand hoppers are taken from Kommetjie (where they orient up and down the beach by using the sun) and are released at Fish Hoek, they continue to orient the same way and thus migrate in the wrong direction and never locate their normal zone on the beach.

in the faeces. Part of the absorbed energy is also spent on chemical reactions and therefore lost as heat. Because oxygen is normally used in these reactions, measurement of respiration allows us to estimate the amount of energy lost in this way: and it is usually a substantial fraction of the energy intake. Only about 10 percent of the energy is actually used for growth and reproduction, the two functions that matter most to the animal in terms of survival. However, in the process of converting energy from kelp to flesh, the sand hoppers also fulfil a vital function: each year they consume up to 315 kg of dry kelp per metre of beach and produce 151 kg of faeces. The importance of this is that they help recycle the kelp, breaking it down into a form more quickly acted on by bacteria, and also returning it to the sea to be used by particle feeders.

Talorchestia is also very important to some shore birds, being a major source of food for the sanderling. Thus the humble sand hopper plays a central rôle in the ecology of beaches. It is aided by the isopod *Ligia* (Plate 55) which has similar feeding habits, and to a lesser extent by the larvae of kelp flies (such as *Fucellia capensis*) which also eat kelp.

Kelp flies are of course terrestrial and, because the larvae spend their short lives on washed-up kelp, they run the risk of being flooded at high tide. For this reason the flies lay their eggs on kelp high on the shore just after the spring tide, and the development of the larvae takes 22 to 28 days, so that they pupate and the pupae hatch before the high spring tide a month later. This reduces the chances of flooding because the neap tides fail to reach as high as the spring tides. However, if the pupae are submerged, they float until washed up on to the drift-line where they can safely hatch.

Another kelp-eating animal is the giant isopod *Tylos,* of which there are two species: *T. granulatus* (Fig. 75) on the west coast and *T. capensis* on the south coast. Like all other high-shore species, *Tylos* is nocturnal, remaining buried all day. The advantage of this is that while the surface of the sand may heat up enormously during the day, at a depth of 20 to 30 cm, temperatures remain almost constant. Nocturnal activity may also reduce predation.

Tylos granulatus has three interrelated rhythms of activity: firstly, it only emerges at night, so that it has a daily (circadian) rhythm; and secondly it emerges only at the time of low tide so that it also has a tidal rhythm superimposed on the daily rhythm. Emergence during low tide ensures the animals are not swept away by the waves. There are of course two low tides each day but only one of these falls during the night. Since the night-time low tide occurs about 50 minutes later each day, the emergence of *Tylos* is delayed by this much as well and becomes later and later as the days pass. Eventually the low tide during which they have been feeding occurs in daylight and the animals must then 'switch back' to the early evening tide (Fig. 76). This pattern of emergence, delayed 50 minutes each day and switching back every 14 days, is faithfully maintained for up to 30 days in the laboratory under constant conditions, so the animals must maintain this rhythm on their own, independent of environmental conditions.

Fig. 75 The isopod *Tylos granulatus* (30 mm).

Tylos has, in addition, a third rhythm: great numbers of animals emerge during the neap tides and very few over the spring tide period. This may be to minimise the dangers of being washed away by the higher spring tides but it also relates to the animals' feeding habits. *Tylos* has a strong preference for eating kelp that has dried on the beach for about a week. Since most of the kelp is deposited high on the shore during spring tides, emergence during the neap tide a week later gives the kelp time to mature to a suitably soft consistency: vintage kelp!

Measurements have been made of the respiration rate of *Tylos granulatus* and even under constant conditions this too is rhythmic, being low during the day and during the high tide, but increasing nearly tenfold during the night-time low tide. Thus for most of the day the animals keep their respiration very low which will mean a considerable saving of energy.

While seeking food, *Tylos* moves over much of the beach and must crawl back to the high-tide mark to bury itself. To navigate the animals seem to use the slope of the beach and are able to detect slopes as small as one degree. If the sand is wet, they crawl up the slope, but if it is dry they move down it, thus locating the correct zone to bury in.

In the eastern Cape little material is deposited at the top of the beaches, mainly because there are no kelp beds in this region, and practically no high-shore scavengers occur here. This fact changes the whole arrangement of animals on the beaches for while on the west coast the highest number of individuals and the greatest number of species live very high along the drift line of the shore, on the eastern Cape beaches the pattern is reversed, and most animals are found low on the shore where physical conditions are not so harsh. On the Natal coast, too, it is true that little food is stranded high on the shore but here a single high-shore scavenger makes its appearance. The ghost crabs, *Ocypode,* are quite common on these shores and dig holes as much as a metre deep, reaching down to the water-table. There are three species of ghost crab, *Ocypode madagascariensis* (Plate 81) and *O. ryderi* (Fig. 77), being commonest on exposed sandy beaches, while *O. ceratophthalmus* (Plate 75) occupies more sheltered

A Activity rhythms of *Tylos*

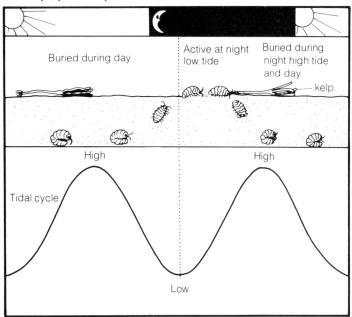

B Timing of activity rhythms of *Tylos*

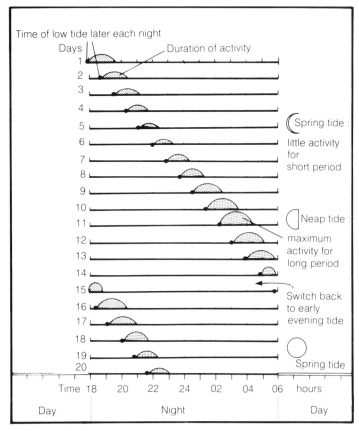

Fig. 76 A. The giant isopod *Tylos* has regular rhythms of activity, only being active during low tide at night. Fig. 76 B. As low tide becomes later each night, so does the period of activity. Activity is greatest at neap tides.

Fig. 77 The ghost crab *Ocypode ryderi* (50 mm) digs deep holes high on sandy beaches on the east coast.

rhythms of activity like those of *Tylos*, usually emerging at night as the tide falls and scurrying over the sand in search of food. They will eat almost any animal life, from young turtles to isopods, and scavenge on dead animals as well. Their enormous eyes, mounted on erect stalks, are an obvious adaptation to nocturnal life. The animals' legs are unusually long and account for the remarkable speed at which these crabs can run. An *Ocypode* may become very aggressive when close to its burrow and it threatens other crabs with a mock display if they approach. The crabs stretch out their legs and lift the first pair, tipping the body up at the front to make themselves appear as big as possible. They then jump at the intruder, swinging their nippers downwards in the process. This threat is sufficient to chase off other ghost crab intruders without a fight even taking place. All ghost crabs have ridges on the palms of their nippers (stridulating organs) which are rubbed against the claw to produce a rasping sound used to communicate aggression or courtship with other crabs.

The high-shore air breathers on sandy beaches are notably similar in their habits. All are scavengers, all are nocturnal, and all have rhythms of activity related to the tides. Nearly all are isopod or amphipod crustaceans that carry their young in a brood pouch and have no free-living larval stage. This releases the animals from requiring any direct contact with the sea. It is partly for this reason that the amphipods and isopods are among the few crustaceans to have successfully colonised land.

Smaller animals – the meiofauna

Our attention is invariably captured by the larger animals, but sandy beaches abound in tiny animals never exceeding 0,5 mm in size and referred to as the meiofauna. They live

shores. All three have special tufts of hair at the bases of their last two legs which can suck up water even from damp sand, thus allowing the crabs to keep their gills wet while they scurry around the shore. Ghost crabs have

between the sand grains where small size is obviously essential. There are far more species of meiofauna on most beaches than there are of larger (macrofaunal) animals, including representatives of most of the major groups of animals. However, two groups are commonest: the slender wire-like nematode worms (Fig. 222) and tiny crustaceans known as harpacticoid copepods (Fig. 78).

We cannot ignore the meiofauna simply because it is microscopic in size. For every single large animal such as a *Bullia*, there will be up to 15 000 individuals of the meiofauna. The mass of these is of course minute, but taken collectively the meiofauna accounts for 20 to 45 percent of the living flesh on sandy shores. Another consideration is that these tiny organisms grow, reproduce and die in a short space of time, with perhaps 10 to 20 generations per year. This means the rate at which they convert food into meiofaunal meat is also high, perhaps three to four times higher than that of larger animals.

The meiofauna faces three basic problems: firstly, the sand in which it lives can dry out too much; secondly, the lower layers of sand can become stagnant and as a result there may be too little oxygen in the sediment; finally, there must be sufficient food to support the meiofauna. The first two problems relate partly to the nature of the sand, particularly the size of the grains. Maximum numbers of meiofauna are found where the mean size of the sand grains is about 0,284 mm. Above this size, water drains too rapidly leaving the sand dry, while below this size the space between the sand grains becomes too small for the animals to move easily, and the fine particles reduce water-flow to the point where oxygen is not renewed very quickly. Near the surface of the sand the problem of desiccation is greatest, while deeper down the lack of oxygen is a limiting factor. The greatest numbers of meiofauna therefore occur at the happy medium between these two extremes and it is not unusual to find up to 160 000 of these tiny animals in a square metre of sand. Nematode worms seem more tolerant of extreme conditions and dominate the dry upper layers and the lower, oxygen-deficient layers, while crustaceans are commonest in the middle layers.

Naturally the problems of desiccation and lack of oxygen will change with the tide, and so the meiofaunal animals migrate up and down in the sand to keep pace with these changes. At high tide they are found nearer the surface where oxygen is readily available but, as the water drains away during low tide, they migrate downwards. This movement probably covers 10 to 20 cm which is a considerable distance for animals that are less than 0,5 mm in length.

Meiofaunal species seem to be involved in a food web of their own, independent of the larger animals, for none of them are eaten by the macrofauna. Most of the meiofaunal species depend on organic particles, which are usually colonised by bacteria, as a food source. However, in miniature they have the same sort of food web we associate with larger animals. Some are herbivorous, grazing on microscopic plant life, many feed on detritus or scavenge, while others are carnivores, feeding on other meiofauna or on protozoa. Thus at a microscopic level the web of life is re-enacted.

The meiofauna, by breaking particles down to sizes that are more easily colonised by bacteria, plays an important rôle in helping with the decomposition of organic matter. In recent years the meiofauna has been used to monitor the effects of pollution of sandy beaches. The larger animals tend to be few in number so that their responses to pollution are difficult to detect, but the vast numbers of meiofauna make the task much easier.

Higher predators

Just as sandy-beach animals depend on an input of plant material from the sea to supply the first step of their food chain, so the food chain ends with the higher predators which live outside the beach system but visit it to feed on sandy-beach animals. The most important of these are the black-backed gull, the black oystercatcher, the white-fronted plover and the sanderling. In the eastern Cape, birds are known to consume about 8 percent of the flesh-weight of invertebrates present on the beaches. Oyster-catchers alone are responsible for eating almost one third of the white mussels each year. Gulls tend to scavenge, although some have learnt to break white mussels on the rocks. The white-fronted sand plover and the sanderling consume huge numbers of *Talorchestia*, individual birds eating as many as 300 sand hoppers per hour. Sanderlings may also eat *Gastrosaccus* and can nip the siphons off the white mussel *Donax serra*. Strangely, *Bullia*, despite being such an obvious animal, is not eaten by birds, suggesting that it is unpleasant tasting. It is therefore interesting to find that *Bullia* concentrates cadmium and may have as much as a million times more cadmium in its tissues than in the surrounding sea-water. Cadmium is, of course, a poison but whether this makes the animals taste unpleasant to predators is not known.

At high tide the fishes swim over the submerged beaches and take their toll. Galjoen (*Coracinus capensis*) feed on

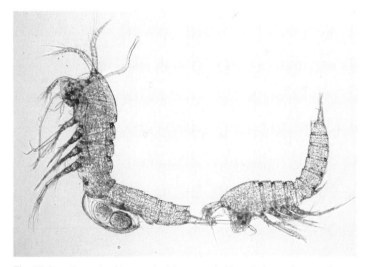

Fig. 78 A mating pair of harpacticoid copepods (1 mm), the male grasping the female with his antennae.

crustaceans and at times their guts are swollen with large numbers of sand hoppers. The white steenbras (*Lithognathus lithognathus*) is able to direct a jet of water to uncover crustaceans in the sand, and is even capable of blasting sand prawns out of their burrows. White mussels are eaten by many fish, and *Bullia* are often consumed by rays and skates.

THE FOOD WEB

A picture of the food web on sandy shores is summarised in Fig. 79. Plant material imported from the sea may be stranded near the high-tide mark where it is eaten by the air-breathing species such as *Talorchestia, Tylos, Ligia* and the kelp fly larvae. Much of this plant material is fragmented and colonised by bacteria and then, together with phytoplankton, can be eaten by the particle-feeding animals such as *Donax* and *Gastrosaccus*. Particulate organic matter is also filtered out as the water trickles through the sand and supports a vast number of bacteria occurring in sandy beaches. This forms the basis of the meiofaunal food chain which has its own particle feeders as well as herbivores and carnivores, but seems to function independently of the larger animals. Bacterial action breaks down the organic matter, releasing nutrients which are returned to the sea where they can help fertilise the growth of phytoplankton in the surf zone. Animals are also stranded on the shore where they can be eaten by scavengers such as *Bullia* and the ghost crab *Ocypode*. Top predators such as birds and fish coming in from outside the beach area are the major predators. An interesting fact that emerges is that relatively few of the animals resident in the beach eat one another.

The sandy beach is a harsh habitat, unstable, wave-beaten and dependent on an outside source of food and it is occupied by only a few species which have either turned the problems of the habitat to their advantage, making use of the waves for transport and food, or which live high enough on the shore to avoid the problems of wave action while still capitalising on the food deposited by the waves. All the animals have lifestyles intimately linked with the rise and fall of the tides, and almost without exception they have developed remarkable rhythms of activity and methods of orientating up and down the beach to make the best and safest use of the tides. It is these fascinating adaptations that reward our study of the few species which have successfully colonised the sandy beaches.

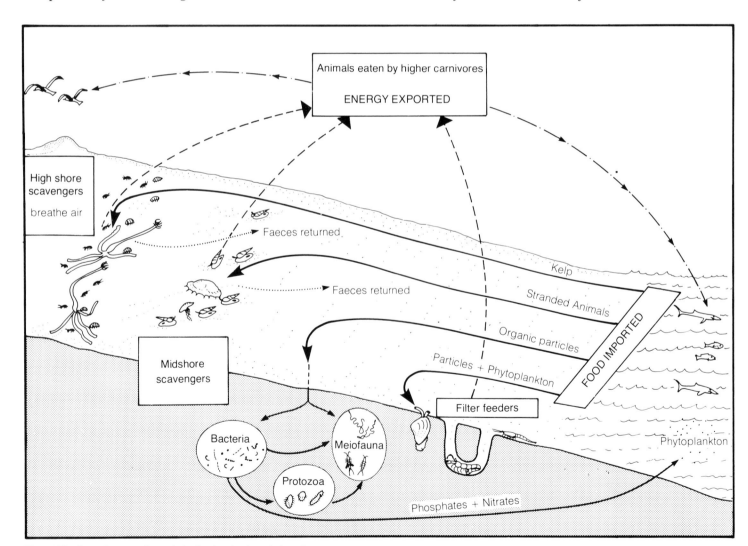

Fig. 79 The flow of energy through the food web of sandy beaches.

REFERENCES
Popular articles and books
Berry, P. F. 1976. Natal's Ghost Crabs. *African Wildlife*, Vol. 30 (2): 34-37.

Brown, A. C. 1964. Food relationships on the intertidal sandy beaches of the Cape Peninsula. *S. Afr. Journal of Science*, Vol. 60 (2): 33-64.

Brown, A. C. 1978. Life on marine sandy beaches. *African Wildlife*, Vol. 32: 22-24.

Eltringham, S. K. 1971. *Life in Mud and Sand.* English Universities Press, Oxford. 218 pp.

Scientific references
Brown, A. C. 1961. Physiological-ecological studies on two sandy-beach Gastropoda from South Africa; *Bullia digitalis* Meuschen and *Bullia laevissima* (Gmelin). *Zeitschrift für Morphologie und Oekologie der Tiere*, Vol. 49: 629 – 657.

Brown, A. C. 1964. Blood volumes, blood distribution and sea-water spaces in relation to expansion and retraction of the foot in *Bullia* (Gastropoda). *Journal of experimental Biology*, Vol. 41: 837-854.

Brown, A. C. 1971. The ecology of the sandy beaches of the Cape Peninsula, South Africa: 2. The mode of life of *Bullia* (Gastropoda: Prosobranchiata). *Transactions of the Royal Society of S. Afr.*, Vol. 39 (3): 281-319.

Brown, A. C. 1973. The ecology of the sandy beaches of the Cape Peninsula, South Africa: 4. Observations on two intertidal Isopoda, *Eurydice longicornis* (Stüder) and *Exosphaeroma truncatitelson* Barnard. *Transactions of the Royal Society of S. Afr.*, Vol. 40 (5): 381-404.

Brown, A. C. 1981. An estimate of the cost of free existence in the sandy-beach whelk *Bullia digitalis* (Dillwyn) on the west coast of South Africa. *Journal of experimental marine Biology and Ecology*, Vol. 49: 51-56.

Brown, A. C. & Da Silva, F. M. 1979. The effects of temperature on oxygen consumption in *Bullia digitalis* Meuschen (Gastropoda, Nassaridae). *Comparative Biochemistry and Physiology*, Vol. 62 A: 572-576.

Kensley, B. 1974. Aspects of the biology and ecology of the genus *Tylos* Latrielle. *Annals of the S. Afr. Museum*, Vol. 65: 401-471.

McLachlan, A. 1977. Composition, distribution, abundance and biomass of the macrofauna and meiofauna of four sandy beaches. *Zoologica Africana*, Vol. 12: 279-306.

McLachlan, A. 1979. Volumes of sea water filtered through Eastern Cape sandy beaches. *S. Afr. Journal of Science*, Vol. 75: 75-79.

McLachlan, A. 1980. Exposed sandy beaches as semi-closed ecosystems. *Marine Environmental Research*, Vol. 4: 59-63.

McLachlan, A., Erasmus, T. & Furstenberg, J. P. 1977. Migrations of sandy beach meiofauna. *Zoologica Africana*, Vol. 12 (2): 257-277.

McLachlan, A., Wooldridge, T. & Van der Horst, G. 1979. Tidal movements of the macrofauna on an exposed sandy beach in South Africa. *Journal of Zoology, London*, Vol. 188: 433-442.

4. KELP BEDS

The west coast of southern Africa is dominated by dense beds of sea bamboo or kelp which are almost like underwater forests and extend from the shore to as much as 3 km offshore. These kelps are extremely productive; not only are they a major source of food for animals, but their dense growth breaks the force of waves, thus providing shelter for calm-water animals and plants (Plate 164).

Kelp beds have been the subject of a detailed study, centred at Oudekraal on the west coast of the Cape Peninsula, and undertaken jointly by the Zoology Department of the University of Cape Town and the Sea Fisheries Institute, under the leadership of Professor John Field. One of the aims of this study has been to determine the extent to which kelp contributes to the food chains of inshore waters. Marine biologists have long accepted phytoplankton as the only significant primary producer in the sea, and only relatively recently have the seaweeds been considered of any importance in terms of the productivity of inshore waters.

This study of kelp beds is not simply to satisfy academic curiosity, for kelp beds support several commercially important species. These include rock lobsters, worth R30 million each year, the kelp plants themselves, and the perlemoen (*Haliotis midae*). Therefore if we can trace the food webs and work out how the species affect one another, then rational recommendations can be made about the exploitation of these resources.

KELP SPECIES
The most familiar of the kelp species is *Ecklonia maxima*, which is a large plant with a cylindrical stipe reaching up to 12 m in length and forming a flat, palm-like 'hand' bearing strap-shaped fronds (Fig. 81). *Ecklonia maxima* has a hollow gas-filled stipe with a buoyant swollen bulb at the top which holds the plant upright, allowing its fronds to float near the surface of the water. This fact is of great importance in the ecology of the system: firstly, it means that *Ecklonia* always forms the top canopy of the kelp bed, shading other species; secondly, it means that the plants float when torn free and can thus be washed ashore where they are of central importance to the ecology of sandy beaches on the west coast, as described in the previous chapter.

Laminaria pallida achieves a length of about 5 m. Like all kelps it has a tangled mass of haptera that form the holdfast, attaching the plant to rocks. The stipe is solid and stiff, holding erect the fan-shaped blade which is split into segments resembling straps. Although it grows under the canopy of *Ecklonia, Laminaria* often extends much further offshore into water as deep as 30 m. As a result, it may

contribute more to the total mass of kelp. North of St Helena Bay, *Laminaria pallida* is replaced by a similar species, *L. schintzei*.

The fourth west coast species is *Macrocystis angustifolia*, a slender plant with a rope-like stipe that forms blades all along its length, each with a small gas-filled float (Fig. 81). *Macrocystis* is only found in sheltered waters and contributes little to the total amount of kelp.

On the south and east coasts there are no massive kelp beds equivalent to those on the west coast, but a much smaller kelp plant does occur there. This is *Ecklonia biruncinata*, which seldom grows more than 1 m in height and has a typical prickly edge to the blades by which it is readily identified.

All these species have a similar but complex life-cycle (see Chapter 22). The familiar kelp plant is but one phase in this life-cycle and, in this asexual phase (the sporophyte), it produces millions of tiny spores that settle and give rise to microscopic male and female gametophytes. Gametes are then produced by the gametophytes and, after fertilisation, the embryo grows into the large sporophyte so familiar to us.

THE STRUCTURE OF KELP BEDS
The organisms that inhabit kelp beds and their relative abundance change from the shore out into deeper waters, and we can usually recognise three characteristic zones: inshore, intermediate and offshore. Inshore, in shallow water, *Ecklonia* is common, although the plants are small; and many other species of algae are found living under the canopy of *Ecklonia* (Fig. 81). Very few animals occur in this inshore zone. In the intermediate zone *Ecklonia* reaches its greatest mass (per unit area of rock) and forms a dense canopy under which *Laminaria* grows. Attached to the rocks below is an under-storey of smaller seaweeds, many of which are flat red algae whose growth is largely controlled by the amount of light penetrating the canopy. When light penetrates water, the red end of the spectrum is filtered out first, blue penetrating to the greatest depths: since red pigments absorb blue light, this is perhaps why many of the under-storey algae are red (see Chapter 22). If the plants forming the canopy are removed, this often has dramatic effects on the algae below. Firstly, young kelps that are struggling to develop now grow much faster: a fact that is important when considering the implications of commercial harvesting of kelp. In addition to this, kelp gametophytes, although they are able to remain dormant for up to 20 days in total darkness, depend on light to develop. Removal of the canopy may thus stimulate their

development and initiate the growth of new kelp plants. Removal of the canopy may also cause changes in the under-storey species. For example one common species, *Bifurcariopsis,* is often overgrown and replaced by a faster-growing species, *Pterosiphonia cloiophylla,* when more light becomes available.

Beneath the kelp canopy, light is dim. Some algae live attached to the kelps and thus closer to the surface where the light is brighter. These include *Suhria vittata* and *Carradoria virgata* (Plate 174). Two others have taken this relationship further and have become parasitic on the kelps. *Carpoblepharis flaccida* sends out haptera into the stipe of *Ecklonia* and by this means extracts photosynthetic products from the kelp (Plate 174). A close relative, *Carpoblepharis minima,* parasitises *Laminaria.* Other plants and many encrusting animals may also grow attached to the kelp and in doing so rob it of sunlight and can reduce its growth.

The intermediate zone clearly supports a massive growth of algae, but as is the case with the inshore zone, relatively few animals occur here, although mussels and sponges are quite common.

The offshore provides a complete contrast. Here *Ecklonia* is largely replaced by patches of *Laminaria.* Between these patches are dense animal communities, so the offshore zone is really an animal-dominated zone. Among the creatures, a few species are particularly common, including sea urchins, mussels, sponges, sea cucumbers, anemones and the rock lobster. A striking feature is that most of the animals are filter-feeders (Fig. 81).

Not only does the offshore zone support much less kelp, but the size and arrangement of the plants is different: most of the plants are large and mature and are arranged in clumps, largest kelps being found at the centre of each clump. This contrasts with the situation inshore where the beds are continuous and contain numerous young plants.

What explains these differences? It seems that fewer *Laminaria* manage to develop in deeper areas but, once they are established, they are more likely to survive, possibly because wave action is reduced in deeper waters. Why then are the kelps not more abundant in deeper waters? To answer this we must turn to the interaction between kelp and animals.

One of the dominant animals, the urchin *Parechinus angulosus,* feeds mainly on broken pieces of kelp that sink to the floor of the kelp bed. However, it also scrapes the surface of rocks and, in the process, removes all young plants including kelp sporelings. If the urchins are experimentally removed, about three times as much kelp can develop (Fig. 80). Filter-feeders may also consume waterborne sporelings and so prevent kelp spores from settling. Animals thus reduce the settlement and growth of young kelp. On the other hand, once they are established, the adult kelp plants are largely immune to herbivores, for water movement prevents the animals from climbing the kelp stipes. Adult plants of *Laminaria* also have an important effect on the animals, for their fronds drape downwards and waves lash them around with a whip-like action. This sweeps all the animals away from the base of the plant. The stipes of older kelps become stiffer so that while the fronds still lash around the rock they cannot reach the base of the plant where a zone is left in which juvenile kelps can settle, and where they will be sheltered from the grazing urchins by a curtain of lashing fronds. Once a clump of plants begins to form it will continue to enlarge outwards. This accounts for the largest plants always being found at the centre of these clumps (Fig. 82).

This interaction between kelp and animals may also explain why the inshore zones are dominated by plants while the offshore zone supports more animals. In deeper waters plant-growth and the formation of sporophytes from gametophytes will be slower because less light

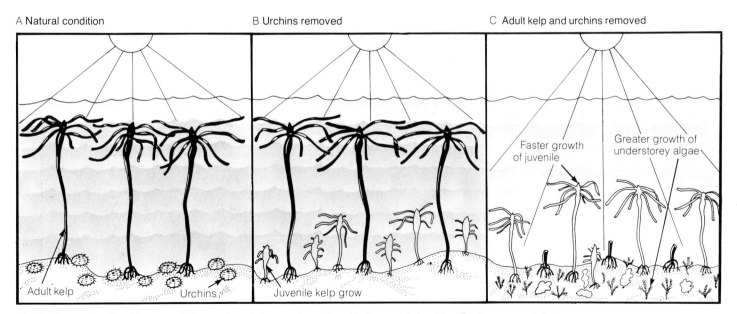

A Natural condition   B Urchins removed   C Adult kelp and urchins removed

Adult kelp   Urchins   Juvenile kelp grow   Faster growth of juvenile   Greater growth of understorey algae

Fig. 80 The grazing of urchins normally keeps down kelp sporelings (A), so that removal of urchins (B) allows young kelp to develop. The growth of this juvenile kelp is greater if the canopy of adult kelp is removed (C).

Fig. 81 **The underwater kelp forests teem with life.**

Inshore, beneath the canopy of the kelp *Ecklonia maxima,* algal plants dominate.

1. Kelp, *Ecklonia maxima;* 2. Limpet, *Patella cochlear;* 3. *Patella argenvillei* trapping kelp; 4. Red-bait, *Pyura stolonifera.*

5 – 21: Algae 5. *Gigartina stiriata;* 6. *Cladophora;* 7. *Champia lumbricalis;* 8. *Gymnogongrus dilatata;* 9. *Trematocarpus;*
10. *Codium isaacii;* 11. *Codium stephensiae;* 12. Large, flat, red alga e.g. *Pachymenia;* 13. Encrusting pink coralline alga;
14. *Pterosiphonia;* 15. Kelp, *Macrocystis angustifolia;* 16. *Botryoglossum platycarpum;* 17. *Epymenia obtusa;*
18. *Botryocarpa prolifera;* **19-21: Algae growing on** *Ecklonia;* 19. *Carradoria virgata;* 20. *Suhria vittata;* 21 *Carpoblepharis flaccida:*

Offshore, amid clumps of the kelp *Laminaria pallida,* animals dominate.
22. Limpet living on kelp, *Patella compressa;* 23. Octopus jets in to eat rock lobsters; 24. Turban shell, *Turbo sarmaticus;*
25. Black mussel, *Choromytilus meridionalis;* 26. Klipvis, *Clinus;* 27. Sea anemone; 28. Feather-star; 29. Sea urchin,
Parechinus angulosus, eats kelp fragments; 30. Starfish, *Marthasterias glacialis,* eats mussels; 31. Sea cucumber,
Pentacta doliolum; 32. Perlemoen, *Haliotis midae,* traps kelp; 33. Carnivorous whelk, *Nucella;* 34. Ribbed mussels,
Aulacomya ater; 35. Rock lobster, *Jasus lalandii,* eating mussels; 36. Anemone, *Corynactis;* 37. Soft coral; 38. Horny coral;
39. Six different sponges; 40. Ball sponge, *Tethys;* 41. Hottentot, *Pachymetopon;* 42 Kelp, *Laminaria pallida;* 43. Jellyfish.

Fig. 82 The sweeping action of *Laminaria* fronds excludes animals (A), allowing young *Laminaria* to settle (B) and grow, forming outwardly-expanding clumps of the kelp (C).

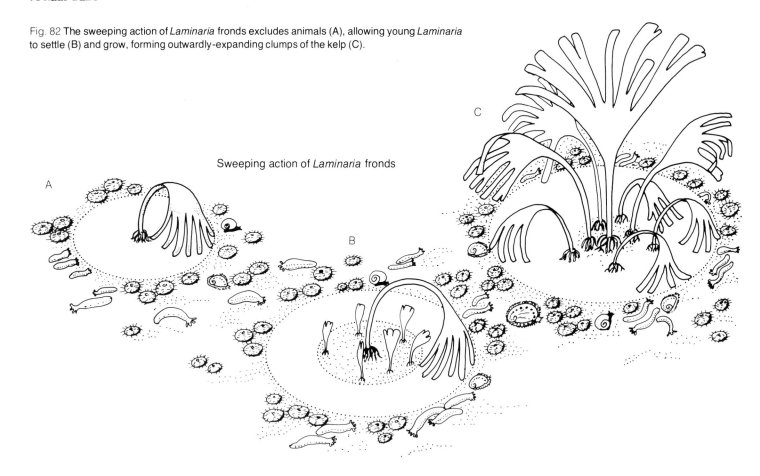

Sweeping action of *Laminaria* fronds

reaches the floor. At the same time wave action is reduced in the deeper waters, so that the activities of animals are less hindered by water movement. Thus offshore animals are likely to gain the upper hand in the interaction, and only the occasional kelp plant will escape their attention and grow large enough to form the nucleus of a new clump of plants. In shallower areas higher light levels will promote kelp growth, making it more likely that a greater percentage of sporelings will grow fast enough to escape being eaten. The greater wave action may in turn prevent animals from feeding efficiently. Perhaps these are the reasons why algae dominate the inshore zone.

ENERGY FLOW
A central theme in the study of kelp beds has been the way in which energy flows through the system, starting with the amount of sunlight trapped by the plants for their growth and following the fate of this energy as it passes on to successive animals. The use of energy is not the simplest way to measure the quantities of animals and plants, but it is certainly the most informative. We could simply count the organisms, but numbers are not in themselves very useful because some species are far larger than others. If we know the energy content of an animal, we not only have a better measure of its value to other organisms, but we can also determine at what rate that animal turns over energy. Food, which represents the input of energy into the animal, is consumed at a certain rate and used to produce body tissues and to reproduce. The animals may be eaten or die

and decompose. All these processes can be measured by the rate at which energy flows along food chains.

The production of kelps and phytoplankton
Kelp plants increase in size by slowly lengthening their stipes which continue to grow until the plant reaches the surface. At the same time their fronds are continually growing at a much faster rate. To measure the amount of organic material kelps produce each year we need to know not only the total growth but the mortality rate of the plants, for when they die they can still be eaten and thus contribute to the food chain. Mortality is assessed by labelling a sample of plants and following their fate over a year. About 5 percent die each year, mostly through being torn free during winter storms.

Growth cannot be measured by simply finding out how much the plant increases in size, for as fast as the fronds grow they are eroded away at their tips. In this way they are able to yield a substantial amount of food while remaining essentially the same size. To overcome this problem, divers punched holes at regular intervals along the fronds, and then followed the rate at which these moved along each frond in order to measure its growth (Fig. 83). In this manner it was shown that the fronds grow between 1 and 13 mm each day. The amount of growth is greatest in summer, closely following the average amount of sunlight received each month (Fig. 84). Plants that grow in deeper water receive less light and grow more slowly. Light also influences how deep the kelps can grow. As one moves

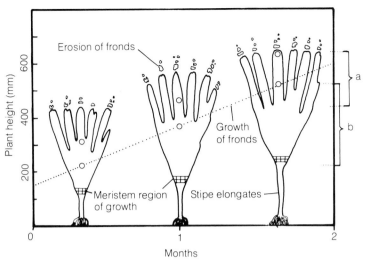

Fig. 83 Holes are punched in the *Laminaria* fronds to measure their growth. In two months the lower hole grows 250 mm (from 200 to 450 mm: b) although the height of the whole plant only grows 200 mm (from 440 to 640 mm: a) because it is eroded away at the tip.

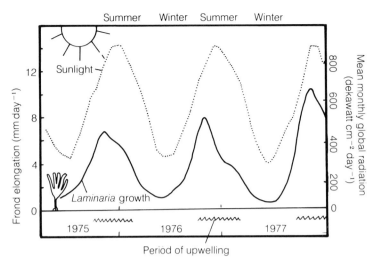

Fig. 84 The growth rate of the kelp *Laminaria* is closely related to the amount of sunlight received, which is greatest in summer when upwelling is supplying nutrients to the plants as well.

northwards along the coast from Cape Point to Saldanha Bay, the water becomes more murky and kelps are therefore limited to shallower waters. This has an important effect on the whole ecology of the coast, for the total amount of kelp is reduced more than tenfold between Cape Point and Saldanha, although this pattern changes again beyond Saldanha (Fig. 85).

During summer the kelps benefit from the increased sunlight, and also from the increase in south-easterly winds, which cause upwelling (see Chapter 1). Cold, nutrient-rich water is thus brought up to the surface and into the kelp beds where it fertilises their growth. Experiments on the microscopic gametophytes of kelps show that they fail to mature unless the water is enriched with nutrients. Perhaps more than anything else, the upwelling of nutrients on the west coast accounts for kelp beds being limited to this coast. Although upwelling is not unique to the west coast of southern Africa, it is more intense here than anywhere else in the world. By comparison, upwelling in Peru and California brings deeper waters to the surface at a rate of between 1,9 m and 2,3 m per day, but on the west coast of southern Africa upwelling occurs at 30 m per day! The west coast is also pounded by powerful waves and this, too promotes rapid growth of the kelps, by ensuring that nutrients are replaced as fast as the plants use them.

With a sunny climate, a rich supply of nutrients and wave action to circulate the water, it is no surprise to find that these kelp beds are amongst the most productive in the world, exceeding even the productivity of most agricultural land! Each frond of kelp will produce about 6,16 times its own mass in detritus each year: a major contribution to the food chain.

We are still not certain how much the microscopic phytoplankton contributes to the productivity within kelp beds. In terms of mass we would be inclined to overlook the phytoplankton, since it is minute compared with the kelp

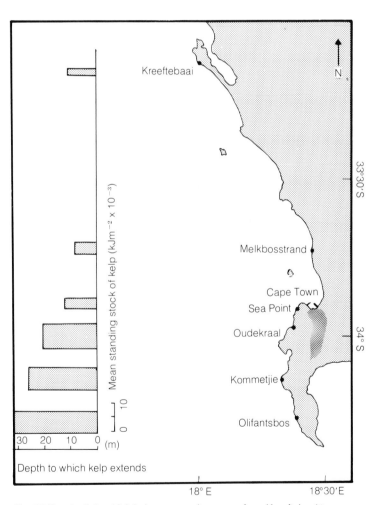

Fig. 85 The depth to which kelp can grow increases from Kreeftebaai to Olifantsbos, and the amount of kelp (measured as the energy content, kilojoules per square metre) also increases. This is probably because the water is much clearer in the south.

plants and other large algae. However, phytoplankton is able to turn over at an incredible rate when conditions are suitable, producing up to nine times its own mass per day. The amount of phytoplankton present in the water is also strongly seasonal and, as we would expect, it peaks in summer when sunlight and nutrient levels are at their highest.

The amount of phytoplankton available in kelp beds depends on the winds. With offshore south-easterlies, upwelling is promoted, but it takes several days for the phytoplankton to build up and take advantage of this fresh supply of nutrients, so freshly upwelled water contains little phytoplankton. However, as the water is blown offshore, the phytoplankton blooms and very high levels of production have been recorded. If the winds continue to blow offshore for several days the phytoplankton may exhaust the nutrients and begin to age and die, contributing to the detritus in the water. More often the winds reverse after a few days and the bloom of phytoplankton is then blown back into the kelp bed where it contributes to the food available to animals. However, even under these conditions the levels of phytoplankton are never as high in the kelp beds as they are offshore, possibly because the phytoplankton must compete with kelp plants for light and nutrients, but also because they are consumed rapidly by the dense, filter-feeding animal community.

Consumption by herbivores

In spite of the wealth of plants there are very few herbivores in kelp beds. Only three species are of any importance. The small alikreukel, *Turbo cidaris*, is quite common, but is very seldom able to climb the kelp plants and feed on them because of wave action. This probably pin-points the main reason for the relative scarcity of herbivores in the kelp beds. The remaining two herbivores have overcome the problem of wave action in different ways. The limpet *Patella compressa* is specially adapted to live directly attached to *Ecklonia* and is never found elsewhere. Its muscular foot allows firm attachment and its shell is wrapped around the stipe and streamlined to provide minimal resistance to water movement. *Patella compressa* never reaches high densities. This is partly explained by its territorial behaviour. Juveniles are found clustered together in the folds along the edges of fronds, but as they grow they move on to the hand and then down to the stipe (Fig. 86). In the process their behaviour changes and they space out from one another and become territorial. Each stipe is normally only occupied by one adult limpet which defends its stipe against any intruding limpets, pushing against them until they move off (Fig. 87). Yet, if we analyse the energy required by each limpet it seems as if the kelp can supply so much food that it could support dozens of limpets. Why then the need for limpets to spend time and energy defending their territorial stipes? We can only guess at this, but it may be that if several limpets were to eat on one stipe, they might weaken it to such a degree that storms could sweep the plant and the limpets to their destruction.

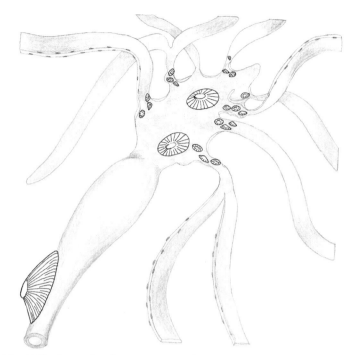

Fig. 86 The limpet, *Patella compressa,* only occurs on the kelp *Ecklonia maxima.* Tiny specimens shelter in the folds between the fronds; medium-sized animals move onto the hand; while adults are always found singly on the stipe, which they will defend territorially.

The final herbivore that eats kelp is the perlemoen *Haliotis midae*, which uses waves to its advantage. It attaches firmly on to rocks, where it feeds in a novel way by lifting its shell and part of its foot to trap fronds that are swept under it by the waves (Fig. 81). Again the rôle of

Fig. 87 Attached to the stalk of a kelp plant, two specimens of the limpet, *Patella compressa,* push against one another in territorial contest.

Fig. 88 Mountainous piles of the kelp *Ecklonia* washed ashore after a winter storm.

wave action in the functioning of the kelp bed system is evident. In most kelp forests *Haliotis* is not very common but in a survey done at Betty's Bay in a marine sanctuary, perlemoen had a biomass (mass per unit area) 8,7 times as much as in any other area. This is a reflection of the heavy commercial exploitation of *Haliotis* in most other areas. Perlemoen are slow growing, a legal sized animal of 115 mm being about 12 years old, and they only begin reproducing when about eight years old, which makes them vulnerable to over-exploitation.

Debris-feeders

Strong waves continually break pieces off kelp plants and sometimes tear whole plants from their attachment. Whole *Ecklonia* float to the surface and are often washed on to the shore (Fig. 88) where they form the main food for a number of sandy beach crustaceans such as the sand hoppers *Talorchestia capensis* (see Chapter 3). On rocky shores these stranded kelps are eaten by the isopod *Ligia* (Plate 55). The rate at which kelp is stranded is strongly seasonal, with a winter peak (Fig. 89) coincident with winter storms and onshore winds. The life-cycles and growth rates of *Ligia* and *Talorchestia* are closely linked to the stranding of kelp. Their reproductive development occurs in winter and growth is nearly three times higher in winter than in summer. Thus in many ways the lives of these animals are dominated by the amount of kelp washed up. Stranded

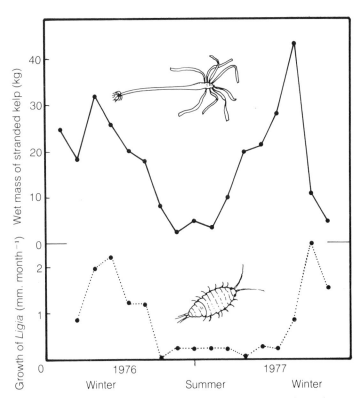

Fig. 89 The amount of kelp washed ashore is greatest during winter when storms are common, and the growth rate of the beach louse, *Ligia dilatata*, is controlled by the amount of kelp available.

kelp is not lost to the sea, for a large proportion is returned in the form of faeces produced by these scavenging crustaceans.

Laminaria does not float and so, together with fragments of *Ecklonia* fronds, it sinks to the floor of kelp beds when conditions are calm enough. Here this debris is eaten by large numbers of the spiny urchin *Parechinus angulosus*. Young urchins are too small to trap these fragments and depend on a detrital soup of smaller organic particles. Judging by the slow growth of these young urchins this seems an inadequate diet, and the urchins grow more quickly only when they are large enough to handle kelp fragments. Waves have a strong influence on *Parechinus*. On one hand strong wave action increases the amount of kelp debris that is torn free and becomes available to the urchins, but on the other hand it prevents them from climbing up and eating the living kelp plants.

We know that about 5 percent of the kelp production is used by these debris-feeders. We also know that herbivores are of little significance in kelp beds, and this raises the question of what happens to the rest of the kelp material that is produced in such large quantities each year.

The fate of kelp material

Kelp fronds have been likened to 'moving conveyor belts of living tissue' for they grow from their bases but are eroded away at the tips. The particles that fragment off the ends of fronds account for about 70 to 80 percent of the material kelp contributes to the food chain.

In addition to this, considerable quantities of mucus are released from the fronds and contribute to the dissolved organic matter in solution in the sea-water. This is the fate

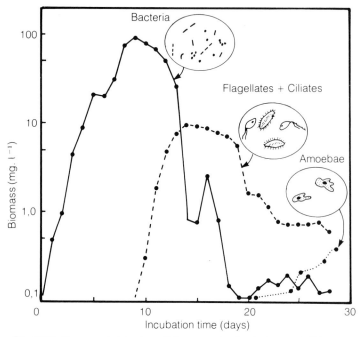

Fig. 90 If kelp mucus is introduced into sea-water, bacteria soon build up, decomposing the mucus in the process. They decline when unicellular ciliates and flagellates develop and start eating them. Amoebae appear later on.

of 20 to 30 percent of the material derived from kelps. The mucus contains many compounds, including proteins, simple sugars and alcohols, particularly mannitol which is one of the products of photosynthesis and plays a key rôle in the ecology of kelp beds. There are also more complex molecules such as alginates and laminarins which form part of the structure of cell walls in kelp plants. Small amounts of fats are also present.

The fats are important for several reasons. Firstly, although they contribute only 0,2 percent to the dissolved compounds, because the production of kelps is so high, the total amount of fats becomes significant. Secondly, there are among the fats certain fatty acids that cannot be manufactured by animals but which are essential to their physiological processes. Finally, when whipped by waves, the fats help in the formation of foam. We may turn up our noses at foam when it coats the beaches, but ecologically it is extremely important, for it concentrates organic materials and has a high protein content. Some animals feed directly on this foam, but it is the bacteria that really capitalise on it, building up in large numbers in the foam where they thrive on the concentrated organic matter.

The fate of mucus from kelp fronds can be studied in laboratory cultures. If dried mucus is introduced into sea-water, bacteria soon attack the organic compounds, using them as an energy source. Within seven to 10 days the numbers of bacteria build up enormously to almost one hundred times their original levels. Following this, successive waves of other organisms develop, starting with tiny flagellate protozoans that feed on the bacteria, then larger ciliated protozoans, and finally, on occasion, amoebae. As the flagellates develop, so the numbers of bacteria decline (Fig. 90).

If the numbers of bacteria are counted, it is possible to calculate their mass. Bacteria are far too small to weigh directly, but by using an electron microscope we are able to measure their sizes and therefore estimate their mass. Along with the measurement of bacterial build-up, we can record the depletion of various components of mucus used by the bacteria. Mannitol is used up very quickly, being a simple compound, and disappears from the cultures within 48 hours. More complex substances take longer. Sugars last about 144 hours and alginates almost 440 hours before they are broken down by the bacteria. This timing is quite important, for when upwelling occurs, all the water in the kelp bed may be replaced as often as three to seven times a day. Thus if the bacteria are to build up within the system they need a food source such as mannitol that can be utilised quickly.

If we know how fast the organic materials are used, and how quickly the bacterial populations build up, then the efficiency with which mucus is converted into bacterial tissue can be calculated. This efficiency is greater in summer than winter, but averages 10 percent.

The growth of bacteria on eroded particles of kelp can also be studied in laboratory cultures, in the same way as the effects of bacteria on mucus were examined. We find that the same succession of organisms develop on particles

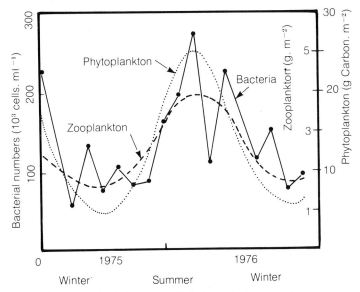

Fig. 91 Bacteria in the kelp beds reach their greatest numbers in summer, when the kelp is growing faster and phytoplankton and zooplankton are also at a peak.

consume up to 60 times their own body-mass per day. Since the Protozoa use bacteria with an efficiency of about 10 percent, each gram of bacteria will produce only 0,1 gram of Protozoa. If higher animals are then to eat the Protozoa instead of using the bacteria directly, they stand to lose 90 percent of their potential food source. As it takes the protozoans about 20 to 30 days to build up their populations to high levels (Fig. 90), the faster the bacteria are eaten by higher animals, the less chance there is of energy being wasted by introducing large numbers of Protozoa as an extra link in the food chain. It is therefore interesting to find that one of the major filter-feeders in kelp beds, the ribbed mussel, *Aulacomya ater,* is abundant enough to filter a column of water 10 metres deep in only 7,5 hours: so perhaps the animals *can* keep ahead of the Protozoa in consuming bacteria.

Some of the compounds released by kelps, such as laminarin and alginates, resist bacterial breakdown for several days and almost certainly are swept away from the kelp beds during upwelling and are blown offshore. Once there, they will move northwards along the coast and may

of kelp: bacteria followed by protozoans. In this case, however, the bacteria must rely on the complex chemicals that make up the structure of kelp, and they use these materials with an efficiency of only 5,5 percent. By combining these figures we estimate that for every 100 grams of kelp eroded from the fronds, about 6,4 grams of bacteria can grow.

As the bacteria are so dependent on the erosion of kelp, their numbers rise in summer when the kelp plants grow fastest (Fig. 91). Many of the bacteria float free in the sea water, each millilitre containing about 275 000 bacteria. In addition, huge numbers grow on the kelp fronds (Fig. 92), each square centimetre supporting over 10 million bacteria! Because of this, large quantities of bacteria are released as the frond erodes away. At the very least these add 10 percent to the mass of material released, and more probably they double the mass.

Why should we be so interested in the way bacteria use the particles and mucus from kelp, and in the details of how efficiently and fast they do so? The main reason is that bacteria are the agents by which kelp is made available to animals. There are two problems for animals that try to use the kelp particles and mucus directly. Firstly, animals have no means of concentrating the dissolved mucus, and they must rely on bacteria to use the mucus, and then eat the bacteria. Secondly, the kelp particles have relatively little nitrogen. Since animals depend on nitrogen to produce protein, an energy source such as particulate kelp is useless to them if they cannot obtain enough nitrogen as well. Bacteria contain high levels of nitrogen. Kelps have between 10 and 14 carbon atoms for every nitrogen atom, but this ratio drops to between 2 and 5 after kelp particles are colonised by bacteria, because of an increase in nitrogen. Thus bacteria act as a vital link in the food web between kelp and animals.

The bacteria are of course also eaten by Protozoa, which

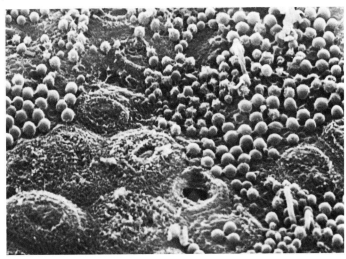

Fig. 92 Freshly-grown kelp soon develops a covering of cocci – small spherical bacteria, but as it ages a dense coat of filamentous rod-like bacteria and oval diatoms smother the frond (electron micrographs: magnification about x1 500).

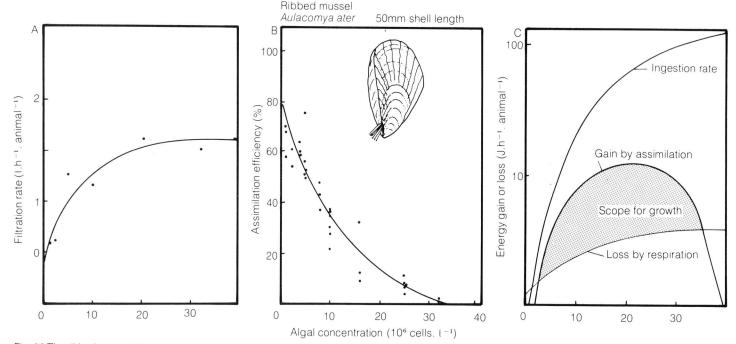

Fig. 93 The ribbed mussel, *Aulacomya ater,* feeds faster when more phytoplankton is present (A), but the efficiency with which it absorbs food drops dramatically (B). As a result the energy it gains reaches a peak and then declines (C). Since the animal loses energy by respiration, the difference between gain (assimilation) and loss (respiration) gives a measure of energy available for growth (the scope for growth).

well sink, only to be upwelled again further along. This northward transport of particles and resistant compounds may be very important. A survey of the kelp beds between Saldanha Bay and Cape Point has shown that the beds in the south have rich kelp growths that often extend into deep water and seem more than adequate to feed the animals there. However, in the north the pattern changes, kelps being limited to shallows by the murky water, and here the total mass of animals is nearly four times that of plants. Perhaps in the north the animals depend more on phytoplankton and on kelp particles that are swept up the coast from the south.

Filter-feeders

Filter-feeders and detritus-feeders, which eat tiny particles such as kelp fragments, bacteria and phytoplankton, make up 70 to 90 percent of the animal life in kelp beds. Among the most important species are the ribbed mussel *Aulacomya ater,* sea cucumbers *Thyone aurea* and *Pentacta doliolum,* sponges, and the red-bait *Pyura stolonifera.* These filter-feeders form dense communities, often covering the rock face completely. The two sea cucumbers sometimes even lie piled one on top of the other with only their crowns of tentacles surfacing to feed.

One species, the ribbed mussel *Aulacomya,* is so common that it has been selected for a special study of energy flow through its populations. If the mussels are fed on a culture of phytoplankton, it is possible to measure the rate at which they filter it from the water. At low levels of phytoplankton *Aulacomya* filters slowly, presumably

because there is no benefit in trying to feed rapidly on a limited food supply. As the phytoplankton levels are increased, so the rate of filtration increases (Fig. 93A). The only problem with this is that the efficiency with which the mussels absorb food then drops: as much as 80 percent of the food is absorbed when the filtration rate is low, but this drops rapidly when there is more food available and the animals are filtering fast; it may even fall to zero (Fig. 93B). Another problem is that as the animals speed up filtration, they respire more quickly. Respiration results in a loss of energy, so the animal is balancing what it gains by absorbing food against what it loses by respiring. Only if the gain is greater than the loss does the mussel profit from feeding, and thus has energy to devote to growth and reproduction. *Aulacomya* actually loses energy at very low food levels (when too little is absorbed to offset the cost of respiration). It also loses energy if food levels are very high, for it filters so rapidly that the food is absorbed inefficiently: in fact phytoplankton can travel right through the mussel's digestive system and be passed out alive in the faeces! However, at normal food levels the mussels make a profit, referred to as the 'scope for growth', when the energy absorbed is more than enough to meet the needs for respiration (Fig. 93C). One interesting feature is that the scope for growth becomes less and less as the mussels age, so that growth also slows down in larger mussels. Since *Aulacomya* is commercially cultured (in South America), this decrease in productivity as the animals age is obviously important: small animals will give a quicker yield than larger mussels.

The scope for growth is a measure of how much energy the mussel has for growth and reproduction. The mussel can devote all of its excess energy to growth, or all to reproduction, or part to each of these functions. Evolution determines which of these choices is best. Young mussels devote nearly all of their energy to growth which is comparatively rapid. This has two advantages: firstly, by growing bigger, the mussel is more likely to escape being eaten; secondly, a larger mussel is able to produce more gametes and thus leave more offspring. Almost 26 percent of the energy used for growth is put into forming the shell, and 8 to 15 percent into producing the byssus threads that attach the animal to rocks. At first sight it seems wasteful to spend such a high proportion of the energy on structures that do not directly increase the production of eggs or sperm. However, a strong shell and attachment are vital to reduce predation and to survive wave action. The east coast brown mussel *Perna perna* increases the number of byssus threads it produces in wave-beaten areas and reduces them on sheltered shores. It also positions the threads so that most of them point in the direction of the on-coming waves. Thus it produces an organ of attachment which is both efficient and involves a minimum expenditure of material and energy.

In large *Aulacomya ater*, energy is used differently. Almost all surplus energy is channelled into eggs or sperm, and practically none into growth (Fig. 94). Again this gives the best return, for there is little need to grow even larger and, as the animal ages, its chances of living another year are not very great so it may as well produce as many offspring as possible. The black mussel, *Choromytilus meridionalis*, takes the situation so far that it spawns several times a year, releasing up to four times its own body-mass as eggs or sperm each year.

Carnivores

The rock lobster *Jasus lalandii* is the most important predator in kelp beds (in spite of being heavily exploited). Whelks, anemones, octopus, dogfish, cormorants and the

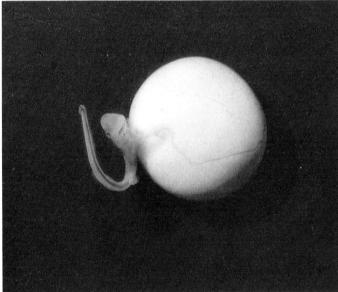

Fig. 95(A) The egg-case of a dogshark entwined with a kelp plant. (B) Cut open, the egg-case reveals a miniature dogshark embryo nourished by a massive supply of yolk.

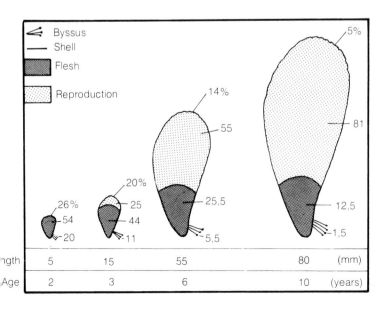

	Byssus
	Shell
	Flesh
	Reproduction

	5%
14%	81
55	
20%	25,5
26% 25	12,5
54 44	1,5
20 11	5,5

ngth	5	15	55	80	(mm)
Age	2	3	6	10	(years)

Fig. 94 As the ribbed mussel grows, it puts proportionately more energy into reproduction than into body growth, shell growth, or formation of the beard-like byssus threads.

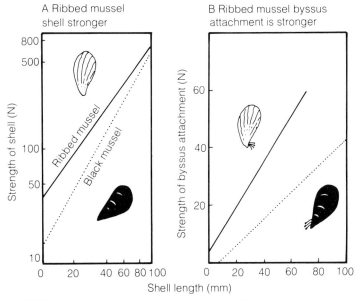

Fig. 96 Ribbed mussels have much stronger shells (A) and are more strongly attached (B) than black mussels, which is probably why rock lobsters prefer to eat black mussels.

hottentot fish, *Pachymetapon blochii* are also present. The egg cases of sand sharks are often found tangled in the seaweeds of kelp beds (Fig. 95A). If they are cut open these are found to contain perfectly-formed miniature sharks, which will even actively swim around while still attached by a cord to the massive yolk sac that nourishes them in this embryonic stage (Fig. 95B).

Rock lobsters feed on many animals including the urchin *Parechinus*, but it favours mussels. If given a choice in an aquarium, rock lobsters show a strong preference for the black mussel, *Choromytilus meridonalis*, over the ribbed mussel, *Aulacomya ater*, although it is far more

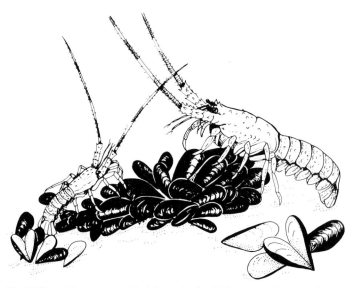

Fig. 97 Rock lobsters select their favourite food, black mussels, on the basis of size. Small rock lobsters select small mussels, being unable to crush larger ones, while larger rock lobsters prefer large mussels since they give a greater yield of food for the effort put into crushing them open.

likely to meet the ribbed mussels in kelp beds. What can explain this preference?

To test for differences in the strength of the shells of the two mussels, rock lobster mandibles were mounted on to a tensometer compression tester and used to crush the shells until they broke. These tests showed that the shells of *Aulacomya* are nearly twice as strong as those of *Choromytilus* (Fig.96A). *Aulacomya* also has a broader shell which makes it difficult for rock lobsters to get a grip with their mandibles. The weakest point on *Choromytilus* shells is near the top posterior margin: and it is at precisely this point that the lobsters usually attack the mussels. *Aulacomya* also attaches itself much more firmly with its byssus than *Choromytilus* (Fig. 96B), and is therefore more difficult for the rock lobsters to tear free. Thus there are at least two good reasons why lobsters should prefer black mussels.

Experiments also show that as mussels become larger, they also become increasingly immune to attack. Small *Jasus* can only handle small mussels, while larger rock lobsters are able to eat larger mussels. Thus for rock lobsters of any particular size mussels above a critical size are safe from attack (Fig. 97). This must explain why it is important for the mussels to grow rapidly when they are small, rather than channelling energy into reproduction.

If they are given a choice, large lobsters will always choose large mussels rather than small ones. In terms of rewards this is the better choice, for although more effort must be spent in pulling a large mussel off the rocks and cracking it open, the yield in terms of food is proportionally greater.

Jasus probably has an important effect on the nature of the animal community in kelp beds. If ropes are suspended in kelp beds, or if vertical pillars are built, black mussels often settle on these and can become the dominant animals, yet they are quite uncommon on natural rocks within the kelp beds. Probably the rock lobsters eat young black mussels so quickly that they never have a chance to establish themselves except on ropes and pylons where the lobsters cannot easily get at them.

Aulacomya is more resistant to attack but even it is affected. Its populations consist largely of two size groups: very small newly-settled animals, and a much smaller number of very large mussels which have, over the years, escaped predation for long enough to grow to a size where they are safe from the rock lobsters.

This fact has important repercussions, influencing even the exploitation of rock lobsters. It has been known for some time that the growth of rock lobsters is somewhat different in different areas, and researchers at the Sea Fisheries Institute of South Africa have shown that the growth rate is related to the amount of food present at each locality. The only difficulty with this is that the total amount of food has always seemed more than adequate for the rock lobsters' needs. For example, at Robben Island in Table Bay the mussels reach about 1,75 kg of flesh per m², and the rock lobsters in theory only require about 1,53 kg per m² for their annual needs. But when we analyse the

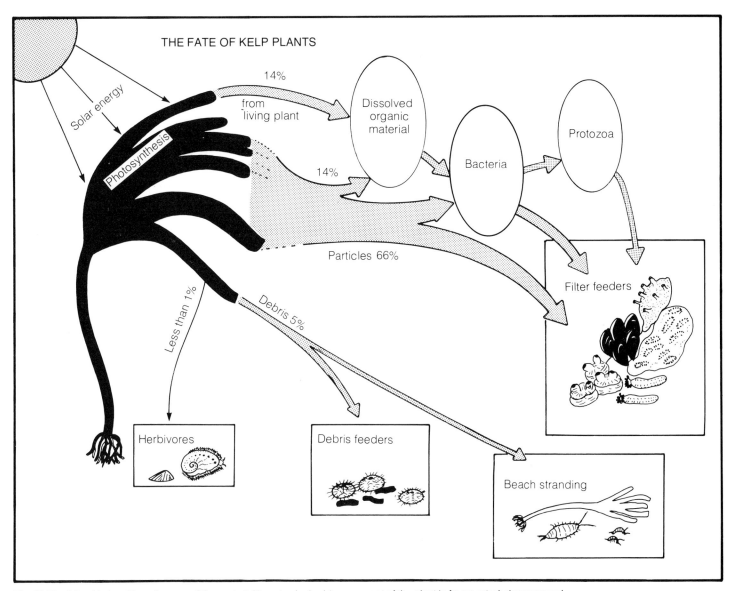

THE FATE OF KELP PLANTS

Solar energy

Photosynthesis

14% from living plant

14%

Dissolved organic material

Bacteria

Protozoa

Particles 66%

Less than 1%

Debris 5%

Filter feeders

Herbivores

Debris feeders

Beach stranding

Fig. 98 The fate of kelp: although some of the material is eaten by herbivores, most of the plant is fragmented, decomposed by bacteria and then eaten by filter-feeders such as mussels, sponges and red-bait.

population structure of the mussels, this paradox is resolved. Only about 22 percent of the mussel mass is actually available to the rock lobsters: the remaining mussels are too large to be eaten. Thus the rock lobsters are indeed short of food and their growth is stunted as a result.

Interactions of this sort between predator and prey have been described elsewhere and in at least two cases disturbance of the natural interaction has had far-reaching consequences. For instance in eastern Canada outbreaks of urchins have been associated with drastic local reductions in the kelp beds. In some areas the urchins have become so numerous that they climb the kelp plants and weigh them down, devouring the whole plant and leaving bare *Lithothamnion*-covered white rocks. The question is: What has caused the almost epidemic outbreaks of urchins? The most likely suggestion is that heavy commercial exploitation of lobsters (the natural predators of urchins) has allowed the urchin populations to expand.

A parallel case has occurred in California where harvest-

ing of the kelp *Macrocystis* is the basis of a rich industry. In some areas kelp beds have dwindled because of increases in urchin populations and so quicklime has been used to control the urchins. Although quicklime does not harm the kelp plants it kills most forms of animal life. A less ecologically disastrous method of control, but one certainly Herculean in execution, has been to employ Scuba divers with hammers!

The elimination or reduction of urchins certainly did increase the growth of kelps, as we would expect from small-scale experiments in South Africa (Fig. 80C). The outbreaks of Californian urchins may be linked to the near elimination of sea otters which have been hunted for their pelts, for these animals are the natural predators of urchins. Incidentally they hunt them in a most unusual way, swimming on their backs so that they can balance a rock on their chests, to be used as an anvil to smash the urchin's spiny case.

Could urchins similarly take over kelp beds in South

Africa because of interference with predators? It seems unlikely, mainly because wave action is so strong along this coast that the urchins never have a chance to damage the kelps the way they do in North America. If anything, kelp beds have increased around the Cape Peninsula, for there are many anecdotes of the "when I was a boy" kind, describing such an increase in False Bay, although there is no scientific evidence that this is so.

THE VITAL PROCESSES

The kelp bed is obviously an enormously productive system with fast-growing plants fuelled by upwelled nutrients. As we have seen, most of the kelp is not eaten by herbivores but is fragmented or given off as mucus. Both fragments and mucus support rich bacterial populations and the major flow of energy is through the filter-feeding organisms that use this resource and are in turn eaten by the rock lobsters and other carnivores (Fig. 98). The high productivity depends on the offshore south-easterly winds which cause upwelling, but it is also clear that the strong wave action along the west coast is central to kelp bed ecology. Waves break off fragments of kelp that are used by the debris-feeding urchins, and are able to tear free whole plants and deposit them on beaches where they support large populations of sand hoppers and isopods. Waves also prevent all but a few specialised herbivores from getting a chance to eat the kelp, and the wave-driven, whip-like action of kelp fronds keeps grazers at bay and allows clumps of kelp to form. There can be no question that the massive kelp beds, powered by winds and waves, are of major importance to the inshore ecology of the west coast.

REFERENCES

Popular articles and books
Field, J. G. et al. 1977. Sun, Waves, Seaweed and Lobsters: the dynamics of a west coast kelp bed. S. Afr. Journal of Science, Vol. 73: 7-10.

Scientific references
Branch, M. L. 1974. Limiting factors for the gametophytes of three South African Laminariales. Investigational Report of the Sea Fisheries Branch, South Africa, Vol. 104: 1-38.

Dieckmann, G. S. 1980. Aspects of the Ecology of Laminaria pallida (Grev) J. Ag. off the Cape Peninsula (South Africa). 1. Seasonal Growth. Botanica Marina, Vol. 23: 579-585.

Field, J. G. et al. 1980. Variations in structure and biomass of kelp communities along the South-west Cape Coast. Transactions of the Royal Society of S. Afr., Vol. 44: 145-203.

Fricke, A. H. 1979. Kelp grazing by the common sea urchin Parechinus angulosus Leske, in False Bay, Cape. S. Afr. Journal of Zoology, Vol. 14: 143-148.

Griffiths, C. L. & King, J. A. 1979. Some relationships between size, food availability and energy balance in the ribbed mussel Aulacomya ater (Molina). Marine Biology, Vol. 51: 141-149.

Griffiths, C. L. & King, J. A. 1979. Energy expended on growth and gonad output in the ribbed mussel Aulacomya ater. Marine Biology, Vol. 53: 217-222.

Griffiths, C. L. & Seiderer, J. L. 1980. Rock-lobsters and mussels – limitations and preferences in a predator-prey interaction. Journal of experimental marine Biology and Ecology, Vol. 44: 95-109.

Koop, K. & Field, J. G. 1980. The influence of food availability on population dynamics of a supralittoral isopod Ligia dilatata Brandt. Journal of experimental marine Biology and Ecology, Vol. 48: 61-72.

Newell, R. C., Lucas, M., Velimirov, B. & Seiderer, L. J. 1980. Quantitative Significance of Dissolved Organic losses following fragmentation of Kelp (Ecklonia maxima and Laminaria pallida). Marine Ecology, Progress Series, Vol. 2: 45-59.

Velimirov, B. & Griffiths, C. L. 1979. Wave-induced Kelp movement and its Importance for Community Structure. Botanica Marina, Vol. 22: 169-172.

5. ESTUARIES

Estuaries are the meeting-places of rivers and the salt waters of the sea and their character is determined by this interplay. Because of this, estuaries are extremely variable: each rise and fall of the tide causes changes while seasonal rainfall brings even more radical fluctuations. The flooding of the Karoo in 1981 is still vivid in our minds and testimony of the forces unleashed by flooding rivers. Often estuaries bear the brunt of such floods which can transform them overnight from tranquillity to raging muddy torrents.

Such fluctuations in mood and character lie at the heart of estuarine ecology and demand special adaptations in the organisms that live there. Those species that overcome

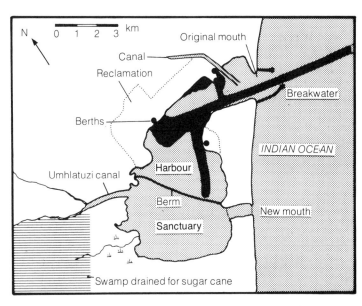

Fig. 99 Aerial photograph and plan of the development of Richards Bay, showing the berm that divides the harbour from the nature sanctuary. The darkly shaded area is dredged. (A) Canalised river. (B) The flood of silt that has smothered the sanctuary. (C) Flood-gate in middle of berm. (D) New mouth cut to sea.

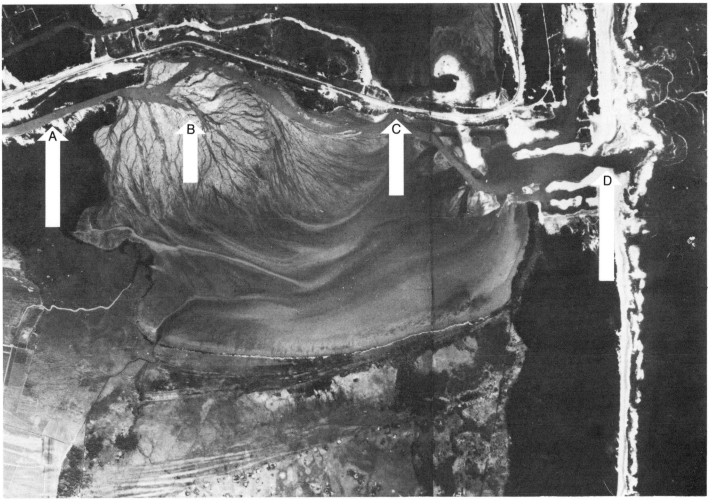

these problems thrive on the nutrients and food provided by both rivers and the sea, making estuaries among the most productive systems in the world.

Because estuaries depend on the interaction of sea and river, they are also extraordinarily vulnerable and easily damaged by man's activities. The Richards Bay Harbour is a case in point. Here careful planning went into the attempt to separate the ecologically important shallows from the deeper lagoon where the harbour was built. An earth embankment or berm was constructed to divide the estuary in half, and a new mouth was cut so that the river and upper reaches of the estuary still maintained direct contact with the sea (Fig. 99). This planning allowed the conservation of the sanctuary area, and also served to prevent river silt from washing down into the harbour.

For once a compromise between conservation and harbour development appeared to have served both interests. However, having gone to all this trouble, much of the sanctuary has since been ruined by the canalisation of the Umhlatuzi swamp which formerly acted as a filtering-bed of reeds, protecting the estuary. The reclaimed land was planted with sugar-cane and the siltation of the estuary, predictably, increased. Instead of silt building up at an average of 0,7 mm a year as previously recorded, the 1974 floods alone brought down enough silt to smother half the sanctuary area (Fig. 99) so that now almost two-thirds is exposed at low tide and the rest is only a few centimetres deep.

The story of Richards Bay Harbour is but one of many in southern Africa which illustrates how important it is to understand the many and complex ecological interactions that take place in estuaries if we are to prevent them all from being irrevocably spoilt.

This chapter is concerned with three important aspects of estuaries: their variable nature and the ingenious adaptations of life to the changeable conditions; the high level of plant production and how animals capitalise on this rich food source; and the sensitivity of estuaries to interference by humans.

PHYSICAL CONDITIONS: STRESSES AND SOLUTIONS
Salinity

Since sea-water flows in at the mouth and river water at the head of an estuary, a gradient of salinity (salt content) is established with the saltier water near the mouth. This gradient is the most obvious factor that changes along the length of most estuaries and allows us to define estuaries as 'those parts of a river that experience variations in salinity due to the effects of sea-water'. Salinity is usually measured in parts per thousand (grams of salt per litre of water) and in scientific shorthand this is expressed as ‰. Sea-water has a salinity of about 35‰.

As the tide rises, salt-water is pushed higher up the estuary, only to retreat on the ebb (Fig. 100). In some estuaries the sea and river waters do not mix uniformly, for sea-water is heavier and tends to sink, so that the river-water flows over the top of a wedge of sea-water (Fig. 100). Such layering (stratification) protects bottom-dwelling organisms that are intolerant of low salinities. There is, however, always the danger that sea-water trapped beneath a freshwater layer may become stagnant and too short of oxygen to support animal life.

In general, however, every tide brings a change in salinity. This in itself may be enough to prevent many marine or freshwater animals from occupying estuaries, but there may also be more radical changes of salinity between times of drought and flood. During droughts there may not be enough inflowing fresh water to counteract evaporation so that the salinity of the estuary becomes more concentrated, and may even exceed that of sea-water (become hypersaline). Floods have the opposite effect, filling the estuary with fresh water.

Faced with the stresses of changing salinity, estuarine creatures have come to cope in different ways. Some species avoid stressful salinities by migrating when conditions become unpleasant: the fish and prawns are obvious examples. Others that are less mobile must tolerate the changes. For instance, the tolerances of three common estuarine crabs are related to how far they penetrate estuaries. *Cyclograpsus punctatus* (Plate 83) is most at home on rocky shores and is limited to the lower reaches of estuaries because it cannot survive in salinities below 20‰; *Sesarma catenata* penetrates further up the estuaries and can tolerate 7‰; while *S. eulimene* lives even nearer to the heads of the estuaries and only succumbs when salinities drop below 2,7‰.

Tolerance to salinity is not the sole factor governing where various organisms live in estuaries. Tests on one of

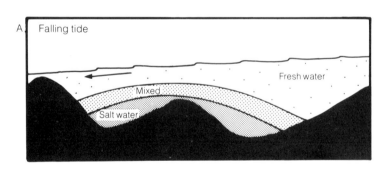

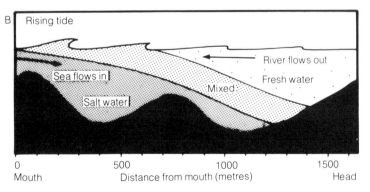

Fig. 100 In some estuaries the lighter fresh river-water lies on top of the heavier salty sea-water. As the tide falls, fresh water penetrates further down towards the mouth, while with the rising tide sea-water fills the estuary and pushes the fresh water back. The situation in the Palmiet estuary is shown here.

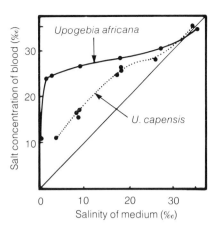

Fig. 101 If the salinity of the medium is varied, the estuarine mud-prawn *Upogebia africana* can control the ionic concentration of its body tissues, while a marine species, *U. capensis,* has little control.

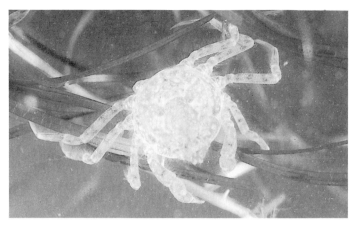

Fig. 102 **The membrane-bodied crab, *Hymenosoma orbiculare* (2 cm).**

Fig. 103 **The mud-prawn, *Upogebia africana* (4 cm).**

the planktonic copepods, *Pseudodiaptomus stuhlmanni,* have shown that it tolerates an exceptional range of salinities, from fresh water to twice the concentration of sea-water, although its survival rate is greatest in sea-water. It is thus surprising to find it largely confined to the low salinities of the upper reaches of estuaries. What prevents it from living further down estuaries or in sea-water? Perhaps marine species provide such overwhelming competition that it only lives in low salinities which exclude the marine plankton.

Floods often result in very low salinities which have been known to kill estuarine bivalves such as *Macoma litoralis* and the pencil baits *Solen capensis* and *S. corneus.* One bivalve, *Dosinia hepatica,* overcomes this problem by clamping its shell tightly shut, excluding the water when salinities drop below 14‰. So efficient is this device, that one animal placed in distilled water was still alive 23 days later and within the clamped shell the salinity was still 22‰.

Another way of surviving low salinities is for the animal to regulate the concentration of salts in its tissue fluids quite independently of the salinity level of the water around it. We can test for this ability by immersing animals in different dilutions of sea-water and seeing if their body tissues simply equilibrate with the water or if their concentration can be kept above that of the surrounding water. Bivalves are incapable of regulating the salt content of their body fluids and are said to be osmoconformers, but most crustaceans can osmoregulate – adjust the salt content of their tissues. The ability of an estuarine mud-prawn *Upogebia africana* (Fig. 103) to regulate its body fluids has been dramatically illustrated by comparing it with the ability of a closely-related animal, *U. capensis,* which never occurs in estuaries. Even when the salinity of the surrounding water dropped as low as 1,7‰ *Upogebia africana* maintained normal salt levels in its blood, but *U. capensis* failed to regulate tissue salts at salinities below 18‰ and died when exposed to less than 15‰ (Fig. 101). *Upogebia africana* is obviously better adapted for an estuarine existence where it even survives floods when salinities are extremely low.

The crab *Hymenosoma orbiculare* (Fig. 102) is another estuarine animal that regulates the concentration of salt in its body fluids, and does this so effectively that it even lives

in the fresh water of Lake Sibaya in Tongaland (Fig. 138). This lake is of great interest, for it was originally an estuary but due to changes in sea level in past ages, has been cut off from the sea and is now filled with fresh water. Despite this, several estuarine species continue to thrive there, including crabs, amphipods and planktonic copepods: all relics of the previously estuarine nature of the lake.

We can classify organisms found in estuaries according to their responses to salinities. *Stenohaline* marine species are intolerant of low or high salinities and only enter the lower reaches of estuaries where salinities are similar to those of the sea. However, most species in estuaries are *euryhaline* marine species that tolerate a wide range of salinities. A few animals and plants are truly *estuarine,* being confined to estuaries and not found in the sea. At the heads of estuaries *freshwater* species may also penetrate from the river but are seldom found in salinities of over 5‰ and are not important in most estuaries. Finally, some species such as fish and prawns form a *migratory* component that moves up and down estuaries as conditions change.

Temperature

The sea has a relatively constant temperature, but because of their smaller volumes, rivers are warmer than the sea in summer, and colder in winter. It follows quite naturally that the head of the estuary experiences a far wider range of temperatures than the mouth. These temperature changes pose yet another form of stress on organisms living in estuaries. Some species are more tolerant of temperature extremes than others, and we can compare their tolerances by experimentally heating (or cooling) batches of animals and noting the temperatures at which they succumb. For example, experiments on five estuarine bivalves have shown that only temperatures over 40 °C kill them; such temperatures would be exceptional in southern African estuaries. The mud-prawn *Upogebia africana* (Fig. 103) is less tolerant, beginning to show signs of discomfort at temperatures over 30 °C. Even this temperature exceeds normal conditions in southern African estuaries. However, increases in temperature below the 30 °C mark may have a beneficial effect, and mud-prawns living in the hot water effluent of a power station on the banks of Knysna Lagoon actually grow faster than normal and produce more eggs. Mud-prawns also have a means of avoiding lethal temperatures: if the temperature rises over 32 °C they stop pumping water through their burrows. As the sediment is a good insulator, heat penetrates it slowly and the mud-prawns remain comfortably buried in the cooler sediments.

It appears that along most of the southern African coastline temperature extremes present no difficulties under normal estuarine conditions. However, high temperatures are more of a problem in the tropics, especially for crabs that feed out of water. For instance, there are five species of fiddler crabs (*Uca* species) that live on Inhaca Island in Moçambique. Only those species with the highest tolerance to heat occur high on the shore and on open bare sands, while the others are limited to shaded or cooler areas. The temperature of the sandflats on which these crabs feed often exceeds 45 °C, well over the lethal body temperatures of all five species. In spite of this, they man-

Fig. 105 The common shore crab *Cyclograpsus punctatus* blowing a froth of bubbles.

age to spend much of their time feeding there because they cool their bodies by evaporation of body water, thus reducing their temperatures by about 6 °C. To make up this water-loss they must periodically scuttle back to their burrows, which extend down to the water-table.

Water-loss

Because estuarine muds are normally saturated with water, desiccation does not trouble creatures that burrow. However, many crabs spend time feeding out of water. This may help them avoid low salinities, but periods out of water create another problem: that of respiring in air without losing too much water. Crabs must keep their gills wet: while submerged they do so by continually circulating water through their gill chambers (see Chapter 13). This is more difficult in air, and *Cyclograpsus punctatus* and *Sesarma* species (Fig. 273) have evolved two adaptations to solve this problem. Firstly, like the fiddler crabs and their sandy-beach kindred, the ghost crabs, they have water-absorbent hairs at the bases of their back legs, that absorb water from the film of moisture on damp sand and pass it into the gill chamber. In addition, their chests are covered with a beautiful array of tiny ridges and a coating of hairs. As water is pumped out of the gill chamber it runs between the ridges and rapidly passes over the hairy chest as a thin film, to be gathered at the base of the legs and reabsorbed into the gill chamber (Fig. 104). The thinness of this film allows oxygen to diffuse into the water, while the speed of its movement minimises water-loss by evaporation. Furthermore, when it is cornered out of water, *Cyclograpsus* is also able to blow a froth of bubbles from its gill chamber, possibly as a defence (Fig. 105).

It is an over-simplification to look at factors like temperature or salinity in isolation. For example, work on juvenile stumpnose (*Rhabdosargus holubi*) shows they can survive a wide range of salinities (5‰ to 65‰) at 20 °C but at temperatures below or above this the juveniles are much less tolerant of salinity extremes. At 12 °C they survive only between 20‰ and 35‰. Thus while neither factor alone may be lethal, in combination they may become intolerable. We can speculate that this is the reason why the

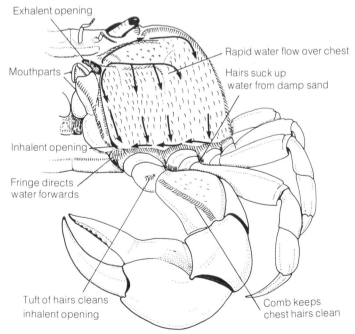

Exhalent opening

Rapid water flow over chest

Mouthparts

Hairs suck up water from damp sand

Inhalent opening

Fringe directs water forwards

Tuft of hairs cleans inhalent opening

Comb keeps chest hairs clean

Fig. 104 The circulation of water over the chest of the crab *Cyclograpsus punctatus* allows rapid oxygenation of the water without much loss of water to the air.

warmer tropical and subtropical estuaries of Natal and Mocambique teem with many species of crab, while the colder south and west coast estuaries support only a handful of different crabs.

Vulnerability to physical extremes also changes at different stages in an organism's life-cycle, the early stages being most at risk. For instance, the zoaea larvae of the giant mud crab *Scylla serrata* (Fig. 127) are killed by temperatures over 25 °C and salinities of less than 17,5‰, and therefore cannot survive in estuaries although adults thrive there. As a result, mature females migrate out to sea to release their eggs, and only after the vulnerable larval stages are completed do the young crabs return to the estuaries.

WATER FLOW AND THE NATURE OF SEDIMENTS

Estuarine animals also face the problem of water flowing out to sea. Floating or planktonic forms have particular difficulty in maintaining their position in the estuary. It is therefore interesting to find that the sand-prawn *Callianassa kraussi* (Fig. 119) has an abbreviated life-cycle in which the usual planktonic stages have been eliminated. Its eggs hatch into larvae that resemble miniature adults and initially dig tiny side tunnels from the parent's burrow. Another common estuarine animal, the snail *Nassarius kraussianus* (Fig. 106), broods its eggs inside its shell, only releasing larvae at a late stage so that the planktonic phase is brief. On the other hand many estuarine animals do have planktonic larvae. In a way, estuarine animals are caught in a cleft stick, for while planktonic larvae are at a disadvantage because they may be carried out to sea and lost, in the event of a catastrophe eliminating most of the adult population, planktonic larvae can in turn be washed in from elsewhere to recolonise the area. Since estuaries are extremely variable and catastrophes by no means unusual, perhaps the need for recolonisation outweighs the disadvantages and is the reason that so many estuarine animals still retain a planktonic larval stage.

Most species of estuarine zooplankton have strong rhythms of activity, coming up to the surface only at night and descending to the bottom and sometimes even burrowing into the mud during the day. This migration may help the animals maintain their position in the estuary. While they are in the fresher surface waters they will tend to drift out towards the sea, but by sinking down into the more saline deeper water they will tend to be carried back up the estuary (Fig. 100). It is especially interesting that upward migration is inhibited if the zooplankton meets with very fresh water lying over the salty lower layers. This is a safety device that prevents the animals from moving upwards in times of flood when they would almost certainly be swept out to sea.

Adult copepods migrate up and down more strongly than juveniles and seem better equipped to maintain their position. For example, the adults of one common estuarine copepod, *Pseudodiaptomus stuhlmanni*, were found to be very common at the head of Richards Bay, while the juveniles seemed unable to hold their position there and

Fig. 106 **The whelk *Nassarius kraussianus*,** with siphon held erect (1 cm).

were spread over the estuary right down to the mouth where many must surely have been lost to the sea.

This raises another point. If zooplankton is to survive in estuaries it must reproduce fast enough to replace losses to the sea. Most estuarine species are small, grow quickly to maturity and reproduce rapidly. It is not easy to measure just how quickly zooplankton is able to regenerate, but an opportunity to do so arose when floods flushed Richards Bay in May 1971, eliminating most of the zooplankton. The rate at which populations built up again could then be followed. By July of the same year the numbers of the copepod, *Pseudodiaptomus stuhlmanni*, were back to normal and we estimate that it has the potential to replace its numbers about 14 times a year.

Another important issue in the ecology of estuaries is the rate of water flow. Most estuaries in southern Africa are roughly onion-shaped, the river expanding into a broad bulb-like lagoon with a narrow mouth to the sea (Fig. 107). Currents within estuaries are caused by a combination of tidal action and river-flow: at the narrow head, the river often flows rapidly and currents are strong, but as the water enters the broad lagoon it slows and loses its force. At the mouth the tidal flood and ebb of sea-water may create very strong currents, which are especially dangerous when the tide falls, sea and fresh waters surging out together.

Currents directly affect the substratum; strong currents erode the sediment leaving coarse heavy particles at the head and mouth, while in calm lagoons fine muddy sand is deposited. Quiet waters also allow lightweight organic particles to settle and accumulate, so that fine sediments have a higher organic content. While sandy beaches seldom contain more than 1 percent organic matter, lagoons usually have 5 percent to 10 percent. This organic matter is an important source of food and contributes to the abundance of life in estuaries.

The mingling of river and sea-water also aids the accumulation of organic matter in estuaries. River water contains many negatively-charged organic compounds that remain suspended as colloids because they repel one

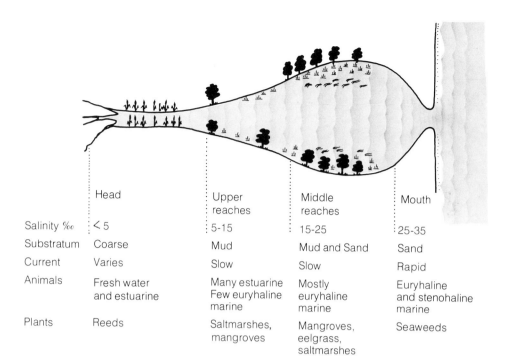

Fig. 107 The four typical zones of an estuary, showing changes of physical and biological conditions, as first described by Prof. J. H. Day.

	Head	Upper reaches	Middle reaches	Mouth
Salinity ‰	< 5	5-15	15-25	25-35
Substratum	Coarse	Mud	Mud and Sand	Sand
Current	Varies	Slow	Slow	Rapid
Animals	Fresh water and estuarine	Many estuarine Few euryhaline marine	Mostly euryhaline marine	Euryhaline and stenohaline marine
Plants	Reeds	Saltmarshes, mangroves	Mangroves, eelgrass, saltmarshes	Seaweeds

another; but when these meet the saline estuarine water, their negative charges are neutralized by the salts and they then join together (flocculate), forming larger particles that sink to the bottom, adding to the organic pool of the estuary.

In the south-western Cape many rivers carry 'black water', which is stained dark brown by humic acid and other organic compounds from the fynbos vegetation. This reduces light penetration, thus inhibiting plant growth. In Palmiet estuary, which is strongly stratified, it is an uncanny experience to dive through the black upper layers in which you cannot even see your hand if it is held out at arm's length, and then to emerge into perfectly clear sea-water beneath.

If we analyse the species that occur in estuaries, few of them are actually restricted to estuaries; the majority are marine species adapted to living in calm waters. Estuaries share almost no species with wave-beaten sandy beaches, their fauna and flora being more closely related to those occurring offshore in deep calm waters, or to species that shelter in nooks on rocky shores to avoid waves.

Neither Langebaan Lagoon nor Durban Bay are estuaries for they have no rivers entering them and they are simply sheltered arms of the sea. Despite the fact that their salinity is the same as sea-water, these bays have typically estuarine fauna and flora. It would therefore seem that calm water and not salinity is the critical factor controlling which species live in estuaries.

Calm waters are a mixed blessing: they allow the formation of stable, organically rich sediments which support many species, but they also result in rocks being covered with silt, preventing plants from settling and at the same time smothering animals that are accustomed to living on a hard clean surface. Thus while the sediments of estuaries often support a much richer fauna than that of sandy

beaches, estuarine rocks are impoverished compared with the rocky shores of open seas.

RAINFALL – FLOODS AND DROUGHTS

Changes in salinity, temperature, oxygen, currents and substratum make estuaries formidable enough, but there are two additional problems that are exceptionally acute in southern African estuaries. Much of the sub-continent receives a low and strongly seasonal rainfall: a river may be no more than a trickle for several months – even years – and then comes down in raging flood, Such floods sweep down, scouring the river beds and banks, gathering up huge amounts of silt which they carry to the estuaries, transforming the environment, either by depositing blankets of silt or by the rush of water scouring the lagoon. Often the entire body of normally brack water is swept before the flood out to sea and freshwater fills the estuary. The animals and plants risk either being flushed out to sea or smothered by silt, and if they do survive they must be able to tolerate the freshwater until the flood abates. Furthermore, the muddiness (turbidity) of floodwaters cuts down penetration of light, which may limit or prevent photosynthesis, making this an even more trying episode for estuarine life.

Siltation is perhaps the single overriding danger in southern African estuaries. Small amounts of silt are welcome for they herald the arrival of fresh organic material and nutrients, but excessive silt smothers and fills in the estuary. As discussed later in this chapter, various human activities have greatly increased this problem.

A striking example of the effect of siltation is Onrus Lagoon, near Hermanus, where a relatively deep and large estuary existed until the 1940s, when heavy floods brought down huge quantities of silt that filled almost a third of the lagoon. Since then the river entering this lagoon has been dammed upstream so that now there are no annual floods to sweep the estuary clear: the mouth is closed most of the time, the water is now essentially fresh, and dense growths of the reed *Phragmites* have colonized the silt and have taken over almost half of the lagoon. The reeds trap further silt in turn, and so are creeping slowly across the lagoon and will choke it completely unless action is taken. Figs. 108A and B contrast conditions in 1921 and 1979.

A second problem arises from the seasonal pattern of rainfall. The mouth of an estuary is kept open by tidal currents and by the escaping river waters which scour the mouth. On the other hand, waves and coastal currents build up sandbars across the estuary mouth. There is often a fine balance between this sand deposition and its removal and, during the dry season, there may not be enough river flow to prevent the mouth from closing.

When the rains do arrive, water builds up within the closed estuary until it finally breaks through the sandbar and scours the mouth clean. This is a natural seasonal occurrence in many of our estuaries. Unfortunately, estuary mouths are often opened prematurely by artificial means to prevent flooding of properties and lands on the banks. The outflow is then less than normal and fails to open the mouth to the same extent. An unfortunate chain of events follows: the mouth closes again more quickly and may then become progressively sanded up until it closes almost permanently.

Prolonged closure of an estuary mouth can have disastrous effects. Tides cease to affect the salinity and the water level so that salt-marsh vegetation near the high-tide zone dies if the water level drops. Nutrients previously supplied from the sea are no longer replenished. Larvae that colonise estuaries from the sea cannot be recruited. Species that return to the sea to breed are prevented from doing so. It is hardly surprising that estuaries like Mngazana in Transkei, Morrumbene in Moçambique, and Knysna, that are always open, have between five and ten times as many species as estuaries such as Milnerton and the Bot River which close for long periods.

FOOD: SUPPLY AND DEMAND
Estuaries can be extremely productive. For instance, where shellfish are harvested from estuaries in Europe and North America an annual yield of 7 800 kg of mussels, 3 700 kg of cockles and 400 kg of oysters may be gleaned from each hectare. By comparison, stock-farming yields about 18 kg of mutton per hectare. Small wonder that estuaries are sought-after for the mariculture of oysters, prawns and other shellfish.

Fig. 109 compares the productivity of different types of ecosystems. Estuaries rank highest, together with the most intensive agriculture, coral reefs, kelp beds and areas of strong upwelling. By comparison, most of the open sea is ten to 20 times less productive.

Production by Plant Life
Estuaries are so productive in large part because they act as 'nutrient traps', gaining nutrients from both rivers and the

Fig. 108 Two photographs of Onrus Lagoon, taken in 1921 (A) and 1977 (B), showing how the lagoon has been choked by reeds.

sea. Organic particles carried down rivers settle in estuaries where they are decomposed by bacteria, releasing nutrients that in turn fertilise plant growth. With every tide fresh nutrients wash in from the sea. The estuarine muds absorb phosphates which are then extracted by rooted plants such as *Spartina* and the eelgrass *Zostera*, which release any excess phosphate from their leaves and thus further enrich the water. Such plants are described as 'phosphate pumps'. Estuarine waters are consequently often rich in phosphates while nitrates are more likely to be in short supply and to limit plant growth.

What plant life capitalizes on the calm waters and rich nutrient supplies of estuaries? Phytoplankton is obviously at a disadvantage here: firstly, it is always in danger of being washed out to sea, and secondly, many estuaries are so muddy that only the top few centimetres of water enjoy sufficient light for photosynthesis. In addition, large rooted plants (macrophytes) may inhibit the growth of phytoplankton. Mangroves, for instance, release tannins that suppress phytoplankton and all macrophytes can compete with phytoplankton for nutrients. In Langebaan Lagoon, for example, the level of nitrate in the water drops dramatically from the mouth of the lagoon to the head (presumably because the rich growths of salt-marsh plants use it as fast as it is supplied) and phytoplankton therefore declines up the length of the lagoon with this drop in nitrates.

Two other examples of this effect relate to the practical

Production (10³ k cal/m²/yr)

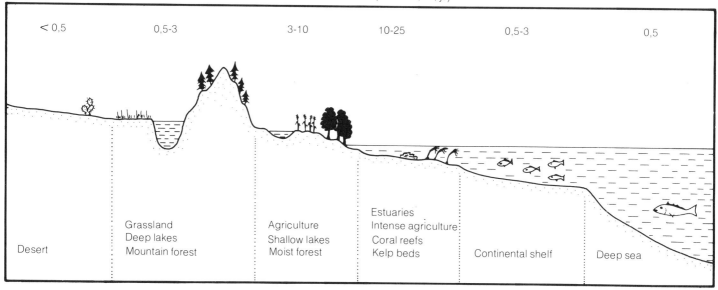

| < 0,5 | 0,5-3 | 3-10 | 10-25 | 0,5-3 | 0,5 |

Desert

Grassland
Deep lakes
Mountain forest

Agriculture
Shallow lakes
Moist forest

Estuaries
Intense agriculture
Coral reefs
Kelp beds

Continental shelf

Deep sea

Fig. 109 The high productivity of estuaries is compared here with that of other habitats in the sea and on land.

management of lagoons and estuaries. Zeekoevlei in the Western Cape has been cleared of many of its reeds to allow boats to reach the water easily, but their removal has allowed phytoplankton to thrive on the nutrients that flow in from agricultural lands, and the vlei is now like pea-soup. In Sandvlei, also in the Western Cape, the weed *Potamogeton* has also been removed to allow yachting. Provided only the top layers of the weed are cut back this has few repercussions. However, a small part of the estuary was dredged deeper in an attempt to stop the weed growing. Into these deeper trenches salt water sank, effectively excluding weeds which cannot tolerate high salinities, but allowing phytoplankton to bloom. Once again (if only on a small scale) the elimination of competing macrophytes allowed phytoplankton to thrive.

There are thus several reasons why phytoplankton is seldom abundant in estuaries. Before we dismiss the phytoplankton out of hand, it must be remembered that it is able to grow very fast and, if conditions are suitable, can double its mass as quickly as once a day, so that low levels of phytoplankton may still produce significant quantities of food.

Resting on the surface of estuarine muds and sands are a surprisingly high number of microscopic diatoms, each looking like a tiny pill box with beautifully sculptured surfaces (Fig. 110). Their numbers are greatest in quiet muddy areas where they may reach 2 000 million per square metre! More interesting is that large numbers occur within the sediments, as much as 10 to 20 cm below the surface. Obviously they are unable to photosynthesize here, for light penetrates only the top 2 or 3 mm of the sand, yet these deeper diatoms seem healthy and contain chlorophyll. Experiments have revealed the astonishing fact that they can survive three months of total darkness. We guess that the activities of sand- and mud-prawns bury the diatoms and they remain there until eaten, or until they manage to surface and begin photosynthesizing once more. These diatoms may be an important source of food and are eaten in large quantities by mullet.

Another intriguing aspect of diatoms is their ability to migrate up and down through the top few millimetres of sand. In estuaries with murky waters they remain on the surface of intertidal banks only while the tide is out, migrating down into the sediments as the water rises over them. Perhaps this reduces the chances of their being eaten by mud-grubbing fish. In clear-water estuaries no such migration occurs: perhaps enough light penetrates the water to make it worthwhile for the diatoms to remain on the surface all the time, even if they risk being eaten.

Most seaweeds cannot tolerate low salinities and are excluded from estuaries, although one exception is the stringy green *Enteromorpha* (Plate 166) which survives an amazing range of salinities from fresh water to three times the concentration of sea-water! It does, however, need a firm substratum on which to attach itself. *Enteromorpha* can become a pest in estuaries, as the developers of Marina

Fig. 110 The exquisite pattern on the surface of pill-box diatoms is revealed in this electron micrograph, magnified 2500x life size.

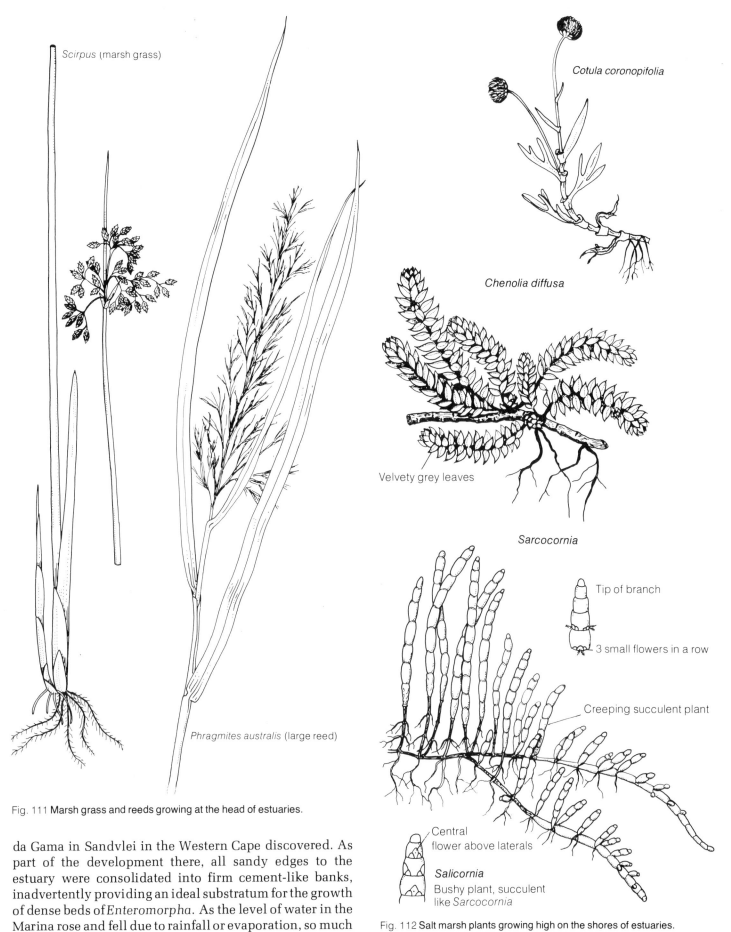

Scirpus (marsh grass)

Phragmites australis (large reed)

Fig. 111 Marsh grass and reeds growing at the head of estuaries.

Cotula coronopifolia

Chenolia diffusa

Velvety grey leaves

Sarcocornia

Tip of branch

3 small flowers in a row

Creeping succulent plant

Central flower above laterals

Salicornia
Bushy plant, succulent like Sarcocornia

Fig. 112 Salt marsh plants growing high on the shores of estuaries.

da Gama in Sandvlei in the Western Cape discovered. As part of the development there, all sandy edges to the estuary were consolidated into firm cement-like banks, inadvertently providing an ideal substratum for the growth of dense beds of Enteromorpha. As the level of water in the Marina rose and fell due to rainfall or evaporation, so much

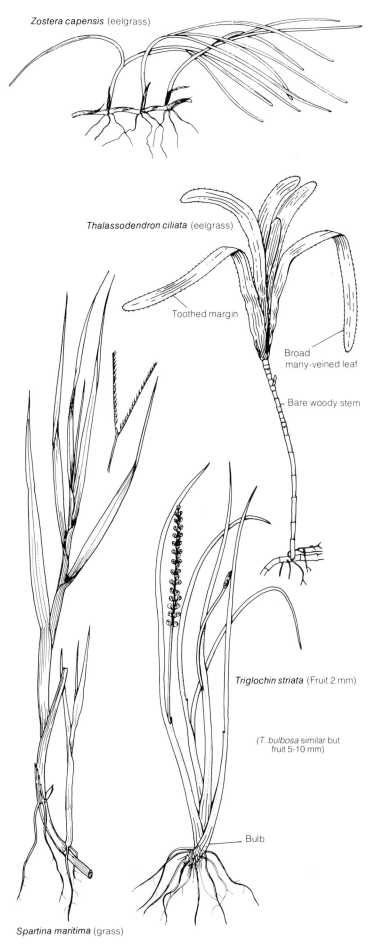

Zostera capensis (eelgrass)

Thalassodendron ciliata (eelgrass)

Toothed margin

Broad
many-veined leaf

Bare woody stem

Triglochin striata (Fruit 2 mm)

(T. bulbosa similar but
fruit 5-10 mm)

Bulb

Spartina maritima (grass)

Fig. 113 Eelgrasses *(Zostera* and *Thalassodendron)* grow in estuarine lagoons and sheltered waters, while rice grass *(Spartina)* occurs near the top of the shore in open estuaries.

of this weed died and rotted, creating a foul smell and an oozy slime. This was unpleasant enough, but when a pet dog ate some of the algae and died, the problem could no longer be ignored. The solution was simple but ironical: cover up the consolidated banks with coarse, shifting sand to prevent *Enteromorpha* from settling. The developers had taken the progressive step of appointing an ecologist to aid their venture, and in solving practical problems such as this he more than earned his keep.

Even in Langebaan Lagoon, which is filled with sea-water, most seaweeds are excluded because silt coats the rocks. Only one species thrives here: the commercially-important *Graciliara verrucosa* (Plate 177n) from which agar is extracted (see Chapter 7).

Rooted plants such as salt-marsh plants, mangroves, sea grasses and reeds thrive in estuaries for they are in no danger of being flushed away and, since they grow around the edges or on intertidal sand banks, they receive enough light even if the water is muddy. They are also able to extract nutrients directly from the muddy sand, while algae and phytoplankton must rely on nutrients dissolved in the water. At the heads of estuaries where salinities are low, reeds such as *Phragmites* and *Scirpus* (Fig.111) often line the banks where they may form dense beds that con-solidate the soil and act as filters, trapping silt and using nutrients in the river-water trickling through them. In this manner reed-beds fill a vital function keeping the estuary clean and preventing excess fertilisation. A case in point is Sandvlei estuary. When the Marina da Gama was developed there, the reed-beds at the head of the estuary were reclaimed and canalised – despite protests from ecologists and conservationists. As a result, fertilisers washed from surrounding farms entered directly into the lagoon, increasing the growth of the weed *Potamogeton*, much to the annoyance of yachtsmen. Mosquitos thrived in the open pans left by the removal of the reeds. The irony is that the developers had appointed an ecologist to their staff, but were too impatient to await his arrival before going ahead with the reclamation of the reed-beds. The outcome of removing the reeds would have been predicta-ble enough to an ecologist. The final twist to this sad tale has been the decision not to go ahead with the develop-ment of the reed-bed area, so that its destruction was unnecessary. Over the last six years, the beds have slowly regrown, though they are still not restored to their original condition. In fairness, it must be admitted that Sandvlei was already degraded even before the marina was deve-loped.

The salt-tolerant plants that form broad salt-marshes around the edges of estuarine lagoons are of great impor-tance. These include plants such as *Sarcocornia, Salicor-nia, Chenolea, Cotula, Spartina* and *Triglochin* (Fig. 112). Below these salt-marshes, beds of eelgrass grow: *Zostera* (Fig. 113) occurs in many southern estuaries while *Cymodocea* (Fig.113) replaces it in Mocambique. Salt-marshes and eelgrasses account for 60 percent to 90 percent of the plant production in the temperate south and west coast estuaries. In Transkei and Natal and even more particularly in tropical Moçambique they are still important, but are often eclipsed by dense mangrove forests.

Mangroves are the only trees adapted to living in salty tidal waters. Here they face two main problems. First, they are rooted in water-saturated soil and in danger of being drowned – for all root systems need air. As a solution they have evolved special aerial roots (pneumatophores) that stick out of the mud. *Avicennia marina* has pencil-shaped pneumatophores that stick straight up out of the ground; *Bruguiera gymnorrhiza* has knobbly elbow-like projections; and *Rhizophora mucronata* has strut-roots that grow from high on the trunk and serve both as pneumatophores and as stabilizers to the tree (Fig. 116).

Mangroves are vulnerable to changes of water level, for they drown if the pneumatophores are submerged for too long. Consequently they are seldom found in closed estuaries in which there is no tidal action. Kosi Bay is normally open to the sea and supports rich mangroves, but on one of the rare occasions when the mouth was closed and water levels rose, there was a mass mortality of the mangroves.

The second problem facing mangroves is that they live in brack water and, like all higher plants, rely on transpiration of water from their leaves to draw water and nutrients up from their roots. If mangroves draw up salt water and evaporate it from their leaves, what do they do with the salt left behind in their tissues? *Bruguieria* has roots that actively exclude most salt and the salt that is taken up accumulates in old leaves which are subsequently shed. *Rhizophora* is less successful in preventing salt uptake and its tissues contain about 3‰ salt, over 100 times more than most land plants. It has special salt glands on its leaves that exude a very concentrated salty fluid (of about 20‰ to 40‰) and help rid the plant of salt.

Germination of mangrove seeds poses problems of its own. Mangroves have unusual seeds that germinate while still attached to the flower. In some, each seedling forms a long cigar-shaped fruit (the hypocotyl) which hangs beneath the remnants of the flower. When mature, this plummets to the ground and usually plunges straight into the mud, thus reducing the chances of it being swept out to sea (Fig. 115). *Avicennia* is the only species that drops round seedlings that are not immediately embedded in the mud, but wash around before taking root. Not surprisingly, this species is a pioneer that initiates the nucleus of new

Fig. 114 A cigar-shaped hypocotyl grows from the attached mangrove fruit.

Fig. 115 When the mangrove fruit drops, the sharp tip of the hypocotyl plunges into the mud, embedding the fruit so that it is not likely to be washed away.

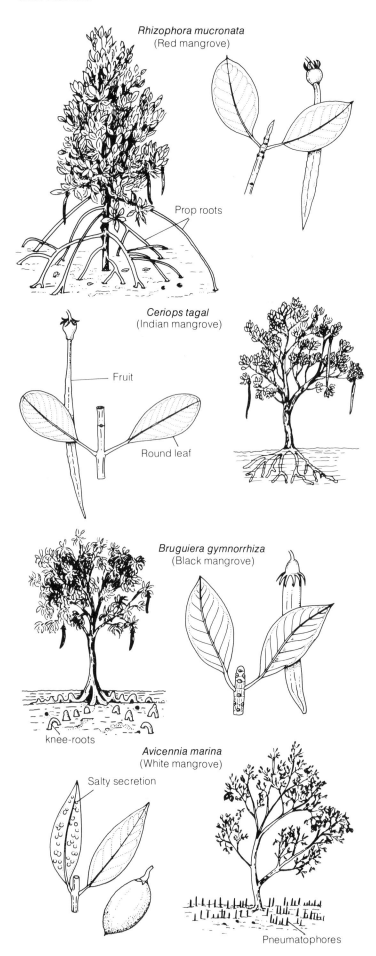

Fig. 116 Four mangrove trees found in tropical and subtropical estuaries.

Rhizophora mucronata
(Red mangrove)

Prop roots

Ceriops tagal
(Indian mangrove)

Fruit

Round leaf

Bruguiera gymnorrhiza
(Black mangrove)

knee-roots

Avicennia marina
(White mangrove)

Salty secretion

Pneumatophores

mangrove stands. *Bruguiera* and *Rhizophora* can only settle in sediments which have already been stabilised by other plants such as *Avicennia*. In addition, *Bruguiera* seedlings thrive in the shade of other trees while those of *Avicennia* are sickly when shaded. Because of this, *Bruguiera* replaces *Avicennia* in the heart of more mature mangrove swamps, while *Avicennia* is commonest at the fringes.

Mangroves play important rôles. They are very productive and shed large quantities of leaves which can be eaten by animals such as the crab *Sesarma meinerti* (Fig. 125), or add to the detritus so important in estuaries. Mangroves also have a tremendous capacity for trapping silt because their rootlets form a dense web which stabilises mud banks and cleanses the water of silt.

Mangroves are not the only plants to suffer when estuary mouths close and the water level changes drastically. Salt-marshes are either left high and dry or are submerged and drowned; eelgrasses disappear. If the salinity rises beyond 50‰ due to evaporation, almost all aquatic plants die. However, if the salinity of the water becomes more diluted, a whole new suite of aquatic weeds may take over. Between salinities of 5‰ and 20‰ *Chara* and *Potamogeton* (Fig. 117) thrive and are common near the heads of estuaries. At higher salinities, between 15‰ and 25‰, *Ruppia* (Fig. 117) takes their place. A special study has been made of these plants in Swartvlei estuary and lake in the eastern Cape. The lake has a low salinity and is fringed by *Chara* in the shallows. In deeper waters of 0,8 to 2,3 m *Potamogeton* replaces it and forms a dense band around the lake. It cannot flourish in water deeper than this because the stained 'black water' cuts out too much light. *Chara* owes its existence to the *Potamogeton* because it does not tolerate wave action and thrives only where sheltered by the dense *Potamogeton*.

Both a bridge and a causeway have been built between Swartvlei Lake and its estuary. These reduce tidal flow into the lake by 40 percent and the resultant drop in salinity in the lake has allowed *Potamogeton* to take over more of the lake. Below the bridge *Ruppia* dominates in the higher salinities, although it is replaced nearer the mouth by the eelgrass *Zostera* which forms luxuriant beds. *Ruppia* is able to live in much higher and much lower salinities than it ever experiences in Swartvlei, which makes one wonder why it does not occur higher in the lake or further down near the mouth. It has been suggested that it is sandwiched between *Zostera* and *Potamogeton*: one out-competing it near the mouth, and the other preventing it from penetrating the lake.

Salt-marsh plants, eelgrasses, mangroves, reeds and aquatic weeds obviously have different requirements so each predominates in a particular region and in different types of estuaries. Taken together they are by far the most important plant life in estuaries and the source of most of

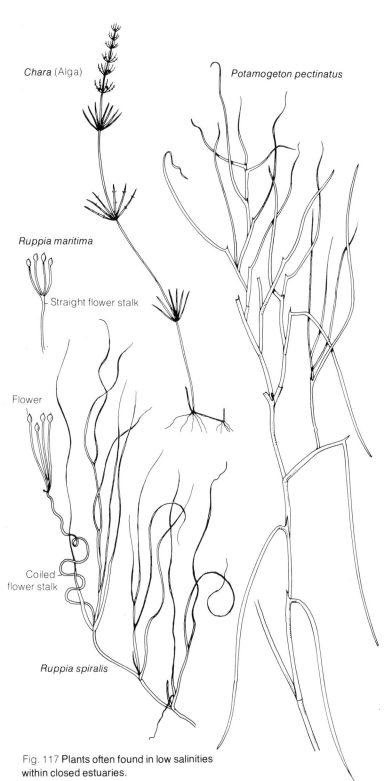

Chara (Alga)

Potamogeton pectinatus

Ruppia maritima

Straight flower stalk

Flower

Coiled flower stalk

Ruppia spiralis

Fig. 117 Plants often found in low salinities within closed estuaries.

the food that sustains the prolific organisms living there. The implications of 'reclaiming' the wetlands that support these plants are obvious; the term 'reclaiming' in itself displays the arrogance of man and his attitude to areas such as salt-marshes which lie at the heart of estuarine food-webs.

Herbivores

Very few herbivores feed directly on the plants growing in estuaries. At one time the hippopotamus may have been a major consumer of aquatic weeds, but only in Lake St Lucia and the Kosi Lakes is it still important. The dugong, that ugliest of beasts whose sighting has been blamed for mariners' visions of mermaids, eats quantities of estuarine weeds, but it is very rare although occasional specimens are still sighted in Moçambique. Only the red-knobbed coot (Fulica cristata) is common enough to be considered important as a herbivore, and this bird eats large quantities of Potamogeton.

The juveniles of both species of stumpnose (Rhabdosargus sarba and R. holubi) feed on Zostera and Ruppia, but although their guts can be crammed with these plants they seem to derive little nourishment from them, for when the plants pass out in the faeces their cells are still intact. It seems the fish digest only the tiny animals and plants that coat these two plants. Thus, as in kelp-beds, there are few animals that feed directly on the plants.

The detrital food chain

Most aquatic weeds, reeds and salt-marsh plants grow fastest in summer and then die back. Eelgrass grows continuously but, somewhat like kelp, the tips of its blades erode away as fast as they grow. Mangrove trees are longer-lived than most other estuarine plants but shed large quantities of leaves. Detritus accumulates from all these sources, and is added to the organic matter introduced from the rivers and the sea, to become the major source of food for animals in estuaries.

It is always difficult to estimate how much material comes from each of these sources, but an attempt has been made at the Palmiet estuary. Nets were laid at the mouth and across the river to catch large plants being washed in or out of the estuary; water samples were taken hourly over full tidal cycles to see how much particulate organic matter was washed in and out at the mouth; and measurements over the course of a year determined how much plant life was produced within the estuary. In this case, estuarine plants produced about one-fifth of the detritus, while three-fifths was imported as particles of organic matter from the river and sea; the rest was introduced in the form of kelp or riverine vegetation that washed into the estuary. Incidentally, the sheer agony of obtaining these estimates can only be appreciated by those stalwarts who huddled at the Palmiet mouth taking samples throughout the day and night while the weather first scorched and then froze us.

Because large quantities of detritus accumulate in estuaries, bacteria occur abundantly in the sediments, and their densities are directly related to the organic content of the sediments. In Langebaan Lagoon, for instance, there may be 600 million bacteria per gram of sediment!

Much of the detritus consists of complex compounds that make up the structural elements of plants, which are a poor food source for animals, being difficult to digest and having little nitrogen. Bacteria, however, decompose these materials to a more digestible blend, multiplying their own numbers in the process. The rich soup of bacteria and partly decomposed detritus is then a more palatable food source for animals.

Fig. 119 The detailed structure of the sand-prawn *Callianassa kraussi*, showing how its body is modified for life within a sandy burrow.

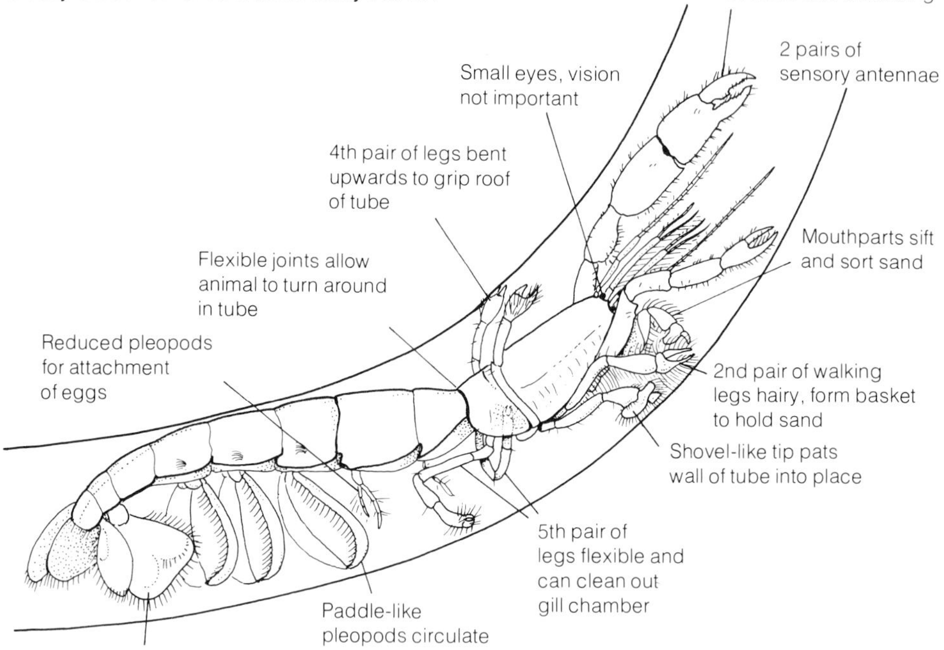

Fig. 118 Apparently lifeless estuarine mud teems with life and is continually disturbed by burrowing prawns (forming large holes), and worms and snails (smaller holes). These animals are eaten by birds whose footprints and peck-marks also imprint the mud.

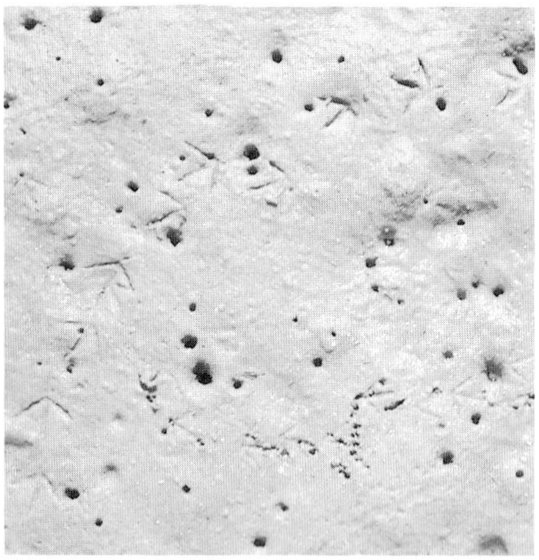

Small eyes, vision not important

Nipper for defence and burrowing

2 pairs of sensory antennae

4th pair of legs bent upwards to grip roof of tube

Mouthparts sift and sort sand

Flexible joints allow animal to turn around in tube

Reduced pleopods for attachment of eggs

2nd pair of walking legs hairy, form basket to hold sand

Shovel-like tip pats wall of tube into place

5th pair of legs flexible and can clean out gill chamber

Paddle-like pleopods circulate water through tube

Uropods wedge animal in tube

It comes as no surprise that over 80 percent of the invertebrates in estuaries, including the zooplankton, are detritus feeders. Mud-prawns *(Upogebia africana)* and sand-prawns *(Callianassa kraussi)* abound in many of our estuaries, although only the sand-prawn survives in closed estuaries. Both species form burrows in the sediment (Fig. 118), and the way in which the body of *Callianassa* is adapted for life in a burrow is shown in Fig. 119.

At first sight detritus-feeders seem to have a simple enough method of feeding, grubbing through the sediment gulping detritus but, since much of the detritus is not nutritious, most species have some means of enriching or concentrating this food. For example, the sand-prawn *Callianassa* circulates water through its burrow where it traps suspended particles. To do so, its first pair of legs and mouthparts are covered with a net of fine hairs forming a basket that holds and sifts the sediment so that the fine organically-rich particles are separated out and eaten. Although some of this organic matter is digested and absorbed by the sand-prawn, much of it is passed out neatly packed up in their sausage-like faeces. Each sand-prawn may produce 3 grams of faeces per day. This sounds insignificant until we begin multiplying by the number of days in a year and the density of sand-prawns: in a small estuary like the Palmiet, which is only 1,5 km in length, sand-prawns may produce more than 200 tonnes of faeces each year. Since the faeces are very rich in organic matter they must be a prime food source for bacteria, and possibly for some animals as well.

Assiminea, a tiny snail that sometimes occurs in countless thousands near the high-water line, and its close relative *Hydrobia,* are also detritus-feeders (Fig. 120). Studies on European *Hydrobia* show that its faeces contain almost as much organic carbon as the detritus originally eaten by the snails, but much less organic nitrogen. From this it seems that *Hydrobia* does not digest or absorb much of the detritus as such, but strips off the bacteria attached to the organic particles. Since bacteria have a high nitrogen content, they provide the nitrogen necessary for protein synthesis and body growth. Removal of the bacteria from the detritus leaves the snails' faeces with little nitrogen but still laden with organic carbon. New bacteria soon colonize these faeces, increasing the nitrogen again, and the snails will then happily consume their own faeces. Thus the faeces are literally being recycled. Weird though this idea may be, it reveals an important principle: 'detritus-feeders' may really be bacterial feeders. This re-emphasises the important role of bacteria in making the energy locked in the detritus available to animals.

Another detritus-feeder is the humble bloodworm, *Arenicola loveni* (Fig. 121), so popular as bait. *Arenicola* forms U-shaped tubes in the sand, drawing water down one side and pumping it out the other, so that at one end a depression forms in the sand while the other end is raised (Fig. 121). In the case of the European *Arenicola*, this circulation of water achieves three things: firstly, suspended organic matter is trapped by the sand and so enriches the sediment; secondly, the circulation supplies oxygen to the worm; finally, the normally stagnant sediments immediately around the burrow are oxygenated. This supply of oxygen allows bacteria to decompose the organic matter more efficiently, and soon dense bacterial populations build up. Protozoa eat the bacteria, and both may form a food source for the bloodworm. In this way the bloodworm cultures its own supply of micro-organisms. We still do not know if our local species 'garden' micro-organisms in this manner.

The pea-shaped snail *Nassarius kraussianus* is a

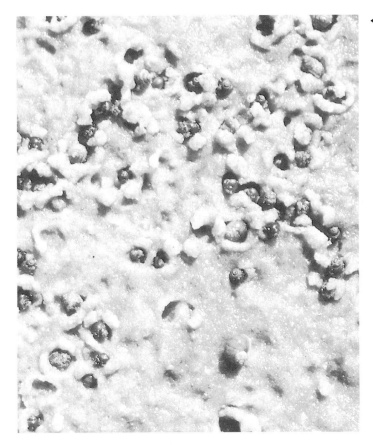

Fig. 122 One of the commonest estuarine prawns, *Penaeus japonicus* (10 cm).

detritus-feeder, too, but supplements its diet by scavenging on dead animals. As it marches over the sediment, it holds its siphon erect like an elephant's trunk, sensing for decaying animal matter (Fig.106).

Edible prawns occur in many east coast estuaries, *Penaeus indicus* being the commonest species (Fig. 122). In Moçambique, the Zambesi Delta and adjacent estuaries once supported a large prawn industry. Prawns are mainly detritus-feeders and thrive in such areas because of the detritus from rich mangrove forests, but are not above scavenging or even eating small animals as well. Adult prawns migrate from estuaries to spawn and their larvae develop at sea, but the juveniles then return for an extended period to feed and grow in the same way as many fish use estuaries as nursery grounds.

Filter-feeders

Although the sediments of estuaries are usually the richest source of detritus, the water itself carries suspended particles and phytoplankton that may be exploited by filter-feeders. For example, the common estuarine hermit crab, *Diogenes brevirostris*, in addition to being a scavenger, has a fine net of hairs on its antennae which it sweeps through the water to catch particles (Fig. 266B).

There are several filter-feeding bivalves in southern African estuaries. The mussels *Arcuatula (Lamya) capensis* and *Musculus virgiliae* attach onto weeds and rocks, *Musculus* being especially common at the heads of estuaries. *Dosinia, Eumarcia, Mactra* and the pencil-bait *Solen* (Plates 110 & 111) all dig into the sediment but extend their siphons to the surface to feed. Burrowing bivalves are a feature of European estuaries and some are very common in Moçambique where they are gathered for the local market. Further south they are seldom abundant. Part of the reason for this may be that they compete unsuccessfully with mud-prawns. Swartkops estuary well illustrates this point for the bivalve community stops abruptly where the mud-prawns become dominant. However, after floods eliminated most animal life in this estuary, several bivalve species began to settle in areas previously

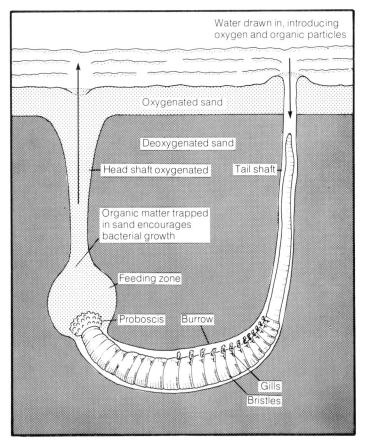

Fig. 121 The bloodworm *Arenicola* circulates water through its burrow, aerating the sand and encouraging the growth of micro-organisms on which it feeds, thus cultivating its food supply.

Water drawn in, introducing oxygen and organic particles

Oxygenated sand

Deoxygenated sand

Head shaft oxygenated

Tail shaft

Organic matter trapped in sand encourages bacterial growth

Feeding zone

Proboscis   Burrow

Gills

Bristles

Fig. 123 Embedded knee-deep, biologists sample glutinous mangrove mud for animal life.

Fig. 124 The mangrove snail, *Cerithidea decollata* (4 cm) clings to mangrove trunks, together with the smaller *Littorina scabra*.

occupied by the mud-prawn. This suggests that they are capable of living in such areas but are normally kept out by the mud-prawns. Perhaps the burrowing activities of the prawns smother newly-settled bivalves.

The projecting siphons of bivalves are tempting morsels for predatory fish such as grunters, white steenbras and river bream. The pencil-baits (*Solen capensis* and *S. corneus*) have developed special weak planes in their siphons, and are able to voluntarily sacrifice part of the siphon to a predator rather than risk being dragged out of the mud.

Two other burrowing bivalves, the horse mussel *Atrina squamifera* and the white clam *Mactra glabrata* (Plate 110 & 111), are common in some of our estuaries. The horse mussel has a long wedge-shaped shell and digs vertically down into the sediment, leaving only the sharp back edges of the shell exposed, so that it is liable to cut one's feet. Living inside the shell of these bivalves there are often one or more small blind crabs (*Pinnotheres dofleini*), which are semi-parasitic and sit astride the gills of the bivalve, cleaning off all the hard-earned food the horse mussel has filtered from the water.

Mactra occurs in incredible densities in some lagoons, particularly in areas where currents are strong. The ani-mals are so numerous in the channel entering Langebaan Lagoon that they orient parallel to one another in order to fit in side by side: there are up to 400 per m² with a wet flesh weight of over five kilograms! Another indication of their density is the fact that juveniles are never found mixed with adults: presumably the larvae never have a chance of settling where the densely-packed adults are vacuum-cleaning the water. At such high densities, *Mactra* must filter enormous volumes of water, and is surely partly responsible for the clarity of the water in Langebaan Lagoon.

The mangrove fauna

Mangroves trap silt and the mud beneath them is accordingly very fine, oozy and highly organic (Fig.123). Although this mud contains a potentially rich source of food, very few species can live permanently buried in it, for it is glutinous, black and sulphurous, and almost lacking in oxygen. Yet a few species manage to avoid or overcome these disadvantages and thrive on this organic mud.

The tiny snail *Assiminea bisasciata* avoids the problems of a muddy substratum by living and feeding on the surface, but it pays a price, for when the tide comes in it is

Fig. 125 One of the larger estuarine crabs, *Sesarma meinerti* (12 cm),
occupies hooded holes from which it dashes to collect mangrove leaves (below).

heavily preyed upon by fish and crabs. *Cerithidea decollata* (Fig.124) feeds on the surface of the mud only during low tide and, by climbing up mangrove trunks as the tide rises, escapes these predators. During spring-tides, when the tidal range is at its greatest, fewer of these snails descend to feed, and at these times climb higher than normal on the trees. This is of particular interest, as the snails must have some in-built rhythm that induces them to climb higher during spring-tides, for they are never in contact with water and their upward migration starts long before the water reaches them.

A number of crabs frequent mangroves. *Sesarma catenata* may occur in vast numbers, scuttling around feeding on the mud and diving into holes when alarmed. A much larger species, *S. meinerti* (Fig. 125), lives near the top of the shore and digs deep holes that have raised hooded entrances and extend down as much as 2 m to the water-table. This habit allows these crabs to live inland and holes are sometimes found hundreds of metres from the estuary. They feed on coarse detritus, leaf litter, fungi and lichens, and avidly collect the leaves that fall from mangroves, scuttling from their holes to grab leaves within seconds of their falling, and dashing back to their burrows with the leaf triumphantly gripped in nipper (Fig. 125).

The most appealing of all the mangrove animals are the fiddler crabs, *Uca* species, which live in dense colonies on the edge of mangroves and in sandbanks (Plates 76 & 77). It requires patience and a statue-like stillness to really appreciate these crabs, for they are shy, wary creatures that

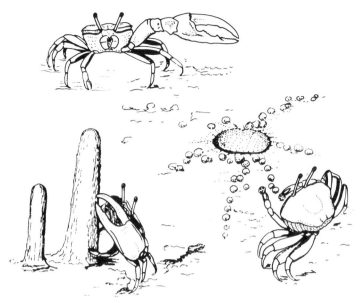

Fig. 126 A male fiddler crab *(Uca)* waves his enlarged nipper to attract a female, which is feeding by rolling sand-balls in her mouthparts. Discarded pseudo-faeces radiate from her hole. A second male scrapes algae from the aerial root of a mangrove tree.

scuttle down their holes at the least jitter. At low tide they emerge to feed, and their antics can keep one entertained for hours. They feed by scooping up blobs of mud with their nippers and with their mouthparts they roll these into balls, extracting what food they can, before discarding the balls as pseudofaeces which form trails radiating outwards from each crab's hole. Much time is spent on the most amusing ritualised pantomime with other individuals: either as territorial defence of the hole or in courtship. Each male has one enormously-enlarged vivid nipper, and this is waved rhythmically in the air like a signalman's semaphore flag to communicate with other crabs. Since several species may live together, some means is needed of recognizing whether a potential mate is kith or kin, which is probably why the precise manner and timing of these signals differ from species to species. During the summer breeding season the crabs become more vivid and the males spend most of their time in frenzied gesturing at females, swinging the nipper in a beckoning manner that, in human terms, is unmistakably a seductive invitation.

Males also fight other males (and even females of other species) if they come too close to their holes, chasing them with nipper aloft and waved threateningly like a sword. Large males prevent small ones from building holes near their own burrows, and even if an intruder does succeed in making a burrow the larger male will repeatedly flatten and fill it in until its occupant concedes and gives up its position (Fig. 126).

The fiddler crabs' deep burrows serve several purposes, the most important being shelter against predators. Before the advancing tide covers them, the crabs retire into their holes neatly blocking off each hole with a plug of mud. Because the burrows are firm, they allow air or oxygen-laden water to percolate down to the crabs so that they are able to survive the anoxic mangrove muds.

Hard substrata are in short supply in estuaries, and mangrove trunks and pneumatophores therefore often support animals more usually found on rocks – including oysters and barnacles. In Australia, most of the oyster harvest is gleaned from mangrove estuaries, and rafts have been built to increase the settlement of oysters.

Littorina scabra (Fig. 124) spends most of its life feeding on the surface of mangrove trunks, but since it has a planktonic larval stage it is not freed from its ancestral aquatic existence and must descend to the water to reproduce. These descents are rhythmic, coinciding with the fortnightly high spring-tides, so that the snails only need to move a short distance to spawn in the water.

Invertebrate predators

Estuaries support few invertebrate predators. The snail *Natica* drills holes through the shells of bivalves to feed on the animal: and crabs such as *Hymenosoma* (Fig. 102) eat small crustaceans. Perhaps the most significant invertebrate predator is the giant mud crab *Scylla serrata* (Fig. 127), which reaches 40 cm across and has massive pincers the size of a man's fist. These formidable weapons are capable of cutting off a finger, yet *Scylla* feeds mainly on minute molluscs including the pea-sized *Nassarius kraussianus*.

Birds

Many birds use estuaries as feeding grounds, including weed-eating species such as the red-knobbed coot and fish-eaters such as pelicans, herons and cormorants.

The waders are perhaps the most interesting of the estuarine birds, for most of them breed in the arctic regions during the brief but productive summer there and then migrate south as the black arctic winter approaches. For large numbers, the end of the journey south is Langebaan Lagoon, which supports up to 55 000 waders in summer: over 40 percent of the total wader population in the south western Cape. Most are curlew sandpipers (Fig. 128). Sandwich Harbour and Walvis Bay also support large

Fig. 127 The giant mud crab *Scylla serrata* (30 cm) threateningly waving its nippers amongst the aerial roots of a mangrove.

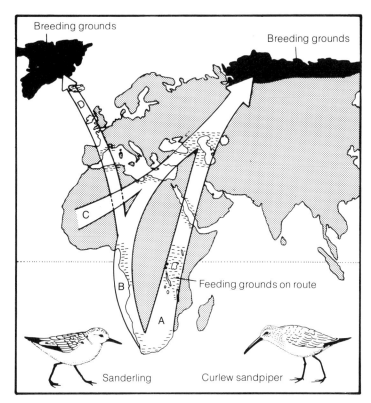

Fig. 128 Migratory routes of the curlew sandpiper and sanderling.
(A) Route of curlews on southward and northward journeys, and the
southward route of the sanderling. (B) Sanderling northward route.
(C) Movement of West African curlew population. (D) Sanderling migration
to Greenland. Feeding grounds on route are shaded.

Fig. 129 Greater flamingos feed by treadling the mud and scooping up
invertebrates that float out (A). Circular impressions are left in the mud (B).

numbers of waders. Areas like these are clearly of great
significance and in need of conservation, as has been recognised by the international Ramsar Convention on Wetlands of International Importance. Huge tracts of land in
Siberia and Greenland have been set aside as nature
reserves where birds can breed in peace, but this is a futile
action unless similar wetland reserves preserve their feeding grounds in the southern hemisphere: so it is encouraging that Langebaan Lagoon has now been declared a
reserve.

Waders eat quantities of invertebrates, particularly
worms, shrimps and the tiny snail *Assiminea*. In Langebaan Lagoon alone, the waders consume 150 tonnes a year:
13 percent of the annual invertebrate production and equivalent to about 500 million invertebrates.

In preparation for their arduous return to the Arctic,
migrant birds must increase their rate of feeding to fatten
themselves. Juvenile birds, not having mastered the art of
picking out prey that is often hidden in the sand, feed
inefficiently and, perhaps because of this, many over-
winter in southern African lagoons and estuaries, and only
migrate the following year.

Despite being so abundant, waders make up only about
5 percent of the biomass of bird life in estuaries, the larger
pelicans, cormorants and flamingos making up 85 percent.
Pelicans alone may reach a biomass of 55 kg per km². Since
this is equal to the combined biomass (per square
kilometre) of *all* top terrestrial carnivores such as the big
cats and hunting dogs, their impact on fish populations
must be considerable.

The lesser flamingo is a filter-feeder, sieving water

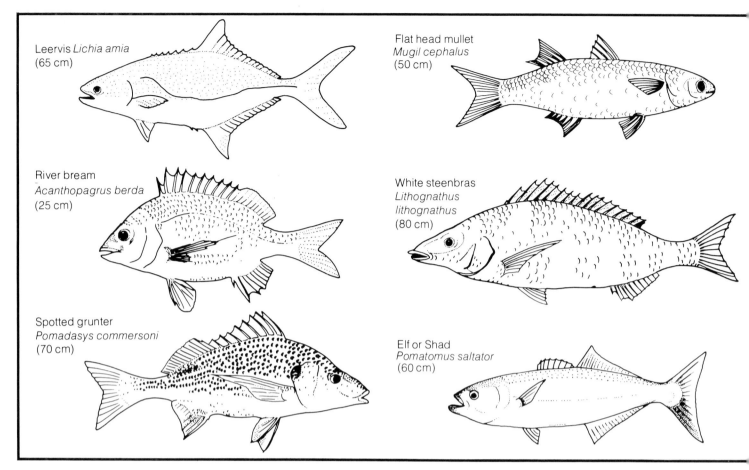

Fig. 130 **Some of the common estuarine fishes** (from J. L. B. Smith: *Sea Fishes of Southern Africa*).

through its moustache-lined beak to capture plankton. The greater flamingo (Fig. 129) feeds in a different manner; each bird treadles the mud in a circular jog, and then sieves through the muddy water to catch invertebrates that swarm out of the disturbed mud. The birds leave circular depressions, like the imprints of tyres left lying on the sand, which cover the mudflats and testify to how much the sediment is disturbed (Fig. 129).

Birds may remove large quantities of food from estuaries, but they also return about 20 percent in the form of faeces. In Langebaan Lagoon it has been calculated that the waders alone deposit about 20 tonnes of faeces each year. Donkergat peninsula, which separates Langebaan Lagoon from the sea, is dotted with hills that were originally islands when the sea level was higher.

Here lived great populations of seabirds and as a result the hills are laden with thousands of years of faecal accumulation which is mined as guano, one of the purest sources of phosphate.

Fish

Estuaries provide a sheltered food-rich haven for many fish. Over 400 species, including 20 percent of the southern African marine species, frequent estuaries at some time in their lives. Fig. 130 shows the more important species. A few, such as round herring and silverside (*Gilchristella aestuarius* and *Hepsetia breviceps*) eat zooplankton, but

most species are carnivorous. The kob, steenbras, stumpnose and others, grub in the sediment for mud- and sandprawns and molluscs. Elf, leervis and sharks are highspeed swimmers that hunt other fish, particularly whitebait and small mullet. Although most of the species are carnivorous, the most abundant fish in estuaries are often the mullet (haarders), which are detritus-feeders. This again emphasises the importance of detritus in the estuarine food web (Fig. 130). Furthermore, different species of mullet select different-sized particles on which to feed, and thus feed in different parts of estuaries. It has been suggested that this prevents competition between the different species.

Some fish such as the sand goby (*Psammogobius knysnaensis*), various species of white-bait, glassies (*Ambassis*), pipefish (*Syngnathus*) and needle-fish (*Hyporhamphus*), may spend their entire lives in estuaries. These species are faced with the problem of preventing their eggs and young larvae from being swept out to sea and they have coped with this in various ways. In Natal, for instance, most of these species breed in winter, when rainfall is low and flooding least likely. Many gobies in turn have sticky eggs which they fasten to rocks, while yet others stand guard over burrows in which they lay their eggs. Female pipefish must gladden the heart of any women's libber; as with sea horses, it is the male pipefish that carries the fertilized eggs in a brood pouch on his belly, and it is he

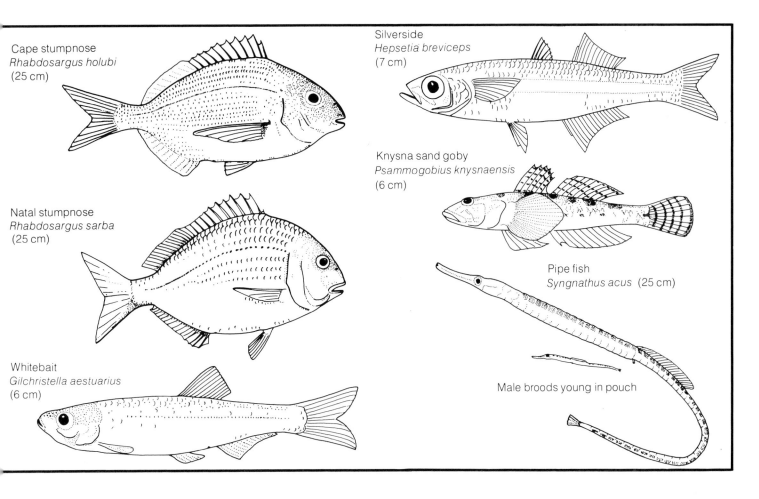

Cape stumpnose
Rhabdosargus holubi
(25 cm)

Natal stumpnose
Rhabdosargus sarba
(25 cm)

Whitebait
Gilchristella aestuarius
(6 cm)

Silverside
Hepsetia breviceps
(7 cm)

Knysna sand goby
Psammogobius knysnaensis
(6 cm)

Pipe fish
Syngnathus acus (25 cm)

Male broods young in pouch

who literally gives birth to the young. Again, retention of the young in a brood pouch protects the vulnerable early stages.

Most fish which occur in estuaries breed in the sea, presumably because estuaries are too harsh for the eggs and young larvae. However, large numbers of their juveniles then return to the estuaries and develop there until mature enough to breed. This pattern is typical of stumpnose, steenbras and mullet. The grunter (*Pomadasys commersonni*) is well-known for its 'runs' when juveniles and recently-spawned adults pour back into estuaries in spring and summer. After a year here the grunter are mature enough to return to the sea to breed, but other species such as the flat-head mullet (*Mugil cephalus*) remain in estuaries for three to four years before venturing out to sea to reproduce.

To give an indication of the numbers of juvenile fish entering estuaries, a single pull of a seine net across the mouth of the Klein Rivier estuary in the Western Cape (Fig. 131) yielded 24 703 fish with a total mass of 275 kg!

Estuaries are thus nursery grounds for many fish (as well as prawns), providing shelter and rich feeding grounds for the juveniles. This is often given as a reason why estuaries must be conserved. How important is the 'nursery' function of estuaries? This is a difficult question to answer, for there is no easy way of finding out whether these estuarine-dependent fish have marine nursery grounds as

well, and if so, what proportions of their populations depend on estuaries. Recently an intensive sampling programme was launched jointly by the Port Elizabeth Museum and the University of Cape Town to see if there are any marine nursery grounds for these fish. Despite sampling over 130 localities between Port Elizabeth and Cape Town, only a handful of juveniles of these fish was located

Fig. 131 A rich haul of fish from the Klein Rivier estuary gives some indication of the numbers of fish entering estuaries.

Fig. 132 Cultivation of sugar-cane right to the edge of the Umhlatuzi River has led to extensive erosion of the bank.

in the sea, while hundreds of thousands could be netted in estuaries.

Many of the Natal estuaries close in winter and break open only in spring, while in summer they are prone to flooding. Therefore most of the fish that use these estuaries as nurseries breed in winter and enter the estuaries in spring when they are open but not yet in full flood. They also have quite long breeding periods so that at least some of the offspring will be produced when conditions are suitable. Many species gather inshore and spawn near estuary mouths. Thus the breeding cycles seem geared to giving juveniles the best chance of invading Natal estuaries: but we still need to know what happens in Namibia and the Cape where conditions are very different.

The danger of artificially opening an estuary mouth too early in the year is well illustrated at Mhlanga where, if the estuary is opened between February and April, only two or three species of fish manage to occupy the estuary, while a November opening allows a recruitment of four times as many species.

Many estuarine-dependent fish are important angling species and their recreational importance must not be underestimated. Even in South Africa, people spend more time on sport-fishing than playing rugby! Angling is a major factor in Natal's tourist industry (worth some R200 million a year) and it is a matter of concern that, according to angling records, the numbers of all estuarine-dependent fish have declined in Natal over the last 21 years. The decline of riverbream *(Acanthopagrus berda)* has been particularly drastic. While there seems to be no evidence that these fish have been over-exploited, there has been a serious degradation of estuaries in Natal which would seem to underscore the link between fish populations and the condition of estuaries. Fish that hunt by sight have declined badly, perhaps because increased siltation has made many estuaries murky: species that grub on the mud and rely on smell have been less affected.

The importance of estuaries goes beyond the species directly linked to them, for much detritus may be swept out of productive estuaries, contributing to the coastal food web. The most dramatic demonstration of this has been in Viet-Nam, where military use of chemical defoliants destroyed many forests, including mangroves, leading to the collapse of the previously rich coastal fishery.

OUR FRAGILE ESTUARIES

Estuaries are not independent systems. Their structure depends on rainfall, geology, waves and tides; they are fed by nutrients from rivers and the sea and in turn yield detritus to the sea; they house migrant birds, and act as nurseries for marine fish and prawns. It is clear that the very existence and dynamic nature of estuaries is closely bound to that of both rivers and the sea. This very fact makes them vulnerable. Any activity within the catchment may eventually affect the estuary.

Estuaries depend on an interplay of different physical factors so that alteration of one factor can influence others and, since estuaries are more intensively exploited by man than any other marine habitat, this delicate balance has often been disturbed. Estuaries are used for transport, harbours, mariculture of oysters, mussels and the like, marina development, fishing, watersports and even sometimes as open sewers for effluents. In southern African the fate of estuaries is particularly critical, for the pattern of rainfall often results in the closure of estuary mouths or in flooding, compounding the problems that may arise from man's actions.

Of the many human activities influencing estuaries, the following four are of special importance.

Agriculture

Southern African estuaries are prone to becoming silted up, and over 50 years ago it was pointed out that 'owing to soil-deterioration by overgrazing in the Karoo . . . the southern rivers are muddy when in flood, and . . . the silting up of estuaries may now proceed with increasing rapidity'. It is not only in the Karoo that overgrazing bares the ground so that surface soil is eroded by rain and washed down rivers. Even more serious, but more easily overcome, is the practice of cutting down the marginal vegetation lining river-banks in order to cultivate land right down to the water's edge (Fig. 132). Marginal vegetation consolidates the banks and reduces erosion, and it has been suggested that removal of this vital vegetation is the major cause of erosion and siltation in southern Africa. South Africa has legislation against the removal of this vegetation but it is often ignored – particularly by the sugar-cane industry of Natal – and offenders have seldom been prosecuted. Under pressure of population, forests on steep hillsides in Transkei have been stripped for firewood and cleared for fields – an unfortunately short-sighted action. Crops can only be grown on the slopes for a season or two before rains wash away the unprotected topsoil, adding to the silt in rivers and further impoverishing the land.

The legacy of these actions is clearly seen in estuaries such as the Umzimvubu at Port St Johns and the Umzimkulu at Port Shepstone. Within living memory these were

Fig. 133 Bridges across the Buffels River hindered the floods of February 1981, and were extensively damaged (A). They also contributed to the spread of floodwaters that ravaged Laingsburg (B).

deep estuaries that could be used as harbours by coastal steamers: now they can be waded across and are only called 'ports' out of nostalgia.

The most obvious effect of silt on estuaries is to fill them in, but it also smothers animals and cuts down light penetration so that growth of aquatic plants is limited to very shallow water. The suspension of silt in the Umzimvubu is so great that if a secchi disc (a black and white disc 45 cm in diameter) is lowered into the water to measure light penetration, it disappears 5 cm below the surface.

Reed-beds at the head of estuaries and in marshes filter out silt and protect estuaries, yet it is common practice to canalise reed-beds and reclaim them for agriculture. As an example, Professor J. H. Day and his co-workers, in 1954, described how the lower reaches of the Umfolozi River had been canalised and then used to grow sugar-cane. At that time the Umfolozi joined Lake St Lucia near its mouth. Canalisation led to large quantities of silt flooding down the Umfolozi, to be trapped by the rising tides and pushed up into St Lucia where it smothered most life and decreased the size of the mouth and channel, making dredging necessary to keep St Lucia open. Subsequently a new mouth had to be cut for the Umfolozi, diverting it away from St Lucia to prevent further damage.

Fig. 134 River and tidal flow are hindered at the mouth of the Umkomasi estuary by a narrow-span bridge. The flood of silt pouring into the sea is clearly visible as a chocolate-brown stain, sharply delimited from the clean sea-water on the right.

Fig. 135 A healthy mangrove stand at Beachwood on the Umgeni estuary, photographed in 1971 (A) and then again in 1975 (B) after total destruction of the mangroves by the construction of a causeway. Resultant erosion of the banks and the murky colour of the silted water are obvious.

Modern agriculture depends on fertilizers and pesticides, both of which often wash down rivers and accumulate in estuaries. Small amounts of fertilizer, just as small amounts of domestic sewage, may increase the productivity of estuaries, but there is always a danger of excessive plant or phytoplankton growth choking the system: a condition called eutrophication. Pesticides are more dangerous because each predator accumulates the pesticides that have built up in its prey: so the higher up the food-chain an organism is, the greater the concentration of pesticide it may retain in its tissues. Fortunately, so far, neither fertilizers nor pesticides appear to be a major problem in southern African estuaries; but it would be as well to heed their effects in North America, where for example, pesticides have reduced the thickness of eggshells making the embryos more vulnerable and thus threatening pelican populations. In Texas a multi-million-dollar prawn industry collapsed because the prawns became unfit to eat.

Bridges and causeways

Bridges sometimes radically alter the rate of water-flow in rivers and estuaries. A remarkable illustration of this was provided when the old London Bridge was removed, increasing tidal flow by 25 percent and threatening to wash away some of the remaining bridges in the process. In South Africa, the bridges across the Buffels River contributed towards hindering the recent floods in the Karoo and spreading the floodwaters across Laingsburg (Fig. 133).

Bridges with long spans and narrow pylons have little effect on water movement but they are expensive to build. More often, solid embankments are built out from each bank, often cutting across the reed-beds or salt-marshes of estuaries, and are then spanned by a small bridge (Fig. 134). This severely limits the penetration of tidal waters up estuaries and so reduces salt-marshes. A classic example can be found on the Bietou River which flows into Plettenberg Lagoon. The first bridge built here squeezed the river between embankments but was washed away in floods. The embankment still remains there and no lessons were learnt from it, for the new bridge built downstream has a similar pair of embankments, creating a double barricade. A survey undertaken there reveals that the flora and fauna is much richer below the bridges where tidal action is greatest.

Even tiny bridges may have dramatic effects. A short causeway penetrated by eleven 1 m pipes was built over the Mgobezeleni estuary in Zululand, preventing upstream movement of tidal water and impounding river water so that the water level rose by about 50 cm. This was sufficient to drown almost all of the mangroves in the estuary. Figs. 135A & B dramatically show the death of drowned mangroves and the subsequent erosion of the estuary banks.

It is clear that bridges and causeways should be designed so that they hinder river and tidal flow as little as possible.

Harbour construction

Our sheer and wave-beaten coastline is graced with very few sheltered embayments, placing a premium on estuaries as possible sites for harbours. Durban Bay, once a rich mangrove forest, is now South Africa's largest harbour and the mangroves reduced to a pitiful remnant. Mngazana, the richest estuary in Transkei, and an obvious choice for a nature reserve, was at one time also threatened with harbour development. Saldanha Bay and Richards Bay have been developed as harbours more recently, although in both cases attempts have been made to minimize the damage done to ecologically-sensitive areas. Despite this, dredging, blasting, reclamation and pollution inevitably take their toll, and there is always the spectre of oil pollution. At Saldanha it was necessary to dredge much of the bay, partly to build a breakwater between Marcus Island and the mainland, and partly to deepen the bay to allow ships of 200 000 tonnes to berth. Because of the breakwater, predators such as water mongoose, genet, bat-eared fox, meerkat and rats, have invaded the island and threaten the bird life – despite eight years of warning and pleading for a predator-proof fence. Dredging also totally changed the fauna of the bay, reducing it to a few fast-growing species that quickly recolonized the area. Even five years later, the fauna was still recovering. Dredging also increased the silt suspended in the water, reducing light penetration and oxygen levels. The subsequent deposition of silt is the most likely cause of decline in the seaweed *Gracilaria verrucosa* which, prior to 1974, grew copiously in the bay and hundreds of tonnes were washed ashore each year. *Gracilaria* is a rich source of agar, so stranded weed was collected and exported, earning a revenue of about R1 000 000 in 1973. Since 1974 the weed has failed to yield even a tenth of its original crop.

Underwater blasting was necessary to deepen the approach channel (Fig. 136A), and inevitably killed large numbers of fish. What could have been avoided was the simultaneous slaughter of hundreds of sea-birds. Penguins and cormorants soon learnt that a blast signalled a wealth of food in the form of dead, floating, fish, and poured into the area: only to be caught by the next blast (Fig. 136B). These episodes were initially hushed up but, subsequently, blasting was permitted only twice a day, at times when the birds were least likely to be feeding, and with sufficient time between blasts for the birds to feed on the dead fish and return to land before the next blast. Forethought and consultation with ecologists could so easily have minimised the initial slaughter.

Richards Bay, as discussed on p. 82, is another example of the ecological problems which may arise from harbour development.

Dams
The shortage of water in many parts of southern Africa makes water-storage essential. In addition, two of the biggest dams in the world, Lake Kariba and Cabora Bassa, were built for hydro-electric purposes. In South Africa, 40 percent of the total river run-off is impounded. In terms of estuaries this has led to the danger of river-flow becoming insufficient to scour out the marine sand swept in and across the mouths by wave action. For example, dams built above the Bushman's River estuary have led to marine sand penetrating 4 km upstream, covering eelgrass and mud-prawn beds in the process. Another effect from damming rivers is that the reduced flow may no longer compensate

Fig. 136 Blasting to deepen the approach channel in Saldanha Bay (A) killed many penguins (B).

for evaporation in the estuary, and salinities may rise. The Palmiet estuary is threatened by the proposed damming of the river, which has been much opposed by conservationists because it will flood the Kogelberg State Reserve with its unique flora. The estuary has been studied and the following recommendations made: if the dam is built, firstly, sufficient fresh water must flow into the estuary to balance evaporation and, secondly, a minimum of one flood a year must be allowed to take place to scour the mouth open. Even these steps are unlikely to keep the estuary in its present pristine state.

Lake St Lucia, one of South Africa's largest estuaries and internationally known for its animal and bird-life, as well as being popular for sport-fishing, is a classic example of the problems arising from water extraction. Even in its natural state Lake St Lucia has a precarious existence for, in times of drought, evaporation from the shallow lakes exceeds the input of fresh water. Under these circumstances the water level may drop so much that sea-water flows into the lakes and makes them yet more salty. Further

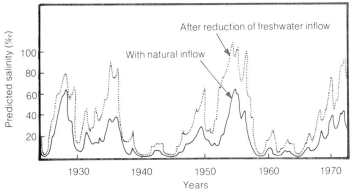

Fig. 137 **Changes in the salinity of Lake St Lucia.** The dotted line shows the actual salinities that have been recorded, while the solid line indicates the salinities that probably would have occurred if the natural inflow of fresh water had not been reduced by irrigation, dams and the planting of forests.

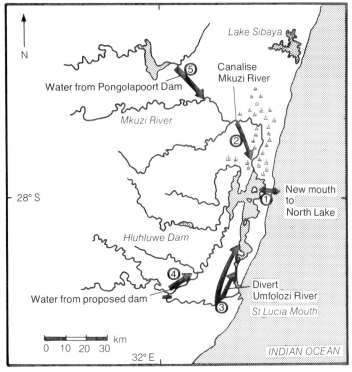

Fig. 138 **Map showing five possible ways of increasing flow of water into the Lake St Lucia system to counteract the high salinities that occur in times of drought.**

evaporation then concentrates the sea-water and, in the northern lake, salinities have reached 120‰ – almost four times the concentration of sea-water. Practically all life is eliminated under these conditions. The mouth may also close, worsening the situation. When floods come down, the mouth bursts open again and the whole estuary is flushed out, eventually restoring normal salinities.

Lake St Lucia receives fresh water from rain falling directly on to the lakes, through run-off from the surrounding lands, and from four rivers. Three activities have reduced this flow: the diversion of river-water for irrigation, storage of water in dams, and the planting of forests of introduced trees that draw water from the soil.

The resultant reduction of water-flow into St Lucia increases the severity of droughts and also slows the subsequent recovery of the estuary. To test the impact of this and to investigate ways of improving the situation, a mathematical 'model' has been developed. 'Models' are simply equations which allow calculations of factors such as water-level or salinity, given the necessary information about rainfall, river-flow, run-off, transpiration, evaporation and tidal flow. Such equations are often very complex and need to be run on computers. To test the model it is compared with known data and adjusted until the predictions it makes are realistic. At this stage it may be used to predict the unknown. The model developed for Lake St Lucia shows that if the flow of water had been left untouched, then the effects of drought would only have been half as severe as they are now (Fig. 137). In other words, instead of experiencing the catastrophic salinities of 120‰, they would not have exceeded 55‰: a condition most estuarine species are able to survive.

This same model was also used to predict the future, and revealed that we can expect catastrophic conditions in St Lucia six times a century if no action is taken to improve current matters. In addition, the model tested the effectiveness of possible measures that might improve the state of the estuary. Fig. 138 shows five ways of increasing the amount of water entering St Lucia and in this way preventing excessively high salinities:
1. Open a new mouth from north lake to the sea
2. Canalise the Mkuzi River so that it by-passes the swamps
3. Divert the Umfolozi River to enter St Lucia
4. Transfer some water from the proposed Umfolozi Dam
5. Transfer water from Pongolapoort Dam to a tributary of Lake St Lucia

The computer model predicts that opening a new mouth would be of little assistance. Canalisation through the swamps is a risky proposition since it is likely to increase silt in the estuary. We know from previous experience that the Umfolozi silted up St Lucia when it originally joined the estuary and so this too is no answer. Thus the most promising possibility is to divert some water from the storage dams to the estuary in times of drought.

This is a complicated example, but it illustrates two points: that a decrease in river-flow will have adverse effects on estuaries and, secondly, that we have the sophisticated technology to accurately predict these effects and to take steps to minimise them.

THE FUTURE

Estuaries are obviously extremely productive but also extremely vulnerable, but we cannot expect all development to halt because we wish to conserve estuaries. At the same time two things are necessary. Firstly, any development should not proceed without sincere effort to minimise the damage it may do to estuaries. Many of the examples in this chapter reveal quite clearly that lack of foresight, often coupled with lack of knowledge, and sometimes lack of goodwill, have resulted in needless damage in the past. Consultation between engineers and ecologists must become accepted as necessary from the earliest planning stages of major developments that may affect estuaries. A change of attitude is also necessary; the idea that 'every drop that enters the sea is wasted' is surely an anachronism today when we are increasingly aware of the importance of our estuaries.

Secondly, there is a need for an over-all plan as to how estuaries should be used in the future. Some must be set aside for conservation: others may be developed to various degrees. Conservation of an estuary is more far-reaching than it seems at first for it should ideally also mean conservation of its catchment, which is most practical if the catchment is small. Mngazana estuary in Transkei and Knysna Lagoon are obvious candidates for conservation. To aid this decision-making, Professor J. H. Day's book on southern African estuaries is a timely summary of 40 years' experience in the field and provides a fund of information for biologists and planners alike. A more specific study has been made by George Begg on the state of Natal's estuaries. Finally, Dr Allan Heydorn is presently leading a programme on the condition of Cape estuaries. We can but hope that our fragile estuaries will receive more protection in the future than they have in the past, for we are still in the fortunate position of having some rich, clean, permanently open estuaries worthy of protection.

REFERENCES

Popular articles and books

Anonymous. 1978. Marcus Island – killers hit at the sea birds. *African Wildlife*, Vol. 32 (2): 24-26.

Barnes, R. S. K. 1974. *Estuarine Biology*. Studies in Biology No. 49. Edward Arnold, London.

Berjak, P., Campbell, G. K., Huckett, B. I. & Pammenter, N. W. 1977. *In the Mangroves of Southern Africa*. Natal Branch of the Wildlife Society of Southern Africa. 74 pp.

Day, J. H. 1979. Estuaries. *Environment R. S. A.*, Vol. 6 (12): 1-2.

Grindley, J. R. & Heydorn, A. E. F. 1979. Man's impact on estuarine environments. *S. Afr. Journal of Science*, Vol. 75 : 554-560.

Heydorn, A. E. F. 1977. Agriculture and earthworks – death knell of Natal's estuaries. *African Wildlife*, Vol. 31 (6): 27-30.

Heydorn, A. E. F. & Tinley, K. L. 1980. *Estuaries of the Cape, Part 1: Synopsis of the Cape Coast*. C. S. I. R. Research Report 380, 1-97.

Hutchison, I. P. G. 1977. Lake St. Lucia – the computer points the way. *African Wildlife*, Vol. 31 (2): 24-27.

Percy Fitzpatrick Institute of African Ornithology. 1975. Langebaan Lagoon. *African Wildlife*, Vol. 29 (4): 10-13.

Identification guides

Smith, J. L. B. 1965. *The Sea Fishes of Southern Africa*. Central News Agency, South Africa. 580 pp.

Scientific references

Alexander, S. J. & Ewer, D. W. 1969. A comparative study of some aspects of the biology and ecology of *Sesarma catenata* Ort. and *Cyclograpsus punctatus* M. Edw., with additional observations on *Sesarma meinerti* Deman. *Zoologica Africana*, Vol. 4: 1-35.

Begg, G. 1978. *The Estuaries of Natal*. Natal Town and Regional Planning Commission Report, Vol. 41: 1-657.

Bruton, M. N. 1975. Survey of the Mgobezeleni lake-system in Zululand, with notes on the effect of a bridge on the mangrove swamp. *Transactions of the Royal Society of S. Afr.*, Vol. 42: 283-293.

Cockroft, V. G. & Forbes, A. T. 1981. Tidal activity rhythms in the mangrove snail *Cerithidea decollata*. *S. Afr. Journal of Zoology*, Vol. 16 (1) (in press).

Day, J. H. 1951. The ecology of South African estuaries: Part 1. General considerations. *Transactions of the Royal Society of S. Afr.*, Vol. 33: 53-91.

Day, J. H. 1959. The biology of Langebaan Lagoon: a study of the effects of shelter from wave action. *Transactions of the Royal Society of S. Afr.*, Vol. 35: 475-576.

Day, J. H. 1981. *Estuarine Ecology – with particular reference to Southern Africa*. (J. H. Day editor) A. A. Balkema, Cape Town. 411 pp.

Day, J. H., Millard, N. A. H. & Broekhuysen, G. J. 1954. The ecology of South African estuaries: Part 4. The St. Lucia System. *Transactions of the Royal Society of S. Afr.*, Vol. 34: 129-156.

Edney, E. B. 1961. The water and heat relationships of fiddler crabs (*Uca* sp.) *Transactions of the Royal Society of S. Afr.*, Vol. 36: 71-91.

Forbes, A. T. & Hill, B. J. 1969. The physiological ability of a marine crab, *Hymenosoma orbiculare* Desm., to live in a subtropical freshwater lake. *Transactions of the Royal Society of S. Afr.*, Vol. 38: 271-283.

Grindley, J. R. & Wooldridge, T. 1974. The plankton of Richards Bay. *Hydrobiological Bulletin*, Vol. 8: 201-212.

Heydorn, A. E. F. 1978. Coastal zone management and conservation. *Ocean Management*, Vol. 4: 303-317.

Hill, B. J. 1971. Osmoregulation by an estuarine and a marine species of *Upogebia* (Anomura, Crustacea). *Zoologica Africana*, Vol. 6 (2): 229-236.

Hill, B. J. 1974. Salinity and temperature tolerance of zoeae larvae of the portunid crab *Scylla serrata*. *Marine Biology*, Vol. 25: 21-25.

Howard Williams, C. & Liptrot, M. R. M. 1980. Submerged macrophyte communities in a brackish South African estuarine-lake system. *Aquatic Botany*, Vol. 9: 101-116.

Wallace, J. A. & Van der Elst, R. 1975. The estuarine fishes of the east coast of South Africa. Parts I-IV. *Investigation Report of the oceanographic Research Institute*, Vols. 40: 1-72, 41: 1-48, 42: 1-63.

Begg, G. 1981. Marina da Gama. A case study of the interdependence of property development and ecology. *Planning and Building Developments* Sept./Oct. 1981: 75-87.

6.THE OPEN SEA

The average beach visitor only glimpses the life that exists in open waters, for the flotsam that washes up is but a memento of all that dwells there. Animal life in the open sea ranges from microscopic single celled protozoans to the whales – the largest animal the earth has ever known. Curiously, all these animals depend on the tiniest forms of plant life, the phytoplankton. Few species of phytoplankton exceed the size of a pinhead and most are very much smaller: yet they are often very beautiful when seen under the microscope, having elegant sculptured surfaces or dainty spines that may link one cell to the next (Fig. 139).

The growth of phytoplankton

Phytoplankton may account for as much as 90 percent of the total plant production on earth, but its growth is limited to the surface skin of the sea (the euphotic zone), where there is sufficient light for photosynthesis. Much of the sea is also deficient in nutrients and this too limits the growth of phytoplankton.

Obviously some measurement of the growth of phytoplankton is an essential first step to understanding food chains of the open sea. We can determine the rate of photosynthesis by measuring how fast the phytoplankton takes up radioactive carbon dioxide or the speed at which it gives off oxygen. Nowadays it is even possible to use satellite photographs (with special colour filters) to measure how green the sea-water is, giving an index of the concentration of phytoplankton, and allowing seasonal changes to be tracked.

In temperate seas there are well-developed annual cycles of phytoplankton growth, relating to the availability of sunlight and nutrients. In spring, increased sunlight allows the phytoplankton to bloom, but as a result the nutrients available in the upper layers of the sea are used up. As summer approaches, the surface water heats up and a layer of warm water forms over the cooler deep water, so that there is a sharp change in temperature – a thermocline – between the two water masses. This thermocline serves as a barrier, preventing exchange between the two layers. Thus the nutrients in the upper layer cannot be replenished from below once they are used up. As a result the phytoplankton fades away in summer, for although light is at its most intense, plants cannot grow without nutrients. As winter approaches the surface layers become cooler, the thermocline breaks down, and once again deep water mixes with that nearer to the surface, restoring nutrients. Thus there may be a brief bloom of phytoplankton in autumn, before light becomes inadequate in winter (Fig. 140A).

This seasonal pattern is most obvious in the temperate regions of the Atlantic Ocean, but in the tropical and subtropical regions of the sea off Moçambique and Natal, light is continually available and phytoplankton levels are more constant. In the Antarctic Southern Ocean, sufficient light is only available in mid-summer, so that a single massive bloom of phytoplankton occurs during this time of year. On the west coast of southern Africa, the upwelling described in Chapter 1 has an overriding effect on the availability of nutrients. The south-easterly winds blow the surface waters offshore during summer, and they are replaced by deep nutrient-rich waters which rise to the surface, making nutrients available at a time when sunlight is also intense, and thus allowing remarkably rapid growth of phytoplankton (Fig. 140B). We cannot, however, predict the day-to-day frequency or strength of this wind, and the phytoplankton is equally unpredictable and can fluctuate greatly.

Red Tides

Particular species of phytoplankton can bloom so densely that they colour the water red, and these red tides are of great interest because they may cause mass mortalities of marine animals. The first written record of a red tide appears in *Exodus*, Chapter 7, verses 20-21, where it is described as one of the plagues that struck the Egyptians.

The colour of red tides is due to red pigment spots within these unicellular organisms, which shield their light sen-

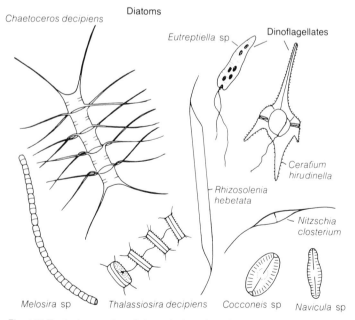

Diatoms

Chaetoceros decipiens

Eutreptiella sp

Dinoflagellates

Ceratium hirudinella

Rhizosolenia hebetata

Nitzschia closterium

Melosira sp   *Thalassiosira decipiens*   *Cocconeis* sp   *Navicula* sp

Fig. 139 Typical examples of phytoplankton found in southern African waters. Greatly magnified.

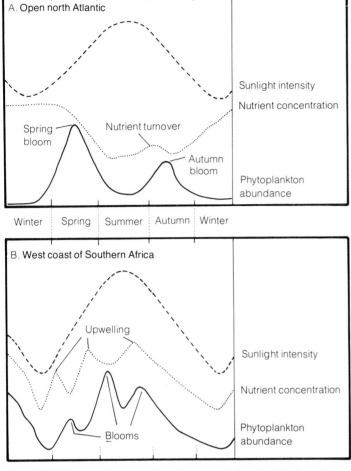

Fig. 140A. In temperate oceans there is a peak of phytoplankton in spring and a lesser peak in autumn, related to the availability of nutrients and sunlight.

Fig. 140B. On the west coast of southern Africa, phytoplankton blooms in summer, when pulses of upwelling bring nutrients to the surface.

sors and allow them to detect the direction of a light source. Only a few species of plankton cause red tides. The commonest is a round-celled organism called *Noctiluca*, which reaches a surprisingly large size for a unicellular creature, being about 1 mm in diameter (Fig. 141B), and is famous because it often causes phosphorescence.

Why do red tides occur? Although they come and go unpredictably, their frequent appearance on the west coast of southern Africa usually follows a pattern. Firstly, when upwelling occurs the phytoplankton bloom begins. If north-westerly winds then ensue, the plankton is concentrated inshore and, if calm weather follows in turn, the dense bloom multiplies to produce a red tide.

Noctiluca is usually harmless, but as with all red tides its blooms may consume all available nutrients and then die leaving masses of decaying phytoplankton which deplete the water of oxygen, killing fish and other marine life, as happened in False Bay in the Cape in 1962. Various species of *Gonyaulax* are also common in red tides. These too are usually harmless but, in 1966, they caused massive mortalities of fish when a huge red tide, 50 km long, washed the coast near Elands Bay. More than eight years afterwards the white mussel population in this area had only begun to

recover from this decimation. In this case, oxygen levels remained high throughout the red tide, and it seems that the plankton only became lethal because it was so dense that it clogged the gills of marine animals.

One species, *Gonyaulax catenella* (Fig. 141A), has a far more drastic effect for it contains poisons that are amongst the most potent of any known biological toxins. Some forms of life are immune to these toxins, but filter-feeding animals such as black and white mussels, which eat the *Gonyaulax*, concentrate the toxins in their tissues and become lethal to anyone who subsequently eats them. Fatalities due to mussel poisoning are almost unheard of on the south and east coasts, but have been recorded several times on the west coast (Fig. 141A). The potency of poisoned mussels may be assessed from the fact that 100 grams of mussel have a toxicity of 42 000 'mouse units' (i.e. they can kill this number of mice). Two or three poisoned mussels can be enough to kill a man. Raw mussels are particularly dangerous, for boiling reduces, but does not eliminate, the toxicity of the poison. Unfortu-

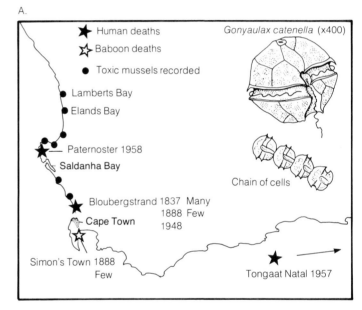

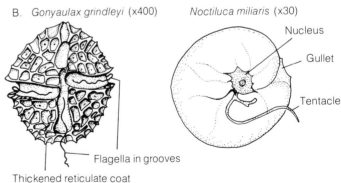

Fig. 141A. The dinoflagellate *Gonyaulax catenella* (shown magnified x100) is the probable cause of deaths from mussel-poisoning. Dots on the map show where toxic mussels have been found, and stars show where deaths have occurred.

Fig. 141B. Two other organisms, *Gonyaulax grindleyi* (x100) and *Noctiluca miliaris* (x30) cause red tides but are not responsible for mussel-poisoning.

nately mussels retain their toxicity for up to four months after a red tide. The Sea Fisheries Institute now routinely tests the toxicity of mussels on the west coast. Only filter-feeders accumulate the toxins from *Gonyaulax catenella*, so that herbivores like perlemoen *(Haliotis)* and even the crayfish which may eat toxic mussels, can be consumed without fear.

Mussel poisoning attacks the nervous system and first produces a tingling of the lips and tongue, then slowly affects the rest of the mouth, the arms, hands and feet, until paralysis progressively sets in. There is no antidote, although an alkaline stomach wash (e.g. bicarbonate) may help break down the toxins. Failure of the respiratory system may follow and measures must be taken to counteract this. The first 12 hours after poisoning are the most critical and after this period the patient is likely to recover.

Zooplankton

A host of small animals feed on phytoplankton. In open seas these include the tiny unicellular Radiolaria and Foraminifera which are related to *Amoeba*, but are encased in beautiful symmetrical shells (Fig. 142). In some areas of the sea they are so abundant that their minute dead shells rain down on the sea bed and form an ooze. This accumulates at a rate of about 2mm each year, and in parts of the sea the ooze is over 100m deep. Such deposits of micro-

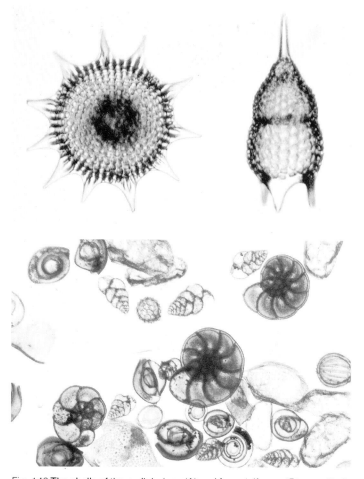

Fig. 142 The shells of tiny radiolarians (A) and foraminiferans (B) magnified 50 times.

scopic fossils are of great importance, for they reveal to geologists the nature of the sea bed and the conditions under which it was laid down. Oil is formed by the bacterial decomposition of marine organisms. Normally it diffuses away and is lost, but if it is trapped under impermeable rocks it may form an exploitable reserve. Micro-fossils can be used to indicate the origin and nature of such sites and have been used to pinpoint the sea bed between Port Elizabeth and Mossel Bay as the most likely area for oil deposits off the South African coast.

The micro-fossils of Foraminifera have been used to measure prehistoric sea-bed temperatures, using a recently developed technique. Oxygen exists as three different isotopes (O_2^{16}, O_2^{17} and O_2^{18}). The ratios at which these are incorporated into the calcium carbonate foraminiferan shells depend on the temperature. Thus we can measure the ratios of these isotopes in fossil shells to determine the temperatures of the long gone past. This technique has shown that 32 million years ago the deep sea was a relatively warm 10,5 °C (compared with 1,8 °C today), and has also confirmed the rise and fall of sea temperatures between and during the Ice Ages.

The copepods (Fig. 143) are probably the commonest of all planktonic organisms and in fact it has been calculated that not only are they the most abundant animals in the world, but that although they are tiny their combined mass is greater than that of any other group. They are of enormous importance as food for higher forms including many commercially-important fish.

The euphausids are much larger shrimp-like beasts reaching 60mm in length and are better known as krill. Krill has recently caught the imagination of fishing concerns, following the discovery of huge stocks of these animals in the Southern Oceans. There is at the moment an intense international research programme investigating the biology and magnitude of these stocks, and South African scientists have been among the world's leaders in applying echo-location methods to detect and measure the size of krill swarms. At present, estimates of the potential harvest vary widely from 25 million to 1 000 million tonnes per year (the former estimate being more likely!), but in any case the resource is huge and may well be greater than the 70 million tonnes currently gleaned from all other fisheries combined.

Very recently the largest school of animal life ever recorded by man was reported near Antarctica: a single shoal of krill many square kilometres in area, with a depth of up to 200m and a total mass of 10 million tonnes.

The reason why such rich krill stocks exist relates partly to the high productivity of the upwelled Antarctic water. The elimination of many of the whales that used to feed on krill has probably also contributed to their current vast numbers. Krill could be a valuable source of human food, for it consists of 64 percent protein, but at present it is not marketed in a palatable form and is used only as an animal feed.

Zooplankton consists mainly of resident species that permanently float around in open seas, but there are times

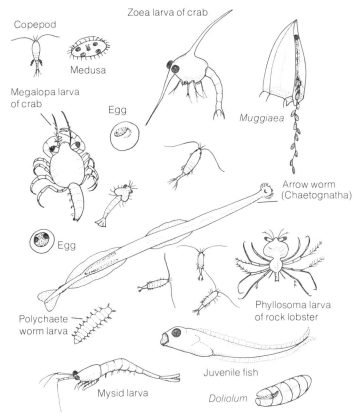

Fig. 143 Examples of zooplankton common in southern African seas.

when the plankton is added to by swarms of the larvae of animals such as barnacles, crayfish and crabs.

All of these smaller organisms are preyed upon by larger animals such as jellyfish, small fish, and the arrow worms (Chaetognatha). Floating on the surface of the water is a whole community of carnivores, including the bluebottles that fish with their long tentacles, and their relatives *Vellela* and *Porpita* (see Chapter 9 and Plates 9 & 10). Feeding on these is the purple bubble shell *Janthina* (Plate 105) and the nudibranch *Glaucus atlanticus* (Plate 131). The goose barnacle *Lepas* hangs from any firm, floating structure, whether it be a plank or cast-out apple, and filters the smaller plankton from the water (Fig. 144). Fish such as the anchovy and pilchard have specially developed gill rakers on their gill arches and, as they swim through the water, they are able to filter out plankton continually.

Adaptations of plankton
Planktonic organisms have two basic problems: they must swim continuously to prevent sinking; and they have nowhere to hide. They can reduce the rate at which they sink by increasing their surface area, and a wide range of species have bizarre spines, long hairs, or frilled appendages, and very flattened or ribbon-like bodies (Fig. 143). These elaborate projections may also make it more difficult for small predators to capture planktonic organisms. Most species reduce the heavy structural elements of their bodies to a minimum and are often jelly-like. The body may be further lightened if heavy ions such as calcium or sul-

phate are excluded and replaced by lighter ions such as sodium. Ammonia – the normal breakdown product of proteins in aquatic animals – may be accumulated in the form of light ammonium ions, increasing the buoyancy of the body. If food reserves are stored in the form of oil, this too decreases the density of the body, and oil reserves are found in diatoms, many planktonic Crustacea and in fish eggs.

Another ploy is to create gas bubbles that allow the animal to float. Bluebottles (Plate 11) have a gas-filled float; the bubble-raft shell *Janthina* produces a frothy raft of bubbles to which it clings (Plate 105) and on which it lays its eggs; and the beautiful nudibranch *Glaucus* gulps bubbles of air to keep it afloat. Many of the siphonophorans have reduced the float that is so prominent in their bluebottle relatives, and instead contain one or two pulsating individuals in the colony to prevent them from sinking. Cuttlebones and the spiral white shells so often washed ashore are the internal shells of cuttlefish and a squid-like animal called *Spirula*: they contain gas and can be used to regulate the buoyancy of these animals (see Chapter 19). The control of buoyancy reaches its zenith in the swim bladders of fish which are like inflated balloons that lie in the gut cavity beneath the backbone. The gas content of a swim bladder can be regulated by the fish so that the animal has a neutral buoyancy and neither sinks nor floats but remains suspended at a chosen depth. Gas is pumped into the bladder by secreting an acid (lactic acid) into the blood that supplies the bladder. Acidity reduces the solubility of oxygen in the blood so that it forms gaseous bubbles that can be pumped into the bladder. In the absence of the acid, the oxygen is redissolved and the buoyancy of the fish decreases.

During the Second World War when underwater echoes (sonar) were used to locate submarines, a puzzling sound-reflecting layer was regularly detected at depths of about 300m, giving the appearance of a ghostly false bottom to the sea floor. These 'deep scattering layers' are actually due to dense accumulations of planktonic animals or fish which contain gas in their bodies and thus reflect sounds. Off the South African coast, lantern fish (Myctophidae) are sometimes so common that they create deep scattering layers (Fig. 145): at present their relatively large stocks are scarcely exploited. Deep scattering layers are so prevalent in most seas that it was once remarked that there must be a 'zone of mid-water predators – a living net – stretched across the world's oceans'.

Many species of zooplankton undertake a well developed daily migration, congregating near the surface of the water at night and then sinking down to deeper layers during the day. This is so marked that it is reflected in the movements of the deep scattering layer. Some fish follow this pattern as well and this is why anchovies are more readily captured at night, as discussed in Chapter 7. Different species of zooplankton migrate to different degrees. For instance the larger shrimp-like euphausids may migrate over 600m each day, whilst small copepods scarcely change their position.

Fig. 144 A plank carrying a cluster of goose barnacles *(Lepas)*, cast ashore next to the burrow of a ghost crab, provides a convenient meal.

What advantage does this migration have? There are several possibilities. Anchovies and pilchards, for instance, may descend by day to avoid predatory birds. Zooplankton may move up and down to sample different patches of phytoplankton. Perhaps between bouts of feeding at the surface, the zooplankton saves energy by descending into deeper cooler waters to digest its food. When currents move in opposite directions in deeper layers and at the surface, zooplankton may maintain its position by alternating between these layers. These are all possibilities, but we must admit we are not really sure why plankton migrate in such a manner. In any case, it is perhaps of greater interest that much of the zooplankton off

the west coast reacts quite differently and does not migrate but remains in the surface layers most of the time. Scientists speculate that this unorthodox behaviour is an adaptation to the unusual and fluctuating conditions that exist there. We recall that upwelling promotes dense phytoplankton blooms but that these are unpredictable in time and space and last for a few days or weeks, being blown offshore by the south-east winds. This pattern presents great problems for the zooplankton that feeds on the phytoplankton, for the build-up of zooplankton populations lags about 10 days behind that of the phytoplankton, so there is every chance that the two will not coincide sufficiently for the zooplankton to capitalise on this rich but tantilizingly unpredictable food source. Under these conditions it may be important for the zooplankton to seize every opportunity and not risk losing contact with the phytoplankton by migrating. As it is, most phytoplankton on the west coast dies not because it is eaten, but because the upwelled water eventually sinks down below the euphotic zone, so that the plants perish through lack of sunlight.

To avoid detection, most zooplankton is almost transparent. Often only the eyes (which must have pigments to function) are visible and these seemingly disembodied eyes at times present a ghostly spectacle. Animals living near the surface are frequently blue or purplish in colour so that they blend in with the blue water when viewed from above. Bluebottles and their kin, bubble-raft shells *(Janthina)* and the nudibranch *Glaucus*, blue goose barnacles and even a tiny blue crab form a floating community and are often washed ashore together. Since this 'blue community' is always associated with bluebottles and is hence dangerous to swimmers, the Australians have taken to announcing their arrival at beaches by warning bathers that 'the blues are in'.

Closer examination of the nudibranch *Glaucus* shows that it is not uniformly blue but silvery-white below (in fact it hangs upside down from the surface of the water so that it is the dorsal surface that is lowermost and coloured white). This two-tone coloration is known as counter-shading and ensures that the animal is camouflaged both from above and below. Looking down, one sees a blue animal against blue water, but looking up from beneath, as any diver knows, the surface of the water is silvery, so that once again *Glaucus* blends in with its background.

Perhaps the most remarkable feature of plankton is that many species are luminescent. This production of light is under the control of the animal and can be switched on or off at will. It is usually caused by the oxidation of a chemical substrate controlled by enzymes, but some animals cheat a bit by housing luminescent bacteria that do the job for them. Luminescence is found in almost all groups of zooplankton and can cause spectacular phosphorescence at night. One of our most vivid memories is of a red tide of *Noctiluca* lighting up the waves in False Bay, each wave flashing like green fire as it broke on the shore.

We may know how bioluminescence is produced, but its purpose remains in most cases an enigma. Some species

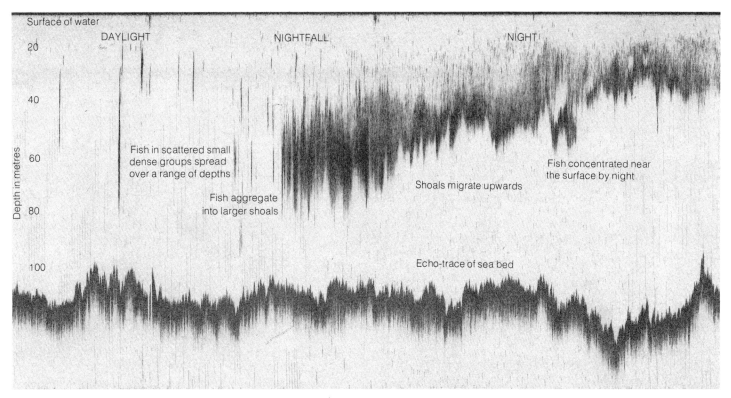

Fig. 145 Sounds emitted from a ship's echo-sounder bounce off the sea bottom and return to the ship where they can be recorded as a trace that shows the shape and depth of the bottom. Shoals of pelagic fish can also be detected; on the left of this trace, fish are shown clumped together during the day, in small groups (paaltjies) in relatively deep water, while at nightfall they aggregate in larger shoals (showing up as a dense trace) and, as the night progresses, they migrate up into the surface waters.

use it as a defence. For instance, one prawn and a deep-sea squid are able to squirt out luminescent clouds to confuse predators. Other species may use it to attract their prey. Sexual attraction and recognition may also be involved. As an example, one tiny syllid worm produces luminescent eggs. The worms tend to mature at the same time and appear simultaneously at the surface of the water in mating swarms. The females squirt out puffs of brightly-lit eggs which spur the males into a frenzy of sperm release.

Perhaps the most remarkable use of luminescence is as a form of countershading in hatchet and lantern fish, which have special light-producing organs (photophores) along their ventral surfaces. If you think of a predator sitting immediately under a fish, its prey will be silhouetted against the light that filters down from the surface. But if the prey has its own ventral light source, this can be used to obliterate the silhouette. The most incredible thing is that the photophores have a half-mirror surface which lets out light of different intensities at different angles. Thus light passing straight downwards from the photophores is at maximum intensity to match the bright sunlight from straight above, while light passing obliquely downwards from the photophore is fainter, and that passing out sideways is very dim, matching the increasingly dimmer sunlight that a predator will see if it looks up at an angle or horizontally through the water.

This remarkable example makes us appreciate that although the open water habitat may be very uniform, compared, for example, with a rocky shore, its inhabitants have adaptations that are just as subtle and amazing as those found in other habitats.

Larger predators

The larger active hunters such as the cuttlefish, squid (Plate 136), the paper nautilus *Argonauta* (Plate 134), and fish such as tunny, hake and elf feast on the smaller open-sea animals.

Sea birds also take their toll, but in a sense they are visitors to the scene, for although they feed from the sea they are compelled to return to land to breed. Huge numbers of gannets, cormorants and penguins may gather on offshore islands. Living and breeding in high-density communities, the birds compete for space and nesting materials. There are few more comical sights than a penguin sneaking over surreptitiously to steal nesting materials from a neighbour, only to have its own nest plundered in its absence. Gannets (Fig. 146) have more sophisticated behaviour patterns that ease the problems of high-density living. Since they need a long runway to allow them to work up enough speed to launch themselves into the air, part of the island is always set aside for this purpose. To reach this area, the birds must thread their way between the nests of other gannets, risking attack from defensive occupants. Their progress is slow and cautious and as they move the birds point their beaks straight upwards, 'sky-pointing' in a ritual that displays their non-aggressive

Fig. 146 Densely packed gannets on their nesting grounds. Some of the birds are 'sky-pointing' in appeasement as they thread their way through the colony.

Fig. 147A. A cluster of jackass penguins takes to the water to feed.
Fig. 147B. Female jackass penguins protect their fluffy offspring from marauding gulls. Penguins normally have two chicks of different ages: if food is scarce the larger chick is preferentially fed and survives at the expense of the smaller one.

Fig. 148 Cape cormorants bask in the sun, drying their wings after feeding.

intentions and appeases the other birds. To emphasise their sky-point the birds' white throats are marked with a vertical dark stripe. When the birds fly in after feeding at sea, they land adjacent to their own nests, although how they manage to identify their particular nests in the seethe of birds is still unknown. Immediately they land, the birds once again sky-point to pacify neighbours and then perform an elaborate series of recognition signals with their partners. They repeatedly bow to each other, their long necks crossed to the left and then to the right; and they also indulge in 'fencing', with bills crossed and clacked one against the other. All these rituals are means of communication and of recognition which are important in the crowded colonies.

Penguins (Fig. 147), cormorants (Fig. 148) and gannets feed largely on fish or squid and, as discussed in the next chapter, human competition for food may have reduced seabird numbers. Seals are also confined to land when they breed and often displace birds from islands. They, too, are major consumers of fish (see Chapter 7).

The dolphins and whales are surely the most highly evolved of the predators in open seas. Their methods of feeding allow us to classify them into two orders. The first of these, the order Odontoceti, includes the dolphins and all toothed whales which are active hunters of fish and squid. The sperm whale is one of the toothed whales and feeds mainly on giant deep-sea squid, eating specimens of up to 200kg in mass. Dolphins hunt in a sophisticated manner, often co-operating in packs to drive shoals of fish into a confined area. Since sight is little help in murky water, dolphins and whales rely on sonar to navigate, and emit high-pitched squeaks which bounce back from solid objects (including prey). These reflected sounds are detected by canals on the lower jaw which are connected to the ear. This process of echo-location also allows dolphins to communicate with one another and there are known examples of dolphins 'telling' one another of the whereabouts of fish. Dolphins trained to release fish into their aquarium by pushing a lever have also been known to communicate this trick to a newly captured dolphin, despite the fact that it was separated from them in such a way that it was out of sight though not out of sound. We are still very ignorant of just how sophisticated this communication is, but we do know from work at the Port Elizabeth Oceanarium that each dolphin has a distinctive 'voice' with its own frequency and timing. In spite of this, dolphins at Port Elizabeth have never learnt to receive or repeat any words. Since sound behaves very differently under water, dolphins may be tone deaf but very sensitive to the intensity of sound, and possibly communicate by changing the loudness of a narrow range of tones. In addition, dolphins have no voice box and their whistles are produced by blowing through their nasal passages. These differences make direct communication with humans impossible, but the complex brain structure of dolphins, their intelligence and highly evolved social organization, all point to an advanced form of communication among themselves.

Humpback whales produce slow, booming songs while they are in their breeding grounds. Although all members of a local population sing the same song, the songs are continually changed so that new songs are composed as the days pass. The wavelength and volume of these sounds is such that they can probably be detected many tens of kilometres away.

The reliance of dolphins and whales on echo-location may be responsible for the periodic mass strandings of these animals: parasites are often found in the ears of stranded animals and may have impaired their ability to navigate.

Most of the great whales belong to a second order, Mystacoceti, and feed further down the food chain by gulping water and then expelling it through the sieve-like baleen plates that lie in the mouth, capturing plankton in the process. Krill (Fig. 149) is their main prey, and a large blue whale may eat four tonnes of krill a day. Recent work on humpback whales has shown that they have a unique method of feeding. They dive deep and then circle around blowing bubbles that froth towards the surface, forming a ring. Krill that are encircled retreat from the bubbles and concentrate in the centre of the ring so that when the whale erupts at the surface with its mouth agape, it engulfs this dense swarm (Fig. 149).

In the southern hemisphere, whales spend their summers in the Southern Ocean, taking advantage of the sunlight and upwelling which provide the necessary ingredients for dense phytoplankton blooms that in turn support the vast quantities of krill required by the whales. In winter they migrate to warmer climes where they give birth and mate, but where food is seldom abundant enough to support their needs. Many species do not feed at all in winter, relying on their thick blubber to tide them over. Thus it is in winter and spring that sperm, fin, sei, right and minke whales gather in the waters off southern Africa, and the humpback whale migrates to Moçambique and Angola.

One of my own unforgettable experiences was the birth of a right whale, close inshore at Kommetjie in September

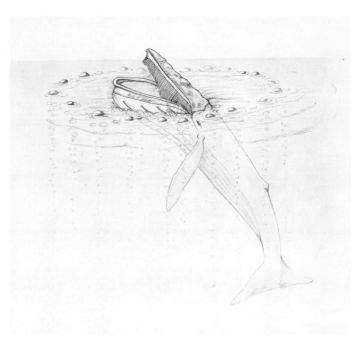

Fig. 149A. The humpback whale erupts at the surface in the centre of a circle of bubbles it has blown to concentrate its prey, the krill.

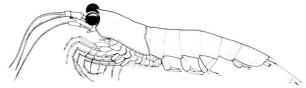

Fig. 149B. The commonest species of krill, *Euphausia superba* (x2).

1976. Being able to snorkel close to the solitary female and her calf brought home the sheer size of whales, for although in reality she was about 15m in length, she seemed to stretch from horizon to horizon and dwarfed her new-born calf – itself about 2m long!

Nutrient availability: Riches vs. poverty
Just as offshore winds may cause upwelling of nutrient-rich water, so onshore winds push surface waters against the coastline and force them downwards. Currents that travel parallel to the coast will deflect the surface waters to the left of their path in the southern hemisphere and to the right in the northern hemisphere, due to Coriolis forces (described in Chapter 1). Because of this, currents off Antarctica and on the west coast of Africa and North and South America cause upwelling. Conversely, on the east coasts of Australia, Africa, North and South America and the Austro-Asian islands, currents have the opposite effect and cause downwelling.

Wherever upwelling occurs, growths of phytoplankton usually develop. On the other hand, in the surface waters of open oceans, or in areas where water is downwelled, nutrients will be in short supply. Only small numbers of tiny flagellates survive in these nutrient-deficient waters, for they can at least swim around to seek out the limited nutrients. In areas of upwelling, on the contrary, nutrients are so abundant that large non-motile diatoms are able to thrive. Diatoms are large enough to store oil as a food

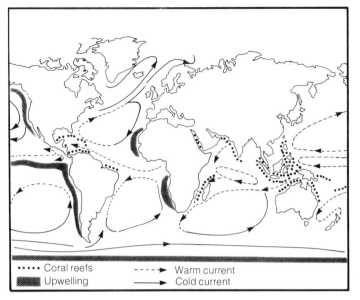

····· Coral reefs   ‒ ‒ ‒→ Warm current
▓▓▓ Upwelling   ——→ Cold current

Fig. 150 Coral reefs are concentrated on the eastern seaboards where temperatures are high and nutrients often low, while upwelling is common on western coasts and in the Antarctic and is associated with rich fisheries.

reserve, which can tide them over the intervals between upwelling. This simple fact is important, for these oils find their way into the anchovies that feed on the diatoms and are thus the basis of the fish oil industry.

Diatoms have also evolved a process that increases their growth. All plants possess chlorophyll a for photosynthesis, but diatoms have chlorophyll c and other auxiliary pigments in addition. These pigments are not able to photosynthesise but they can trap blue light and transmit this energy to the chlorophyll a. We will remember that light is filtered out by water but that blue light penetrates deepest (see Chapter 6). Because diatoms are able to use this blue light, they can live deeper in the water than the simple flagellates found in nutrient-poor water, and because of this they further increase the high productivity of upwelled water.

Since phytoplankton in areas of downwelling is very small, only tiny species of zooplankton, such as the single-celled radiolarians and foraminiferans (Fig. 142) can feed on it. These are in turn eaten by tiny crustaceans.

Thus if fish are to enter the food chain they do so fourth or fifth hand. Since there is an ecological principle that about 80 percent to 90 percent of the energy contained in living organisms is lost at each step of the food chain, precious little is left by the time the fish find something large enough to feed on. This is probably why jellyfish and corals thrive in such waters, for relatively little energy is required for their simple needs. So it is that we find coral reefs dominating the eastern coasts of Australia, Africa and the Americas, where downwelling prevails (Fig. 150).

Upwelled waters are a contrast. Not only do they support dense phytoplankton populations, but these consist mainly of large diatoms which may even link up to form chains, thus further increasing their size. Thus they are large enough to be eaten directly by fish such as anchovies and pilchards, without first going through a series of energy-wasting steps in the food chain. Because fish are active, complex animals that hunt their food, their energy needs are almost seven times those of the simple jellyfish and corals: it is not surprising therefore that the tiny strips of coastal upwelling, which occupy only 0,1 percent of the surface area of the sea, should support almost half the fish production of the oceans!

Whales, apart from demanding huge quantities of food because they are so large, are also warm-blooded. Maintaining body warmth is an expensive process in terms of energy, and whales need 30 times more energy (per unit body mass). Small wonder that many whales only feed during the highly productive summer in the upwelling zones of the Antarctic, while during winter they cease feeding and migrate north to breed in warmer areas where they will spend less of their food reserves on keeping their bodies warm.

Thus we can see that the availability of nutrients not only influences the amount of phytoplankton growth, but even dictates the nature of animal communities living in different areas. It is a curious thought that the mighty whales would probably never have evolved if it had not been for the diatoms, for it is only due to their efficiency and size that the nutritive potential of upwelling zones is translated into a form that can support both the huge krill stocks needed by whales and the richest fisheries in the world.

REFERENCES

Popular articles and books

Boney, A. D. 1975. *Phytoplankton.* Studies in Biology No. 52. Edward Arnold, London. 116 pp.

Earle, S. 1979. Humpbacks: the gentle whales. *National Geographic,* Vol. 155 (1): 2-17.

Payne, R. 1979. Humpbacks: their mysterious songs. *National Geographic,* Vol. 155 (1): 18-25.

Scheffer, V. B. 1976. Exploring the lives of whales. *National Geographic,* Vol. 150: 752-767.

Tietz, R. M. & Taylor, C. K. 1964. Dolphin talk. *Scientific South Africa,* Vol. 1: 385-390.

Wickstead, J. H. 1976. *Marine Zooplankton.* Studies in Biology No. 62. Edward Arnold, London. 60 pp.

See also Best P. 1982. Whales: Why do they strand? *Afr. Wildlife* 36 (3): 96 – 101.

Scientific references

Andrews, W. R. H. & Hutchings, L. 1980. Upwelling in the southern Benguela current. *Progress in Oceanography,* Vol. 9: 1-81.

Day, J. H. 1970. The biology of False Bay, South Africa. *Transactions of the Royal Society of S. Afr.,* Vol. 39: 211-221.

Grindley, J. R. & Sapeika, N. 1969. The cause of mussel poisonings in South Africa. *S. Afr. Medical Journal,* Vol. 43: 275-279.

Parsons, T. R. 1979. Some ecological, experimental and evolutionary aspects of the upwelling ecosystem. *S. Afr. Journal of Science,* Vol. 75: 536-540.

Ryther, J. H. 1969. Photosynthesis and fish production in the sea. *Science,* Vol. 166: 72-76.

7. MAN AND THE SEA

For centuries the sea has entranced poet, painter and priest but, long before this, man's primary interest in the sea has been to glean food. Not all marine organisms are, however, beneficial to man. Some are a direct danger and others hinder our use of the sea. Many human activities are, in turn, harmful to life in the sea; pollution, in particular, threatens many shores. Thus it is that we focus here on four aspects of man's involvement with the sea; exploitation, problem species, pollution and finally marine biology as a career.

THE HARVEST OF THE SEAS
Prehistoric man
Man has gathered food from the seas of southern Africa for over 150 000 years and the remains he has left have built up, layer upon layer, in 'kitchen middens', which provide archaeologists with a wealth of information about the habits of long-dead men and the use they made of sea life. We can learn other things from these middens as well, for they reflect changes of climate that have transformed the nature of southern Africa over the ages.

A detailed study has been made of one such midden that lines the floor of a cave overlooking Elands Bay on the west coast – a cave that has been occupied by man for about 40 000 years.

Digging down from the surface to the deeper, older layers reveals striking changes in the composition of the midden. The lower layers, deposited more than 11 000 years BP (Before Present), contain remains of rhinoceros, giant horse, giant buffalo and eland – mostly species that are extinct today. Yet the more recent upper layers contain totally different remains – mainly limpets and mussel shells.

What could have caused such a transformation in the diet of prehistoric man? It seems that the older layers were deposited during the last glacial period, when much of the world's sea-water was locked up as ice and the sea-level was about 100 m lower than at present. The Elands Bay cave would then have been about 25 km from the sea. At that time cool moist conditions supported grasslands and a rich fauna of large mammals. But as the ice caps melted the sea advanced; at the same time the west coast became drier and hotter. The extinction of many of the large mammals forced man to switch diet and take advantage of marine life which, by 10 000 years B.P., was within easy walking distance of the Elands Bay cave. Initially limpets formed the major part of this new diet, but within 1 000 years black mussels became equally important.

During this period changes were also taking place on the south coast, faithfully recorded in another midden, 'Nelson's Cave' at Plettenberg Bay. Here black mussels disappear about 8 000 BP and are replaced by brown mussels. It seems possible that as the seas warmed up after the glacial period, brown mussels penetrated further down the south coast while the black mussels, preferring moderately cold temperatures, were displaced from the south coast and colonised the west coast.

We can even deduce from these middens that prehistoric man normally used coastal caves as a winter retreat, living inland during summer when vegetable foods were readily available. What evidence is there to support this conclusion? Firstly, the sizes of seal jaw-bones found in the middens are such that the seal pups must have died when they were about six months old. Since seal pups are born in summer, these animals must have died in winter. Secondly, a sophisticated technique can be used to measure the ratio of different oxygen isotopes within limpet shells that have been taken from middens. These ratios change according to the temperature at which the shell was laid down by the living animal, and indicate that most of the limpets died in winter, again suggesting that the caves were occupied by man during this season.

The middens also reveal that exploitation of sea life by prehistoric man had a considerable effect on some species. The larger limpets evidently soon disappeared from the shore so that the more recent deposits in the midden contain much smaller limpets. It seems that modern man is not the first of his kind to over-exploit marine resources.

Even today, limpets, mussels and oysters are collected in Transkei, and in some areas this has had a dramatic effect on these species. The maximum size of one limpet, *Patella*

Fig. 151 A Transkeian woman delights in the capture of an octopus.

concolor, has declined from 66 mm to 38 mm, equivalent to lowering the maximum flesh weight from 5,4 g to 1,5 g and reducing the reproductive potential of the species by more than 95 percent.

Primitive societies also used, and still use, extracts of marine organisms as medicine. The Topnaar Hottentots of the west coast treat wounds with powdered kelp; a sound practice considering the high iodine content of kelp. They also have more bizarre remedies such as using the egg yolk of Joseph sharks to treat venereal diseases; and smearing the eggs of fish-lice (Plate 59) onto the pubic region to stop bed-wetting!

Aquaculture

Man is still essentially a hunter of the sea: less than 5 percent of his harvest is actually farmed. Yet most marine life is already being fished to the limit or even over-exploited, and marine farming or aquaculture is likely to become more important. Southern Africa has an unenviably hostile wave-beaten coast, with few calm lagoons like those of Langebaan and Knysna where aquaculture can take place – all the more reason for preserving these in a healthy state.

The Fisheries Development Corporation (F.D.C.) has developed the art of culturing oysters at Knysna, using an imported species, *Crassostrea gigas*, which is preferred to local species because it is hardier and fast-growing. Oysters can be persuaded to spawn by suddenly raising the temperature, making artificial fertilization possible, and allowing the production of large quantities of tiny swimming larvae. These are fed on cultures of phytoplankton until they settle, fasten themselves to the trays in which they are grown, and metamorphose into miniature oysters (spat). When the spat are large enough they are transferred to wire racks in the open lagoon, which are elevated from the mud-banks to prevent mud-prawns from smothering the oysters. There they are left until they grow to a marketable size. The most difficult phase of the process is the successful rearing of larvae and at present the F.D.C. undertakes this and then supplies the spat to a commercial company.

Langebaan Lagoon has been the site of recent and very successful cultivation of oysters. Unfortunately there has been some controversy about the future of commercial oyster culture here, since the lagoon is likely to become a new national park. It seems to me that the culturing of oysters is not incompatible with a nature reserve, for natural populations are not disturbed in the process – and in fact many organisms find a home on the oyster racks. The oysters can also be used to monitor any future pollution of the lagoon for they accumulate heavy metals in their tissues.

Oyster cultures in South Africa have been mercifully free of some of the pests that plague overseas oyster beds. The slipper limpet *Crepidula fornicata* was accidently introduced to Britain together with imported oysters, and is now so dense that it smothers and competes with oysters and has practically brought the industry to a standstill. The oyster drill *Urosalpinx* also decimates oysters, boring through their shells to feed on them. Spanish oyster beds suffer from a more unusual problem – growths of the gas-filled alga *Colpomenia* (Plate 167n) float the young spat off settlement racks. All of these pests, or close relatives, occur in southern Africa but none has yet become a problem.

Attempts have also been made to culture prawns at Amatikulu in KwaZulu. Hawaii and Japan each produce more than one hundred thousand tonnes of prawns each year, but local experiments have not yet reached the point where a commercial venture is possible.

Other animals which could be cultured in southern Africa are the black and brown mussels and the mullet (*Mugil cephalus*), but the whole concept of farming rather than harvesting the sea is in its infancy and only luxury items are likely to yield commercial returns in the near future.

Pelagic fish

The fishing industry of southern Africa dates back to 1895 when John D. Gilchrist was appointed Government Biologist and charged with investigating fish stocks on the Agulhas Bank. In 1907 he was also appointed Professor of Zoology at the University of Cape Town, and in tribute the University later named its first research ship after him. The

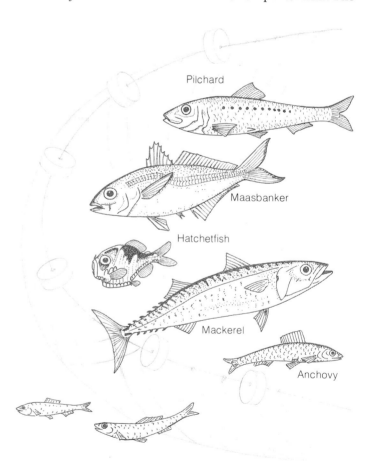

Fig. 152 The commonest pelagic fish caught in purse seine nets are the pilchard *Sardinops ocellata*, maasbanker *Trachurus trachurus*, mackerel *Scomber japonicus*, and anchovy *Engraulis capensis*. The hatchet-fish, *Polyipnus spinosus*, is a mid-water fish only occasionally caught at the surface.

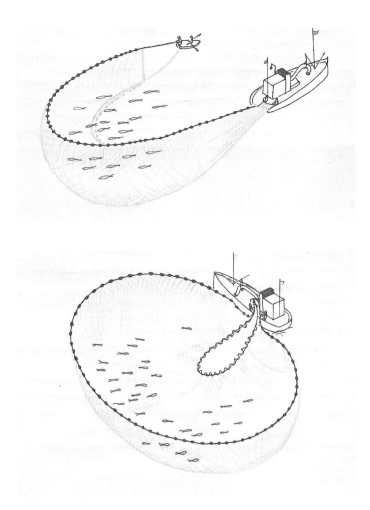

Fig. 153 A purse seine net is laid around a shoal of fish. The top is buoyed by floats and the net hangs like a curtain. Once the shoal is encircled the net is pulled in, closing the bottom of the net like a purse, and the fish are pumped on board through a broad hose.

Fig. 154 The silver harvest comes on board.

'Gil' was used with mixed feelings of affection and trepidation, for she was an old trawler 'sold' to the University for £1 and her seaworthiness was at times suspect. After several years of loyal service to the University, she was finally sold to a company which fitted her with soft carpets and planned to use her as a pleasure cruiser. One dark night she quietly opened up and sank at her dockside moorings – and biologists who had known her in more functional days felt she had died of shame at her new role.

From Gilchrist's solitary position the Sea Fisheries Institute was born and has since grown to a staff of over 550; and is now responsible for advising on the multi-million rand fishing industry. Of the stocks they manage, the pelagic fish are amongst the most important, earning about R50 million a year.

Pelagic fish – the commonest are shown in Fig. 152 – occur in the upper layers of the open sea, and are most abundant off the west coast where upwelling enriches the water, as described in Chapters 1 and 6. Purse seine nets are laid from boats that circle around a shoal of pelagic fish (Fig. 153). In the past, most fishing took place at night, for

the fish are then feeding and as a result are concentrated at the surface and are easier to detect because of the phosphorescence they stimulate in the plankton. In recent years, however, echo-sounders and sonar have enabled skippers to locate shoals at any time of the day (Fig. 145).

Spotter planes also direct boats to areas where the fish are shoaling. The fish usually gather along the edge of the dense phytoplankton blooms that lie close to the coast; satellite photographs can even reveal the limits of the phytoplankton and thus the zone in which the fish are most likely to occur.

Most of the pelagic catch is used to make fishmeal which is fed to farm animals, although fish oil is an important by-product. Only 3 percent to 5 percent of the fish is canned for human consumption, and it is one of the paradoxes of modern economy that so much fish is used to feed animals while much of the world's human population is short of protein.

Practically throughout the world, pelagic fisheries have developed along a common pattern. In each case, pilchards (or some equivalent species) have been the most important

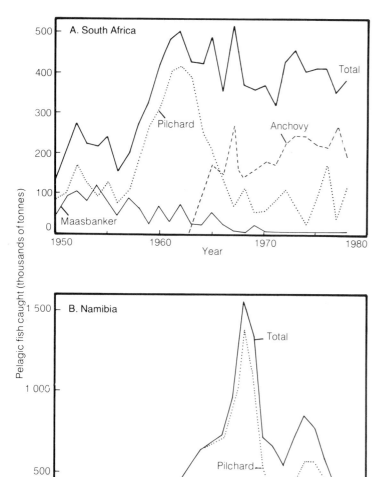

Fig. 155 **Pelagic fish catches in (A) South Africa, and (B) Namibia, over the period 1950-1980. In both cases the lucrative pilchard has declined due to over-fishing and the fishing industry has now turned to the anchovy.**

fish in the early stages of the fishery, but over-fishing has soon led to their virtual extinction and the fishing fleets have turned to less valuable fish such as the anchovy. The total collapse of the once rich Californian pilchard industry has haunted other pelagic fish industries all over the world, including those in South Africa and Namibia, and a great deal of research has been done in an attempt to prevent a similar outcome here. Fig. 155A shows what has happened. From 1956 to 1962 the South African pilchard catch quadrupled to a peak of 400 000 tonnes per year, only to collapse over the following years to an all-time low of 16 000 tonnes in 1974. During this decline, the industry was permitted to reduce the mesh-size of its nets from 32 mm to 12,7 mm, thus allowing the capture of much smaller species, including anchovy, and Fig. 155A shows just how important to the industry the anchovy has become as a substitute for pilchards.

Even while the pilchard stocks were dwindling in South Africa, the Namibian industry was being granted ever-increasing quotas of pilchards (Fig. 155B), rising to an all-time record of 1,4 million tonnes in 1968 – despite dire warnings that such enormous catches could only lead to a decimation of stocks. The downward slide began in 1969 and was horrifyingly precipitous. By 1971 catches had decreased by 73 percent. An intensive research project, the Cape Cross Programme, was launched by the Sea Fisheries Institute, and quotas were slashed year after year. The pilchards recovered briefly in 1974 and 1975 before declining so disastrously that a total ban has now been placed on direct fishing of pilchards and all canning factories in Walvis Bay have had to be closed.

What was responsible for the crash? Undoubtedly over-fishing took its toll. The Sea Fisheries Institute often bears the brunt of criticism for this, but very often their cautions were not heeded by the authorities who granted ever-increasing quotas. In particular, the South African Government 'unleashed a tremendous new force onto the fishing scene' in the late 1960s when they licensed factory ships that could operate outside the (then) 12-mile limits off both South Africa and Namibia. The latter country was strongly opposed to such a development, since the ships annually captured over 300 000 tonnes of fish – and at a time when great concern was being expressed about the escalation of catches. In essence, the factory ships were a means of 'circumventing the established conservation means'.

The legacy of over-fishing pilchards is only too apparent today. But at the same time it must be appreciated that the correct management of pelagic fish is one of the most difficult tasks confronting fisheries biologists, and nowhere in the world has a solution been found.

Part of the problem is that the fish are quick-growing and short-lived, so they are often caught before they have even had a chance to reproduce. Because of this, recruitment of juveniles for next year's catch is always chancy. In the upwelled waters of the west coast there is an additional problem. As outlined in Chapter 6, winds cause upwelling, upwelling promotes phytoplankton blooms, and these allow the zooplankton to develop. The unpredictability of each step is a feature of the system. Pilchard and anchovy juveniles feed entirely on zooplankton, although the adults are filter-feeders and consume both zooplankton and phytoplankton. Thus the success of the juveniles depends very much on the prevailing environmental conditions, which can at times be catastrophic.

Adult pilchards and anchovies undertake spawning migrations each year. For example, the stocks in South Africa migrate south during summer to spawn between Cape Point and Cape Agulhas. The larvae then drift northwards to their normal grounds off St Helena Bay where most of the fishing takes place. If the timing of this cycle does not coincide with suitable physical conditions and sufficient food, recruitment of juveniles to the fishing grounds will be poor.

We suspect that intrusions of warm off-shore water into

growth-rate can be determined. More importantly, they tell us how far the fish migrate. This has shown that the Namibian stocks are largely separate from those of South Africa – an important point when considering how much fishing should be allowed in these two countries.

The size of a population can be gauged from the size of the annual catch, but of course this depends on the time and effort put into fishing. For instance, by allowing for the number of days' fishing and the number of boats, researchers can use the 'catch per unit effort' (CPUE) as an index of abundance. Once the CPUE starts dropping, the stocks are declining and the intensity of fishing should be reduced. Counts can also be made of the number of eggs or larvae caught in plankton nets: again an index of the reproducing stock and perhaps an indication of future stocks.

A more original idea has been to employ very sensitive low-light-level television mounted in aircraft that crisscross the fishing grounds at night and record the number and size of fish shoals, as indicated by areas of phosphorescence (Fig. 156).

Another imaginative approach has been to check back on the amounts of guano harvested annually from bird islands on the west coast. The rationale behind this analysis is that sea birds feed on pelagic fish, so that if the fish have declined, fewer birds will have survived and less guano will have been deposited. The production of guano has indeed declined, reaching the lowest levels ever recorded during the 1962-1967 period, precisely when the pilchard catch was declining so disastrously in South Africa (Fig. 157).

This analysis also yields two further important conclusions. Firstly, it is often supposed that although the pilchards have been substantially reduced, that anchovy populations have expanded to fill the vacancy. This impression is gained because of the increased importance of anchovy to the fishing industry since 1964 (Fig. 155A). It must, however, be remembered that it is only since then that the fishing industry has been allowed to use small mesh nets and has been able to catch anchovies. The data

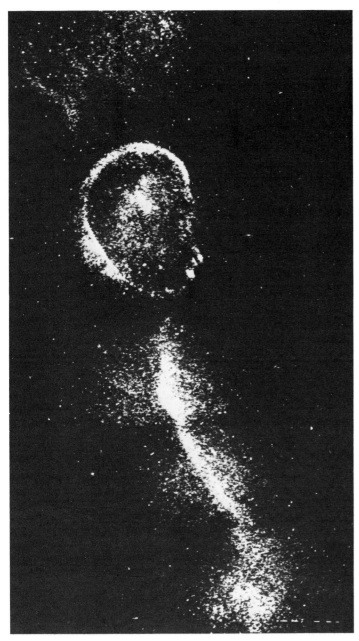

Fig. 156 A remarkable composite photograph, taken from the air at night, using a low light level T.V. camera, showing the phosphorescence left by a huge shoal of fish, part of which has been encircled by a seine net. The detail is so good that even the cork-line of the net is visible, where the fish bulge the net outwards.

the coastal zone can inhibit spawning migrations and that even intensive fishing can turn migrating fish back. The survival of larvae is also influenced by temperature and oxygen levels. All these factors make the success of recruitment more unpredictable.

Thus the vexing question is whether it is possible for the fisheries biologists, in the face of all these unpredictable factors, to foretell the size of the population in the year to come and how much may be harvested without endangering the fish stocks.

To aid in this task, researchers have a variety of techniques at their disposal. Firstly, the fish can be tagged with tiny metal tags. If these animals are recovered later their

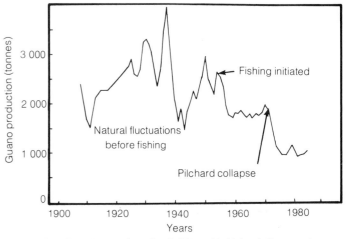

Fig. 157 The yield of guano from South African bird-islands fluctuated naturally even before fishing, but was always low once commercial fishing was initiated and reached lowest-ever levels after the collapse of the pilchard stocks.

on guano production suggest that the numbers of anchovy have not expanded greatly to fill the void left by the pilchards' demise. Certainly in Namibia, the pilchard crash has not been followed by a boom of anchovies (Fig. 155B). Secondly, Fig. 157 shows that even prior to fishing, there were wide fluctuations in the guano harvest, lending support to the idea that environmental conditions change from year to year and have a strong influence on the size of the pelagic fish stock.

No matter how good these various techniques are, they cannot predict the future. Four methods which may assist in this have, however, been developed. Firstly, a correlation has been found between the oil content of fish in any given year and the abundance of fish four years later. It is argued that if the fish are fat and have a high oil content, the environment must be favourable so that reproduction should be successful and larval survival high. If it takes four years for those larvae to grow to a size where they can be caught, then four years after a high oil yield the industry should be able to expect another bumper year. Unfortunately we now know it takes only one year – not four – for the larvae to grow to a catchable size so the validity of this argument has been questioned.

The second and third methods also rely on correlations: both high water temperatures and constant temperatures during the spawning season result in good catches a year later, probably because high temperatures speed larval growth and constant temperatures increase their survival. The value of these correlations is that if they stand the test of time they may give advance warning about the state of the fishery.

The final method of prediction is that of Dr J. P. Lochner, and is certainly the most novel and controversial. He has developed a 'model' of the pelagic fishery based on electrical circuitry. For instance, the current passing through the circuit is made proportional to the number of fish which spawn each year, and resistance to the current represents mortality due to predators and to fishing. By varying the size of the model population and the catch, Lochner maintains he can describe 'the natural control system . . . exactly' – a brave boast considering the many unpredictable factors of which he does not take account.

Scientists often disagree, but rarely has there been such a barrage of criticism as was evoked by Lochner's theories. Shortly after the publication of his method no less than seven scientists – including fisheries biologists, mathematicians and electrical engineers – wrote a damning critique, and overseas experts also considered his theory contributed nothing to the management of pelagic stocks. I agree with their conclusions.

While we may argue about the merits and demerits of different means of assessing fish stocks, taken together they provide a powerful repertoire of methods. Yet despite this, some important fish stocks have declined catastrophically, possibly because, as a deputy director of Sea Fisheries once remarked, 'The advice of scientists has been regarded as being too careful and there have been supposed short-term social and economic difficulties associated with the reduction of fishing effort required by scientific recommendations'. It is thus disturbing that the current quota for the Cape pelagic fishery remains as high as 380 000 tonnes in spite of the recommendation by fisheries biologists that it be reduced by 55 000 tonnes. As one letter to the press comments: 'Is the lesson of the South West African catastrophe yet to be learned?'

Trawled fish

Demersal fish that live on or near the ocean bottom are netted by trawlers towing behind them sturdy trawl nets (Fig. 158). By far the most important of the demersal fish is the hake (Fig. 158), which accounts for about 70 percent of South Africa's annual catch totalling about 136 000 tonnes and worth about R100 million. Until recently the hake was regarded as a single species of fish but we now know that there are two closely related species, distinguishable only by subtle differences of gill structure and the number of vertebrae. Both are widespread, being caught abundantly off the coasts of Angola, Namibia and the west and south coasts of South Africa, but while *Merluccius capensis* occurs close to the coast, normally never deeper than 500m, *M. paradoxus* is a deep-water animal extending down to 750 m. An interesting feature is that in both species the young animals are found closest inshore and the size of the fish increases offshore. When we examine the diet of hake, the advantage of this is obvious, for large hake feed almost entirely on small hake! In fact, this is one case where reduction of large hake by the fishery may actually promote survival of the juveniles.

Both species of hake undertake daily migrations, rising by night from the bottom to feed in mid-water so that trawling usually takes place by day. However, during the spawning season in August and September the fish disappear from the bottom grounds and are difficult to net.

The age of a hake can be determined accurately by examining its otoliths ('ear-bones'), because transparent rings are laid down on the otoliths once a year (during the spawning period), much like the growth-rings of a tree. Hake grow fairly slowly, becoming sexually mature only after about four years, but can live 14 years and reach a length of 110 cm.

This pattern is quite different from the rapid growth, early maturity and short life of the pelagic fish. The contrast is an important one, for it means that the hake stocks are far more stable from year to year, that recruitment of young is more predictable and that the trawling industry has far more warning of any changes in the availability of fish.

Prior to 1960 South Africa was the only country fishing intensively for hake but, from 1961 to 1965, foreign vessels almost trebled the catch, and by 1970 the stocks were clearly being over-fished. A measure of this over-fishing is clearly illustrated by looking at just one sector of the fishery: the Cape Division that runs from just south of the Orange River to Cape Agulhas. Fig. 159A shows that from the inception of this fishery there has been a steady increase in the amount of effort put into fishing (measured

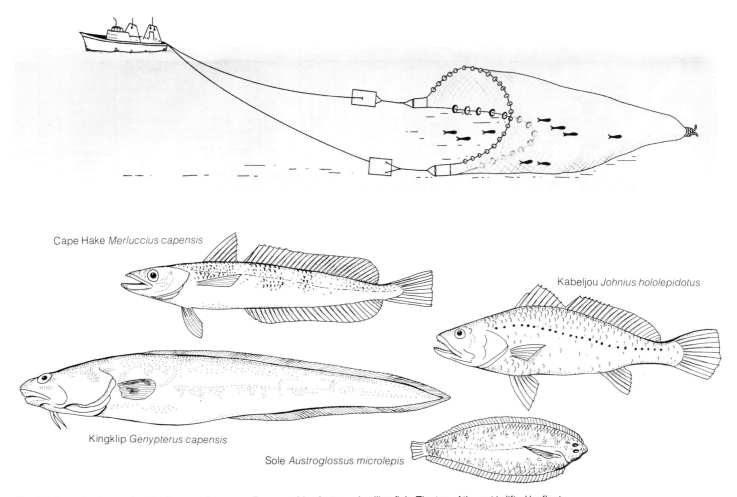

Cape Hake *Merluccius capensis*

Kabeljou *Johnius hololepidotus*

Kingklip *Genypterus capensis*

Sole *Austroglossus microlepis*

Fig. 158 A trawler drags a trawl net across the ocean floor, catching bottom-dwelling fish. The top of the net is lifted by floats while the foot-rope rolls on weighted bobbins. The net is held open by two 'otter-boards', forced apart by the pressure of water. The commonest trawl-fish are shown below.

as the number of trawlers multiplied by the number of days spent fishing), but on the other hand the catch per unit effort (CPUE) has declined alarmingly (Fig. 159B). This information on CPUE allows us to calculate how much sustainable (long-term) yield can be anticipated from any particular fishing effort. Fig. 159C shows that up to an effort of about 25 000 trawler-days, increasing effort produces an increasing yield, but that once this figure is exceeded, diminishing catches can be expected. Even in 1973, fishing effort was almost double the desired level. A 50 percent reduction in effort could, within five years, theoretically improve the catch rate by about 130 percent.

By 1970 grave doubts were expressed about the future of the hake fishery, for over 15 countries were by then exploiting the fish. Fortunately two events have forestalled the collapse of the fishery. Firstly, there was unusual agreement between the participating countries that fishing was too intense, and this led to the formation of the International Commission of the South-East Atlantic Fisheries (ICSEAF). Working with commendable speed considering the difficulties, ICSEAF divided the coast of Africa into eight regions and allocated quotas of fish to the participating countries. In 1975, ICSEAF also increased the minimum mesh-size of nets from 102 mm to 110 mm: a measure that immediately reduced the catch by about 20 percent, but is likely to increase the long-term yield by about 5 percent to 13 percent as the stocks recover.

Secondly, in November 1977 South Africa implemented a 200-mile (360 km) exclusive fishing zone within which all foreign fishing was banned except for small quotas granted to a few countries. Since almost half the hake previously captured in these waters was taken by foreign vessels, and since South African waters contain almost half the total hake stocks, this step brought welcome relief to the hake. If the trawling industry in South Africa can now resist the temptation to step in immediately and take up the slack, the future of the hake stocks should be assured.

Rock lobster

Three species of rock lobster are exploited in southern Africa. By far the most important is the west coast species, *Jasus lalandii*, yielding about 6 500 tonnes annually. Ninety percent of the catch is exported and brings in a foreign exchange of about R25 million each year. Smaller catches of 300 tonnes of *Palinurus gilchristi* are made in deeper waters of 100 to 200 m off the coast of Port Elizabeth, and *Palinurus delagoae* yields about 90 tonnes per annum off Natal and Moçambique.

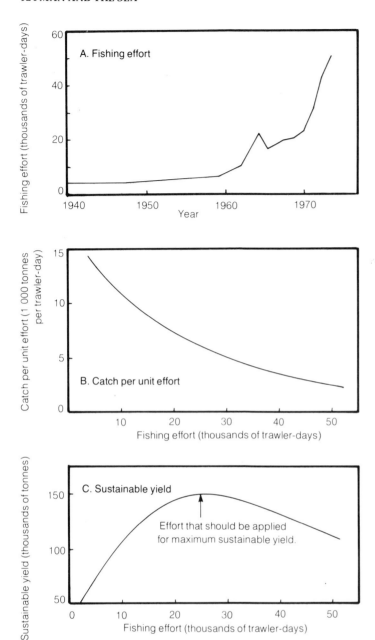

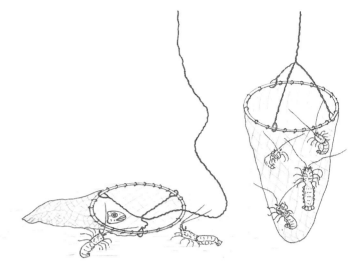

Fig. 160 Rock lobster hoop-nets are laid on the sea floor and are baited with fish-heads.

Fig. 159 The effort put into catching Cape hake has steadily increased (A), but the amount caught per unit effort has declined (B), and the maximum long-term catch would actually be achieved at a much lower effort (C).

Rock lobsters are usually caught in traps that are baited with dead fish and left lying on the sea bed. There they attract rock lobsters which clamber in but cannot escape easily when the trap is hauled to the surface (Figs. 160 & 161). *Palinurus delagoae* is, however, caught by trawling.

At one time rock lobsters abounded on the west coast and could be caught in knee-deep water, but the lucrative commercial fishery has considerably reduced their numbers. To determine the 'maximum sustainable yield' (the greatest number that can be caught without endangering the stocks) the Sea Fisheries Institute has for many years undertaken research on rock lobsters, a leading role being played by Drs Garth Newman and Dave Pollock.

To manage a fishery of this nature it is necessary to

Fig. 161 The rectangular trap, shown here being hauled on board with a load of rock lobsters, is a more efficient device than the hoop-net.

know, amongst other things, the size of the natural population, mortality rate, growth rate, size and sexual maturity, diet and life-cycle. Much of this information is gained by tagging and releasing large numbers of animals. The tags resemble miniature strips of spaghetti, armed with a plastic barb that is thrust into the top of the tail of the rock lobster, where it remains embedded for months without harming the animal. Animals that are recaptured later, allow calculations of growth and an estimation of mortality and the influence of the fishery on the size of the total population.

In South African waters, *Jasus lalandii* grows agonisingly slowly. The animal may only be legally harvested when its carapace (the 'shell' covering the head and the thorax) is over 89 mm in length, which the rock lobster achieves at an age of about nine years. Males are sexually mature at 70 mm and females at 80 mm, so that the minimum size limit of 89 mm ensures that the animals have an opportunity to reproduce before being captured. Once they are mature, female rock lobsters grow only about 1 mm a year and males 3 mm a year so that the monsters of 150 mm occasionally caught could be as old as 30 to 40 years. This means that it is very easy to over-fish the populations and that the stocks are slow to recover.

As described in Chapter 4, rock lobsters grow slowly in some areas because they are short of the right sized food, and very recently the suggestion has been made that if some of the small rock lobsters could be caught, more food would be left for the rest to grow more quickly to a reproductive condition. Can this be done without endangering the stocks? We cannot answer this directly, nor can we risk going ahead with such an experiment in case it fails and destroys the fishery. What can be done is to use a computer to 'model' a hypothetical situation. Such modelling throws an interesting light on this possibility. Growth rates of young rock lobsters would indeed increase if the young were thinned out: and the total yield to the fishery could actually be increased by an estimated 15 percent. What the model cannot tell us is what effect this would have on the reproductive potential of the population, which is likely to drop if fewer rock lobsters are allowed to reach a reproductive age. Until this question is answered it woud be unwise to lower the legal size of rock lobsters.

In Namibia *Jasus lalandii* matures at a smaller size: 62 mm in males and 70 mm in females. Consequently the legal size has always been lower there than in South Africa. In the early 1960s the Namibian industry had difficulty in catching enough tail weight to fill the annual quota of 1 632 tonnes to which it was then entitled, and made representations to the Government to decrease the legal size of rock lobsters. Despite the concern of fisheries biologists, the legal size was lowered from 76 mm to 70 mm in 1964. Furthermore, by simultaneously increasing the quota to almost 2 500 tonnes, the authorities opened the door to the exploitation of large numbers of small rock lobsters. By 1969 almost five times as many rock lobsters were being caught compared with 1959. This caused a rapid reduction of the average size of rock lobsters and even by the end of the 1964 season between 60 percent and 70 percent of the animals were smaller than 76 mm. The danger of this is obvious when we realise that a female lobster of 76 mm produces about 50 000 more eggs than one of 70 mm. These moves only worsened the problem. But instead of curbing fishing and allowing the stocks to recover, the authorities then actually lifted the size restriction completely so that from 1968 to 1969 rock lobsters of any size could be caught. By 1968, over 60 percent of the female rock lobsters that were caught were so small that they could never have had the opportunity to breed! It was only in 1970 that, due to strong pressure from fisheries scientists, a minimum size was reinstated and the total quota lowered to 1 360 tonnes. Despite this, the rock lobsters have still not recovered.

Nevertheless, at least precautions are being taken to protect the west coast rock lobster. In addition to quotas and size restrictions, certain areas have been set aside as rock lobster sanctuaries. Along the entire coastline no fishing is allowed between 1 July and 31 October, which is when most of the females are bearing eggs. After moulting the rock lobsters are soft and helpless and cannot feed, so that they are never found in crayfish nets, and in any case it is illegal to capture soft rock lobsters. Female rock lobsters are legally protected while they are 'in berry' – carrying eggs on their abdominal limbs (Figs. 262 & 263). All these restrictions have ensured that although there are signs of over-fishing, the stocks are now relatively well-managed and certainly in no danger of extermination.

Seal culling

The South African fur seal (*Arctocephalus pusillus*) is more at home in the sea than on land but it must return to shore to breed. Bulls haul up on to islands and secluded beaches along the west coast of South Africa and Namibia in spring and fight fiercely to establish territories. Successful bulls will occupy their territories continuously for several weeks while they attract and mate with a harem of up to 28 cows (Fig. 162). Seals have an interesting reproductive cycle. The cows mate almost immediately after giving birth, but they have the ability to delay pregnancy by postponing the implantation of the embryo in the uterus. This unusual system ensures that the young are born a year later although the period of pregnancy is less than a year.

The young are confined to land to begin with and congregate in large nursery groups, often so densely packed that they form a squirming mass, scratching, biting and mock-fighting while awaiting the daily return of their mothers, who must take to the sea to feed. Growth is rapid and females are able to reproduce by their second year – no doubt a factor contributing to the rapid expansion of undisturbed seal colonies.

There has always been controversy about seal culling, partly because the method of culling – by clubbing the young pups – is abhorrent to many people, including myself. In 1978 there were threats to sue the Minister of Economic Affairs for cruelty to animals when he granted a private concession for the culling of seals in False Bay. At the same time, even the SPCA considers clubbing the most

Fig. 162 A bull fur seal with his harem of females.

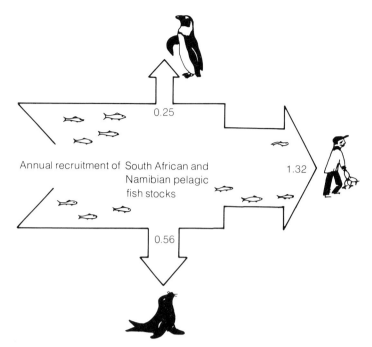

Fig. 163 The relative amounts of pelagic fish that are caught by man, eaten by seals, and consumed by birds. The figures given are millions of tonnes for South Africa and Namibia combined.

Fig. 164 Fur seals dive over the float line of a purse seine net to feed on the captive fish.

humane way of killing pups, for their partly-formed brain cases are scant protection against a club, so that the animals die instantly. Furthermore, an international commission to South Africa agreed that culling was practised in the most humane way possible.

But why should seals be culled? Pups are hunted mainly for their pelts, which are worth R10 each, but oil from the blubber brings in another R1,50 an animal and the flesh can be used as animal food. About 75 000 pups are harvested annually in southern Africa. Culling takes place between June and September – being timed to minimise its impact on the breeding season. In addition to the pups, small numbers of bulls are shot. Though their hides are tattered from territorial battles and worth little, they yield a great deal of oil and their reproductive organs are much desired in the Far East as a reputed aphrodisiac. The total southern African seal harvest realises about R1 million annually.

There are, however, other reasons for culling. Since their decimation by sealers in the nineteenth century, South African fur seals have been increasing steadily in number. Seal Island in False Bay, for instance, was not inhabited by seals at the turn of the century but now supports a colony of 35 000. The rapid growth of this colony has all but displaced the once-rich bird population that lived on the island. There have also been suggestions (though no proof) that sharks are increasingly attracted into the bay to feed on the seals.

Seals also come into direct competition with the fishing industry. The amount of fish they eat is a significant proportion of the potential catch (Fig. 163). More importantly,

seals have learnt that a boat casting a seine net signals that food is available and they swarm over the net in their hundreds (Fig. 164) consuming the fish and often damaging the costly net in their efforts to escape from it afterwards. Attempts to keep the seals out of nets have not yet proved completely successful. Tape recordings of killer whales played back under water do scare them away but they soon learn that the recording is a false alarm. Underwater explosions of thunder flashes seem the most effective means of deterring them at present, but in sheer frustration many skippers have illegally taken to shooting the seals.

It is in view of these problems that the Sea Fisheries Institute holds that the seal populations must be controlled, that they are an exploitable resource, but that their exploitation must be as humane as possible and must ensure their long-term conservation. Certainly the quotas that are currently permitted present no threat to the species.

The whaling industry

Of all the sea animals, the whale is most symbolic of man's early plunder of the seas and of his more recent awareness of conservation. The hey-day of whaling is long past, having reached a peak between 1820 and 1860. But the plight of the whale today is a telling reflection of the effects of over-exploitation during most of the history of whaling. One species after another has been drastically depleted as the industry has turned to smaller and less and less profitable species (Fig. 165). The blue whale *(Balaenoptera musculus)* – the largest animal the world has ever known, reaching 30 m and weighing nearly 100 tonnes – has been hunted to the verge of extinction. Perhaps only 3 percent of the original population remains today.

Herman Melville foresaw the demise of whales when he wrote in 1851, in *Moby Dick*, 'the moot point is whether leviathan can long endure so wide a chase . . . so remorseless a havoc; whether he must not at last be exterminated'.

Concern over the plight of whales has led to the creation of the International Whaling Commission (IWC) which meets annually to decide the quotas that should be set for various species. It is through this body that total protection from commercial whaling has been granted to the blue, right, bowhead, grey and humpback whales. The fin and sei whales have been totally protected in the southern hemisphere and the sperm whale has only this year joined these. The IWC has fixed the 1980-81 quotas as shown in Fig. 165. These are divided between the various whaling countries, Japan and Russia accounting for about 85 percent of the whales. South Africa used to operate two whaling stations, one at Donkergat near Saldanha and the other at Durban, but these closed down in 1967 and 1975 respectively. In its final year the Durban station processed 1 817 whales, almost all of which were sperm whales: a catch worth R3-4 million. Today, almost all the great whales are protected because their numbers are so low and attention has shifted to the smaller species such as Bryde's whale and more particularly to the Minke whale. Incidentally, the name 'Minke' originated in jest from the name of a Norwegian whaler who confused the small whales with the giant blue whales – and was never allowed to forget it!

Minke whales are hunted largely for their meat and are the major source of this form of protein in Japan, which being a small country cannot afford to farm sheep and cattle. An additional product is the oil derived from the whale's blubber. In the early nineteenth century whale oil was an important source of fuel but its significance declined with the discovery of petroleum in 1859.

Sperm whales have an extremely high haemoglobin content in their flesh, which gives the meat a metallic taint because of the iron in the haemoglobin. As a result, the meat is not eaten and sperm whales are hunted mainly for their oil. Sperm oil (and spermaceti, the solid wax form) is an almost perfect lubricant for refined machinery: no synthetic oils approach its efficiency or its long life in high-speed, high-temperature machines. Only very recently has a substitute, the oil of the jojoba bean, been discovered.

The protection of many species, the creation of an Indian Ocean sanctuary and the allocation of quotas to control hunting, have ensured that none of the whale populations is now threatened by whaling. Despite this, there has been strong pressure from conservation bodies for a total ban on whaling – a proposal hotly debated at the IWC in 1980. At this meeting the South African delegation from the Sea Fisheries voted against the proposed ban on whaling, and repeated criticism appeared in the local press, some of it constructive but a good deal of it misinformed, including the accusation that the South African vote had been made on the basis of political expediency to curry favour with Japan. I do not believe this. If anything, they have been pressurised to vote in favour of the ban. Their standpoint arises from the fact that there is no scientific reason why whale stocks should not continue to be ex-

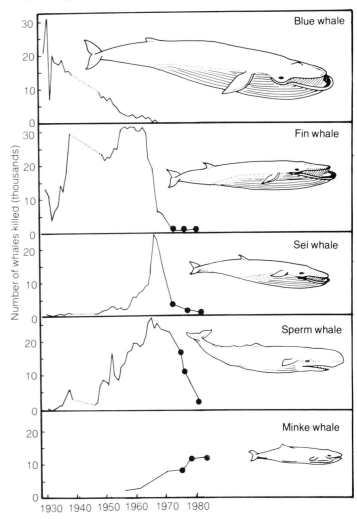

Fig. 165 The numbers of whales captured each year during the period 1930-1981. As the larger species have dwindled, hunters have turned to smaller and smaller species. Whaling was interrupted during World War 2 (dotted lines). Dots indicate quotas set by the International Whaling Commission.

ploited as long as whaling presents no threat to any of the species. Furthermore, the IWC has no power to enforce quotas and depends on the mutual co-operation of its members to ensure that quotas are not exceeded. A total ban on whaling would probably have driven Japan and Russia to withdraw from the IWC and continue whaling, uncontrolled by international scientific opinion.

The whale now hunted most intensively – the Minke – is abundant, and actually increased its numbers between 1930 and 1975. Furthermore, Dr Peter Best of the Sea Fisheries Institute finds that this species now grows faster, becoming sexually mature at an age of about 7½, compared with 11½ years in 1935. These facts raise important questions. Why should the Minke be increasing in number and growing faster? The likely answer is that as the large whales have become reduced in number, so there has been more food for the Minke. Other whales also show heartening signs of maturing more quickly, thus speeding the recovery of their populations. But if Minke whales increase in number, there is a danger that they will compete with the depleted great whales and prevent their hoped-for recovery. We know that the blue whale competes directly with the Minke for its food, the krill *Euphausia*. We also know that the right whale which was intensively hunted in the nineteenth century began to recover quite suddenly in the 1960s, only once the sei whale had been reduced in number. Both species feed on copepods and presumably compete for food.

These are all tenuous threads, but they cannot be ignored if we are to manage the recovery of the great whales: it may not be in their interests to impose a total ban on whaling, allowing the smaller whales to multiply unchecked. This question is even more critical when we realise that man is likely to enter the scene as a further competitor for the whales' main food, krill.

The rational decision seems to be to continue hunting whales in a controlled manner; but of course the issue of whaling goes beyond the rational. Are we as a human race entitled to hunt what is obviously a highly evolved and intelligent animal, using explosive harpoons that must inflict torture to the beasts before they die? Only our emotions are involved in answering this question. Sir Alistair Hardy, one of the world's leading biologists, once said that if the brutality of whaling took place on land for all to see, it would never be allowed.

Similar emotions drive people to protest about the capture of dolphins for oceanariums. No one should deny such emotions, for they are central to our changing attitudes to conservation. I myself cannot be purely objective about the dolphin controversy, for the experience of diving and surfing amongst dolphins leaves a bond. Yet I must agree with the Wildlife Society's recent stand, that the capture of a few dolphins is of small import compared with the threats posed to some species or even to whole ecosystems. And the performing dolphins at Durban surely justify their existence. Not only do they give obvious pleasure to many people, but they also are the subjects of valuable research, and the money they bring promotes research at the

Fig. 166 A playful dolphin breaks the water.

Oceanographic Institute – most of it directed towards the conservation of threatened species and habitats.

The utilization of seaweeds

The average person's reactions to the thought of eating seaweed is to wrinkle up his or her nose. Yet almost all of us have at some time eaten extracts from seaweeds, for they are used in an amazing range of products, including jelly, soup, icecream, instant puddings, cheese, sausage casing, cereals, icing and even as a stabilizer for beer foam!

Seaweeds have been utilised since 1720 as a source of soda, potash and iodine; but none of these substances is commercially obtained from algae any more. Nowadays there are three main uses of seaweeds: as a food or food supplement, as a source of gels, and as a fertilizer.

Seaweeds are an important source of food in the Far East. *Porphyra* (Plate 172b), or *nori* as it is called in Japan, is the most valuable species, being rich in protein and, like all seaweeds, containing a complete range of trace elements and high levels of iodine. Because of this latter property, seaweeds are often used in the treatment of goitre and other thyroid complaints. *Porphyra* is common in South Africa, being the most characteristic seaweed high on the shore. In Japan it is cultivated on nets in calm lagoons. Good quality *nori* sells for $100 a kilogram and the industry in Japan is worth $700 million a year.

Seaweeds are seldom eaten in southern Africa, but they are used to supplement the diets of domestic animals. As an example, traces of the kelp *(Ecklonia maxima)* increase the butter-fat content of milk by 15 percent and relieve eczema in dogs.

Two important gel-forming chemicals are derived from algae. The red algae yield agar-agar, which has the property of dissolving when warm but forming a gel when cool. Its most important use is in pharmaceutical and bacteriological work. *Gracilaria verrucosa* (Plate 177n) was at one time collected in vast quantities when it washed ashore at Saldanha Bay, and was exported for the extraction of agar, but this lucrative practice has ceased since dredging virtually eliminated the weed-beds (see p. 105). More recently an agar industry has been founded in Transkei, based on *Gelidium* (Plate 176), a small red alga that grows on rocky shores.

Alginic acid is another compound which can only be obtained from algae. It, too, serves as a gel widely used in food products, but it has the additional property of forming salts with a wide range of metals such as sodium, calcium, copper and iron, which have different solubilities that can be altered by changing conditions. They can therefore be used in an insoluble form to bind materials together, but at any stage of the process their solubility can be changed and the alginate removed. They are used to waterproof cement, to seal fine papers, to stabilize toothpaste, paint, ink and explosives, as well as in a wide range of other products. Alginic acid also fixes radioactive strontium, allowing it to be passed out of the body; at many United States nuclear power stations daily doses of seaweed or alginate are given for this reason.

Alginic acid is obtained from the brown algae. The kelp *Ecklonia maxima* is a particularly rich source. Kelps that wash ashore on the west coast are at present collected, dried and exported. Smaller quantities are processed locally to produce a crude alginate employed to stabilize soil, successfully binding earth embankments and thereby encouraging the growth of plant cover.

It is as a 'fertilizer' that seaweeds have very recently captured the imagination of local agriculturists. Two adventurous zoologists – both graduates of the University of Cape Town – have launched a company to market kelp as a growth stimulant for crops. The project is still in the developmental stage, but already farmers' cooperatives in Transvaal and the Free State describe the product as 'the most exciting they have handled in 20 years'.

There is nothing new to the use of seaweed as fertilizers: even the Romans used it, and Irish potatoes were nourished with kelp for centuries. The great potato blight of 1846, which resulted in the emigration of over two million Irish, was caused partly because it became more profitable to extract iodine from seaweeds than to use them as a fertilizer. Previous to this, the natural fungicidal action of seaweed had kept the blight in check. What *is* new about the local plant stimulant is its method of preparation – a 'cold process' that involves neither heat nor any strong chemical treatment. The kelp is simply macerated, liquidized under pressure and a preservative is added. This cold process has been a major breakthrough, for it preserves the hormones in the kelp. It is these hormones – gibberellins, auxins and cytokinins – that enhance plant growth. The kelp is thus not a fertilizer but a growth stimulant. Experimental trials show that the local kelp product, which is normally applied at only 2 litres per hectare in conjunction with an ordinary fertilizer mix, increases wheat production anything from 20 percent to 300 percent, can raise the production of beans by 300 percent and improves the germination and production of at least 12 other crop plants. Its application seems especially valuable in marginal farming areas or in times of drought; several times it has saved crops that would otherwise have been abandoned.

This venture depends on freshly harvested kelp, cut by divers and brought in by small boats (Fig. 167). At the moment it is restricted to an experimental 250 tonnes per year (rising to 3 000 tonnes over the next three years). Since this is a tiny proportion of the estimated 60 000 tonnes available, the ecological effects of this harvest are likely to be small. One advantage of harvesting large kelp plants is that it encourages growth of young kelp plants normally shaded by the canopy of larger kelps (see Chapter 4). Thus, after the kelp has been harvested, rapid regrowth occurs and the kelp stands recover within a year. So far no adverse effects of harvesting have been detected. Local complaints of an increase in the kelp cast ashore and fears that harvesting will drive away rock lobsters have been allayed by on-the-spot investigations.

For all the excitement of a breakthrough in using kelp as

Fig. 167 Harvesting of freshly cut kelp for kelp products.

a plant stimulant, local usage of seaweed is still in its infancy. The United States government has recently embarked on a project to farm kelp, grown on giant underwater racks and fertilized by drawing up deep nutrient-rich water to the surface by wave-powered pumps. Used to produce methane, such kelp farms could eventually meet the entire United States demand for natural gas. A grandiose scheme – and one which illustrates the enormous potential of seaweeds.

SPECIES THAT CONFLICT WITH MAN
Fouling organisms
Every man-made surface submerged in the sea is quickly coated with marine life (Fig. 168). Ships become covered with barnacles and algae, which increase the drag of the ship as it moves through the water. Even six months of growth calls for an 80 percent increase in power to maintain the same ship's speed. The increased fuel consump-

Fig. 168 Experimental stainless steel plates were coated with barnacles within three months of being submerged (below) while after 12 months they were almost unrecognisable and covered with 25 kg of red-bait and other organisms (above).

tion costs shipping companies millions of rands, and to this must be added the expense of scraping down and repainting the ship periodically. Anti-fouling paints, which contain a toxic metal such as copper or zinc, are widely used to slow down the rate of fouling, but their effect is temporary.

Another problem is the fouling of intake pipes transporting sea-water to factories or power stations. These pipes are soon coated with animal life, particularly with barnacles and mussels, slowing the flow of water and sometimes blocking the entire system when shells of dead animals accumulate or flush through to narrower pipes. There are various ways of combating the problem. Pipes may be made large enough to avoid clogging, but this is an expensive process and the increase in the size of the pipes means a reduction in the rate of water-flow, encouraging more life to settle in the pipes. Alternatively, intake pipes can be constructed in pairs. While one pipe is in use the other can be closed down and the water in it left to stagnate, killing off the organisms. Table Bay power station operates on this basis. Experiments on the fouling organisms there show that after 60 hours without oxygen, most animals succumb but barnacles survive up to eight days, and mussels for an astonishing 21 days.

Quite recently the Electricity Supply Commission has funded research on the use of chlorine to reduce fouling, having in mind the intake pipes at Koeberg Nuclear Power Station. At a continuous very low dose of 0,1 parts per million, chlorination effectively prevents fouling. But if chlorination is interrupted long enough for animals to settle, they are then much more difficult to remove. Adult black mussels can, for instance, survive a 50-fold increase in the concentration of chlorine for 14 days. Continuous applications of low concentrations of chlorine thus seem the best way to prevent fouling and, as chlorine is rapidly lost from the discharge of sea-water, its effect on other marine life is minimal.

Dangers of the sea
As an adaptation against predators, many marine animals bear venomous spines. Others have poisonous flesh. The blaasops (Fig. 169), belonging to the fish family Tetraodontidae, have extremely poisonous flesh, capable of killing a man. The livers of red steenbras (Petrus rupestris), seals and sharks may at times be dangerous to eat because they contain high concentrations of Vitamin A which causes a range of unpleasant symptoms from nausea, vomiting and a tingling of the lips, through to severe paralysis of muscles, respiratory failure, coma and death. Loss of skin and hair may occur. In none of these cases is there an antidote. However, the stomach should be evacuated as soon as possible and the patient hospitalized. Other cases of poisoning are usually due to eating spoiled seafoods or species contaminated by the toxins from a red tide (see Chapter 6). Allergies to seafoods are quite common and can be dangerous, but are usually in specific response to a particular type of animal.

The sea snake, Pelamis platurus (Fig. 63C), deserves

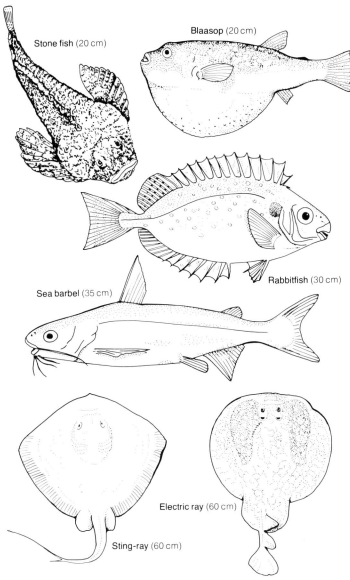

Fig. 169 Dangerous fish. The blaasop *Amblyrhynchotes honckenii* and its relatives are highly poisonous and should not be eaten. Rabbit fish *(Siganus canaliculatus)*, sea barbel *(Arius feliceps)* and the deadly stonefish *(Synanceja verrucosa)* have venomous fin-spines, while sting rays (such as *Dasyatis*) have spines on their whip-action tails. The electric ray *(Torpedo marmorata)* discharges a high voltage shock from the organs on either side of its eyes, which can knock a man over but is never lethal.

are the stingrays which carry a spine at the base of the tail; the sea barbel or catfish *Arius feliceps* which has serrated spines supporting its dorsal and pectoral fins, and can lock these into an upright position; the scorpionfish (family Scorpaenidae) and the exquisitely beautiful firefish *(Pterois volitans,* Plate 25) which is armed with venomous dorsal spines. The rabbit fishes (family Siganidae) also give an extremely painful stab. With typical whimsical humour the Australians refer to rabbit fish as 'happy moments' – it was only when one of us hooked a rabbit fish and our short-lived ecstasy ended with the violent pain of a stabbed finger that we realised why!

The stone fish, *Synanceja verrucosa,* which is an ugly beast so perfectly camouflaged that it looks like a seaweed-covered stone (Fig. 169), is probably the most venomous fish in the world. It bears stout spines that are hollow like hypodermic needles and forcibly discharge a highly toxic venom. Stabs from the spines cause excruciating pain and can result in death within 20 minutes. Margaret Smith, in her informative booklet *Sea and Shore Dangers* describes how her famous ichthyologist husband was stabbed in the thumb by a stone fish in Moçambique and suffered fiery pain, which even injections of morphine failed to quell; only immersing the hand in very hot water of about 55 °C – as hot as could be borne – brought any relief. Immersion in very hot water for about 30 to 90 minutes seems to be the most practical treatment for any fish stabs, since it destroys the proteins of the venom. The wound should also be cleaned and any fragments of the spine removed. Treatment with antibiotics and anti-tetanus agents may also be necessary to prevent secondary complications.

Despite this long list of dangers, much of the coast of southern Africa houses mercifully few really dangerous species. But in tropical waters such as those of Moçambique and northern Natal there are many more species with unpleasant stings or spines – a reflection of the more intense predation in these warmer waters.

Sharks and shark control

Of all the fears man has of the sea, shark attack ranks high. Yet this fear of sharks is out of all proportion to the danger, for the chances of being attacked are extremely small. Lightning claims many more people, and the statistics for motor accidents make shark attack insignificant. But one has only to look at the effect of a shark scare to appreciate how fearful man is. Black Christmas of 1957, when five attacks occurred on the Durban South Coast, caused tourists to flood almost hysterically away from the coastal resorts, leaving virtual ghost towns. For a year the R300 million tourist industry of Natal was all but crippled.

The horror of shark attack is partly because the beasts can inflict such fearsome wounds. Armed with several rows of lacerating teeth, which are renewable so that they are perpetually razor sharp, a shark can exert a force of some 3 000 kg/cm² when it strikes. A single bite can cut a seal in half. Tim Wallett, in his book *Shark Attack*, stresses the horrifying nature of shark wounds – not because he wishes to be

special mention as one of the most venomous animals, for although it is not aggressive it is often washed ashore after storms and attracts children because of its bright colours. Fortunately it is easy to recognize, having an orange or yellow spotted tail flattened like an oar. It has an extremely potent venom and there is no specific anti-venene for it, although polyvalent anti-serum neutralises its effects.

Other less dangerous but still unpleasantly venomous creatures include the long-spined urchins, bluebottles *(Physalia)*, fireworms *(Eurythoe)* and the cone-shells *(Conus* spp.) – all mentioned elsewhere in this book.

Many fish (Fig. 169) have venomous spines and all fish should be handled with caution. Particularly dangerous

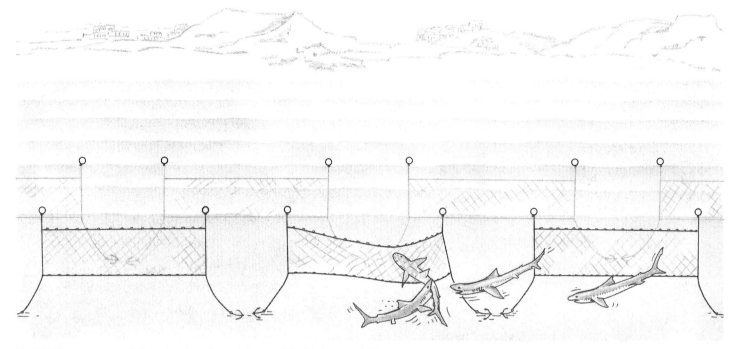

Fig. 170 The arrangement of shark-nets is like an interrupted double barrier of gill nets. The nets are serviced daily to remove trapped sharks.

sensational but to emphasise that victims can survive such brutal wounds provided they are given immediate and correct treatment.

The greatest danger to a shark victim is loss of blood and the first thing to do is to stem the flow of blood by using a pad or tourniquet or by pressing on pressure points. Always lie the patient head downwards to maintain a flow of blood to the brain. It is important not to move the person for at least 30 minutes, for during the initial period of shock the blood system adjusts; blood-flow to the skin and body extremities decreases and the arteries contract, thus improving the circulation to the vital organs. If medical help is at hand, a 4 percent albumen solution (or electrolyte solution if this is not available) should be administered intravenously. Dilute morphine hydrochloride may be given to relieve pain.

Only once the blood system has been stabilized should the patient be moved, and again the head should be kept lowermost. Food and drink should not be given and alcohol is particularly damaging since it dilates the blood-vessels and encourages bleeding. For a similar reason the body should be kept cool.

As Tim Wallett remarks in his book, many shark victims have died simply because these elementary rules were not followed.

Why should there have been such a concentrated series of attacks in Natal during 1957/58? Considering the large number of sharks off the coast of southern Africa, the few attacks on man are clearly the exception rather than the rule. But 'rogue' sharks break this rule and turn repeatedly to feeding on man. A single rogue may be responsible for spates of attacks such as those of 1957/58. Rogue sharks seem rare, and most attacks are of quite a different nature

and can be termed 'investigatory attacks'. Sharks have poor eyesight but have sensitive lateral lines along their bodies that perceive vibrations. A swimmer kicking through the water is readily detectable to the shark, but it may then need to investigate the source of the vibrations, and does so by gliding past, nudging, bumping or even mouthing the swimmer. These approaches may be pure inquisitiveness but the scaly skin still lacerates and the teeth tear into the bather.

The resulting wounds are usually mild compared with those of a full-scale attack, but the shark may then return in earnest. Since such 'investigation' is most likely when the shark cannot see its victim, attacks of this nature are most frequent at night or in murky water. Lone bathers are more liable to attack since sharks shun groups. Other features which attract sharks are bright colours, shiny ornaments, blood from a wound or from a speared fish and panic movements like the struggling of a dying fish or a frightened swimmer. Thus, there are obvious steps one can take to reduce the chances of being attacked.

Most shark attacks take place when the sea is over 24 °C and very seldom when it less than 18 °C. This is more a function of human behaviour than of shark behaviour because more people enter warm water, and they remain in it longer. Thus cold water does not grant immunity from attack, as witnessed by the several occasions on which boats have been attacked in False Bay and on the cold west coast. The summer peak of attacks is also a reflection of the number of bathers in the water.

One curious statistic, difficult to explain, is that men are attacked far more often than women. In Natal over 17 men are attacked for every one woman. The most likely explanation is that men behave differently, often swimming further out, on their own, and are more active in the water.

Divers are at much greater risk than swimmers, and are frequently 'buzzed' by curious sharks. But at least divers often have the benefit of seeing the shark before it attacks and many a shark has been scared off by shouting at it or by punching it on the nose. Gouging the shark's eyes or gills may deter it if it does attack.

The dramatic effect shark attacks have on tourism has made it essential to keep sharks away from popular swimming beaches in Natal, and in 1964 the Natal Anti-Shark Measures Board was given the responsibility of providing this protection.

Various anti-shark methods have been tried in other parts of the world. Curtains of bubbles have proved ineffectual. Dolphins can be trained to attack sharks, but they avoid large sharks. Electric fields are currently being tested at Durban and hold great promise: an 'eddy current electrode system' – a single core of insulated cable through which large pulses are directed – causes large animals to lose voluntary control over their muscles, turning away, although smaller creatures (including man) are unaffected.

By far the most effective method has been the erection of shark nets. Contrary to popular belief, these do not form a continuous barrier, but are positioned in two rows with gaps between the 190 metre-long nets. The nets are anchored in water about 12 m deep and buoyed so that they hang suspended about 3 m from the surface and a similar distance from the sea floor. Thus the sharks can – and do – swim over, under or around the nets. How then do they protect swimmers? The answer is that they do not provide direct protection: their effectiveness lies in entangling the sharks and thus reducing the numbers of large sharks to a point that attack is unlikely. Since the installation of nets along the Natal coast in 1966 not a single attack has taken place behind undamaged nets and, in 11 years of netting, 11 700 sharks have been caught. The once-famous '1000 Club' – members of which had caught a shark weighing over 1 000 lbs – has long been disbanded, for there are no large sharks to catch. The numbers of sharks being caught in the nets and the numbers of attacks have also declined (Fig. 171).

Shark nets act like giant gill nets, enmeshing the sharks. Sharks must keep swimming to circulate water over their gills so they soon 'drown' in the nets, but before they die their threshing attracts other sharks, which in their haste to feast off their helpless compatriots, become entangled themselves.

The success of shark nets in reducing attack is proven beyond doubt. What is still questionable is the possible ecological effect of removing large numbers of top predators from the coastal waters. In Tasmania, where shark nets were employed for a number of years, reduction of sharks led to an enormous increase in the numbers of octopus, with the consequent collapse of the crayfish industry since octopus feed on crayfish.

Have there been any such changes in Natal? Only two possible effects have been detected so far. Firstly, because large sharks prey on smaller sharks, their elimination

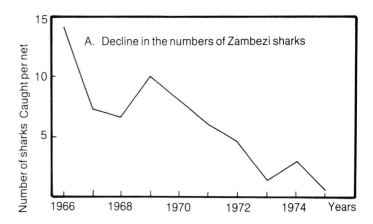

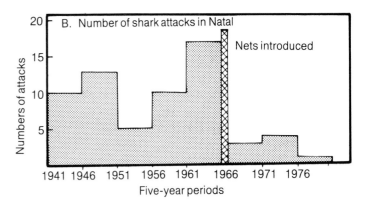

Fig. 171 Since the shark nets were installed in Natal in 1966, the numbers of large sharks such as the Zambezi shark have declined (A), as has the number of attacks (B). All attacks since this date have been on beaches that are not protected by nets or when swimming has been banned.

seems to have led to a population explosion of the smaller dusky sharks. The Director of the Natal Anti-Sharks Board has denied such increase, but angling records show quite clearly that while most fish are declining, small sharks are on the increase. It has been estimated that there could now be 2,8 million more dusky sharks off the coast of Natal. At present these are mostly immature, since duskies only reproduce once they are about 11 years old, but in the early 1980s they will start multiplying. How many sharks will we have then?

Another possible effect of shark nets may be linked only indirectly (and inconclusively) to the eradication of large sharks: it is the decline in the numbers of angling fish and particularly of the shad or elf (Pomatomus saltator). This issue is a far more contentious one, for while it seems indisputable that shad have become scarce, an increase in dusky sharks is only one of several factors that may have caused the decline. Pollution and over-fishing may also have played their part.

The reduction in shad was first demonstrated when Rudy van der Elst, a young marine biologist at Durban's Oceanographic Research Institute, came across the invaluable records kept by the Natal Coastal Angling Union since 1956. Van der Elst's analyses confirmed anglers' fears; the much sought after shad had indeed declined and the average mass in 1966 was about half that in 1958. As a result of his findings, a limit of 10 elf per day per angler, and a minimum size were imposed in 1973. In 1977 the daily bag was lowered to two fish and a closed season was introduced during the breeding season from September to December. Currently, four elf can be taken a day.

Unfortunately, a solitary scientist was strongly critical of Van der Elst's methods, and in particular that he had based his assessment of shad abundance on the catch per unit effort (i.e. the number caught per angler per 100 hours of angling). The smouldering fire of this criticism was soon fanned by a small sector of the press – to the point that doubt was cast on the validity of Van der Elst's findings and on his scientific integrity. The situation developed to the point that an independent committee of enquiry, consisting of the Director of the J.L.B. Smith Institute of Ichthyology, a Deputy Director of Sea Fisheries, and a Professor of mathematical statistics, was appointed to evaluate Van der Elst's findings. They were unanimous in their approval of his methods and endorsed his recommendations for a shad ban – a finding that did a good deal to restore the trust Van der Elst had built up with the angling fraternity. But best of all, it must be gratifying for Natal's anglers to see that since the ban was initiated, the size and numbers of shad have steadily increased so that the 1979 season was the best in decades.

It is worth stressing that Van der Elst had the interest of anglers at heart. The practical result of his work in Natal, and the use he has made of the catch-records kept there must surely be an incentive to other angling clubs. Van der Elst has recently been given the task of introducing a system of anglers' catch-returns on a national basis and deserves active support from all sport anglers.

POLLUTION

For years man has used the sea as a sink and assumed that its vast size would grant it immunity to the effects of pollution. Only in the 1950s when mercury poisoning killed 46 people in Japan and left another 141 permanently paralysed from Minimata disease, was serious attention given to the fate of marine pollutants.

Almost any substance in excess can be a pollutant. Even ordinary table salt, the commonest compound in the sea, kills most forms of life at a concentration only double that of sea-water. Different types of pollutants do, however, have quite different effects and we can recognise at least five groups of pollutants: toxic metals and pesticides, oil products, radioactive substances, excessive heat or thermal pollution, and organic effluents such as sewage.

Heavy metals and pesticides

Heavy metals and pesticides are, of course, poisonous, but they have one unfortunate additional property: they are concentrated up food chains. Thus herbivores accumulate all the heavy metals or pesticides present in their food plants and predators further concentrate these chemicals from their prey. It is for this reason that the Sea Fisheries Institute runs tests on the blubber of seals to monitor these pollutants in southern African waters. And they find that seals have surprisingly high levels of pesticides in their tissues, considering that they are far from any obvious source of these pollutants. It seems that most of the pesticides reaching our seas are probably air-borne, having been wafted into the atmosphere from America and Europe which make extensive use of pesticides. Even seals in the Arctic are not free of contamination, so widespread is the effect.

The accumulation of heavy metals in animals can be dramatic. For instance, although sea-water contains only minute quantities of the toxic metal cadmium, the plough snail *Bullia* may contain 400 parts per million, concentrating the metal 10 million-fold in its tissues!

In spite of these problems, southern African seas are still reasonably untainted by heavy metals and pesticides, and the banning of DDT and other long-lasting pesticides in 1976 will go a long way to maintaining this position.

Oil pollution

Oil is probably the greatest threat to the southern African coastline. Some 600 million tonnes of oil is shipped around the tip of Africa annually (Fig. 172). Between 1968 and 1981 there have been 24 tanker accidents, spilling over 250 000 tonnes of oil into our seas. In addition, old-fashioned tankers must flush their empty bunkers with sea-water before taking on a new cargo and often illegally discharge this waste near the coast, fouling beaches with the tar residue. Northern Natal and Zululand suffer particularly from this practice and there are areas where up to 80 percent of the ghost crabs are smeared with tar. More modern tankers have a 'load-on-top' system which eliminates the need to flush the bunkers at sea.

Freshly spilt oil is extremely toxic but its toxicity is mainly due to smaller molecules which are volatile and soon lost from the sea to the air. As an oil slick ages it thus loses its toxicity, but the thick 'chocolate mousse' that is left behind can still be ecologically disastrous. The recent collision of the *VenPet* and *VenOil* in 1977 is a case in

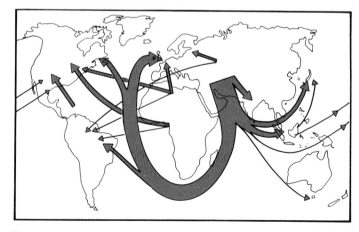

Fig. 172 The transport of oil by sea. Six hundred million tonnes are transported around the Cape each year.

point. The 31 000 tonnes of oil released into the sea drifted at the whim of wind and current for 13 days before beaching between Plettenberg Bay and Still Bay. By this time its toxicity had largely been lost, but even so it devastated the more sensitive animals such as urchins. More seriously, about 5 000 tonnes of the oil entered the Little and Great Brak estuaries, smothering salt marshes and destroying almost all bottom-dwelling life.

Left to its own devices at sea, oil will form tar balls and slowly decompose through natural processes. Currently, strains of bacteria are being experimentally developed, which may hasten the decomposition of oil. Oil can be dispersed by detergents, but sometimes these are more poisonous to marine life than the oil itself. It must, however, be admitted that the dispersant Corexit, used on the west coast after a spill from the *Esso Essen,* was remarkably non-toxic: even concentrations of 20 000 parts per million proved harmless to a wide range of animals. It is now official policy to use dispersants only at sea and to mop up beached oil with straw, which can later be burnt, leaving nature to eliminate the residue.

Of all marine life, the birds – and particularly penguins – suffer most obviously from oil. Oil fouls their feathers, destroying their insulating ability, so that water then wets and chills the birds and they die of exposure. It was in response to this threat that the South African Foundation for Conservation of Coastal Birds (SANCCOB) came into being. Since 1968 SANCCOB has treated over 10 000 oiled penguins, sponging the feathers with detergent to remove the oil and then tending the birds for up to 80 days while the natural plumage oils are restored and become water-repellent once more. The 70 percent success rate of the treatment is by far the highest in the world. In one case, badly oiled penguins from St Croix Island near Port Elizabeth were treated in Cape Town and released at Robben Island; within a year 80 percent were back on St Croix, having swum the 1 000 km to get there.

Can penguins be prevented from entering oil spills? They do flee from a boat broadcasting recordings of killer whales: but further experiments are needed to test if this is a practicable method of chasing them from an oil slick.

In recent years tough regulations have been introduced in South Africa in an attempt to reduce oil spills. Loaded oil tankers are obliged to remain certain distances from the coast, never approaching closer than 40 km. Owners of ships that cause oil pollution are responsible for all cleansing operations and may in addition be fined up to R100 000. Two of the most powerful tugs in the world, the John Ross and Wolraad Woltemade are on continuous standby and the five Kuswag boats, each carrying 110 tonnes of dispersant, patrol the coast. Even with these precautions, the violent seas around southern Africa continue to take their toll of shipping, and oil spills are an ever-present threat.

Radioactivity

Radioactivity is due to the disintegration of atoms that have unstable nuclei, releasing helium nuclei (alpha radiation), or electrons (beta radiation) or simply electromagnetic (gamma) radiation. These products are able to penetrate the body and cause cellular or molecular damage. Their cumulative effect on body cells may lead to cancer and, if reproductive cells – eggs or sperm – are damaged, genetic abnormalities may arise in the next generation. Small wonder there is a fear of radioactive processes and controversy about nuclear installations. Yet it should be appreciated that radioactivity is a natural phenomenon we are subjected to all the time. Sea-water contains tiny quantities of a number of alpha emitters. One of the commonest is polonium-210 which occurs in micro-micro trace quantities, of one part of polonium-210 to a thousand trillion parts of water.

There are thus only minute quantities of radioactive materials present in the environment and it requires the most sensitive of modern methods to detect most of them. But radioactive materials can be accumulated in living organisms. Phytoplankton concentrates polonium-210 up to a million times more than the normal level in sea-water. Could seafoods thus become dangerously contaminated? To answer this question, experiments have been carried out on economically important species occuring near the Koeberg Nuclear Power Station at Cape Town. As examples of the results, red-bait accumulates iron 135 000 times and black mussels and crayfish build up zinc to about 14 000 times the level found in sea-water. Of course iron and zinc are not radioactive, but they are safe to work with and the animals concentrate them in the same way they would comparable radioactive isotopes. But even if radioactive materials were concentrated to this extent in seafoods they would still present no threat to man, for the actual levels of radioactivity released into the water from a nuclear power station such as Koeberg are extremely small; only a fraction of the natural background radiation, which is in itself extremely low. The increased dosage to the average man will be less than that received from a luminous watch or from drinking beer.

The question that still remains unanswered is whether we can guarantee the safe storage of the intensely radioactive nuclear waste fuel during the thousands of years necessary for it to disintegrate into harmless products. The past practice of dumping wastes into the sea, even inside formidably constructed lead-lined concrete blocks, is no long-term solution. Molten glass provides a more stable tomb for the wastes, but even so, can we be sure such an encasement will be sufficiently durable, bearing in mind the natural catastrophes that periodically shake the earth? The possibility that wastes should be shot into outer space in satellites has even been seriously considered, but at present there is no solution to this problem.

Thermal pollution

All power stations require water for cooling and the return of this heated water to rivers or estuaries may have serious effects. One such power station, on the Swartkops estuary near Port Elizabeth, pumps out water that is well over 30 °C – the lethal temperature for mud-prawns, amongst other species (see Chapter 5). Koeberg Nuclear Power Station will require enormous quantities of cooling water. By 1984 when both reactors should be operative, some 100 m³ of sea-water will circulate through the plant each second and be returned to the sea about 10 °C hotter. Fortunately this hot water will soon mix with the cooler sea, but even so a large area will be warmer by about 5 °C.

Research has been undertaken to establish the best position for the water pipes circulating the water. During summer, cold upwelled water travels northwards so the intake pipe has been placed north of the outlet confining recirculation to that time of the year when it is least problematical.

Research on the ecological effects of hot water effluent has been funded by the Electricity Supply Commission as well. Amongst other things, this has shown that rock lobsters grow almost twice as fast, reproduce earlier in the year and carry more eggs when the adults are kept in water that is 6 °C hotter than normal sea temperatures. On the other hand their larvae suffer a much greater mortality, as do both adult and juvenile mussels. Kelp plants also grow faster but die earlier in the hotter water. Thus we can anticipate ecological changes in the vicinity of the hot water effluent, but it seems they are unlikely to be drastic. In fact, it may be possible to turn this hot water to good use. In Australia, Europe and America, cooling water from power stations is used to culture tropical species such as prawns and oysters, and speeds the growth of rock lobsters so that they reach a commercial size in half or even a quarter of the normal time.

Organic pollution

In 1972 there was a mass mortality of marine life in Saldanha Bay and within the rock lobster sanctuary in St Helena Bay. Over 100 000 clams and 10 000 rock lobsters died, as well as thousands of other animals. The cause of this was soon traced to the fish factories which were processing bumper catches of anchovy.

At that time, fish were sucked from the boats in sea-water – a system known as wet off-loading – and of course the water had later to be returned to the sea, laden with blood, scales and fish remains. Such organic matter is not in itself harmful, but when the amounts are excessive, bacterial decomposition proceeds so rapidly that all the oxygen in the water is used up, causing the death of most marine life. Even some time after the mass kill, when conditions had returned more or less to normal, surveys showed that very little lived in the vicinity of these fish factories, and that as one moved away from the factories the number of species and their biomass rose progressively.

In 1974 regulations were introduced compelling factories to change to a dry off-loading system. This process damages the fish more but it does result in a higher yield and less wastage. It resulted in an immediate improvement in environmental conditions and since then there have been no further mortalities of sea life due to pollution from the fish factories.

A far bigger problem is the disposal of sewage. Each day 80 million litres of richly-organic effluent pours into the

Fig. 173 A rock lobster is wired with electrodes to monitor its heart-beat and the rate it pumps water through its gill chamber (A). The normal heart-beat (B) is radically transformed by tiny traces of crude oil (C).

sea off Durban alone. Prior to 1968 most of Durban's sewage was pumped – often scarcely treated – out of the pipe at the mouth of the harbour and constituted a health hazard, apart from being aesthetically unpleasant.

The quality of such water can be monitored by counting the bacteria (particularly *Escherichia coli* and *Salmonella typhi*) and the eggs of human parasites. At times the pollution at Durban was so bad that there were 5 million bacteria per 100 ml of sea-water. Since then, the sewage has been treated to allow partial breakdown of organics and two submarine pipes installed to lead the treated effluent away and to diffuse it into the sea, far from the shore. The resulting improvement in sea-water was spectacular, and was described by the Marine Pollution Unit as 'a formidable achievement for an industrial port'. But with the memory of the old polluted state of Durban harbour, and the unsightliness of raw solids from sewage pipes washing ashore at Port Elizabeth, it is scarcely surprising that there has been public outcry about the Durban Corporation's recent experimental pumping of raw sewage sludge out to sea.

Recently there has been much critical comment about the plume of sewage that sometimes extends into False Bay from the Strandfontein sewage pans – a plume so extensive that it can be seen on satellite photographs. In actual fact this is not sewage, but an algal bloom that thrives on the nutrients released by decomposing organic matter. When we investigated the source of these nutrients, we found that the thousands of birds that roost on and around the sewage pans were actually contributing substantially – and the Cape Town City Council could scarcely be held responsible for them.

Very refined and acceptable methods for treating sewage do exist but of course they cost more than simply pouring the sewage into the sea. One method is to spray the sewage over large boulder-beds (trickling filters) which provide a large surface area for the growth of bacteria and keep the sewage oxygenated as it trickles through the bed. This speeds the natural biological decay of sewage and is so efficient that up to 95 percent of the sewage is broken down by the time it reaches the bottom of the trickling filter. The treated sewage could also be used to fertilise the growth of unicellular algae, which in turn can feed more desirable organisms. The effluent from 10 000 people could in theory grow 10 million oysters a year. Experiments at Richards Bay show that it is possible to grow up to 1 400 kg of prawns and 2 900 kg of mullet and river bream per hectare, using 25 percent sewage effluent in sea-water. More importantly, these animals have also proved free of bacterial infection and human parasites and have no more than the normal levels of heavy metals and pesticides in their tissues, so there is no reason why they should not be safe for human consumption. Possibilities such as this may only be for the future, but they open up the exciting vista that we may be able to use problem wastes such as sewage to produce food rather than allowing it to pollute our seas.

Monitoring marine pollution
In 1973 the Council for Scientific and Industrial Research in South Africa created a special Marine Pollution Unit charged with monitoring pollution and its effects on the sea. They have at their disposal sophisticated techniques which can detect even micro-micro traces of most pollutants. But while it is useful to know what pollutants are present in sea-water, animals themselves accumulate and concentrate materials such as heavy metals and pesticides, so that we obtain a much more representative picture of environmental conditions if we sample their tissues. Routine tests are therefore done on mussels and oysters in areas such as Langebaan and Knysna lagoons, and (as described above) on the blubber of seals.

Even these measurements are, however, of little use if we do not know what levels of pollution marine life is able to tolerate. One widely used method of determining this is to find out the concentration of a pollutant that will kill 50 percent of a sample of animals: a measure known as the LC_{50}. A high LC_{50} indicates that only a high concentration

is lethal and suggests that the pollutant in question is relatively harmless. As an example, the sand-prawn *Palaemon pacificus* (Plate 62) is used to test toxicity of oil dispersants and no dispersant with an LC_{50} of less than 3 300 parts per million is considered sufficiently non-toxic for permission to be given for its use.

This type of test is convenient but somewhat crude, for it assumes that all other species will react in a similar way. Furthermore it assumes that the test animal is equally tolerant at all stages of its life-cycle. One example will suffice to show that this is not so. Experiments on the toxicity of ammonium nitrate (a waste product released into the sea by many industries) reveal that adult black mussels (*Choromytilus meridionalis*) are able to tolerate as much as 1 600 parts per million; but the embryos are extremely sensitive, as little as 0,5 parts per million causing abnormal development. It seems that the young stages of most species are more vulnerable to pollution, which is the reason why the eggs, sperm and developing larvae of the common sea urchin *Parechinus angulosus* are now being used to test pollutants.

Pollutants may of course have adverse effects without actually killing an animal. They can, for instance, slow its growth, or retard reproduction. The most sensitive and meaningful way of testing a pollutant is to see whether it has any of these 'sub-lethal' effects. The Sea Fisheries Institute is at present investigating the response of the heart-beat of rock lobsters to physical conditions and pollutants. Sensitive electrodes are fastened to the animal (Fig. 173A), allowing its heart-beat to be recorded continually (Fig. 173B, C).

In many ways we are fortunate in southern Africa, for heavy industry with its potential pollution is still relatively new and we have before us the clear warning of ecological disasters in other more industrial countries. Even so, there is no room for complacency, for while our open shores are relatively healthy, many estuaries have already been irreparably damaged. We do have the refined technology necessary to detect and restrict pollution to acceptable levels. And we have a responsibility to do just this.

MARINE BIOLOGY AS A CAREER
I was once accused of having the perfect job, combining marine biological research with the stimulus of lecturing to students – and I cannot deny it. Yet there is a danger of glamorising marine biology as a career. It is extremely varied and interesting, ranging from outdoor activities such as diving and sampling from ships, through analyses of ecological collections, to sophisticated biochemical and bacteriological work. But, like any job, there is often tedious routine as well. The main problem is that employment opportunities are limited, although graduates with promise are still able to find good positions. The following institutes all offer employment to marine biologists in various capacities: the Sea Fisheries Institute; Fishing Industries Research Institute; the Department of National Parks;

Fig. 174 Marine biologists exploring the sea-floor.

Natal Parks Board; Cape Provincial Nature Conservation; a number of museums; the Anti-Shark Measures Board; the Oceanographic Research Institute at Durban; Fisheries Development Corporation; the National Research Institute of Oceanology; botany, zoology, ichthyology and ornithology departments at a number of universities; the Department of Environmental Conservation and various branches of the Council for Scientific and Industrial Research. Marine biology is also a useful auxiliary subject for teachers, particularly in these times of increased environmental awareness.

Training in marine biology
To do research in marine biology a B.Sc. degree is a starting point. This normally involves a three-year degree course, usually including zoology as a major subject, although for students more interested in plants, botany is an obvious choice. In addition to the major course a number of auxiliary courses will be required, varying from university to university. As an example, students at the University of Cape Town normally do four courses in their first year and then two more advanced courses in each of the second and third years. Thus the first year could include zoology, botany, chemistry, physics and mathematics. In addition to zoology in the second and third years, students interested in marine biology usually select two other courses in any of the following: oceanography, chemistry, statistics, computer science, physiology, microbiology, biochemistry or botany. A first-year course in chemistry is usually compulsory and for this reason it is advisable for scholars to do science as well as biology at school. A pass in matriculation level mathematics is necessary for acceptance in any science faculty. A few schools still unfortunately have to make their pupils choose between science and biology, and in this case it is better to elect to do the science. Anyone with an interest in biology will cope with university zoology and botany without difficulty, but chemistry more often provides a stumbling block for students who have not taken science at school.

At present the Zoology Department at the University of Cape Town is the only department in southern Africa to offer an undergraduate course specifically in marine biology, and this is normally taken in the third year together with a major couse in zoology. The zoology departments of Rhodes, Durban and Port Elizabeth universities also have particular interests in marine biology.

After obtaining a B.Sc. degree, most students who are seriously interested in zoology as a research career will continue with a one-year B.Sc. Honours course in their chosen subject – say, for example, zoology. The honours year is designed as a training in research and usually involves independent projects in addition to more formal tuition. Many people take a job after completing their honours degree, but research work leading to a thesis that can be presented for a Masters Degree or eventually for a Doctorate, may follow at a later stage.

While these degrees are important for the research scientist, it must be stressed that for those with a more practical bent, there are technical posts available in most marine institutes; good technical officers are much in demand. No research scientist can function without technical support.

For those with a real love of the sea, there are few careers which offer as much job satisfaction as marine biology, despite the fact that no marine biologist will ever become a millionaire.

REFERENCES

Popular articles and books
Anon. 1979. Dusky shark problem. *African Wildlife*, Vol. 33 (6): 5-6.
Anon. 1979. What the Shad Commission found. *African Wildlife*, Vol. 33 (6): 4.
Anon. 1979. Processors cut live seaweed in experimental harvest. *S.Afr. Shipping News and Fishing Industry Review*, Vol. 34 (12): 29-31.
Avery, G. & Siegfried, W. R. 1980. 150 000-year tradition. *Oceans*, Vol. 13 (4): 32-37.
Best, P. B. 1973. Seals and sealing in South and South West Africa. *S.Afr. Shipping News and Fishing Industry Review*, Vol. 28 (12): 49-57.
Botha, L. 1973. Migration and spawning behaviour of the Cape hakes. *S. Afr. Shipping News and Fishing Industry Review*, Vol. 28 (4): 62-63, 65, 67.

Brown, A. C. 1976. Toxicity studies on marine animals. *S.Afr. Journal of Science*, Vol. 72: 197-199.
Chapman, P. & Watling, R. G. 1980. Oil pollution studies in South Africa. *S.Afr. Journal of Science*, Vol. 76: 534-535.
Chittleborough, R. G. 1974. How to double growth rate of captive rock lobsters. *S.Afr. Shipping News and Fishing Industry Review*, Vol. 29 (12): 40-45.
Cook, P. A. 1977. Prevention of marine fouling in coastal installations. *S.Afr. Shipping News and Fishing Industry Review*, Vol. 32 (1): 38-40.
Cram, D. L. 1978. Comprehensive research into SWA fisheries. *S.Afr. Shipping News and Fishing Industry Review*, Vol. 33 (2): 36-39.
Cram, D. L. & Agenbag, J. J. 1974. Low light level television – an aid to pilchard research. *S.Afr. Shipping News and Fishing Industry Review*, Vol. 29 (7): 52-53.

Davies, B. 1979. The travelling dusky shark. *African Wildlife*, Vol. 23 (6): 5-6.

De Villiers, G. & Du Plooy. 1979. Seereservate in Suid-Afrika. *Environment R.S.A.*, Vol. 6 (4): 6-7.

Gitay, A. 1972. Marine farming prospects on the South African west coast. *S.Afr. Shipping News and Fishing Industry Review*, May 1972: 50-53.

Graves, W. 1976. The imperilled giants. *National Geographic*, Vol. 150: 722-751.

Grindley, J. R. 1969. *Riches of the Sea*. Caltex, Cape Town.

Grindley, J. R. 1979. South Africa's marine fisheries. *S.Afr. Journal of Science*, Vol. 75: 202-205.

Hey, D. 1975. The conservation of dolphins. *Environment R.S.A.*, Vol. 2 (9): 3.

Holmes, M. 1973. Oil and penguins don't mix. *National Geographic*, Vol. 143 (3): 384-397.

King, D. P. F. & Robertson, A. A. 1973. Methods of pelagic fish egg and larval research in South West Africa. *S.Afr. Shipping News and Fishing Industry Review*, Vol. 28 (5): 57, 59, 61.

Linehan, E. J. 1979. The trouble with dolphins. *National Geographic*, Vol. 155 (4): 506-541.

Mallory, J. R. & Cook, P. 1974. Nuclear power and the sea. *S.Afr. Shipping News and Fishing Industry Review*, Vol. 29(8): 52-55.

Newman, G. & Crawford, R. J. M. 1979. Long-term trends of stock size and fishing effort in the W. Cape purse-seine fishery. *S.Afr. Shipping News and Fishing Industry Review*, Vol. 34 (1): 25-29.

Randall, R. M. & Randall, B. M. 1980. Black death for penguins. *Environment R.S.A.*, Vol. 7 (9): 1-2.

Shannon, L. V. 1971. Radioactivity in the marine environment of South Africa. *S.Afr. Shipping News and Fishing Industry Review*, Vol. 26 (4): 58-59.

Smith, M. M. 1978. *Sea and Shore Dangers*. Time Printers, Durban. 78 pp.

Stander, G. H. & Negpen, C. S. de V. 1968. Some facts about linefish – with special reference to False Bay. *S.Afr. Shipping News and Fishing Industry Review*, Vol. 23: 108-111.

Van der Elst, R. P. 1979. A proliferation of small sharks in the shore-based Natal sport fishery. *Environmental Biology of Fishes* (in press).

Van der Elst, R. P. 1981. *A Guide to the Common Sea Fishes of Southern Africa*. C. Struik, Cape Town. 368 pp.

Wallett, T. 1978. *Shark Attack and Treatment of Victims in Southern African Waters*. Purnell, Cape Town. 176 pp.

Watling, R. J. 1980. Don't touch. Tanker traffic around the Cape of Good Hope. *Oceans*, Vol. 13 (4): 62-64.

Vary C. 1983. *Diving for crayfish in South Africa* (in preparation) C. Struik 1983.

Scientific references

Branch, G. M. 1975. Notes on the ecology of *Patella concolor* and *Cellana capensis*, and the effects of human consumption on limpet populations. *Zoologica Africana*, Vol. 10 (1): 75-85.

Cook, P. A. 1978. A prediction of some possible effects of thermal pollution on marine organisms on the west coast of South Africa, with special reference to the rock lobster, *Jasus lalandii*. *Transactions of the Royal Society of S. Afr.*, Vol. 43: 107-118.

Crawford, R. J. M. & Shelton, P. A. 1978. Pelagic fish and seabird interrelationships off the coasts of South West and South Africa. *Biological Conservation*, Vol. 14: 85-109.

Christie, N. D. & Moldan, A. 1977. Effects of fish factory effluent on the benthic macrofauna of Saldanha Bay. *Marine Pollution Bulletin*, Vol. 8: 41-45.

Grindley, J. R. & Sapeika, N. 1969. The cause of mussel poisoning in South Africa. *S. Afr. Medical Journal*, Vol. 43: 275-279.

Lochner, J. P. A. 1980. The control of a pelagic resource. *S. Afr. Journal of Science*, Vol. 76: 15-25.

Newman, G. G. & Pollock, D. E. 1974. Biological cycles, maturity and availability of rock lobster, *Jasus lalandii*, on two South African fishing grounds. *Investigation Report of the Division of Sea Fisheries of S. Afr.*, Vol. 107: 1-16.

Newman, G. G. et al. 1980. A critique of 'The control of a pelagic resource'. *S. Afr. Journal of Science*, Vol. 76: 453-464.

Parkington, J. 1981. The effects of environmental change on the scheduling of visits to the Eland's Bay cave, Cape Province, S.A. In: *Patterns of the Past : Studies in Honour of David Clarke* (Eds. I. Hodder, G. Isaac & N. Hammond). Cambridge University Press. pp. 341-359.

Van der Elst, R. P. 1976. Game fish of the east coast of southern Africa. 1. The biology of the elf, *Pomatomus saltatrix* (Linnaeus), in the coastal waters of Natal. *Investigational Report of the Oceanographic Research Institute*, Vol. 44: 1-59.

MARINE INVERTEBRATES AND ALGAE

INTRODUCTION TO PART 2

This section of the book focuses on the main groups of marine invertebrates and algae; quite deliberately we have omitted the fish and birds, because excellent guides to these groups already exist. The purpose of this part of the book is two-fold. Firstly, it deals with the characteristic features of each group, their life-cycles and the modifications of body structure that adapt animals to their particular environments. Secondly, it allows the identification of the most common species of marine life.

As an introductory guide, the visual key on pages 8 & 9 shows the major groups of marine animals and plants and cross-refers to the colour plates and the text pages that deal with each group. It has obviously been impossible to show all the animals and plants in colour, although the shells and seaweeds are covered more comprehensively than the other groups. After referring to the colour plates, turn to the relevant text pages and consult the text and black and white drawings which expand and complement the colour plates.

For each group of organisms, their general nature is described first, including their basic structure and life-cycle. This preliminary material can be glossed over by anyone who is already familiar with the groups, but it serves to introduce the animals and the key features used in their identification. Following this introduction, the biology of particular species, or groups of species, is described in more detail.

Whole books are written about the identification of single groups of animals and plants, so it is not possible within the scope of this book to cover all the known invertebrates and algae. Nevertheless it should be possible to identify most of the common species, for over 700 species have been illustrated, either in colour or by way of line drawings that accompany the text. More specific scientific guides are listed at the end of each chapter for those readers who require more detailed texts. Particular mention must be made of Professor J. H. Day's *A Guide to Marine Life on South African Shores*, which although it does not deal with the biology of animals in any detail, is the most comprehensive scientific guide to their identification. *Invertebrate Animals* by R. J. Lincoln and J. G. Sheal (Published by the British Museum) is a useful guide to methods of collection and preservation.

At the end of the book the scientific index doubles as a distribution list, giving the known coastal distribution of each species, so that it is possible to check whether an animal you have identified normally occurs in the locality in which you have found it.

The use of scientific names

Where common names are available we have used them in the text as well as giving the scientific names, but unfortunately there are not very many widely accepted common names, and those that do exist may often be misleading because they change from time to time and from one part of the world to another and can sometimes refer to more than one species. Scientific names need not scare you, for they usually have a logical meaning and once you begin to understand and remember a few names it becomes easier to remember others.

Each species has two scientific names. For example the white mussel is called *Donax serra*. In this case, the first name refers to the genus *Donax* which includes several types of white mussel, but the specific name *serra* applies to only one particular species, so that the two names are a unique combination. This binomial nomenclature dates back to the biologist Carl von Linné who first adopted the system in the eighteenth century.

The oldest binomial scientific name given to a species is always accepted as being its correct name, in preference to any other names that may subsequently be given it. Very often an older name is rediscovered after being 'lost' in the scientific literature. In the meanwhile, however, the species has been given a second name; but the older name is the one that must be applied to the species. This is the main reason for scientific names having the annoying habit of altering just when one has got used to them! Scientific names also change when an authority revises a group of animals and decides that some species have previously been placed in the wrong genus. In this case the specific name remains the same but becomes linked to a different generic name.

Despite these problems, scientific names are still essential. At least we should eventually get back to one correct and final name for each species, while common names not only change at the whim of the local populace but have no bearing on the relationship between different species. As an example, sea 'lice' are crustaceans totally unrelated either in body structure or in habit to the body lice which are insect parasites on man.

Similar species are grouped together in a genus, which implies that they are all closely related. In the same way related genera are grouped into families, families into orders, orders into classes, and finally classes into phyla. At each of these steps, more and more distantly related groups of animals are linked together. As an example, a glance at Fig. 244 will show the steps by which the Crustacea are classified. Appendix 1 tabulates the major animal phyla and classes, together with brief descriptions of the characteristics of each of these groups. Some of the larger phyla are classified in more detail within the relevant chapters.

The classification of animals and plants should in theory reflect their evolutionary origins, linking each species with its relatives. As we learn more about the relationships of animals and plants, so our classification should become more refined. And to obtain this knowledge, we need to delve not only into the structure of animals and plants, but into their life-cycles, physiology and ecology; for only with this balanced view can we hope to understand why a particular species is what it is and from where it may have originated.

8.PORIFERA THE SPONGES

The sponges are the least animal-like of all marine animals. Even in the nineteenth century, naturalists were still arguing whether sponges were plant or animal. They are the simplest of all the metazoan (multi-cellular) animals and, because they have no muscles or nerves, they are unable to move about. In spite of this they can be of considerable ecological importance, for their bodies are beautifully adapted for one central function: that of circulating water through the body cavity to allow capture of suspended food particles.

At its simplest, a sponge's body is like a tall vase with a single large opening at the top (the osculum) and numer-

A. Section through simple sponge

B. Detail of body wall

C. Complex sponge

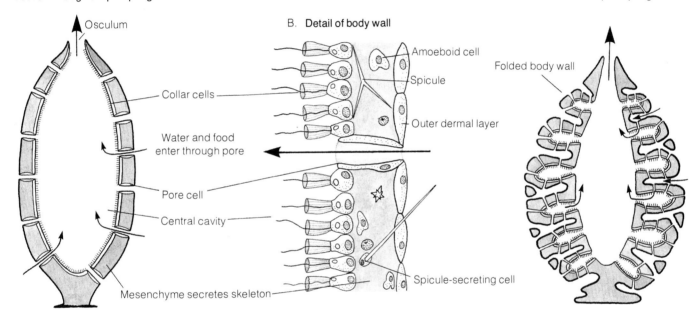

D. Structure of single collar cell

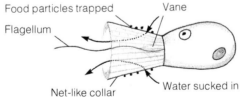

E. Sponge spicules

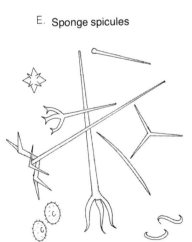

F. Spongin skeleton of Demospongiae

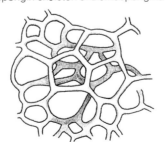

G. Silicon skeleton of glass sponges

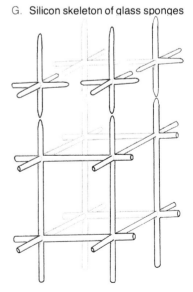

Fig. 175 The structure of sponges and the detailed form of various types of sponge skeletons.

Fig. 176 The range of body shapes adopted by sponges is clearly illustrated in this photograph, taken at a depth of 50 m. The sponge on the left is *Clathrina* (x ¼).

Fig. 177 A simple tubular calcarean sponge, *Leucosolenia arachnoides* (x 2).

ous tiny pores which penetrate the side walls (Fig. 175A, Plate 2). Since sponges grow throughout their lives they often spread across the substratum and may give rise to a series of such vase- or turret-like bodies, but these are united at their bases and so interconnected that it is better to regard the whole structure as a single colony rather than as a group of individuals (see Plates 5 & 6). The body wall is three-layered, with an outer covering of flat cells, a middle jelly-like mesenchyme with a few amoeba-like cells, and an inner layer lining the central cavity (Fig. 175B). The middle and inner layers are the most interesting. The cells of the central mesenchyme produce a skeleton that supports the sponge, and this skeleton is all that is left of the animal when we use it as the familiar bath-tub sponge. The body shape may be flat and encrusting, tubular, vase-like, globular, branching or leaf-like, and is so variable that when it comes to classifying sponges, body form is meaningless. Fortunately, the skeleton is more constant and can be used to classify and identify sponges. Even then, sponges can make fools of taxonomists, for some species

overrun others and can incorporate bits of their victims' skeletons into their own bodies.

The Calcarea are simple tubular sponges (Fig. 177) with a skeleton made of calcium carbonate spicules, which are beautifully symmetrical and resemble miniature javelins, pick-axes and tridents (Fig. 175E). The next group, the Hexactinellida (glass sponges) bear spicules made of silicon, many of which are six-pointed and joined together to form a rigid but elegant skeleton (Fig. 175G). Venus' flowerbasket *(Euplectella)* is a well-known example (Fig. 178). However, most sponges fall into the class Demospongiae and, in addition to silicon spicules, produce an organic skeleton of spongin, which forms an intricate web of flexible wiry threads, and has a chemical composition like that of silk (Fig. 175F).

These skeletons provide more than support, for the spicules are usually spiky and give the sponge a cactus-like appearance when it is seen under a microscope. Since these spicules are often fiercely irritant, few animals eat sponges, and their almost psychedelic colours may serve as a warning to predators (Plates 2–7 & 49).

All sponges reproduce sexually. Cells in the central mesenchymal layer give rise to sperm and eggs. The eggs are usually retained in the parent until they have been fertilized, when they divide into a blastula stage which is like an oval ball of many small flagellated cells, which propel the body through the water. Later in the development of the larva, larger cells cap the ball, growing over and enveloping the flagellated cells, so that they come to form the inner lining of the gastrula stage that soon settles, attaches to a rock and grows into the adult sponge.

Sponges are also able to reproduce asexually by budding off pieces. Some species (particularly those living in fresh water) enclose batches of cells in a protective coat of spicules, forming gemmules which can survive adverse conditions. One of the most amazing things about sponges is their power of regeneration. Not only can small pieces regenerate into whole animals, but if a sponge is forced through a sieve, or all the cells are separated by chemical means, the cells are able to reaggregate and form a complete sponge again. This is like asking bits of boerewors to get together and form cows!

The innermost layer of the sponge body consists of flagellated cells, whose whip-like action drives water through the sponge and out of the osculum (which is thus an exhalant opening and not a mouth, in spite of the fact that 'osculum' is Latin for 'little mouth'). To replace this water, more is sucked in through the pores in the body wall. Since these pores are very small, only tiny particles are able to enter with the water and form the food of sponges. The flagellated cells each have a funnel-like collar surrounding the flagellum which gives the name 'choanocytes' to these cells (Greek for 'funnel-cells'). The collars are made up of tiny thread-like microvilli closely applied and connected by strands, forming an extremely fine net. As water is driven through the sponge, particles are sieved out by these nets and are passed down to be engulfed by the cells (Fig. 175D). So efficient is this filtra-

Fig. 178 The beautiful skeleton of a Venus flowerbasket, *Euplectella* (x ½).

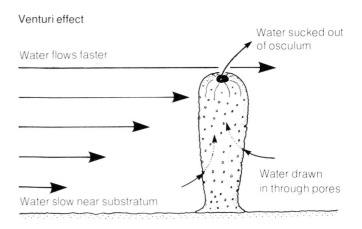

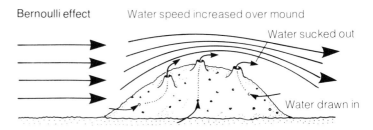

Fig. 179 Water is passively drawn through the bodies of sponges if their turrets project into faster flowing water (Venturi effect) or if the water is deflected over their bodies (Bernoulli effect).

tion process that particles as small as one micron (one-thousandth of a millimetre) may be caught and eaten. Even bacteria are captured.

Since the circulation of the water through the body is so important to sponges, it is not surprising that many have complex body walls that are folded back and forth to increase the area of collar cells (Fig. 175C).

Sponges may also make use of two physical phenomena to aid water circulation. If water flows over a surface it is slowed down, but further from the surface it continues to flow faster (Fig. 179). Therefore, if a sponge can sit with its osculum in faster-moving water than is experienced by its body, the faster current will draw water out of the osculum (by the *Venturi effect*) and in this way increase circulation through the sponge. Mound-shaped sponges make use of a second phenomenon for they are able to deflect water that is flowing smoothly, causing it to move faster over the top of the mound. This *Bernoulli effect* will produce the same result, sucking water through the sponge (Fig. 179). Since sponges are often mound-like and have tall turrets that hoist the osculum above the rest of the body, they can take advantage of these two physical effects and, at the same time, reduce the chances of waste water being recirculated.

The efficiency of their filtration is one reason why sponges are of great ecological importance, for in shallow calm waters they can completely clear the water of all suspended particles. In some areas sponges have rhythms of activity and only pump water through their bodies in the morning when sea breezes stir the water and bring in fresh food: by the night they have cleared the water of food and further filtration is futile.

Sponges are also important because they often cover subtidal rocks and exclude other species. Some have evolved chemicals that actually inhibit the growth of competitors: others are less subtle and simply grow over their opposition (Plate 4). In spite of this, many species of sponge can occur in the same area, for no one sponge ever manages to master all the other species. As a simple example, Species A may overgrow B, and B overgrow C, but C may still outcompete A. These 'hierarchical networks' can thus be added to the processes described in Chapter 2, which prevent any one species from monopolising the habitat.

REFERENCES
Popular articles and books
Doublet, D. 1977. Consider the sponge. *National Geographic*, Vol. 151: 392–407.

Identification guide
Day, J. H. 1969. *A Guide to Marine Life on South African Shores*. A. A. Balkema, Cape Town. pp. 16–22.

9. CNIDARIA JELLYFISH, ANEMONES, CORALS AND THEIR KIN

The Cnidaria have a simple body structure but have been singularly effective in adapting this to different needs. Two basic types of body plan are found in the group: a polyp and a medusa. Polyps have cylindrical bodies attached to the substratum and are crowned by tentacles surrounding the mouth. Medusae have bell-shaped bodies with a fringe of tentacles and a central mouth that hangs down like the clapper of a bell. Although different in form, it is not difficult to imagine a medusa as an upside-down free-floating polyp which has been flattened (Fig. 180A).

The Cnidaria are typically radially symmetrical – having no definite left or right side – and have but a single entrance to the body cavity or coelenteron. The body wall is simple and diploblastic – having only two layers of cells – an outer ectoderm and an inner endoderm, separated by a jelly-like mesogloea (Fig. 180B). All Cnidaria have muscles and a nervous system and can move actively, belying their often flower-like appearance. However, they have no organs of respiration, circulation or excretion, and individual cells must fulfil these functions.

Despite their simplicity, the Cnidaria have a unique and very specialised group of cells: the stinging cells or nematocysts (from which the name Cnidaria is derived, being Greek for 'nettle'). These cells are like round or oval sacs, each housing a tightly coiled and pleated thread that can be shot out of the cell. When they discharge, these threads are actually everted, being turned inside out like the finger of a glove (Figs. 180C & 186B), and they elongate enormously so that they can be over 100 times the length of the cell when fully discharged. Nematocysts fall into three types: one releases a sticky glue, another coils tightly to entangle prey, while the commonest type is armed with barbs and can tear into the flesh and release a venom. A few species have very potent venoms lethal to man, and many can be mildly irritant.

What controls the discharge of stinging cells? This is something anyone can investigate using sea anemones. Prodding the tentacles with a clean microscope slide will discharge only a few nematocysts. However, if the slide is first wetted with saliva, which contains protein and is thus a potential food, it will then explode large numbers of nematocysts (which stick to the slide and are best viewed using a compound microscope). It seems that both mechanical and chemical stimuli are necessary before the stinging cells will discharge, thus avoiding the futility of blasting the cells at every passing inanimate object. But how does the anemone actually bring about discharge? Micropipettes can be used to extract the fluid from stinging cells, which we find is more than three times the ionic concentration of sea-water. Once discharge occurs the

fluid is, however, much diluted. It seems that the cell wall must alter its permeability just prior to discharge, allowing water to rush into the cell by osmosis to dilute the concentrated fluid. This intake will increase pressure in the cell and explosively discharge the thread.

CLASS HYDROZOA

The hydrozoans are the most primitive of the Cnidaria. Most species belong to the order **Hydroida,** and typically their complex life-cycle involves both a polyp and a medusa. The medusa is the sexual phase in the life-cycle and produces eggs or sperm. Fertilization leads to swimming larvae which eventually settle and form polyps. These repeatedly bud off new polyps to form colonies, which are usually branched in an orderly and elegant fashion, forming dainty plumes (Fig. 181 and Plate 8). The regular shape of colonies is maintained because the polyps produce a sheath or perisarc of chitin and protein (chemically very like the exoskeleton of insects), and this perisarc encases the stems of the colony. In the sub-order Gymnoblastea, the polyps themselves are left naked (Fig. 182), but in the Calyptoblastea, they are sheltered in cup-like expansions of the perisarc. The life-cycle is completed when some of the polyps develop medusae that bud off and swim away (Fig. 183). Thus asexual reproduction by the polyp alternates with sexual reproduction by the medusa. The ability to multiply by budding gives the hydrozoans their name, after the multi-headed Hydra of Greek mythology, which Hercules struggled to slay because it grew two heads in place of every one he cut off.

The polyp has an outer layer of cells that acts like a skin or epithelium, but these cells also have elongated muscle tails that stretch along the length of the body (Fig. 180B). The inner cells are musculo-digestive, having muscle tails that run circularly around the body, and also secrete digestive enzymes. Thus many of the cells are not highly specialized but have dual functions.

Although simple in structure, this body plan introduces two important advances over the sponges. Firstly, because they can secrete digestive enzymes, the Cnidaria are able to handle large prey, and most of them are predators. Prey are captured by the tentacles, subdued by stinging cells and swallowed whole, to be slowly digested. Indigestible remnants are cast out of the mouth which thus doubles as an anus. Secondly, the development of longitudinal and circular muscles which can act antagonistically allows active movement and changes of body shape. For muscles to act against one another the body must have a skeleton or it will collapse. Of course the Hydrozoa have no bones, but

A. Polyp

Medusa

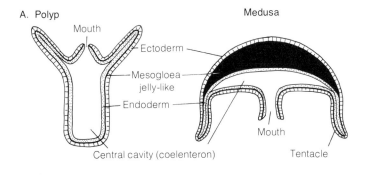

Mouth

Ectoderm

Mesogloea jelly-like

Endoderm

Central cavity (coelenteron)

Mouth

Tentacle

B. Body wall of polyp

Circular muscle

Longitudinal muscle

Nematocyst

Discharged nematocyst

Musculo-epithelial cell

Sensory cell

Nerve cell

Musculo-digestive cell

Gland cell

Food particle

Ectoderm

Mesogloea

Endoderm

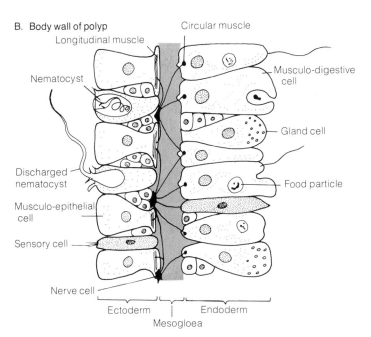

C. Nematocyst types

Sea anemone

D. Balancing organ of medusa

Edge of bell

Ball of lime

Sensory cells record movement of ball

Wall of statocyst

Tentacle

Coral

Hydroids

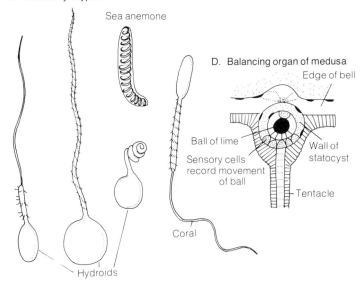

Fig. 180 A. The typical structure of a polyp and a medusa. B. A section of the two-layered body wall of a polyp showing cell types. C. Various types of nematocysts. D. The balancing organ (statocyst) of a medusa.

Fig. 181 A cluster of plume-like *Thecocarpus formosus* growing on an alga (x 1).

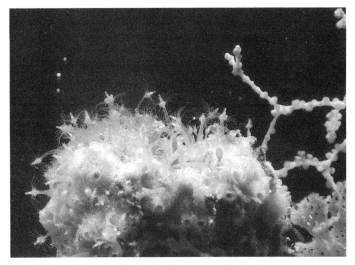

Fig. 182 One of the naked hydroids, *Tubularia solitaria,* always characteristically embedded in a sponge (x 2).

they do have a central body cavity filled with sea-water. Provided the mouth is kept closed this bag of incompressible fluid maintains the body shape and acts as a hydrostatic skeleton. This is like having a water-filled balloon as a skeleton: the squeezing of circular muscles will make it

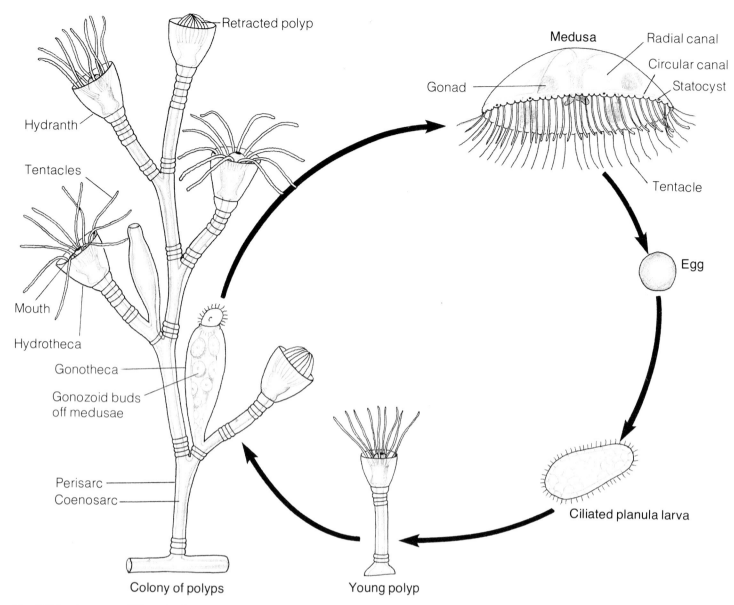

Fig. 183 **The structure and life-cycle of a typical hydroid,** *Obelia dichotoma.*

long and narrow while the longitudinal muscles can shorten it.

Hydroid colonies consist mainly of feeding polyps, but some of the polyps can be modified into protective individuals called nematophores. These are usually smaller than the feeding polyps and lack a mouth, but are powerfully armed with stinging cells. The colonies may also bear gonophores, which are sac-like and specialised to bud off medusae (Fig. 183). In some species the gonophores are grouped together into a structure that looks somewhat like a miniature pine-cone, called the corbula (Fig. 184B).

Medusae are made up of the same two layers of cells as the polyps, but in this case the mesogloea is much thicker, making up 95 percent of the body. Although this jelly-like mass is almost inert, containing 99 percent water and only 1 percent organic matter, it performs a vital function, for it is elastic and maintains body shape. Circular muscles line the inside of the bell and, by contracting, they pulse the bell, expelling the water beneath and gently propelling the

medusa upwards in the water. When these muscles relax, the elastic mesogloea restores the body shape and the medusa then slowly sinks again. Thus continual pulsing is necessary to keep the medusa in the surface water where there is most food.

Since the medusa swims actively, it needs sensory organs that are lacking in the polyp. These include tiny light-sensitive ocelli and balancing organs (statocysts), both situated at the edge of the bell (Fig. 180D). Statocysts contain a small stalked ball of calcium carbonate that sways to one side if the bell tips, leaning on sensory cells which signal the muscles on the lower side of the medusa, causing them to contract more vigorously to keep the animal upright.

From the central mouth of the medusa four canals radiate to the edge of the bell to distribute food around the body. Gonads hang from each of these canals and produce eggs or sperm that are released into the sea.

In some species the medusae are stunted and never

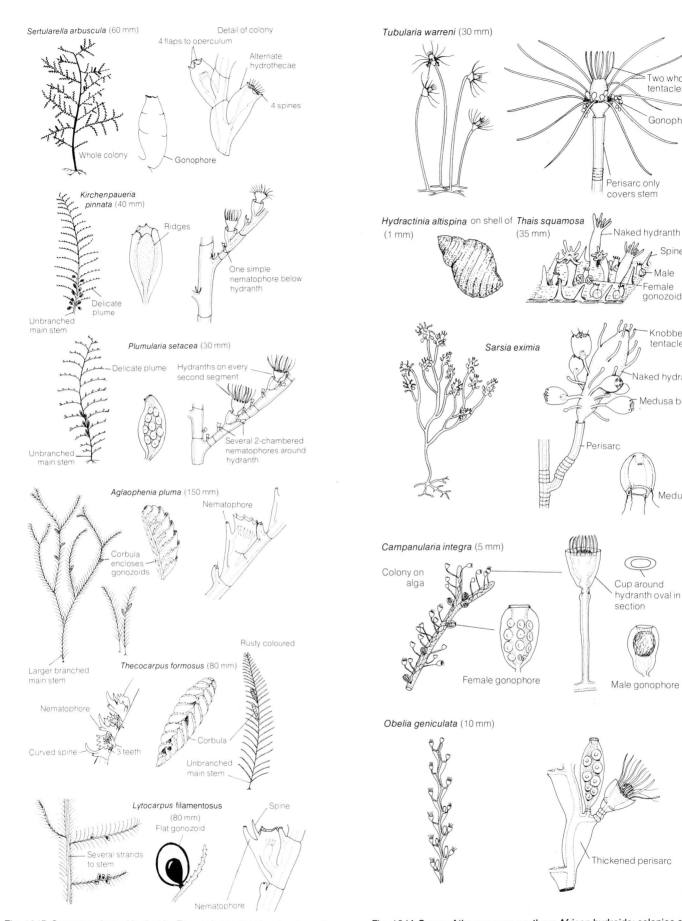

Fig. 184B Common plumed hydroids. For each species the structure of a whole plume, and details of the hydranths and gonozoids are shown: Whole plumes natural size except where indicated.

Fig. 184A Some of the common southern African hydroids: colonies are shown on the left and details on the right.

Fig. 185 The massive coral-like skeleton of *Allopora nobilis* dotted with the tiny holes in which the live polyps occur (x 1).

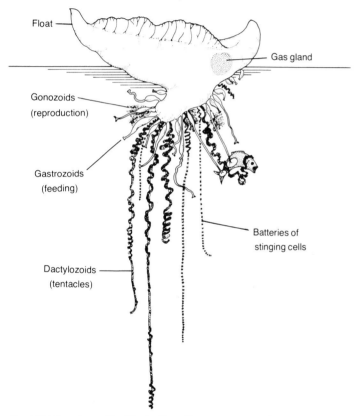

Float

Gas gland

Gonozoids
(reproduction)

Gastrozoids
(feeding)

Batteries of
stinging cells

Dactylozoids
(tentacles)

Fig. 186A Structure of the bluebottle or Portuguese man-o'-war, *Physalia*.

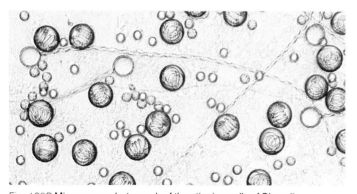

Fig. 186B Microscope photograph of the stinging cells of *Physalia*. Undischarged cells contain tightly coiled threads, while four of the cells are empty, having discharged their long barbed threads.

escape from the gonophore, so that fertilization of the eggs occurs within the gonophore. This is the case in *Hydractinia*. Incidentally, all species of *Hydractinia* live commensally on the shells of specific gastropods (Fig. 184A), gaining a unique hard substratum and possibly scraps of the snail's food, and in turn deter the snail's predators. In that most famous of all hydrozoans, the freshwater *Hydra*, the medusoid phase is reduced to such an extent that it consists only of a blob of gonads that grows on the polyp (and for this reason *Hydra* is a poor example of the group).

The order Hydroida is a large one, and over 250 species are known from southern Africa. A few of the commonest are shown in Fig. 184A & B, but Dr N. A. H. Millard's monograph on the group should be consulted by those needing a more detailed guide.

A small number of hydrozoans secrete a massive hard skeleton of lime (calcium carbonate), superficially like that of the true corals; this is characteristic of the order **Milleporina.** Of the local species, *Allopora nobilis* (Fig. 185) is much in demand for carving and jewellery and is sold commercially. Unfortunately it grows only a few millimetres a year, so that large specimens are probably over 100 years old. This makes it vulnerable to overexploitation, and it is now protected by legislation and only the deep-water beds off Port Elizabeth are currently harvested under special permit.

The third hydrozoan order, **Siphonophora,** includes species that float or pulse through the water and consist of complex colonies containing both polyps and medusae fused together as a unit. Of all of these, none is so well known and so strange as the bluebottle or Portuguese man-o'-war, *Physalia* (Fig. 186A and Plates 11 & 12) that floats in the open waters of most oceans and is often cast ashore in vast numbers after onshore storms. *Physalia* is not a single animal but a colony of animals living permanently attached to one another. What is more remarkable is that the individuals are very different from one another, and have specialised functions. Thus one individual forms the float, another group is concerned only with catching prey, a third group with digesting it, and a final group is involved only with reproduction. There is no better example of the concept of a 'super-organism', for the individuals are all interdependent, and are so specialised that each individual cannot function on its own.

The float that buoys the colony is gas-filled. The gas is not simply air but consists of up to 90 percent nitrogen and, more remarkably, between 5 percent and 20 percent carbon monoxide which is produced by a special gas gland on the side of the float. Although the float looks like a passive balloon, it is capable of movement; at regular intervals of about three minutes it twists sideways, flopping to submerge alternate sides of the float to prevent it from drying out. Trailing below the float are the long tentacles (dactylozoids) which can reach 10 m in length. They bear batteries of the stinging cells used for defence and to immobilise the prey.

The tentacles are capable of the most astonishing contraction, shortening from as much as 10 m down to 10 cm, and pulling the prey up to the feeding individuals (gastrozoids). Each one of these consists of a cylindrical enzyme-secreting body and a terminal mouth that can expand up to 100 times its normal area and fastens like a sucker onto the prey. The digested food is transmitted by a series of internal canals to other individuals in the colony, including the reproductive gonozoids which are concerned solely with producing eggs and sperm. Fish are often eaten, yet curiously one fish, *Nomeus*, has a special relationship with *Physalia* and shelters unharmed in the protective canopy of its tentacles.

The venom from bluebottle nematocysts can be acutely painful or even dangerous to man. A bather stung by a bluebottle should resist rubbing the wound and avoid washing the site with fresh water, since this causes any remaining stinging cells to swell and discharge. Alcohol (including methylated spirits or liquor) fixes the cells and also sterilises the wound, and meat tenderiser changes the proteins in the venom and thus destroys it. As with many other venoms from sea animals, very hot water (as hot as can be borne, and with a pinch of Epsom salts or even table salt to prevent swelling of the nematocysts) often brings relief. Despite their formidable stinging power, bluebottles are eaten by a few animals, including the nudibranch *Glaucus* (see Chapter 2 and Plate 131), the purple-shelled snail *Janthina* (Plate 105) and the plough shells.

Two other siphonophorans are often seen stranded on the beach. One of them, *Vellela*, has a flat oval float with a vertical sail (Plate 9), from which hangs a single central gastrozoid surrounded by gonozoids and a fringe of stinging tentacles. The other, *Porpita*, has a similar structure but its disc-like float lacks a sail (Plate 10). Both species are harmless to man.

CLASS SCYPHOZOA:
The jellyfish
In the life-cycle of a jellyfish, the sexually reproducing medusa is the dominant phase and may reach a diameter of 4 m and have tentacles 30 m long – although most species are about 25 cm in diameter. By contrast, the polyp is reduced to a tiny larval stage (the scyphistoma) which divides and buds off one ephyra larva after the next (Fig. 187). These are like dainty versions of the medusae into which they mature.

The jellyfish are aptly named, for although they are very bulky, almost all of their mass consists of the jelly-like mesogloea, covered inside and out by a thin layer of living tissue. Probably this is because the Scyphozoa lack circulatory and respiratory systems and would have no way of supplying oxygen to deeper tissues.

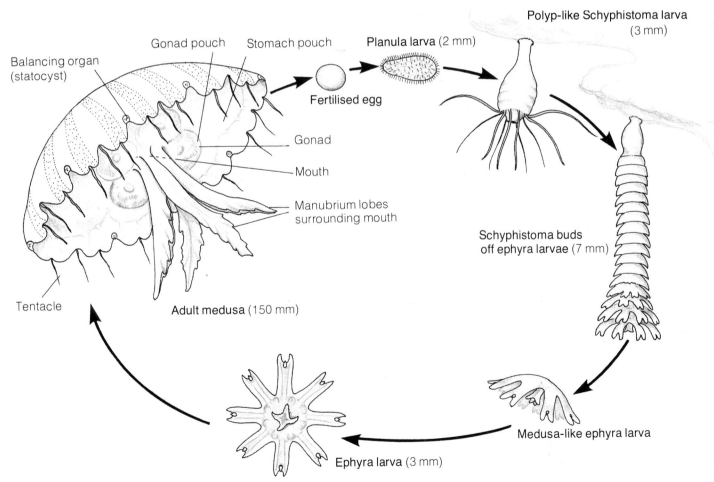

Fig. 187 **The structure and life-cycle of a jellyfish,** *Chrysaora,* **of the order Semaeostomae.**

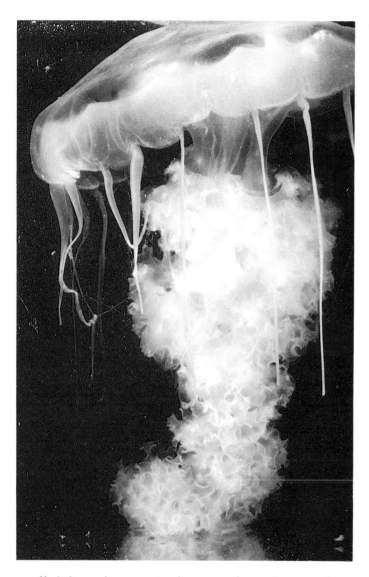

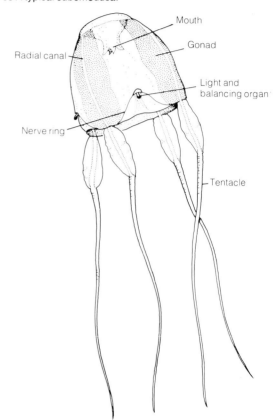

◄ Fig. 188 A typical semaeostoman jellyfish, with scalloped margin and frilly lips hanging below the mouth (x ½).

Fig. 189 A typical cubomedusa.

Jellyfish medusae swim by muscular pulsation of the bell, much as in the Hydrozoa. When they stop pulsating they slowly sink, spreading their tentacles to capture prey. Because of its composition, it is the mesogloea that prevents large medusae from sinking too rapidly. Ninety-nine percent of the mesogloea consists of fluid identical to sea-water, except that it contains fewer sulphate ions, so that its specific gravity is 1,025, fractionally less than that of sea-water (1,026), thus making it slightly buoyant. The mesogloea is also criss-crossed by fibres of collagen that are linked to one another, making the mesogloea elastic so that the body always returns to its original shape after muscular contractions. This unique system saves the animal the energy which would normally be spent by antagonistic muscles working one against the other.

Most jellyfish belong to the order **Semaeostomae** in which the umbrella has a scalloped edge bearing numerous tentacles (Fig. 188). The mouth, which is drawn out into four frilly lips that drape below the umbrella, opens into a stomach with four pouches. These house the gonads and also give rise to radiating branched canals that distribute food throughout the umbrella. The edge of the umbrella bears a series of light-sensitive ocelli, and balancing statocysts which have a different structure but similar function to those in the Hydrozoa.

The second order, **Rhizostomae,** contains medusae that are quite different, for they have no tentacles and use their mouths to capture minute zooplankton (Plate 13). Because of this, the mouth is drawn into elaborate folds through which numerous narrow ducts open. These are like tiny sucking mouths that hold and digest the prey externally before absorbing its fluids. The Rhizostomae are amongst the largest jellyfish and are often stranded on our beaches.

A final order, the appropriately named **Cubomedusae,** consists of box-shaped medusae with four very long tentacles that hang from the lower corners of the box (Fig. 189). Although the tentacles are few in number, the Cubomedusae make up for this by having particularly virulent venom. One Australian species, the sea wasp *Chironex fleckeri*, is amongst the most dangerous of animals and can kill a man in three minutes. Fortunately none of the southern African species is known to be as potent as this.

Very recently the Cubomedusae have been placed in a new class of their own, Cubozoa, because their life-style is different from all other jellyfish, the polyp changing directly into a medusa without budding off ephyra larvae.

Fig. 191 The sea fan *Wrightella,* which is usually white, yellow or orange, is closely related to *Acabaria,* a cherry red species (x 1).

Fig. 190 Detail of a sea fan (see Plate 33) showing the eight pinnate tentacles typical of the subclass Octocorallia.

CLASS ANTHOZOA:
Sea fans, anemones and corals
All the sea anemones, corals and sea fans fall into the class Anthozoa in which the polyp is large and elaborate but there is no medusoid stage in the life-cycle. Eggs and sperm are released by the polyp. In most species fertilization is external and results in oval ciliated planula larvae which soon settle and form polyps. A few species, such as *Actinia equina* (see Chapter 2 and Plate 16), develop the eggs inside the body cavity, and juvenile anemones eventually crawl out of the mouth. Multiplication often takes place by budding and many species form colonies of interconnected individuals. Even solitary forms such as anemones can multiply by dividing: the two halves of the polyp literally walk apart to split the animal in two.

The Anthozoa are divided into two subclasses: the Octocorallia (sometimes called Alcyonaria) all have polyps with eight tentacles which are pinnate and feather-like (Fig. 190), while the Zoantharia have more than eight tentacles, all of which are simple and unbranched (Fig. 196).

Subclass Octocorallia:
Sea fans and soft corals
Nearly all the octocorals are colonial. They include some of the most exquisitely coloured animals in the sea, the most familiar of which are the sea fans (order **Gorgonacea)** which have a tree-like branching structure. The colony is supported by a tough but flexible horny central core. This skeleton, the hallmark of all gorgonians, is covered with a continuous fleshy coenenchyme which connects the polyps, allowing food to be transferred from one polyp to another.

The delicate flexible structure of gorgonians confines them to relatively calm, deeper water or to rocky caves and

Fig. 192 The bright red skeleton of a dead organ-pipe coral, *Tubipora* (x 1).

crevices. Smaller species like *Wrightella* (Fig. 191) often shelter in the folds of bryozoan colonies. Several of the sea fans are common in deeper water and the vivid red *Lophogorgia flammea* (literally 'gorgeous flamed tentacles') adorns many a diver's walls (Plates 33 & 149). In some areas it grows to a height of over 3 m and can form underwater forests, but such large colonies must be extremely old, for *Lophogorgia* grows only about 15 mm a year.

The order **Stolonifera** has only one common species, the organ-pipe coral *Tubipora,* which is best known from skeletons often washed ashore (Fig. 192). Another order, **Alcyonacea,** contains the soft corals, which have no skeleton and form rubbery branched colonies of soft polyps with long droopy tentacles. Many of them are spectacularly coloured. *Xenia,* which is common in Natal, is found in

Fig. 193 The sun-burst soft coral, which is often found by divers, has a crown of polyps on a broad stalk and can completely withdraw these into the stalk (x 1).

colours ranging from grey to royal blue (Plate 35); *Pareryth-ropodium purpureum* is a shocking-purple (Plates 34 & 37), although its larger relative, *Parerythropodium wilsoni*, is a shabby brown; *Alcyonium* ranges from delicate pink to luminescent orange (Plate 38). These vivid colours have a purpose for they advertise to predators that these animals should be left alone because of their stinging cells. Apart from this, the soft corals cannot be very nutritious, for much of their bulk is made up of watery mesogloea and their energy content is among the lowest of all animals.

Subclass Zoantharia: Anemones and corals

Anyone who has dabbled in sea-shore pools will be familiar with the sea anemones, which are classified in the order **Actiniaria**. All of them are solitary animals, and their polyps are much larger than those of the dainty Hydrozoa, resulting in some modifications of the body structure (Fig. 194). Firstly, the mouth now forms a pharynx that hangs down into the body cavity like a circular curtain and functions as a valve, allowing food to be engulfed without loss of water from the body cavity. This is of vital importance since this water acts as a hydrostatic skeleton, and the animal cannot afford to collapse every time it opens its mouth. In spite of this, water is periodically lost, particularly when the anemone is threatened and contracts all its muscles simultaneously, squirting out water and collapsing into a huddle. It then faces the problem of how to refill

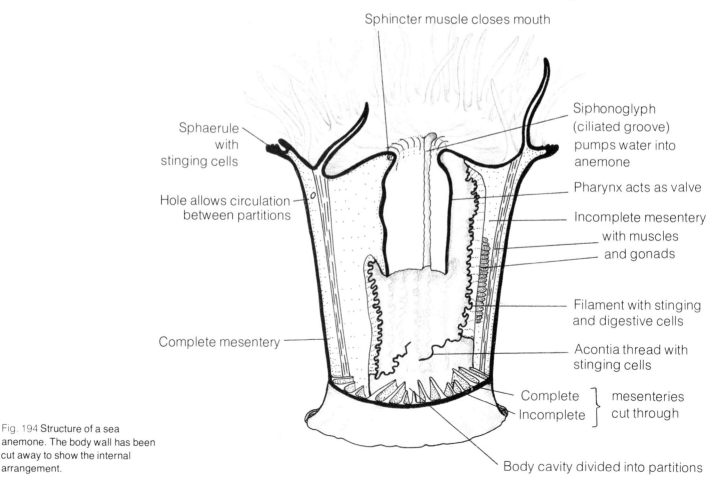

Sphincter muscle closes mouth

Sphaerule with stinging cells

Hole allows circulation between partitions

Complete mesentery

Siphonoglyph (ciliated groove) pumps water into anemone

Pharynx acts as valve

Incomplete mesentery with muscles and gonads

Filament with stinging and digestive cells

Acontia thread with stinging cells

Complete } mesenteries
Incomplete } cut through

Body cavity divided into partitions

Fig. 194 Structure of a sea anemone. The body wall has been cut away to show the internal arrangement.

Fig. 195 The giant anemone *Stoichactis,* which reaches a metre in diameter, amongst eelgrass *(Thalassodendron).* The anemone hosts a commensal shrimp, seen sheltering in the tentacles towards the centre left.

the body cavity with water. It cannot use its muscles to do this for they are helpless without the skeleton; however, the pharynx has two ciliated grooves (the siphonoglyphs) and the flickering of these cilia drives water back into the body cavity. Although the cilia are weak, they slowly build up enough pressure to pump up the anemone.

The body wall is also modified in sea anemones, the inner layer being folded to form partitions (mesenteries) that stretch vertically down the body cavity (Fig. 194). Some mesenteries join the pharynx and are said to be 'complete'. Between these are 'incomplete' mesenteries that project only a short distance so that their inner edges lie free in the body cavity (see cross-section of mesenteries in Fig. 194). The mesenteries have several functions. First-ly, they increase the area for digestion. Secondly, muscles are attached to them, thus, improving muscular action. Thirdly, the free edges of mesenteries are lined with three twisted ridges called filaments: two of these are digestive in function, but the third is armed with batteries of stinging cells and extends beyond the mesentery as a stringy loose coil. Each of these coils (acontia) can be ejected out of the mouth in times of threat, and in one species, *Anthothoe stimpsoni,* they can be discharged directly through the body wall (Fig. 316). Finally, the mesenteries make the hydrostatic skeleton more efficient. A single water-filled cavity has one disadvantage as a skeleton: every time a muscle contracts, water is displaced throughout the cavity, so that all the other muscles must respond to this increased pressure. By dividing the cavity with mesenteries, the action of any one muscle can be localised, limiting its effect on the body as a whole. The mesenteries clearly have many functions, and although they are most obvious in the anemones, they are a characteristic feature of all anthozoan polyps.

Most anemones are carnivorous, catching quite large

prey or dead animals with their tentacles (Fig. 39), but curiously the very largest of anemones are often filter-feeders and use mucus to entangle tiny particles. *Stoichac-tis,* which is common in the estuaries of Moçambique, can reach a metre in diameter, and often shelters the com-mensal shrimps, *Saron* and *Periclimenes* (Fig. 195 and Plate 6), or even fish. In tropical waters the clownfish *Amphiprion* (Plate 21) is always found sheltering in anemones. The mucus on the fish evidently reduces dis-charge of nematocysts, but the relationship is not simple, for the anemones somehow recognise fish that they have sheltered for some time and avoid stinging them, but will attack new clownfish that take liberties. The resident fish reciprocate by protecting the anemone from predators, by removing damaged tissues, and by preventing silt from settling on the anemone.

Surrounding the tentacles of many anemones is a row or two of round tubercles called sphaerules (Fig. 194). Only recently has their function been discovered: they are armed with special nematocysts used against other anemones. The thought of sedentary anemones being aggressive seems absurd, but aggressive they are. For example, *Actinia* will lean across and rake adjacent anemones with its inflated sphaerules, leaving great weals across its oppo-nent. Because of this, the anemones space themselves out, preventing overcrowding. However, there is a further remarkable refinement to this behaviour. Anemones can reproduce by budding but they are never aggressive to members of their own clone. Obviously they somehow 'know' when they are dealing with genetically identical individuals.

The commonest southern African anemones are shown in Fig. 196 and Plates 16–20. *Pseudactinia* (Plate 18) is bright red, smooth and floppy and is readily recognised because it is the only species that lacks a sphincter muscle around its mouth so that it is unable to withdraw its tenta-cles quickly into its mouth when prodded. *Actinia equina* occurs in the high-shore and is smooth and plum-coloured

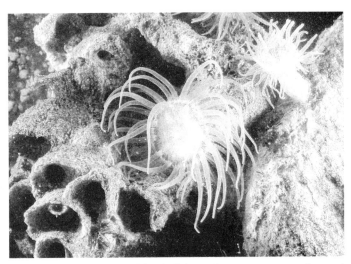

Fig. 196 The sea anemone *Halianthella* is a pale cream or green colour and has long drooping tentacles. It is common in very sheltered pools (x 1).

(Plate 16); *Bunodosoma capensis* has over 200 tentacles and a column that is warty (Plate 19); *Bunodactis reynaudi* is similar, but has a sticky column to which sand grains always stick (Plate 17); while *Anthopleura michaelseni*, too, is bedecked with sand but has only 96 tentacles. *Anthothoe stimpsoni* is another smooth-columned species and has characteristic stripes of various colours running down the column – these may be grey, green, brown or pink (Plate 20).

Closely related to the anemones are members of another order, **Coralliomorpha.** The only common representative in southern Africa is *Corynactis annulata* (Plates 14 & 15), which is a tiny but exquisitely beautiful pink animal that often forms clusters, and can be recognised by its several rings of knobbed tentacles.

The order **Zoanthidea** also includes anemone-like forms, but can be distinguished by their single siphono-glyph groove on the pharynx. Furthermore, they are all colonial, the polyps being linked together by a fleshy coenenchyme. Several species are very common in sub-tropical Natal and Moçambique, where they form slippery carpets on intertidal rocks. These are illustrated in Plates 27–32 and in Fig. 197.

Although zoanthids are carnivorous, they seem to obtain most of their nourishment from tiny algae that live sym-biotically within their bodies.

The most spectacular and biologically important anthozoans are the hard corals belonging to the order **Mad-reporaria,** which sometimes form continuous reefs in tropical waters. Coral reefs are the most exciting of all marine environments (Plate 26). The sheer range of coral form and colour is in itself overwhelming. In addition, more species are packed into coral reefs than in any other habitat, and somehow they also seem to interact in a more intimate manner than elsewhere.

A few corals such as *Balanophyllia* and *Caryophyllia* (Fig. 199) are solitary or, like *Dendrophyllia* (Plate 24 & back cover), form small clusters. They look much like anemones perched on top of a hard skeleton. However, most corals are colonial and secrete a massive lime skele-ton: the bulk of these corals is actually inanimate limestone overlain by a thin veneer of interconnected living polyps. Each polyp is usually sunken into a crater in the skeleton, which has radiating ridges or septa that project upwards between the mesenteries of the polyp (Fig. 198). Different species are distinguished by the size and structure of these craters which are seen most clearly if the skeleton is boiled in potassium hydroxide and then bleached to reveal the detailed structure (Figs. 200–214).

The stag horn corals are all branched. *Acropora* grows like a flat-topped thorn tree and is distinguished by its porous coral and the cup-like projections that house polyps (Fig. 201). *Stylophora* has flat branches (Fig. 202). *Pocillopora* is very common in Moçambique and northern Natal and has much more solid branches with projecting knobbles that carry the polyps (Fig. 203). The tips of the branches often form little caves, housing commensal crabs. Eventually the coral grows almost completely over the crab, leaving only a slender opening (see Chapter 13).

Another group of corals forms encrusting balls, the sur-faces of which are covered by cup-like craters housing the polyps (Figs. 204–210). These species are sometimes dif-ficult to separate, their identification depending on the size of the cups and whether their septa are smooth or roughened by projecting prickles, and whether or not these prickles join one septum to the next. In yet another group of species, the brain corals, the polyps are elongated and have several mouths so that they form a pattern on the coral head that looks like the surface of a brain (Figs. 211–212).

Galaxia does not have cups but projecting turrets, crowned with spine-like septa (Fig. 213) which in life are so covered by the polyps that one cannot even see the skeleton (Plate 24). *Pavona* forms scroll-like plates (Fig. 214) and its cups all interconnect in an exquisite pattern (Plate 22).

The reef-building (hermatypic) corals owe their success to unicellular algae called zooxanthellae living within their tissues. Both the algae and the corals are able to live without each other but are so mutually beneficial that they are seldom found apart. As much as 50 percent of the protein present in coral tissues is due to the inclusion of these algae. What advantage do the algae gain from the relationship? They certainly gain protection and can use

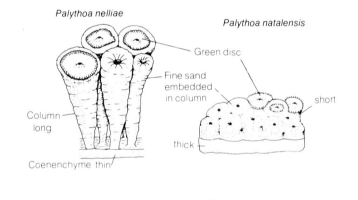

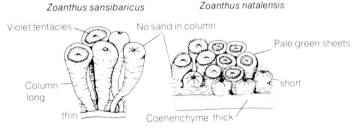

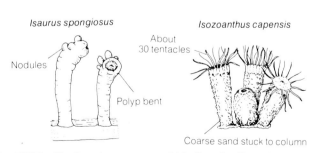

Fig. 197 Identification of common zoanthids. See also Plates 27-32.

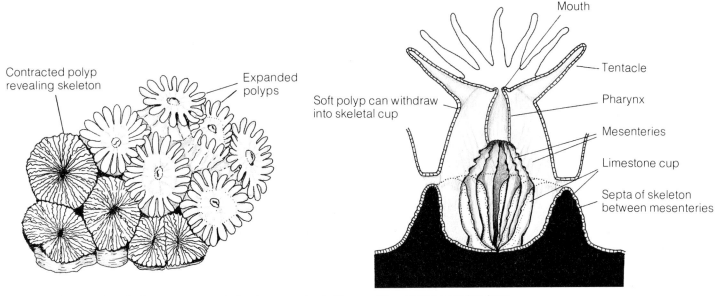

Fig. 198 A. A group of coral polyps, some expanded and some contracted to reveal the underlying coral skeleton.
B. Section of a coral polyp showing internal structure and skeleton.

the carbon dioxide given off by the coral. But most of all they rely on nitrogenous waste products from the coral, for tropical waters are often deficient in nutrients.

We might expect the corals to benefit by digesting the algae (as does the giant clam *Tridacna*), but in fact they never do so. Even if starved and kept in the dark, corals will extrude the algae rather than digest them. However, corals do profit in other ways from the association. The algae remove their waste products; they also produce organic materials that diffuse from the algal cells and can be absorbed by the coral. Experiments show that up to 50 percent of the carbon dioxide used during photosynthesis by the algae finds its way into the coral in the form of compounds such as glycerol, glucose and alanine. Perhaps most importantly, the algae help in the formation of the coral skeleton, which is made of calcium carbonate. Corals absorb calcium from the water, and this combines with carbon dioxide and water to form calcium bicarbonate, which is soluble in water and dissociates into calcium and bicarbonate ions. If the algae in turn use up the carbon dioxide during photosynthesis, this chemical reaction shifts so that the calcium bicarbonate breaks down into carbonic acid and calcium carbonate. Since calcium carbonate is insoluble, it deposits to form the skeleton of the coral (Fig. 215).

Because corals depend to such an extent on their zooxanthellae, they are limited to shallow water where photosynthesis can occur, and to tropical waters where the high temperatures hasten the rate at which the coral skeleton is laid down, allowing it to grow fast enough to outpace its erosion by waves.

There are three main types of coral reefs: fringing reefs around islands, barrier reefs further offshore, and ring-like atolls which occur in deep water far from any land. This raises a puzzle: if corals must live in shallow waters, how do these atolls ever come into being? It was Charles Darwin who suggested the solution. Corals may form a fringing

Fig. 199 A. Three live solitary corals, *Balanophyllia*. B. The dead skeletons of *Balanophyllia* (centre) and *Caryophyllia* (left and right) (x 1).

Fig. 200 Fungus coral, *Fungia*.

Fig. 201 Staghorn coral, *Acropora*.

Fig. 202 *Stylophora*.

Fig. 203 *Pocillopora*.

Fig. 204 Whole colony and detail of *Favia*.

Fig. 205 Whole colony and detail of *Anomastrea irregularis*.

Fig. 206 Whole colony and detail of *Porites solida*.

SKELETONS OF COMMON SOUTHERN AFRICAN CORALS

Fig. 207 Detail of *Acanthastrea*.

Fig. 208 Detail of *Favites*.

Fig. 209 Detail of *Symphyllia*.

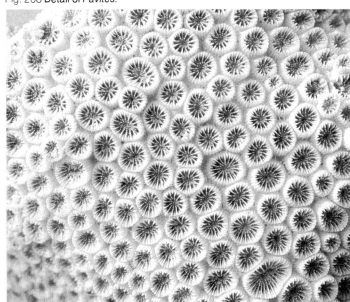

Fig. 210 Segment of *Solenaster*.

Fig. 211 Surface of brain coral.

Fig. 212 Small portion of *Lobophyllia*.

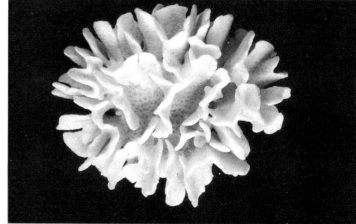

Fig. 213 Whole colony and detail of *Galaxia*.

reef around a volcanic island that subsequently subsides into the ocean and, if the coral reef continues to grow up towards the surface as the island disappears, it will form a circular atoll of coral surrounding a lagoon that marks the original position of the island (Fig. 216). Only very recently has Darwin's suggestion been confirmed. Very deep cores taken through the Pacific atoll of Eniwetok have demonstrated that coral extends an incredible 1 000 m down to where it perches on an underwater volcanic mount, 3 200 m above the ocean floor. It must have taken about 60 million years for this mount to have subsided from the surface to its present position, while the coral grew apace to keep the living polyps in sunlit shallow water.

To increase the photosynthesis of their symbiotic algae, many species, such as staghorn corals, have branched tree-like colonies that can catch as much as possible of the diffuse light that dances around in the water. The only problem with such structures is that they are brittle and easily broken, so these colonies are confined to quiet lagoons. Other species such as the brain corals have mas-

Fig. 214 Whole colony and detail of *Pavona*.

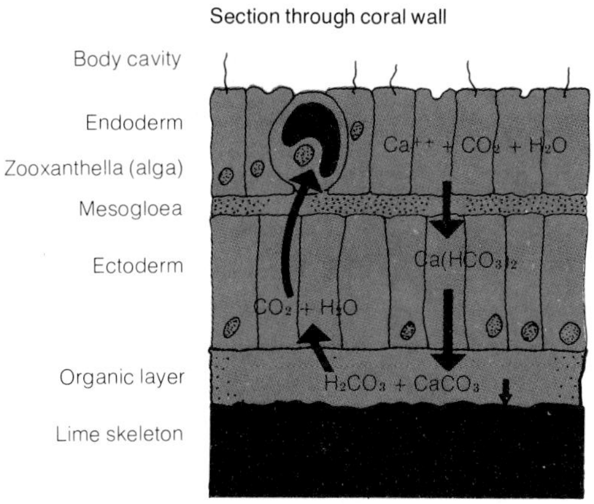

Section through coral wall

Body cavity
Endoderm
Zooxanthella (alga)
Mesogloea
Ectoderm

Organic layer
Lime skeleton

$Ca^{++} + CO_2 + H_2O$

$Ca(HCO_3)_2$

$CO_2 + H_2O$

$H_2CO_3 + CaCO_3$

Skeleton formation

1. Calcium ions from sea water in body cavity combine with:
2. Carbon dioxide from respiration of coral tissues and water to form:
3. Soluble calcium bicarbonate which breaks down to deposit:
4. Calcium carbonate (lime), thus adding to the coral skeleton.
5. The soluble by-product, carbonic acid, forms carbon dioxide and water.
6. By removing carbon dioxide during photosynthesis the zooxanthellae in the coral tissues assist further deposition of calcium carbonate.

Fig. 215 Section through the body wall of a coral polyp showing how the symbiotic algae (Zooxanthellae) increase the rate of deposition of the skeleton.

sive round heads that resist wave action. These are mainly filter-feeding carnivores and their polyps emerge only at night to feed on plankton when it migrates to the surface of the water.

Corals often compete for space, aggressively stinging opponents to death or overgrowing them. To reduce this problem, some species have a narrow 'trunk' that allows them to settle in a small space, but they expand upwards and outwards like a thorn tree, growing above possible competitors. Quite clearly there are various ways in which body form is functionally related to the needs of particular corals.

When we think back on the impact of coral reefs, the intimacy of their relationship with zooxanthellae, the massive size of some medusae, the specialised nature of stinging cells and the complexity of some hydrozoan colonies, we realise that the Cnidaria have been remarkably successful in spite of their simple body structure. In fact simplicity does have one great advantage, for very little food is required to supply the energy needs of such animals.

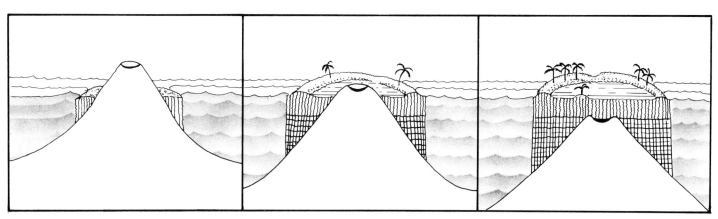

Fig. 216 The processes leading to the formation of coral atolls.
A. A fringing coral reef forms around a volcanic island.
B. When the island begins to subside, the reef continues to grow to remain near the surface, forming a barrier reef separated from the island.
C. Finally the island disappears from sight, leaving a circular atoll surrounding a lagoon.

REFERENCES

Popular articles and books
Lane, C. E. 1963. The deadly fisher. *National Geographic,* Vol. 123 (3): 388-397.
Sisson, R. F. 1973. Life cycle of a coral. *National Geographic,* Vol. 143 (6): 780-793.

Identification guides
Boshoff, P. H. 1981. List of southern African Scleractinia Bourne, 1900. Investigational Report, Oceanographic Research Institute, Durban, Vol. 49: 1-45.

Crossland, C. 1948. Reef corals of the South African coast. *Annals of the Natal Museum,* Vol. 11: 169-207.
Day, J. H. 1969. *A Guide to Marine Life on South African Shores.* A. A. Balkema, Cape Town. pp. 22-45.
McNae, W. & Kalk, M. 1958. *A Natural History of Inhaca Island, Moçambique.* Witwatersrand University Press, Johannesburg. pp. 46-56.
Millard, N. A. H. 1975. Monograph on the Hydroida of Southern Africa. *Annals of the S. Afr. Museum,* Vol. 68: 1-513.

10. CTENOPHORA COMB JELLIES

The ctenophores are round jelly-like animals often washed ashore where they lie glistening in the sun like transparent marbles. They are sometimes referred to as sea gooseberries or sea walnuts, depending on their size, but the name 'comb jelly' is more descriptive. At one time the ctenophores were linked with the Cnidaria in a single phylum, Coelenterata, but they are so different that the two groups are now separated.

The basic structure of the Ctenophores is not unlike that of a jellyfish. The body is round and has an outer ectodermal layer of cells covering the jelly-like mass of the mesogloea, and an inner endodermal layer that lines the gut. The mouth opens at one pole of the ball and leads into a stomach with eight radiating canals that extend through the mesogloea. Gonads line each of these canals.

Eight bands of cilia run down the length of the body like lines of longitude on a globe. Each band consists of row upon row of tiny cilia that beat in rhythmic sequence, providing the animal with its only means of movement and propelling it, mouth forwards, through the water (Fig. 217). These comb rows, characteristic of the group, give them their name (Cteno = comb; phora = bearing). They are astonishingly beautiful for, as they beat, all the colours of the rainbow flicker down their length. At night they can be even more spectacular, for the canals of the gut luminesce, lighting up the comb rows.

At the apex of the body is a balancing organ or statocyst, consisting of a ball of lime balancing on four tufts of cilia connected to the nerve net. If the animal tips over, the ball of lime rests more heavily on the lower tufts, stimulating the adjacent nerves, which increase the activity of the cilia in the comb rows on that side, so that the animal rights itself.

Most ctenophores fall in the order Tentaculata, and have a distinctive pair of long dainty tentacles that emerge from deep sheaths on either side of the body and trail behind the animal. These lack stinging cells, but are armed with adhesive cells (colloblasts) that stick to small prey, which can then be hauled up to the mouth. In addition, these adhesive cells bear coiled filaments embedded in the jelly of the tentacle (Fig. 217), providing the cell with the necessary 'give' so that it is not torn out by struggling prey. While most comb jellies have tentacles, these are lacking in the order Nuda, which includes one species of *Beroe* that is very common on the west coast, particularly in Langebaan Lagoon.

In one aberrant genus of comb jellies, *Coeloplana*, the body is completely flattened and the animals creep around like flatworms. These strange creatures have been found living quite commonly on one particular species of soft coral in rock pools near Durban; the only place where they have been recorded in the whole of Africa.

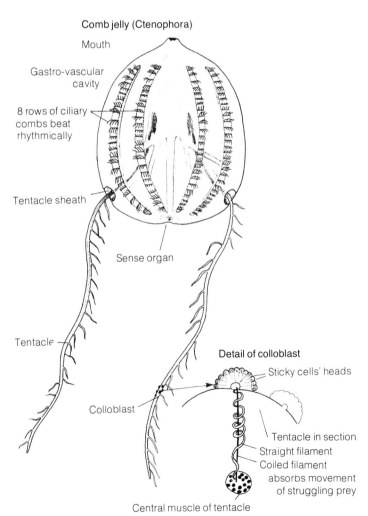

Comb jelly (Ctenophora)

Mouth

Gastro-vascular cavity

8 rows of ciliary combs beat rhythmically

Tentacle sheath

Sense organ

Tentacle

Colloblast

Detail of colloblast

Sticky cells' heads

Tentacle in section
Straight filament
Coiled filament absorbs movement of struggling prey

Central muscle of tentacle

Fig. 217 **The body structure of a comb-jelly.**

REFERENCES

Scientific references
Pople, W. 1959. The occurrence of *Coeloplana* in Natal, South Africa. *S. Afr. Journal of Science*, Vol. 56: 39-42.

PREVIOUS PAGE:
1. Rich growths of animals and algae vie for space on low-shore rocks on the Natal coast.

SPONGES
2. The tube-sponge, *Grantessa* sp. (x5).
3. In deeper waters a variety of sponges coats the rocks. Photographed at a depth of 60 m.

4. Three encrusting sponges compete for space, overgrowing one another. Sitting on them is a brittle star, *Ophiothrix fragilis* (x1).
5. A colonial sponge, *Haliclona* sp. (x5).
6. A common intertidal sponge, *Hymeniacedon perlevis* (x1).
7. Seemingly growing on rock, this *Haliclona* actually formed a protective cloak carried by a sponge-crab, *Cryptodromiopsis spongiosa* (x2).

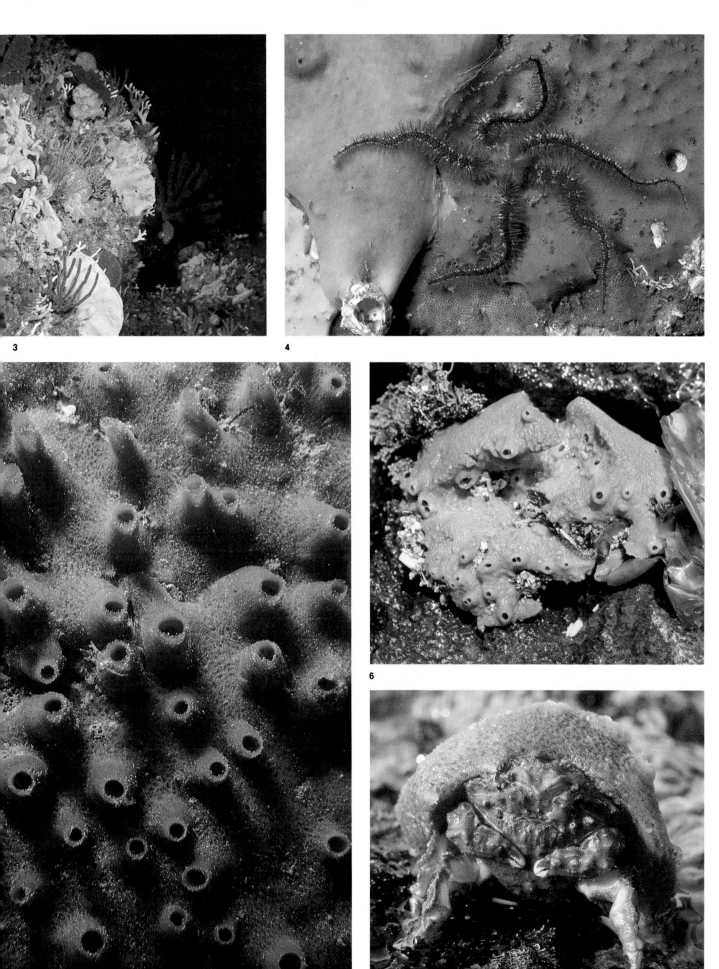

3

4

5

6

7

8

9

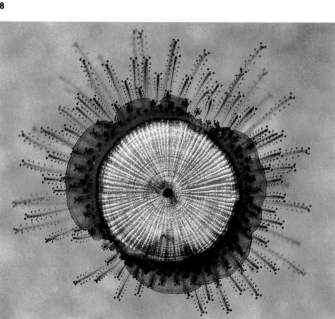

10

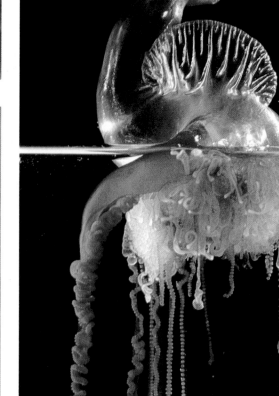

HYDROIDS AND BLUEBOTTLES

8. Two plumes of the hydroid *Thecocarpus formosus* with oval reproductive bodies (corbulae) attached (x6).

9. By-the-wind-sailor, *Vellela,* floats on the surface and has a vertical sail (x2).

10. The raft-hydroid, *Porpita pacifica,* has a round flat float from which hang the stinging tentacles (x1).

11. The bluebottle, *Physalia physalis* (x1).

12. Detail of the bluebottle showing the bottle-like feeding polyps and the extensible tentacles, laden with batteries of stinging cells (x5).

11   12

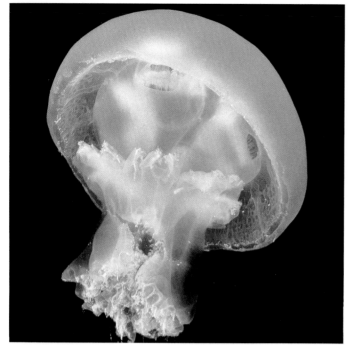

13

14

15

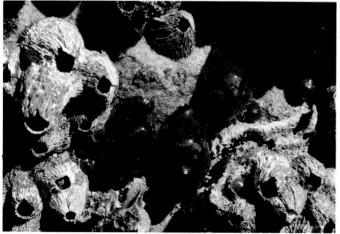

16

17

JELLYFISH AND ANEMONES

13. A jellyfish medusa, belonging to the order Rhizostomeae, in which the lobes surrounding the mouth have tiny pores through which food is filtered. The umbrella lacks the tentacles found in most other medusae (x1).

14. A colony of strawberry anemones, *Corynactis annulata* (x3).

15. A single polyp of *Corynactis* showing the successive rings of knobbed tentacles that characterise the animal (x3).

16. Plum anemones, *Actinia equina,* occur high on the shore and bear their young live. Here they are seen surrounded by several newly-born juveniles and the barnacle *Tetraclita serrata (x1).*

17. Sandy-anemones, *Bunodactis reynaudi,* are characterised by having a sticky column to which sand-grains adhere. As shown here, sandy-anemones often compete with mussels for space (x½).

18. *Pseudactinia flagellifera* is a common intertidal anemone on the south and west coasts. Unlike most anemones, it lacks a sphincter muscle around the mouth and therefore cannot withdraw its tentacles easily (x1).

19. *Bunodosoma capensis* comes in a wide range of colours such as red, purple or cream and may be mottled. Although it has dense papillae all over its column, like its close relative *Bunodactis,* sand never adheres to it (x2).

20

22

21

23

ANEMONES AND CORALS

20. The striped anemone, *Anthothoe stimpsoni* (x1).

21. Clownfish, *Amphiprion* sp., seek shelter within the stinging tentacles of an anemone (x1).

22. Detail of the lime skeleton of a coral, *Pavona* sp. (x12).

23. Live polyps of a coral, *Galaxea* sp. (x6).

24. Expanded polyps of the coral *Dendrophyllia* sp. (x1).

25. The firefish, *Pterois antennata,* swims in front of a *Dendrophyllia* which has contracted its polyps (x1).

26. A splendid coral reef in northern Zululand. Three species of *Acropora* can be seen in the foreground with *Porites solida* behind.

24

25

26

ZOANTHIDS
27. Patches of barnacle-covered brown mussels, *Perna perna*
break the green sheets of zoanthids which carpet the rocks in
Natal.
28. *Palythoa nelliae* (x2).
29. *Zoanthus natalensis* (x2)
30. *Zoanthus natalensis* (x2).
31. *Zoanthus sansibaricus* (x2).
32. *Isozoanthus capensis* (x5).

28

29

30

31

32

33

35

34

36

SOFT AND HORNY CORALS

33. A small segment of the sea fan, *Lophogorgia flammea:* (x3) see also Plate 149.

34. Purple soft coral, *Parerythropodium purpureum* (x1).

35. The blue soft coral, *Xenia florida,* ranges in colour from grey to royal blue (x1).

36. *Eunicella papillosa,* one of the sea fans, is normally branched irregularly, but where the current direction is constant, it forms a flat fan at right angles to the current (x1).

37. An unusual colour variety of *Parerythropodium purpureum* (x2).

38. Soft coral, *Alcyonium* sp. (x10).

37   38

FLATWORMS

39. A tropical polyclad flatworm (x2).

40. This polyclad flatworm crawling over glass reveals the repeatedly branched gut and pair of gonads (x1).

41. All polyclads swim gracefully like this one (x2).

42. *Thysanozoon* is covered with finger-like papillae which increase the surface area for oxygen uptake and also blend the animal into its background. Here it matches the coralline alga *Lithothamnion* which encrusts the rock (x1½).

POLYCHAETE WORMS

43. *Pomatoleios kraussii* forms dense masses of calcareous blue-tinged tubes, from which the animals' delicate fans extend to filter food from the water (x3).

44. A fan worm, *Sabellastarte longa* (x1).

45. *Protula bispiralis* in its calcareous tube which is secreted by the bright red collar behind the fan of feeding tentacles (x1).

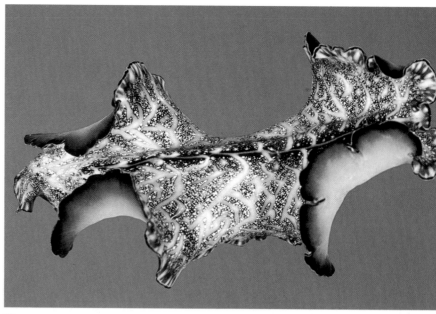

39

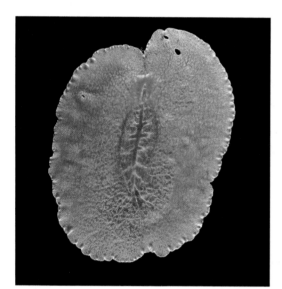

40

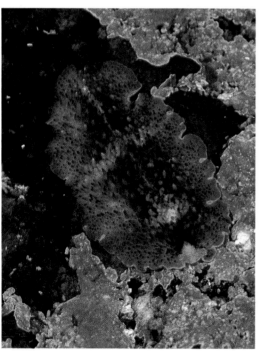

42

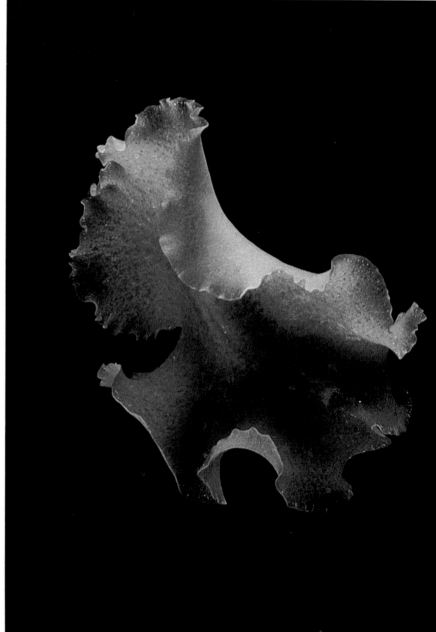

41

43

44

45

46

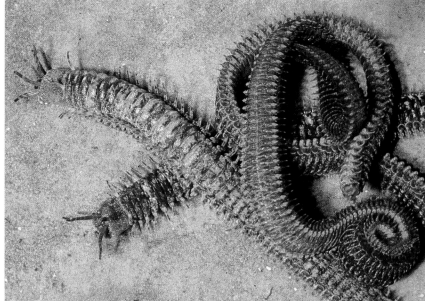

48

47

49

POLYCHAETE WORMS

46. *Serpula vermicularis.* Note the colour resemblance to the purple soft coral which the worm may mimic (x1).

47. A dainty colony of *Filograna implexa* (x3).

48. A pair of intertwined *Eunice aphroditois* living up to their name. The well-developed parapodia on the sides of each segment are typical of all such polychaetes (x1).

49. The fireworm *Eurythoe complanata* bears irritant bristles (x1).

50. *Amblyosyllis formosa* holds its cirri rolled up tightly until it is disturbed, when it shoots them out (x3).

51. *Eunice antennata* has five antennae on its head which are characteristically beaded. Feathery gills grace the front end of the body (x4).

50   51

BARNACLES

52. Goose barnacles, *Lepas,* attached to a floating shell of a squid-like animal, *Spirula* (x2).
53. *Lepas* sp. with its net of cirri extended.
54. Acorn barnacles, *Chthamalus dentatus,* and the snail *Littorina africana africana* live high on the shore where few other animals survive (x5).

ISOPODS AND AMPHIPODS

55. The sea louse, *Ligia dilatata,* scavenges on the high-shore, feeding on rotting seaweeds (x2).
56. A caprellid, *Caprella* sp. clinging to the seaweed *Dictyota* (x3).
57. A female caprellid, her brood-pouch bulging with embryos (x6).
58. A typical amphipod, *Ceradocus rubromaculatus* (x5).
59. A male and female pair of parasitic fish-lice, *Anilocra capensis,* feeding on a stumpnose, *Rhabdosargus* (x1).
60. Teeming sand hoppers, *Talorchestia capensis,* feeding on kelp at night (x4).

52

53

54

55

56

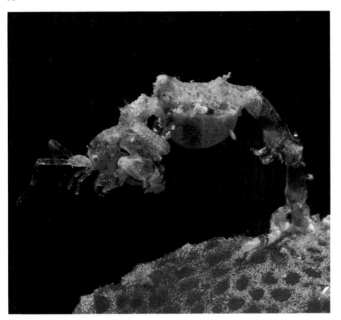

57

58

59

60

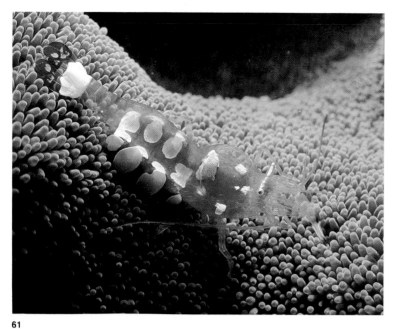

61

62

SHRIMPS AND ROCK LOBSTERS

61. The shrimp *Periclimenes brevicarpalis* lives commensally among the tentacles of the giant anemone *Stoichactis* (x1½).

62. The sand-shrimp, *Palaemon pacificus,* is normally almost transparent with vertical bars that break up its outline so that it blends into the sand, but it can change its colour and darken if kept on a dark background (x1½).

63. A young rock lobster, *Jasus lalandii* (x1). This is the west coast species which is of such commercial importance, realising about R30 million each year. Adults grow very slowly and probably take about 30 years to reach their maximum length of 40 cm.

64. The cleaner shrimp *Stenopus hispidus,* which cleans fish by removing parasites and old tissues. Because of its bright colours, fish recognise it readily and forgo a meal for the sake of the cleaner shrimp's services (x1½).

65. The shoveller crayfish, *Scyllarides elisabethae* (x½).

63

64

65

66

68

MANTIS-SHRIMPS AND HERMIT CRABS

66. The mantis-shrimp *Gonodactylus chiragra*, like a preying mantis, has a massive pair of grasping limbs shown here folded under the thorax. It is a voracious predator (x2).

67. A pagurid hermit crab with two anemones on its shell. Many hermit crabs prise anemones off the rocks and transplant them onto their shells, the stinging cells on the anemones' tentacles providing the hermit with protection, while the anemones benefit from scraps of the hermit's food.

68. *Dardanus arrosor* is found right round the coast of southern Africa and is distributed from Japan to Brazil. This handsome example occupies a helmet-shell, *Phalium labiatum zeylanicum* (x1).

69. The beautiful blue-eyed hermit, *Calcinus laevimanus,* is common in Natal (x3).

70

71

HERMIT CRABS

Clibanarius virescens is one of the most abundant hermit crabs on the east coast of southern Africa. Because of its abundance, and because it never ejects living gastropods from their shells, *Clibanarius* competes fiercely for empty shells. As the hermits grow they must find larger shells, and this remarkable sequence of photographs shows a *Clibanarius* in search of a new one.

Clearly cramped in a shell that is so small that the hermit cannot even retreat completely into it (70), a *Clibanarius* locates a larger shell (71), inserts its nipper to test if the shell is empty (72) and rapidly hops into it (73), only to be accosted by another hermit and to have to fight for possession of its new home (74).

74

72

73

75

76

77

78

CRABS

75. An alert ghost crab, *Ocypode ceratophthalmus* (x1½).
76. A mature male fiddler crab, *Uca urvillei:* males have one very enlarged nipper, used in courtship and territorial battle (x1).
77. A young *Uca urvillei* male, showing how much the colour can vary within the species (x2).
78. The red-eyed crab, *Percnon planissimum* (x4).

79. A swimming crab, *Ovalipes punctatus,* feeding on a plough snail, *Bullia,* after crushing its shell (x1).
80. A xanthid crab, *Eriphia smithii* (x1).
81. Pink ghost crab, *Ocypode madagascariensis,* making a meal of a turtle hatchling (x½).
82. Masked crab, *Mursia cristimanus* (x1).
83. Common shore-crab *Cyclograpsus punctatus* (x1).

79

80

81

82

83

84

85

86

87

SPIDERS AND PYCNOGONIDS

84. A pair of spiders, *Desis formidabilis,* in courtship (x2).
85. The spider *Amaurobioides africanus* at the mouth of its nest of eggs (x2).
86. A pycnogonid or 'sea spider' (x4).
87. Like a creature from another world, this pycnogonid *Nymphon signatum* picks its way over a yellow sponge. Its four pairs of long stilt-like legs are typical of the group. Male pycnogonids have an additional pair of shorter legs to which they attach egg-masses which hang beneath the body (x5).

CHITONS

88. An overturned rock reveals two chitons *(Chiton tulipa),* a rayed limpet *(Helcion pruinosus)* and a cushion starfish *(Patiriella exigua)* – the latter beautifully camouflaged at the lower right of the photograph (x3).

BIVALVES

89. The giant clam *Tridacna* with its beautiful mantle fully expanded to catch light for the symbiotic algae in its tissues (x¼).
90. Detail of the mantle of *Tridacna* (x1).
91. *Donax serra,* the white mussel, digging into sand. Its siphons, partly extended, show the 'sieve' that protects the inhalant siphon (x1½).
92. A bed of brown mussels, *Perna perna* (x½).

88   89

91

90

92

93

94

MOLLUSCS

93. Egg-cases of a whelk, each containing about 12 eggs (x4).

94. The perlemoen *Haliotis midae* trapping a frond of kelp *(Macrocystis),* one of the algae it eats (x½).

95. Helmet shell, *Phalium labiatum zeylanicum* (x1).

96. The angel-wing bivalve, *Lima* sp. is free-living and propels itself through the water by clapping its shells together (x1½).

97. Helmet shell, *Cypraecassis rufa,* roving amongst sea-grass in a coral reef lagoon (x½).

98. The pear limpet, *Patella cochlear,* with its fringe of algal 'garden' (x1).

99. A false limpet, *Siphonaria,* with egg ribbons (x1½).

100-102 A unique sequence showing how the long-spined limpet, *Patella longicosta,* reacts to a *Patella oculus* that intrudes on its territorial garden, thrusting strongly against it until it retreats (x½).

95

96

97

98

99

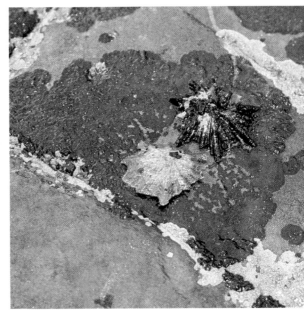

100

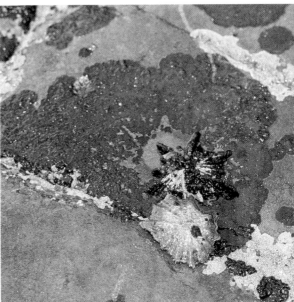

101

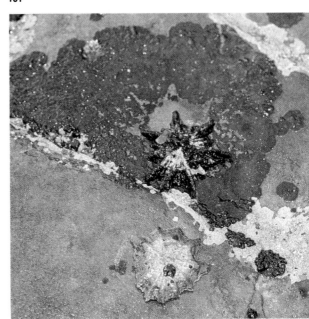

102

103

104

105

106

107

108

109

MOLLUSCS

103. The egg cowrie, *Ovula ovum* with its mantle partly withdrawn.
104. This photograph shows the same animal with its mantle expanded to cover its shell (x1).
105. The bubble-raft shell, *Janthina* sp., secretes a froth of bubbles which keeps the animal floating at the surface of the sea, where it feasts on bluebottles and their kin (x4).
106. The tiger cowrie, *Cypraea tigris,* with its mantle partly expanded to cover the shell, camouflaging the animal (x1).
107-109 This sequence shows a keyhole limpet leaping away from the predatory *Marginella rosea.* The *Marginella* then captures a winkle *(Gibbula zonata),* and finally attaches the winkle to the tip of its foot (109) where it carries it around until hungry (x2).

110. BIVALVES

a. *Saccostrea cuccullata*   b. *Crassostrea margaritacea*   c. *Pinctada capensis*   d. *Barbatia obliquata*   e. *Choromytilus meridionalis*
f. *Aulacomya ater*   g. *Perna perna*   h. *Septifer bilocularis*   i. *Arcuatula capensis*   j. *Atrina squamifera*   k. *Venus verrucosa*   l. *Limaria rotundata*
m. *Solen capensis*   n. *Solen cylindraceus*   o. *Trachycardium flavum*   p. *Trachycardium rubicundum*   q. *Thecalia concamerata*
r. *Cardita variegata*

111. BIVALVES

a. *Eumarcia paupercula*   b. *Macoma litoralis*   c. *Macoma litoralis*   d. *Dosinia hepatica*   e. *Loripes clausus*   f. *Chlamys tincta*   g. *Sunetta contempta bruggeni*   h. *Sunetta contempta bruggeni*   i. *Tellina gilchristi*   j. *Tellina apelina*   k. *Tellina alfredensis*   l. *Tellina trilatera*   m. *Venerupis corrugatus*   n. *Donax lubricus*   o. *Donax faba*   p. *Donax serra*   q. *Donax bipartitus*   r. *Donax madagascariensis*   s. *Donax sordidus*   t. *Scissodesma spengleri*   u. *Tivela compressa*   v. *Tivela polita*   w. *Mactra glabrata*

112. GASTROPODA

a. *Cellana capensis*   b. *Patella concolor*   c. *P. granatina*   d. *P. oculus*   e. *P. tabularis*   f. *P. cochlear*   g. *P. longicosta*   h. *P. argenvillei*
i. *P. barbara*   j. *P. compressa*   k. *P. miniata*   l. *P. granularis*

113. GASTROPODA

a. *Calyptraea chinensis*   b. *Crepidula porcellana*   c. *Haliotis parva*
d. *Haliotis spadicea*   e. *Haliotis midae*   f. *Amblychilepas scutellum*
g. *Fissurella mutabilis*   h. *Fissurella natalensis*   i. *Helcion pectunculus*
j. *Helcion pruinosus*   k. *Helcion dunkeri*   l. *Patellioda profunda*
m. *Siphonaria aspera*   n. *Siphonaria concinna* (= *S. deflexa*)
o. *Siphonaria anneae*   p. *Siphonaria oculus*   q. *Siphonaria capensis*

114. SMALL GASTROPODA

a. *Gibbula zonata*   b. *Gibbula capensis*   c. *Gibbula cicer*   d. *Gibbula cicer*   e. *Tricolia kochi*   f. *Tricolia capensis*   g. *Tricolia neritina*
h. *Assiminea ovata*   i. *Assiminea globulus*   j. *Nodilittorina natalensis*
k. *Littorina kraussi*   l. *Littorina scabra*   m. *Littorina africana africana*
n. *Littorina africana knysnaensis*

115. GASTROPODA

a. *Oxystele tabularis*   b. *Oxystele tigrina*   c. *Oxystele sinensis*   d. *Oxystele variegata*   e. *Turbo cidaris cidaris*   f. *Turbo sarmaticus*
g. *Turbo coronatus*   h. *Turbo cidaris natalensis*   i. *Clanculus atricatena*   j. *Clanculus puniceus*   k. *Clanculus miniatus*   l. *Monodonta australis*
m. *Trochus nigropunctatus*   n. *Calliostoma ornatum*   o. *Nerita textilis*   p. *Nerita polita*   q. *Nerita albicilla*   r. *Nerita plicata*   s. *Heliacus variegatus*
t. *Serpulorbis natalensis*   u. *Janthina janthina*

116. GASTROPODA

a. *Turritella sanguinea*   b. *Turritella capensis*   c. *Turritella carinifera*   d. *Epitonium coronatum*   e. *Cerithidea decollata*   f. *Nucella dubia*
g. *Nucella cingulata*   h. *Mancinella alouina*   i. *Thais bufo*   j. *Nucella squamosa*   k. *Purpura panama*   l. *Thais capensis*   m. *Burnupena cincta*
n. *Burnupena catarrhacta (= B. delalandii)*   o. *Burnupena pubescens*   p. *Burnupena lagenaria*   q. *Burnupena papyracea*   r. *Bullia annulata*
s. *Bullia pura*   t. *Bullia mozambicus*   u. *Bullia natalensis*   v. *Bullia rhodostoma*   w. *Bullia digitalis*   x. *Bullia diluta*   y. *Bullia laevissima*
z. *Demoulia ventricosa*   a'. *Nassarius speciosus*   b'. *Nassarius arcularius*   c'. *Nassarius variegatus*   d'. *Nassarius coronatus*
e'. *Nassarius plicatellus*   f'. *Nassarius kraussianus.*

117. GASTROPODA

a. *Fusinus ocelliferus*   b. *Peristernea forskalii forskalii*   c. *Peristernea forskalii leucothea*   d. *Fasciolaria lugubris heynemanni*   e. *Fasciolaria lugubris lugubris*   f. *Pyrene filmerae*   g. *Mitrella floccata*   h. *Pteropurpura capensis*   i. *Pteropurpura uncinaria*   j. *Morula granulata*   k. *Vexilla vexillum*   l. *Drupa ricinus*   m. *Gyrineum pusillum*   n. *Ranella australasia gemmifera*   o. *Charonia lampas pustulata*   p. *Cymatium cutaneum africanum* (= *C. dolarium*)   q. *Argobuccinum pustulosum* (= *A. argus*)   r. *Bursa granularis.*

118. COWRIES ETC.

a. *Polinices didyma*　b. *Natica tecta*　c. *Polinices tumidus*　d. *Cypraea moneta*　e. *C. annulus*　f. *C. citrina*　g. *C. felina*　h. *C. lamarcki*
i. *C. erosa*　j. *C. mauritiana*　k. *C. fuscodentata*　l. *C. helvola*　m. *C. caputserpentis*　n. *C. carneola*　o. *C. capensis*　p. *C. edentula*
q. *C. arabica immanis*　r. *C. vitellus*　s. *C. tigris*　t. *Trivia pellucidula*　u. *Trivia ovulata*　v. *Trivia aperta.*

119. GASTROPODA

a. *Phalium labiatum zeylanicum*   b. *Strombus mutabilis*   c. *Melapium lineatum*   d. *Olivia caroliniana*   e. *Amalda obtusa*   f. *Amalda obesa*   g. *Ancilla fasciata*   h. *Mitra litterata*   i. *Mitra picta*   j. *Clionella sinuata*   k. *Clionella rosaria*   l. *Trigonostoma foveolata*   m. *Conus algoensis simplex*   n. *Conus algoensis scitulus*   o. *Marginella rosea*   p. *Marginella ornata*   q. *Marginella capensis*   r. *Marginella nebulosa*   s. *Hastula diversa*   t. *Duplicaria capensis*   u. *Conus ebraeus*   v. *Conus natalis*   w. *Conus mozambicus*   x. *Conus tinianus*   y. *Callipara bullatiana*   z. *Harpa major*

121

122

125

NUDIBRANCHS
Many of the nudibranchs are vividly
coloured, advertising their unpalatable nature.
120. (Previous page) *Cyerce nigra* (x10).
121. *Casella* sp.(x1½).
122. *Cratena capensis* (x2).
123. *Godiva quadricolor* (x1½).
124. *Aplysia parvula* sitting on its egg mass (x1).
125. *Hypselodoris capensis* (x3).
126. *Polycera capensis* (x2).
127. *Melibe rosea* with its cowl inflated and about
to pounce on an isopod (x5).

126

127

123

124

NUDIBRANCHS

128. *Phyllodesmium serratum* astride the sponge it is feeding on. Tiny coiled tubeworms, *Spirorbis* sp. cover the rock (x3).

129. A tectibranch, *Berthellina citrina,* and its egg ribbon (x1).

130. The nudibranch *Hypselodoris* sp. rapidly retreating from a bubble-shell, *Hydatina physis* (x1).

131. *Glaucus atlanticus* floats on the surface of the sea (x2).

132. Tough-skinned *Phyllidia varicosa* is extremely toxic, capable of killing fish kept in the same aquarium (x1½).

OCTOPUS

133. The octopus, *Octopus granulatus* (x¼).

134. A paper nautilus, *Argonauta argo* (x½).

135. Detail of an octopus arm and suckers (x1).

128

129

130

131

132

133

134

135

136

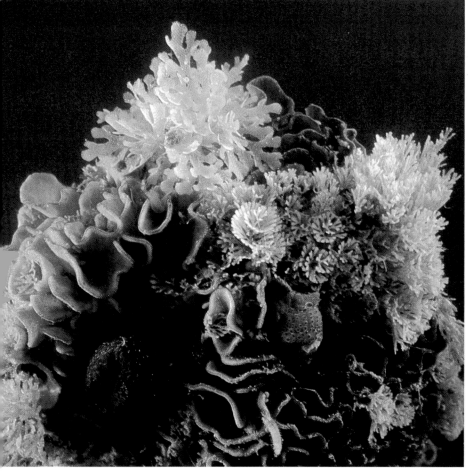

137

138

139

SQUID
136. A pair of squid, *Loligo* sp., hover around a diver's shot-line at a depth of 20 metres, their irridescent surfaces rippling with continually changing colours (x1).

BRYOZOANS
137. A group of bryozoans. Scroll-like *Chaperia* on the left, frond-like *Onchoporella buskii* at top, spiral *Menipea triseriata* in the centre and branching *Menipea crispa* upper right (x1).
138. *Chaperia* sp. with a purple soft coral growing in it (x4).
139. Lace-coral, *Schizoretepora tesselata,* with the red horny coral *Acabaria capensis* growing in amongst the colony (x1).
140. A juvenile top-shell, *Calliostoma ornatum,* climbs over a colony of *Onchoporella buskii.* The tiny individuals making up the colony are clearly visible (x30).

140

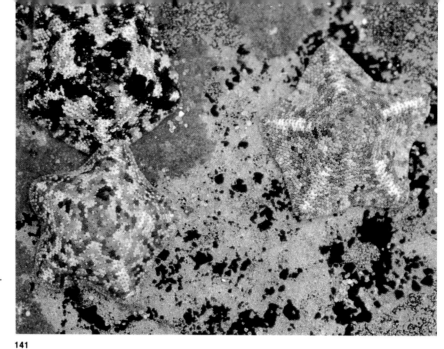

STARFISH AND BRITTLE STARS

141. Three cushion stars, *Patiriella exigua*, showing how the colour varieties blend into the colour of the rock (x1½).

142. *Pentaceraster mammillatus* in a bed of tropical sea-grass (x½).

143. A juvenile of *Marthasterias glacialis* (x2). Adults reach 200 mm in diameter.

144. *Patiria granifera* (right), *Patiriella exigua* (centre) and *Henricia ornata* (left) (x1).

145. *Asterina burtoni* (x2).

146. The brittle star, *Ophiarachnella capensis* (x1).

147-148. Unique pictures of the birth of a brittle star, *Ophioderma wahlbergi.* The young is seen emerging from the genital slit at the base of the upper leg (x3).

142

141

143

144

147

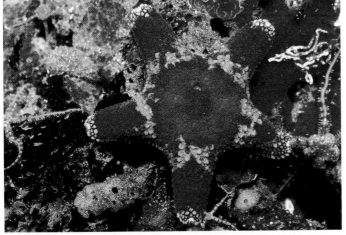

145

146

148

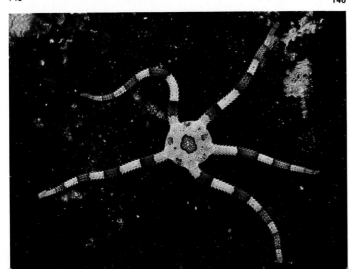

150

151

152

BRITTLE STARS AND SEA-URCHINS

149. Gorgon's head or basket star, *Astrocladus,* is an unusual brittle star with repeatedly branching arms. It is frequently found clinging to horny corals or sea fans – *Lophogorgia flammea* in this instance (x1).

150. The urchin *Stomopneustes variolans* shelters in hollows in rocks and often settles inside holes, where it may grow too large to ever leave. There, it feeds on algal debris that accumulates in the hole (x½).

151. The pencil urchin *Heterocentrotus mammillatus* (x1).

152. A group of *Parechinus angulosus,* the only common south and west coast urchin. Because it is abundant, its grazing curtails the growth of algae, often leaving only the coralline *Lithothamnion* to form a white paint-like crust on the rocks (x1).

FEATHER-STARS AND SEA CUCUMBERS

153. *Comathus wahlbergi,* the common south coast feather-star (x1).

154. A tropical feather-star bearing eggs in the swollen central pinnules (x1).

155. *Tropiometra carinata* (x1½).

156. The red-chested sea cucumber, *Trachythyone insolens* (x4).

157. A colonial sea-squirt, *Botrylloides* sp. The individuals are embedded in a jelly-like matrix and clustered in star-shaped groups (x1).

155

153

154

156 157

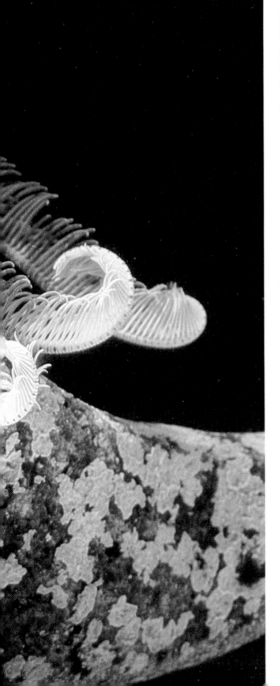

158

159

COMMUNITIES

158. Zonation is clearly demonstrated on this vertical rock face. Zones of red-bait, kelp, seaweeds and barnacles are visible.

159. High on the shore in the spray zone, vivid lichens coat the rocks.

160. Low-shore rocks on the east coast are richly coated with algae.

161. *Scaevola thunbergi* colonises and stabilises dunes on the east coast.

162. Oysters, *Saccostrea cuccullata,* form a characteristic mid-shore community on the east coast.

163. The limpet, *Patella cochlear,* dominates the low-shore of the south coast; algae only flourish below the Cochlear zone.

164. Dense subtidal kelp beds on the west coast.

OVERLEAF

165. The sea in tranquil mood in the Tsitsikama Coastal Park.

161

162

163

164

11. UNSEGMENTED WORMS
FLATWORMS, RIBBON WORMS, ROUNDWORMS, PEANUT WORMS AND TONGUE WORMS

Many of the lower worm-like animals are little known because they belong to minor groups with few species or because they are tiny and as a result seldom noticed. But some of them are of major ecological importance and all of them are of great interest on account of the evolutionary trends that have been developed in each group and because of the links they provide between the lower and higher invertebrates. For convenience they are considered together in a single chapter, although they belong to five different phyla, each with its own unique adaptations of body structure.

PLATHYHELMINTHES:
Flatworms

Translated literally from the Greek, 'Plathyhelminthes' means 'flat worms' and this is an apt description of these animals. The phylum contains three very different groups: the parasitic flukes such as bilharzia, tapeworms (classes Trematoda and Cestoda) and the free-living flatworms (class Turbellaria). Only the flatworms are dealt with in this chapter, since the other classes are generally small and are not found free-swimming in the sea.

The body structure of flatworms shows two advances over that of the Cnidaria. Firstly, the body is bilaterally symmetrical with a definite front and back, and with left and right sides. The radial symmetry that we saw in the Cnidaria is ideal for floating or sessile animals which need to detect what is happening all around them. By contrast, the flatworms are mobile, creeping animals in which it is an advantage to concentrate sensory organs at the front of the creature so that it can perceive the conditions that lie ahead. Thus simple eyes and sensors of chemicals, currents and temperature are found on the head.

The nervous system is concentrated into an anterior cerebral ganglion: the first signs of a 'brain' in the invertebrates. Flatworms can even be taught simple responses and have been popular subjects for investigations into the nature of memory. For instance, batches of worms were once conditioned to turn in a particular direction when faced with a choice in a simple maze. The fact that flatworms have a simple memory is interesting in itself, but more controversial research followed this finding. In one experiment a group of animals was taught a particular response and then cut up and fed to a second group of animals, which were shown to have inherited the memory. Even extracts of ribonucleic acid (RNA) from the cells of 'taught' worms increased the learning power of worms into which the RNA was injected. This result has never been verified, but at least one profiteering company benefited from the finding by selling students RNA at exam times!

The second development in the flatworms, compared to Cnidaria, is that the body has three layers of tissues, a central mesoderm of cells separating the outer ectoderm and the inner endoderm. This has important consequences. The central layer now forms the reproductive and excretory organs, so that the flatworms are the lowest grade of animal life with specialised organs. The mesoderm also serves as a firm skeleton on which the muscles can act, so that the gut fluids no longer have to perform this function. The outer and inner layers of the body are now free to become more specialised for locomotion and digestion. The lower surface is covered with cilia that are adequate to propel small species, while larger flatworms move by a rippling muscular action and can even swim by an elegant undulation of the body margin (Plates 39–42).

All flatworms have a well-developed long, tubular pharynx which opens on the mid-ventral surface of the body: being strongly muscular it can reach out and capture prey which includes crustaceans and small snails.

The structure of the gut varies from one order to another. Flatworms in the order Acoela lack a gut. The only common southern African representative, *Convoluta*, is famous for the symbiotic algae it contains within its tissues and which make it bright green. *Convoluta* occurs in damp areas on sandy beaches and can become so abundant that it colours the sand green. In the order Tricladida the gut has three main branches, while in the Polycladida it has many branches (Plate 40). Most of the larger flatworms, including all those described below, are polyclads. The repeated branching of the gut allows food to be distributed throughout the body.

Flatworms store food reserves in their cells and can go without food for long periods. However, when starved, they begin to digest their own tissues, starting with their reproductive organs. This 'self-cannibalism' may be carried so far that the animal may be reduced to less than one-hundredth of its original size. Flatworms are, however, also famous for their powers of regeneration and can regrow parts of their body – even after drastic mutilation or severe starvation.

For such lowly creatures, flatworms have surprisingly complex reproductive organs and practise internal fertilization. They are all hermaphroditic, producing eggs and sperm, thus guaranteeing that mating can occur between any two animals and that every animal has the potential to produce offspring: both important advantages for such slow-moving animals which may seldom meet and mate. In many species the transfer of sperm occurs in the most peculiar manner: the penis is armed with a stout barb and is injected through the body wall of the mate. The sperm then

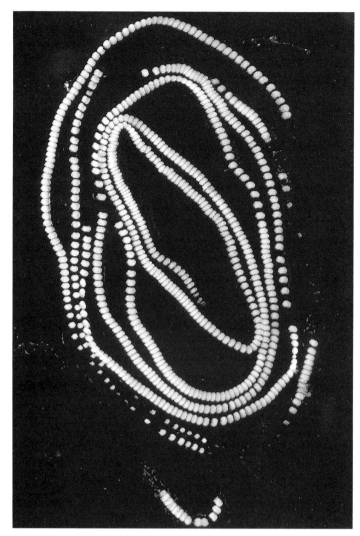

Fig. 218 The delicate necklace-like egg mass of a flatworm (x 2). The animal that laid these eggs is shown in Plate 40.

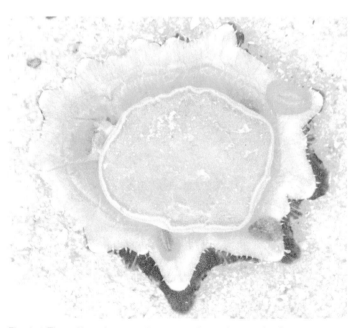

Fig. 219 Three *Notoplana patellarum* crawl over the mantle of an overturned limpet, *Patella oculus,* which is the normal host for these commensal flatworms (x 1).

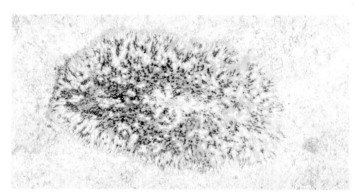

Fig. 220 A common free-living flatworm, *Planocera gilchristi* (x 1½).

passes between the cells of the recipient to reach the ovary and fertilize the eggs. This seemingly brutal method has been developed to extremes in one species, which has about 30 penis bulbs: only one is used for reproduction and the rest are to deter predators!

Fertilized eggs are supplied with yolk from a special yolk gland and are encased in jelly before being laid in an elegant coil which resembles a beaded necklace (Fig. 218). Small ciliated larvae hatch from the eggs and are dispersed in the water before they sink to the bottom and metamorphose into young flatworms.

Several flatworms occur commonly along the coast of southern Africa. Best known is *Notoplana patellarum,* which lives commensally under the limpet *Patella oculus* (Fig. 219). As many as 16 of these flatworms may be housed under a single large limpet. *Notoplana* is very particular in its choice of limpet and shows great preference for *P. oculus,* only occasionally being found under other limpet species.

This preference can easily be demonstrated in the laboratory by offering the worms a choice of different species and leaving them overnight to make their selection. We still wonder why they should prefer one particular species of limpet. *Notoplana* preys on small crustaceans and often eats the tiny copepods that also live commensally under limpets.

Planocera gilchristi is a larger free-living flatworm reaching 30 mm, and recognizable by its speckled greybrown colour, frilly margin and pair of tentacles on the head (Fig. 220). It, too, is predatory, feeding on crustaceans, worms and small molluscs. *Thysanozoon* is a more attractive animal, pinky-brown, with a profusion of finger-like papillae all over its back (Plate 43). In tropical waters one encounters yet more spectacular flatworms which measure up to 100 mm in length and are often vividly coloured (Plate 39).

NEMERTEA:
Proboscis worms
Proboscis or ribbon worms are long ribbon-like creatures which often coil their bodies into irregular twisted bundles. They can extend and contract to a remarkable degree, being capable of forty-fold changes of body length. One

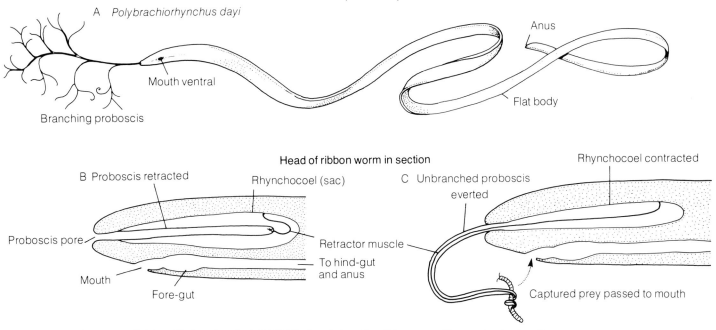

Fig. 221 A. The ribbon worm *Polybrachiorhynchus dayi*. B & C. The head of another ribbon worm, *Lineus*, showing how the proboscis is completely separate from the gut, and can be shot out to capture prey.

specimen we collected in Moçambique had a body 1 mm wide but a length of 5 m! In some respects the proboscis worms are like long thin flatworms, having the same three body layers, but their structure is more specialised. Firstly, the gut now has an anus, situated at the posterior end of the body. This means that the gut can become specialised, different parts being set aside for prey capture and ingestion, digestion of the food, absorption into the body and the voiding of waste materials. A simple blood system has also been added to the nemertean body plan, so that the gut no longer needs to branch in a complicated fashion to distribute food around the body, as it does in the flatworms. Finally, the proboscis worms have an innovation all of their own: a long extensible proboscis which is unique in that it lies in its own cavity (the rhynchocoel, which means 'snout-space') and is not connected to the gut. When the muscles around the rhynchocoel contract, they build up a pressure which shoots out the proboscis to capture prey, which must then be passed to the separate mouth to be eaten (Fig. 221). Some species have a barbed stylet and poison glands at the tip of the proboscis, while others rely on an incredibly sticky mucus that exudes from the proboscis and enslimes the prey.

The best known of the southern African species is the 'tapeworm' *Polybrachiorhynchus dayi*, which is so sought-after as a fish bait that it is currently sold at R12 per half-jack — where else in the world would bait be sold in such measures! It is one of the larger nemerteans, being as thick as a pencil and reaching 30 cm in length, and is common in some estuaries, particularly Swartkops near Port Elizabeth. *Polybrachiorhynchus* has a delightfully descriptive name, meaning 'many-branched snout', an allusion to its distinctive proboscis, which branches again and again to form a tree-like structure which can cover a man's hand when fully everted (Fig. 221). The proboscis produces a mucus that hardens instantly and entangles even quite large prey. Its favourite meal is the mud-prawn *Upogebia* but it will eat other crustaceans, worms and snails as well.

All other southern African nemerteans have a simple tubular proboscis and are distinguished by their colour and whether or not they have eyes. *Cerebratulus fuscus* is a white species, common on sandy beaches. Several species of *Lineus* occur on rocky shores: all lack eyes and are purple-brown with white patterns on the head. *Zygonemertes capensis* has several eyes on the head, which is marked off from the rest of the body by a V-shaped groove. *Amphiporus* species also have groups of eyes on the head, but lack the V-shaped groove.

NEMATODA:
Roundworms

Many people are not even aware of the existence of roundworms because most species are very tiny, being 1 to 5 mm in length and perhaps 0,05 mm in diameter. However, they can be incredibly abundant: for instance, sandy beaches and estuarine muds in southern Africa may support between one and four million roundworms per square metre! Nematodes are actually so common that an authority on the group once remarked that should all earthly substance vanish in a moment, leaving only the roundworms, we would still be able to discern the ghostly outlines of the world and its life because roundworms are so abundant.

Many plants and animals play host to parasitic roundworms. The guts and body cavities of fish often contain

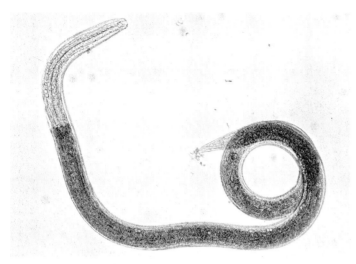

Fig. 222 A typical roundworm, photographed through a microscope and enlarged about x 70.

large numbers. Marine nematode parasites are relatively harmless to humans but, on land, species such as the eelworm infest cultivated plants, while in the tropics man himself suffers desperately from roundworms which can cause river blindness, elephantiasis and several other severe diseases.

Although different species vary in length from 0,2 mm to over 600 mm, all nematodes have a remarkably consistent body form, which makes it impossible for anyone but the expert taxonomist to identify one species from another. The main reason for this uniformity is that roundworms are unique in maintaining a high pressure of about 1,1 to 1,3 atmospheres in the internal body-space or pseudocoel. This factor dominates and restricts the architecture of the body. It accounts for the fact that all roundworms are shaped like long, very thin, tightly-blown balloons and are circular in cross-section (Fig. 222). It explains the worms' unorthodox muscular system, which consists solely of longitudinal muscles broken into two dorsal and two ventral blocks. Contraction of either block will bend the animal up or down, but after the muscles relax, the high body-pressure will snap the animal back into its original position: rather like a full balloon which is bent over and then released. It is thus unnecessary to have circular muscles to oppose the longitudinal muscles. As a result of this muscular arrangement, nematodes move in a characteristic manner – a dorso-ventral snake-like wriggling that throws the body into a series of S-bends (Fig. 223). For this action to move the animal forwards, the body must be thrust

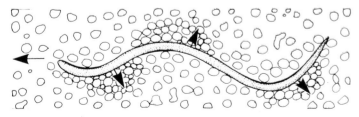

Fig. 223 Roundworms locomote through wet sand or mud by pushing sideways against the sand in a series of S-bends.

sideways against something firm, and on a slippery surface nematodes simply writhe up and down without making any progress. Snakes have much the same problem, prompting the following erudite exposition from the well-known snake expert, Sirion Robertson:

> The Mamba can't travel
> On slippery gravel,
> And makes an ass
> Of itself on glass.
> To achieve forward propulsion
> From a sigmoid convulsion,
> It needs lateral reaction
> For complete satisfaction.

While roundworms need 'lateral reaction' to be able to move, they also require a medium fluid enough not to prevent forward movement. This is probably why they are so successful as gut parasites and in damp sandy or muddy sediments, and also why they prefer sediments which are firm and yet sufficiently fluid to allow locomotion.

To maintain a high pressure in the body cavity, the outside of the body is covered with a cuticle within which bands of inelastic fibres spiral in opposite directions up the body, like a lattice. Since these fibres cannot stretch, the body can only change shape if this lattice is folded or expanded (like a clothes-horse).

The reproductive organs are long and tubular and have thick walls, presumably to prevent their collapse under the high body-pressure. The male bears spicules with which he grips the female while sperm is being transferred. Fertilized eggs are covered with a tough protective cuticle and are released from the female. They hatch into miniature roundworms very like the adults in appearance. A unique feature of their development is that the worms hatch with a finite number of cells, and grow by enlarging the cells rather than by the usual process of cell division and multiplication.

The gut has had to be specially modified to handle the high body-pressure. A muscular pharynx is essential to pump in food against the body pressure, while a circular sphincter muscle tightly closes the anus and only relaxes during defaecation. Without this muscle, food would be squirted out as fast as it entered the gut. The diet is limited to liquids (in parasitic or detritus-feeding species) or to small prey such as bacteria or protozoans that can be sucked up.

Quite obviously, the high body-pressure inside the body cavity is a key feature and dictates much of the body structure, the method of feeding, locomotion and even the type of environment in which roundworms are likely to be successful.

SIPUNCULIDA:
Peanut worms

Peanut worms are so-called because when they are fully contracted they look remarkably like peanuts. Their most characteristic feature is the enormously extensible front part of the body (the introvert) which can be shot out or rolled back into the body with equal facility. To force out the introvert, the muscles in the body wall squeeze the body cavity, exerting a pressure. Withdrawal is brought about by four massive retractor muscles that run from the head through the body cavity to the hind part of the body (Fig. 224).

The body cavity in peanut worms is a true coelom (the origin and significance of which is discussed in the following chapter), but peanut worms are unusual in that the coelom is not divided into compartments but forms a single continuous cavity, perhaps to allow the in-and-out movement of the introvert.

The introvert is used for a somewhat tedious and inefficient form of locomotion. First it is extended, then its tip swells to provide a grip on the substratum, and finally the body is drawn up behind as it shortens. Since this is rather clumsy, it is not surprising that most sipunculids move little and are usually found wedged under stones.

The mouth, at the tip of the introvert, is surrounded by a frill of tentacles which collect detritus. The gut has had to be adapted to cater for the extraordinary extension and contraction of the introvert. A normal gut would be alternatively stretched to the limit or concertinaed by the action of the introvert, but in the case of the sipunculids it is coiled so that it can unravel or coil up as needs be. In addition, the anus is not situated in the usual posterior position, but is placed halfway along the body so that the coils of the gut lie in a U-shape that can be straightened when the introvert is thrust out, without stretching the gut itself (Fig. 224B).

Fig. 225 A group of peanut worms, *Golfingia capensis*. Some of the worms are contracted, others have protruded their introverts (x 1).

Since the body cavity is one continuous bag, there is need for only one pair of excretory organs (nephridia) to rid the coelomic fluid of waste products. The nervous system is simple, with a small brain and a pair of long nerves running back to the muscles of the body (Fig. 224B).

The sipunculids seem quite different from other worm-like creatures, yet their life-cycle is so similar to that of the segmented worms (Chapter 12), that the two groups must be related.

The commonest southern African species is *Golfingia capensis* (Fig. 225), recognised by its smooth body surface. This worm is usually found in clusters, for it aggregates under stones on rocky shores, particularly where gravel accumulates. Various species of *Phascolosoma* occur in a similar habitat but can be distinguished by the tiny cone-like papillae that cover their bodies. *Siphonosoma* species also have papillae on their bodies, but they are much larger animals, reaching a length of 60 mm, and are found only in the muddy sands of estuaries and lagoons.

ECHIURIDA:
Tongue worms

The echiurids are common in many southern African estuaries and lagoons, burrowing through the mud and quite often being found deep within the sediments. They are most closely related to the peanut worms, also having a sac-like body with a single large body cavity, but where the peanut worm has an introvert, the head of a tongue worm is distinctively expanded into a hood-like proboscis that spreads out to collect detritus. Just behind the mouth is a characteristic pair of hooks (Fig. 226).

The gut coils from the mouth to a posterior anus where it is joined by two glands which seem to have an excretory function. As in the peanut worms, because the body cavity is continuous, there is but a single pair of excretory nephridia to process all the wastes accumulating in the coelom. These nephridia also serve to release the gametes into the water. Fertilized eggs develop into top-shaped swimming

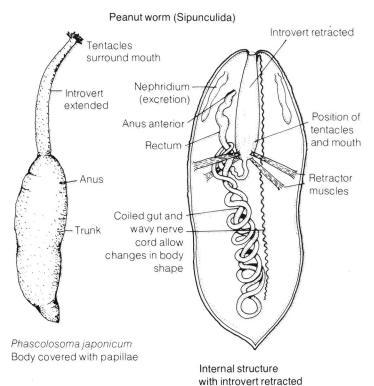

Peanut worm (Sipunculida)

Tentacles surround mouth

Introvert retracted

Introvert extended

Nephridium (excretion)

Anus anterior

Rectum

Anus

Position of tentacles and mouth

Retractor muscles

Trunk

Coiled gut and wavy nerve cord allow changes in body shape

Phascolosoma japonicum Body covered with papillae

Internal structure with introvert retracted

Fig. 224 A. The peanut worm *Phascolosoma japonicum*. B. Dissection of a peanut worm showing how the gut is modified to allow the introvert to be extended or contracted.

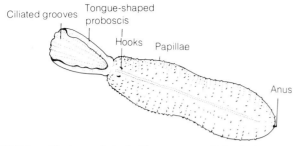

Fig. 226 External features of a typical tongue-worm, *Ochaetostoma capense*.

larvae known as trochophores. These are remarkably like the larvae of polychaetes for, as they develop, their bodies divide up into segments. Only when the larvae metamorphose into adults do these segments disappear, leaving the adult with a single undivided body cavity. The life-cycle is thus of great interest in linking these animals to the phylum Annelida (the segmented worms) since their

development hints that the echiurids may once have been segmented, but have lost their segmentation in the course of evolution.

Two common species are found in southern African estuaries. *Ochaetostoma capense* occurs on the west and south coasts and is recognised by its opaque body wall which is covered with numerous papillae. *Ochaetostoma formulosum* is an east coast species with an almost transparent body wall through which the gut can be seen and which is dotted with only a few isolated papillae.

REFERENCES

Scientific references
Branch, G. M. 1975. The ecology of *Patella* from the Cape Peninsula, South Africa: v. Commensalism. *Zoologica Africana,* Vol. 10 (2): 133-162.
Wesenberg-Lund, E. 1963. South African sipunculids and echiuroids from coastal waters. *Videnskabelige Meddelelser fra Dansk naturhistorisk Forening,* Vol. 126: 101-146.

12.ANNELIDA SEGMENTED WORMS

All segmented worms are grouped together in the phylum Annelida. Like most other soft-bodied creatures, these worms use their fluid-filled body cavities as a hydrostatic skeleton against which the muscles of the body wall act. The principles of such fluid skeletons have already been outlined in Chapter 9, but their unique development in the annelids will be discussed later in this chapter.

The phylum Annelida is divided into three major classes. Earthworms fall into the class Oligochaeta, but there are so few marine species that they are not considered any further in this book. The class Hirudinea contains the leeches; and the class Polychaeta includes the bulk of marine worms, characterised by having numerous bristle-like chaetae which give the group its name.

CLASS HIRUDINEA
The Leeches
Most marine leeches are parasitic, and use their characteristic anterior and posterior suckers to attach to the outer surfaces of fish and other creatures, either sucking their host's blood or scraping at its flesh. Leeches move by a characteristic looping action, using their two suckers alternately.

All leeches are hermaphroditic, each individual having

a complex double set of male and female reproductive organs. Hermaphroditism is an advantage in a slow-moving beast such as a leech, for it ensures that every time another individual is encountered, it is possible to mate with it. Many leeches practise internal fertilisation by 'hypodermic impregnation', the penis being violently thrust through the body wall of the partner to inject the sperm. Fertilised eggs are packed into mucous cocoons and are then abandoned to eventually hatch as miniature leeches.

Of the local species, *Branchellion* is commonly found attached to skates and rays and is recognised by the flap-like gills that project from the sides of each segment. *Pontobdella* (Fig. 227) is a free-living species that preys on small Crustacea. Most divers are familiar with a third species, still only tentatively identified as *Helobdella*, which is very common on the rock lobster *Jasus lalandii*, and found crawling all over the soft underbelly of its tail.

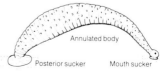

Fig. 227 The leech *Pontobdella*.

CLASS POLYCHAETA

The Class Polychaeta is one of the most important groups of marine animals and contains over four thousand species. Polychaetes are extremely varied in structure but most of them have soft lobe-like appendages (parapodia) projecting from the sides of each segment and carrying long bristles or chaetae. These parapodia are used almost like legs, pushing against the substratum to pole the animal along.

Reproduction and development

Polychaetes usually practise external fertilisation, sperm and eggs being shed by the breeding polychaetes into the water. After fertilisation, each egg develops into a top-shaped larva, the trochophore (Fig. 228A), which swims around in the water where it begins its transformation into a juvenile worm. This transformation begins with the formation of segments at the posterior end, after which parapodia and chaetae gradually form on the sides of each segment (Fig 228B). Eventually the swimming larva settles on a suitable substratum and completes its metamorphosis there.

During the development of the larva, we can trace the origin of the coelom or body cavity that will eventually form the essential hydrostatic skeleton of the adult. From an early stage the larva has three layers of tissues: an outer skin-like ectoderm, an inner gastric endoderm, and a central layer or mesoderm (Fig. 228D). As the larva begins to bud off segments, two blocks of mesoderm are cut off in each segment and a cavity is formed within each block (Fig. 228E). It is this cavity which expands to form the coelom of the adult (Fig. 228F).

There are two reasons why this whole process is of the greatest significance. Firstly, the formation of a fluid-filled cavity (coelom) leads to the most efficient hydrostatic skeleton so far developed in the animal kingdom. Secondly, the innermost portion of the mesoderm now comes to surround the gut, giving rise to independent muscles which are able to control the action of the gut (Fig. 228F). Segmentation of the body has been a further evolutionary breakthrough for the annelids; it allows the individual segments to function as separate hydrostatic units. This means that when the muscles are at work changing the shape of a particular part of the body, the muscular forces can be localised and not dissipated throughout the body.

The possession of a segmented coelom allows the annelids much more powerful and controlled muscular activity. For this reason they are much more efficient at burrowing or swimming than most of the animals examined in the previous chapters.

On the other hand, because the body is divided up into segments, it has been necessary to develop a complete set of organs for each segment (Fig. 229). Thus in the primitive annelids there is a pair of nerve ganglia to control the muscles of each segment, a pair of excretory ducts (nephridia) and a pair of reproductive organs (gonads).

External fertilisation is always a risk, and vast quantities of eggs and sperm need to be produced to allow for the

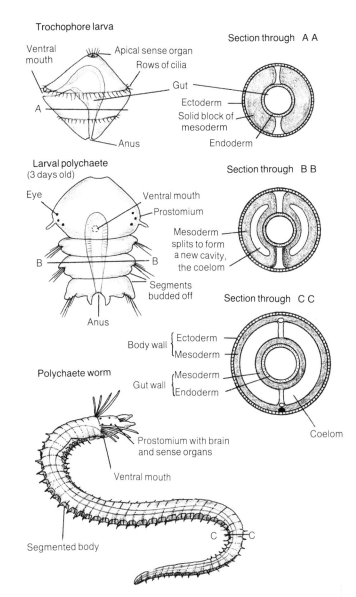

Fig. 228 A - C: The larval development and metamorphosis of a polychaete worm. D - F: The formation of the coelomic body cavity, as seen by cutting transverse sections through the developmental stages shown in A - C.

inevitable wastage. The entire body cavity can become jam-packed with gametes, and in some species the only way to release the eggs or sperm is to rupture the body wall, so that the worm subsequently dies. Perhaps to overcome this sacrifice, one family of polychaetes, the Syllidae, undergoes asexual 'budding' – dividing the body into a posterior individual that becomes sexually mature while the original front end remains asexual and is capable of budding off other individuals later. Often chains of tiny worms can be created in the process as worm after worm is budded off (Fig. 230A).

To reduce the wastage of eggs and sperm, polychaetes synchronise their breeding season, so that an entire population reaches a reproductive peak at the same time. Some species release hormones (gamones) from their gametes which stimulate the opposite sex to spawn. Thus if one female releases her eggs, the gamones from these will

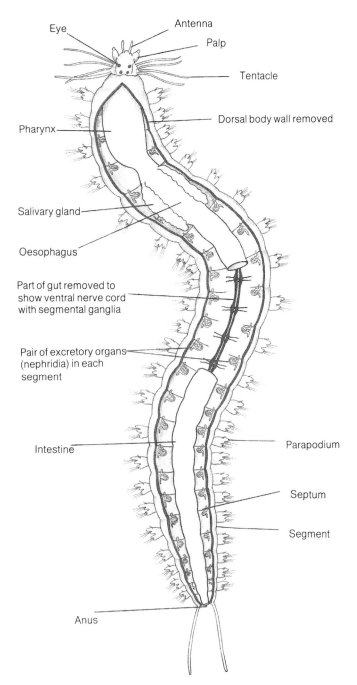

Fig. 229 A partially dissected polychaete worm, revealing the segmented body and the repetitive arrangement of organs within the segments.

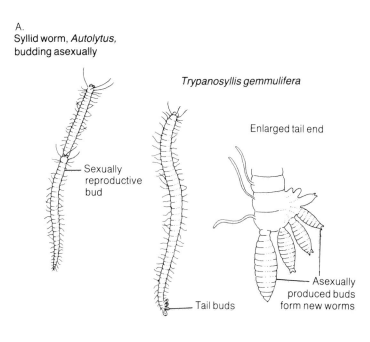

A.
Syllid worm, *Autolytus,* budding asexually

Trypanosyllis gemmulifera

Enlarged tail end

Sexually reproductive bud

Tail buds

Asexually produced buds form new worms

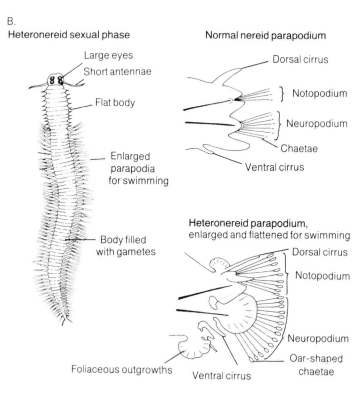

B.
Heteronereid sexual phase

Large eyes
Short antennae

Flat body

Enlarged parapodia for swimming

Body filled with gametes

Foliaceous outgrowths

Normal nereid parapodium

Dorsal cirrus

Notopodium

Neuropodium

Chaetae

Ventral cirrus

Heteronereid parapodium, enlarged and flattened for swimming

Dorsal cirrus

Notopodium

Neuropodium

Oar-shaped chaetae

Ventral cirrus

Fig. 230 A. Various methods of 'budding' that take place in syllid worms. B. A sexually mature 'heteronereid' worm, with eyes and parapodia enlarged to aid swarming. On the right the detailed structure of a heteronereid's parapodium is compared with that of a normal worm.

stimulate males; while their sperm will in turn trigger off more females, which induce more males to spawn – and so before long the whole population will with gay abandon be showering the sea with gametes. With unintended humour scientists call this process 'hysterical spawning'. One of the syllid worms, *Odontosyllis,* has luminous eggs which also attract and stimulate males, swarms of spawning females sometimes presenting a vivid spectacle in tropical waters.

Many species, in a further attempt to synchronise spawning, form swarms during the breeding period, rising from their normal bottom-dwelling habit and swimming up into the water in dense clouds to release their gametes.

Often their bodies are specially modified to aid swarming, the parapodia being enlarged and the chaetae becoming flattened to act as paddles, improving the animals' ability to swim. The eyes are enlarged to allow detection of other worms while the palps on the head are reduced in size to streamline the body. These modified individuals are known as 'heteronereids' (Fig. 230B).

One of the most famous worms, the palolo worm *(Eunice*

fucata), swarms once a year, timed to coincide precisely with the third quarter of the moon in July, when millions of the worms flood to the surface of the water. So regular and well-known is this phenomenon that Pacific Islanders lay nets at this time of the year to harvest the worms as a food source.

Classification of polychaetes

The polychaetes are broadly divided into two groups: Errantia, including those that are active and mobile and thus have well developed parapodia, sensory tentacles and palps on the head and, usually, a large pair of jaws; and Sedentaria, containing species that are immobile and usually tube dwelling.

Common species of Errantia

The families and species most likely to be encountered in southern African waters are summarised in Fig. 232 and Plates 48–51.

The family Nereidae (Figs. 231 & 232K-Q) is typical of the errant polychaetes, having a uniform body that is long and cylindrical, with obvious bi-lobed parapodia projecting laterally, each armed with two tufts of stout chaetae. The head bears a pair of broad palps used to detect chemicals, and a series of sensory tentacles. As in all annelids, the gut extends the length of the body from the mouth to an anus situated on the last segment. This permits one-way traffic of food through the gut and different regions have as a result become specialised for different functions. The front end of the gut forms an eversible proboscis armed with a pair of stout jaws and can be shot out to capture prey. It is also dotted with a variable number of tiny teeth called paragnathes. These paragnathes are in fact the most useful feature on which we can base the identification of different species of nereids (see Fig. 232M-Q). They are not always easy to see, for unless the animal dies with its pharynx everted, it must be dissected to reveal the paragnathes. Alternatively, freshly dead animals may be gently squeezed, stroking from the tail towards the head, and this pressure is often enough to evert the proboscis.

The family Eunicidae (Fig. 232H-J) contains very large worms which may reach 60 cm in length. All eunicids have two pairs of large serrated jaws that can inflict a painful bite. The commonest species belong to two genera. *Marphysa* species have five antennae on the head (Fig. 232J) while *Eunice* species, in addition to these five antennae, have a tiny pair of tentacles (Fig. 232I). *Eunice aphroditois* (Fig. 232H, Plate 48) is a spectacular creature with a dull purple-brown body shot with iridescent glints, and can be distinguished by its smooth antennae; *Eunice antennata* (Plate 51) has characteristic beaded antennae.

Almost all members of the family Syllidae are tiny worms about 10 mm in length, but they are so common that they cannot be ignored. Most of them are recognised by the long beaded filaments (cirri) that project from the top of their parapodia (Fig. 232D, E). One of the more spectacular species, the hair-curler worm *Amblyosyllis formosa*, has long cirri normally held tightly curled up but which may

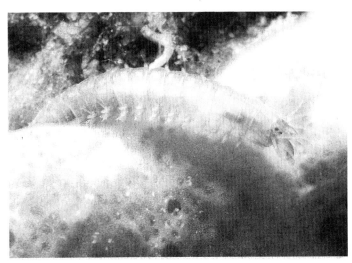

Fig. 231 *Pseudonereis variegata,* one of the commonest nereid worms found on rocky shores (x 1).

be shot out, like an uncurling spring, if the animal is threatened (Plate 50).

The scale worms, family Aphroditidae, are amongst the most distinctive polychaetes, having a series of plate-like scales that cover the dorsal surface (Fig. 232A-C). The function of these scales is unknown, but they are readily shed if the worms are attacked by a predator. The number and size of the scales are most useful in identifying the various species. *Lepidonotus semitectus* (Fig. 232A, B), the common Cape scale worm, has 12 pairs of scales that cover the whole body and each is dotted with tiny cone-like tubercles. *Lepidonotus durbanensis*, its Natal counterpart, is very similar except that the tubercles on the scales are like tiny spheres. *Antinoe lactea* (Fig. 233) lives commensally in the tubes of the sand prawn *Callianassa* and has 15 pairs of milky-white scales, again covering the whole body. *Polynoe scolopendrina* is a longer, thinner worm with grey scales that cover only the front end of the body; *P. erythrotaenia* is almost identical, but is recognised by the colour of its scales which are half black and half white (Fig. 232C).

The family Amphinomidae contains species with a peculiar sensory organ, known as the caruncle, that lies on the dorsal surface immediately behind the head (Fig. 232F, G). *Euphrosine capensis* is a very common example, found sticking to the under-surface of boulders, but it is often overlooked because it is slow-moving and a dull orange colour. Row upon row of short erect spines cover its dorsal surface. Another species, *Eurythoe complanata*, is known as the fireworm (Plate 49), for its bristles are long and sharp and fiercely irritant. The easiest way to remove these bristles from a wound is gently to apply sticky tape or masking tape and then peel it away.

Glycera tridactyla, a very common representative of the family Glyceridae (Fig. 232R, S), is an aggressive predator found in sandy sediments. Its very long proboscis is tipped with four characteristic jaws, each associated with a large poison gland.

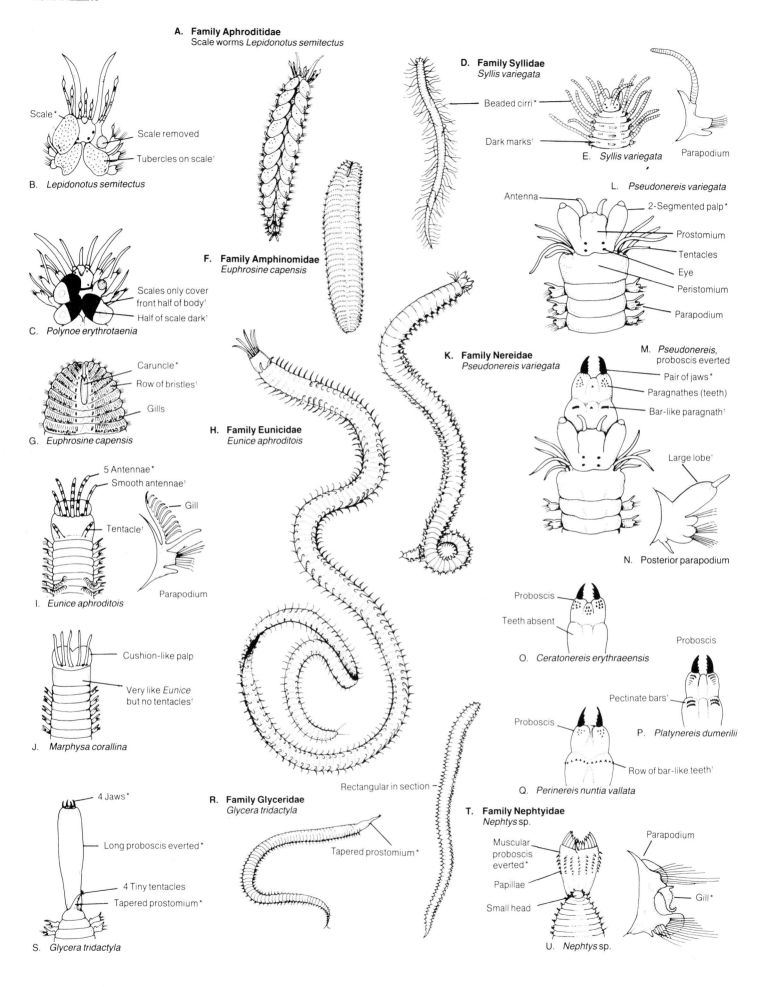

A. Family Aphroditidae
Scale worms *Lepidonotus semitectus*

Scale*
Scale removed
Tubercles on scale†

B. *Lepidonotus semitectus*

Scales only cover front half of body†
Half of scale dark†

C. *Polynoe erythrotaenia*

Caruncle*
Row of bristles†
Gills

G. *Euphrosine capensis*

5 Antennae*
Smooth antennae†
Gill
Tentacle†
Parapodium

I. *Eunice aphroditois*

Cushion-like palp
Very like *Eunice* but no tentacles†

J. *Marphysa corallina*

4 Jaws*
Long proboscis everted*
4 Tiny tentacles
Tapered prostomium*

S. *Glycera tridactyla*

F. Family Amphinomidae
Euphrosine capensis

H. Family Eunicidae
Eunice aphroditois

D. Family Syllidae
Syllis variegata

Beaded cirri*
Dark marks†

E. *Syllis variegata*
Parapodium

L. *Pseudonereis variegata*

Antenna
2-Segmented palp*
Prostomium
Tentacles
Eye
Peristomium
Parapodium

K. Family Nereidae
Pseudonereis variegata

M. *Pseudonereis*, proboscis everted
Pair of jaws*
Paragnathes (teeth)
Bar-like paragnath†

Large lobe†

N. Posterior parapodium

Proboscis
Teeth absent

O. *Ceratonereis erythraeensis*

Proboscis

Pectinate bars†

P. *Platynereis dumerilii*

Proboscis
Row of bar-like teeth†

Q. *Perinereis nuntia vallata*

Rectangular in section

R. Family Glyceridae
Glycera tridactyla

Tapered prostomium*

T. Family Nephtyidae
Nephtys sp.

Muscular proboscis everted*
Papillae
Small head
Parapodium
Gill*

U. *Nephtys* sp.

◀ Fig. 232 *Errant polychaetes:* Typically active, with uniformly segmented bodies, large parapodia, internal jaws and well-developed sensory organs on the head. Representatives of the common families are shown life-size in the centre (except for *Syllis,* shown x 4), while on the left and right details of the common species are given. Features diagnostic of each family are marked*, while those that allow identification of individual species are marked†.

Fig. 233 The milky scale-worm, *Antinoe lactea,* which lives commensally with the sand prawn (x 2).

Common Sedentaria and their adaptations

The Sedentaria include a wide range of worms, the most common of which are identified in Figs. 234–241 and Plates 43–47.

Many of these species produce tubes, which may be manufactured from mucus, mud, sand, lime or by binding together pieces of algae. Since these worms spend their entire adult life in these tubes, they must face various difficulties, in particular, how to obtain food, how to respire within the confines of the tube, and how to get rid of waste products in such a way that the tube is not continually fouled. It is the solutions to these issues that make the sedentary polychaetes amongst the most fascinating of worms.

Some of the Sedentaria are not confined to tubes but burrow in sand or mud. As a result, their body structure is not highly specialised. An example is the bloodworm, *Arenicola loveni* (Fig. 235), which is discussed in more detail in Chapter 5. The bamboo worms (family Maldanidae) make fragile sandy tubes in estuarine sand banks, and are recognised by their exceptionally long segments (Fig. 234D). In the family Spionidae (Fig. 234C) the head is more specialised, bearing two very long food-gathering tentacles.

The family Cirratulidae includes worms such as *Cirriformia capensis* (Fig. 234A), a golden-orange worm

Fig. 234 *Sedentary polychaetes:* Normally inactive, tube dwelling, with ▶ small parapodia; head often modified with elaborate appendages for particle feeding, jaws lacking. Typical representatives of the common families are shown here and in Figs. 235-241.

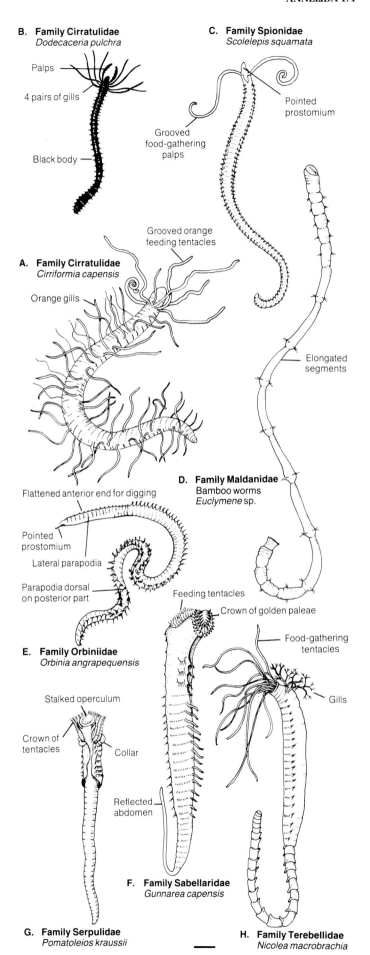

B. Family Cirratulidae
Dodecaceria pulchra
Palps
4 pairs of gills
Black body

C. Family Spionidae
Scolelepis squamata
Pointed prostomium
Grooved food-gathering palps
Elongated segments

A. Family Cirratulidae
Cirriformia capensis
Grooved orange feeding tentacles
Orange gills

D. Family Maldanidae
Bamboo worms
Euclymene sp.

Flattened anterior end for digging
Pointed prostomium
Lateral parapodia
Parapodia dorsal on posterior part

E. Family Orbiniidae
Orbinia angrapequensis

Feeding tentacles
Crown of golden paleae

F. Family Sabellariidae
Gunnarea capensis

Stalked operculum
Crown of tentacles
Collar
Reflected abdomen

Food-gathering tentacles
Gills

G. Family Serpulidae
Pomatoleios kraussii

H. Family Terebellidae
Nicolea macrobrachia

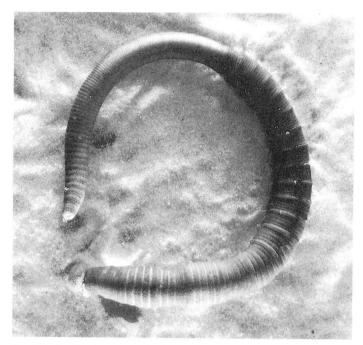

Fig. 235 The bloodworm, *Arenicola loveni* (x ¼).

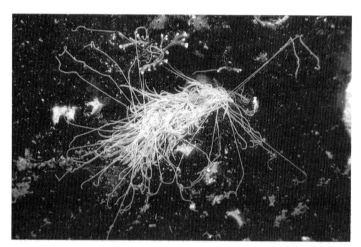

Fig. 236 The golden-orange tentacles of *Cirriformia capensis* are often seen protruding from crevices, but the body remains hidden (x 1).

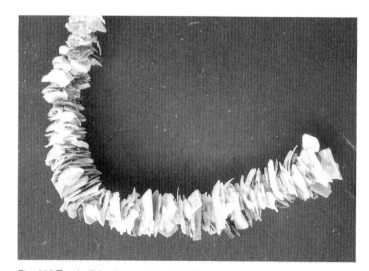

Fig. 238 Terebellids glue sand and shell fragments together to manufacture their tubes (x 1).

Fig. 237 All terebellids have long feeding tentacles, but in this species they are exceptionally long, reaching a metre in length, and lie like tangled white threads of string over the surface of the rock.

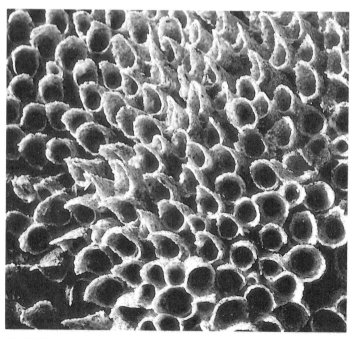

Fig. 239 Cape reef-worms, *Gunnarea capensis,* cement sand grains into massive reefs of tubes (x 1).

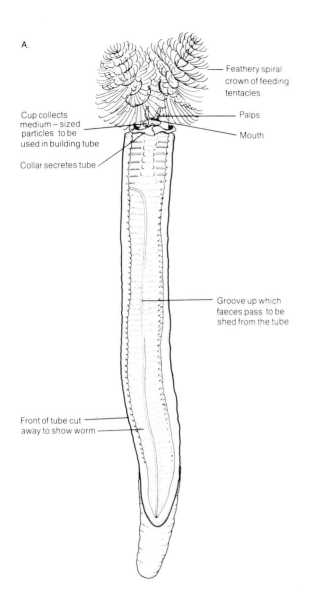

A.

Feathery spiral crown of feeding tentacles

Palps

Mouth

Cup collects medium – sized particles to be used in building tube

Collar secretes tube

Groove up which faeces pass to be shed from the tube

Front of tube cut away to show worm

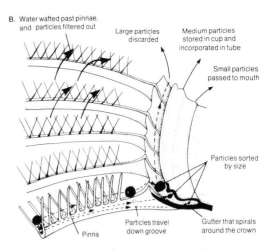

B. Water wafted past pinnae, and particles filtered out

Large particles discarded

Medium particles stored in cup and incorporated in tube

Small particles passed to mouth

Particles sorted by size

Particles travel down groove

Gutter that spirals around the crown

Pinna

Fig. 240 The fan-worm *Sabellastarte longa* (A) lives in a parchment-like tube. Its crown of tentacles, a portion of which is shown in detail (B), traps particles and carries them to the gutter that spirals down the centre of the crown to the head. In the gutter, particles are sorted by size (see text for details).

which has extremely long filamentous cirri. While the worm remains buried in gravel or sand, these long cirri extend out and creep over the surface of the sediment, allowing extraction of oxygen from the water (Fig. 236). *Cirriformia* has an additional series of softer tentacles that arise from the head and gather food. Another member of this family is the much smaller pitch-black *Dodecaceria pulchra* (Fig. 234B) which always lives in large groups and drills tunnels through the encrusting white alga *Lithothamnion*. When the worms extend their tentacled heads they give the appearance of tiny black stars studding the *Lithothamnion*.

In the family Terebellidae (Fig. 234H), the food-gathering tentacles are concentrated on the anterior part of the body and may be exceptionally long. One very well known species, common at Reunion Rocks near Durban, has tentacles over a metre in length (Fig. 237). These appendages are spread-eagled over the substratum and are shaped like long thin gutters, so that any food falling on them can be driven by cilia along the groove to the mouth. If a particle is too large for the cilia to handle in this manner, the whole tentacle can curl around it and with-

draw to the mouth. In addition to these tentacles, Terebellidae have bright red gills that hang from the head, extending out of the worm's tube, which is formed by cementing pieces of sand together (Fig. 238).

One of the most characteristic west coast polychaetes is the Cape reef worm, *Gunnarea capensis* (family Sabellaridae), which forms massive banks of sandy tubes, so solidly cemented together that a man can stand on them (Fig. 239). *Gunnarea* has a neatly arranged double row of shining gold chaetae (called paleae) at its anterior end, and these form a horny plug to the tube. An effective barrier to most predators, this structure is readily breached by the snail *Argobuccinum pustulosum* which pours sulphuric acid down the tube, dissolving both sandy tube and the paleae (Fig. 42). Like the other sedentary species, *Gunnarea* has simple tentacles that hang from the tube and gather food particles as well as catching the sand-grains from which the tube is constructed. To avoid fouling its tube, *Gunnarea* has an elongation at the end of its body, which is bent back on itself (Fig. 234F) and which can stretch forwards to the mouth of the tube where faeces can safely be shed.

Gunnarea extends round the coast to Natal, but it is never abundant on the warmer coasts. Further north it is replaced by another member of the same family, the Natal reef worm (*Idanthyrsus pennatus*) which is distinguished by having feather-like chaetae on its head.

The fan-worms, such as *Sabellastarte longa* (family Sabellidae), are amongst the best known and most beautiful of worms, for they have a striking double crown of spirally-arranged feathery filaments on the head (Plate 44, Fig. 240A). Since the colour of the crown can be white, purple, pink or brown, a group of these dainty creatures is a photographer's delight – although at the slightest disturbance they shoot back into the protection of their leathery tubes. Apart from their beauty, the feathery crowns fulfil a double purpose: they extract oxygen from the water, and

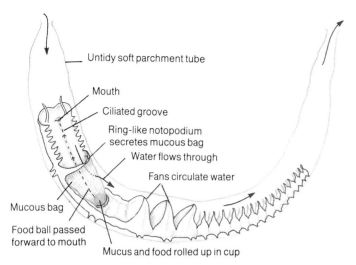

Fig. 241 One of the most specialised of all worms, *Chaetopterus,* spins a mucous web which it uses to sieve particles from water circulated through the tube.

they capture particles of food. Each filament that radiates out from the crown carries tiny 'leaflets' or pinnules along its length, and flickering cilia on these pinnules drive particles into a gutter that runs along the filament before linking up with a similar groove that spirals down the crown to the mouth (Fig. 240B). The extraordinary thing about this arrangement is that the gutter and spiral groove are able to separate particles on the basis of size. Smaller particles fall deepest into the groove and are driven by cilia to the mouth (Fig. 240B). In this way the smallest, and hence most digestible, fragments are singled out for consumption. Medium-sized particles are wedged halfway down the gutter and are transported to a special sac which stores them. At a later stage they are mixed with mucus to produce the leathery tube so typical of the whole family. Finally, large particles balance on the top of the groove and are led to two long palps which discard these apparently useless particles outside the tube.

Members of another family, Serpulidae, have similar feathery crowns of feeding tentacles, but they can be distinguished by their hard lime tubes and, in most cases, by a stalked operculum that blocks off the tube when the animal retreats (Fig. 234G). *Protula bispiralis* (Plate 45) is a particularly striking example, with its vivid red crown. A smaller species, *Serpula vermicularis* (Plate 46), is of interest because it has a variety of colour forms, and often tones in with background animals, particularly if they are poisonous or unpleasant to eat. Thus, by mimicking inedible species, the worm may gain some protection from its predators. Plate 46 shows one example of this: the worm could easily pass for one of the purple soft corals that surround it.

The genus *Spirorbis* also belongs to the family Serpulidae and includes several species that are minute but extremely abundant. Practically every stone, most large shells, and even algae will have a sprinkling of their tightly-coiled tubes (Plate 128). The different species are

difficult to tell apart, but are very particular about the habitats they choose. Some occur only on particular algae; others are sun-lovers and grow on top of rocks, while yet others seek dark crevices. A single mussel-shell may support as many as three different species of *Spirorbis:* one near the outer edge, another buried underneath the shell, and a third sandwiched between them. This sharing of space is an example of an important ecological principle: closely-related species may be very selective about their different habitats in order to reduce competition between the species.

Pomatoleios kraussii (Plate 43, Fig. 234G) forms dense colonies so that its blue calcium carbonate tubes intermesh into coral-like masses. Like all other serpulids, *Pomatoleios* filters particles from the water, using its feathery crown. Because it is so common on the south and east coasts it is one of the organisms that dictate what sort of community develops on rocky shores: for its filtering activities prevent algal spores from settling wherever it grows.

Filograna implexa is one of the daintiest of the serpulids (Plate 47), forming fragile intertwining masses of tubes from which the bright red tentacular crowns project. Another species which builds colonies of interwoven tubes is *Ficopomatus enigmatica,* which is restricted entirely to estuaries and commonly encrusts bridge pylons. Its tubes are distinctively jointed like bamboo.

The final family dealt with here, Chaetopteridae, contains one species that is probably the most remarkably specialised of all the sedentary polychaetes: *Chaetopterus varieopedatus.* Its body is beautifully designed to capture particles from the water that it circulates through its parchment-like tube (Fig. 241). Near the middle of its body three parapodia have become fused to form paddle-like structures which pump water through the tube. In front of these pumping structures there is a pair of horn-like appendages that loop over the animal's back, forming a ring. These 'wings' produce a sheet of mucus that is billowed out into a net by the pressure of the circulating water, and sieves particles from the water. The tip of this mucous net is held in position by a cup-shaped organ which continually rolls up the end of the net as fast as it is produced by the 'wings'. Periodically it cuts off portions of the mucous net which are then rolled forwards along a dorsal groove to the mouth, where they are ingested along with the captured particles.

It is difficult not to admire the elaborate and efficient mechanisms the sedentary polychaetes have evolved to capture food, thus overcoming their main limitation – that they cannot actively seek out food but must bring it to themselves.

REFERENCES

Popular articles and books
Dales, R. P. 1963. *Annelids.* Hutchinson University Library, London, 200 pp.

Identification guides
Day, J. H. 1967. *A Monograph of the Polychaeta of Southern Africa.* British Museum (Natural History), London. 878 pp.

13.CRUSTACEA CRABS AND THEIR KIN

Of the many advances that have taken place in different groups of animals, one of the most significant has been the evolution of a hard skeleton. Only the vertebrates, with their internal bony skeleton and the arthropods (including the Crustacea, insects, spiders and so on), which have an external horny skeleton encasing the body, have achieved this grade of sophistication. A hard skeleton allows several developments which are impossible with a fluid hydrostatic skeleton. In the first place, the skeleton provides leverage for muscles so that they can act far more quickly, powerfully and efficiently. It is no coincidence that all flying animals have hard skeletons, that the insects make up more than three-quarters of all known species and that the Crustacea are amongst the most important of marine animals.

The arthropod exoskeleton must of course be jointed to allow movement, so the body is segmented to allow flexure between one segment and the next and the limbs have joints at which they can be bent. However, since the Crustacea make no use of their body cavity as a fluid skeleton, there is no reason why the body should be internally divided into segments and, in fact, the body space is continuous. For this reason there is no internal repetition of organs as occurs in the segmented worms.

A hard exoskeleton has other advantages. It is a protection against predators and can reduce water-loss. It also makes it easier for different regions of the body to become specialised for particular functions. In the Crustacea, the head serves as a sensory centre bearing two compound eyes and two pairs of antennae, and contains a concentration of nerve cells that forms the cerebral ganglion which is a fairly sophisticated brain. The head is also involved in feeding. The first pair of limbs which it carries are the stout mandibles that crush the food and behind them lie two pairs of maxillae that manipulate the food.

The central portion of the body – the thorax – houses the reproductive, digestive and excretory organs, and gives rise to a series of walking legs (pereiopods). The abdomen usually carries paddle-like swimming appendages. Since the front end of the body does not need to be flexible, it is often consolidated into a single fused unit. This is achieved by an outgrowth of the skeleton (the carapace) which expands backwards from the head to cover portions of the body which thus lose all external signs of segmentation. In some groups of Crustacea practically the whole body is encased by the carapace, but more usually it covers over part or all of the head and thorax, while some groups lack a carapace altogether (see Figs. 242 & 244).

While the exoskeleton is clearly a great asset it carries with it one penalty: a hard external skeleton prevents con-

Fig. 242 A remarkable picture of the rock lobster *Jasus lalandii* in the act of moulting. The old carapace has been fractured and lifted, and the animal is in the process of crawling out of it (x ½).

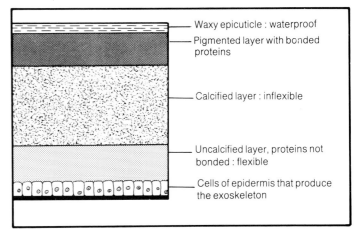

Fig. 243 Diagrammatic representation of the different layers in the crustacean exoskeleton.

tinual growth. As a result the Crustacea must periodically moult, shedding the exoskeleton; then, while the animal is soft and helpless, the body can be expanded rapidly, usually by the uptake of water which 'balloons' the animal, and a new exoskeleton is then deposited over the enlarged animal and later hardens.

To understand the process of moulting, we need first to examine the detailed structure of the skeleton (Fig. 243). Most of it is made up of protein, but by altering the nature of the protein, the animal can change the properties of different layers of the cuticle. The outermost layer, the epicuticle, contains lipoproteins (fat molecules combined with protein) and these provide the crustaceans with a waterproofing, which is particularly important in terrestrial and high-shore species. Even so, the Crustacea are not nearly as efficient at controlling water-loss as the insects.

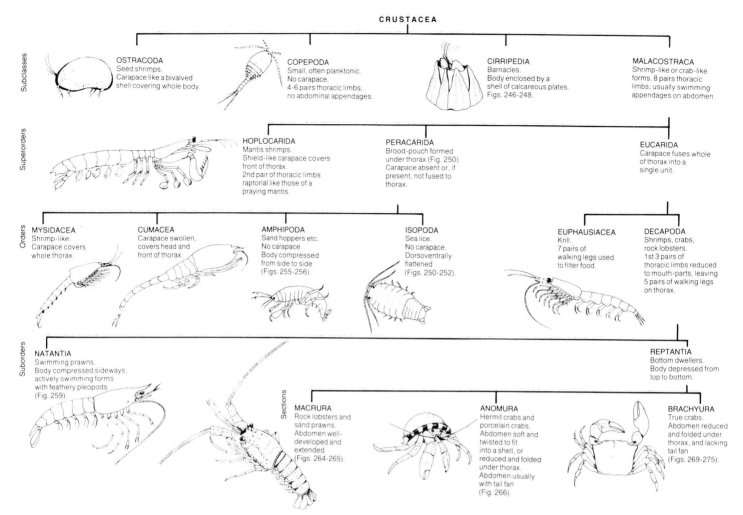

CRUSTACEA

Subclasses

OSTRACODA
Seed shrimps.
Carapace like a bivalved
shell covering whole body.

COPEPODA
Small, often planktonic.
No carapace.
4-6 pairs thoracic limbs,
no abdominal appendages.

CIRRIPEDIA
Barnacles.
Body enclosed by a
shell of calcareous plates.
Figs. 246-248.

MALACOSTRACA
Shrimp-like or crab-like
forms. 8 pairs thoracic
limbs; usually swimming
appendages on abdomen.

Superorders

HOPLOCARIDA
Mantis shrimps.
Shield-like carapace covers
front of thorax.
2nd pair of thoracic limbs
raptorial like those of a
praying mantis.

PERACARIDA
Brood-pouch formed
under thorax (Fig. 250).
Carapace absent or, if
present, not fused to
thorax.

EUCARIDA
Carapace fuses whole
of thorax into a
single unit.

Orders

MYSIDACEA
Shrimp-like.
Carapace covers
whole thorax.

CUMACEA
Carapace swollen,
covers head and
front of thorax.

AMPHIPODA
Sand hoppers etc.
No carapace.
Body compressed
from side to side
(Figs. 255-256).

ISOPODA
Sea lice.
No carapace.
Dorsoventrally
flattened
(Figs. 250-252).

EUPHAUSIACEA
Krill.
7 pairs of
walking legs used
to filter food.

DECAPODA
Shrimps, crabs,
rock lobsters.
1st 3 pairs of
thoracic limbs reduced
to mouth-parts, leaving
5 pairs of walking legs
on thorax.

Suborders

NATANTIA
Swimming prawns.
Body compressed sideways;
actively swimming forms
with feathery pleopods
(Fig. 259).

REPTANTIA
Bottom dwellers.
Body depressed from
top to bottom.

Sections

MACRURA
Rock lobsters and
sand prawns.
Abdomen well-
developed and
extended
(Figs. 264-265).

ANOMURA
Hermit crabs and
porcelain crabs.
Abdomen soft and
twisted to fit
into a shell, or
reduced and folded
under thorax.
Abdomen usually
with tail fan
(Fig. 266).

BRACHYURA
True crabs.
Abdomen reduced
and folded under
thorax, and lacking
tail fan
(Figs. 269-275).

Fig. 244 Classification of the main groups of Crustacea.

Beneath the epicuticle is a broader pigmented layer in which the protein molecules are chemically bonded to one another to strengthen the exoskeleton. The breaking and re-creation of such protein bonds is precisely the process that women rely on when they 'perm' their hair. Below this pigmented layer the protein is saturated with calcium carbonate, and it is this lime that gives the skeleton its rigidity. Finally, the innermost layer consists entirely of loosely arranged proteins that are not bonded to one another, so that this part of the skeleton is flexible. By varying the thickness of these different layers, a crustacean is able to regulate the skeleton so that some parts are rigid while others, such as the joints, may be flexible.

When moulting takes place, the skeleton must be softened to the point that it can be fractured and shed. During moulting it is obviously desirable for as much as possible of the old skeleton to be reabsorbed by the animal, to avoid wastage. Enzymes are therefore released from the skin-like epidermis, which digest the proteins. The breakdown products, including most of the calcium carbonate, can then be taken up by the body. It is this accumulation of lime in the body that taints the flesh of 'soft' rock lobsters. Once softened, the skeleton is fractured along weak planes and the animal crawls out of it (Fig. 242). Cast-off skeletons are

virtually intact and are often washed ashore where they are mistaken for dead animals.

While moulting takes place, a new skeleton is formed beneath the old skeleton, although it is initially soft and floppy, allowing the body to expand. Only later is this new skeleton hardened by the release of enzymes that bond the proteins and by the redeposition of calcium carbonate. Whilst the skeleton is soft, the animal is of course helpless, for it has no skeleton on which the muscles can act. This is why soft rock lobsters are never caught in traps and also why rock lobsters and other crustaceans migrate into sheltered bays before moulting.

Obviously crustaceans must be able to regulate the complex process of moulting. This is achieved by two hormonal glands, unimaginatively described as X and Y glands. The Y glands usually lie at the bases of the antennae and their hormones stimulate moulting. The X glands, which are situated in the eye-stalks, block the action of the Y glands, thus inhibiting moulting. Their secretions also prevent the development of the ovaries in females. A knowledge of these processes can have practical applications. For example, female prawns kept in commercial cultures can be induced to produce eggs at any stage, by optic ablation (which is a polite way of saying the prawns' eyes are cut off to remove the inhibitory effect of the X gland).

KINDS OF CRUSTACEA:
Of all the marine animals, the Crustacea are the most diverse, and in keeping with this they are classified in a more than usually complex manner. Fig. 244 isolates the commoner groups of Crustacea and illustrates their classification and how they are related.

Copepoda:
The copepods rank amongst the smallest and yet the most significant of all crustaceans, for they are extremely abundant and dominate most open-sea planktonic communities. Not only are they abundant, but their combined biomass probably exceeds that of any other animal group. The copepods provide a vital link between the phytoplankton, which they eat, and the higher animals such as the herring, sardine, pilchard and anchovy, as well as larger beasts including basking sharks, whale sharks and some of the great whales themselves – all of which feed directly on copepods. Copepods probably represent the largest stock of animal protein in the world, but because they are so small it is impractical to try to harvest them – let alone try to persuade people to eat them. As a result, this protein only reaches man by way of chickens fed on fishmeal, produced from fish that eat copepods. Because of the large number of steps in this food chain, man eats only about one ten-thousandth of the potential protein provided by the copepods.

Copepods have elongated bodies (Fig. 244) which are very flexible since there is no carapace covering the anterior segments. In planktonic forms, the head bears two very long antennae, the whiplike action of which helps propel the animal. The thoracic appendages are flat and paddle-like and are not only the major organs of locomotion but create vortices of water that pass through the hairy, filtering mouthparts, allowing food particles to be sieved out. Thus swimming is automatically linked with filter-feeding. However, copepods can also seize larger prey and shred it, and this versatility is one of the reasons for their success.

Although the copepods are best known for their abundance in the plankton, a group of them – the Harpacticoidea – are found burrowing in sediments and are often amongst the commonest of the meiofaunal animals living in sandy beaches (see Chapter 3 & Fig. 78).

Cirripedia – the barnacles:
Anyone can be forgiven for asking why the barnacles should be considered Crustacea at all, for with their hard plate-like shells they seem more like molluscs than anything else. It is only in tracing a barnacle's life-cycle that its crustacean affinities become obvious. It begins life as a nauplius larva – a small triangular creature with a characteristic pair of frontal horns and a longer dorsal spine (Fig. 245). The whole body consists essentially of a head, with a single simple eye, two pairs of antennae and a pair of mandibles. At this stage these limbs serve mainly as organs of propulsion, although they are destined to form the mouthparts of the adult animal.

The nauplius larva is soon transformed into a cyprid larva – so named because superficially it looks like one of the ostracods called *Cypris* (Fig. 244). The cyprid is enclosed in a bivalved carapace from which a pair of stubby antennae protrude at the front end while six pairs of thoracic limbs project ventrally and drive the larva through the water (Fig. 245).

When the cyprid is ready to metamorphose into an adult barnacle, it attaches onto the substratum by suctorial pads at the ends of its antennae. Since the adult is sessile, it is critical that the larva selects a suitable site to settle, and it repeatedly tests the substratum before finally doing so. The substratum must receive sufficient light, the correct amount of current, and must be rough enough to ensure that the adult can attach its shell securely. Cyprids are strongly drawn to adults of their own species, being attracted by proteins within the adults' exoskeletons. Despite this attraction, larvae usually space themselves out

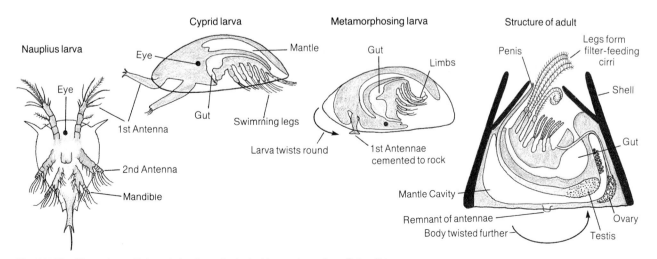

Fig. 245 The life-cycle and internal structure of a typical barnacle such as *Tetraclita*.

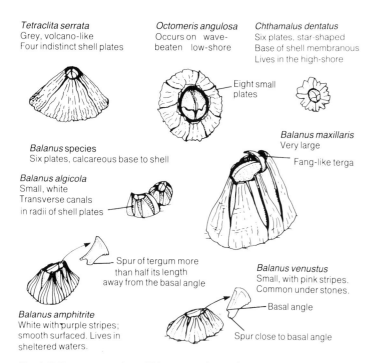

Tetraclita serrata
Grey, volcano-like
Four indistinct shell plates

Octomeris angulosa
Occurs on wave-beaten low-shore

Eight small plates

Chthamalus dentatus
Six plates, star-shaped
Base of shell membranous
Lives in the high-shore

Balanus species
Six plates, calcareous base to shell

Balanus maxillaris
Very large

Fang-like terga

Balanus algicola
Small, white
Transverse canals
in radii of shell plates

Spur of tergum more
than half its length
away from the basal angle

Balanus venustus
Small, with pink stripes.
Common under stones.

Basal angle

Balanus amphitrite
White with purple stripes;
smooth surfaced. Lives in
sheltered waters.

Spur close to basal angle

Fig. 246 Common southern African acorn barnacles.

Fig. 247 The grey volcano barnacle, *Tetraclita serrata*, is one of the dominant mid-shore animals on the south and east coasts, but in Moçambique and northern Natal it is replaced by a very similar but rosy-pink species, *Tetraclita squamosa rufotincta* (x 1).

Fig. 248 Small and often star-shaped, *Chthamalus dentatus* occurs mainly on the high-shore. Here it is being drilled by a whelk, *Nucella dubia*, while one of the empty barnacle shells provides shelter for a second whelk (x2).

from any adults or other settled larvae, thus ensuring there is room for subsequent growth (see Chapter 2). It is the attraction of larvae to remnants of adults that make barnacles such a curse when they attach to ships, for unless the old growth is completely stripped away, new larvae are soon stimulated by the bases of old shells to settle.

Having selected a suitable site, the cyprid literally stands on its head and, pouring cement from special glands inside the antennae, it firmly glues its anterior end to the substratum. The whole body is then twisted around so that the legs project up into the water. The bivalved carapace is shed, leaving a fleshy mantle that deposits the calcareous plates which finally surround the adult body (Fig. 245). A conical series of six or eight plates encase the body leaving an apical opening, which can be blocked off by an operculum of four additional plates if the animal is threatened or exposed to the air at low tide. The internal structure of an adult barnacle is shown in Fig. 245, and the long flexible legs (cirri) are a feature. These cirri can be extended through the apical opening of the shell and are stroked through the water, collecting particles of food on their hairy fringes (Plates 52 & 53).

Barnacles are hermaphroditic, but most species practise cross-fertilization between different individuals. Being sessile, the creatures can only accomplish this if they can reach an adjacent barnacle; hence the need for the extraordinarily long penis which can be three times the length of the animal (Fig. 245). Barnacles store their fertilized eggs in a mantle cavity beneath the body, and early larval development takes place there. In some cases the release of larvae is triggered by a bloom of phytoplankton in the surrounding water, thus ensuring an adequate supply of food for the larvae.

Common species of barnacles
Two groups of barnacle are easily distinguished: acorn barnacles (suborder Balanomorpha) have shells that are cemented onto the substratum, while goose-barnacles (suborder Lepadomorpha) have a fleshy stalk. Only one common goose-barnacle is found in southern Africa. This is *Lepas*, an open-sea creature which attaches itself to any floating object and is frequently found on logs cast ashore (Fig. 144, Plates 52 & 53). The common acorn barnacles, shown in Figs. 47A & 246–248 and Plates 16 & 54, are distinguished largely by the number and structure of their shell plates.

In addition to these species there are two oddities of interest. Some barnacles occur exclusively on whales. Amongst them is a goose-barnacle, *Conchoderma aurita*, which has lost almost all its calcareous plates but has developed two 'ears' that project like siphons from the back of the body. These are actually a device that allows water to flow right through the mantle, so that the barnacle's legs can be held passively in position while the whale provides the necessary water current as it swims along (Fig. 249).

The other unusual species is one that can scarcely be recognized as a barnacle. It is a parasitic beast, *Sacculina* by name, and sac-like in appearance. *Sacculina* has normal

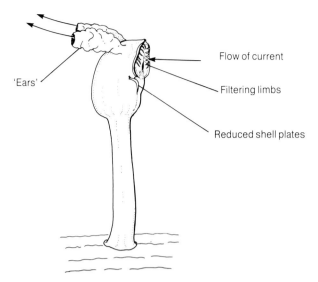

Fig. 249 *Conchoderma aurita*, a goose barnacle that attaches to whales, has evolved two 'ears' that allow currents, set up by the swimming whale, to flow through the barnacle's mantle where it can passively filter food from the water (x 1).

naupliar and cyprid larval stages, but the cyprid cements itself to a crab, and its entire body contents are then poured through the antennal tube to penetrate the crab. Like a giant branching amoeba it ramifies through the crab's tissues, only to emerge again under the crab's abdomen where it forms a bulbous reproductive bag and produces copious quantities of eggs. From this, a root-like anchorage extends into the crab and not only nourishes the parasite's eggs at the cost of the crab but also affects the crab's own sexual status. Male crabs infected by *Sacculina* lose their copulatory organs and develop swollen abdomens like those of females. It seems that the parasite interferes with the androgenic glands (described below, p. 194) which control sexuality in crabs, thus feminising males and causing what is called 'parasitic castration'.

Hoplocarida – mantis-shrimps:

Mantis-shrimps are so named because of their resemblance to praying mantises. This is due to the development of their second pair of thoracic legs to massive grasping (raptorial) limbs (Fig. 244). The mantis-shrimps are aggressive predatory animals, and use their raptorial limbs to strike out at prey.

Mantis-shrimps live in holes in sandbanks or under rocks, and are intensively competitive, fighting fiercely to defend their holes against others of their kind. Their abdominal limbs (pleopods) are broad and paddle-like so that the animals can swim efficiently, but their thoracic limbs are barely adequate for walking; apart from the second pair being modified into raptorial organs, the first pair is used to hold food and the third to fifth pairs are hook-like (subchelate) and used to shred the prey.

Three southern African species are fairly common. *Gonodactylus chiragra* (Plate 66) has stiletto-like terminal joints to its raptorial limbs, which it uses to stab its prey, while of the other two species, the banded mantis-shrimp

Harpiosquilla harpax has eight or nine spine-like teeth on this same joint and is brightly banded, and *Lysiosquilla capensis* has 15 to 16 teeth and is the only species found commonly on the south coast.

Peracarida – sand hoppers and sea-lice:

The super-order Peracarida includes a curious assemblage of animals, having in common the possession of a thoracic brood pouch in the females.

This pouch consists of a series of plate-like sheets that project across the underside of the thorax to form a secure basket into which the eggs are deposited (Fig. 250). None of the peracarids have a larval stage, the embryos developing into juveniles within the brood pouch. Of the four orders of the Peracarida summarised in Fig. 244, the Isopoda and Amphipoda are the most important and contain some extremely common species that can be found in virtually every tuft of seaweed and under almost every stone. In both orders the animals lack a carapace, so that all the segments of the thorax are clearly visible, but where the isopods tend to be flattened from top to bottom, the amphipods are compressed from side to side.

Isopoda:

The common southern African isopods are identified in Figs. 250–254 and Plates 55 & 59. Kensley's *Guide to the Isopods of Southern Africa* provides a more comprehensive means of identifying isopods.

Cirolana cranchii (Fig. 250) is a typical example, with a broad thorax (peraeon) fused to the head, and a stubbier abdomen (or pleotelson). The head bears two compound eyes which are sessile (i.e. fused to the head and not

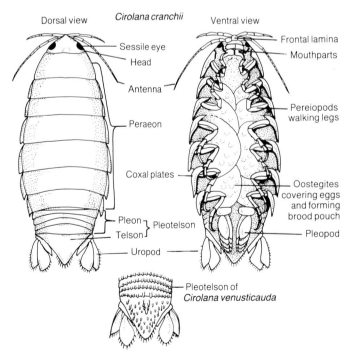

Fig. 250 The structure of a typical isopod – *Cirolana cranchii*. Below it is the distinctively spined tail-region of another species, *Cirolana venusticauda* (x 10).

A. *Eurydice longicornis*

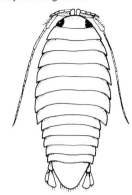

B. *Excirolana natalensis*

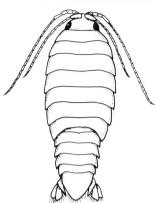

◄ Fig. 251 **Common southern African Isopoda: I. (all x3).**

C. *Pontogeloides latipes*

D. *Dynamenella huttoni*

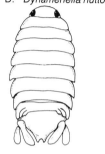

E. *Dynamenella australis*

F. *Dynamenella scabricula*

G. *Exosphaeroma truncatitelson*

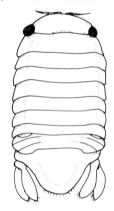

H. *Exosphaeroma kraussii*

I. *Exosphaeroma laeviusculum*

J. *Parisocladus perforatus*, male

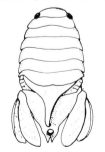

K. *Parisocladus perforatus*, female

L. *Parisocladus stimpsoni*, male

M. *Parisocladus stimpsoni*, female

stalked), two pairs of antennae, and a series of mouthparts. The peraeon bears seven pairs of walking legs (pereiopods) while the abdomen carries five pairs of flap-like pleopods which serve both as swimming appendages and as gills. The abdomen ends in a pair of uropods and a central telson which make up a tail fan.

Genera that have a similar body plan to that of *Cirolana* include *Euridice* (previously discussed in Chapter 3), *Excirolana* and *Pontogeloides* (Fig. 251A-C). The fish-louse *Anilocra capensis* (Plate 59), a much larger beast reaching 5 cm in length, has strongly hooked pereiopods to allow it to cling tightly to its host, from which it sucks blood.

From this basic body plan, at least five other groups of isopods are derived. The family Sphaeromidae contains many of the commonest isopods, characterised by the fact that the abdomen is telescoped into two or three segments (Fig. 251). All have the ability to roll into tight balls when alarmed. Most of the sphaeromids are free-living animals that feed on algae, but *Dynamenella australis* (Fig. 251E) lives commensally in the mantle groove of various limpets, seemingly causing the limpets no discomfort but gaining protection from desiccation.

The various species of sphaeromids are distinguished mainly by the structure of the telson (Fig. 251D-M).

In another family, Idoteidae, the posterior end of the body is modified, and the uropods are folded underneath the telson so that they are not visible from above, and form a chamber under the tail which houses the thin-walled pleopods (Fig. 252A). The functional significance of this is two-fold. Firstly the flapping of the uropods circulates water over the pleopods to promote uptake of oxygen and, secondly, in times of threat this flapping can be intensified to jet-propel the animal through the water. *Paridotea ungulata* (Fig. 252A) is one of the commonest representatives of the family. *Paridotea reticulata* is very similar, but is larger and has a distinctive net-like pattern all over its body (Fig. 253). Other members of the family are shown in Figs. 252B & C.

All members of the family Anthuridae depart radically from the basic isopod plan, being long and thin, perhaps because many of them burrow in sand. *Mesanthura catenula* is the most distinctive species, strikingly patterned with black squares on its yellow body (Fig. 252D). Another species, *Cyathura estuaria*, is found abundantly in estuarine sandbanks, and is a uniform off-white.

The final family of isopods, Oniscidae, includes the wood-lice and semi-terrestrial species which scuttle around near the high-tide mark (Fig. 252E-I). Since they are never submerged, their second antennae (which are normally used for underwater detection of chemical stimuli) are much reduced or absent. The most familiar species is the sea cockroach, *Ligia dilatata* (Fig. 252E, Plate 55), which swarms over kelp and other stranded algae and is one of the animals hastening decomposition of algae (see

A. *Paridotea ungulata*

side plates distinct

Pleopods
Uropod
Ventral view

B. *Glyptidotea lichtensteini*

Ridged body

C. *Synidotea variegata*

Side plates fused to body

D. *Mesanthura catenula*

E. *Ligia dilatata*

F. *Deto echinata*

Dorsal spines

Terminal uropods

G. *Tylos granulatus*

Granular

I. *Tylos capensis* ventral view of tail

H. *Tylos granulatus* ventral view of tail

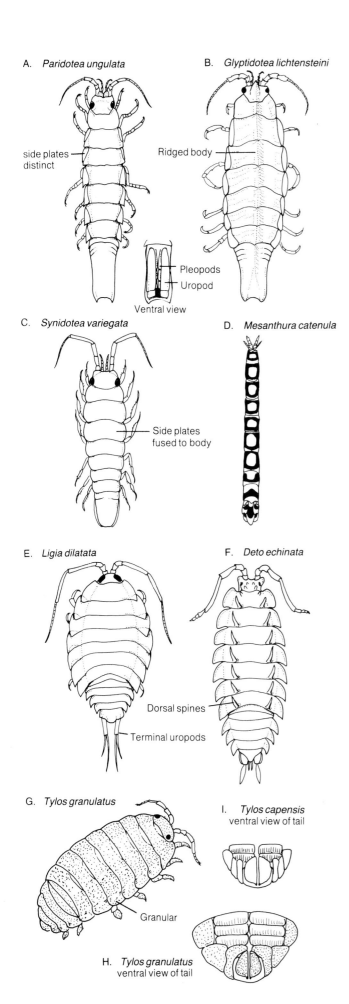

◀ Fig. 252 Common southern African Isopoda: II. (all x 1½ except D, x 3).

Fig. 253 *Paridotea reticulata* is characteristically marked with a net-like pattern, and its colour blends in with the kelp on which it is often found (x 1).

Fig. 254 The spiny-backed sea louse, *Deto echinata,* feeds on rotting seaweeds but is not above eating other isopods, or in this case, the sand hopper *Talorchestia capensis* (x 2).

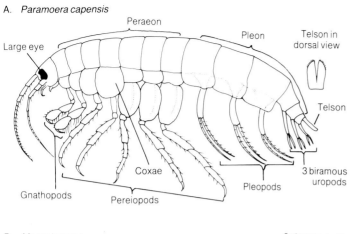

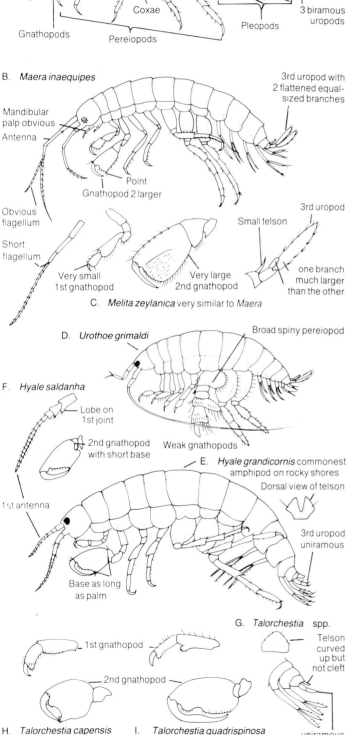

A. *Paramoera capensis*

Peraeon
Pleon
Telson in dorsal view
Large eye
Telson
Coxae
3 biramous uropods
Gnathopods
Pleopods
Pereiopods

B. *Maera inaequipes*

3rd uropod with 2 flattened equal-sized branches
Mandibular palp obvious
Antenna
Point
Gnathopod 2 larger
Obvious flagellum
Small telson
Short flagellum
3rd uropod
Very small 1st gnathopod
Very large 2nd gnathopod
one branch much larger than the other

C. *Melita zeylanica* very similar to *Maera*

D. *Urothoe grimaldi*
Broad spiny pereiopod

F. *Hyale saldanha*
Lobe on 1st joint
2nd gnathopod with short base
Weak gnathopods
1st antenna
Base as long as palm

E. *Hyale grandicornis* commonest amphipod on rocky shores
Dorsal view of telson
3rd uropod uniramous

G. *Talorchestia* spp.
Telson curved up but not cleft
1st gnathopod
2nd gnathopod

H. *Talorchestia capensis*   I. *Talorchestia quadrispinosa*
Similiar to *Hyale* but occur on sandy beaches
uniramous 3rd uropod

p. 73). A similar animal, *Deto echinata* (Fig. 252F), recognizable by the long spines projecting from its back, has quite different habits, for although it may feed on algae, it often preys on other crustaceans including the sand hoppers (Fig. 254).

On sandy shores of the west coast, the giant isopod *Tylos granulatus* (Figs. 75 & 252G) digs into the beach near the high-tide mark, emerging only at night during low tide to feed on washed-up kelp (as described in more detail in Chapter 3). On the south coast it is replaced by a smaller species, *Tylos capensis* (Fig. 252I).

Amphipoda:

The order Amphipoda is the second largest order of crustaceans, with over 4 700 species. Figs. 255–257 and Plates 56–60 illustrate species most often found in southern African waters, but for those who require a more detailed guide, Griffiths's *Guide to Marine Amphipods* should be consulted.

Paramoera capensis (family Eusiridae) is one of the most abundant and typical of amphipods – so typical that it is difficult to identify because it lacks any distinctive features (Fig. 255A). The body is laterally compressed (flattened from side to side) and the head bears two pairs of long sensory antennae and a pair of sessile compound eyes. The mouthparts consist of a pair of mandibles and three other pairs of limbs, the third of which is actually the first pair of thoracic legs. As in the isopods, the thorax is termed a peraeon (Fig. 255A) and has seven pairs of walking legs all of which have enlarged plate-like bases (coxae) that hang down, thereby increasing the apparent size of the body (Fig. 255A). The first two pairs of walking legs are usually enlarged into grasping limbs referred to as gnathopods (gnath = jaw, -pod = leg), while the remaining five pairs of legs are called pereiopods. The abdomen (pleon), which is much smaller than the peraeon, has three pairs of biramous, (two-branched) slender pleopods and three pairs of stubbier biramous uropods. At the end of the abdomen is a short telson which, in *Paramoera*, is deeply cleft.

Calliopiella michaelseni is a very similar animal, belonging to the same family, but distinguished by the fact that its telson is scarcely notched and never deeply cleft. It is an interesting creature for it is usually found living under limpets, and eats their faeces. Since this source of food is limited, only a certain number of amphipods can be supported beneath each limpet, and in fact one never finds more than a male and female under each large limpet. Newly-released juveniles may linger on under the same shell as their parents, but soon disperse. This arrangement is maintained because the resident pair of amphipods defends 'their' territorial limpet, reacting aggressively towards intruders.

Another commensal species is *Polycheria atolli* which lives in slit-like cavities that it creates in compound ascidians (minute colonial relatives of red-bait). It is a filter-

◀ Fig. 255 Common southern African Amphipoda: I. Free-living species (all x 10).

feeder and continually flickers its legs to draw a current of water into the cavity.

Maera inaequipes, a common representative of the family Gammaridae, is recognised by the two large flattened branches of its third uropods (Fig. 255B). *Melita zeylanica*, the most frequent amphipod in estuaries, is closely related to it and is identified by the structure of the male's gnathopods and by the reduced size of one of the branches of the third uropod (Fig. 255C). Also belonging to the same family is one of the most striking amphipods, *Ceradocus rubromaculatus*, which is a distinctive vivid red colour (Plate 58).

Members of the family Haustoriidae all live in the intertidal sands of estuaries and sheltered bays and are beautifully adapted for a burrowing life. They have broad bodies and their pereiopods are expanded (Fig. 255D) to create a ventral space under the animal through which a current of water is propelled by the beating of the abdominal pleopods. This jet of sand-laden water drives the animal through the sand. *Urothoe grimaldi* (Fig. 255D) is the commonest species and is so abundant in Langebaan Lagoon that it forms one of the most important prey items for the thousands of curlew sandpipers that congregate there in summer.

The family Talitridae contains two of the most familiar amphipods. On intertidal rocky shores, *Hyale grandicornis* accounts for about 80 percent of the amphipods found there and is recognized by its enlarged second gnathopods and deeply-cleft telson (Fig. 255E). A very similar species, *Hyale saldanha,* is distinguished from it only by subtle differences in the shape of the gnathopods and antennae (see Fig. 255F). The other common talitrid is the sand hopper *Talorchestia capensis* (Fig. 255G, H), which occurs in vast numbers high on sandy beaches and emerges at night to feed on stranded algae (see Chapter 3 for more details about its biology). *Talorchestia quadrispinosa* belongs to the same genus and often occurs on the same beaches, but although it lives in a similar habitat it has a totally different diet, for it preys upon its relative, *Talorchestia capensis.* The two species can be told apart by the shape of their gnathopods (Fig. 255H, I).

A number of amphipods build tubes of sand or mud mixed with mucus, including various species of *Ampelisca* which are easily recognized by their two pairs of simple eyes (Fig. 256A). *Cymadusa filosa* and *Ampithoe* species are tube dwellers as well and belong to the family Ampithoidae, characterized by the recurved spines situated at the tip of the third uropods (Fig. 256B, D). Only subtle differences in the lengths of the two branches of the uropods help distinguish *Cymadusa* from *Ampithoe* (Fig. 256C, D).

A frequent inhabitant of estuaries is *Corophium triaenonyx* (Fig. 256E) which builds muddy tubes all over rocks or the stems of plants and has long stout hairy antennae and second gnathopods which are used to filter parti-

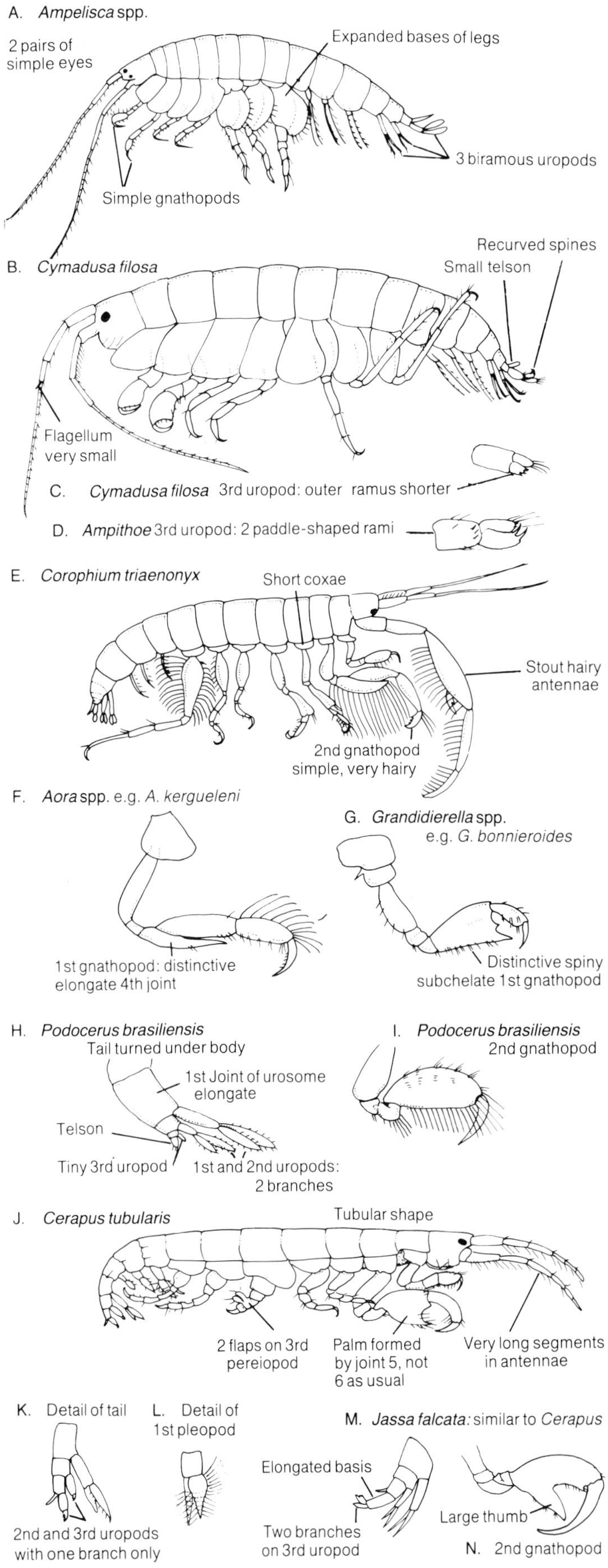

Fig. 256 Common southern African Amphipoda: II. Tube-dwelling species ► (all x 10).

A. *Ampelisca* spp.
2 pairs of simple eyes
Expanded bases of legs
Simple gnathopods
3 biramous uropods

B. *Cymadusa filosa*
Recurved spines
Small telson
Flagellum very small

C. *Cymadusa filosa* 3rd uropod: outer ramus shorter

D. *Ampithoe* 3rd uropod: 2 paddle-shaped rami

E. *Corophium triaenonyx*
Short coxae
Stout hairy antennae
2nd gnathopod simple, very hairy

F. *Aora* spp. e.g. *A. kergueleni*
1st gnathopod: distinctive elongate 4th joint

G. *Grandidierella* spp. e.g. *G. bonnieroides*
Distinctive spiny subchelate 1st gnathopod

H. *Podocerus brasiliensis*
Tail turned under body
1st Joint of urosome elongate
Telson
Tiny 3rd uropod
1st and 2nd uropods: 2 branches

I. *Podocerus brasiliensis* 2nd gnathopod

J. *Cerapus tubularis*
Tubular shape
2 flaps on 3rd pereiopod
Palm formed by joint 5, not 6 as usual
Very long segments in antennae

K. Detail of tail
2nd and 3rd uropods with one branch only

L. Detail of 1st pleopod

M. *Jassa falcata*: similar to *Cerapus*
Elongated basis
Two branches on 3rd uropod
Large thumb

N. 2nd gnathopod

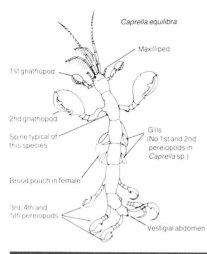

Caprella equilibra

Maxilliped

1st gnathopod

2nd gnathopod

Spine typical of
this species

Brood pouch in female

3rd, 4th and
5th pereiopods

Gills
(No 1st and 2nd
pereiopods in
Caprella sp.)

Vestigial abdomen

Fig. 257 The caprellids, such as *Caprella equilibria* shown here (x 5), are most unusual amphipods with much modified bodies.

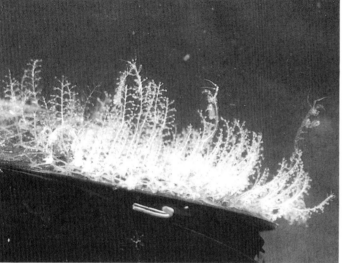

Fig. 258 This caprellid mimics the hydroid it lives on, presumably gaining protection because the hydroids are laden with stinging cells and are avoided by predators. There are actually six caprellids in this photograph, but only three are obvious (x 2).

cles from the water. Other members of the family Corophiidae include *Aora* and *Grandidierella* which have distinctive first gnathopods (Fig. 256F & G). Closely related is the family Podoceridae, readily identified by an elongation of the segment carrying the first pair of uropods (Fig. 256H): one of the well-known species is *Podocerus brasiliensis* which has extremely hairy second gnathopods, the palms of which also, characteristically, lack teeth (Fig. 256I).

Another species that forms muddy worm-like tubes is *Cerapus tubularis* (family Ischyroceridae) which has a long narrow body that fits the confines of its tube (Fig. 256J-L). *Jassa falcata*, also a member of this family, has massive second gnathopods with a diagnostic thumb-like knob (Fig. 256M & N).

The last group of amphipods is also the oddest. It consists of the suborder Caprellidea in which the animals are greatly elongated and slender, but have abdomens that are reduced to a tiny stub (Fig. 257, Plates 56 & 57). The last three pairs of pereiopods are modified to grasp the substratum while the remaining pereiopods are reduced. The

second pair of gnathopods is massive. Caprellids spend much of their time quietly attached to algae waiting for passing prey such as small worms or crustaceans at which they strike. For their minute size they are surprisingly aggressive. I have, for example, seen them repulsing nudibranchs five times their size. Several species mimic other animals. One, for instance, looks remarkably like a white feathery hydroid, presumably gaining protection from predators because it shelters amongst the hydroids which are laden with stinging cells (Fig. 258).

Superorder Eucarida – prawns, crabs and their kin:
The most widely known crustaceans such as krill, crabs and rock lobsters belong to the superorder Eucarida, and have in common the fact that the carapace is well developed and covers the whole of the thorax, fusing it into a solid unit. Two orders are distinguished: the order Euphausiacea (Fig. 244), containing the krill, and the order Decapoda, which includes a more diverse assemblage of animals such as the swimming prawns, crabs, hermit crabs and lobsters.

The euphausids are quite large considering that they are permanently planktonic, and reach 6 cm in length. They congregate in huge swarms which may in the future form the basis of an important fishery (see Chapter 6). Euphausids swim more or less continuously, using their plumed abdominal pleopods for propulsion. Their long and spindly thoracic pereiopods which are heavily armed with stiff hairs, form a ventral basket through which the water is sieved as the animal swims along, thus allowing the capture of smaller planktonic organisms. Many species are luminescent and have special light-producing organs on their ventral surfaces. While the function of this luminescence is unknown, it has been speculated that luminescence keeps the shoals together and may also aid with reproduction.

Order Decapoda:
The prawns, rock lobsters and crabs:
By far the largest order of crustaceans, the Decapoda contain some 9 000 species: about one-third of all known Crustacea. All of them have only five pairs of walking legs on the thorax, hence the name Decapoda (Deca = ten, -poda = legs). There are in fact eight pairs of limbs on the thorax, but the first three pairs are reduced in size and now form mouthparts, so they are referred to as maxillipeds.

Because the order is such a large one it is necessary to divide it up further, and two sub-orders (Fig. 244) are recognized. The Natantia include all swimming prawns in which the body is compressed from side to side and the abdominal pleopods are large and feathery and used for swimming. The second suborder, Reptantia, contains the rock lobsters, crayfish, crabs and hermit crabs, all of which are bottom-dwelling (the word 'reptant' means 'crawling') and have bodies that are dorso-ventrally flattened.

The suborder Reptantia is further subdivided into three sections (Fig. 244). Firstly, the Macrura all have well-developed extended abdomens like those of the rock lobsters. Secondly, the Anomura, comprising the hermit crabs and their kin, typically have a soft twisted abdomen that can fit into an empty snail shell. Some of the Anomura look more like crabs than anything else, having a reduced abdomen bent under the thorax; but they differ from the true crabs in that the last pair of walking legs is always reduced in size and turns upwards. The final section, Brachyura, contains all the true crabs, in which the abdomen is small and reflexed beneath the thorax and always lacks a tail-fan, while the first pair of walking legs forms a massive pair of pincers.

Natantia – swimming prawns:

The sand-shrimp *Palaemon pacificus* (Plate 62) is typical of the swimming prawns, having a laterally flattened body and a long-toothed rostrum projecting forwards between the eyes like an elongated nose; and large feathery pleopods on the abdomen which are used for swimming. Sand-shrimp are almost transparent but striped with delicate bars of black, so they blend beautifully into the background. They also have the ability to change their colour. Embedded in the epidermis beneath the exoskeleton is a series of chromatophores: cells specially designed to regulate colour. Each of these cells contains one or more pigments and can either expand the pigments to reveal the colours or contract them to an almost invisible pin-point. Such chromatophores are common in many crustaceans, but the shrimps seem to make the most spectacular use of them. *Palaemon* can change from being almost completely transparent when swimming in clear water or sitting on a pale sandy background, to a dark brown with a marked zebra patterning when faced with a dark backdrop. This change of colour is controlled by hormones, and if the blood is taken from a dark animal and injected into a pale one, the latter rapidly darkens.

Macrobrachium equidens (Fig. 259B), the smooth river-prawn, which is an estuarine species frequently found in rivers, can be recognized by its extremely long second pair of walking legs which end in nippers. A close relative, *M. scabriculum*, is distinguished by its granular carapace and hairy second walking legs. Both species occur in estuaries in Natal and Transkei. Several attempts have been made to culture *Macrobrachium equidens*, since related species have been successfully reared in Hawaii and, more recently, on Mauritius.

The pistol or cracker shrimps, *Synalpheus anisocheir* (Fig. 260) and *Alpheus crassimanus* (Fig. 259A), are so named because one of their nippers is enlarged and can be used in the same way as a finger and thumb to produce a loud snapping sound. The nipper has a protruding knob against which the movable finger builds up a pressure before slipping over to slap against the other half of the nipper. Divers sometimes hear an almost continuous crackling produced by these animals. The function of the loud snapping has long aroused curiosity. Certainly it scares predators, and it may also be used to generate shock waves that stun prey. Experiments have, however, shown that it is used in addition to settle contests for territorial

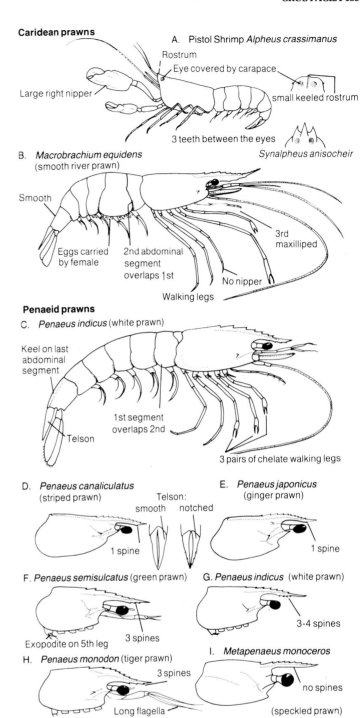

Fig. 259 Common swimming prawns found in southern Africa. The upper two belong to the group Caridea, in which the sides of the second abdominal segment overlap the first, and the third pair of legs never ends in nippers; the lower animals belong to another group of prawns, the Penaeidea, in which the first three legs end in nippers and the second abdominal segment never overlaps the first. Penaeids are all similar to *Penaeus indicus* but are distinguished by the number of teeth on the upper and lower edges of the rostrum above the eyes. All life-size.

holes. The underwater shock waves generated by snapping are proportional to the size of the shrimp, so that an intruding individual can gauge the size of a resident opponent without embarking on physical battle.

Fig. 260 The pistol shrimp, *Synalpheus anisocheir* (x 1½), which produces a loud clicking noise by snapping together the finger and thumb of its nipper. It is similar to another pistol shrimp, *Alpheus crassimanus*, but may be distinguished by the three spines projecting in front of its eyes (see Fig. 259A).

Fig. 261 A pair of zebra shrimps, *Gnathophyllum fasciolatum*, begin their courtship (x 1).

Alpheus crassimanus is commonly found in coral heads, or sharing sandy burrows with gobies. In other parts of the world commensal cooperation between such shrimps and gobies is well known: the shrimp excavating and maintaining a hidy-hole for both beasts, while the more alert goby serves as an early warning system for the shrimp.

Some of the most interesting swimming prawns are the cleaner shrimps, *Stenopus hispidus* (Plate 64) and *Periclimenes*, which perform the useful function of cleaning the surfaces of fish, removing dead scales and tending wounds. *Periclimenes* often shelters in the tentacles of the giant anemone *Stoichactis* (Plate 61). The bright colours of these shrimps probably allow easy recognition by fish, which soon learn to enjoy the shrimps' ministrations rather than attempting to eat them. Cleaner fish fulfil a similar function.

Symbiotic relationships such as this have in the past been treated as interesting curiosities, but quite recently it has been shown that they have a more profound influence. Experimental removal of cleaner shrimps and cleaner fish from a coral reef leads to other fish shunning the area,

which in turn means that algae flourish, unchecked by herbivorous fish, and soon smother and kill the coral. Thus the whole nature of the community changes in the absence of these cleaner organisms.

Another brightly coloured prawn is the zebra shrimp, *Gnathophyllum fasciolatum*, which has a white body with vertical black stripes and yellow and black bands on its white legs. Fig. 261 shows two of these zebra shrimps in a ritual dance – possibly part of their courtship. Zebra shrimps are common in Natal, but are very shy.

The best known of the swimming prawns are placed in a separate division, Penaeidea – recognized because their first three pairs of walking legs terminate in nippers and because the sides of the second abdominal segment do not overlap the first segment as they do in all other prawns – which are placed in another division, Caridea (compare Fig. 259B & C). The penaeids are famous for being amongst the most delicious of all crustaceans and are commercially trawled off Moçambique and Natal. Of the many species, the most common are illustrated in Figs. 122 & 259 C-I.

Penaeids are widely cultured in various parts of the world and a proposal was once put forward to fence off part of the Kosi Bay lakes and to fertilise them to increase the productivity so that prawns could be farmed there. However, on investigation, the lakes proved to be mildly eutrophic – that is to say they already have fairly high levels of plant and phytoplankton growth. The implication of this is that if further nutrients were to be added in the form of fertilisers, the aesthetically pleasing clear waters of Kosi could easily be transformed into a pea soup. The idea of farming prawns there was thus shelved.

Rock lobsters and sand-prawns:

The Macrura include both the rock lobsters (or spiny lobsters as they are called in other parts of the world) and the sand prawns and mud-prawns, all of which have well-developed extended abdomens.

The rock lobsters, which are of such commercial importance (see Chapter 7), have a very complex life-cycle that takes about ten months to complete. After mating has taken place, the fertilised eggs are attached by curly stalks to hairs on the female's pleopods (Figs. 262 & 263). These hatch after 80 to 90 days into flat spider-like naupliosoma larvae (Fig. 263), helpless creatures that are barely motile and drift with the currents. Once these larvae moult they are transformed into phyllosoma larvae (Fig. 263) with flat leaf-like bodies and long spindly legs armed with feathery hairs: all adaptations that reduce the rate at which the larvae sink in the water and thus minimise the energy spent on swimming. The phyllosoma larvae go through no fewer than 11 moults, becoming larger and more elaborate at each step. Finally, after seven and a half months of floating around in the sea, they metamorphose into puerulus larvae, which settle on the bottom in shallow waters. It is only at this stage that the larvae begin to look like miniature rock lobsters although they are both soft and almost transparent (Fig. 263).

It is because this life-cycle is so prolonged and complex

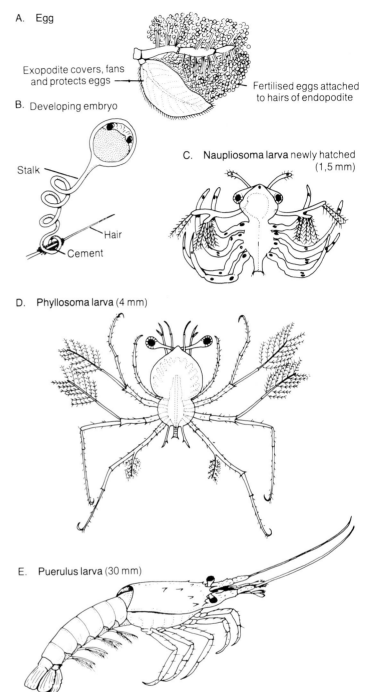

A. Egg

Exopodite covers, fans and protects eggs

Fertilised eggs attached to hairs of endopodite

B. Developing embryo

Stalk

Hair

Cement

C. Naupliosoma larva newly hatched (1,5 mm)

D. Phyllosoma larva (4 mm)

E. Puerulus larva (30 mm)

Fig. 263 The life-cycle of a rock lobster, *Jasus lalandii*.

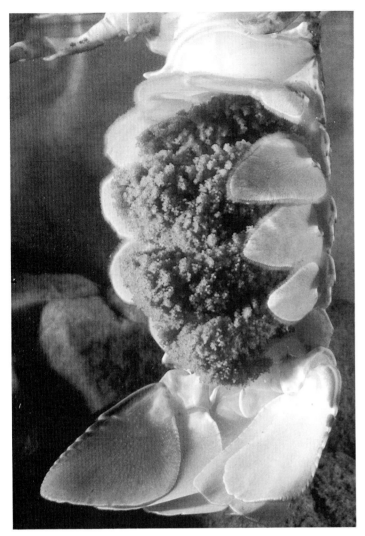

Fig. 262 The abdomen of a rock lobster, heavy with 'berry' (x 1).

that no-one has yet succeeded in rearing any of the southern African species – despite the obvious financial rewards such a breakthrough would bring.

The actual process whereby the eggs are fertilised is still the subject of argument. The east coast rock lobster (*Panulirus homarus*) mates shortly after the female has moulted, but only after her skeleton has hardened. The male plasters a mass of sperm in a jelly-like matrix onto the ventral surface of her thorax. This hardens and remains stuck to the female until she is ready to deposit the eggs, and only then does she scrape at the spermatophoric mass to release the sperm. As in all decapods, the reproductive organs of the female open at the base of the third walking leg (Fig. 264) and the eggs are wafted from there over the sperm mass, so that they are fertilised just before they attach to the pleopods.

In the case of the west coast *Jasus lalandii*, no spermatophoric mass has ever been found on a female, but on the other hand sperm has been located internally in the oviducts. It is still a puzzle as to how it reaches there, for the male has no organ that could act as a penis to bring about internal fertilisation. Mating seems to occur immediately after the female has moulted and while she is

still soft. When she sloughs off her old skin, part of the ventral surface of the thorax tears away, leaving a narrow opening almost like a wound; and it has been suggested that the sperm finds its way through this to the oviduct – although not all researchers agree that this is possible.

One interesting observation that urgently needs more research is that males are strongly stimulated and attracted by females that have just moulted. Even water that is taken from a tank containing a moulting female is enough to make a male literally climb out of an aquarium in excitement. It seems that some chemical (pheromone) is transmitted from the female. Insect pheromones have been

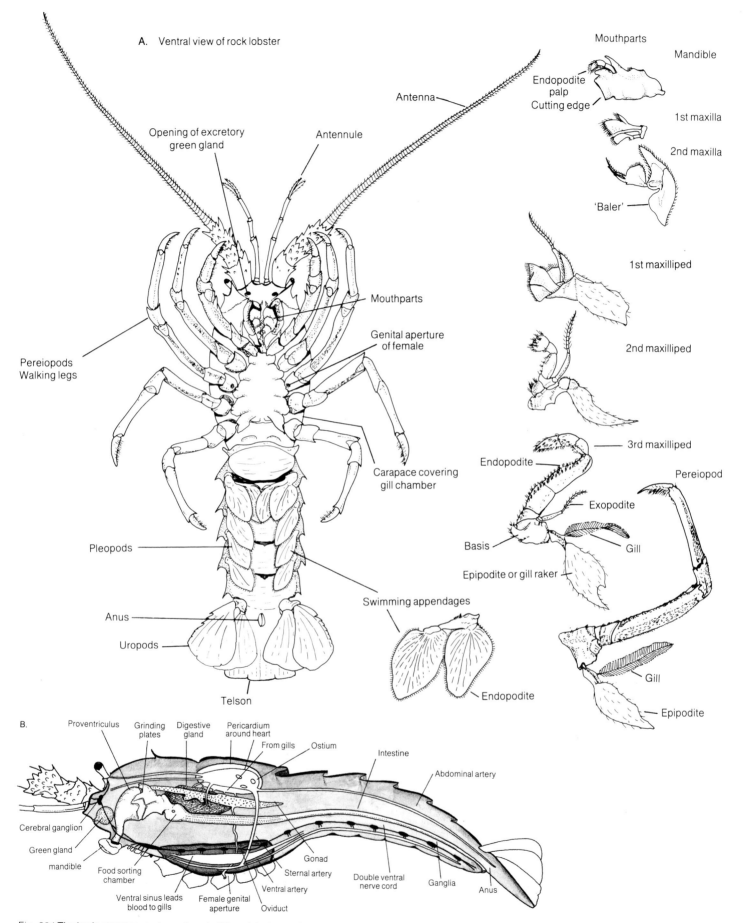

Fig. 264 The body structure and mouthparts (A) and the internal organs (B) of the west coast rock lobster, *Jasus lalandii*.

extensively studied and even artificially synthesized and used to lure the males of pest species into baited traps. The possibility of a similar sex attractant in rock lobsters should be investigated further.

The body structure of the west coast rock lobster *Jasus lalandii* is typical of most Macrura (Fig. 264A). The thorax and head are fused into a solid unit by the overlying carapace, which overhangs the sides of the thorax as well to form gill chambers. The mouth is flanked by very strong mandibles. Behind these are two pairs of maxillae and, in addition, three pairs of maxillipeds – all concerned with manipulating the food. The second maxillae have become modified for an additional function, their inner faces being expanded into paddle-like 'balers' (scaphognathites) serving to pump water through the gill chambers (Fig. 264A).

The maxillipeds are worth examining in more detail, for of all the limbs they come closest to the primitive plan of the supposed ancestral crustacean limbs. Each of them consists of a basal joint from which a stout jointed endopodite and a slender sensory exopodite arise. Since such a limb has two branches it is termed biramous, and all Crustacea are characterised by having at least one pair of biramous limbs. The appendages of the abdomen (pleopods) contain both these branches, although they are flattened into paddles. The walking legs have only one branch, the sensory expodite having disappeared in the course of evolution.

The internal organs of the rock lobster are shown in Fig. 264B. The gut is specialised into regions, a short oesophagus opening into a swollen proventriculus which is lined by hard plates of teeth that grind one against the other to macerate the food. These can easily be seen if the proventriculus is cut open. The macerated food is then sieved by filters at the back of the proventriculus and small particles are passed into the digestive gland. Larger particles are macerated once again, or are moved on to the intestine to be voided. The thorax is largely filled by the yellowish finger-like lobes of the digestive gland. The reproductive organs, too, are concentrated in the thorax and open onto the bases of the third walking legs in the female and the bases of the fifth legs in the male.

The blood system is quite different from that of any of the lower invertebrates. The heart pumps blood out of a series of arteries, but from these the blood accumulates in a diffuse body space (the haemocoel) so that it bathes all the organs. There are thus no veins and the blood is sucked back into the heart through little valve-operated holes (ostia) on the sides of the heart. Since the body cavity is one continuous space, none of the organs is segmentally repeated and a single pair of excretory organs – the green glands – near the base of the antennae, cleanses the blood and eliminates waste products. Segmentation is only visible in the abdomen, where the muscles are arranged in segmental blocks and the nerve cord has segmental ganglia. The tail is capable of a powerful flapping which drives the animal backwards in an escape response.

Rock lobsters occupy crevices and holes under rocks and defend these against others of their kind: a hierarchy exists,

with the largest animals occupying the choice holes. *Jasus* is a silent creature, but the east coast *Panulirus* and most other rock lobsters can stridulate – emit a rasping sound by rubbing parts of the body together. In doing so, they communicate with one another. Rock lobsters normally retreat into their holes and wedge themselves in when threatened, a reaction well known to divers. But if an octopus approaches, they behave entirely differently, abandoning their holes and swimming away – presumably because an octopus has little difficulty in extracting a rock lobster from its hole.

On the east coast, *Panulirus homarus* has established an interesting relationship with moray eels which prey on octopuses and share holes with rock lobsters – as many a diver has learnt to his cost. Thus an unwary octopus attacking a rock lobster is liable to be attacked itself. Furthermore the morays are attracted by the stridulation of threatened rock lobsters.

There are many species of rock lobster around the coast of southern Africa. *Jasus lalandii* (Plate 63) is the common west coast species. On the south and east coasts live a host of *Panulirus* and *Palinurus* species. *Panulirus homarus* is the commonest and has a distinctive groove that runs across the top of each abdominal segment. *Panulirus versicolor* is a beautiful black and green creature with a conspicuous white band across the back edge of each abdominal segment and white stripes running down its legs, while *Panulirus ornatus* is bluish green with a conspicuous white spot on each of the spurs that project from the side of the abdomen. In Moçambique, young specimens are very common on rock faces where they live in tight-fitting holes from which only their astonishingly long and conspicuous white antennae protrude. In deeper waters, *Palinurus delagoae* is trawled off the coast of Moçambique and Natal, while *Palinurus gilchristi* is caught only off the south coast. A somewhat different type of animal is the shoveller or Port Elizabeth crayfish (Plate 65), with its broad flat antennae.

The sand prawns and mud-prawns *Callianassa kraussi* (Fig. 265 and see Fig. 119 for more details) and *Upogebia africana* (Fig. 103) are familiar inhabitants of estuaries. But

Fig. 265 The sand prawn *Callianassa kraussii* (x 1), extracted from its burrow and left on the sand, instantly begins digging. The single enlarged nipper distinguishes sand prawns from their mud-prawn relatives, *Upogebia* species (see Fig. 103).

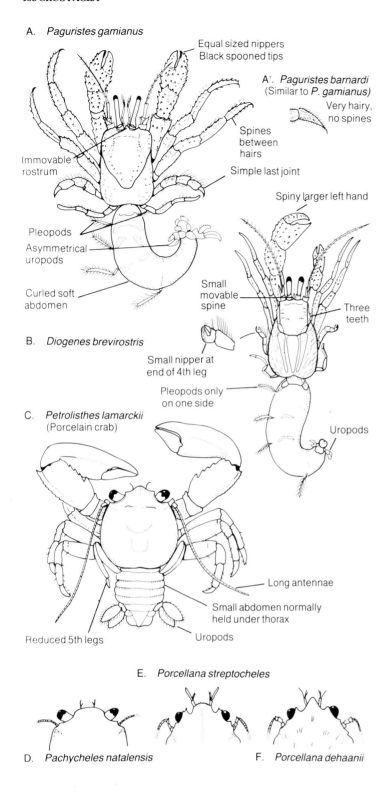

A. *Paguristes gamianus*

Equal sized nippers
Black spooned tips

A¹. *Paguristes barnardi*
(Similar to *P. gamianus*)

Very hairy,
no spines

Spines
between
hairs

Immovable
rostrum

Simple last joint

Spiny larger left hand

Pleopods
Asymmetrical
uropods

Small
movable
spine

Three
teeth

Curled soft
abdomen

B. *Diogenes brevirostris*

Small nipper at
end of 4th leg

Pleopods only
on one side

Uropods

C. *Petrolisthes lamarckii*
(Porcelain crab)

Long antennae

Small abdomen normally
held under thorax

Reduced 5th legs

Uropods

E. *Porcellana streptocheles*

D. *Pachycheles natalensis*

F. *Porcellana dehaanii*

Fig. 266 Two of the common hermit crabs removed from their shells:
(A) *Paguristes gamianus* and (B) *Diogenes brevirostris*. *Paguristes
barnardi* is almost identical to *P. gamianus* but the tips of its legs are less
spiny and the tiny spines it does have are hidden in the denser hairs. Shown
below (C) is a porcelain crab, *Petrolisthes lamarckii*, related to the hermit
crabs (despite superficial resemblance to the true crabs) because its fifth
legs are reduced and its abdomen ends in a tail fan. The abdomen is
normally reflected under the thorax but has been drawn extended to show
the tail fan. Other porcelain crabs are similar, but can be distinguished by
the shape of the carapace between the eyes (D-F).

where *Callianassa* extends onto sandy beaches and also
lives in closed estuaries, *Upogebia africana* is confined to
muddy, permanently open, estuaries. Another species,
Upogebia capensis, is a very similar creature and is distinguished from *U. africana* because it bears tiny spines which
project inwards from the bases of its first two walking legs;
furthermore, it lives in a different habitat, burrowing under
mud-embedded stones and never being found in estuaries.

Anomura – the hermit crabs
Hermit crabs are well known for their habit of living in
empty shells, and their bodies are extensively modified to
suit this curious life-style (Figs. 266A & B). The abdomen is
soft and twisted to one side to fit the curvature of the coiled
snail shell, and ends in a set of horny uropods that are also
asymmetrical and wedge the animal in the shell. The
pleopods are reduced on the inner side of the curved
abdomen but are still retained on the outer side and used to
hold the eggs in the case of the female. The first pair of legs
form nippers; one of these is often much larger than the
other and acts as a door-stop to the shell when the crab
withdraws. The second and third legs function as normal
walking legs, but the fourth and fifth are reduced in size
and are used to grip the mouth of the shell. In most species,
the tip of the fourth leg is modified into a tiny nipper and
this, too, helps the animal to grasp the shell (Fig. 266B)
although in the genus *Paguristes* (Fig. 266A) the tip forms a
simple point.

As a hermit grows, it becomes too big for its shell and
must find a larger one. For a female, a larger shell also
means that she can carry more eggs and thus increase her
reproductive potential. Thus it is not surprising that hermits are intensely competitive about shells. Every large
shell is carefully examined, first by thrusting a nipper into
it to check whether it is uninhabited and then by swiftly
transferring across to try it for size (see Plates 70–74). These
behavioural responses may be observed in the laboratory
by keeping a group of hermits in an aquarium, or by removing one of them from its shell and then offering it a choice
of other shells. Removing the beast from its shell is no easy
task, but by gently heating the apex of the shell with a
match one can make things uncomfortably hot for it so that
it abandons its home.

Diogenes brevirostris (Fig. 266B) is one of the commoner
species found on sandy banks or in sandy pools in sheltered areas. Like other hermits, it is able to scavenge for
food but it sweeps its long feathery antennae through the
water as well, filtering out particles. Its mouthparts also
keep up a continuous high-speed flickering which circulates water past the antennae.

During the breeding season in December and January,
Diogenes emerges from the sea to run around the sand in a
frenzy of courtship. Males pursue females, grasp their
shells in their enlarged nippers, and drag them forcibly
down to the water. The comical nature of the whole performance is heightened because males seem unable to recognize the sex of another animal until they have captured

it. Two or more males will often fight over a female while she nonchalantly leaves them squabbling. Males are not in the least faithful and even once a male starts dragging a female down the shore he will readily abandon her if a larger female appears. This apparent fickleness pays dividends if the male succeeds in finding a larger mate, for her size (and the size of her shell) will determine the number of progeny he will sire. It is difficult not to interpret this courtship in human terms and even Hollywood stars would be hard put to match the marital squabbling and infidelity of these creatures.

Fig. 266 and Plates 67–74 illustrate the common local species of hermit crabs. On rocky shores along the east coast, *Clibanarius virescens* is by far the most abundant species, easily recognized by the yellow bands on its legs (Plates 70–74). In estuaries its place is taken by *Clibanarius longitarsus* which has blue stripes on its legs. In addition to these typical hermit crabs, there are a few species not so readily assigned to the Anomura. They include the mole crabs or sea lice *Emerita austroafricana* (discussed in greater detail in Chapter 3 and shown in Fig. 69) and *Hippa adactyla* (Fig. 268A & B).

Lithodes (Fig. 267), the giant deep-sea crab (or stone crab) looks more like the popular image of a crab than it does a hermit crab, having its abdomen tucked under its thorax. We surmise that the stone crab was at one stage in the past a hermit crab, but that in the course of evolution it has simply grown too big to be able to find shells and has been obliged to tuck its soft tail between its legs. It still carries with it reminders of its hermit crab ancestry, for its fifth pair of walking legs are reduced and its abdomen is unsegmented.

The porcelain crabs (Fig. 266C) are even less obviously related to the hermit crabs: only their reduced fifth legs, very long antennae and the presence of uropods at the tip of the abdomen indicate that they should be classified among the Anomura. Four common species occur in southern African waters; all are similar to *Petrolisthes lamarckii* (Fig. 266C) but differ from one another in colour and in the

Fig. 267 A small example of a deep-sea stone crab, *Lithodes*, which is also related to the hermits, having small fifth legs and a soft unsegmented abdomen (x ¼).

Fig. 268 The sea lice or mole crabs, (A) *Hippa adactyla* and (B) *Emerita austroafricana* (see also Fig. 69).

shape of the carapace between the eyes (see Figs. 266D-F). Porcelain crabs are so named because they are fragile and shed their legs when threatened by a predator. The nippers in particular are readily cast off, and distract the predator by continuing to snap repeatedly while the crab makes its escape. Many crustaceans have this ability to voluntarily shed limbs (autotomy) and must then regrow the limbs over the next few moults.

Brachyura – the true crabs

Amongst the best known of all marine animals, the crabs have been remarkably successful in occupying practically every marine habitat.

The basic structure of a crab is shown in Fig. 269. The most obvious feature is the much reduced abdomen tucked tightly under the thorax. The uropods that form a tail fan in most other Crustacea have been lost. The pleopods on the abdomen are retained as slender feathery structures in the female; no longer functional as swimming appendages but used to hold the eggs under the abdomen when the female is 'in berry'. For this reason females have much broader abdomens than males. The male has lost all the pleopods except for the first pair and these are radically modified for an unusual function. Each of the male's pleopods now forms a hollow tubular structure, open at both ends. When reproduction occurs, the pleopods are connected by way of soft tubes to the male's genital pores on the bases of the fifth legs. In this way each pleopod can now function as a penis, transferring sperm from the male to the female's genital

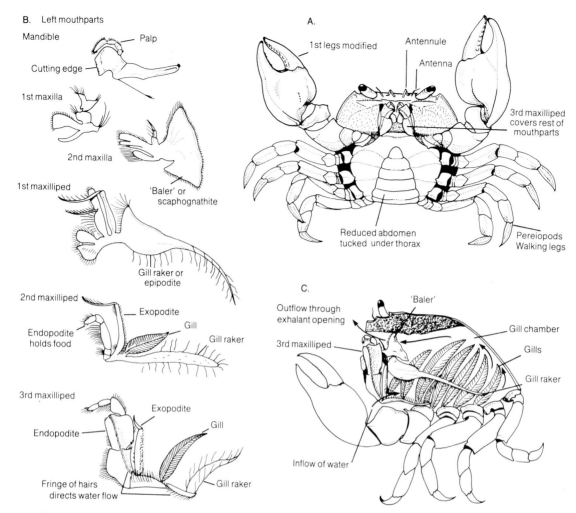

B. Left mouthparts
Mandible — Palp
Cutting edge
1st maxilla
2nd maxilla
1st maxilliped
'Baler' or scaphognathite
Gill raker or epipodite
2nd maxilliped
Exopodite
Gill
Endopodite holds food
Gill raker
3rd maxilliped
Exopodite
Endopodite
Gill
Fringe of hairs directs water flow
Gill raker

A.
1st legs modified
Antennule
Antenna
3rd maxilliped covers rest of mouthparts
Reduced abdomen tucked under thorax
Pereiopods Walking legs

C.
Outflow through exhalant opening
'Baler'
Gill chamber
3rd maxilliped
Gills
Gill raker
Inflow of water

Fig. 269 Ventral view (A) of the crab *Cyclograpsus punctatus,* showing its structure, mouthparts (B) and the arrangement of the gill chamber, gill rakers, and the flow of water pumped by the 'baler' through the gill chamber (C).

aperture (at the base of her third legs). This means that the crabs are amongst the few crustaceans able to practise internal fertilisation: and no doubt this contributes to the success of the group.

The thorax, consolidated into a solid unit by the carapace, has five pairs of walking legs – the first forming massive nippers and being termed chelipeds. Crabs are well known for walking sideways and one wonders why this should be. The answer to this is that if they were to walk forwards, each leg could only take a short stride before becoming entangled with the one in front or the one behind. By moving sideways the stride of each leg is greatly increased. Some of the crabs, such as ghost crabs, *Ocypode* species (Plates 75 & 81), are amongst the fastest running animals.

The carapace overhangs the sides of the thorax to form gill chambers, and water is circulated through these by the beating of the 'balers' on the second maxillae (Fig. 269B). The basic plan is much the same as that described for the rock lobster, but in crabs the gill chamber is more securely enclosed, allowing them to hold water in the chamber so that they are able to emerge onto land. The first three pairs of thoracic limbs, which lie in front of the walking legs, are small and modified to form mouthparts. In addition to

manipulating and shredding food, they have long flat gill rakers (epipodites) that stretch back into the gill chamber and lie between the gills, which they cleanse by gently wiping them in an up and down movement (Fig. 269B).

Crabs have an elaborate life-cycle. The eggs hatch into planktonic zoeae larvae (Fig. 270), comma-shaped creatures with two characteristic and extraordinarily long spines, one on the thorax and the other forming a rostrum like a prolonged nose. These spines are once again adaptations that reduce the rate of sinking, helping the larvae keep afloat in the plankton, but at the same time, making it more difficult for other planktonic animals to eat them. The zoea larva metamorphoses into a megalopa which looks very much like a miniature crab except that its stubby abdomen projects backwards, not yet being folded under the thorax as in the adult. Perhaps this reflects the ancestral history of crabs, for they probably evolved from crayfish-like creatures with an extended abdomen.

Most of the well-known southern African crabs can be identified from Figs. 271–275 and Plates 75–83. We are able to recognise at least five groups of crabs on the basis of their general biology, and these tend to correspond with the major families.

The common rock crabs that scuttle actively around the

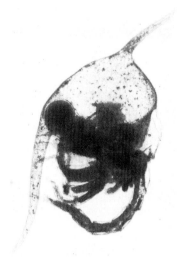

Fig. 270 The zoea larva of a crab (x 25).

Fig. 271 The green rock crab, *Grapsus fourmanoiri* (x ²/₃).

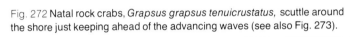
Fig. 272 Natal rock crabs, *Grapsus grapsus tenuicrustatus,* scuttle around the shore just keeping ahead of the advancing waves (see also Fig. 273).

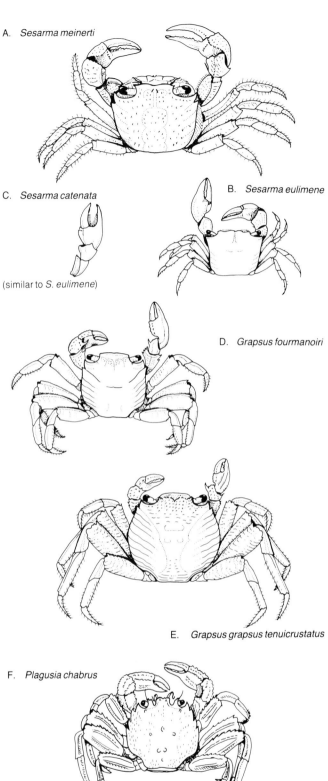

A. *Sesarma meinerti*

C. *Sesarma catenata*

(similar to *S. eulimene*)

B. *Sesarma eulimene*

D. *Grapsus fourmanoiri*

E. *Grapsus grapsus tenuicrustatus*

F. *Plagusia chabrus*

G. *Percnon planissimum*

shore all belong to family Grapsidae and have an almost square carapace and very long legs. On the Natal and Moçambique coasts there are two abundant species. *Grapsus grapsus tenuicrustatus* (Fig. 273E) is a beautifully coloured animal with a dark green body that is mottled with red, yellow and black. Larger males develop lavish colours during the reproductive season. These crabs are a familiar sight as they follow the advancing tide up the shore, always remaining just above the water-level and clinging tightly as waves crash over them (Fig. 272).

A second common species is the mottled green and yellow *Grapsus fourmanoiri* (Figs. 271 & 273D). In the

Fig. 273 Common southern African crabs: I. The rock crabs, family Grapsidae. All x ½. ▶

estuaries of Natal and Moçambique a third species, *Metopograpsus thukuhar*, is found living under stones: it is very similar to *Grapsus fourmanoiri* in structure, but the sides of its carapace taper towards the back of its white-spotted, distinctively purple body.

One of the most attractive east coast grapsids is the red-eyed crab, *Percnon planissimum* (Plate 78, Fig. 273G), which is extremely difficult to capture as it is fast-moving and scuttles around the sides of boulders, in gullies and deep pools. Its very spiny legs and its two-toned eyes make this animal impossible to confuse with any of the other crabs.

Right round the coast of southern Africa, the shore crab *Cyclograpsus punctatus* (Fig. 105, Plate 83) is one of the commonest species. It shelters under stones on the high shore. As is the case for most grapsids, populations of *Cyclograpsus* establish an order of dominance between the individuals. Dominant crabs are aggressive and are avoided by others, and they usually win any fights in which they become involved. Dominance increases the chance that a male will mate and secures for him the best available crevice in which to hide. But what determines dominance? In vertebrates, male androgenic hormones are implicated. Could a corresponding system operate in crabs? To test this idea, operations have been performed on *Cyclograpsus* in order to remove the androgenic glands which line the male reproductive organs and produce hormones. In every case, removal of these organs reduces the dominance of a male, while if the same organs are then implanted into another male that was previously subordinate, he then becomes more dominant. Thus it seems that in crabs, too, the level of male hormones determines how dominant an individual will be.

Another abundant grapsid is the Cape rock crab, *Plagusia chabrus* (Fig. 273F), which occurs subtidally and is an active swimmer, having fringes of hairs on its legs to make them more efficient for swimming. *Plagusia* is the favoured prey of octopuses and it is not unusual to see them scuttling out of the water to escape these beasts – the only time they are found on dry land. On the Natal coast, this species is replaced by a less common member of the genus, *Plagusia depressa*, which is very similar but has flat tubercles all over its carapace, while *P. chabrus* has a smooth velvety carapace.

In south and east coast estuaries are found several species of *Sesarma*, also members of the family Grapsidae. *Sesarma mienerti*, the red mangrove crab (Fig. 273A), is very common in mangrove swamps but scavenges widely and digs deep holes down to the water table (Fig. 125). Like *Cyclograpsus*, it has special adaptations allowing it to recirculate the water in its gill chambers without excessive loss of water, and thus can remain out of the water for long periods (see Chapter 5, p. 84). *Sesarma catenata* and *S. eulimene* (Fig. 273B & C) are both detritus feeders, rolling

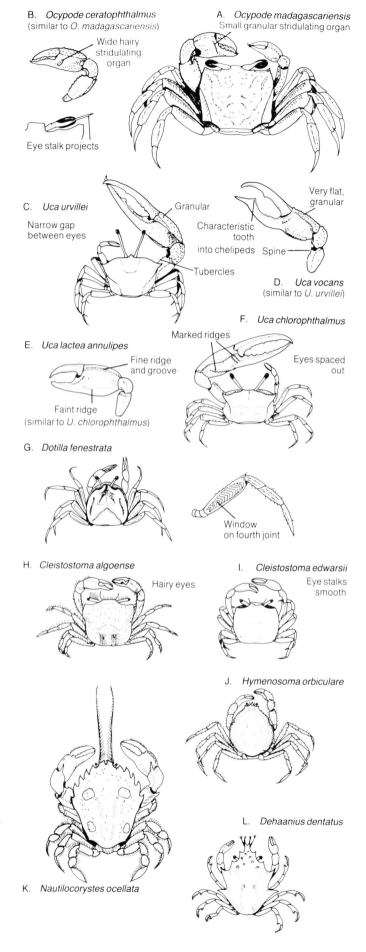

Fig. 274 Common southern African crabs: II. Burrowing crabs, families Ocypodidae (A-I), Hymenosomatidae (J), Corystidae (K); and the seaweed crab *Dehaanius* which decorates itself with algae (see Fig. 48). All x ½ except G-I, x 1½.

balls of mud in their mouthparts to extract organic materials and micro-organisms. Both species are often found in salt marshes and for this reason are loosely known as marsh crabs. Perhaps to avoid competition between the two, *S. catenata* occurs in the lower regions of estuaries while *S. eulimene* lives nearer the head and is more tolerant of lower salinities (as discussed in Chapter 5).

The family Ocypodidae contains the burrowing crabs, most of which make distinctive tunnels in the sand or mud. All of them are characterised by their very long eye-stalks which can fold along the front of the carapace where they fit into grooves (see Figs. 274A-I). In addition, they all have a cavity on either side of the body between the bases of the third and fourth legs, which is fringed with hairs: these hairs serve to suck water from damp sand and pass it through the cavity to the gill chamber. They also serve to filter the water to exclude sand or mud. The ghost crabs and fiddler crabs, familiar examples of the family, are illustrated in Figs. 274A-F and Plates 75–77 & 81. Their biology is discussed in greater detail in Chapters 3 and 5.

Only distantly related to the ocypodids, but also found living in sand and mud banks, is an assemblage of other crabs. None, however, actually forms burrows, for they all simply shuffle into the sand or make use of burrows other animals have created. *Thaumastoplax spiralis* is the most easily recognized of these species because it has only three pairs of walking legs in addition to the nippers, instead of the usual four pairs. It lives commensally inside the burrows of the sand-prawns *Callianassa*.

The membrane-bodied crab *Hymenosoma orbicularis* (Figs. 102 & 274J) is also found in estuaries, its flat mottled body blending into the sand. The shame-faced crab *Matuta lunaris* (Fig. 275A) – so called because its nippers are moulded to fit the front of the carapace and hide the 'face' – has specially flattened tips to its legs to help it to dig into the sand. Like many mud-dwelling species it has fringes of hairs along its legs and mouthparts to exclude the smothering mud particles as much as possible. *Mutata* is closely related to another shame-faced crab, *Mursia cristimanus* (Plate 82), a rock-dwelling subtidal species. Both species have two ridges on the inner surfaces of their nippers, which can be rubbed against ridges on the mouthparts (the third maxillipeds) or on the chest, and this stridulation produces a squeaking noise.

The most striking of the sand-dwellers is the masked crab *Nautilocorystes ocellata*, which has an elongated carapace marked with four spots resembling the eyes and mouth of a mask. Its most significant feature is its unusually long second antennae (Fig. 274K). Once again its limb-tips are flattened to allow it to dig efficiently and it burrows backwards into the sand until only the tips of its antennae project from the sediment.

Each of the long antennal shafts is lined with two rows of hairs oriented at right angles to each other, so that when the two shafts are held together they form a hair-lined tube. It is through this that the buried animal sucks water to supply food and oxygen. The water is filtered through the mouthparts so that organic particles can be extracted, and then

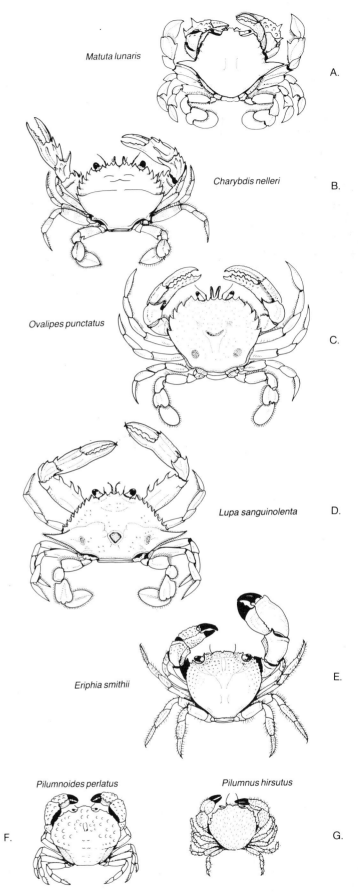

Matuta lunaris — A.

Charybdis nelleri — B.

Ovalipes punctatus — C.

Lupa sanguinolenta — D.

Eriphia smithii — E.

Pilumnoides perlatus — F.

Pilumnus hirsutus — G.

Fig. 275 Common southern African crabs: III. The shame-faced crab, family Calappidae (A), swimming crabs, family Portunidae (B-D), and the family Xanthidae (E-G). All x ½.

circulated through the gill chambers and passed out at the back of the body. Thus the striking elongation of the antennae allows the animal to remain concealed while still obtaining food and oxygen.

The family Portunidae contains the swimming crabs, all of which have the tips of the back pairs of legs flattened into paddles (Fig. 275B-D). Although they are able to swim efficiently, portunids spend much of their time buried in sand or mud and emerge at night to capture prey. All of them are ferocious predators with powerful, strongly-toothed nippers (Fig. 276), attacking molluscs, other crustaceans and even fish. The three-spotted swimming crab, *Ovalipes punctatus*, lives in the breaker zone off sandy beaches and is often caught in trek nets. It feeds mainly on the plough snail *Bullia*, smashing its shell open before shredding the flesh (Plate 79). On the east coast, *Lupa pelagica* occupies a similar habitat. Apart from preying on other species, it is also cannibalistic, as Fig. 277 reveals.

In Natal and Moçambique, several common swimming crabs live on rocky shores. These include *Charybdis nelleri* (Fig. 275B) and a very similar genus of crabs, *Thalamita*, distinguished from *Charybdis* by having only five teeth along each side of the carapace behind the eye, instead of six. *Thalamita admete* is recognized by the two broad lobes on the front of the carapace between its eyes, while *T. woodmasoni* has four somewhat indistinct lobes.

Included in the family Portunidae is the Knysna mud crab, one of the largest crabs in southern Africa (Fig. 278), which despite its massive chelipeds feeds on surprisingly small prey such as the tiny snail *Nassarius kraussianus*.

A totally different type of body structure is found in the family Xanthidae, members of which have an oval, often nodular, body and a pair of massive nippers, usually with characteristically dark tips to the finger and thumb. All xanthids are slow-moving and cumbersome, using their massive nippers to crush open the shells of gastropods. The xanthids become increasingly common in tropical waters, and it is probably in response to their presence that many tropical gastropods have evolved thick, narrow-mouthed shells and spines (see Chapter 2 and Fig. 51).

On the east coast various species of *Eriphia* are fre-

Fig. 277 The swimming crab *Lupa sanguinolenta* is a vicious predator. Here two animals turn on a third, which had previously been injured, and devour it – starting with the eyes (x½). *Lupa pelagica* is a very similar species but lacks eye spots on its back.

Fig. 278 The giant mud-crab *Scylla serrata* is also one of the swimming crabs, and reaches a size of 30 cm.

quently encountered. *Eriphia smithii* (Plate 80, Fig. 275E) is the largest and has dense nodules on its smaller nipper; while the surface of both nippers of *Eriphia laevimanus* is smooth. *Eriphia scabricula* has a distinctive but sparse covering of hairs all over its body and nippers. *Eurycarcinus natalensis* is an unusually smooth-surfaced member of the family Xanthidae; additional features enabling identification of this species are its unusual deep purple colour and the three teeth projecting from the edge of its carapace behind each eye.

One of the few common west coast xanthids is the kelp crab, *Pilumnoides perlatus* (Fig. 275F). Another species, *Pilumnus hirsutus* (Fig. 275G), recognized by its golden-brown coat of short hairs, has a wider distribution from Saldanha Bay to Durban, but both species are suspected of having been introduced to South Africa. Neither was found in South Africa by early collectors and both were first recorded from ports, so possibly they were introduced on the bottom of ships. This theory gains credence from their habit of clinging to the dense growths of organisms which develop on fouled ships. Presumably because they are transported in this manner specimens have been recorded all over the world.

The family Dromiidae is the final important family and consists of the sponge crabs, all of which have specially

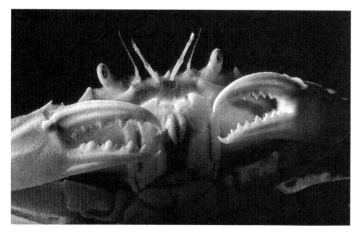

Fig. 276 Face to face with the massive cutting nippers of the three-spotted swimming crab, *Ovalipes punctatus* (x 1½).

modified fifth legs bent upwards over the back of the carapace. There these legs perform the curious function of holding a mantle of sponge or some other distasteful animal. Dromiids will actually cut a piece of sponge from the parent colony, then hold it over the carapace, where it grows to fit the crab. The sponge may even overgrow the animal to the extent that only its nippers can reach out to grasp food.

One of the clearest examples of the family is *Cryptodromiopsis spongiosa* (Plate 7) which has fine velvety hairs all over its body and knobby legs. A more spectacular beast is *Dromidia hirsutissima*, the shaggy sponge crab, which is covered by a dense mat of hairs (hirsute = hairy, issima = the most). A tropical species, *Dromidia unidentata*, has a coat of short hairs and is further distinguished by having no marginal teeth on the outer edge of the carapace behind the eyes. Unlike most other species it carries a cloak of colonial anemone-like zoanthids.

By hiding beneath a mantle of some distasteful animal, the dromiids are not only camouflaging themselves, but make themselves unattractive to predators even if they are detected. In keeping with this, they are very slow-moving, heightening the deception. As far as is known, most of them are detritus feeders, although their feeding habits are little known. At least one species, *Pseudodromia latens* (easily recognized because it is the only dromiid with a carapace that is longer than it is broad), has been seen feeding on the polyps of sea fans, sluggishly clambering up the fan to nip off the polyps with its pincers.

The art of deception is not confined to the dromiids. The seaweed crab *Dehaanius dentatus* (Figs. 274L & 48) has evolved hooks on the front of its carapace, to which it attaches algae. These seaweeds then actually grow on the crab, effectively hiding it. *Dehaanius dentatus* also has the ability to slowly change its colour to match the background algae. A close relative, *Dehaanius 4-dentatus* (which has four teeth on the margin of the carapace and not three as in *D. dentatus*) has hooks scattered all over its carapace and may become so covered with algae and other animals that it is impossible to distinguish it until it moves. On one crab I found 17 different species growing on its carapace, including algae, sponges, bryozoans, hydroids, barnacles and protozoans – a veritable community all on its own.

Several species of crab have developed a protective relationship with cnidarians. One lives inside anemones, although how it avoids being stung and digested is not known. Another, the boxer crab *Lybia plumosa* (Fig. 48), carries an anemone in each nipper and uses these to repel predators and to stun prey. The members of one whole family of crabs, Hapalocarcinidae, form galls in corals. Almost every head of the staghorn coral *Pocillopora* bears two or three such galls induced by female crabs which cling to the tips of coral branches. Here their respiratory currents influence the growth of the coral, which slowly develops arms around the crab and eventually completely encases the animal in a cage, leaving only a narrow slit through which the animal draws water (and thus food) and through which the larvae escape. The coral seems unharmed by the process and the crab gains protection.

No crabs are truly parasitic, but one species, the pea-crab *Pinnotheres dofleini*, lives inside the shells of the horse mussel *Atrina squamifera*, or in oysters, and there they strain off the food the bivalve has filtered from the water. Large pea-crabs stunt the growth of their hosts, so that in this sense perhaps they may be regarded as parasites.

The crabs are the pinnacle of crustacean evolution. Proof of their achievements is that there are more species of crab than in any other equivalent group. Moreover they have radiated to fill practically every conceivable niche, being found on rocky shores, in sand and mud, on land and in estuaries and rivers. They have adapted to feed on a wide range of materials including detritus, micro-organisms, plants and animals; not least of all, they have developed some remarkable relationships with other animals.

REFERENCES

Popular articles and books

Green, J. 1961. *A biology of Crustacea*. Quadrangle Books, Chicago.

Silberbauer, B. I. 1971. The biology of the South African rock lobster. *S. Afr. Shipping News and Fishing Industry Review*, Vol. 26: 56-63.

Starbird, E. A. 1973. Friendless squatters of the sea (barnacles). *National Geographic*, Vol. 144 (5): 623-633.

Scientific references

Berry, P. F. 1970. Mating behaviour, oviposition and fertilisation in the spiny lobster *Palinurus homarus* (Linnaeus). *S. Afr. Association for Marine Biological Research, Oceanographic Research Institute, Investigational Report*, Vol. 24: 1-16.

Berry, P. F. 1971. The spiny lobsters (Palinuridae) of the east coast of southern Africa : distribution and ecological notes. *S. Afr. Association for Marine Biological Research, Oceanographic Research Institute, Investigational Report*, Vol. 27: 1-23.

Berry, P. F. 1973. The biology of the spiny lobster *Palinurus delagoae* Barnard, off the coast of Natal, South Africa. *S. Afr. Association for Marine Biological Research, Oceanographic Research Institute, Investigational Report*, Vol. 31: 1-27.

Branch, G. M. 1975. The ecology of *Patella* from the Cape Peninsula, South Africa: v. Commensalism. *Zoologica Africana*, Vol. 10 (2): 133-162.

Caiger, K. M. & Alexander, A. J. 1973. The control of dominance in the brachyuran crustacean, *Cyclograpsus punctatus* M.Edw. *Zoologica Africana*, Vol. 8: 138-140.

Silberbauer, B. I. 1971a. The biology of the South African rock lobster, *Jasus lalandii* (H. Milne-Edwards) I. Development. *Investigational Report, Division of Sea Fisheries, South Africa*, Vol. 92: 1-10.

Silberbauer. B. I. 1971b. The biology of the South African rock lobster, *Jasus lalandii* (H. Milne-Edwards) II. The reproductive organs, mating and fertilisation. *Investigational Report, Division of Sea Fisheries, South Africa*, Vol. 93: 1-46.

Identification guides

Barnard, K. H. 1924. Contributions to the crustacean fauna of South Africa. No. 7 – Cirripedia. *Annals of the S. Afr. Museum*, Vol. 20: 1-103.

Barnard, K. H. 1950. Descriptive catalogue of South African decapod crustacea (crabs and shrimps). *Annals of the S. Afr. Museum*, Vol. 38: 1-837.

Barnard, K. H. 1950. Descriptive list of South African Stomatopod Crustacea (Mantis Shrimps). *Annals of the S. Afr. Museum*, Vol. 38: 838-864.

Day, J. A. 1975-1980. South African Cumacea: Parts I – IV. *Annals of the S. Afr. Museum*, Vols. 66: 177-220, 75: 159-290, 76: 137-189, 82: 187-292.

Day, J. H. 1969. *A Guide to Marine Life on South African Shores*. A. A. Balkema, Cape Town. pp. 68-118.

Griffiths, C. L. 1976. *Guide to the Benthic Marine Amphipods of Southern Africa*. S. Afr. Museum, Cape Town. pp. 1-106.

Kensley, B. 1972. *Shrimps and Prawns of Southern Africa*. S. Afr. Museum, Cape Town. 65 pp.

Kensley, B. 1978. *Guide to the Marine Isopods of Southern Africa*. S. Afr. Museum, Cape Town, pp. 1-173.

McNae, W. & Kalk, M. 1958. *A Natural History of Inhaca Island, Moçambique*. Witwatersrand University Press, Johannesburg. pp. 64-83.

14.INSECTA THE MARINE INSECTS

Fig. 279 The collembolan *Anurida maritima* floats on the surface of pools because it is covered by waxy hairs (x 5).

The insects are true masters of the land and air, making up more than three-quarters of all known species, and so it is curious that they have never succeeded in becoming marine. The question of why this should be so has vexed many a biologist and there is still no satisfactory answer; however, some hints are implicit in the structure and life-cycles of insects.

Insects' bodies are divisible into a head, thorax and abdomen. The head carries a pair of antennae, a pair of compound eyes and a series of mouthparts, which in their most basic form consist of a pair of maxillae and a labium which hold the food while it is macerated by the biting mandibles. The abdomen bears no limbs and serves mainly as a housing for the reproductive organs. The thorax has three pairs of legs and, in many species, one or two pairs of wings. Here we have the first hint of why the insects are unsuccessful in the sea: a six-legged body is relatively unstable and unsuited to the rigours of water movement, and the wings that stand insects in such good stead on land are useless in the water.

Insects respire by trachea, which form ramifying tubules throughout the body and carry oxygen from spiracles on the sides of the body to the tissues. Since this system depends on gaseous oxygen, it too is unsuited for life in the sea.

Insect life-cycles are also radically different from those found in marine organisms, for none of the insects have anything like a planktonic stage that could allow dispersion in the sea.

Yet, despite all these restrictions, insects do live successfully under water in freshwater rivers and lakes, so that none of these limitations really explain their absence from the sea. Perhaps the crustaceans, which evolved long

before the insects, have provided too much competition in the sea.

A number of insects scavenge in the intertidal zone. For example, a host of beetles may be found under cast-up kelp (Fig. 280A-D). These include *Pachyphaleria capensis*, a fat oval yellow beetle about 8 mm in length, which eats decaying algae; a number of tiny staphylinid beetles with long narrow bodies and exceptionally short wing cases that cover only the first two segments of the long abdomen; *Platychila pallida*, a predatory species with massive jaws; and *Acanthoscelis ruficornis*, a shiny black oval beetle about 15 mm long, which may occur in great clusters under kelp and feeds on isopods and amphipods. Scurrying around on sandy beaches are the ferocious tiger beetles – aptly named because they are aggressive creatures, seizing their prey in large mandibles that project forwards from the head. Tiger beetles (Fig. 280E) have streamlined bodies and long legs and can run at speed, although they take to the wing if alarmed. Two common species occur in southern Africa: *Cicindela capensis* occurs on the south coast and is replaced by a smaller darker brown species, *Cicindela brevicollis*, on the west coast. Technically the two are distinguished from one another by the labrum (the 'lip' that hangs down in front of the mouthparts), that of *C. brevicollis* having three teeth while that of *C. capensis* is smooth.

Clouds of kelp flies are often seen around stranded kelp, on which they lay their eggs. The larvae feed on the rotting kelp and pupate under the seaweed. As described in Chapter 3, kelp flies have monthly cycles of egg-laying and hatching to make best use of kelp stranded high on the shore by spring tides, and to minimise the chance of the larvae being swept away by rising tides. Of the two common flies, *Fucellia capensis* is distinguished by two white stripes on the thorax of the adult fly, while *Coelopea africana* lacks the stripes. There are, however, several other species with the same habits.

Another fly with a similar life-cycle is the midge *Telmatogeton minor* (Fig. 280F), which lays its eggs on living algae low on the shore. At times the larvae are very abundant and are feasted upon by tide-pool fish. The 7 mm larvae are cylindrical and worm-like in shape, with a well-marked chitinised head behind which a single stubby proleg projects. The posterior end is armed with a ring of hooks used to cling to the seaweed on which the larvae feed. *Telmatogeton* has marked rhythms, ensuring that it hatches from the pupae only during the low spring tide when the low-shore is exposed.

All these species are associated with the sea but can only barely be considered marine. Curiously, it is one of the

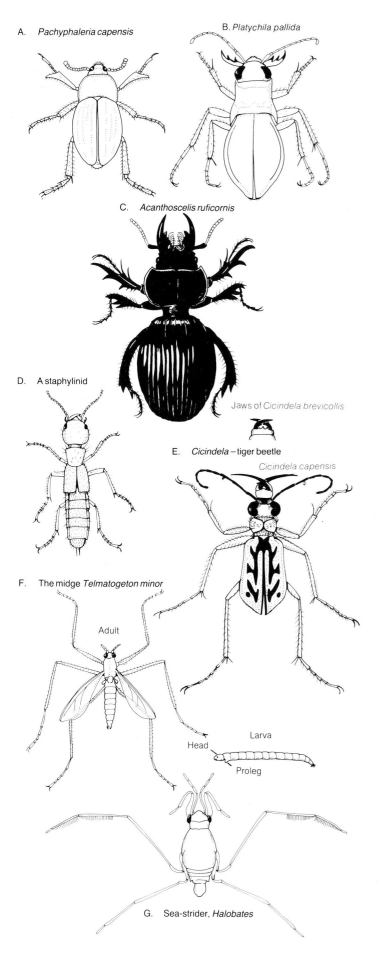

A. *Pachyphaleria capensis*

B. *Platychila pallida*

C. *Acanthoscelis ruficornis*

Jaws of *Cicindela brevicollis*

D. A staphylinid

E. *Cicindela* – tiger beetle

Cicindela capensis

F. The midge *Telmatogeton minor*

Adult

Larva

Head

Proleg

G. Sea-strider, *Halobates*

most primitive insect-like creatures – *Anurida maritima* – which has succeeded in living permanently in the intertidal zone. *Anurida* belongs to the class Collembola, normally called springtails because they have a forked appendage bent under the abdomen and which can be used to kick the animals off the ground; but, being marine, *Anurida* has little use for this mechanism and has, accordingly, lost the appendage. The Collembola were once classified as insects, but some of their features are so unlike those of other insects that they are now considered as a separate class.

Anurida scavenges during low tide, gathering scraps left behind by larger predators, while at high tide it shelters under shells or stones, or in the empty cases of dead barnacles. Masses of the tiny 2 mm long *Anurida* are often seen floating on the surface of the pools (Fig. 279), supported there by surface tension and by the short waxy hairs covering their bodies.

A most unlikely creature to have made a success of marine life is the sea-strider *Halobates* (Fig. 280G). It is closely related to the pond-skaters or water-striders, which are a familiar sight on the surface of ponds. Like its freshwater kin, *Halobates* has developed two pairs of particularly long legs which distribute its weight and allow it to sit on the surface skin of the sea. The first of these is fringed with hairs and provides propulsion by rowing the animal over the surface of the water. In front of these is a small pair of legs which serves to grasp prey. The mouthparts form a long jointed beak (as they do in all members of the order Hemiptera) and through this the animal sucks the juices of its prey. *Halobates* spends its entire life skating over the surface of the open sea, where it is often found hundreds of kilometres from the shore. It completes its life-cycle at sea; the eggs are laid on floating objects and the nymphs begin their life on the skin of the sea from the moment they hatch.

Of all the insects, *Halobates* comes closest to being fully marine, which returns us to the enigma posed at the beginning of this chapter: that not a single one of the almost one million species of insect has become sufficiently adapted to the sea to spend its whole life under water.

REFERENCES
Popular articles and books
Gess, F. W. & Gess, S. K. 1981. The insect mariner: *Halobates. The Naturalist,* Vol. 25 (1): 25-26.
Skaife, S. H. 1979. *African Insect Life* (2nd edition revised by J. Ledger). C. Struik, Cape Town. 279 pp.

Scientific references
Cheng, L. 1976. *Marine insects.* North-Holland Publishing Company, Amsterdam. 581 pp.
Hesse, A. J. 1934. Contributions to a knowledge of S. African marine Clunionine-Chironomids. *The Transactions of the Royal Entomological Society of London,* Vol. 55: 27-40.
Stenton-Dozey, J. & Griffiths, C. L. 1980. Growth, consumption and respiration by larvae of the kelp-fly *Fucellia capensis* (Diptera : Anthomyiidae). *S. Afr. Journal of Zoology,* Vol. 15: 280-283.

◀ Fig. 280 A number of beetles shelter and feed under stranded kelp (A-D). The tiger beetle, *Cicindela* (E), is an active fast-running predator on the high-shore of sandy beaches. Larvae of *Telmatogeton* (F) frequent algae low on rocky shores. The sea-strider, *Halobates* (G), floats on the surface of the open sea.

15. ARANAEA THE TRUE SPIDERS

Almost all spiders are terrestrial, but a few have adapted their body structure and behaviour to allow them to occupy intertidal rocky shores. In fact they are so dependent on conditions there that they are never found anywhere else.

Spiders have a body that is divided into an anterior prosoma (roughly equivalent to the head and thorax merged into a single unit) and an opisthosoma (or abdomen). The prosoma carries four pairs of long walking legs, fronted by mouthparts that are modified to form hollow hypodermic fangs which can inject poison from special glands in the head. Immediately behind the fangs is a pair of short leg-like palps (pedipalps) which serve as sensory organs and, in the case of the male, they are swollen into complex organs which are also used to transfer sperm to the female. Prior to mating, the male deposits his sperm on a silk web and then picks it up in the sac-like structures that lie within the pedipalps; from these he is able to deposit the sperm into the genital aperture of the female. When we remember that spiders are voracious animals, and that as likely as not the male will end up a meal for his erstwhile mate, the purpose of this devious method of sperm transfer becomes apparent, for it allows internal fertilisation without involving the male in the risky procedure of copulation with a potentially cannibalistic female. Most spiders have a complex courtship which ensures that mating only takes place if the two spiders belong to the same species and if the female is sufficiently mature and receptive – and pacified. Some male spiders have evolved the trick of wrapping food in silk and presenting this to the female to suppress her cannibalistic instincts; others have gone even further and, instead of a tasty morsel, they simply bind up a bit of dead stick to keep her occupied while they mate. It seems that spiders were way ahead of man in inventing the chocolate box gift!

Spiders have an unsegmented abdomen which contains the reproductive organs, the respiratory book lungs (much like internal folded sheets that allow uptake of oxygen), and a set of spinnerettes near the posterior end, which produce the silk from which webs are manufactured. The

evolution of spinning organs has probably been a major contribution to the success of spiders.

Two southern African spiders are particularly common on rocky shores. *Desis formidabilis* (Plate 84) is the largest, with a uniform brown body up to 20 mm in length. *Desis* has formidable fangs that are almost one-third the body length (hence its specific name). *Amaurobioides africanus* (Plate 85) is slightly smaller, with a distinctive chevron pattern on the back of its opisthosoma (abdomen); in addition, its fangs are much smaller than those of *Desis* (a factor of some importance, which influences the relationship between the two species).

Both species make web-lined nests under limpet shells or in empty barnacles, cementing the shell securely to the rock so that a bubble of air is trapped there during high tide. In these nests the eggs are laid (Plate 85) and here the juveniles spend their early life. Little is known of the mating habits of *Amaurobioides*, but *Desis* mates readily while out on its feeding forays. The courtship is fairly simple, the male approaching the female and first tapping her with his legs (Plate 84) and then with his pedipalps to test if she is prepared to mate. If she is, he crawls under her to deposit the sperm from his pedipalps into her abdominal reproductive aperture (Fig. 281) – a seemingly perilous position, and yet no cases of cannibalism have been recorded. Females which are not ready to mate simply brush the male away.

Since empty shells are often in short supply, the spiders compete fiercely for them. Larger spiders evict smaller ones from shells; and females are particularly exclusive and never share their shell with another female – presumably because ultimately they will brood their young under it. Experiments have shown that the availability of shells largely determines the population density of the spiders.

The spiders emerge at night during the low tide to feed, and to prey on isopods and amphipods. An interesting feature is that the two spiders feed on different species of prey: *Desis* eats sphaeromid and idoteid isopods (Figs. 251 & 252) and the amphipod *Hyale*; while *Amaurobioides* preys on different isopods, including *Ligia* and *Deto* (Fig. 252) and on the sand hopper *Talorchestia*. At first glance, it seems curious that they should be so particular about the animals they eat. Experiments have, however, shown that this preference is not simply a question of the two spiders feeding on what is most available to them: in aquaria they faithfully maintain their diets even when given a choice of different species of prey. Possibly they feed on different species to reduce competition for food, although there is no evidence that their food is ever in short supply.

Both species are sometimes stranded from their nests

Fig. 281 Sketch showing the position a male *Desis* adopts during mating, while he transfers sperm from his pedipalps to the female. The male is shaded black and the pedipalps are arrowed.

by the advancing tide, but even without the air-filled nests they are able to live many hours under water. Their survival under water is as a result of a velvety mat of waxy hairs which covers the abdomen and keeps it dry, creating a film of air beneath the hairs (Figs. 282 & 283). From this film, oxygen may be supplied to the animal. But the air film is more than a simple reservoir of oxygen: it functions as a physical gill allowing the animal to extract oxygen from the water. The principle it operates on is as follows: air contains about 20 percent oxygen and 80 percent nitrogen. As the animal uses up the oxygen in the air film, the percentage of oxygen drops, leaving a higher percentage of nitrogen. If the surrounding water is saturated with air (and it usually is in the turbulent intertidal zone), then it too will contain 20 parts of oxygen to 80 parts of nitrogen. After the spider has used some of the oxygen in its air space, the air film will thus have a lower percentage of oxygen than the surrounding water. As a result, oxygen diffuses from the water across the surface of the bubble into the air film. Thus the film provides a means of extracting oxygen from the water. Of course, by the same token, the air film will slowly lose nitrogen into the water and eventually it will collapse – but it provides a vital means of tiding the spider over periods of submergence.

Apart from having different diets, the two spiders also occupy different places on the shore. *Desis* lives low on the shore where desiccation is reduced and where food is more abundant. It seems likely that being more aggressive and larger fanged, it excludes *Amaurobioides* from the low shore, for when kept together in aquaria, *Desis* soon kills and eats *Amaurobioides*.

This does not, of course, answer the question of why *Desis* should not colonize the high-shore as well, and eliminate *Amaurobioides* altogether. Its tolerances to desiccation, heat and low humidity have been experimentally tested and all are so great that physical factors cannot alone explain the absence of *Desis* from the high-shore. So we are left with no really satisfactory explanation as to why *Desis* is restricted to the low-shore – except possibly that the prey it prefers are all low-shore species.

In localities where shells accumulate and become wedged between boulders, *Desis* may become very abundant and thus have an important effect on its prey. This is not its only influence on the low-shore community. The tiny scavenging collembolans, *Anurida maritima* (see Chapter 14, Fig. 279) are frequently found in the nests of *Desis* where they feed upon the remnants of prey left by the spider. On the other hand, *Desis* is parasitised by a tiny wasp, *Echthrodesis lamorali*, which lays its eggs inside those of the spider. It is the only known intertidal member of the wasp family Scelionidae and, in keeping with its semi-marine habitat, it is wingless and covered with a pile of hairs which probably prevents wetting and forms a physical gill. The wasp is named in honour of Bruno Lamoral, who first worked out its relationship with the spider, and to whom we owe almost all our knowledge about southern African intertidal spiders.

It was he, too, who discovered an undescribed mite in

Fig. 282 Water sometimes floods a spider's nest, as has occurred under this limpet shell, but the waxy hairs that coat the spider create an air film which can keep the animal alive until the following low tide (x 3).

Fig. 283 Details of the hairs surrounding one of the respiratory openings of a *Desis*. Electron micrograph, magnified x 100.

the nests of *Desis*. The mite does the spider a favour by preying on the wasp, as well as feeding on the scavenging *Anurida*.

Thus it is that the few spiders that have succeeded in inhabiting the intertidal zone have not only developed remarkable habits and specialised respiratory adaptations to allow them to live in this challenging habitat, but their very presence has a profound influence on a number of other species.

REFERENCES

Scientific references

Lamoral, B. H. 1973. On the ecology and habitat adaptations of two intertidal spiders, *Desis formidabilis* (O. P. Cambridge) and *Amaurobioides africanus* Hewitt, at "The Island" (Kommetjie, Cape Peninsula), with notes on the occurrence of two other spiders. *Annals of the Natal Museum*, Vol. 20: 151-193.

16.PYCNOGONIDA
'SEA SPIDERS'

The pycnogonids are often referred to as 'sea spiders' because superficially they resemble spiders, having four pairs of long legs; but in fact they are totally unrelated and are quite different in structure. Pycnogonids have a comparatively small body made up of a head and a trunk of four segments. The abdomen is vestigial, being reduced to a stub. The head usually bears a long bulbous proboscis, a pair of nipper-bearing chelifers and a pair of sensory palps (Fig. 284A). Arising from the trunk are the animals' most characteristic features – the four pairs of long spindly legs which give the creatures an other-world appearance. Some deep-sea species such as *Colosendeis colossea* have bodies 5 cm long supported by 30-cm legs which are spread-eagled around the body. Because the body is so small the legs actually contain the major part of the reproductive and digestive systems.

Pycnogonids move sluggishly, their stilted slow-motion action heightening their bizarre appearance. Armed with claws at the tips of their legs, they are able to cling tightly to the substratum. Most of them feed on sessile animals such as sponges, hydroids or sea anemones, using their chelifers to cut off pieces, or the suctorial proboscis to slurp up the softer parts of the prey.

The reproductive system has a series of openings, one at the base of each leg – more reproductive apertures than in any other arthropod, which is why the animals were given the name Pycnogonida (pycnos = great or multiple, gonas = reproduction). Fertilisation is external, but in almost all species the males gather up the egg masses and carry them mounted on a special pair of miniature legs – the ovigerous legs (Fig. 284A) – until they hatch. In some species, the females lack these legs altogether, but even those that do possess ovigerous legs are liberated from the task of tending the eggs.

The larvae are like miniature stunted versions of the adult except that initially they have only three pairs of appendages. Many of them are parasitic on the animals their adults prey on, clinging to them or forming galls in them while sucking their tissues. In one as yet undescribed species, the parasitic habit lingers on and the adults live inside mussels, and have feeble thin legs but an enlarged proboscis which is permanently embedded into the mussel on which it feeds.

Several species are encountered around the coast of southern Africa, including various species of *Nymphon* and *Pycnogonum* (Plates 86 & 87), but by far the commonest species is a small insignificant creature, *Tanystylum brevipes* (Fig. 284B), only 15 mm across the span of its legs. Its characteristic round body and its possession of palps but no chelifers make this animal easy to identify.

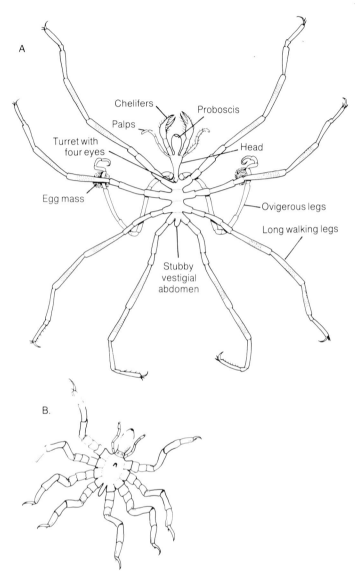

Fig. 284A. A typical pycnogonid such as *Nymphon* (see Plate 87).
B. The commonest southern African species, *Tanystylum brevipes,* which lacks chelifers.

REFERENCES

Popular book
King, P. E. 1973. *Pycnogonids.* Hutchinson University Library, London. 144 pp.

Identification guides
Barnard, K. H. 1954. South African Pycnogonida. *Annals of the S. Afr. Museum,* Vol. 41: 81-159.
Day, J. H. 1969. *A Guide to Marine Life on South African Shores.* A. A. Balkema, Cape Town. pp. 120-121.

17. BRYOZOA MOSS OR LACE ANIMALS

Bryozoans are amongst the least-known and yet most exquisite of marine animals. The reason they are unfamiliar is not because they are rare. In fact there are over 4 000 species and many are very common; practically every overturned stone, most large algae and a great many shells are encrusted with bryozoans. They are unfamiliar because they resemble a wide range of other organisms and are easily confused with corals, seaweeds, hydroids and even with encrusting lichens (see Plates 137–140). The name Bryozoa means 'moss-animals' and refers to the fact that many are moss-like. At different times other names have been applied to this unique group of animals and they are still sometimes called Polyzoa or Ectoprocta.

All the bryozoans form colonies of numerous individuals. Each colony is started by a single larva that settles and metamorphoses into an adult. This solitary adult then divides to produce two individuals, which divide into four, and so a colony is soon established and continues to grow at its edges throughout its life. The colony lays down an external skeleton of chitin or calcium carbonate, each animal being encased in a coffin-like skeletal box known as a zooecium. The body structure of a pair of individuals, or zooids, is shown in Fig. 285. The head bears a ring of tentacles (the lophophore) which serves to filter particles from the water. The mouth lies at the base of this lophophore and the gut is bent back on itself so that the anus opens outside the ring of tentacles and the faeces may be shed externally, so that neither the tentacles nor the zooecium is fouled (Fig. 285).

The body structure described above applies to the normal feeding individuals in a colony, called autozooids; but in some species a certain number of the zooids are specialised. Some have a reduced body and gut, but are modified into structures that look much like a bird's head – hence their name, avicularia, from aves = birds (Fig. 290C, D). This resemblance is heightened when the avicularia are seen in action, for the 'beak' snaps open and shut to protect the colony and to prevent fouling organisms from settling on it. Other individuals are even more drastically modified into long slender spines (vibracula) that sweep across the colony to prevent sediment from settling. The Hydrozoa is the only other group to match such specialisation of individuals within a colony (see Chapter 9).

In the most primitive bryozoans, a frontal membrane which is flexible and chitinous covers the outer surface of the zooecium, leaving only an aperture through which the lophophore projects. The tentacles can, however, be withdrawn by the contraction of retractor muscles. Naturally this increases the volume inside the zooecium, and the flexible frontal membrane bows outwards to make room for the lophophore. To bring about the extension of the lophophore, parietal (or protractor) muscles pull the frontal membrane downwards, increasing the pressure on the body cavity and forcing the tentacles out again.

The only problem with this arrangement is that the body gains little protection from the fragile frontal membrane. Most of the bryozoans have developed one of three different kinds of armature to protect the body more efficiently. Some, such as *Electra* and *Beania vanhoeffeni* (Fig. 286D, E & G), have long spines that project over the frontal membrane. Others have a light calcium carbonate sheet (called a cryptocyst) that lies underneath the frontal membrane (Fig. 285B).Of necessity this must be penetrated by pores which allow the parietal muscles to extend through the

Fig. 285 (A) The structure of two typical bryozoan zooids, one withdrawn into its box-like zooecium, the other expanded. Simplified drawings show the development of a protective cryptocyst beneath the frontal membrane (B), and the formation of a calcified frontal membrane together with a compensation chamber or ascus (C).

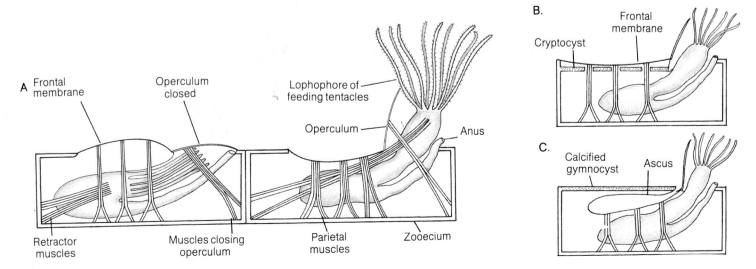

GROUP I

Fig. 286 **Species that encrust algae.**

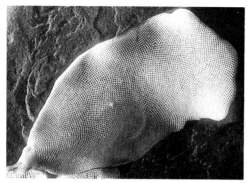

A. *Membranipora* species grow on flat algae (x1)

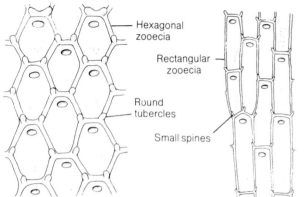

Hexagonal
zooecia

Rectangular
zooecia

Round
tubercles

Small spines

B. *Membranipora tuberculata*   C *Membranipora membranacea*

D *Electra verticellata* grows on narrow-bladed algae (x1)

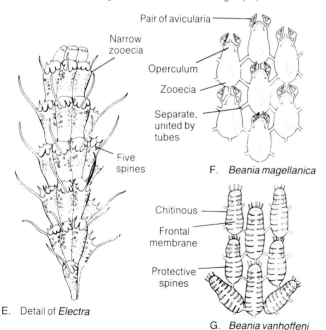

Pair of avicularia

Narrow
zooecia

Operculum

Zooecia

Separate,
united by
tubes

Five
spines

F. *Beania magellanica*

Chitinous

Frontal
membrane

Protective
spines

E. Detail of *Electra*

G. *Beania vanhoffeni*

cryptocyst to the frontal membrane so that they are able to fulfil their vital function of extending the tentacles.

The final solution, and the one adopted by most species, has been to form a calcified (calcium carbonate) frontal membrane (called a gymnocyst), which is rigid and much stronger so that it protects the body more efficiently (Fig. 285C). Of course this eliminates the original function of the flexible frontal membrane. To make up for this, a special sac-like ascus has been evolved, and acts like a compensation chamber. When the lophophore withdraws, water is expelled from the ascus. When the parietal muscles tug on the ascus they expand it, sucking water in; and the ensuing increase of pressure inside the body once again forces the tentacles out.

These different adaptations are interesting in their own right, but they also provide us with the basis of the modern classification of the bryozoans, which is discussed in J. S. Ryland's excellent introductory book on the group.

The Bryozoa are commercially important because they are amongst the most frequent of fouling organisms (see Chapter 7) and often they are the early colonisers of any clean surface. Part of their success results from their ability to exclude many other animals, although the ascidians (sea squirts), mussels and barnacles usually triumph over them. Those species which have avicularia and vibracula seem more effective in preventing other animals from settling on them.

Many bryozoans grow on algae, and they have evolved several methods for reducing competition with other plant-dwelling organisms. Firstly, their larvae show a preference for young algal tissues over old tissues, thus ensuring they settle on a fresh growth which is not likely to have other organisms on it. Secondly, their colonies often spread towards the growth point in algae, thus continuing to occupy the newest tissues. Finally (and this applies to bryozoans in general), different species are very particular about the species of alga or the nature of the substratum on which they settle, and this must reduce competition between different species. As an example, *Alcyonidium* (Fig. 287) is only found on one particular whelk, *Bur-*

GROUP II

Fig. 287 **Species that encrust shells of molluscs. Here** *Alcyonidium nodosum* forms a purple covering on the whelk *Burnupena papyracea* (x1).

nupena papyracea, on which it forms a purple knobbly crust.

Bryozoans have been used to test one of the basic ecological concepts about competition. It has been hypothesised that if a species is crowded and therefore suffering from competition from its own species (intraspecific competition) it should expand its niche, perhaps to occupy a wider range of habitats or to eat a wider range of food. On the other hand, if it is competing with other species (interspecific competition), it is suggested that the animals do

GROUP III
Fig. 288 Species that form flat crusts on rocks.

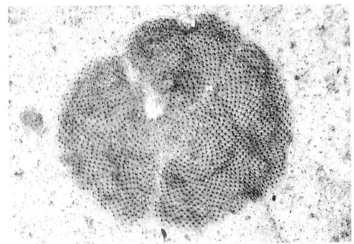

A. *Watersipora subovoidea* (x1½)

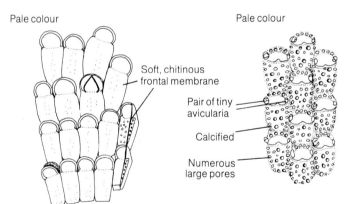

Pale colour

B. *Steganiporella buskii*

Pale colour

Soft, chitinous frontal membrane

Pair of tiny avicularia

Calcified

Numerous large pores

C. *Escharoides contorta*

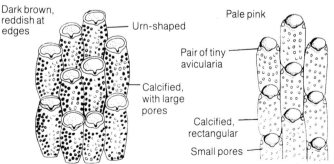

Dark brown, reddish at edges

Urn-shaped

Calcified, with large pores

D. *Watersipora subovoidea*
Very common

Pale pink

Pair of tiny avicularia

Calcified, rectangular

Small pores

E. *Cryptotheca nivea*

GROUP IV
Fig. 289 Upright, branching or cylindrical forms that resemble coral.

A. *Gigantopora polymorpha* (x1)

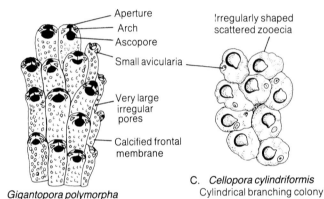

Aperture
Arch
Ascopore
Small avicularia

Very large irregular pores

Calcified frontal membrane

B. *Gigantopora polymorpha*

Irregularly shaped scattered zooecia

C. *Cellopora cylindriformis*
Cylindrical branching colony

better to restrict themselves to a smaller part of their niche – say by occupying a more limited part of the habitat or by specialising on certain items of food.

Do animals really conform to this concept? By using bryozoans that live on algae, it has been possible to measure how much of the alga is occupied in relation to competition from other colonies. Obligingly, the creatures conform to the predicted trend: if their density is high and they have to compete with their own species, they spread out to occupy more of the alga than would be expected purely on the basis of their numbers; but if other species provide the competition, they specialise on only a small part of the alga.

Several species of bryozoans form scroll-like sheets that project from the rock face and these frequently have horny corals or soft corals growing in amongst them (Plates 138 & 139). This seems curious, for the bryozoans exclude most other fouling organisms. At first it was thought that the stinging cells of the soft and horny corals kept the bryozoans at bay, but in fact no damage is done to them. There is a suspicion that the two types of animals may be of benefit to each other. The bryozoan skeleton may provide extra protection for the soft corals whose stinging cells in turn could deter other fouling organisms. The association

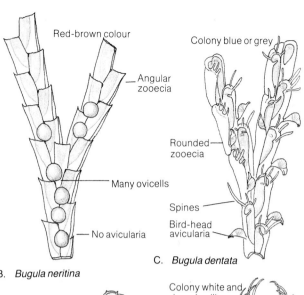

Red-brown colour

Angular zooecia

Many ovicells

No avicularia

B. *Bugula neritina*

Colony blue or grey

Rounded zooecia

Spines

Bird-head avicularia

C. *Bugula dentata*

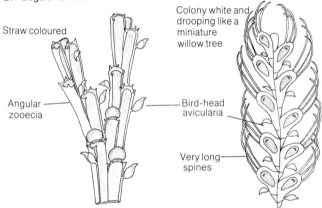

Straw coloured

Angular zooecia

Bird-head avicularia

Very long spines

Colony white and drooping like a miniature willow tree

D. *Bugula avicularia*

E. *Bicellariella ciliata*

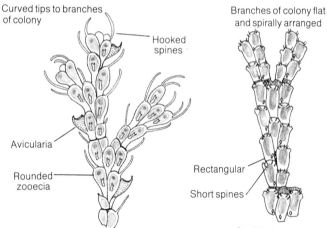

Curved tips to branches of colony

Hooked spines

Avicularia

Rounded zooecia

F. *Menipea crispa* (see Plate 137)

Branches of colony flat and spirally arranged

Rectangular

Short spines

G. *Menipea triseriata* (see Plate 137)

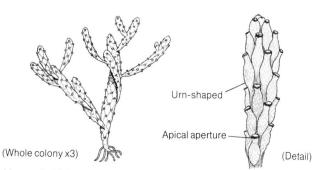

(Whole colony x3)

H. *Margaretta triplex*

Urn-shaped

Apical aperture

(Detail)

I. *Margaretta triplex*

◀ GROUP V
Fig. 290 Bushy branched colonies, fern-like or cactus-like.
▼

A. *Bugula dentata* (x2)

GROUP VI
Fig. 291 Species that form scroll-like, twisted coralline plates.

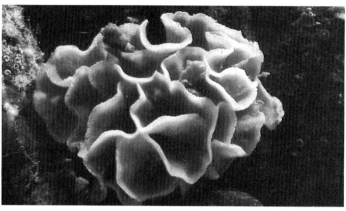

A. *Laminopora bimunita* (x½)

Colony punctured with holes, lace-like

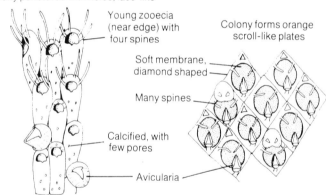

Young zooecia (near edge) with four spines

Calcified, with few pores

Avicularia

B. *Schizoretepora tesselata* (see Plate 139)

Colony forms orange scroll-like plates

Soft membrane, diamond shaped

Many spines

Avicularia

C. *Chaperia* spp. (See Plate 137)

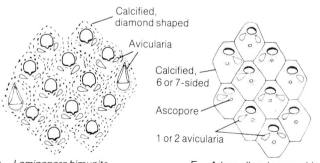

Calcified, diamond shaped

Avicularia

D. *Laminopora bimunita*

Calcified, 6 or 7-sided

Ascopore

1 or 2 avicularia

E. *Adeonellopsis meandrina*

is too frequent to be due to chance, but more work is needed to test whether the animals really are mutually beneficial.

Identification of local species

A large number of species occur in southern African waters, many as yet not named. To identify most of the species it is necessary to examine the shape and nature of the zooecia, and particularly whether they are covered by a thin and flexible chitinous frontal membrane or closed over by a rigid calcified roof. These features can only be seen properly by using a dissecting microscope or at least a powerful magnifying lens, but the effort is well worth it since many of the animals are delicately sculptured and very beautiful. Figs. 286 – 291 have, however, been arranged so that the bryozoans are divided into six groups purely on the basis of their habitats and gross structure. A preliminary identification can thus be made by deciding to which group an animal belongs and then comparing it with the photographs or the notes that are given about each of the species that fall into that group. These groups are, however, artificial in the sense that they bear no relationship to the accepted classification of the Bryozoa. Within each group the species can only be identified with any certainty by examining the detailed structure of the zooecia, and for this reason more detailed illustrations are given of their arrangement and nature.

REFERENCES

Introductory book
Ryland, J. S. 1970. *Bryozoans.* Hutchinson University Library, London.
Identification guide
Day, J. H. 1969, *A Guide to Marine Life on South African Shores.* A. A. Balkema, Cape Town. pp. 124-131.

18. BRACHIOPODA LAMP SHELLS

Lamp shells are superficially so like bivalve molluscs that uninitiated shell collectors quite naturally place them amongst the bivalves. It is only when the animals are opened up that the radically different body structure is revealed. In the first place, lamp shells have dorsal and ventral shell valves so that the body is flattened from top to bottom. The uppermost shell has a round opening near the back of the shell, through which a fleshy stalk or pedicle extends to attach the animal to the substratum. The general shape of the shell is like an Aladdin's lamp, hence their popular name. Bivalve molluscs such as mussels have quite a different arrangement, being compressed from side to side and having left and right shell valves.

If the dorsal valve of a brachiopod's shell is removed, the first thing to strike one is the pair of horseshoe-shaped arms, feathery with tentacles, which make up the lophophore (Fig. 292). The tentacles filter particles from the water and transmit them along a groove on the arms to the mouth. It is these arms that give the group their name – 'arm-footed'.

The remaining organs are quite small and cramped near the back of the shell. The mouth opens into a small stomach which is blind-ending, there being no anus. Two thin mantles cover the whole of the body and are responsible for laying down the shell. The gonads branch throughout both mantle lobes.

The remarkably large size of the lophophore obviously improves the animal's ability to filter-feed. In addition, it

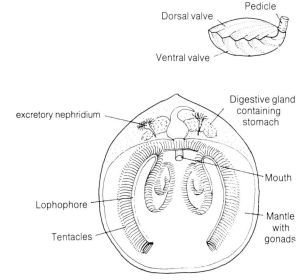

Fig. 292 The internal structure of a brachiopod, as revealed by the removal of the dorsal shell valve.

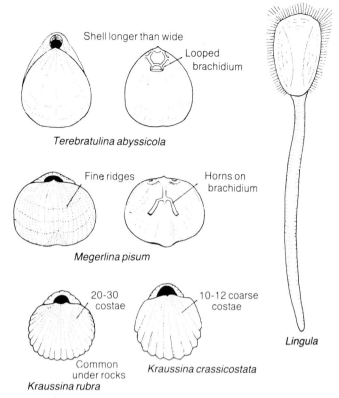

Fig. 293 Southern African species of lamp-shells (all life size).

Terebratulina abyssicola

Shell longer than wide

Looped brachidium

Megerlina pisum

Fine ridges

Horns on brachidium

Kraussina rubra

20-30 costae

Common under rocks

Kraussina crassicostata

10-12 coarse costae

Lingula

has been shown that it contains digestive enzymes as well that break down the food before it even reaches the gut. There has also been suggestion that it has the ability to extract dissolved organic molecules from the water, and if this is the case, this perhaps explains why the lamp shells have such a small gut and no anus.

The phylum Brachiopoda is of little significance today and there are only a handful of species in southern Africa. But the fossil record shows that there was a time when they were amongst the dominant animals, and over 30 000 species have been described. The brachiopods reigned during the Palaeozoic era, about 450 million years ago, but their number declined after this, possibly as they came into competition with the bivalves. One of the limitations of the lamp shells is the lophophore which is not very efficient at ridding the body of unwanted particles (while the bivalves have evolved sophisticated means of eliminating wastes) and this is possibly the reason that lamp shells are often found growing beneath overhanging rocks where siltation is reduced.

The identification of southern African species depends on the structure of the shell. In the more advanced class Articulata the two shell valves are linked by articulating teeth which restrict the extent to which the shells can gape. Inside the dorsal valve there is also a skeletal support for the lophophore, called the brachidium. In *Terebratulina*, a

pearly-white species with an elongated shell, the brachidium forms a complete loop while in all other species it forms a pair of horns. The width and number of ridges (costae) on the outside of the shells also allow identification of the four common species (Fig. 293). The second class, Inarticulata, contains the more primitive species that lack articulatory teeth. There is only one southern African species, *Lingula*, which is common at Inhaca Island in Mocambique but is not recorded further south in South African waters. It burrows into sandbanks, leaving only the tip of its shell exposed to siphon in water. *Lingula* is something of a living fossil, for its body structure has remained almost unchanged since the Ordovician period, that is, for a period of 400 million years.

Fig. 294 A group of the commonest lamp shell, *Kraussina rubra,* clinging to the lower surface of a rock (x1).

REFERENCES

General reading
Rudwick, M. J. S. 1970. *Living and Fossil Brachiopods.* Hutchinson University Library, London.

Identification guide
Jackson, J. W. 1952. A revision of some South African Brachiopoda, with descriptions of new species. *Annals Natal Museum,* Vol. 41: 1-40.

19. MOLLUSCA

SNAILS, MUSSELS, OCTOPUS AND THEIR KIN

Shells have attracted man for centuries, both because of their beauty and because of their extraordinary diversity. They have inspired architects, poets, painters and composers, all of whom have incorporated the shell motif in their work. This fascination is not new, for buildings over 3 000 years old are decorated with shell patterns and even today various societies use shells as currency, as jewellery, trumpets, cutting tools, cooking utensils and even as bridal dowries.

Shell collecting is a popular hobby for, apart from the attractive nature of the shells, they are easy to store and do not deteriorate. Some of the rarer ones are extremely valuable and there is a regular international trade in shells – often to the detriment of mollusc populations. The Conchological Society of Southern Africa, founded in 1958, produces a regular bulletin, *The Strandloper*, which contains articles about shells and a guide to the identification of particular groups of molluscs; it is a valuable aid to anyone with an interest in shell collecting.

Although the shell is the hallmark of molluscs, the phylum contains several very different groups such as chitons, snails, bivalves and squids. Some of these either lack shells or only have small internal shells. Nevertheless, these divergent groups do share various other features. They are all soft-bodied creatures that are unsegmented, although the body can be divided into a foot, head and a visceral mass containing the gut and other organs. The body is cloaked by a fleshy sheath of skin, the mantle, which is responsible for laying down the shell and which overhangs part of the body to create a cavity (the mantle cavity) in which the gills are housed. Another distinguishing feature of creatures in this phylum is the gills which are covered with cilia that drive water over their surfaces. This makes them different from the gills of most other animals which cannot generate their own currents – and justifies a special name for mollusc gills: ctenidia.

Most species are protected by a shell, which is made up of three layers (Fig. 295). The outer layer consists of organic compounds, notably proteins, and forms a shaggy coat – known as the periostracum – over the shell. It is this layer that often camouflages the animal. It may even contain chemicals derived from the animal's food plants, so that the creature not only looks but may also taste like its background. Beneath the periostracum is the prismatic layer consisting of calcium carbonate crystals that are oriented at right angles to the surface of the shell. The innermost or nacreous layer is also made up of calcium carbonate but the crystals run parallel to the shell surface and form a smooth mother-of-pearl lining to the shell. The two calcified layers thus have a two-ply arrangement, strengthening the shell and making it less brittle.

The three layers need to be deposited in an orderly fashion as the shell is built up, and to achieve this the edge of the mantle is made up of three different types of glandular cells (Fig. 295A). Around the margin, short squat shells produce the periostracum, which is the first part of the shell to be laid down. Immediately adjacent to these cells is a second group which deposits the prismatic layer beneath the periostracum. Finally, a third type of glandular cell, which is more elongated, covers the rest of the mantle and is responsible for producing the nacreous layer, which being innermost, is the last to be deposited.

If a shell is fractured it is possible for the animal to repair it by plastering a new nacreous layer over the break. In the same way, if an irritating grain of sand lodges inside the shell it is coated with nacreous layers, and this is how pearls are formed.

The extraordinary variety of colour and shape displayed by shells is, of course, what makes them so attractive to collectors. Even within a single species, individual shells differ from one another. As an example, no two individuals of the bivalve *Venerupis corrugatus* seem to share the same patterning and colours (Fig. 295B).

Shell colouration seems to be determined by diet. Herbivorous molluscs are able to extract pigments (usually porphyrins) from their food plants and build these into the shell. Experiments show quite clearly that a change of diet, or even a change in the quantity of food, brings about corresponding alterations in the colour of the shell.

Very recently it has been demonstrated that the organic

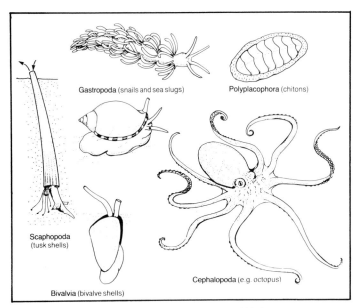

Fig. 294 **Representatives of the five major classes of Mollusca.**

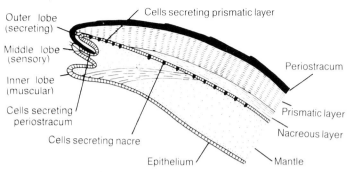

Fig. 295A. **A section through the margin of the shell and mantle of a mussel.**

Fig. 295B. Variation in shell pattern in the bivalve *Venerupis corrugatus*.

compounds derived from food plants and incorporated into the shell may have a novel function: they confuse predators that rely on smell to detect their prey.

Shell shape is, if anything, more variable than colour and this prompts us to ask what advantages various shapes, textures, sizes and proportions may have for different species.

There are obvious differences in shell structure between the five major classes of mollusc discussed in more detail below, and it is clear that these relate to the biology of each class. But there is sufficient variability even within the classes for us to focus, for example, on the gastropods in an attempt to relate shell structure to function.

Gastropods typically have spirally coiled shells, but the

degree to which they coil varies. In some, the spire is long and pointed, streamlining the shell so that it offers minimal resistance to water movement. Species that burrow in the sand, such as the plough snails *(Bullia)*, also have pointed shells that are easy to drag through the sand. Most intertidal species such as the winkles (Plate 115) tend to have more globular shells which allow storage of more water inside the shell, in this way reducing the risk of desiccation.

In the cones (*Conus* sp) the spire has been greatly shortened, and in the cowries it is eliminated altogether because each new whorl is wrapped around the previous one as the shell grows (see Plates 118 & 119, and Fig. 302). In both groups, the reduction of the spire strengthens the shell against attack, for a jutting spire is vulnerable and easily crushed.

The familiar perlemoen (*Haliotis*) has evolved a shell which is flat and has only a trace of a spire near the back end of the shell. This has been achieved by an enormous expansion of the mouth of the shell, to the extent that it covers practically the whole of the lower surface. This trend is carried further in the limpets which, although they begin life as tiny coiled shells, soon expand the mouth to the point where the shell becomes flat and cap-shaped (Plates 112 & 113). Both the perlemoen and the limpets live in areas of strong wave action and their shells reflect their adaptation to these conditions, for flatness reduces resistance to waves, while a wide mouth allows the development of a very broad foot to cling securely to the substratum.

These flat shells are a mixed blessing, for while they may be beautifully adapted for wave action, they are practically the worst design for an intertidal animal faced with the blazing sun at low tide. A flat shell receives more radiation from the sun than does a globular or spiral one, and the large foot also results in considerable uptake of heat by conduction from the rock.

A second intriguing aspect of shell structure is the texture of the external surface, which may be smooth, rippled, nodular or spiny. Any projections on a shell will help intertidal species keep cool when they are heated by the sun, for they increase the surface area from which heat can be reradiated. As discussed in Chapter 2, many high-shore or tropical species have textured shells as a means of avoiding over-heating.

Elaborate ridges or spines are a disadvantage in wave-beaten localities, for they increase the resistance to water movement. Intriguingly, low nodules or ridges actually decrease the drag exerted by water flowing over the shell, compared to that passing over a completely smooth shell. This is because these slight projections reduce the turbulence behind the shell (see Chapter 2, p. 36). The ripples on the surface of a perlemoen and the nodules or ridges on many limpets (see Plates 94, 112 & 113) function in this manner.

Spines projecting from shells reduce predation, both by making the shell uncomfortable to mouth and by increasing its diameter so that only a large-mouthed predator can

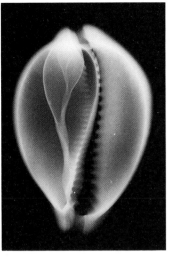

Fig. 296 X-rays of the whelk *Fasciolaria heynemanni* and a cowrie, *Cypraea tigris*. The whelk's long spire and open mouth contrast with the reduced spire and toothed slit-like mouth of the cowrie, which make it less vulnerable to predation.

get the shell between its jaws to crush it. Completely smooth shells may also be very effective deterrents to predators, for they, too, are difficult to grasp.

In at least one species, flanges jutting from the shell have a novel function. In this case, if the shell is dislodged and falls free in the water, the flanges ensure that it lands mouth-downwards. Thus the animal seldom needs to right itself, a process that is not only a waste of time but exposes the vulnerable foot to attack.

A final aspect of shell shape is the nature of the mouth. For instance, all herbivorous gastropods have rounded apertures to their shells. Predatory snails, however, have a long siphon and a proboscis, and the shell is modified to accommodate these organs, having an anterior notch or even a long canal through which they project (compare Plates 114 & 115 with Plates 116 & 117). Thus diet influences the shape of the shell as well.

Crabs, often important predators on gastropods, are able to cut their way into shells by scissoring inwards from the mouth. To foil this, many gastropods have thickened lips to their shells and toothed margins to the mouth (see Plate 117). For a similar reason other species such as the cones and cowries have developed long narrow mouths which make it difficult for a crab on the hunt to insert its nipper (Plates 118 & 119).

Quite clearly the shells of molluscs are finely adapted to a wide range of functions, and there is a great deal to be learnt about the biology of molluscs simply from the nature of their shells.

The phylum Mollusca is divided into seven classes, of which only five are commonly represented in southern Africa (Fig. 294). A good deal has been said about the biology of individual molluscs in Chapters 2, 3 and 4, so that the focus of this chapter is to explore the evolutionary trends within each of these classes.

CLASS POLYPLACOPHORA:
The chitons

The chitons are slow-moving creatures adapted to clinging tightly to the rock face. The large flat foot provides a firm attachment but, contrary to popular belief, chitons (and limpets, which operate in a similar manner, as discussed in Chapter 2) do not cling by suction, but by secreting a thin layer of slime that allows adhesion. Anyone who has tried to pull apart two sheets of glass that have a thin layer of water between them will know just how powerful this force of adhesion can be.

Much of a chiton's body is normally hidden from view by the mantle, which produces the dorsal shell and overlaps the sides of the body, forming a broad girdle (Fig. 297). This girdle is usually strengthened by scales, tough hairs or spines, which not only provide protection but are the easiest features by which to identify different species. The shell itself is divided into eight separate plates or valves held together by muscles but which articulate on one another, allowing the animal to flex its body and to fit exactly the often irregular surface of the rock. When chitons are detached, they immediately curl into tight balls, thus protecting the soft vulnerable central surface and the gills.

Concealed beneath the mantle is the broad foot, encircled by a ring of gills. Since the head is permanently hidden, it lacks the eyes and sensory tentacles found in many other molluscs. As if to compensate for this, the chitons have evolved large numbers of the most unusual eyes that penetrate right through the shell to emerge on the dorsal surface of the animal. Although small, these eyes may be remarkably complex, being furnished with tiny lenses, pigmented layers and photo-receptive nerve-endings.

All chitons are herbivorous, grazing algal fronds or scraping diatoms and sporelings from the surface of the rock. In common with almost all molluscs, chitons possess a radula – an elongate tongue-like structure with row upon row of tiny teeth (Figs. 305 & 306) which is projected from the mouth and rasps back and forth to fragment and scrape up food.

They also have an extremely long coiled gut: unwound and stretched out it is about eight times longer than the body. This is in keeping with their diet, for plant material is

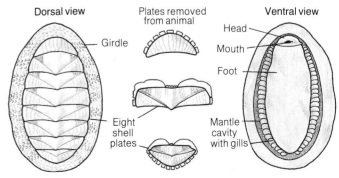

Fig. 297 The structure of a typical chiton, *Chiton tulipa*.

Fig. 298 *Acanthochiton garnoti,* showing its characteristic tufts of spines. *Notoplax productus* has similar but much smaller tufts and a much wider girdle (x 1).

Fig. 299 *Dinoplax gigas,* the largest southern African chiton (x ½).

Fig. 300 *Chiton nigrovirescens* often occurs in clusters under boulders and broods its young under its mantle (x 1).

less digestible than animal matter and a long gut is not only necessary to process the food but to package the wastes into faeces. Many chitons are intertidal and, like the limpets, they store their faeces in the gut until the tide rises over them, so that once the faeces are voided they are flushed away instead of accumulating under the mantle. Like most other molluscs, chitons have a large digestive gland (often incorrectly called a liver), with ducts that connect it to the gut. Small food particles pass up these ducts and are actually engulfed by cells before they can finally be digested. This intracellular method of digestion means that the food must be ground up into small particles before it can be digested and, as we will see later, this is a recurrent problem for the molluscs – particularly those feeding on large prey – for they are obliged to sort their food according to size before they are able to digest it.

Chitons reproduce by external fertilisation. The simple sac-like gonad lies above the gut and produces vast quantities of eggs or sperm which are shed into the sea. Fertilised eggs develop into trochophore larvae, which look almost exactly like the larvae of polychaetes. One exception is *Chiton nigrovirescens* (Fig. 300), an attractive reddish-brown or black animal, which broods its eggs in the mantle cavity where minute but perfectly formed juveniles can be found if the chiton is prised off the rock face and turned over.

Much has been made of the similarity between mollusc and polychaete trochophore larvae, for one school of thought is that this evidences the origin of molluscs from worm-like creatures. The ancestry of molluscs has long been a puzzle, for although they have left a fairly complete fossil record, all the existing classes were established by the Cambrian period, five hundred million years ago, and we know little of the links between them and almost nothing of where they came from – hence the somewhat slender threads grasped by biologists speculating about the ancestry of the Mollusca.

It was therefore with great excitement that living representatives of a primitive group of molluscs, long presumed extinct, were discovered in 1957; an outcome of the Danish Deep-Sea Expedition of 1953 on which a great deal of biological material was collected from the oceanic rifts off the coast of Mexico, at a depth of 5 km. As is so often the case, the material sat in a museum for four years before a somewhat nondescript group of limpet-like creatures was examined. The discovery that these animals were 'living fossils' aroused considerable international interest, for it seemed that at last we might learn something of the origin of the Mollusca.

Neopilina galatheae, as the animal was later named, turned out to be a curious creature. Like the chitons, it has a large flat foot and a simple and obviously primitive nervous system with no ganglia. But its most striking feature is that virtually all its organs are repeated down the length of the body – five pairs of gills, six pairs of excretory organs, two pairs of gonads, a heart with two pairs of auricles, and eight duplicated muscle attachments to the shell. This repetition is unlike anything we find in other living molluscs and, rather than solving the question of molluscan evolution, *Neopilina* has simply aroused more controversy. One line of thought is that the repetition of the organs in *Neopilina* is evidence of segmentation – an almost sacrilegious suggestion considering the Mollusca are defined

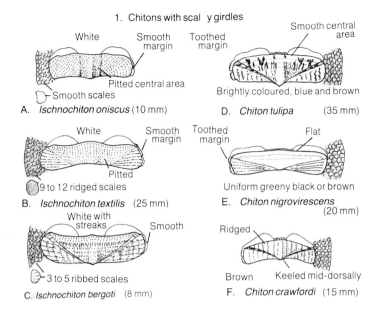

1. Chitons with scaly girdles

A. *Ischnochiton oniscus* (10 mm) — White, Smooth margin, Smooth scales, Pitted central area

D. *Chiton tulipa* (35 mm) — Toothed margin, Smooth central area, Brightly coloured, blue and brown

B. *Ischnochiton textilis* (25 mm) — White, Smooth margin, Pitted, 9 to 12 ridged scales

E. *Chiton nigrovirescens* (20 mm) — Toothed margin, Flat, Uniform greeny black or brown

C. *Ischnochiton bergoti* (8 mm) — White with streaks, Smooth, 3 to 5 ribbed scales

F. *Chiton crawfordi* (15 mm) — Ridged, Brown, Keeled mid-dorsally

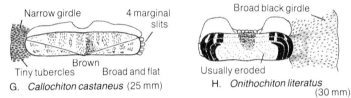

2. Chitons with velvety girdles

G. *Callochiton castaneus* (25 mm) — Narrow girdle, 4 marginal slits, Tiny tubercles, Brown, Broad and flat

H. *Onithochiton literatus* (30 mm) — Broad black girdle, Usually eroded

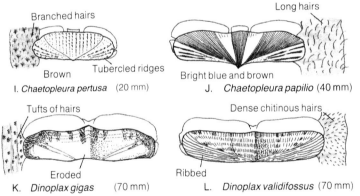

3. Chitons with flexible hairs on the girdle

I. *Chaetopleura pertusa* (20 mm) — Branched hairs, Brown, Tubercled ridges

J. *Chaetopleura papilio* (40 mm) — Long hairs, Bright blue and brown

K. *Dinoplax gigas* (70 mm) — Tufts of hairs, Eroded

L. *Dinoplax validifossus* (70 mm) — Dense chitinous hairs, Ribbed

Fig. 301 **Common southern African chitons: details of one shell valve and a portion of the girdle are shown for each species.**

as being unsegmented. The implication is that the Mollusca had a segmented worm-like ancestor. The majority of zoologists, however, consider the multiplication of organs in *Neopilina* not true segmentation, for the body is not divided into compartments as we saw in the segmented polychaete worms (Chapter 12, Fig. 229). If we return to the chitons, we remember that they too have a series of gills that ring the body – yet no one would suggest that the presence of these numerous gills is a sign of segmentation. Similarly, multiplication of organs in *Neopilina* is not in itself evidence of segmentation.

Thus we must contain our curiosity about the origin of the phylum Mollusca and of the remaining classes.

Local species of chitons:
The chitons are most easily identified by the nature of the girdle which surrounds the shell and, in particular, whether it is scaly or velvety, has stout hairs, or is armed with tufts of spines. On this basis the chitons may be placed in one of four groups. Further separation of the species within these groups depends on the structure of the shell plates, as summarised in Figs. 298 – 301.

CLASS GASTROPODA:
The snails
The class Gastropoda is the largest in the phylum, with some 35 000 species. Most have a spiral shell, and since shape and texture vary widely from one species to the next, the shell provides us with a ready means of distinguishing the species (Plates 112 – 119). However, some of the species lack a shell and are slug-like in appearance, although often very beautiful, as shown in Plates 120 – 132.

All gastropods, including those without shells, have a large foot, a head with sensory tentacles and eyes, and a visceral mass that contains the gut, reproductive organs, blood system and kidney. The visceral mass lies on top of the foot, giving the group their scientific name 'gastropoda' = gut-footed. The single most characteristic feature of all gastropods is that the visceral mass is not symmetrical but is twisted into a spire although, as we shall see later in this chapter, there are slug-like forms which have become almost symmetrical.

To understand why gastropods usually have a coiled body and a spiral shell, we need to trace their larval development. All the primitive gastropods begin life as a trochophore larva, just as the chitons do, but this soon metamorphoses into a much more attractive creature, the veliger larva (Fig. 302), which has two greatly expanded lobes (the velum) that project from the head and are fringed with cilia. The flickering of these cilia gives the microscopic larvae a shimmering, almost ethereal, appearance and serves to propel them through the water and at the same time to capture food particles. Each veliger soon produces a tiny shell into which it can withdraw.

It is at this stage that the most extraordinary development takes place, which leaves its stamp on many aspects of gastropodan biology, and ultimately explains why the adults have coiled bodies. The larva undergoes a twisting process called torsion. We can visualise this if we imagine the head and foot of the veliger being held stationary while the visceral mass above rotates anti-clockwise through 180°. This seemingly torturous process takes place early in the development of all gastropod veliger larvae, and is brought about because the retractor muscles that pull the larva back into its shell are asymmetrical, being larger on one side than on the other, so that they twist the body to one side as it is withdrawn into the shell (Fig. 302).

The results of torsion are profound. All the organs are twisted almost into a figure of eight and the originally posterior mantle cavity with its gills and the opening of the anus is rotated around to lie above the head (Fig. 302). As

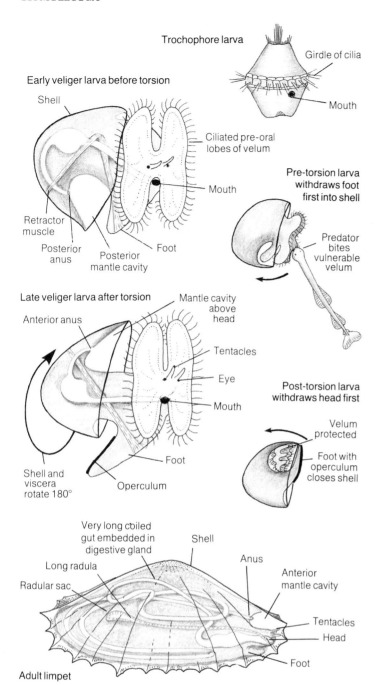

Trochophore larva

Girdle of cilia

Mouth

Early veliger larva before torsion

Shell

Ciliated pre-oral lobes of velum

Mouth

Retractor muscle

Posterior anus

Posterior mantle cavity

Foot

Pre-torsion larva withdraws foot first into shell

Predator bites vulnerable velum

Late veliger larva after torsion

Mantle cavity above head

Anterior anus

Tentacles

Eye

Mouth

Shell and viscera rotate 180°

Foot

Operculum

Post-torsion larva withdraws head first

Velum protected

Foot with operculum closes shell

Very long coiled gut embedded in digestive gland

Shell

Long radula

Anus

Radular sac

Anterior mantle cavity

Tentacles

Head

Foot

Adult limpet

Fig. 302 The life-cycle of a limpet, showing how a gastropod larva twists its body during development (torsion).

discussed below, this has repercussions which account for many of the adaptations found in gastropods.

What advantage can the extraordinary process of torsion have for the gastropods? To begin with, before torsion takes place, the veliger is forced to retreat into its shell foot first, leaving its delicate velum to be withdrawn last of all. After torsion it is the velum that is pulled in first, leaving the horny foot with its protective operculum to block off the shell. Arising from this, one camp of zoologists suggests that torsion is of benefit to the larva, for it makes it more difficult for predators to snap at the delicate and vital velum (Fig. 302).

It was with this in mind that Garstang – who is remem-

bered almost as much for his delightfully humorous writing as for his zoological research – wrote the *Ballad of the Veliger (or how the gastropod got its twist)*:

The Veliger's a lively tar, the liveliest afloat,
A whirling wheel on either side propels his little boat,
But when the danger signal warns his bustling submarine,
He stops the engine, shuts the port, and drops below unseen.

Young Archi-molluscs went to sea with nothing but a velum –
A sort of autocycling hoop, instead of pram – to wheel 'em;
And, spinning round, they one by one acquired parental features,
A shell above, a foot below – the queerest little creatures.

But when by chance they brushed against their neighbours in the briny,
Coelenterates with stinging threads and Arthropods so spiny,
By one weak spot betrayed, alas, they fell an easy prey –
Their preoral lobes in front could not be tucked away!

A fleet of fry turned out one day, eventful in the sequel,
Whose left and right retractors on the two sides were unequal:
Their starboard halliards fixed astern alone supplied the head,
While those set aport were spread abeam and served the back instead.

Predaceous foes, still drifting by in numbers unabated,
Were baffled now by tactics which their dining plans frustrated.
Their prey upon alarm collapsed, but promptly turned about,
With the tender morsal safe within and the horny foot without!

In this way, then, the Veliger, triumphantly askew,
Acquired his cabin for'ard, holding all his sailing crew –
A trochosphere in armour cased, with a foot to work the hatch,
And double screws to drive ahead with smartness and despatch.

(An extract from Garstang, W. 1951, *Larval Forms*, Oxford Press.)

Not all zoologists agree that the larva benefits from torsion. They point out that anchovies and pilchards engulf veligers by the mouthful and will hardly be influenced by which part of the body the tiny creatures withdraw first.

Could it be that it is the adult snail instead that benefits from torsion? The mantle cavity, which comes to lie in front of the head after torsion, contains the gills and also a pair of osphradia, which look much like tiny gills. Osphradia are sensory organs able to detect remarkably small traces of chemicals in the water. This was first proved by Professor A.C. Brown, who showed that if he operated on the plough snail *Bullia* he could eliminate its sense of smell by cutting the nerves running from the osphradia.

It can be argued that it is an advantage to have the gills and osphradia at the front end of the body instead of in their pretorsional posterior position. The gills must receive cleaner water in their new position – instead of that stirred up by the passage of the snails; and anterior osphradia are certainly better placed to warn the animal of what lies ahead. These are several possible benefits from torsion.

Once torsion has brought the anus forwards to lie over the head, the snail can no longer conveniently grow by simply elongating, as a worm might do, and an increase in body size must now involve an upward growth, humping the body. It is because of this that the visceral mass of most gastropods coils into a tight spiral to make the 'humpback' structure as compact as possible (Fig. 296). Almost all species spiral in a right-handed (dextral) manner (so that if the shell is held spire upwards with the mouth towards you, the opening is on the right of the shell). A few contrary species have left-handed (sinistral) coils, and one of them is the bilharzia-transmitting *Bulinus africanus* which occurs in many of the northern rivers in the African sub-continent.

Torsion is thus a key feature in understanding the biology of gastropods, but they are such a huge group that to explore them further they must be divided into three sub-classes: Prosobranchia, Opisthobranchia and Pulmonata.

SUBCLASS PROSOBRANCHIA:
The winkles, whelks and limpets

Torsion leaves the gastropods with an anterior mantle cavity, and this arrangement remains typical in the Prosobranchia (Proso = front; branch = gills). The subclass embraces a wide range of molluscs, from winkles to whelks, and this gives us the opportunity to compare primitive forms with more highly evolved species, revealing three important trends within the group.

The first of these is a direct consequence of torsion. Because the gut is now looped and the anus opens anteriorly, the animal is confronted with a sanitary problem, for the faeces are now squirted out over the head where they may contaminate the sensory organs as well as the gills and osphradia (Fig. 303A, B). The faeces are consolidated by mucus from a pair of hypobranchial glands in the mantle cavity and are then released, but although this eases the problem it does not solve it.

The prosobranchs have adapted in one of two ways to improve matters. Some have evolved holes in their shells to direct the faeces away from the gills. The best example is the keyhole limpet which has a hole at the apex of the shell (Fig. 304 A – C). Water drawn into the mantle under the front of the shell supplies oxygen to the gills, and then passes backwards to flow out of the keyhole. The anus projects into this exhalant stream of water and the faeces are thus carried away. The holes in the shells of perlemoen or Venus ear shells *(Haliotis)* serve a similar purpose, being exhalant exits for the water (Fig. 304 D & E).

If the shell of a keyhole limpet is removed, the primitive arrangement of its gills is clearly visible – a pair of plume-like gills on either side of the mantle cavity, with the anus lying between them (Fig. 304C). Most other prosobranchs have modified this arrangement in response to their sanitary problem. The limpets, for example, have no gills in the mantle cavity over the head but have evolved a frill of gills right around the foot instead. In many more species, including most winkles and whelks, the right-hand gill is reduced and the anus is shifted over to the right hand side of the mantle cavity (Fig. 303C). In this way water can be drawn in on the left of the head, over the single gill, and then past the anus to carry away the waste on the right side. The only problem with this arrangement is that the gills have a central axis from which plate-like lamellae project on either side. This is known as a bipectinate arrangement, and leaves the gill scarcely supported and prone to clogging because particles stick between the gill platelets and the mantle wall. To avoid this, the most advanced whelks have monopectinate gills with platelets only on one side of the axis, while the other side is firmly united with the mantle wall, strengthening the gill and avoiding clogging (Figs. 303D & 304F & G).

This clearly reveals a shift from the primitive arrangement of paired gills, through a single bipectinate gill to the specialised monopectinate condition that occurs in the most highly evolved prosobranchs – all to eliminate the

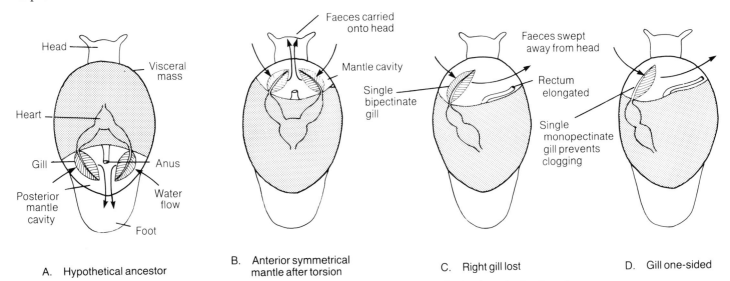

Fig. 303 In the hypothetical ancestor of the gastropods (A) the mantle and gills were posterior, allowing the animal to deposit its faeces behind it without fouling the gills. After torsion (B) the mantle was moved to the front of the animal, creating the problem that the faeces would then have been deposited on the head and could easily foul the gills. As a solution to this, the right gill became reduced and the anus shifted to the right (C), and in more advanced forms the gill became fixed to the floor of the mantle cavity (D) while the water-circulation washed the waste products out to the right of the head.

Fig. 304 As another solution to the sanitary problems created by torsion (see Fig. 303) some species possess modified shells and mantle cavities, allowing respiratory currents to circulate over the gills before carrying away waste products. The key-hole limpet, Amblychilepas scutellum (A, B & C) and the perlemoen, Haliotis (D & E), have holes in their shells while the plough snail Bullia laevissima (F & G) has reduced its right gill and flushes wastes away on the right of its mantle cavity.

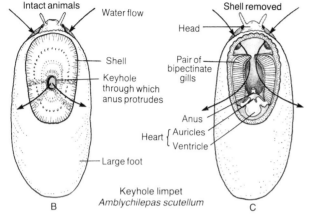

B — Keyhole limpet *Amblychilepas scutellum* — **C**

Intact animals / Water flow / Shell removed / Head / Shell / Keyhole through which anus protrudes / Large foot / Pair of bipectinate gills / Anus / Heart {Auricles / Ventricle}

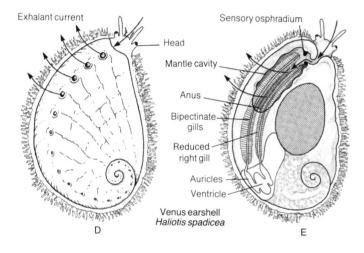

D — Venus earshell *Haliotis spadicea* — **E**

Exhalant current / Head / Mantle cavity / Anus / Bipectinate gills / Reduced right gill / Auricles / Ventricle / Sensory osphradium

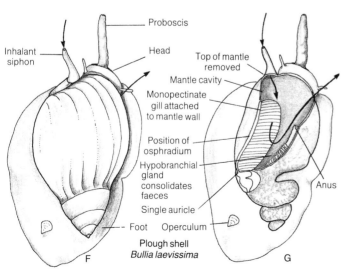

F — Plough shell *Bullia laevissima* — **G**

Inhalant siphon / Proboscis / Head / Mantle cavity / Monopectinate gill attached to mantle wall / Position of osphradium / Hypobranchial gland consolidates faeces / Single auricle / Foot / Operculum / Top of mantle removed / Anus

danger of fouling the gills and osphradia with faeces, which was a direct consequence of torsion.

The second major trend in the prosobranch snails has been a shift from a herbivorous diet in the more primitive limpets and winkles to a carnivorous diet in the more specialised whelks.

Herbivorous species have incredibly long radulae with numerous teeth in each tooth-row (Figs. 305 – 307). For example, the radulae of limpets may be twice the length of the body, and are coiled back and forth within the visceral mass. A long radula has various advantages, the main one being that as the front part is worn away it can be continually renewed. The individual teeth are often capped with an iron oxide which is extremely hard. In the case of limpets and chitons they are particularly remarkable because the leading edge of each tooth contains a high percentage of iron oxide embedded in a silica matrix, while the trailing edge which contains much less iron oxide is much softer. As a result, the back of the tooth wears faster than the front and the teeth act as self-sharpening chisels, keeping the leading edge perpetually honed.

All the herbivorous gastropods also have very long guts – up to eight times the length of the body – to cope with their indigestible diet. Furthermore, they must sort the food according to size, for only the smallest particles can be dealt with by the cells of the digestive gland. As an example, the alikreukel *Turbo sarmaticus* has a tightly coiled tube on the side of its gut. This is readily visible once the animal has been removed from its shell and it evokes curiosity even in those with a purely gastronomic interest in the beast. This structure is actually an extremely long tube arising from the gut, and is coiled like a spring to pack it into the available space. Along its length run three internal grooves which are ciliated and which sort the food particles by size – only the smallest being diverted along one particular groove to the digestive gland while larger fragments are returned to the gut for further processing or to be discarded as faeces.

The manner in which gastropods obtain their food is often fascinating, for some are not content with roaming the rocks to scrape up algae. The limpet *Patella argenvillei*, for instance, raises its shell high off the rock face and then slams it down to trap large fragments of algae, such as kelp fronds; several other limpets go further and maintain territorial 'gardens' of particular species of algae which they defend against other herbivores (as described in Chapter 2). There are other more unorthodox ways of feeding. The worm-shell, *Serpulorbis natalensis*, which has an irregularly coiled shell cemented to the rock face (Fig. 324), and the turret-shells, *Turritella* species (Plate 116a – c), both produce long mucous threads that are spun out into

Fig. 305 A portion of the rasping 'tongue' – radula – of a winkle, *Oxystele*. Microscope photograph x40.

Fig. 306 A seaweed's view of the massive radular teeth of a limpet. Electron micrograph x200.

Fig. 307 The radular marks left by a grazing limpet *(Patella compressa)* on the surface of a kelp frond (x 1).

Fig. 308 A predatory gastropod *(Nassarius capensis)* with siphon erect.

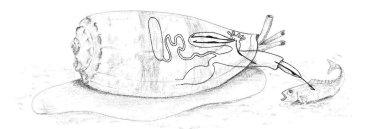

Fig. 309 *Conus geographus* one of the most poisonous cone shells, preys on fish. Its radular teeth have become modified into arrow-like structures that inject poison from the oval poison gland (shown inside the animal).

the current to catch particles and later are hauled in like a fishing line.

The carnivorous gastropods are more specialised, for not only must they capture their prey but, because the prey is usually large, it must be reduced to a size that the cells of the digestive glands can manage and thereby absorb the food. Most carnivorous species have a long proboscis that can be extended to catch the prey. Food is often detected at a distance because the osphradia in the mantle cavity perceive even trace quantities of certain chemicals released by the prey. To aid with location of the prey, a siphon has been evolved, and this directs the water into the mantle cavity and can be moved from side to side, allowing the animal to sample water from different directions and to hone in on the prey (Fig. 308). The proboscis and the siphon extend from the mouth of the shell, and to accommodate them the anterior lip of the shell is notched or even elongated into an anterior canal. For this reason, one can usually tell from a glance at the shell what type of diet an animal has: carnivores have oval mouths with an anterior notch or canal while herbivores have round shell mouths.

Since animal matter is readily digested, carnivores have a short gut, but on the other hand the prey needs to be fragmented. While the radulae of carnivorous gastropods are short, since the prey is soft, the teeth are often hooked or have cutting edges to help break it up. The most specialised radular teeth are those found in the cones *(Conus* species, Plate 119) which are arrow-like and barbed, and serve to inject poison into the prey to subdue it (Fig. 309). The fish-eating species such as *Conus geographicus* and *Conus textile* (both of which occur in Moçambique) are particularly toxic and may even be lethal to man.

The *Marginella* species also have a poison that paralyses prey. They have a curious habit of transporting their stunned prey, attached by mucus to the tail end of the foot, until they are hungry – a portable pantry which is illustrated in Plates 107 – 109.

Natica and the thaid snails (Plates 116f - 1, & 118b) have developed glands that secrete acids, enabling them to drill through the shells of other molluscs. Incidentally, the thaids secrete a yellow mucus which stains one's hands purple; in ancient times they were the source of 'royal purple', used to dye the robes of royalty. The helmet shell *Phalium* bores through the shells of sea urchins and pansy shells. The most remarkable boring gastropod is *Argobuccinum pustulosum,* which produces concentrated sulphuric acid to allow it to break open the sandy tubes of the Cape reef worm (see Figs. 40–42).

Very few gastropods are parasites, although in the tropical waters of Moçambique the limpet-like *Thyca*

Fig. 310 The common nerite, *Nerita albicilla,* lays striking white egg masses which festoon the surfaces of rocks in tide pools.

Fig. 311 The whelk *Burnupena cincta* frequently lays its clumps of egg capsules on the shells of mussels.

Fig. 312 Two whelks *Purpura panama* locked in copulation and sitting astride their egg capsules.

ectoconcha live attached to starfish, while the tiny *Stylifer* embeds itself and forms galls on the arms of starfish. *Heliacus variegatus* (Plate 115s) forces its proboscis through the body wall of zoanthids and feeds on their internal tissues without actually killing the anemone-like creatures, so it too may be considered a parasite.

The final trend we can trace within the subclass Prosobranchia is their increasingly complex methods of reproduction. At the one extreme are the limpets and winkles which practise external fertilisation, shedding sperm and eggs into the water. Since this is a wasteful process vast quantities of gametes need to be produced; up to 60 percent of the body mass of a limpet may be gonad and the production of gametes consumes a great deal of the creature's energy.

These primitive species undergo the typical larval development described above, with a planktonic trochophore and veliger. This does have the advantage of allowing dispersal of the species, but can result in a massive mortality of the larvae because of predation in the plankton.

Nerita species (Fig. 310) are slightly more advanced; they deposit their eggs in round capsules that speckle the under-surfaces of most rocks in the tide pools of Natal. Early larval development occurs within these capsules, and veligers are eventually released and disperse in the plankton.

The highly evolved whelks practise internal fertilisation, reducing wastage of gametes. Their eggs are housed in complex capsules (Plate 93, Figs. 311 & 312), in which much or all of the larval development takes place, so that the planktonic phase is abbreviated or eliminated. This change has involved the evolution of an organ to transfer the sperm and, in the female, a complicated glandular oviduct which provides yolk to nourish the developing embryos, and sheaths the eggs in a capsule that is cemented to the ground.

While this advanced method of reproduction nurtures the embryos and reduces larval mortality, it also reduces the species' ability to disperse. As a result, populations become isolated from one another for it is difficult for individuals to reach other localities. This in turn leads to in-breeding, and populations may diverge from one another in body form. This is why *Nucella dubia* (see Plate 116f), for example, has so many different forms and varies greatly from one locality to another.

Several gastropods are hermaphroditic, carrying both male and female organs. A number become one sex first and then later change to the other sex – consecutive hermaphroditism.

A case in point is the limpet *Patella oculus:* male in its first year, female thereafter. What is the advantage of changing sex? In this instance it may not make much difference to a male whether he is large or small, but a female can only hold a limited number of eggs, and the number depends on her size. Thus it may be better to start off being a male, and only when larger, switch to being female.

Fig. 313 The slipper limpet *Crepidula porcellana* attaches itself to other shells where it forms stacks, one slipper limpet living on the shell of another. The uppermost individual is always male, the lower animals female. A batch of eggs has been removed from one of the females and lies between the two stacks of slipper limpets (x 1).

An even more curious case is the slipper limpet, *Crepidula porcellana* (Fig. 313), which forms piles, one animal on top of the other. The larvae of this species always settle on other molluscs. The first individual to settle on a particular shell becomes a female but, at a later stage, another larva may settle on top of the first and it becomes a male. This ensures that any two animals, sitting one on the other, will be of different sexes. But the story becomes even more intriguing if a third animal perches on the second, for the third becomes a male while the second changes sex and is transformed into a female. This procedure may be repeated – yet the top individual is always male and can fertilise all those under him, which have become females. It amuses me that the British species – which has similar sex habits – should be named *Crepidula fornicata*.

The prosobranchs have been a very successful group and at least part of their success is a result of the trends of increasing specialisation that we have seen in their respiratory adaptations, dietary habits and methods of reproduction.

SUBCLASS OPISTHOBRANCHIA:
Sea slugs and nudibranchs

While torsion is a feature of all gastropods, in the subclass Opisthobranchia the body has become straightened and is nearly symmetrical. It is almost as if the animals have had a change of heart and attempted to reverse the process of torsion – in fact they are referred to as being 'detorted'. While their larvae still undergo torsion and twist their bodies, when the adults develop they untwist, the mantle cavity being moved once again to the back of the body – hence the scientific name for the subclass: ophistho = back, branch = gills. Externally, many of the species look perfectly symmetrical, but internally there are always traces of their previously torted state. For one thing, their nerve cords remain twisted into a figure eight.

If the process of torsion seemed extraordinary, it is even more peculiar that this group of animals should detort. We have no real evidence of why they should do so except that the most primitive members burrow in sand. If the ancestral stock also burrowed, then many of the features displayed by the group are explicable. An anterior mantle cavity with gills and sensory osphradia would instantly have been filled with sand as the animal burrowed through sediment, and this could account for the mantle being shifted back to the posterior end. Most of the group also have reduced, often internal, shells and a large number has no shell at all. Again, a shell may have been a hindrance to the hypothetical burrowing ancestor, and became reduced for this reason. The bubble shells, *Hydatina* species (Plate 130), are amongst those that still have fairly well-developed shells, but even so they are thin and fragile. Most sea hares, *Aplysia* species (Plate 124), have only a small internal shell which does little but protect the gills; while other species, such as *Notarchus leachi* (Fig. 314), have no shell at all.

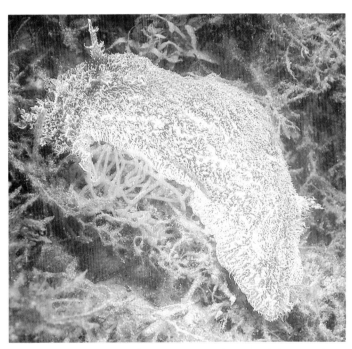

Fig. 314 The sea hare *Notarchus leachi,* shown here astride its egg string, is abundant in many estuaries and grazes on sea grasses and seaweeds (x ½).

This trend is carried to its conclusion by the most specialised members of the group, which have not only lost the shell completely but have also lost the mantle cavity, gills and osphradia. These specialised creatures are known as the sea slugs or nudibranchs ('naked gills'), but neither of these names does anything to prepare us for the spectacular beauty of these animals, for they are amongst the loveliest creatures in the sea, as Plates 120 – 132 reveal.

Once again, a burrowing ancestry could explain the nudibranchs' lack of shell, gills and osphradia – all of which would probably have been clogged by the sand. The only difficulty with this idea is that almost all nudibranchs are no longer burrowers, even if their ancestors were. How then do they manage without the very features that characterise most other molluscs? The answer is that they have evolved other structures which serve the same functions as their discarded organs. The dorsal surface is either thrown into bunches of long papillae (cerata) or has a series of feathery appendages that form a rosette around the anus

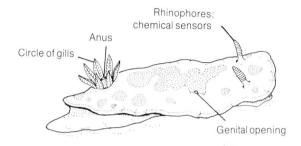

Fig. 315 Nudibranchs do not possess a shell, mantle cavity, sensory osphradia or gills; but have evolved sensory tentacles (rhinophores), and a set of secondary gills – arranged around the anus in the family Doridae.

Fig. 316 Some nudibranchs, such as *Godiva quadricolor* (see also Plate 123), feed on anemones and are able to extract the prey's stinging cells and mount them in their own tissues. When attacked, the anemone shown here (*Anthothoe stimpsoni*) discharges white threads, laden with stinging cells, through its body wall (x ½).

(Fig. 315). In both cases these expansions increase the surface area sufficiently for oxygen exchange, thus acting as gills. On the head, two tentacles with frilled tips (the rhinophores) serve as chemoreceptors in place of the osphradia.

Finally, there is the question of how nudibranchs, unprotected by a shell, survive attack from predators. A few are beautifully camouflaged. *Corambe*, which feeds on the bryozoan *Membranipora*, is flattened and has a reticulate pattern on its back thereby blending with its prey (Fig. 317). However, most nudibranchs possess toxic chemicals – so toxic that species such as *Phyllidia* (Plate 132) will even kill fish kept in the same aquarium. Other species feed on hydroids or anemones (Fig. 316) and are able to extract the stinging cells from these animals and install them in their own cerata, where they can be discharged secondhand at predators. One nudibranch, *Glaucus atlanticus* (Plate 131), feeds on bluebottles and is thus capable of inflicting an unpleasant sting if handled.

The flamboyant colours that nudibranchs flaunt probably advertise their unpalatable nature.

All of the opisthobranchs are hermaphroditic and have very complex reproductive organs. Fertilisation is internal and because each animal possesses both male and female organs, pairs frequently fertilise each other simultaneously. This is one of the benefits of hermaphroditism, for it allows mating between any two individuals and the fertilisation of two animals for the price of one mating – a particular advantage for slow-moving creatures which may not come across many mates in the course of their lifetime. The sea hare *Notarchus* (Fig. 314) makes the most of such meetings and forms long chains of ten or more animals – each fertilising the individual in front while being fertilised by the beast behind.

Most species embed their eggs in a mucous sheath, forming long beaded strings (Plate 124, Fig. 314) or ribbons folded into attractive rosettes (Fig. 318).

The final group of ophisthobranchs is entirely different in life-style, being planktonic. These are the pteropods, which have fragile glassy shells that often litter the high-tide mark on Natal beaches, although sharp eyes are needed to spot them since the shells are tiny and transparent. *Creseis* has a needle-like shell; *Cavolina* a globular

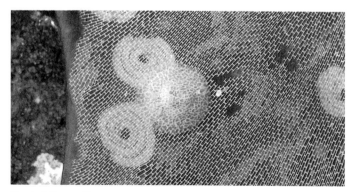

Fig. 317 The nudibranch *Corambe* is flattened and has a reticulate pattern on its back, mimicking the net-like structure of its prey, the bryozoan *Membranipora*. Two of the nudibranch's spiral egg masses are visible (x 4).

Fig. 318 Many nudibranchs lay their eggs in rosette-like ribbons. This bright orange egg mass was laid by *Nembrotha*, a pitch-black nudibranch with a blue stripe down its sides (x 2).

A.

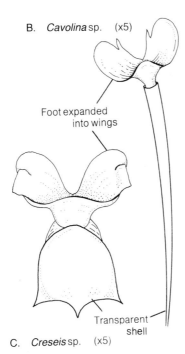

B. *Cavolina* sp. (x5)

Foot expanded
into wings

C. *Creseis* sp. (x5)

Transparent
shell

Fig. 319 The sea butterflies or pteropods have delicate transparent shells (A), and expanded lobes on their feet which allow them to swim (B & C).

shell with three pointed projections (Fig. 319). All pteropods have a foot greatly expanded into wing-like lobes (hence their name – 'wing-footed') and these flap up and down so that the beasts seem to fly gracefully through the water.

SUBCLASS PULMONATA:
Snails, slugs and false limpets

The well-known land snail and their freshwater counterparts nearly all belong to the final group of gastropods – the subclass Pulmonata. In keeping with a terrestrial existence, the pulmonates have lost all signs of gills and, instead, the roof of the mantle is richly supplied with blood vessels and acts as a lung, allowing oxygen uptake from air. To minimise water-loss from this lung, the opening to the mantle is almost closed, leaving only a narrow aperture through which air enters. Since the pulmonates are clearly adapted to a terrestrial life it is not unexpected that there are few marine species. One group does, however, deserve special mention: the genus *Siphonaria* which consists of several limpet-like species which are extremely common on practically every rocky shore around the coast of southern Africa (Plate 99). They can be recognised by the siphon on the right side of the foot which leads into a lung-like mantle cavity. The shell is moulded to fit the siphon and is therefore asymmetrical, bulging slightly on the right (Plate 113m-q). At low tide when individuals of *Siphonaria* are exposed, they take air into their lungs. Like all pulmonates they have lost their original gills, but because they spend much of their time submerged they have re-evolved a set of gill-like outgrowths in the mantle cavity so that they are able to respire under water.

Almost all pulmonates are hermaphrodites and practise internal fertilisation. Terrestrial species produce complex eggs housed in an egg case – with a structure not unlike that of a bird's egg – which reduces water-loss. None of the

terrestrial or freshwater species has a larval stage. *Siphonaria*, however, produces tightly coiled egg-masses which are commonly seen in high-tide pools (Plate 99), and several of the species also have veliger larvae which hatch from the egg-mass and are wafted in the plankton for a week before settling and metamorphosing.

Despite the fact that *Siphonaria* is only distantly related to the true limpets, they have remarkably similar habits. Like the true limpets, *Siphonaria* homes to a fixed scar on the rock, religiously returning to it after each feeding excursion (Fig. 29). The limpets locate their scars by retracing part of their outward trail, and are able somehow to tell in which direction the trail was laid down, so that on re-encountering their outward trail they know which way to turn in order to follow it back to the home scar.

Recent work by Michael Cherry has shown that *Siphonaria* has marked rhythms of activity during which it moves away from its scars to feed. The interesting thing is that these rhythms can be modified under different conditions. For example, populations of *Siphonaria capensis* that live in pools have two periods of activity each day – one during the daytime low tide and one during the nocturnal low tide. On the other hand, individuals of the same species that live on dry rocks move only during the low tide at night.

What possible reasons can there be for such rhythms? We know that all species of southern African *Siphonaria* exude a toxic milky mucus that repels all predators, so that no whelks feed on them. Even the oystercatcher and the giant cling fish (Figs. 45 & 46), both species which readily feed on other limpets, refuse to eat *Siphonaria*. Thus the rhythms are unlikely to be a means of avoiding activity during the period when predators are most likely to be feeding.

Siphonarians attach feebly to the rock face: they are the only limpets that you can dislodge easily with a finger. Perhaps this is why they remain clinging to their scars at high tide, when wave action might rip away a wandering animal.

The rhythms may also be a means of reducing desiccation, for while animals in pools move by day and night, those on dry rocks limit their activity to the night when it is cooler. The limpets' shells fit their scars exactly. Those that live on dry rock soon desiccate to death if moved away from their scars to a position where their shells cannot fit the shape of the rock. Even for animals that live in pools, where desiccation is never a threat, possession of a home scar still has advantages for, when it rains, a close fit between shell and rock allows the animal to seal itself off and exclude the dilute water.

These marine pulmonates demonstrate how adaptable the gastropods are, modifying their body structure, physiology and behaviour to suit prevailing conditions, and this repertoire of adaptations has allowed gastropods to occupy every major habitat on earth – from deep-sea rifts at a depth of 6 km, through shallow waters and the intertidal zone, to rivers, lakes, hot springs, land and even deserts.

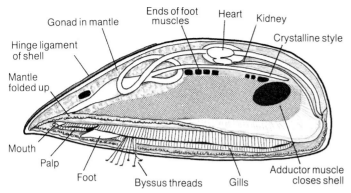

Fig. 320 The black mussel *Choromytilus,* opened to show the internal structure. The upper mantle lobe has been flapped back to show the gills, foot and byssus.

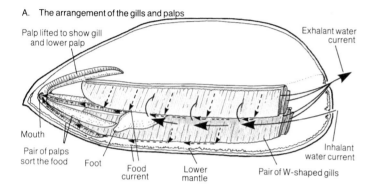

A. The arrangement of the gills and palps

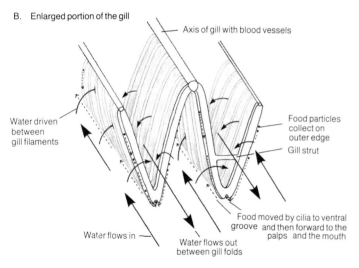

B. Enlarged portion of the gill

C. Detail of palp

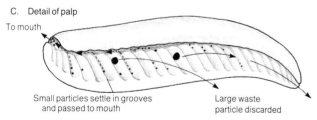

Fig. 321 Black mussels, like most bivalves, use their gills to filter-feed. (A) The gills circulate water through the mantle cavity (solid arrows) using the fine cilia on their surface. The gills extract food particles from the water and pass them to the palps and mouth (dotted arrows). (B) An enlarged portion of one gill illustrates this process. (C) The palps sort particles according to size, discarding large fragments and transferring small particles, via a central gutter, to the mouth.

CLASS BIVALVIA

The clams, mussels and oysters all belong to the class Bivalvia, the second largest molluscan class, containing about 8 000 species throughout the world. The commonest southern African species are shown in Plates 110 & 111.

Bivalves range enormously in size, from a pinhead to the size of the giant clam, *Tridacna* (Plates 89 & 90), which reaches a length of 1,5 m and may weigh as much as 250 kg. As the name Bivalvia implies, all species in this class have a bivalved shell enclosing the body. The two valves are held together by a ligament made of a particularly resilient protein (resilin) which stretches when the animal clamps the shell shut, but shrinks back to its original shape and opens the shell once the animal relaxes its muscles. To keep the two valves aligned, most bivalves have a set of three hinge teeth which lock the two valves together so that they cannot be twisted apart.

As one would imagine, the bivalves have very modified bodies in keeping with life inside a bivalved shell. In the first place, their mobility is limited, and nearly all of them are filter-feeders because of this.

The primitive bivalves (order Protobranchia) have gills that are similar to those of most molluscs and feed by extending a pair of long tentacle-like palps into the sand and picking up organic particles. But most other bivalves belong to a more advanced order, Lamellibranchia ('plate-gills'), in which the gills have become enormously enlarged and elaborated into sheets that are draped down on either side of the body, and which not only allow oxygen uptake but serve as the organ by which the animal filters out its food.

Because of their size, the gills are one of the first things to catch your attention on opening a mussel. Each gill consists of elongated filaments that hang down from the axis of the gill and are loosely held together by cilia (or by firmer fleshy junctions in some species). If a transverse section is cut through the animal, each gill is seen to be W-shaped, thus forming a double curtain on either side of the body (Fig. 321A, B). The cilia on the filaments drive water between them, but particles suspended in the water are captured by a second set of longer cilia, which propels the particles down to the bottom of the filament. Here, yet a third set of cilia carry the particles along the bottom of the gill towards the mouth (Fig. 321B). Before the particles are consumed, they are processed by a pair of leaf-like palps on either side of the mouth. Magnification of their surface reveals corrugations which provide a means of sorting particles according to size (Fig. 321C). Any particles that are sufficiently small drop into the grooves and are carried along them by ciliary action to the mouth. Larger particles rest on top of the ridges, where cilia beat at right angles to the grooves, driving these larger particles to the edge of the palp where they are discarded (Fig. 321C). Waste particles drop down onto the mantle and are carried to the back of the shell where, together with the faeces, they are discarded through a special exhalant opening in the mantle (Fig. 321).

Since bivalves are filter-feeders, they have no radula, nor

do they even have a recognisable head. Internally, the gut is designed to handle small particles. Running into the stomach is a transparent bluish rod, the crystalline style, which is made up of digestive enzymes (mainly amylase). This style is continually rotated, helping to pull a food-laden mucous string into the stomach, while at the same time it is ground against a hard shield to release enzymes. The partly-digested fine particles are then diverted from the stomach into ducts that lead to the digestive gland (Fig. 320). When we recall that in all molluscs digestion can only be completed within cells (demanding that the food particles must be small) we realise the advantages of the complex processes that allow bivalves to sort their food according to size before consuming it.

It is, of course, because the bivalves are filter-feeders that they are prone to poisoning by red tide, for they sometimes consume toxic planktonic organisms (see Chapter 6).

Since the bivalves are generally not very mobile, they all practise external fertilisation, and their large gonads fill much of the visceral mass and even expand into the foot and the lobes of the mantle. People often ask why the flesh of some black mussels is brown while that of others is yellow. This simply depends on the sex of the animals, for the gonads are so large that they influence the overall colour of the animal. Rest assured that both sexes are equally edible.

Fertilised eggs develop into planktonic trochophore larvae and then into veligers, which differ from those of gastropods because they never undergo torsion and are enclosed in tiny bivalved shells. These veligers finally settle and metamorphose into adults. A few bivalves brood their young. An interesting example is *Thecalia concamerata* (Plate 110q) in which the edge of the shell is curled up to form a chamber. Here the larvae undergo their complete development, so that it is possible to find several dozen perfectly formed but miniature versions of the adult inside the brood chamber.

Most bivalves burrow into sand or mud and have a powerful spade-like foot for this purpose (Figs. 66 & 67). The foot is thrust down into the sediment and its tip expanded to provide an anchor. The animal then pulls itself down onto the foot, at the same time closing its shell to make it as narrow as possible, squirting water out of the shell in the process and softening the sand, making it easier for the foot to begin digging once again. Two physical phenomena aid the process of burrowing. Firstly, if a blunt probe is thrust against wet sand, it softens and liquefies the sand. This is precisely the effect experienced when you stand on a wet sandy beach and tread repeatedly in the same spot: the sand liquefies and you sink. This effect – technically known as thixotropism – takes place beneath the probing foot of a bivalve as well. However, the opposite effect is induced if a broad flat surface is pressed on the the sand, for it drives out the water and makes the sand firmer. Thus when the bivalve pushes its shell open and outwards, it firms the sand, allowing the animal to hold its position while it thrusts out its foot.

Many bivalves have circular ridges on their shells – as

Fig. 322 The oyster *Saccostrea cuccullata* grows in dense beds in Natal and is shown here with one of its predators, the drilling gastropod *Morula granulata*.

shown by *Venus verrucosa* (Plate 110k) – and they use these as an aid to burrowing. Each ridge is like a wedge, thin edge facing down, so that if the shell is rocked back and forth the ridges dig in easily but grip the sediment on the upstroke, so that the shell works its way down through the sediment.

Bivalves that burrow into sand must have some means of circulating water through their mantle cavities, and have therefore evolved a pair of long siphons that reach up to the surface – an inhalant siphon to suck down clean water and food and an exhalant siphon returning the water plus waste materials. The tip of the inhalant siphon is often fringed with feathery tentacles that act as a sieve, excluding larger sand particles (Plate 91).

Some bivalves fasten themselves to the substratum. Mussels produce a beard of byssus threads from a gland in the foot. These threads are initially fluid but harden rapidly to form a flexible but very tough attachment. Oysters go a step further, cementing one of the shell valves to the substratum (Fig. 322). The large horse mussel, *Atrina* (Plate 110j), buries itself in sand, leaving only the razor-like apex of its shell exposed. Possibly because of its size, it cannot dig efficiently, and instead it produces long golden byssus threads that spread through the sand and anchor the animal, making it very difficult to wrench it free. These golden threads are reputed to have been the material from which Jason's golden fleece was made.

Only a few bivalves can actually swim. Examples are the angel-wing shell *Limaria* (Plate 96) and the scallops, such as *Pecten*, which clap their shells together to jet out water, propelling them along. Both species use this as a means of rapid escape from predators.

Finally, there are bivalves that bore into substrata. The most famous is *Teredo*, the shipworm, which undermines all but the hardest of woods and has caused the collapse of many a pier (Fig. 323). *Teredo* is a long worm-like creature, capped by a pair of tiny shell valves which perch at one end of the body. These shells no longer have a protective function, but serve as cutting tools that are rocked back and forth to tunnel through the wood (Fig. 234A). One interesting feature is that although dozens of ship worms may drill a single piece of wood, their tunnels never cut across one another. Somehow the shipworms are aware of approaching another tunnel and divert their drilling in a different direction. In the same way they never break through the surface of the wood, so that while a block of wood may be riddled with tunnels, externally it appears sound.

Teredo is able to use the wood shavings as a source of food, storing them in a special compartment of the gut where cellulase enzymes break down the cellulose in the wood. It is still uncertain whether the animal produces its own cellulase enzymes or relies on symbiotic bacteria in the gut. In addition, *Teredo* has two long siphons that extend from the end of the tunnel, sucking up water which is filtered by the gills in the normal bivalve manner to extract phytoplankton and other food.

Relatives of the shipworms, the piddocks, (*Pholas* species), tackle a more formidable substratum, drilling through rock.

Thus we can see that far from being limited by their enclosure in a bivalved shell, the bivalves have succeeded in adapting the structure and function of the shell to allow them a variety of life-styles.

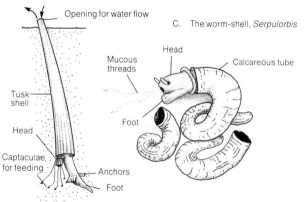

Fig. 323 A section sawn through part of a wooden pier that has been extensively tunnelled by the shipworm *Teredo* (x ½).

CLASS SCAPHOPODA

The tusk shells, which look much like miniature elephant tusks that are hollow and open at both ends, are the homes of unique molluscs, the Scaphopoda (Fig. 324B). Although these creatures are rarely encountered alive, their shells often wash ashore. Two genera occur in southern Africa: *Dentalium*, with longitudinally ridged shells, and *Cadulus* with smooth shells.

Tusk shells dig into sand and occur in fairly deep water. The apex of the shell usually projects from the sand, allowing water to be sucked in and out to supply oxygen. The foot and head extend from the lower end of the shell. The foot is used for digging, being thrust out and then expanded into two lobes to provide an anchorage as the body is pulled down. Extending from the head are a series of clubbed tentacles, the captaculae, which probe the sediment and capture detritus or tiny protozoans, such as the foraminiferans (Fig. 142B).

CLASS CEPHALOPODA:
Squids, cuttlefish and octopuses

The cephalopods, which include the squids, cuttlefish, nautilus and octopus, are the peak of molluscan evolution and are probably the most sophisticated of all the

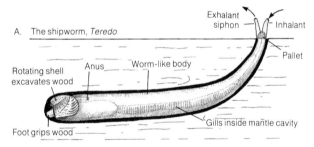

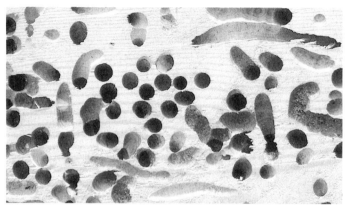

Fig. 324 Three different molluscs that have adopted worm-like bodies for different purposes: (A) The shipworm *Teredo* which forms tunnels in wood; (B) The tusk-shell *Dentalium* which burrows into sand, and (C) the gastropod *Serpulorbis natalensis* which is a filter-feeder and forms an irregularly coiled tubular shell that is cemented to a rock.

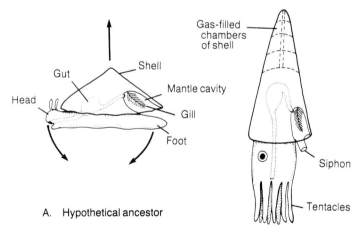

A. Hypothetical ancestor

B. Plan of cephalopod body

Fig. 325 Diagrams showing how the basic body plan of a cephalopod, such as a squid, might have been derived from that of a primitive mollusc.

invertebrates. They include the largest invertebrates the sea has ever known – the deep-sea squids which may have bodies 6 m long, and a total length of 25 m if their tentacles are included. The favourite prey of sperm-whales, these giants of the deep must at times fight fiercely to avoid being eaten, for they leave lacerations on the whales' bodies, and there are records of saucer-sized imprints left by their suckers. Squids are also the fastest marine animals, easily exceeding 20 knots. As we will see below, all cephalopods have complex nervous systems, are capable of learning, and have finely-tuned sensory organs, unrivalled by those of any other invertebrates.

The squids and their kin are so unlike the other Mollusca that early biologists considered them to be a separate phylum. But if we analyse the arrangement of their bodies, it is possible to see how they may have evolved from a primitive mollusc. Fig. 325 shows that if the body of a hypothetical ancestor were to be jack-knifed, by swinging the anterior and posterior ends downwards and fusing them together, while expanding the dorsal surface upwards, then a squid-like body would be created. In all the cephalopods the head and foot are indeed fused together in this manner, which is the reason for their name – 'head-footed'. The head-foot is also extensively modified to form eight or ten long tentacles that surround the mouth and bear suckers, and a siphon that leads out of the mantle cavity.

Buoyancy control

The key to understanding why the cephalopods are so much more sophisticated than the rest of the molluscs lies in their mastery of buoyancy. This is best understood by an examination of a familiar living form such as the cuttlefish, although later in this chapter the possible evolutionary origins of buoyancy control are described.

Almost all living cephalopods have internal shells which in the cuttlefish, *Sepia* (Fig. 326), is reduced to an oval flattened plate, almost like polystyrene foam in texture (Fig. 327). This cuttlebone is light and floats in sea-water, which is why it is so often washed ashore. But the shell is not simply a lightweight object that buoys up the body; its density is under the control of the animal. If a section is cut through the cuttlebone, the many tiny chambers are revealed. In a living animal, these chambers are filled with sea-water, and the whole shell is underlain by a yellow gland.

Originally it was thought that this gland pumped gas into the cuttlebone chambers to alter its buoyancy, but measurements soon showed that there is never any increase in pressure in the chambers, as would be expected if gas were pumped in. Instead, the gland operates in a more indirect manner; it actively withdraws sodium ions from the sea-water in the chambers. Since sodium is positively charged, an excess of positive ions is built up outside the chambers. Soon negatively charged chloride ions begin to flow passively out of the chambers, attracted by the positive sodium ions. This leaves the sea-water in the chambers more dilute, and so by simple osmosis the water

Fig. 326 The cuttlefish *Sepia officinalis vermiculata,* commonly found in sheltered bays and lagoons (x ¼).

Fig. 327 The cuttlebone of a cuttlefish, cut in half below to show the tiny chambers inside (x ⅓).

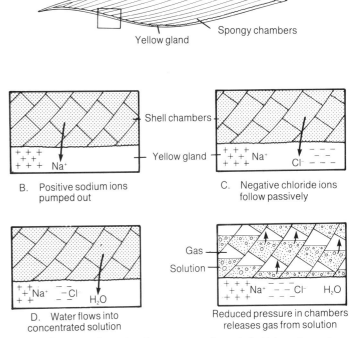

A. Section through cuttlebone

B. Positive sodium ions pumped out

C. Negative chloride ions follow passively

D. Water flows into concentrated solution

Reduced pressure in chambers releases gas from solution

Fig. 328 Diagrams illustrating the sequence of events that takes place when a cuttlefish produces air bubbles in its shell to increase its buoyancy.

molecules in the chambers also begin to move out. The net effect is to reduce the amount of fluid in the chambers. Since strong walls and cross struts support the chambers, they cannot simply shrink as the fluid is lost; instead, the pressure must drop inside the chambers. This is the key to the whole sequence, for when the pressure of a liquid is reduced, gases that are dissolved in it become less soluble and bubble out of it – just as champagne froths when the cork is removed. Thus it is that a reduction in pressure in the cuttlebone chambers causes the air that was dissolved in the fluid to form bubbles of gas, decreasing the density of the cuttlebone (Fig. 328). In this manner, the cuttlefish can control how much gas is produced and can regulate its buoyancy so that it floats in the water, matching its own density against that of sea-water.

The significance of buoyancy control cannot be over-estimated, for it freed the cephalopods from a bottom-dwelling life and allowed them to become active swimming hunters. The fossil record shows that early cephalopods dominated the seas, possibly being the first animals to swim freely and continually.

Locomotion and prey capture

Cephalopods swim mainly by jet propulsion. The mantle is strongly muscular and can swell out to suck in water and then contract suddenly to squirt the water out. It has valves that control the exit of the water so that it jets out of the siphon; and the siphon can be pointed in any direction to control which way the animal moves. This muscular propulsion is also a more efficient way of circulating water over the gills, compared with the cilia on which other molluscs depend. Considering how active the cephalopods are, it is not surprising that they depend on a ready supply of oxygen and they soon die if kept in an enclosed container.

Jet propulsion allows the squids and cuttlefish to escape the attention of all but the fastest fish, but they are often eaten by tunny. The speed of their escape response is partly due to the presence of giant nerves which ensure a rapid conduction of stimuli to the muscles or the mantle. These giant nerves have, incidentally, been of tremendous value to physiologists working on the mechanism of nerve conduction, for they are large enough to allow removal or exchange of their fluid contents and ions in order to explore how ions move across the membrane when an impulse passes down the nerve.

All cephalopods possess ink glands as a defence against predators, squirting out a black cloud to confuse the predator while they escape.

Most cephalopods are active fast-moving hunters. The free-swimming squids and cuttlefish feed mainly on fish or swimming prawns, or on other cephalopods, and have one pair of extremely long sucker-studded tentacles. These are usually kept coiled up and hidden in cavities on either side of the mouth, but can be shot out with unerring accuracy to capture prey. The octopus is a bottom-dweller and feeds largely on crabs, rock lobsters and other crustaceans.

All cephalopods have a powerful beak, shaped much like that of a parrot, with which they shred their prey. Most species also have poison glands and inject toxins when they bite their prey, thus subduing it. The tiny blue-ringed octopus of Australia is notorious for the potency of its venom, being capable of killing a man within minutes, but none of the southern African species is as venomous. In fact, the local octopus is seldom aggressive, and even when it is being manhandled it very rarely bites.

The shredded prey is swallowed and ascends to a stomach; here again we find that the cephalopods are more advanced than other molluscs for they have a muscular stomach that grinds the food. The macerated food passes into a caecum which is lined with projecting leaflets and sorts the food according to size. It is curious that the mighty cephalopods, feeding on large prey, must still reduce the food to a minute size so that digestion can be completed within the cells of the digestion gland.

Reproduction

Squids and cuttlefish have an elaborate courtship before mating. The males take the initiative and approach other individuals head-on, all the while displaying rippling dark stripes of colour on the dorsal surface. As we will see later, cephalopods have a remarkable facility for colour change, and this plays an important role in courtship. If the animal

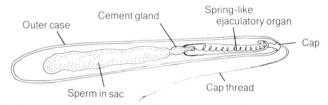

Fig. 329 The squid, *Loligo,* packs its sperm into complicated spermatophores which are transferred from the male to the mantle cavity of the female (x 5).

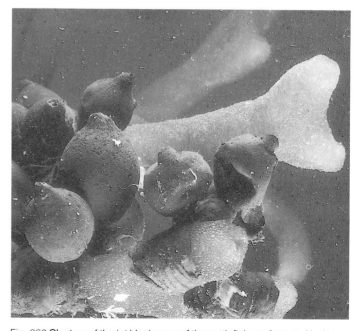

Fig. 330 Clusters of the jet black eggs of the cuttlefish are fastened by loops to algae (x 1).

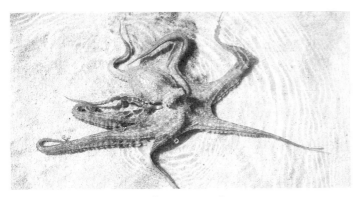

Fig. 331 The common octopus, *Octopus granulatus.*

that is approached happens to be a male as well, he too breaks into a similarly vivid patterning (if he does not, he risks being mated). Females remain pale-coloured if receptive to a male's approaches, thus signalling their willingness to mate. Sperm transfer is a complex procedure, for the male reproductive organs package the sperm into elaborate spermatophores (Fig. 329) and these are picked up by the tip of one of the male's arms and deposited inside the female's mantle cavity. The spermatophores then absorb water and burst open, forcibly releasing the sperm which is ejected by a built-in coiled spring in the cap of the spermatophore (Fig. 329). The female then releases eggs for fertilisation, and later surrounds them with a protective mucous sheath. Octopuses lay their eggs in large groups like bunches of grapes and the female tends the eggs until they hatch, protecting them and blowing fresh water over them. Cuttlefish lay their eggs in clusters, each egg separately enclosed in a black capsule and attached by way of a stalk to an algal frond (Fig. 330).

The arm that the male uses to transfer sperm is specially modified with an adhesive area, or even pocket, to help hold the sperm. This modified arm is known as the hectocotylous arm – and there is a curious reason for this name. The males of some species sacrifice the tip of the arm when they transfer sperm, leaving it behind with its load of sperm in the female's mantle cavity. Early biologists, repeatedly finding these flat suckered structures, thought them to be parasitic flukes (trematodes), and proudly assigned them the generic name *Hectocotylus!*

All cephalopod eggs are richly laden with yolk and the embryo undergoes its complete development within the egg case, hatching as a fully-formed juvenile. Growth is extremely rapid. Research at Durban's Oceanographic Research Institute shows that the common *Octopus granulatus* (Fig. 331) reaches an arm length of 30 cm after a year, and normally reproduces and dies within the first year. Larger beasts are, however, found. The biggest I have ever seen was 3,5 m across the outstretched arms.

Sense organs

The cephalopods have a highly evolved brain and sense organs, unsurpassed by any other invertebrates. The brain is concentrated around the oesophagus and forms a series of lobes which are protected by a cartilaginous brain case. Those lobes lying below the oesophagus control the simpler functions such as the pulsing of the mantle, while the middle brain just above the oesophagus regulates more complex functions including courtship and prey capture. Finally, the uppermost lobes – rather like the cerebellum of vertebrates – are charged with memory and learning.

Octopuses can be taught to distinguish objects of different sizes, shapes, textures and colours. They ignore hermit crabs that have anemones on their shells, soon learning from the stings that their sensitive skins receive from the anemones. Octopuses kept in captivity quickly learn when an approaching handler heralds food and all but clamber out of the aquarium in anticipation.

This learning power is in keeping with creatures that have remarkable sense organs. Their eyes are uncannily like the human eye, complete with cornea, lens, iris, pupil and retina (Fig. 332). Potentially their visual acuity is greater than ours, for the nerve cells run behind the retina so there is no 'blind spot' as in mammalian eyes. The remarkable similarity between the eyes of these two totally different groups of animals is one of the coincidences of evolution, for their eyes have entirely different origins. Vertebrate eyes are formed from outpushings of the brain; those of cephalopods are inpushings of the outer (ectodermal) skin.

Another pair of extraordinary sense organs are the balancing organs or statocysts. Many animals have statocysts and those of cephalopods are functionally like the balancing organs found in jellyfish medusae (Fig. 180), consisting of a cavity lined with sensory cilia that support a ball of lime. Gravity tips the ball to one side or the other, imparting information about the orientation of the animal. The cephalopods have developed the use of statocysts to a

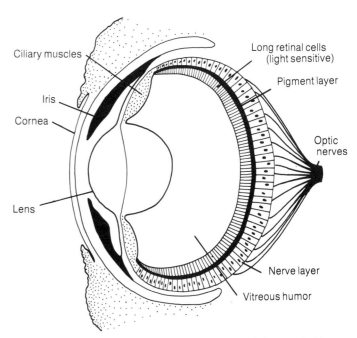

Fig. 332 A section through the eye of an octopus reveals its remarkable complexity and how similar it is to the human eye.

fine art, even being able to tell their angular acceleration from them. In other words, if the animal turns a corner, the difference between the responses of left and right stato-cysts is enough to tell the animal the angle and speed at which it is turning. Vertebrates, with their complicated semi-circular canals, are the only other animals capable of this feat.

Squids, cuttlefish and octopuses can achieve very rapid colour changes. All of them have chromatophores which function like those of crustaceans (see Chapter 13): cells containing various pigments can be expanded to reveal their colour or contracted to concentrate the colour to a pin-point. The cephalopods have further refined this pro-cess because each chromatophore is operated by a ring of tiny radiating muscles, so that colour change is under the control of the nervous system and is practically instanta-neous. Squids, in particular, alter colour with facility, and bands of different colours flicker and ripple across their backs. Yellow, orange and black chromatophores are commonest but a green iridescence may also flood the animal. Colour can be changed to match the background, but the most spectacular colours are produced during courtship or aggression between males – vivid displays

that have excited the attention of biologists since the days of Aristotle.

Kinds of cephalopods

Earlier in this chapter a description was given of the way cuttlefish regulate their buoyancy using their cuttlebones. But this cuttlebone is obviously a very specialised type of shell, which makes one wonder what it originated from and how it relates to the shells of other cephalopods.

The fossil record reveals that two large groups of cephalopods, the Nautiloidea and the Ammonoidea domi-nated the seas during the Carboniferous period, about 250 million years ago. While they had a range of shell shapes, from straight and streamlined to tightly coiled, and a range of sizes from less than a centimetre to over 2 m in diameter, all of these animals had external shells that were divided into compartments (Fig. 333). The animal only occupied the last of these chambers, but maintained contact with the other chambers by a tubular siphuncle which stretched right to the apex of the shell. The function of this siphuncle was probably identical to that of the yellow gland that lies under the cuttlebone – to regulate the amount of gas in the sealed chambers and thus the buoyancy of the animal.

Fig. 333 A fossilised shell of the once abundant ammonites.

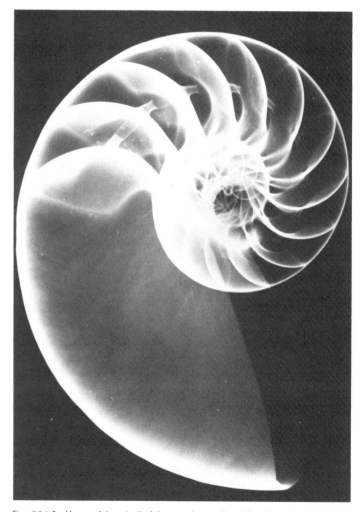

Fig. 334 An X-ray of the shell of the pearly nautilus, *Nautilus*, shows the consecutive chambers and the tubular siphuncle that links the chambers.

Almost 6 000 fossil species of nautiloids and ammonites have been described, mostly from rocks that are more than 70 million years old, and yet only a solitary representative of these once vast groups remains alive today – *Nautilus* (Fig. 334).

While the ammonites became extinct, other cephalopods sprang from them, in which the shell became reduced in size and enveloped inside the mantle. It was these forms that have given rise to almost all the living cephalopods. The spiral ramshorn shells (Fig. 335), that are so often cast ashore, are the internal shells of one of these modern squid-like animals, *Spirula*, which is very abundant in deep waters down to 1 200 m but is rarely seen alive.

In the case of the cuttlefish we have already seen that the shell is oval and greatly flattened, but although the chambers have become compressed we can still equate them with the much larger chambers found in the spiral shells of their ancestors. Several species of cuttlefish are common in southern Africa, including *Sepia officianalis* (Fig. 326) which abounds in calm-water lagoons. A much smaller species, *Sepia tuberculata*, is found in pools on rocky shores and is distinguished by two large oval glands that pucker the ventral surface of the mantle.

The squids (Plate 136) are elegant slender creatures with two triangular fins projecting from the sides of the animal and steering it as it jets through the water. Squids have reduced their shells to a transparent plastic-like 'pen' that no longer has any chambers and serves only for the attachment of mantle muscles. The reason they have reduced their shells is that most of them are deep-sea species. As one descends in the sea, pressure increases, and a depth is eventually reached where it is impossible to get gas out of solution without reducing pressure inside the shell to the point where the shell collapses. Thus in deep waters the buoyancy mechanism described for cuttlefish is useless. Most of the squids have devised a different means of remaining buoyant. Ammonia is their normal excretory product, but instead of excreting it, they store quantities of it in the form of ammonium ions. Since ammonium ions are lighter than water, this reduces the squids' density and keeps them buoyant.

There are enormous stocks of deep-sea squids – perhaps more than the total harvest of fish that man takes each year – and these have probably increased because of a reduction in numbers of toothed whales that feed on them. They are, however, not only inaccessible to man but useless as a food because of their ammoniacal tissues. The shallow-water species such as *Loligo reynaudi*, which swims in large shoals and is often caught by trawlers, have palatable flesh. They are used as fish bait and are sold in South Africa as 'chokker' but in recent years they have become popular for human consumption. Their name – and price – have changed and they are now frozen and sold commercially as 'calamari'.

The octopuses have no shell at all and have abandoned a swimming life, becoming bottom-dwellers. They can still swim, but only do so for short distances. Most of their time is spent hidden in holes, which the animals defend against

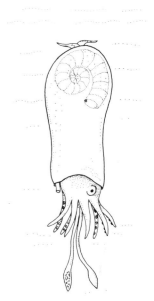

Fig. 335 **The squid-like *Spirula* is a** deep-sea animal that is rarely seen alive, but must be very common if one is to judge by the numbers of its shells that are cast ashore.

other octopuses and which they camouflage by covering the entrance with stones and shells. They emerge from these holes to capture passing crustaceans, particularly crabs, and can be lured out of their holes if tasseled strips of orange inner-tubing are wriggled in front of their dens – evidently sufficiently like a scuttling crab to tempt the octopus to investigate.

Octopus granulatus (Fig. 331) is the common shallow-water species that occurs right round the coast of southern Africa. It is distinguished by having two rows of suckers on each arm, while a rarer species, *Eledone thysanophora*, has only a single row.

While the octopuses have become bottom-dwelling, one of their kind, the well-known paper nautilus *Argonauta argo*, (which is only distantly related to the pearly nautilus), has returned to a pelagic life. Having lost their original shells completely, and thus their means of buoyancy control, female paper nautiluses manufacture a totally new kind of shell to replace it – a very pretty coiled white shell that is much sought-after by shell collectors. This shell is completely different from other molluscan shells in its origin, for it is formed not by the mantle but by two web-like arms that spread on either side of the body. This 'substitute' shell serves partly as a float, but also as an egg chamber in which the female lays her eggs. Males are very much smaller than females and do not produce shells but live inside the female's shell, and sometimes even right inside her mantle cavity. In a sense the male is parasitic on the female, for he feeds on scraps of her food. As far as we know, females normally die after reproducing, although they tend their eggs for some time after laying them.

It seems curious that having evolved an elaborate system of buoyancy control and having mastered the open seas, some of the cephalopods should abandon this way of life and again become bottom-dwellers. But it is even more peculiar that some of these bottom-dwellers, having lost all control over buoyancy, should take to a pelagic life and re-evolve a shell. It is also an unsolved puzzle why the cephalopods, at the pinnacle of invertebrate evolution, should be represented by about 1 000 living species, out of the 6 000 known fossil species that once commanded the seas. We can only guess that the evolution of fishes caused their demise and that we are now left with a remnant of this once dominant group – albeit a remnant that contains some extremely successful species and the most sophisticated invertebrates in the sea.

REFERENCES

Popular articles and books

Morton, J. E. 1962. *Molluscs.* Hutchinson University Library, London. 244 pp.

Russell-Hunter, W. D. 1979. *A Life of Invertebrates.* Collier MacMillan Publishers, London. pp 347-476.

Sisson, R. F. 1971. Octopus-training experiments. *National Geographic, Vol. 140(6):* 788-795.

Voss, G. L. 1967. Squids: jet powered torpedoes of the deep. *National Geographic, Vol. 131(3):* 386-411.

Voss, G. L. 1971. Shy monster, the octopus. *National Geographic, Vol. 140(6):* 776-799.

Walton Smith, F. G. 1956. Shipworms, saboteurs of the sea. *National Geographic, Vol. 110(4):* 559-566.

Yonge, C. M. & Thompson, T. E. 1976. *Living Marine Molluscs.* Collins, London. 288 pp.

Zahl, P. A. 1959. Unsung beauties of Hawaii's coral reefs (Nudibranchs). *National Geographic, Vol. 116(4):* 510-525.

Identification guides

Barnard, K. H. 1951. *A Beginner's Guide to South African Shells.* Maskew Miller, Cape Town. 215 pp.

Barnard, K. H. 1958-1964. Contributions to the knowledge of South African Mollusca. Parts I-V. *Annals of the S. Afr. Museum, Vol. 44:* 73-163. *Annals of the S. Afr. Museum, Vol. 45:* 1-237. *Annals of the S. Afr. Museum, Vol. 47:* 1-199. *Vol. 47:* 201-360. *Vol. 47:* 361-593.

Gosliner, T. 1983. *Nudibranchs of Southern Africa.* Gordon Verhoef Publishers.

Kennelly, D. H. 1969. *Marine Shells of South Africa.* Books of Africa, Cape Town.

Kensley, B. 1973. *Sea Shells of Southern Africa, Gastropoda.* Maskew Miller, Cape Town. pp 1-236.

Kilburn, R & Rippey, E. 1982. *Sea Shells of Southern Africa.* MacMillan & Co., Johannesburg.

Millard, V. G. & Freeman, D. 1979. The Conidae of South Africa. *Strandloper* No. 195: 2-9.

Millard, V. G. 1981. Marginellidae of South Africa. *The Strandloper,* No. 206: 1-12. No. 207: 1-8.

Richards, D. 1981. *South African Shells – A Collector's Guide.* C. Struik, Cape Town. 156 pp.

Scientific references

Several references on the ecology of particular molluscs are given in the reference lists for Chapters 2 to 4.

20. ECHINODERMATA

STARFISH, URCHINS, SEA CUCUMBERS, BRITTLE STARS AND FEATHER-STARS

David Nicholls used the title 'The Uniqueness of the Echinoderms' for his introductory booklet on these animals. Of course every group of animals is unique but, like the equality of communist citizens, some are more unique than others, and the echinoderms do have more than their fair share of singular features.

The phylum Echinodermata includes many of the most familiar seashore creatures, including the starfish, brittle stars, feather-stars, urchins and sea cucumbers. The fact that many of these are called 'stars' is an indication of their first unique characteristic – their five-rayed (pentamerous) radial symmetry. It seems odd that such highly evolved animals should be radially symmetrical, for the primitive cnidarians such as anemones (Chapter 9), are the only other organisms with this body form.

Radially symmetrical animals have no front or back ends but only a top and bottom. Even the terms 'ventral' and 'dorsal' are not easily applied to the echinoderms, for some

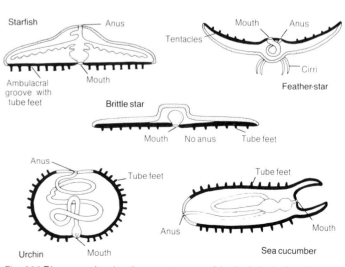

Fig. 336 Diagrams showing the arrangement of the body in the five classes of echinoderms.

of them are orientated mouth uppermost while in others the mouth faces downwards (Figs. 336 & 337). For this reason the term 'oral' is used to describe the surface that bears the mouth, while 'aboral' is used to refer to the opposite surface.

Echinoderms have not always been radially symmetrical: many of the oldest fossil forms are bilateral (with left and right sides and a front and back). Even today, echinoderms start their lives as bilateral larvae, which only late in their development become radial. For this reason echinoderms are said to have a secondary radial symmetry.

Most echinoderms release eggs and sperm into the water where fertilisation takes place. Each fertilised egg divides repeatedly to form a hollow ball of cells (the blastula). Part of the wall of the blastula then folds inwards to form a gut (after which the developing embryo is known as a gastrula). The subsequent development is slightly different in the various classes of echinoderms, but can most easily be traced in the urchins (Fig. 338): in this case the gastrula develops a ring of cilia, and from then on is called the pluteus larva. This ciliary ring expands and becomes thrown into folds or 'arms', first four, then six and finally eight or 12 arms; and two extra ciliary bands (epaulettes) appear on the sides of the body (Fig. 338). The arms often become long and spindly, reaching four to five times the length of the body, and making the microscopic larvae delightfully dainty but fragile. The purpose of these long arms is three-fold: they are used to capture food, they increase the area of the ciliary bands thus improving the larva's powers of locomotion, and they decrease the speed at which the larva will sink – an adaptation we have already seen in other planktonic forms.

Within the developing larva a special group of cells is set aside on the left side of the gut. This 'echinus rudiment'

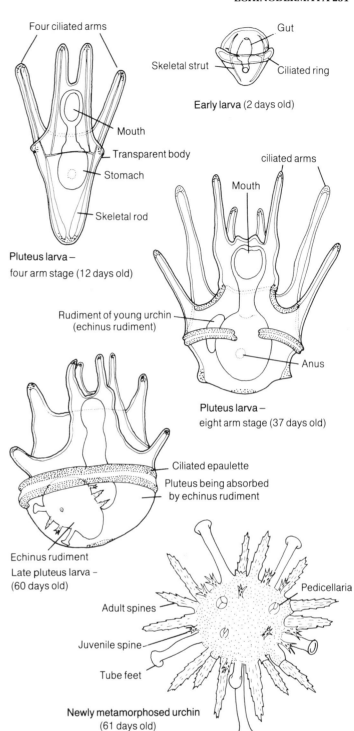

Pluteus larva –
four arm stage (12 days old)

Early larva (2 days old)

Pluteus larva –
eight arm stage (37 days old)

Late pluteus larva –
(60 days old)

Newly metamorphosed urchin
(61 days old)

Fig. 338 The life-cycle of the common Cape sea urchin, *Parechinus angulosus,* (all stages magnified x 50).

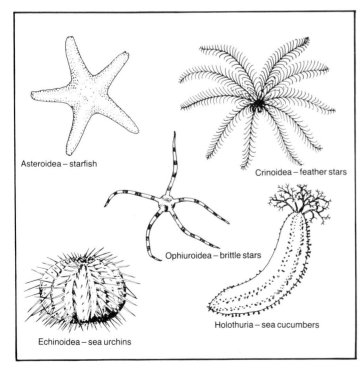

Fig. 337 The five classes of echinoderms.

eventually forms the young urchin, while the rest of the larval tissues are simply absorbed by it during metamorphosis. After about two months of planktonic life the echinus rudiment reaches a size where it begins to break out of the pluteus larva (Fig. 338). It thrusts out a few suctorial tube feet to allow it to attach onto the substratum and then fractures the larval shell and crawls out – and it is only at this stage in the life-cycle that the urchin becomes radially symmetrical.

Fig. 339 *Parechinus angulosus,* mature adult (x 1).

Since echinoderms have bilateral larvae, why should the adults have adopted radial symmetry? All of them are slow-moving animals, and radial symmetry does have the advantage that it allows detection of food or danger wherever it lies, and also allows the animal to respond by moving in any direction. For this reason, one author has likened the echinoderms to 'five-headed creatures'.

While this may explain the benefit of radial symmetry, it does not answer the question of why the symmetry should be specifically five-rayed. Why not three or four or six? If we return to the newly-metamorphosed juvenile urchin, we find that its body is capped by five skeletal plates – about which more is said below. If the young urchin had four or six plates, the weak suture lines between them would run right across the cap of the annimal so that the slightest nudge could displace the plates (Fig. 340). A five-rayed symmetry overcomes this problem, for the suture lines now converge on the centre of the cap instead of running across it, thus strengthening the whole structure. Possibly it is at this critical stage of development that the unique five-rayed arrangement is most needed.

The second unique feature of echinoderms is their skeleton. Embedded in the skin is a layer of tiny platelets (ossicles) which give the skin a spiny texture, hence the name

Echinodermata (echinus = spine; dermal = skin). In some of the echinoderms these ossicles are joined to one another by ligament-like collagen fibres, thus forming a firm skeleton. In the urchins the ossicles are sufficiently densely packed to form a hard internal shell, while in the sea cucumbers they are so sparsely scattered that the body wall is flaccid.

The skeleton is unique because of its composition, for each ossicle is made of a single crystal of calcium carbonate. But, instead of being solid, each crystal is laid down as a network which is intertwined and woven around the cells that secrete it. At first sight we might expect this network to be fragile, but it is in fact very strong, for it can bend and twist without fracturing, and even if some of the strands do become weakened, the cells within the crystal can continually repair it.

Another benefit of this net-like arrangement is that adjacent ossicles can be 'stitched' together by collagen fibres to create a solid skeleton. The nature of the crystals also means that they can slowly be enlarged by the cellular matrix, to keep pace with the growth of the body. Thus, unlike the condition in arthropods, echinoderms can grow continually and are not compelled to moult each time the skeleton must be enlarged.

The third unusual feature possessed by echinoderms is their hydraulic system of locomotion, which is most easily understood in the starfish (Fig. 341). Extending around the mouth is an internal tubular fluid-filled ring, from which a canal extends into each of the animal's five arms (Fig. 342). Along these canals arise numerous tiny tube feet which pass through the skeleton and the skin to form rows

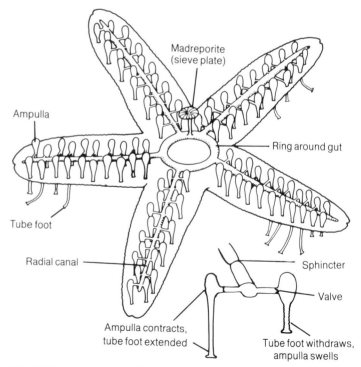

Fig. 341 The arrangement of the water vascular system in a starfish. Sphincter muscles and valves make it possible to isolate any particular portion of the system.

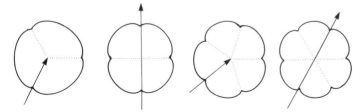

Fig. 340 The five-sided arrangement of scales on a juvenile echinoderm is stronger than a four- or six-sided arrangement because none of the lines of weakness runs directly across the body. Even three scales can be more easily dislodged than five.

of external 'legs', each terminating in a sucker that grips onto the substratum. Associated with each tube foot is a balloon-like ampulla, lying inside the body wall. Contraction of the circular muscles around the ampulla drives its fluid contents down into the tube foot, thus extending it. Longitudinal muscles within the tube foot can then bend the foot in any direction or withdraw it once again. The tube feet possess tiny valves so that it is possible to isolate them from their interconnecting canals, but these valves may also be opened to allow the fluid to be diverted from one part of the body to another. This interlinked hydraulic system is called the water vascular system, for the fluid which drives the tube feet is simply sea-water.

Each tube foot on its own is a puny structure, but applied in concert the feet can exert a considerable force. Furthermore, as the muscles in one tube foot tire, another can be inflated to take its place.

There are, however, two problems with a hydraulic system such as this. The first is that it is incapable of bringing about rapid locomotion; and perhaps this is the secret why echinoderms are such sedentary creatures and, in turn, why they have adopted a radial symmetry.

The second problem is that the whole hydraulic system will collapse if the external pressure is increased or, conversely, becomes inflated if the pressure decreases – and these very changes of pressure must take place when the tide rises and falls, altering the head of water over the animal. In answer to this problem, a tube runs from the circular ring around the mouth to the upper surface of the animal, where it opens to the exterior beneath a shielding sieve-like madreporite (which can clearly be seen near the centre of the starfish's dorsal surface). Through this duct the water vascular system equilibrates with external pressure, either taking in slightly more water or releasing a certain amount, thus maintaining a constant volume inside the water vascular system in spite of external changes of pressure.

In the starfish, the tube feet arise from the lower surface of each arm, and are housed in a groove known as the ambulacral groove. There are thus five of these grooves, one for each arm. While this pattern is less obvious in some of the other echinoderms, they too have a basic pattern of five ambulacrae giving rise to tube feet (Figs. 336 & 337).

During its early development, each echinoderm larva forms hollow out-pockets on the sides of its gut, and these are eventually pinched off from the gut to form five body spaces (coeloms). This process is known as enterocoely, to distinguish it from the schizocoelous development that takes place in most other invertebrates (see Fig. 228). One of these five coeloms (the 'protocoel' at the front of the body) becomes tubular and ring-like and forms the water vascular system. The central two 'mesocoels' form a second tubular system known as the haemal system, while the two posterior 'metacoels' expand greatly to form two massive fluid-filled spaces around the gut and body organs.

This sequence of events is of interest not only because the echinoderms are the only animals to fragment their coelom into such radically different structures, but because the manner in which the coelom is formed links the echinoderms more closely to the vertebrates than to most invertebrates. There has even been speculation that the echinoderm larva was the starting-point for the evolution of all vertebrates.

Finally, the echinoderms are unique in being the only highly evolved animals that lack excretory organs. Waste products are removed by wandering amoeboid cells that engulf unwanted materials and are themselves then cast from the body. Echinoderms also cannot control the concentration of their body fluids, and because of this they are the only major group of animals to be confined entirely to the sea.

Quite clearly the echinoderms are unorthodox in a number of respects, and we can but speculate about their evolutionary origins. Fossil deposits are littered with echinoderms, and at one stage in the history of the earth they were amongst the dominant animals. No less than 12 classes of echinoderm have become extinct, but we are today left with living representatives of five classes. Some are of overriding ecological importance because of their ability to modify the structure of communities by controlling which other species can live there.

CLASS ASTEROIDEA:
Starfish

Starfish are so well known that they are almost symbolic of the seashore. All of them have a central disc which is extended outwards to form tapering arms – usually five in number. Characteristically the arms are not sharply distinguished from the disc but merge into it. The skin is heavily armed with ossicles, but these are not fused into a solid skeleton. Starfish thus have a spiny texture but are able to flex their arms and bodies. Beneath each arm numerous tube feet arise from the ambulacral groove (Fig. 343).

Some starfish are detritus feeders and pick up organic fragments. Of the local species, both *Patiria* and *Henricia* (Plate 144) fall into this category. Others, such as the cushion star *Patiriella exigua* (Plate 141) are micro-algal feed-

Fig. 342 The tube feet of starfish terminate in tiny suckers and can collectively exert a powerful force.

Fig. 343 Ventral view of a cushion star, *Patiriella,* showing the ambulacral grooves that house the tube feet, and the spiny texture of the skin (x 1½).

ers. They feed by extruding the stomach from the mouth, plastering it onto the rock face in order to digest diatoms and algal sporelings. This diet is shared by limpets, and when food is in short supply the two animals come into direct competition. Experiments have shown that limpets are capable of reducing the growth rate of these starfish because their radulae are so much more efficient in scraping the microalgae from the rock face that they leave behind little food for the cushion stars. In addition to competing for food, one species of limpet, *Cellana,* releases a mucus from its mantle which seems to repel the starfish. *Patiriella* actively avoids this limpet, and if they do come into contact the starfish hastily retreats, some-

times trailing a crumpled and seemingly paralysed arm (Fig. 57). The precise effect *Cellana* has on the starfish is not known, but its mucus is probably toxic since it also repels predators.

Starfish are generally thought of as carnivores, but of the local species only *Marthasterias glacialis* – which is also common in Europe – is a voracious predator. *Marthasterias* feeds by humping over its prey and grasping it with its tube feet. The starfish then exudes its stomach to cover the prey and to release enzymes which predigest the animal before it is taken into the gut.

From the mouth of the starfish a short oesophagus opens into a pumpkin-shaped soft-walled stomach. Five pairs of canals (caecae) run from the stomach out into the arms and are bordered by pouches that serve as a digestive gland (Fig. 344).

Marthasterias has a strong preference for mussels, but it will turn to limpets and winkles (both of which have well-developed escape responses to the starfish, as described in Chapter 2 and shown in Fig. 50), or to barnacles, sea urchins or even red-bait (Fig. 43). When feeding on mussels, the starfish's main problem is to open the tightly clamped shell. This it does by slowly pulling apart the two valves of the shell, using its tube feet in relays so that it eventually tires out the mussel. It only needs to open the shell by as little as 0,1 mm to be able to insinuate its floppy stomach into the mussel and begin digestion.

In addition to food that is ingested via the gut, starfish – and all other echinoderms – have the ability to absorb organic molecules that are dissolved in sea-water, directly through the skin. This auxiliary form of food seems important in supplying energy to the tissues lying outside the skeleton.

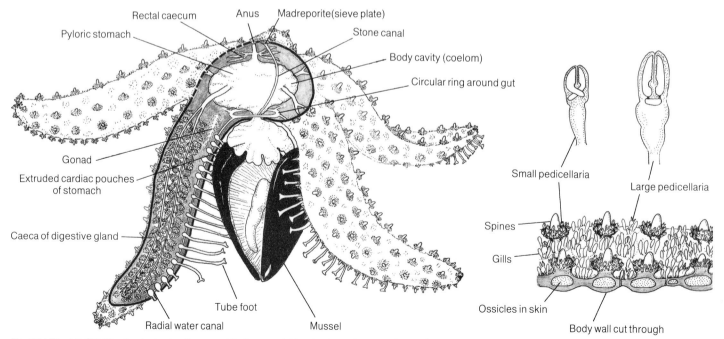

Fig. 344 The starfish *Marthasterias* feeding on a black mussel. Hunched over its prey, the starfish uses its tube feet to force open the shell and then extrudes its stomach into the mussel to digest it. The body and one of the arms have been cut open to reveal the internal structure, and the surface of the skin is shown enlarged.

Apart from the gut, the gonads are the only internal organs, and in the starfish they consist of a pair of sacs in each arm, opening to the exterior via pores at the base of the arms (Fig. 344). Fertilisation is external. Although starfish do not normally reproduce asexually, they do have remarkable powers of regeneration and regularly regrow arms after they have been damaged. Some species even have the ability to discard their arms voluntarily when attacked. The story is often told of how, in the early days of oyster-farming, plagues of starfish descended on the oyster beds. The fishermen harvesting the oysters were naturally outraged, and dragged nets over the oyster beds to entangle the starfish. They then cut up the starfish to kill them and chucked the pieces back into the sea – little realising that most of the pieces would regenerate into whole animals, thus multiplying the number of starfish.

All echinoderms have a simple nervous system consisting of three net-like plexuses at different depths in the body. Since the animals are radially symmetrical there can be no single head and the nervous system is not concentrated into ganglia or into a brain. The echinoderms also lack eyes, although they are very sensitive to changes in light intensity, such as a passing shadow that might herald a predator.

The skeletal ossicles that lie within the skin project sufficiently to form tubercles or scales on the surface, giving starfish a granular texture (Fig. 343). Much more remarkable are specialised ossicles that form trident-like appendages known as pedicellariae (Figs. 344 & 345). These are normally tiny, 2-3 mm long, and consist of a stalk surmounted by two or three jaws which can be snapped shut. In some species these jaws are armed with poison sacs to increase their effectiveness.

Pedicellariae are only found in starfish and urchins – perhaps because they are the only echinoderms with a hard, firm external surface, and thus the only groups in danger of being fouled by settling organisms. It is true that the pedicellariae snap at settling larvae and keep the skin clean but they also serve to repel predators and competitors. In many ways they remind us of the avicularia that bryozoans use in a similar manner (see Chapter 17).

Another line of defence possessed by some starfish is camouflage. The cushion star, Patiriella exigua, comes in a wide range of colours and patterns, seemingly striking when seen in isolation and yet blending into the patchwork patterns in tidal pools (see Plates 88, 141 & 144). In localities where black shale is found, the animals are a uniform dark green, while on beds of sea grass they are khaki green. Thus different populations have different colour patterns, always matching the background colours. In some ways it is puzzling that these animals should go to such lengths to camouflage themselves, for they have no known predators.

Predatory starfish may exert a powerful influence on the structure of communities. As an example, Robert Paine of Washington University has shown that if one particular species (Pisaster) is experimentally removed from intertidal shores, its normal prey – mussels – soon dominate the

Fig. 345 Detail of the upper surface of a starfish arm, showing the gills, spines and pedicellariae (x 3).

shore and exclude many other species. He calls Pisaster a 'keystone' species because its presence radically alters the nature of the intertidal community.

Most starfish can only handle prey of a certain size. As an example, it has been shown by Andrew Penney that small individuals of Marthasterias confine their attention to small mussels while larger individuals select larger mussels. Presumably this behaviour allows the starfish to obtain as much meat as possible without wasting time and energy tackling mussels that are too large to overpower or too small to yield much food. This means that it is possible for the mussels to grow too large to be eaten by the starfish, in the same way that they may escape predation by rock lobsters when they become large enough (see p. 78). However, working on subantarctic Marion Island, William Blankley has discovered a new twist to this tale. There, too, the common starfish Anasterias is unable to capture large individuals of its main prey, the limpet Nacella, when hunting alone. But in this case the starfish have evolved the habit of feeding communally and, by 'ganging up', they are able to capture even the largest of limpets (Fig. 346).

The most notorious of all starfish is the crown-of-thorns, Acanthaster planci (Fig. 347). Over the past few years there have been alarming stories of population explosions of this animal in various parts of the world. The starfish does seem to have increased greatly in number and to have expanded its geographic range. It was first recorded in Moçambique in 1962. The reason for some alarm at the spread of the starfish is that it feeds on corals and has devastated many coral reefs. The crown-of-thorns feeds by extruding its stomach over the coral and releasing enzymes that digest the tiny polyps. Once the polyps are dead, the massive coral skeleton beneath is left exposed to the elements and

Fig. 346 A group of subantarctic starfish, *Anasterias,* collectively captures and feeds on a large limpet, *Nacella* (x ½).

Fig. 347 The crown-of-thorns, *Acanthaster planci,* one of the largest starfish found in Moçambique, feeds on corals.

slowly crumbles. Since each crown-of-thorns may reach 50 cm in diameter and a single animal can consume as much as 2 square metres of coral in a day, large numbers of crown-of-thorns can wreak havoc on a coral reef.

It is still a mystery why the crown-of-thorns should have increased so greatly. One theory is that shell collectors have depleted populations on the giant conches *(Triton)* that feed on the crown-of-thorns. Many countries with coral reefs have now banned the collection and sale of *Triton.* The coral polyps, which feed on planktonic organisms, are known to eat the larvae of *Acanthaster,* and another theory is that dredging, blasting or pollution has damaged coral reefs sufficiently to allow greater number of the starfish larvae to survive, thus allowing the crown-of-thorns to gain the upper hand.

Yet other people argue that the population explosion is a natural phenomenon and point out that many animals have similar outbreaks but sooner or later dwindle again. The expansion of the crown-of-thorns does seem to be halting, but even so, tourist resorts on coral reefs take the threat so seriously that they employ divers to kill the starfish.

Southern African starfish

Most of the common local starfish are shown in Plates 141 – 145 and Figs. 347 – 349. In South Africa there is only a handful of common intertidal species. *Marthasterias glacialis* (Plate 143 & Figs. 43 & 50) is the largest of these. *Henricia ornata* and *Patiria granifera,* smaller orange or reddish animals (Plate 141), may be distinguished from one another by the shape of their arms, for *Henricia* has rounded arms while those of *Patiria* are flattened beneath. *Patiriella exigua* (Plate 141) is probably the commonest of all southern African starfish, extending round the entire coast and occurring abundantly in intertidal pools and in shallow waters. *Asterina burtoni* is a similar but rarer animal with more obvious arms than *Patiriella exigua.* Normally a dull brown, it may sometimes have vivid red patches (as shown in Plate 145).

Divers swimming over sand often encounter large num-

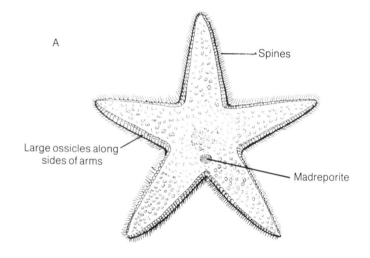

A

Spines

Large ossicles along sides of arms

Madreporite

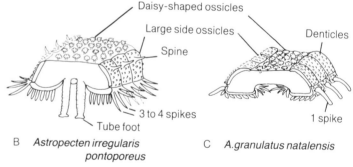

Daisy-shaped ossicles

Large side ossicles

Spine

Denticles

3 to 4 spikes

Tube foot

1 spike

B   *Astropecten irregularis pontoporeus*

C   *A. granulatus natalensis*

Fig. 348 *Astropecten* species are common on sandy bottoms in shallow waters. Detailed drawings of portions of the arms show the features that distinguish two common species.

bers of *Astropecten,* a flat starfish with pointed arms which are edged by a row of large ossicles (Fig. 348). The nature of these large ossicles distinguishes the two commonest species, *Astropecten irregularis pontoporeus,* a west and south coast species, and *Astropecten granulatus natalensis,* which only occurs on the east coast and off Moçambique (Fig. 348).

In the tropical waters of Moçambique and northern Natal

Fig. 349 *Linckia laevigata*, a common bright blue (or sometimes orange) starfish found in Moçambique (x ½).

a new suite of starfish can be found. One of the more spectacular species is *Pentaceraster mammillatus* (see Plate 142) which is found in weed beds in quiet bays and lagoons. *Protoreaster lincki* has a similar structure but is grey-brown with a red pattern and can always be distinguished because it has one or two long spines that stick out on the sides of the arms near their tips.

Various species of *Luidia* also occur in Moçambique, and are instantly recognizable because they have seven (or more) arms. Finally, there are two species of *Linckia* in tropical waters, both with long slender arms. *Linckia laevigata* is bright blue (or less often orange) and has arms about six times longer than the diameter of the central disc (Fig. 349); while in *Linckia multifora* the arms are dull yellow or green and are much longer – between seven and 12 times the diameter of the disc. Probably because its legs are so long, they are often broken and therefore of different lengths.

CLASS OPHIUROIDEA:
Brittle stars

The brittle stars are easily recognized by their round central disc giving rise abruptly to five long slender flexible arms (Fig. 350). It is these arms that propel the animal along with a rapid snake-like movement. Perhaps because the brittle stars have abandoned tube feet as a means of locomotion they are the fastest moving of the echinoderms.

The arms, covered by ossicles which resemble scales, are extremely brittle – hence the name of the group. They can, however, be regrown if they are snapped off, so it is not uncommon to find animals with arms of different lengths.

Each of the 'joints' of the arms bears a pair of tube feet on the lower surface, but these are small and tentacle-like, lack suckers, and can be withdrawn into pockets in the arms where they are protected by tiny ossicles or tentacle

Fig. 350 Common southern African brittle stars. Group I: species in which the disc is covered by dense granules that conceal the scales. Diagnostic features are shown in detail. ▶

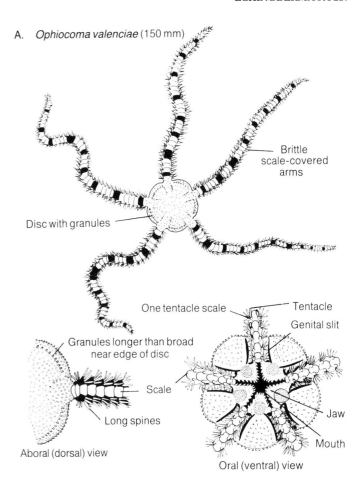

A. *Ophiocoma valenciae* (150 mm)

Brittle scale-covered arms

Disc with granules

One tentacle scale — Tentacle
Genital slit

Granules longer than broad near edge of disc

Scale

Jaw

Long spines

Mouth

Aboral (dorsal) view

Oral (ventral) view

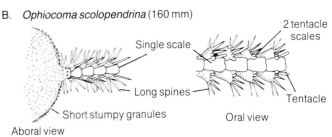

B. *Ophiocoma scolopendrina* (160 mm)

2 tentacle scales

Single scale

Long spines

Short stumpy granules

Tentacle

Oral view

Aboral view

C. *Ophiocoma erinaceus* is similar but has shorter arms and is jet black with orange tentacles.

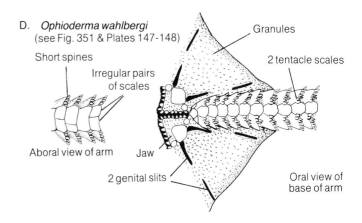

D. *Ophioderma wahlbergi*
(see Fig. 351 & Plates 147-148)

Granules

Short spines

2 tentacle scales

Irregular pairs of scales

Aboral view of arm   Jaw

2 genital slits

Oral view of base of arm

E. *Ophiarachnella capensis* also has short arm spines but its arms are strikingly banded (see Plate 146) and it has only a single genital slit on each side of the arms.

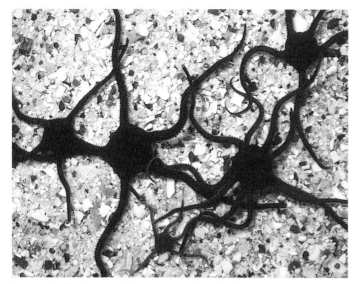

Fig. 351 *Ophioderma wahlbergi,* a large black brittle star reaching 250 mm across the span of its arms, often aggregates on coarse shelly substrates.

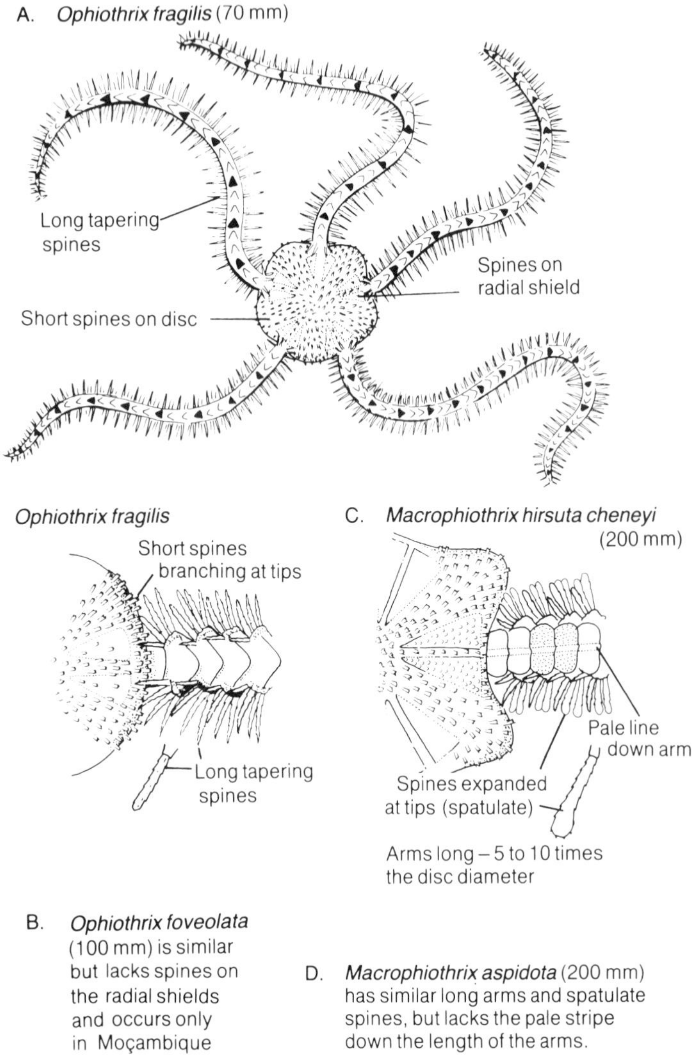

A. *Ophiothrix fragilis* (70 mm)

Long tapering spines

Short spines on disc

Spines on radial shield

Ophiothrix fragilis

Short spines branching at tips

Long tapering spines

C. *Macrophiothrix hirsuta cheneyi* (200 mm)

Pale line down arm

Spines expanded at tips (spatulate)

Arms long – 5 to 10 times the disc diameter

B. *Ophiothrix foveolata* (100 mm) is similar but lacks spines on the radial shields and occurs only in Moçambique

D. *Macrophiothrix aspidota* (200 mm) has similar long arms and spatulate spines, but lacks the pale stripe down the length of the arms.

Fig. 352 Common southern African brittle stars. Group II: species in which the disc is covered with short spines.

scales (Fig. 350). The sides of the arms bristle with long spines, while the central disc is soft and flexible but is covered with scales, granules or spines. Around the edge of the disc at the base of each arm are a series of five pairs of large ossicles, called the radial shields. All these features are of importance when it comes to identifying different species of brittle star.

Most species are detritus-feeders and wave their arms in the water, collecting tiny particles, but some feed on minute animals. Since their food consists of small particles, brittle stars lack an anus, and any wastes are regurgitated through the mouth .The mouth lies in the middle of the lower surface of the disc and is armed with five jaws.

The five gonads are simple and sac-like, and in most species fertilisation is external. A few brittle stars practise internal fertilisation and retain the developing embryos within their bodies so that their young only emerge at an advanced stage of development when they are about 2 cm in diameter. Plates 147 & 148 record the act of birth in a female *Ophioderma wahlbergi*. This particular animal produced no less than seven offspring of this size, and in her pregnant state her body must have been almost totally occupied by the offspring.

Brittle stars are often gregarious and in deeper, calmer, waters dense assemblages may be found. They are, however, secretive animals and hide in crevices – from which they are almost impossible to extricate undamaged, for they grip tenaciously with their snake-like arms and are only too ready to shed an arm rather than be dragged from their shelters.

Local species of brittle stars

Apart from a few distinct species, brittle stars look deceptively alike, and it is necessary to resort to microscopic features to identify them with any certainty. Key features that allow the identification of different species include the nature of the ossicles on the top of the disc, the arrangement of the plates covering the tops of the arms, the size and nature of the spines along the arms, and the number of scales that cover the base of the tentacles.

Without access to a microscope, it is still possible to identify the most striking species which are illustrated in Plates 4 & 146 – 149, and Figs. 350 – 355.

One instantly recognizable species is the Gorgon's head, *Astrocladus euryale* (Plate 149), which has repeatedly branching arms. This animal is often extremely beautiful, sporting yellow, black, grey and white patterns, and hence exciting the interest of divers.

The remaining brittle stars have simple unbranched arms, and they can be divided into three groups depending on the texture of the upper surface of the disc. In Group I the disc is covered with short stumpy granules which are so dense that the underlying scales are scarcely visible. In Group II the disc is scaly but the scales are partly hidden by spines; while in Group III the top of the disc is covered only by flat scales (which are usually quite distinctive but in a

A. *Amphioplus integer* (25 mm)

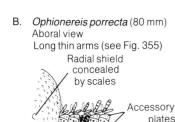

Scales on disc

B. *Ophionereis porrecta* (80 mm)
Aboral view
Long thin arms (see Fig. 355)

Radial shield
concealed
by scales

Accessory
plates

Central plate

Banded arm

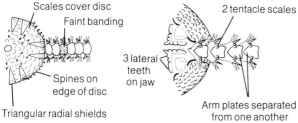

C. *Amphioplus integer*
Aboral view

Radial shields
touch one
another

Single
plate

Only scales
on disc

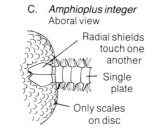

D. *Ophionereis dubia* (Fig. 355)
has similar features but the
scales on its disc are very
small and its white arms
have narrower brown bands.

E. *Amphiura capensis*
(see Fig. 354). Very similar to
Amphioplus integer, but its
radial shields are separated
from one another, and it has
orange arms.

F. *Ophiactis carnea* (25 mm)
Aboral view

Scales cover disc

Faint banding

3 lateral
teeth
on jaw

Spines on
edge of disc

Triangular radial shields

H. *Amphipholis squamata* (10 mm)
Aboral view

2 tentacle scales

Arm plates separated
from one another

G. *Ophiactis savignyi* (22 mm)
A tropical Moçambican species, similar to *O. carnea*, but greenish
and distinguished by having six arms.

Fig. 353 Common southern African brittle stars. Group III: species in which
the disc is covered with flat scales (or appears leathery). Many are small,
5 – 30 mm.

few species are very small, giving the disc a leathery
appearance).

In Figs. 350 – 355 the commonest representatives of
these three groups are illustrated, emphasis being placed
on the key features allowing identification of the species.

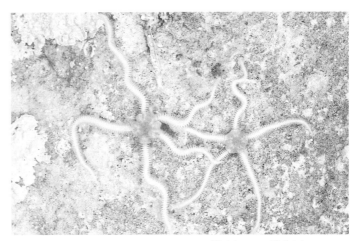

Fig. 354 *Amphiura capensis,* a common small brittle star with bright
orange-yellow arms (x 1½).

Fig. 355 *Ophionereis dubia,* a long-armed brittle star with a blue disc and
striking white arms crossed by narrow brown bands (x ½).

CLASS CRINOIDEA:
The feather-stars

The feather-stars, with long feather-like arms that radiate
from the body (Fig. 356), are the most graceful of the
echinoderms. At one stage of the earth's history, they
ranked among the dominant organisms of the sea, and
during the Carboniferous era (350 million years ago) – if we
are to judge from their abundance in fossil deposits – they
must have carpeted the floor of the sea in certain areas.
Some of the fossil species achieved a length of 20 m, but all
living species are much smaller, the largest being about 30
cm long.

The most primitive members of the group are permanently attached to the substratum by a long stalk, and these
forms are known as 'sea lilies'. Such stalked species are
largely confined to the deep sea. Most shallow-water
species are not stalked but have a series of segmented
hook-like limbs (cirri) on the lower surface of the body,
with which they grasp the substratum (Fig. 356).

Feather stars have comparatively small bodies and
unlike all other echinoderms the mouth is situated on the
upper surface (Fig. 366). From the central disc arise their

Fig. 356 A tropical feather-star clings with its hook-like cirri to the substratum and waves its feathery arms in the water. The lower pinnules branching from the arms are swollen with gametes. (x ²/₃).

most spectacular feature, the long elegant arms. Most species have ten arms, or some multiple of ten. Each arm has a central axis from which extend slender leaf-like pinnules, covered with cilia, which drive particles into a groove that runs down the length of each arm. These grooves join furrows that run across the surface of the disc to the mouth, and food particles captured by the pinnules can thus be transported along the arm to the mouth.

From the mouth, a short oesophagus leads into a stomach which coils around inside the body cavity and ends in an anus which is also situated on the upper surface of the disc close to the mouth. The simplicity of the gut is related to the fact that the arms gather only small, easily digested, food particles.

Since the body is so small, there is little room in it for anything apart from gut, and the gonads are therefore housed in the pinnules on the arms. During the reproductive season these pinnules (Fig. 356) become greatly inflated until the sperm and eggs are released into the water where fertilisation takes place.

Feather-stars remain attached to the substratum for most of their lives, for as filter-feeders they have little need to move. However, if they are detached, they can control the rate at which they sink by spreading or folding their arms and pinnules, and can even swim by slowly undulating their arms up and down.

Southern African feather-stars
Only three common species of feather-stars occur locally. *Comanthus wahlbergi* (Plate 153) is by far the most abundant and is found clinging in large groups to the vertical sides or undersurfaces of rocks in shallow water. *Coman-*

thus is identified by the teeth-like projections that line the tips of the pinnules near the base of its arms, but can also be recognized because it has between 12 and 30 cirri and because its anus is positioned in the centre of its disc while the mouth is pushed towards the side (and is thus termed 'eccentric'). *Comanthus* is found in a wide range of colours, including red, purple, white, brown and orange, or combinations of these colours, so that clusters of the animals present a spectacular sight.

Annametra occidentalis has a similar appearance, but is distinguished by having many more cirri – between 35 and 40. *Tropiometra carinata* (Plate 155) is the most elegant of the local species, with very regularly arranged pinnules tapering towards the tip of the arms. Typically, golden-brownish with yellow tips to its arms, *Tropiometra* is found in a range of pastel colours as well. Like *Comanthus*, *Tropiometra* has between 12 and 30 cirri which are characteristically rounded and smooth, but its mouth is placed centrally on the disc. Although *Tropiometra* extends down the east and south coast as far as False Bay, it is more abundant in tropical waters and is the most frequently encountered feather-star in Moçambique.

CLASS ECHINOIDEA:
Urchins
Sea urchins have globular bodies encased in a calcium carbonate shell (known as a test) formed by the fusion of the ossicles of the skeleton. From the test project a formidable array of long spines. These pivot on ball-and-socket joints so that they can be bent in any direction. Apart from providing protection, the spines also pole the urchin along and are its chief means of locomotion.

The spines of most species provide a purely mechanical defence. They readily puncture the human skin and then break off to form irritating wounds. They can, however, be picked out with a needle, and even if left in the wound they will eventually be absorbed by the body, so that they are little more than a nuisance. By contrast, a few of the long-

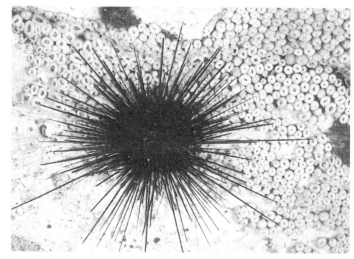

Fig. 357 One of the long-spined urchins, *Diadema savignyi*, crawling over a bed of zoanthids. The spines are hollow and, on fracturing, they release a toxin (x ½).

spined urchins, such as *Diadema* (Fig. 357), possess hollow, needle-sharp spines that have backward-facing barbs which penetrate deeply before fracturing, and release a venom from their hollow shafts. These spines can be fiercely painful and their toxins cause local numbing, nausea, faintness and violent headaches, although the effects soon wear off. The pain is eased by soaking the wound in very hot water. If these long spines penetrate only shallowly they can be softened with vinegar (which contains acetic acid and dissolves the calcium carbonate) which hastens their absorption by the body, but deeply embedded spines may require surgical removal.

Diadema has very mobile spines and quickly rotates them to point in the direction of any danger. The spines may also be rustled against one another and flashed from side to side, to frightening effect. In spite of its fearsome appearance, *Diadema* is still amongst those urchins eaten by the parrot fish, which crushes them with its horny jaws.

Five rows of tube feet run from the apex down the sides of the body to the mid-ventral mouth, like lines of longitude on a globe. These tube feet provide a powerful grip on the substratum and hold algal fragments while they are being eaten. In some species they are also used to hold a canopy of shell fragments – or anything else that is available – over the body. This reaction seems to be a response to light, for if a strip of light is shone over an otherwise darkened animal, it soon rearranges its umbrella of shell fragments to cover the portion of the body that is lit. It has been suggested that this habit protects the urchins from sunburn, but more likely it is simply a means of camouflaging the body.

Between the spines project large numbers of pedicellariae (Fig. 358). The pedicellariae of the common Cape urchin, *Parechinus angulosus*, have been studied in detail (Fig. 359). Most of the time they are held flat against the body, but once the animal is alarmed they are immediately erected. If the pedicellariae are touched on the outside of the jaws they begin to open. Inside each jaw are two sensory 'hillocks' and if these are touched the jaws gape even further. But if the hillocks are touched at the same time as receiving chemical stimulation, they snap shut, biting into the offending object. Since particular chemicals are needed to make the jaws clamp shut, the pedicellariae do not respond to harmless objects, but they can easily be aroused by thrusting a predatory starfish – or even a single tube foot torn from a starfish – at the urchin.

The jaws of some pedicellariae are also armed with large sacs filled with venom; once again only specific chemicals will cause the venom sacs to discharge. A few urchins have extremely potent toxins in the pedicellariae, and *Toxopneustes pileolus*, a short-spined species, is even dangerous to man. Its pedicellariae are particularly large, up to 3 mm in diameter, and when the urchin is alarmed they snap open to cover the whole of the animal, giving it an almost floral appearance (Fig. 366). An extract made from as few as 40 of these pedicellariae is sufficient to kill a rabbit, and the scientist who first worked on the toxins of this species almost lost his life in the course of his researches. Yet,

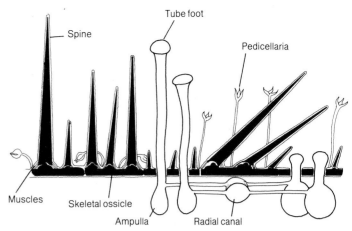

Fig. 358 The surface skin and skeletal ossicles of an urchin, showing how the spines articulate on ball-and-socket joints. On the left the spines are erect, but once the animal is alarmed the spines can be folded back and the pedicellariae erected, jaws agape, as shown on the right.

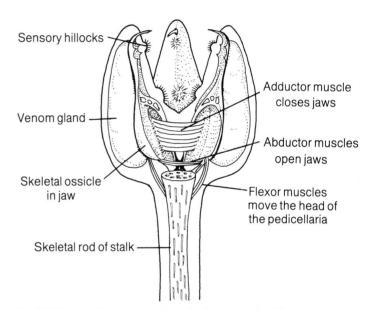

Fig. 359 The detailed structure of a pedicellaria taken from the common Cape urchin, *Parechinus angulosus* (x 100).

Fig. 360 *Toxopneustes pileolus* has short spines but unusually large pedicellariae which cover the animal, giving it a floral appearance (x ²/₃).

because the pedicellariae respond only to particular stimuli, it is possible to handle these animals without suffering any ill-effects – in blissful ignorance of their toxicity I have on several occasions handled these potentially lethal animals, but now treat them with a good deal more respect.

Dead urchins soon shed their spines and pedicellariae and lose their tube feet, leaving the familiar calcium carbonate test, called a 'sea egg' or 'sea pumpkin' (Fig. 361). Detailed examination of the surface of the test reveals the projecting balls on which the spines pivot, and five radiating rows of tiny holes, through which tube feet project in the living animal.

The internal structure of an urchin such as *Parechinus* is most easily seen if the test is cut around the equator and the top half of the shell folded back to reveal the interior of both halves (Fig. 362A).

The mouth lies in the centre of the lower surface and has five massive teeth used to scrape the rock-face and to fragment algae. They form part of an extraordinary complex of 40 calcareous plates arranged in a ring around the mouth, which are as intricately interlocked as any Chinese puzzle (Fig. 362B). This structure is known as Aristotle's lantern – partly because it resembles a Greek five-sided lantern, but also in tribute to Aristotle, who was one of the first scientists to study marine life and who had a particular interest in urchins. The function of Aristotle's lantern is to provide a framework upon which powerful muscles can operate the jaws.

The oesophagus passes through the centre of Aristotle's lantern and joins a loosely-folded stomach that coils once round the centre of the body before entering the intestine which coils back in the opposite direction to join the anus at the upper pole of the body (Fig. 362A).

Nearly all urchins are herbivores and feed on seaweed or microalgae – food plants which often contain an abundance of carbon compounds but little nitrogen, as discus-

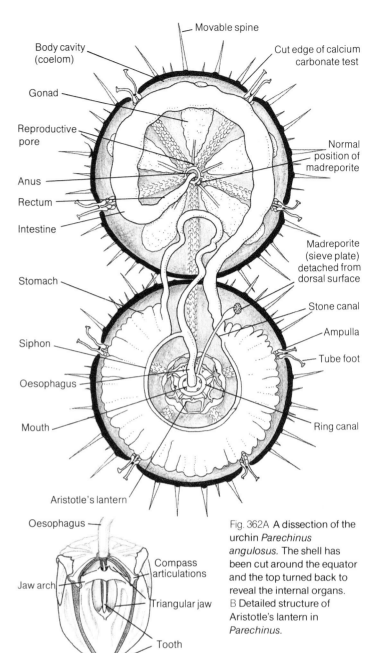

Fig. 362A **A dissection of the urchin** *Parechinus angulosus*. **The shell has been cut around the equator and the top turned back to reveal the internal organs.** B **Detailed structure of Aristotle's lantern in** *Parechinus.*

Fig. 361 The test (or shell) of an urchin, which is formed by the fusion of skeletal ossicles (x 1).

sed in Chapter 4. Urchins are known to 'leak' carbon from their bodies, and this may be because their diet contains an excess of this carbon. However, at least some urchins have the ability to 'fix' nitrogen, converting gaseous nitrogen into nitrogenous organic compounds that can then be used to produce proteins. They owe this ability to nitrogen-fixing bacteria housed in the gut, which allow the urchins to make up for the deficiency of nitrogen in their diet.

Lining the inner surface of the upper half of the test are five gonads which release their gametes via pores arranged around the anus (Fig. 362A). The gonads are edible and are regarded as a delicacy in the Far East, where the urchins are so sought-after that they are imported from all over the world. The gonads are normally eaten raw. To my uneducated palate they taste a bit like sea-water – and frankly it seems a waste to sacrifice an animal for a morsel of meat.

Fig. 363 A dense assemblage of urchins in a coral reef lagoon on Mauritius. Most of the urchins sheltering in depressions are *Echinometra*. Several species have the ability to bore holes in rocks, and one even creates holes in steel pilings. Since the urchins' spines are softer than rock, the method they use to bore into hard substrates is still unknown.

Urchins are popular subjects for embryological studies, for they spawn readily and the eggs can be artificially fertilised by mixing them with sperm. Sexually mature urchins can be induced to spawn if they are suspended upside-down over a bowl of sea-water, with only the top half of the animal submerged in the water. An injection of potassium chloride (at a concentration of 35 grams per litre) will normally persuade less obliging individuals to spawn – and as a last resort the creatures can be cut open and the gonads stripped to obtain eggs and sperm. It is usually easy to rear at least the early larval stages.

Urchins often have a profound influence on the composition of shallow-water communities. Their grazing prevents the establishment of algae, and when they occur densely they leave little but the encrusting *Lithothamnion* that 'paints' rocks white (Plate 152). Experimental removal of urchins usually allows seaweed to flourish.

In various parts of the world urchins have invaded algal beds and stripped them bare. The best documented cases have occurred in North America, where urchins have had a severe effect on kelp beds in several localities.

It seems likely that these infestations occur when human exploitation reduces the urchins' predators – such as sea otters and lobsters (see Chapter 4).

A comparable population explosion of urchins has been recorded in Mauritius by Pierre de Baissac. In this case it seems that over-fishing has drastically reduced the fish which normally eat urchins. Freed from this constraint, the urchins have rapidly multiplied, and most lagoons are now littered with urchins which strip away the seaweed and sea grass (Fig. 363). In the worst-hit areas the urchins reach a density of 250/m².

The identification of southern African urchins

Most urchins are radially symmetrical, resembling pumpkins in shape, and have a mid-ventral mouth and a mid-dorsal anus. These urchins are loosely grouped together as 'Regularia'. Of these, three are large species distinguished by their extremely long spines, which may exceed the diameter of the test (Fig. 357). Adult *Diadema setosum* and *Diadema savignyi* are pitch black and have five pairs of fine iridescent blue lines that run down the body and scintillate between the black spines. The spines of juveniles are banded black and white. The two species are so similar that they have often been confused in the past, and most of the older records of *D. setosum* actually refer to *D. savignyi*. Live animals can be distinguished fairly easily, for *D. setosum* has five conspicuous white spots near the apex of the body and a bright orange or red ring around the fleshy cone that bears the anus; in *D. savignyi* the spots are inconspicuous and the animal never has a bright ring around its anus. Preserved animals lose their colour and it is then necessary to split hairs about their pedicellariae to identify the animals with certainty. *Diadema setosum* has pedicellariae with very long slender teeth, the head of each pedicellaria being 15 to 20 times longer than wide; those of *D. savignyi* are more squat, and about 4 to 5 times longer than wide.

A third long-spined species, *Echinothrix calamaris*, only occurs in Moçambique and is readily recognized because at least some of its spines are banded brown and white, and more particularly because between these long spines are five bands of much shorter, fine, needle-sharp spines. *Echinothrix* varies in colour, but some animals are particularly striking, with emerald green splashes on the body, and pearly white spots on the anal cone, while the shorter spines are golden brown, shot with flecks of green.

In all three of these urchins the long spines are hollow and release a toxin when they break, while all other urchins described here have solid spines.

Stomopneustes variolaris is large, dark and purplish-black with spines which are about half as long as the diameter of the test, and which taper very obviously towards their tips (Plate 150). *Echinometra mathaei*, a common east coast inhabitant found on rocky shores (Fig.

Fig. 364 One of the common east coast urchins, *Echinometra mathaei*, which has purple or black spines, can be recognised by the slightly oval outline of its test (when viewed from above) (x ½).

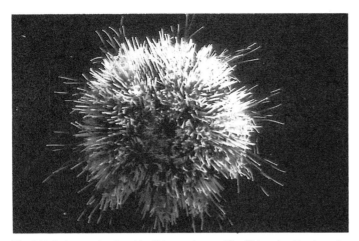

Fig. 365 A short-spined urchin, *Tripneustes gratilla*. This animal is viewed ventrally through the glass wall of an aquarium, and its tube feet are extended as far as they can reach, revealing the five paired rows of ambulacrae from which they arise (x ½).

364), has purple or black spines that are only slightly shorter than those of *Stomopneustes*, but its test is characteristically slightly oval rather than round (when looked at from above).

Parechinus angulosus (Plate 152 and Fig. 339) is the only common south and west coast species, and has much shorter spines – in the order of one-fifth of the test diameter. These spines, vary greatly in length and colour, but are typically green at the base.

Four other urchins with even shorter spines occur on southern African shores. The commonest, *Tripneustes gratilla* (Fig. 365), ranges from the south coast to Moçambique. In contrast to *Parechinus* its spines are all more or less similar in length and are a uniform pale buff colour. *Tripneustes* is also a much larger animal than *Parechinus*, reaching 75 mm in diameter. The remaining short-spined species occur in northern Natal and Moçambique or are restricted to Moçambique. *Toxopneustes pileolus* is unmistakable because its pink or red body is densely covered with pedicellariae (which, as discussed above, contain a potent toxin), and these expand to hide most of the body and the spines (Fig. 360) when the animal is alarmed. Even in death the pedicellariae remain gaping and their triangularly arranged jaws each span 3 mm.

Salmacis bicolor has short spines banded red and yellow or red and green, and the spines near the mouth are slightly flattened rather than cylindrical. In *Temnopleurus toreumaticus* the spines are blackish or may be olive green with purple-black bands. Both these species are additionally distinguished from other urchins by having pits or furrows in the test, in the zone between the spines.

A small group of urchins known as pencil or slate urchins have extremely thick blunt spines. *Heterocentrotus mammillatus* (Plate 151), a Moçambican species, is a typical and unmistakable example. *Eucidaris metularia* has almost cylindrical spines which have a collar of small flat spines fringing their bases (Fig. 366). *Prionocidaris pistillaris*, which extends further south to reach Port

Elizabeth, has tapering spines which are thorny to the touch and have purple spots or lines at their bases.

While all of these 'regular' urchins have round or slightly oval outlines and are radially symmetrical, three species – all referred to as 'Irregularia' – have evolved a bilateral symmetry (with a front and back end to the body). This is brought about because these animals are all burrowers – and it is obviously easier to plough through sand if the body has a definite anterior end. Bilateral symmetry is achieved by a shift in the position of the anus, which instead of being mid-dorsal, as in most urchins, is found on the ventral surface near the posterior end of the body.

The heart urchin, *Echinocardium cordatum*, has an oval test with the mouth near the front of the body. The spines form a dense, brittle, coat to the test and have become specialised for different functions. The lowermost spines are flat and pole the animal through the sand, while the lateral spines are longer and shovel sand aside (Fig. 367). Most of the dorsal spines are short and sharp and have a protective function.

Finally, the most unusual urchins (and certainly the most sought-after) are the pansy shells or sand dollars (see Fig. 368). Two species occur in southern Africa, *Echinodiscus bisperforatus* being the commonest and extending from the south coast to Moçambique, while *Echinodiscus auritus* is confined to Moçambique. The two are easily distinguished, for in *E. auritus* the two narrow slits in the test extend to the edge of the margin, while in *E. bisperforatus* they are closed off short of the margin (Fig. 368).

Both of these pansy shells have extensively modified bodies, being flat and wafer-like. In life they are covered by a short coat of tiny spines, but these soon fall off once the animal is dead, revealing clearly the dorsal 'pansy' that gives the creatures their popular name. This pattern is due to the tiny holes that allow the tube feet to penetrate through the test. On the lower surface, the mouth lies in the centre of the body, and from it five radiating grooves serve to conduct tiny organisms to the mouth. If dead pansy shells are gently shaken it is usually possible to detect the shells of the tiny prey, such as foraminiferans (Fig. 142B), amongst the sand that showers from the mouth.

The two slits in the test have aroused a good deal of curiosity and we are still not sure what use they are put to by our local species. The American 'sand dollar' is known

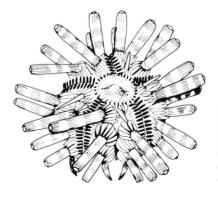

Fig. 366 Like a few other urchins, *Eucidaris metularia* has particularly stout, blunt, primary spines. The base of each spine is ringed by a collar of flat secondary spines (x 1).

Fig. 367 The dorsal (A) and ventral views (B) of a heart urchin, *Echinocardium cordatum* (x 1).

Fig. 368 A pansy shell, *Echinodiscus bisperforatus*, stranded on the beach, and still covered by the coat of spines that soon drop off when the animal dies (x ½).

to up-end itself and wedge its body upright in the sand, so that water currents can flow through these slits. By spanning the slits with tube feet it is able to filter out plankton and particulate matter. This species also weighs itself down by concentrating heavy metals (particulary iron) in certain regions of its body, so that it is not easily disturbed by waves. It is even on record that one entrepreneur displayed an interest in the beasts in the hopes that they might concentrate gold!

A final interesting snippet is that, in Moçambique, pansy shells often harbour the females of a small white commensal brittle star, *Amphylicus scripta*. And while the female brittle stars cling to the undersurface of the pansy shells, they themselves are clung to by their minute dwarf males.

CLASS HOLOTHURIA:
Sea cucumbers

Of all the echinoderms the sea cucumbers come closest to abandoning the star-shaped symmetry that characterises their relatives. The bodies of sea cucumbers are greatly elongated and they lie on their sides. The mouth, situated at one end of the body, is surrounded by a series of ten to 20 tentacles which capture plankton or small organic particles. Down the length of the body run five ambulacral rows of tube feet – practically the only external signs of the five-sided symmetry found in other echinoderms (see Figs. 336 & 337). Like the tube feet of starfish and urchins, those of sea cucumbers usually end in tiny suckers and are operated by internal ampullae which inflate or collapse the tube feet by pumping water into them or draining them. In many sea cucumbers even the five ambulacral rows become ill-defined or are concentrated on the lower surface of the body where the tube feet can most effectively suck onto the substratum. On the upper surface the tube feet often lack suckers and form soft conical papillae randomly dotted over the dorsal surface. In certain species all the tube feet are reduced to papillae which are scattered irregularly over the body, eliminating the last external signs of radial symmetry.

Sea cucumbers have unusually soft pliable skins in comparison with the starfish and urchins – although the skin is laden with tiny ossicles (spicules) which give it a gritty texture. One researcher has calculated that there must be twenty million spicules in the skin of each animal – but, in spite of this, sea cucumbers are regarded as a delicacy in many parts of the world, particularly Japan. The animals are dried in the sun and sold as *trepang* or *bêche-de-mer*. Despite their unappetising appearance, sea cucumbers are delicately flavoured and very nutritious.

Although the skin is flexible it also has the ability to stiffen if the animal is prodded or mouthed by a predator. This ability is unexpected because the skin lacks any trace of muscles. It is, however, criss-crossed by ligament-like collagen fibres. Recently it has been shown that these fibres may become chemically bonded to one another, the amino-acid lysine forming links between the fibres. This bonding crinkles up the collagen fibres, tightening and stiffening the skin. These chemical bonds may also be broken, straightening the collagen fibres once again and restoring the skin to its original pliable state.

Below the skin lie longitudinal muscle bands (Fig. 369) which can withdraw the tentacles and also shorten the body into a stout barrel-shape.

Internal structure

The tentacles around the mouth are in fact modified tube feet, and are connected internally to 'polian vesicles', balloon-like structures equivalent to enlarged ampullae. These are united by a circular canal around the oesophagus (Fig. 369). The polian vesicles are responsible for inflating the tentacles by pumping the fluid into them, and absorb this fluid again when the tentacles are withdrawn into the body.

Sea cucumbers have a single gonad, which resembles a tuft of long yellow threads that unite at their bases and open to the exterior at a dorsal pore just behind the head (Fig. 369). The gonads expand greatly during the reproductive season and may fill much of the body cavity. The possession of a single gonad, instead of five radially arranged gonads, is a further sign that the sea cucumbers

Fig. 370 Many sea cucumbers eviscerate themselves if irritated or threatened. Here the large east coast *Holothuria cinerascens* is seen immediately after disgorging its entire gut. The animals are able to regenerate the gut.

have abandoned the star-shaped symmetry found in other echinoderms.

The gut coils repeatedly back and forth within the body cavity but has a very simple structure. Its most striking feature is at the posterior end where the anus opens into a swollen chamber known as the cloaca. This chamber also receives the trunk of a delicate, much-branched, internal 'respiratory tree' (Fig. 369) which is hollow and contains sea-water. Across its thin walls oxygen enters the body. Muscular pumping of the cloaca periodically replaces the sea-water within the respiratory tree, thus introducing fresh supplies of oxygen.

Several commensal animals shelter inside the anus, including one fish, *Carapus*, which reverses tail first into the anus of at least two species of sea cucumber, including the large bright green *Stichopus chloronotus*.

Some species of sea cucumber have evolved an additional internal organ. This is the organ of Cuvier which consists of numerous long white threads that join the cloaca and can be forcibly discharged from the anus if the animal is irritated or threatened. These threads are formidable structures for not only are they extremely sticky but they are lined with collagen fibres that make them very tough and difficult to snap. As if this were not enough, the threads also contain toxins; and there have even been reports of human deaths following the consumption of species which possess these organs.

Sea cucumbers which lack the organ of Cuvier have a different and even more astonishing method of defence, for when threatened they voluntarily eviscerate themselves, disgorging part or all the gut (Fig. 370). Many a student has puzzled over the identification of strange 'animals' which are the discarded intestines of a holothurian.

This bizarre behaviour has never been fully explained. It has been suggested that by sacrificing a tasty morsel, the sea cucumber loses less than it would if it were ripped apart by a predator. Somehow this begs the question, for having consumed the gut it seems unlikely that a predator will be satisfied and therefore ignore the rest of the animal

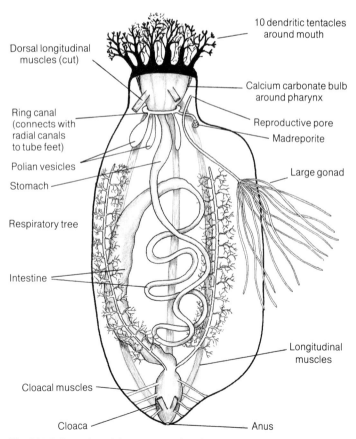

Fig. 369 A dissection of the sea cucumber *Cucumaria stephensoni*. (The five radial canals that run down the length of the body walls and connect with the tube feet have been omitted).

Labels on Fig. 369:
- 10 dendritic tentacles around mouth
- Dorsal longitudinal muscles (cut)
- Calcium carbonate bulb around pharynx
- Ring canal (connects with radial canals to tube feet)
- Reproductive pore
- Madreporite
- Polian vesicles
- Stomach
- Large gonad
- Respiratory tree
- Intestine
- Longitudinal muscles
- Cloacal muscles
- Cloaca
- Anus

– and sea cucumbers are such sedentary creatures that it is not as if they can make good their escape while the predator feasts on the gut. Whatever the advantage of this response, degutted sea cucumbers do have the ability to regenerate their innards.

This extraordinary behaviour only heightens the impression that the echinoderms are indeed unique creatures.

Classification and identification of local sea cucumbers

The tentacles that surround the mouth vary in structure and number and provide a convenient means of recognizing three orders of sea cucumbers (Fig. 371). Creatures in the order Apoda have 12 pinnate (feathery) tentacles; in addition the body characteristically lacks any tube feet. Only two local species need mention: *Epitomapta knysnaensis* is a slender tubular creature about 60 mm in length, and burrows in the sandbanks of lagoons and estuaries; *Synapta oceanica* is an unmistakable animal, for it achieves a length of over 1 m, and is a familiar sight on the sandy bottoms of coral-reef lagoons in Mocambique.

Members of the second order, Aspidochirota (Fig. 373), possess 18 to 20 tentacles arranged in two rings around the mouth. Near the tips the tentacles branch into tight tufts or 'buttons' and are described as being 'peltate' (Fig. 371). Most of the species in this order are large and often rotund animals, about 200 mm in length. While they are most abundant in tropical waters, several species extend down to the east coast of South Africa.

In the final order, Dendrochirota (Fig. 372), the mouth is surrounded by ten dendritic tentacles, which branch irregularly into tree-like structures. Most of the southern African species belong to this order, and all of them are moderate-sized animals, seldom exceeding 80 mm in length.

These three types of tentacles are more than a convenient means of classifying the sea cucumbers, for they reflect different methods of feeding in the three orders. While the feathery (pinnate) and branching (dendritic) tentacles are

| Order Apoda Pinnate (feathery) | Order Aspidobranchia Peltate (buttoned) | Order Dendrochirota Dendritic (branched, tree-like) |

Fig. 371 The three types of tentacles found in different groups of sea cucumbers.

Fig. 372 Common sea cucumbers of the order Dendrochirota, which have ▶ 10 branched dendritic tentacles. Most are moderate sized, 20 – 80 mm, and are limited to the west and south coasts. Details of the spicules found in the body wall are shown.

Group I: Tube feet delicate, scattered randomly over body.

A. **Thyone aurea** (80 mm)
Scattered non-retractile tube feet.
10 dendritic tentacles.

B. *Thyone sacellus* (80 mm)
Very similar but chocolate brown. Restricted to Moçambique.

Very common in sheltered bays, buried in sand with only tentacles extended. Colour ochre-orange.

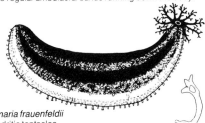

Group II: Tube feet suctorial, retractile and confined to 5 regular ambulacral bands running down the body.

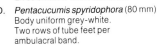

C. *Cucumaria frauenfeldii*
10 dendritic tentacles.
Dark purple-black above.
Pale below.
Body arched. (75 mm)
4 to 6 rows tube feet
per ambulacral band.
Lives on sand-covered rocks.

D. *Pentacucumis spyridophora* (80 mm)
Body uniform grey-white.
Two rows of tube feet per ambulacral band.

E. *Pentacta doliolum* (70 mm)
Dorsally mauve-black,
ventral sole pale and flattened.
Two rows of tube feet per ambulacral band.

Group III: Tube feet retractile and mainly confined to ambulacral bands, but at least some tube feet scattered over the body between these bands (in the interambulacrae).

E. *Cucumaria sykion* (65 mm)
10 dendritic tentacles.
Ambulacral bands with
3 or 4 rows of tube feet.
Scattered tube feet between
ambulacral bands.
Uniformly black.
Dorsal bands of tube feet
irregular but distinguishable.

G. *Cucumaria stephensoni* (70 mm)
Uniformly black.
Six rows of tube feet in
each of the ventral ambulacral
rows; dorsal surface with
irregularly scattered
papillae only.
Aggregates in large numbers
round sides of rocks.

H. *Trachythyone cruciferae* (50 mm)
Uniformly pink-brown to yellow.
Occurs in Moçambique and Natal.
Cross-shaped spicules.

I. *Trachythyone insolens* (40 mm)
'Chest' or whole body red
(see Plate 156).
Two or three rows of tube feet
in each of the 3 ventral bands.
Dorsal surface with a few
scattered papillae only.

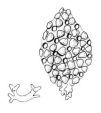

A. *Holothuria cinerascens* (200 mm)
   (see also Fig. 370)
   Scattered tube feet
   forming papillae on
   dorsal surface.

18 peltate tentacles

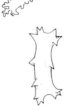

Scattered suctorial tube
feet on ventral sole.
Brown above.
Pink to reddy-brown sole.
Common in Natal on rocky
shores.

B. *Holothuria parva* (130 mm)
   Dark brown, with tips of suckers
   green. Occurs in mangroves and
   on rocky shores.

C. *Holothuria scabra* (150 mm)
   Lives on sheltered sand-banks.
   Mottled grey & black, darker
   above.

D. *Holothuria leucospilota* (220 mm)
   Uniformly black. Very large.
   Occurs from Natal to Moçambique.
   Can be confused with *H. atra*,
   which is also black but is confined
   to Moçambique and lacks the
   'button' spicules of *H. leucospilota*.

E. *Holothuria pervicax* (200 mm)
   Light yellow with large dark brown blotches.
   Can be confused with *Holothuria hilla*, which
   is much smaller (130 mm) and yellow to pink with
   small dark spots. Both restricted to Moçambique.

F. *Neostichopus grammatus* (150 mm)
   Uniformly red or cream to pink
   when alive. Large warts on
   dorsal surface. Internally,
   gonad divided into two tufts.
   Spicules form flat rings divided
   by one to four cross-struts,
   or curved rods.

G. *Actinopyga mauritiana* (200 mm)
   Varied colour, often brown above
   with pink or purple sole below.
   Five calcareous teeth form a
   ring around the anus.

H. *Stichopus chloronotus* (150 mm)
   A distinctive deep green
   colour. Large pointed
   tubercles on the back.

Fig. 373 Common sea cucumbers of the order Aspidochirota, all of which
have 18 to 20 peltate tentacles. Most species are large (up to 200 mm in
length) and are confined to Moçambique and the east coast. Details of the
spicules found in the body wall are shown on the right, while on the left are
notes on the key features for identification.

held aloft to filter plankton and organic particles from the
water, the more robust buttoned (peltate) tentacles can be
shovelled through sediment or through organic debris to
pick up any edible matter the creature comes across.

To identify the various species of sea cucumbers with
certainty, it is necessary to examine the microscopic structure of the spicules embedded in the skin. A snippet of the
skin should be mounted on a microscope slide and then
macerated with either caustic soda or a hypochlorite
bleach to dissolve away the flesh. Since microscopic
examination of the spicules is not always possible, both
Figs. 372 & 373 are annotated to allow identification of
most species purely on the basis of external features.

REFERENCES

Popular articles and books

Nichols, D. 1969. *Echinoderms.* Hutchinson University Library, London.
   192 pp.
Nichols, D. 1975. *The Uniqueness of the Echinoderms.* Oxford Biology
   Readers. 16 pp.
Sugar, J. A. 1970. Starfish threaten Pacific reefs. *National Geographic,*
   Vol. 137(3): 340-353.

Identification guides

Balinsky, J. B. 1957. The Ophiuroidea of Inhaca Island. *Annals of the
   Natal Museum, Vol. 14:* 1-32.
Cherbonnier, G. 1952. Contribution à la connaissance des holothuries de
   l'Afrique du Sud. *Transactions of the Royal Society of S. Afr., Vol. 33:*
   469-509 and plates 35-50.
Clark, A. M. & Courtman-Stock, J. 1976 *The Echinoderms of Southern
   Africa.* British Museum. (Natural History), London. pp 277.
Day, J. H. 1969. *A Guide to Marine Life on South African Shores.*
   A. A. Balkema, Cape Town. pp 180-193.
Diechmann, E. 1948. The holothurian fauna of South Africa. *Annals of the
   Natal Museum, Vol. 11:* 325-376.
McNae, W. & Kalk, M. 1958. *A Natural History of Inhaca Island, Moçam-
   bique.* Witwatersrand University Press, Johannesburg. pp 96-107.

Scientific references

Branch, G. M. & Branch M. L. 1980. Competition between *Cellana
   tramoserica* (Sowerby) (Gastropoda) and *Patiriella exigua* (Lamarck)
   (Asteroidea), and their influence on algal standing stocks. *Journal of
   Experimental Marine Biology and Ecology* Vol. 48: 35-49.
Cram, D. L. 1971. Life history studies on South African echinoids. 1.
   Parechinus angulosus (Leske). *Transactions of the Royal Society of
   S. Afr., Vol. 39:* 321-338.
Cannone, A. J. 1970. The anatomy and venom-emitting mechanism of the
   globiferous pedicellariae of the urchin, *Parechinus angulosus* (Leske)
   with notes on their behaviour. *Zoologica Africana, Vol. 5:* 179-190.
Freinkal, W. D. & Hepburn, H. R. 1975. Dermal stiffness and collagen
   cross-linking in a sea cucumber (Holothuroidea). *S. Afr. Journal of
   Science, Vol. 71:* 280-281.
Paine, R. T. 1974. Intertidal community structure. Experimental studies
   on the relationship between a dominant competitor and its principal
   predator. *Oecologia, Berlin. Vol. 15:* 93-120.
Scott, R. S., Hepburn, H. R., Joffe, I. & Heffron, J. J. A. 1974. The mechani-
   cal defensive mechanism of a sea cucumber. *S. Afr. Journal of Science,
   Vol. 76:* 46-48.

21. ASCIDIACEA

SEA SQUIRTS AND RED-BAIT

The familiar red-bait, *Pyura stolonifera*, which carpets shallow rocks on the south and west coasts, and is much sought-after by anglers, is the best-known representative of the class Ascidiacea. Like red-bait, all ascidians are sessile creatures with barrel-shaped bodies surmounted by a twin pair of turrets or siphons. Since they have the ability to squirt jets of water from their siphons they are often called 'sea squirts' (Fig. 23).

Ascidians have actively swimming larvae which, in many respects, are more complex than the adults, for several of the organs present in the larvae degenerate after metamorphosis. Most ascidians are hermaphroditic and release their sex cells into the water where fertilisation takes place. The young are described as 'tadpole' larvae, for superficially they look much like tadpoles, with a rounded body and an elongated tail fringed by flat fins (Fig. 364). On the front of the larva's body are three glandular papillae, and behind these lies a 'mouth' or inhalant siphon through which water is sucked. This water passes through gill slits (or stigmata) in the walls of the pharynx, then into an atrial cavity which directs the water out of an exhalant siphon. Lying above the pharynx is a balancing organ (otolith) and a group of light-sensitive cells (ocelli). In the tail a rod-like notochord supports the body and provides the long nerve cord with some protection.

When metamorphosis takes place, the larva fastens itself to the substratum by its adhesive papillae, in effect standing on its head. The whole of the tail with its nerve cord and notochord are absorbed into the body, leaving only a rudimentary nerve ganglion. This transformation of the body and internal organs is shown in Fig. 374.

After metamorphosis the body swells and becomes encased in a hard tunic or test, which is made of cellulose (Fig. 374B). In the case of red-bait, this tunic is horny and black and completely conceals and protects the bright orange-red flesh of the animal, which is eaten so avidly by fish. The flesh tastes not unlike that of an oyster but is more strongly flavoured – and very palatable once one has overcome the initial horror at the thought of eating red-bait!

The ascidians have the distinction of being the only animals to synthesise cellulose in large quantities for it is otherwise produced only by plants. It is, however, an ideal choice for a protective coating since scarcely any animals can digest cellulose. The structure of an adult ascidian is most easily seen in those species which have a transparent tunic, such as *Ciona intestinalis* (Figs. 375 & 376). The cylindrical body is surmounted by two siphons. Through the inhalant siphon water is sucked into a large pharynx richly supplied by blood vessels, permitting oxygen uptake from the inhaled water. Its walls are dotted with regular rows of tiny holes, known as stigmata. Through these the water is sieved, entering a larger internal cavity, the atrium, which surrounds the pharynx. From here the water passes out of the body via the exhalant siphon (as shown in Fig. 376).

Running down one side of the pharynx is a groove, known as the endostyle. This continually produces a thin sheet of mucus that forms an internal lining to the pharynx and serves to capture food particles as the inhaled water passes through the stimata. On the opposite side of the pharynx is a ridge known as the dorsal lamina, which is tasselled with finger-like projections called languets. The function of this structure is to gather up the mucus and its entangled particles and to pass them down to the stomach (Fig. 376).

Lying between the coils of the intestine are the testis and ovary, which have separate ducts passing into the atrium, together with the rectum, so that both faeces and gametes are released at a point where they are swept out of the body in the exhalant current.

At the very base of the pharynx is a small heart which, as in all ascidians, functions in a peculiar manner, first pump-

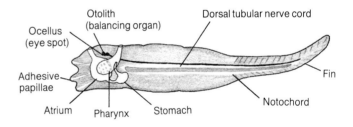

Tadpole larva

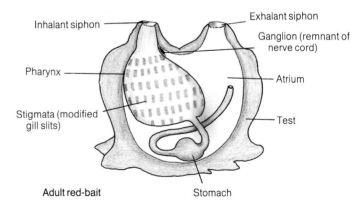

Adult red-bait

Fig. 374 The tadpole larva of a red-bait, *Pyura stolonifera*, and a diagram of the gut and nervous system in an adult red-bait showing how these organs are modified after metamorphosis of the swimming larva into the sessile adult.

Fig. 375 A pair of solitary sea-squirts, *Ciona intestinalis* (x 1).

Fig. 377 *Botryllus* sp., a colonial ascidian – an aggregation of minute sea-squirts which are embedded in a common jelly-like matrix.

ing blood in one direction and then after a few minutes reversing the flow and pumping it in the opposite one.

Ciona occurs very commonly in sheltered harbours and lagoons, particularly on the undersurfaces of jetties, piers and buoys. Its occurrence on the lower surface of these structures ensures that even in the calm waters of its preferred habitat it is unlikely to suffer from silt raining down on it. Its restriction to these sites is explained by the behaviour of its larvae, for when they are ready to metamorphose they secrete gas bubbles, so that they rise upwards and lodge under floating objects.

Red-bait, *Pyura stolonifera*, prefers wave-beaten shores, presumably because the water movement aids the circulation of water through its pharynx and ensures an adequate supply of suspended food particles. Not only does red-bait thrive in turbulent waters, but the size it reaches is directly related to the amount of surge it receives; in certain areas where wave action is particularly strong, it may grow as large as a football.

Both *Ciona* and *Pyura* are solitary ascidians, and although they often live in crowded groups each animal is an independent unit. However, many of the smaller species are colonial, large numbers of minute individuals – usually no more than a few millimetres in size – sharing a common tunic or jelly-like matrix (Fig. 377 and Plate 157). Some species have even evolved common atria and share a single exhalant opening (Fig. 378).

These colonial species – called compound ascidians – abound on the undersurfaces of rock and are among the most important encrusting organisms vying for space with sponges and bryozoans. It is no coincidence that all these animals are colonial, for as a generalisation colonial species nearly always have an advantage over solitary

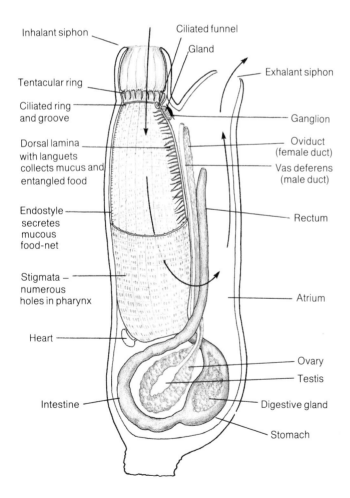

Inhalant siphon

Ciliated funnel

Gland

Tentacular ring

Exhalant siphon

Ciliated ring and groove

Ganglion

Dorsal lamina with languets collects mucus and entangled food

Oviduct (female duct)

Vas deferens (male duct)

Endostyle secretes mucous food-net

Rectum

Stigmata – numerous holes in pharynx

Heart

Atrium

Ovary

Intestine

Testis

Digestive gland

Stomach

Fig. 376 Dissection of the solitary sea-squirt, *Ciona intestinalis*. Part of the body wall has been cut away to show the internal organs and the upper half of the pharynx has been removed to show its internal structure.

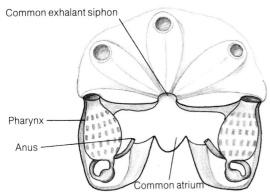

Fig. 378 A partially cut-away view of the compound ascidian shown in Fig. 377.

(labels: Common exhalant siphon, Pharynx, Anus, Common atrium)

creatures, they belong to the phylum Chordata, which includes those most highly evolved of all animals, the vertebrates. Adult ascidians, with their sessile habits, seem far divorced from these élite creatures, yet their larvae bear all the hallmarks of the chordates – a tubular dorsal nerve-cord, a rod-like notochord, gill slits, and a tail that is elongated beyond the anus. These features appear at least during the embryological development of all vertebrates. Walter Garstang was one of the first to suggest that if a larval stage such as the 'tadpole' of ascidians became capable of reproduction (a process called neoteny), it would not be necessary to look further for a suitable ancestor for the early vertebrates (such as primitive fish) and thence, ultimately, perhaps to man himself.

species when they compete for space. Colonial animals can divide asexually and continue to expand the colony throughout their lives, so that it is relatively easy for them to overrun a solitary animal. In addition, the minute individuals in a colony each require only a tiny space and a small amount of food to be able to reproduce. By contrast, solitary animals must grow large enough in order to be able to hold their own against competitors before they can turn their attentions to reproduction.

The ascidians afford us one parting surprise, for despite being immobile, simple, and in some respects, degenerate

REFERENCES

Identification guides
Day, J. H. 1969. *A Guide to Marine Life on South African Shores.* A. A. Balkema, Cape Town. pp. 197-201.

Scientific references
Day, R. W. 1974. An investigation of *Pyura stolonifera* (Tunicata) from the Cape Peninsula. *Zoologica Africana*, Vol. 9: 35-58.
Griffiths, R. G. 1976. The larval development of *Pyura stolonifera* (Tunicata). *Transactions of the Royal Society of S. Afr.*, Vol. 42: 1-9.

22. ALGAE SEAWEEDS

For years the seaweeds were the Cinderellas of marine biology and were regarded as being only of academic interest. It took two world wars to establish seaweeds as vital resources, first as a substitute for the potash produced by Germany and then, later, as a source of agar to replace supplies from Japan. Since then a wider range of commercial applications has been found for seaweeds, some of which are outlined in Chapter 7. In addition, the essential contribution of seaweeds to the ecology of inshore waters has become so obvious that an increasing amount of research is being devoted to them.

Not only are seaweeds a major source of food for marine animals, but they also create unique habitats. They buffer the effects of wave action and provide shelter for a host of animals. In the intertidal zone they offer protection from the heat of the sun and from desiccation, and a single tuft of

seaweed may often support a veritable community of its own. As an example, a solitary growth of the seaweed *Gelidium pristoides* growing on the shell of a limpet was once shown to harbour 132 amphipods, 32 isopods, 1 216 copepods, 79 tiny gastropods, 16 small bivalves, 12 polychaete worms and three bryozoans – an assemblage of no less than 29 different species.

Seaweeds also provide a haven for animals seeking to escape predators, and experiments have proved that the greater the cover of algae, the more difficult it is for predators to locate and capture their prey. Finally, the larger seaweeds provide a firm substratum on which many organisms live. In fact, some animals live only on seaweeds and, furthermore, may be very particular about the species on which they settle.

Apart from the central importance of seaweeds in the

ecology of nearshore waters, they display a remarkable variety of colours and shapes and, as Plates 166 – 177 reveal, many of them are extremely beautiful – a quality that is best appreciated when the plants are seen under water. Their elegance is a far cry from the slimy unappealing vision conjured up in the minds of most people when they think of algae.

PHOTOSYNTHESIS AND ALGAL PIGMENTS

Almost all plants have the ability to produce organic molecules, such as glucose, using only carbon dioxide, water and essential elements, and sunlight as a source of energy. This is why all animal life ultimately depends on plants for food. In the process of photosynthesis, plants release oxygen. Over millions of years they have transformed the earth's atmosphere, for prior to their existence the atmosphere contained very little oxygen. Even today, plants are largely responsible for maintaining the vital balance between carbon dioxide and oxygen.

Photosynthesis may be simplified into two basic steps, known as light and dark phases. During the light phase, solar energy is trapped by pigments, which are usually stored in organelles known as chloroplasts, within the cells of the plant. Chlorophyll is the most familiar of these pigments, but there are several others. Chlorophyll is 'excited' by sunlight, causing each molecule to release an electron which is then transferred along a chain of molecules which act as electron acceptors. Finally they are incorporated into a high-energy molecule (adenosine triphosphate, ATP), thus storing the energy in a chemical form so that it can later be used in a controlled manner to power chemical reactions. One of the molecules in the chain of electron acceptors is nicotinamide adenine dinucleotide phosphate (NADP), which, when it accepts a pair of negatively charged electrons, also pulls two positively charged hydrogen ions (H^+) from water molecules (H_2O) to neutralise the electrons. In the process the water is broken down and the oxygen is released.

The dark phase of photosynthesis may proceed in light or dark conditions for it is not dependent on light. During this phase the energy trapped in ATP and $NADPH_2$ is released and provides the energy necessary for carbon dioxide to be incorporated into carbohydrate molecules. These, in turn, can ultimately be converted into proteins or fats provided certain essential elements are available.

These elements include sulphur, nitrogen, phosphorus and magnesium, and are usually taken up into the plant in the form of salts. Sulphur serves to bind proteins together; nitrogen is essential for the production of proteins; phosphorus is used in compounds involved in energy transfer (such as ATP) and also forms part of the backbone of the genetic double helix, DNA. Magnesium is the central atom in chlorophyll. If any of these elements is in short supply, plant growth is halted by this limiting factor. In the sea, either nitrogen or phosphorus is usually the limiting factor, which is why nitrates and phosphates brought to the surface by the upwelling of nutrient-rich waters greatly enhance plant growth.

All plants possess chlorophyll a, which is known as the primary pigment because it is the only one able to carry out photosynthesis. Since chlorophyll is green, most plants are also green. However, a glance at the algae in Plates 166 – 177 soon reveals that the majority of seaweeds are not green; this is because the chlorophyll a is masked by other pigments.

These pigments are especially important in the classification of seaweeds, and allow us to distinguish three divisions: the green, brown and red algae:

The green algae, division Chlorophyta, are green-coloured because chlorophyll a is their dominant pigment. They do have a second type of chlorophyll known as chlorophyll b, as well as carotenoids such as lutein. This combination of pigments is limited to the green seaweeds and the higher plants. Partly as a result of this it is generally held that the green algae must have been ancestral to the land plants, and this idea is supported by the fact that both groups use starch as a storage product.

The brown algae, or Phaeophyta, possess chlorophylls a and c, as well as many other pigments, including fucoxanthin which gives them their brown colour.

The red algae, division Rhodophyta, are furnished with chlorophyll a (and possibly chlorophyll d) and a range of red and blue pigments called phycobilins. Most of the rhodophytes are red, but some species look like the brown algae, others are purplish black, and a few are even green or bright blue.

In addition to these seaweeds there are several other divisions consisting mainly of microscopic unicellular algae. Two groups deserve particular mention: the divisions Dinophyta and Bacillariophyta which respectively include the dinoflagellates (some of which cause red-tide, see Fig. 141) and the diatoms (Fig. 110). Between them, these two classes account for most of the phytoplankton off South African shores, and the unique contribution of diatoms in areas of upwelling has already been discussed in Chapter 6.

Most diatoms are enclosed in a silicon case which varies in shape but often resembles a pill box. These silicon cases are almost indestructible so that they accumulate at the bottom of the sea, forming a 'diatom ooze' many metres deep. Diatomaceous earth has many commercial applications, including its use as an abrasive toothpaste, as a 'filler' in fine papers, or as a filter to purify water. Quantities of diatomaceous earth occur in various localities in South Africa, but it is commercially mined only in the Ermelo district. The fact that these deposits occur inland is of great interest for it indicates that this area must once have been covered by sea.

The three predominant colours of seaweeds – green, brown and red – have a functional significance, for they absorb different fractions of sunlight. As we perceive sunlight, it contains all the colours of the rainbow mixed to form 'white light'. Each colour has its own particular wavelength. At the red end of the spectrum, light has a wavelength of about 700 nanometres (nm = 1 millionth of a millimetre), while violet, at the opposite end of the spectrum of visible light, has a wavelength of about 450 nm. A green alga appears green because it reflects light that is green (about 540 nm) but absorbs other wavelengths.

We can determine which fractions of light are absorbed by a pigment if we experiment by passing different wavelengths through an extract of the pigment and make measurements of how much of the light passes through the pigment and how much is absorbed. For example, green algae most efficiently absorb light that is violet or red (Fig. 379A).

As light passes through water it is filtered out and at depths exceeding about 50 m to 150 m it is reduced to less than 1 percent of its value at the surface. By convention, this 1 percent level is taken as marking the 'euphotic zone', below which photosynthesis is inadequate to support plant life. This is why seaweeds are mostly limited to shallow coastal waters. But all light is not filtered out at an equal rate by sea-water. Red and violet light disappears first, while blue-green light penetrates deepest (Fig. 379B). Thus green algae which best absorb red and violet may obtain enough light, even though they absorb only a small proportion of the light available to them, provided they live in the intertidal zone where light may be super-abundant. But in shallow waters some of the light is fil-tered out by the sea-water. Brown algae which prevail here have to use an auxiliary pigment, fucoxanthin, which absorbs additional light in the blue-green-yellow wavelengths (Fig. 379C). Fucoxanthin does not have the ability to photosynthesise, but it can pass on the energy it traps to chlorophyll *a*, the only pigment capable of con-verting solar energy to chemical energy.

Turning to the red algae, we find that many of them occur in deep water and suffer even more from the reduc-tion of light and the elimination of red and violet light – the very wavelengths chlorophyll *a* can absorb. Red algae have several auxiliary pigments, collectively known as phycobilins, which absorb blue and green light – the wavelengths most prevalent in deeper waters – and again they transmit this energy to chlorophyll *a* (Fig. 379D).

Not all red algae occur in deep water. Shallow-water and intertidal species, although they are technically 'reds' because of the pigments they contain, tend to be brown in colour, the red being masked by green pigments giving the plants a reddish-brown colour (compare Plate 171 with 173 & 174).

Thus the various pigments are related to the nature and quantity of light each species is likely to receive. There are exceptions, but in general green algae occur in the inter-tidal zone, browns grow lower on the shore and in shallow waters and reds extend from the low-shore down to deeper waters.

Fig. 379(A) Chlorophyll *a* present in green algae absorbs red and violet light. (B) As light passes down from the surface of the sea into deeper water it is absorbed by the water. Red light is absorbed first while blue light penetrates deepest. (C) Brown algae possess chlorophyll *a* and an additional brown pigment, fucoxanthin, which absorbs blue-green light. (D) Red algae living in deep waters depend on auxiliary phycobilin pigments to capture blue light and to transfer the energy to chlorophyll *a*. ▶

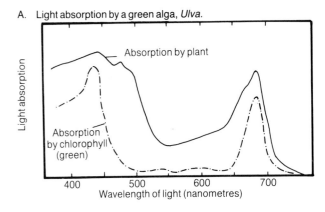

A. Light absorption by a green alga, *Ulva*.

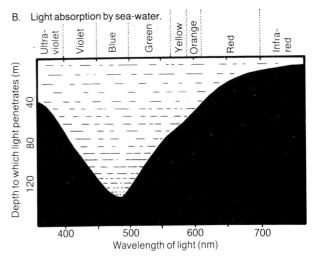

B. Light absorption by sea-water.

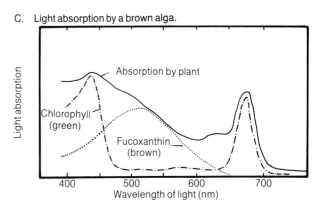

C. Light absorption by a brown alga.

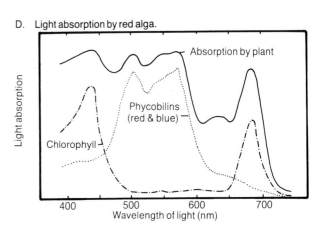

D. Light absorption by red alga.

While deep-water algae may suffer from insufficient light, at high light intensities, such as may be experienced in the intertidal zone, photosynthesis may be inhibited – a process known as photo-inhibition. Intertidal algae actually photosynthesise fastest when they are covered by about 1 m of water, where they are screened from excess light (as described in more detail in Chapter 2, p. 34). The young growing tips of seaweeds seem particularly vulnerable to excess light, and are often protected. *Halopteris* caps the tips of its branches with dark tannin, while in *Padina* the growing edge of the plant is curled over to shield the young cells (Plate 168 a & m).

LIFE-CYCLES

The life-cycles of seaweeds are amongst the most varied and fascinating encountered in any form of life. Since seaweeds are fixed to the substratum, they depend on their spores for dispersal and, as the chances of these spores surviving are very slim, vast quantities are produced. For example, one of the local kelps ('sea bamboo', *Ecklonia maxima*) produced 10 000 spores per hour from each square centimetre of its fertile blades; and the North American *Laminaria* liberates so many spores that it has the potential to cover each square millimetre of substratum with 3,3 million spores!

Most algae have at least two different generations that alternate during the life-cycle. The sea lettuce, *Ulva*, illustrates one of the simpler life-cycles (Fig. 380). It has an asexual phase, known as the sporophyte, which produces abundant spores. These disperse, settle and grow into 'male' or 'female' sexual gametophytes. The gametophytes produce reproductive gametes, which in *Ulva* are morphologically indistinguishable so that they are referred to as 'isogametes'. After fertilisation, the zygote develops into a sporophyte once again.

During this life-cycle, the fusion of gametes unites the nuclei of the 'male' and 'female' parents. Their chromosomes thus become paired in the sporophyte, which is described

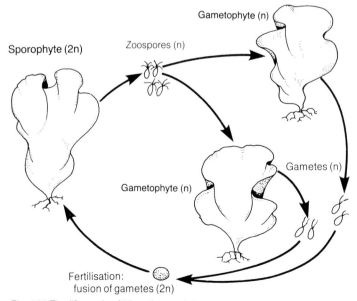

Fig. 380 The life-cycle of *Ulva*, the sea lettuce.

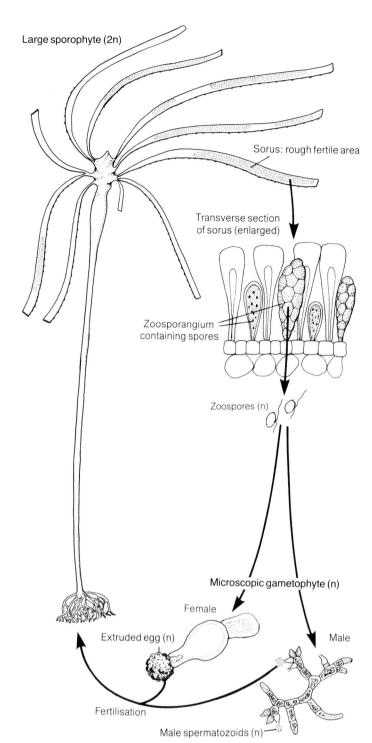

Fig. 381 The life-cycle of the 'sea bamboo', *Ecklonia maxima,* which has a massive sporophyte but a reduced gametophyte.

as being diploid (2n), having two sets of chromosomes. However, during the cell division leading to the production of spores (meiosis) these paired chromosomes are parted, one half going to one spore and the other half to another, so that the spores have only half the number of chromosomes (n) and are termed haploid. When these spores mature they give rise to gametophytes which are also haploid. They in turn produce gametes which have n chromosomes, and only once the gametes fuse is the 2n condition restored.

In the case of *Ulva* the sporophyte and gametophyte appear identical and occupy the same habitat. The sexual phase serves to combine the genes of different pairs, thus maintaining variety amongst the offspring. However, sexual reproduction is a risky procedure for these algae, since many of the tiny gametes may never meet to bring about fertilisation and, even if they do, a large number of the spores may never locate a suitable locality in which to settle. The asexual spores liberated by the sporophyte are a means of dispersing and increasing numbers without some of the risks involved with the sexual gametes. By alternating sexual and asexual phases, algae can have the best of both of these processes.

Some of the brown algae (the Isogeneratae, such as *Dictyota*) have a similar simple alternation of sexual and asexual generations, but in many browns the sexual phase has been reduced to a microscopic plant that lives only long enough to achieve sexual reproduction. An example of these Heterogeneratae is the giant kelp *Ecklonia maxima* (Fig. 381). Kelps have an enormous sporophyte phase which is long-lived and produces huge numbers of tiny spores in certain areas of the surface of its fronds. These settle to form the tiny gametophytes. Female gametophytes consist of only a few cells and usually produce a single gamete – which, unlike those of *Ulva*, is recognisable as an egg as it lacks the ability to move and is much larger than the male gametes. Male spores divide repeatedly to form small much-branched gametophytes, which shed minute spermatozoids. These are free-swimming and are attracted to and fertilise the eggs. The life-cycle is completed by the development of the fertilised egg into a sporophyte.

It is not difficult to culture the gametophytes of kelps. If a snippet of fertile blade is cut from the kelp and suspended over a cover-slip in sea-water, it releases abundant spores which settle on the cover-slip within a few hours. These will, however, only mature if the sea-water is enriched with nutrients, but other than this they need only sunlight to develop.

The life-cycle of *Ecklonia* is more advanced than that of *Ulva*, for the two generations are quite different, with the sporophyte being dominant; and the male and female gametes are also strikingly different.

As a further development of this type of life-cycle, the remaining brown algae – known as the Cyclosporeae – have done away with sexual gametophytes altogether. They have not, however, sacrificed the process of sexual reproduction, for the diploid sporophyte now undertakes meiosis to produce haploid gametes, which fuse and grow into another sporophyte. The development of the British *Fucus* is often described in text books as an example of this type of life-cycle, but the local *Bifurcaria* is just as typical (Fig. 382). Furthermore, *Bifurcaria* gives us a clue as to one of the advantages of this abbreviated life-cycle, for it lives on wave-beaten shores where the chances of spores settling are not good. *Bifurcaria* does not release its eggs into the water but extrudes them on gelatinous stalks, where the eggs are fertilised while still attached to the parent plant. The extruded eggs are visible to the naked eye as feathery

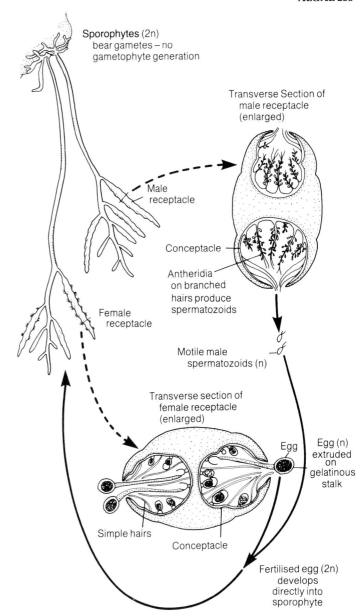

Fig. 382 The life-cycle of an advanced brown alga, *Bifurcaria*, in which the gametophyte generation has been eliminated.

tufts on the sides of the reproductive branches of the plant.

The most complicated life-cycles are found in the red algae. A case in point is *Plocamium* (Fig. 383). In this species the diploid sporophyte is called a tetrasporophyte because its spores are produced in groups of four, following meiosis – each spore once again being haploid with only n chromosomes. The tetraspores are released and develop into sexual gametophyte plants. The gametophytes of *Plocamium* look similar to the sporophytes except for the details of the small fertile branches bearing the spores or gametes (Fig. 383). By contrast, in certain other species of red algae, such as *Gigartina stiriata* (Plate 171b-c), the two generations are rather different in appearance and for many years were considered separate species. *Porphyra* has a large flat-bladed gametophyte generation (Fig. 384), in which the males have a yellow fringe to the blade while the females are edged with pink, and a totally different microscopic filamentous sporophyte.

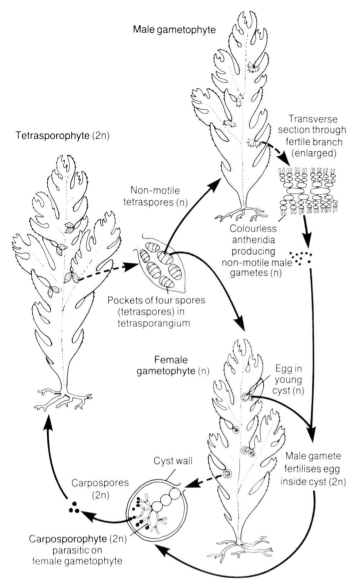

Fig. 383 The life-cycle of a red alga, *Plocamium,* showing the three generations. The carposporophyte generation is parasitic inside cysts on the female gametophyte.

Fig. 384 *Porphyra capensis* forms sheets near the top of the shore and is one of the algae most sought-after in Japan as a food source.

The female gametes produced by *Plocamium* are retained on the gametophyte, where they are fertilised by the male gametes. Once fertilised, each egg becomes encased inside a wart-like cyst and develops into a tiny carposporophyte which is parasitic on the gametophyte. The carposporophyte in turn produces asexual carpospores which are liberated and later settle to grow into tetrasporophytes.

Although the life-cycles of red algae are extremely varied, most follow the pattern described for *Plocamium.* Such life-cycles, with three distinct phases, allow the algae to reap the benefits of sexual reproduction and also provide two opportunities for them to increase their numbers by asexual reproduction. Perhaps because of their complex and varied life-cycles the red algae have evolved almost four times as many species as the green and brown algae put together.

What are the ecological benefits of these diverse life-cycles? Obviously the spores allow dispersal, but this does not explain why there should be an alternation of generations, or why the sexual phase should sometimes be so different from the asexual phase.

One possibility is that the different stages of the life-cycle are able to tolerate different conditions or occupy different habitats. For example, the flat-bladed *Porphyra,* which lives high on the shore, is an annual that thrives in the winter but disappears in the summer when conditions are too rigorous (Fig. 384). It passes summer as a microscopic asexual phase known as the conchocelis which bores into mollusc shells.

In the same way, different phases of the life-cycle of North American *Gigartina* species are not equally tolerant of grazing by herbivores and competition from other algae. One phase is flat and encrusting and resistant to grazing while the other is upright and bushy and less likely to be outcompeted. Different circumstances thus favour one phase or the other.

Species which are poor competitors must continually strive to colonise new habitats as fast as they are ousted by other species. Both *Ulva* and *Enteromorpha* are colonisers of this sort. Both produce prodigious amounts of spores all the year round to ensure that they can capitalise on any unoccupied space as soon as it becomes available. So prolific are their spores that they often create a green scum on the surface of pools. Both these species are seldom found on the low-shore where other species thrive, but if these other algae are experimentally scraped off the rocks their place is almost immediately taken by these opportunistic

166. Chlorophyta – Green algae

a. *Chaetomorpha robusta* b. *Chaetomorpha crassa* c. *Cladophora contexta* d. *Cladophora virgata* e. *Enteromorpha* sp f. *Ulva* sp g. *Microdictyon kraussii* h. *Bryopsis* sp i. *Bryopsis caespitosa* j. Two forms of *Caulerpa racemosa* k. *Caulerpa holmesiana* l. *Caulerpa scalpelliformis* m. *Caulerpa filiformis*. c´ d´ h´ – enlarged details.

167. Chlorophyta – Green algae

a. *Pseudocodium devriesei* b. *Valonia macrophysa* c. *Valonia aegagropila* d. *Halimeda cuneata* e. *Codium fragile capense* (encrusted by *Placophora*) f. *Codium megalophysum* g. *Codium lucasii capense* h. *Udotea orientalis* i. *Chamaedoris delphinii.*

Phaeophyta – Brown algae

j. *Splachnidium rugosum* k. *Chordariopsis capensis* l. *Iyengaria stellata* m. *Leathesia difformis* (fleshy) n. *Colpomenia sinuosa* (hollow and almost transparent).

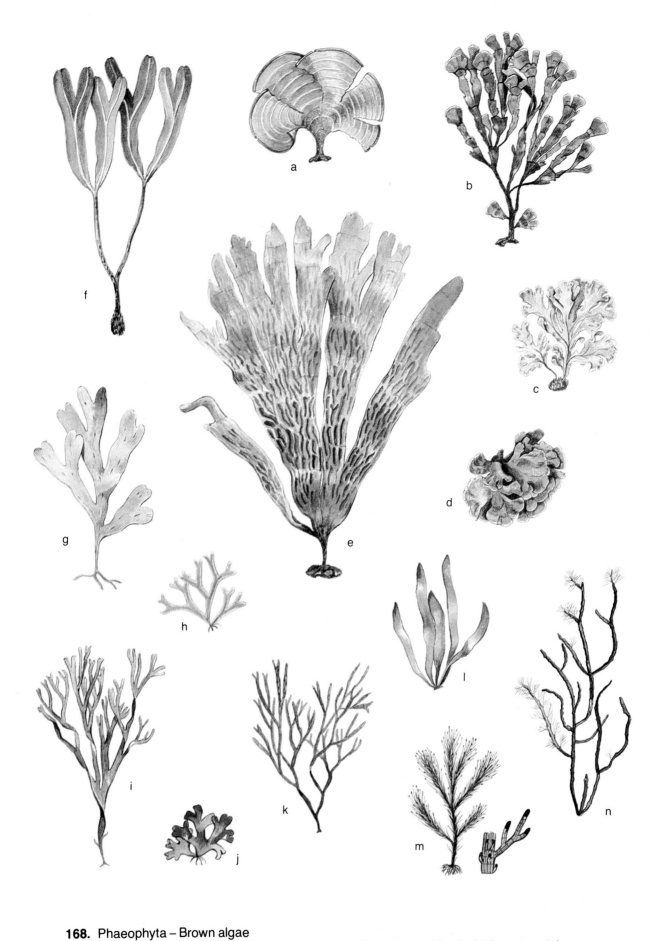

168. Phaeophyta – Brown algae
a. *Padina commersonii* b. *Zonaria subarticulata* c. *Zonaria tournifortii* d. *Homoeostrichus multifidus* e. *Stypopodium zonale* f. *Dictyopteris longifolia* g. *Dictyota liturata* h. *Dictyota* sp
i. *Dictyota dichotoma* j. *Dictyota* sp k. *Chnoospora pacifica* l. *Petalonia debilis* or *Endarachne binghamiae* m. *Halopteris funicularis* – detail enlarged. n. *Phloiocaulon squamulosum.*

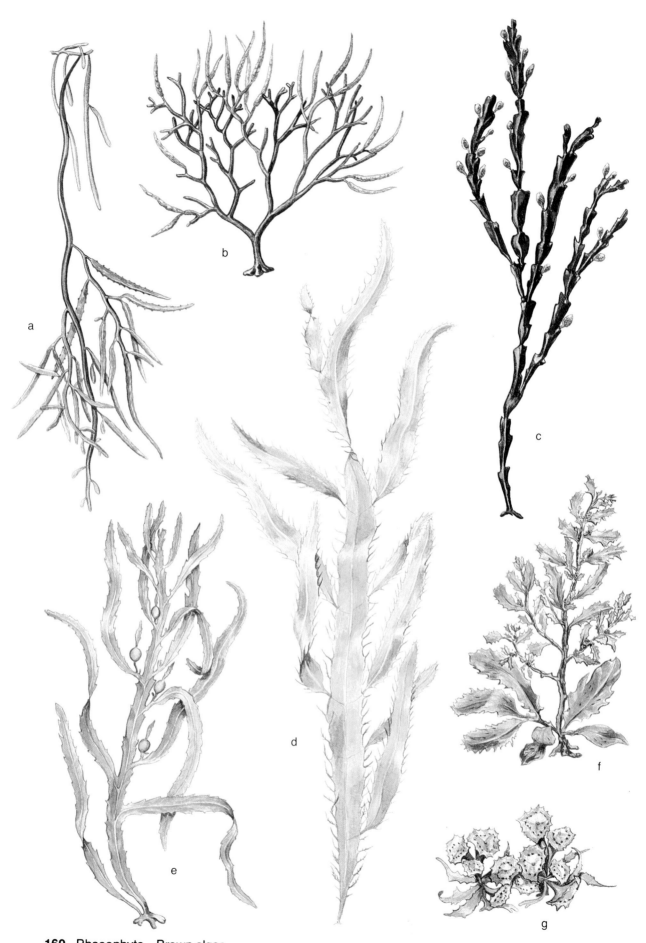

169. Phaeophyta – Brown algae

a. *Bifurcaria brassicaeformis*   b. *Bifurcariopsis capensis*   c. *Axillariella constricta*   d. *Desmarestia firma*   e. *Sargassum longifolium*   f. *Sargassum heterophyllum*   g. *Turbinaria ornata*.

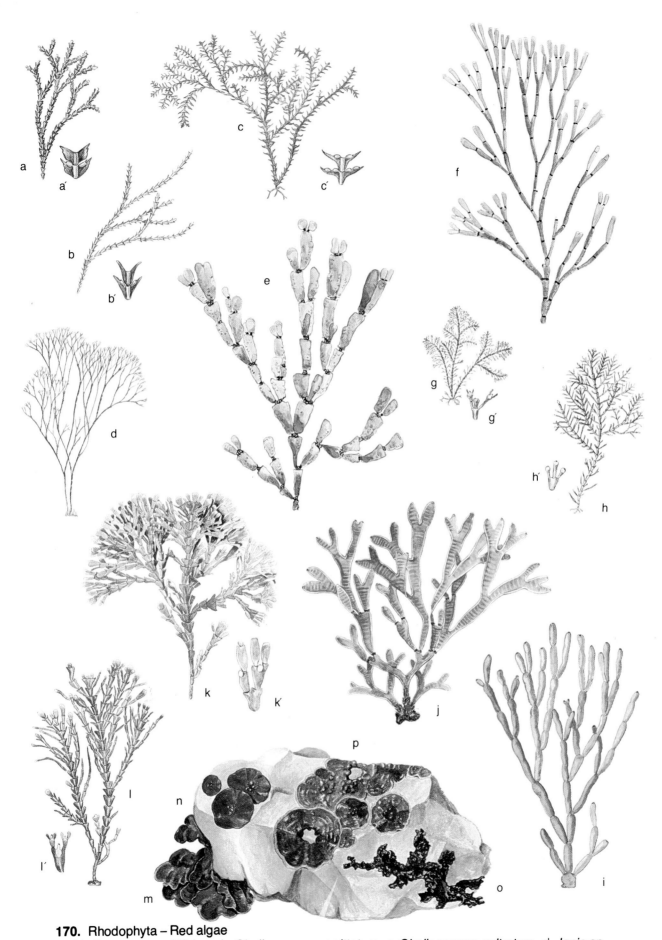

170. Rhodophyta – Red algae
a. *Cheilosporum multifidum* b. *Cheilosporum sagittatum* c. *Cheilosporum cultratum* d. *Jania* sp
e. *Amphiroa bowerbankii* f. *Amphiroa ephedraea* g. *Corallina* sp h. *Corallina* sp i. *Galaxaura corymbifera* j. *Galaxaura diessingiana* k. *Duthiophycus setchelli* l. *Arthrocardia* sp
m. *Peyssonnelia* sp n. *Hildenbrandia rosea* o. *Hildenbrandia pachythallos* a´ b´ c´ g´ h´ k´ l´
enlarged portion with swollen reproductive organs. Phaeophyta – Brown algae: p. *Ralfsia expansa*.

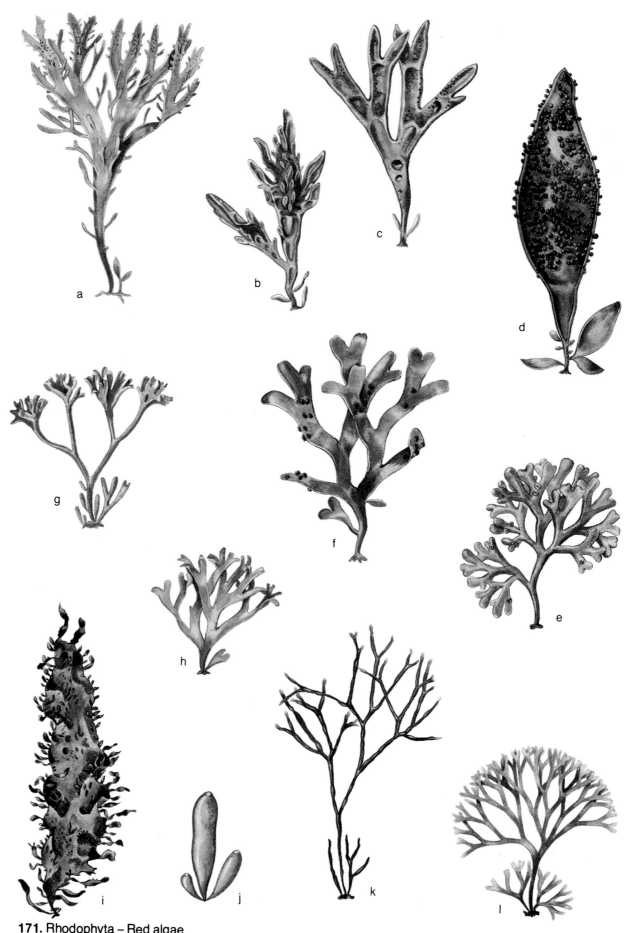

171. Rhodophyta – Red algae

a. *Gigartina paxillata* b. *Gigartina stiriata* gametophyte c. *Gigartina stiriata* tetrasporophyte
d. *Gigartina radula* e. *Gigartina scabiosa* f. *Gymnogongrus dilatatus* g. *Gymnogongrus complicatus*
h. *Gymnogongrus glomeratus* i. *Chaetangium erinaceum* j. *Chaetangium ovale* k. *Polyopes constrictus*
l. *Trematocarpus flabellata.*

172. Rhodophyta – Red algae
a. *Nemastoma lanceolata* b. *Porphyra capensis* c. *Pachymenia cornea* d. *Pachymenia carnosa* e. *Grateloupia longifolia* f. *Grateloupia filicina* g. *Kallymenia agardhii* h. *Aeodes orbitosa* i. *Iridaea capensis.*

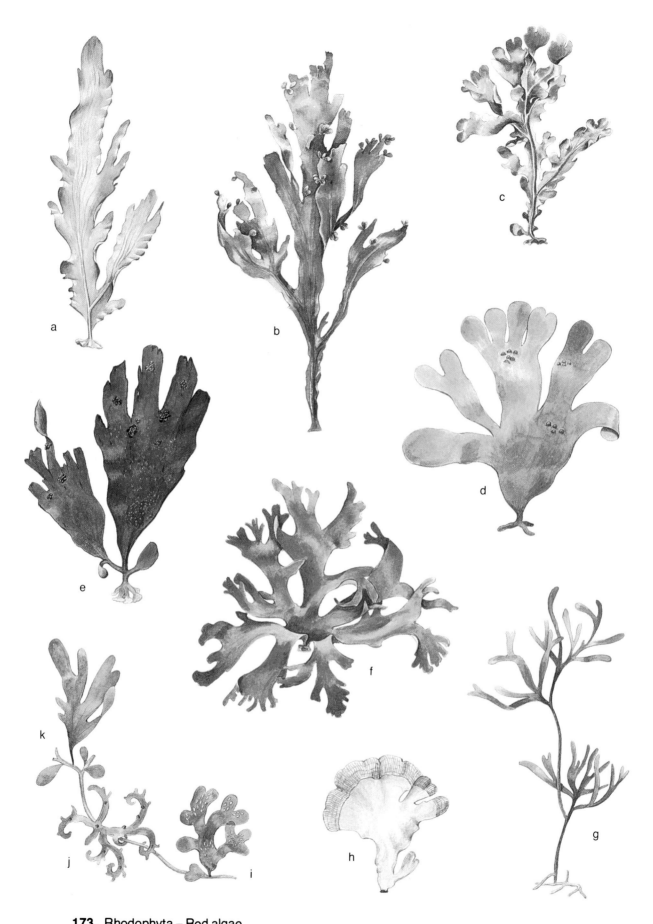

173. Rhodophyta – Red algae

a. *Hymenena venosa* b. *Neuroglossum binderianum* c. *Botryoglossum platycarpum*
d. *Epymenia obtusa* e. *Botryocarpa prolifera* f. *Thamnophyllis discigera* g. *Rhodymenia natalensis* h. *Martensia elegans* i. *Acrosorium maculatum* j. *Acrosorium uncinatum*
k. *Acrosorium acrospermum.*

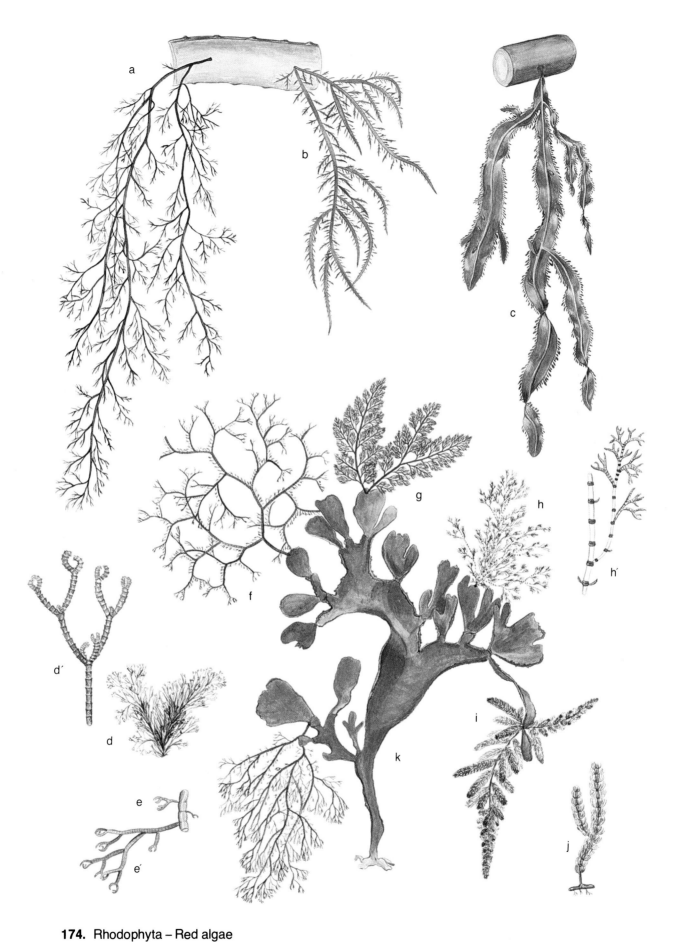

174. Rhodophyta – Red algae

a. *Carradoria virgata* b. *Carpoblepharis flaccida* c. *Suhria vittata* (a, b, c, grow on *Ecklonia maxima* kelp) d. *Centroceras clavulatum* e. *Ceramium capense* f. *Ceramium obsoletum* g. *Ceramium planum* h. *Ceramium* sp (includes *C. diaphanum)* i. *Aristothamnion collabens* (e, f, g, h, i, grow on other algae) j. *Dasya* sp k. *Sarcodia capensis* d´, e´, h´ enlarged to show detail.

175. Rhodophyta – Red algae
a. *Chondrococcus hornemannii* b. *Chondrococcus tripinnata* c. *Plocamium rigidum*
d. *Plocamium suhrii* e. *Plocamium corallorhiza* f. *Plocamium cornutum* g. *Pterosiphonia cloiophylla* h. *Tayloriella tenebrosa* i. *Bostrychia mixta* j. *Hypnea viridis* k. *Hynea rosea*
l. *Hypnea spicifera.* a´ c´ d´ g´ h´ ï enlarged tips of branches.

176. Rhodophyta – Red algae
a. *Gelidium amansii* b. *Gelidium pristoides* c. *Gelidium cartilagineum* d. *Polyzonia elegans*
e. *Calliblepharis fimbriata* f. *Polysiphonia* sp on *Codium* g. *Callithamnion stuposum* h. *Spyridia*
cupressina i. *Spyridia hypnoides.* a′ c′ f′ g′ enlarged details with reproductive bodies, d′ h′ k′
enlarged details of branches.

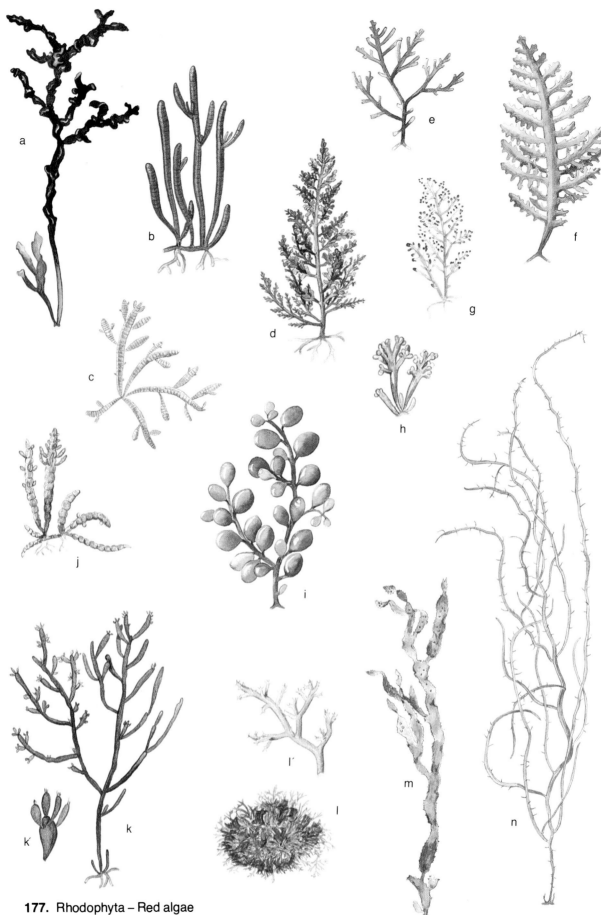

177. Rhodophyta – Red algae
a. *Prionitis nodifera* b. *Champia lumbricalis* c. *Champia compressa* d. *Laurencia glomerata*
e. *Laurencia flexuosa* f. *Laurencia complanata* g. *Laurencia natalensis* h. *Laurencia pumila*
i. *Botryocladia madagascariensis* j. *Chylocladia capensis* k. *Chondria capensis* l. *Caulacanthus*
ustulatus m. *Gracilaria beckeri* n. *Gracilaria verrucosa.* k′ l′ enlarged branch tips.

species, which soon settle and prosper, only to be displaced once superior competitors re-establish themselves.

ALGAL FORM AND FUNCTION

There are two key features that dictate the structure of seaweeds. The first is that the plant needs to present as much as possible of its surface to sunlight to maintain a high rate of photosynthesis. Broad, flat plants are ideally suited for this function. The second key factor is that being attached, algae cannot simply move if the environment proves stressful, so that they must be adapted to withstand the rigours of their habitat and sufficiently tolerant to be able to survive a wide range of conditions. Factors such as wave action and desiccation may dictate that a broad flat form is unsuitable.

Seaweeds vary considerably in form and may be broad and flat, cylindrical, branching, filamentous or encrusting. Each of these body forms is suited to different environmental conditions.

The green algae

The simplest green algae consist of long filaments made up of chains of single cells (Plate 166a – d). Since each cell is bathed by sea-water, and the plants have a large surface area relative to their volume, nutrients are readily absorbed from the water. On the other hand, their large surface area makes filamentous algae susceptible to desiccation, and their simple structure provides no protection against predation. Their size is also limited because they consist of only a chain of cells.

The genus *Chaetomorpha* exemplifies this simple grade of structure: *Chaetomorpha robusta* and *Chaetomorpha crassa* are two of the most easily identified species in this genus, although there are several other species (see Plates 166a, b). The many species of *Cladophora* are also filamentous but branch irregularly (Plates 166c, d). In both genera the cells that make up the filaments are often large and visible to the naked eye, distinguishing them from most other multi-cellular filaments and from non-cellular forms such as *Bryopsis* species (Plate 166h, i) with which they might be confused.

Slightly more complex in their structure are the broad flat-bladed green algae such as the sea lettuce *Ulva* (shown on Plate 166f). *Enteromorpha* (Plate 166e) has a similar structure except that the blade forms a hollow tube and is only one cell thick, while in *Ulva* the blade is two-layered. Although their blades are only one or two cells thick these algae achieve a far greater size than the filamentous algae, and their thin structure allows ready absorption of both nutrients and light. In addition, their cells are simple and unspecialised, and are all capable of cell division. This allows these algae to grow very rapidly, a fact of some importance when we remember that they are opportunist species that must establish themselves as quickly as possible and reproduce before they are outcompeted by other algae. Both species are common in high-shore pools, on unstable sand-scoured rocks, on boulders that are wave-tumbled, in harbours or around freshwater outlet pipes – all localities from which most other algae are excluded by the extreme conditions or by pollution.

Ulva, and even more particularly *Enteromorpha*, are extremely hardy plants that can survive a wide range of conditions. *Enteromorpha* can, for instance, thrive in salinities that vary from 5‰ to 70‰. Because of this the two species grow prolifically under conditions that exclude their competitors.

There are two major disadvantages to a broad flat blade. Firstly, it loses water rapidly during low tide and, secondly, it is easily shredded by waves. As a result *Ulva* only thrives in calm areas or in high-shore pools where it is protected from the pounding of waves. Its flat flimsy blades are also heavily grazed, but because all the cells are capable of growth they can recover quickly.

A completely different growth form is achieved by the so-called siphonaceous green algae. In these the whole plant (thallus) is made up of one or more filaments which have a unique feature: they lack cross walls, so that instead of being divided into cells, each filament is a giant multi-nucleate cell – and is described as being coenocytic. The main advantage of this arrangement is that the tubules are free to transport nutrients from one part of the thallus to another.

The genus *Caulerpa* includes many of the commonest siphonaceous algae (Plate 166j – m). *Caulerpa filiformis* is a particularly striking plant, which blankets sand-scoured gullies (Plate 160). All *Caulerpa* species have creeping rhizomes that grow across the substratum, and give rise to strap-like, feathery or button-like blades.

In some of the Pacific Islands, *Caulerpa* produces toxins which are presumably a deterrent to predators. Even so, some fish eat them, and in turn become poisonous – even lethal – to man. Such ciguatera poisoning is known only from tropical islands and explains why fish that are eaten with impunity in some areas are poisonous in others. The moral of the story is to heed local advice on whether a fish is edible or not.

Another large genus of siphonaceous algae is *Codium* (Plate 167e, g). *Codium* species are particularly interesting because their surfaces are made up of club-like projections (utricles) arising from the intertwined tubules that run the length of the plant. These utricles contain the chloroplasts which carry out photosynthesis, and these can migrate to the outer surface of the utricles or down into the centre of the plant, depending on whether the light intensity is too low or too high (Fig. 32).

All *Codium* species have a dark black-green colour and a spongy texture. Three groups can be distinguished. Species such as *Codium lucasii* and *Codium megalophysum* have an encrusting or cushion-like structure (Plate 167f, g). A second group, including *Codium fragile*, has upright cylindrical branches (Plate 167e). Finally, species such as *Codium platylobium* have flattened branches. There are, however, many other species within these groups which can only be distinguished with any confidence by examining the structure of their utricles under a hand lens (Fig. 385).

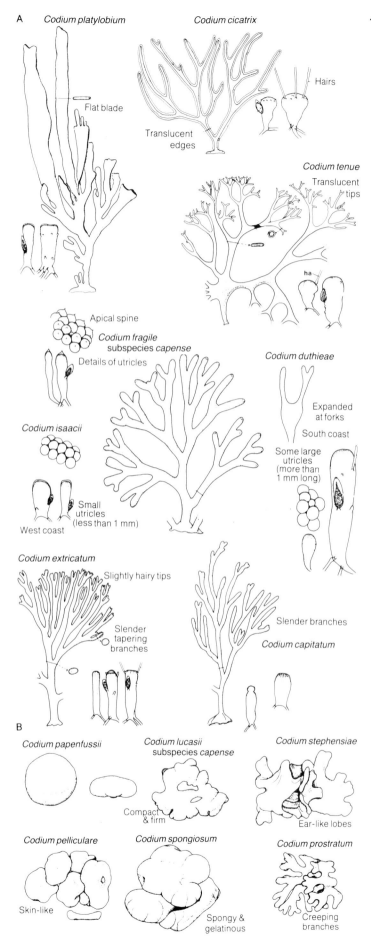

A

Codium platylobium

Codium cicatrix

Flat blade

Hairs

Translucent edges

Translucent edges

Codium tenue

Translucent tips

ha

Apical spine

Codium fragile subspecies capense

Details of utricles

Codium duthieae

Expanded at forks

South coast

Codium isaacii

Some large utricles (more than 1 mm long)

Small utricles (less than 1 mm)

West coast

Codium extricatum

Slightly hairy tips

Slender tapering branches

Slender branches

Codium capitatum

B

Codium papenfussii

Codium lucasii subspecies capense

Codium stephensiae

Compact & firm

Ear-like lobes

Codium pelliculare

Codium spongiosum

Codium prostratum

Skin-like

Spongy & gelatinous

Creeping branches

◀ Fig. 385 Identification of *Codium* species depends largely on the structure of their utricles. (Shown greatly magnified.)

Both *Caulerpa* and *Codium* are eaten by nudibranchs. Because these algae are siphonaceous it is relatively easy for the nudibranchs to suck out their cell contents, and to extract the chloroplasts undamaged and incorporate them into folds on their own dorsal surfaces. This manoeuvre achieves two things: the nudibranch takes on the colour of its food plant and is perfectly camouflaged, and the chloroplasts continue to photosynthesise within the nudibranch, thus supplying organic compounds.

Other siphonaceous green algae include *Halimeda*, *Valonia* with its huge balloon cells, fan-like *Udotea*, the paintbrush alga *Chamaedoris*, and *Pseudocodium* (Plate 167a – i). All of these are distinctive except for *Pseudocodium* which looks like a pale *Codium* but can be recognised because its utricles are fused together and do not separate when the plant is squashed, as they do in *Codium*.

Brown algae

Most of the brown algae grow low on the shore or in shallow water where wave action is often strong. A few of the brown algae counter the effects of wave action by developing cushion-like thalli that are strongly attached to the substratum and offer little resistance to water. *Colpomenia* and *Leathesia* are two common examples that grow attached to other algae (Plate 167m, n). Superficially alike, they can be distinguished because *Colpomenia* is hollow and thin-walled and slightly transparent, while *Leathesia* is much fleshier.

Another cushion-shaped form is *Iyengaria*, which has a tough knobbly surface that traps water and thus minimises the effect of desiccation during low tide. *Splachnidium* has cylindrical branches that are wrinkled and filled with mucus (giving the plant the macabre name of 'dead-man's-fingers'). This mucus helps absorb the shock of wave action and also allows the alga to shrink when desiccated without harming the outer coat of living cells (see Chapter 2, Fig. 28).

Many of the brown algae have fan-like or flat, regularly forked (dichotomous) blades. Even the fan-shaped species such as *Padina*, *Zonaria*, *Stypopodium* and *Homoeostrichus* (Plate 168a – e) soon split their fans, thus reducing resistance to wave action. *Stypopodium* also develops longitudinal ripples on its blade as it ages and these serve to reduce the drag of water on the alga (see Chapter 2, p. 34 for more details).

Brown algae with regularly forked blades include two genera especially common on the east coast – *Dictyota* and *Dictyopteris* – which are easily told apart as only *Dictyopteris* has a mid-rib strengthening the blade (Plate 168f – j). Some *Dictyota* species are amongst the most vivid of algae, with luminescent blue or green blades (see Plate 56).

All the fan-like or dichotomously branching brown algae have growth points (meristems) that are confined to the apex of each branch or around the margin of the fan, where they are vulnerable to grazing. Regular branching or fragmentation of the fans helps offset this problem, making it less likely that a herbivore will succeed in consuming the entire meristem.

The remaining brown algae include some of the largest and most complex seaweeds, such as the giant kelps which may reach a length of 40 m and the *Sargassum* weeds (Plate 169). Curiously, it is these algae that have abbreviated life-cycles; it is almost as if the elaboration of the sporophyte has led to the reduction or elimination of the gametophyte phase of the life-cycle.

In these advanced brown algae, such as the kelp *Ecklonia biruncinata* (Fig. 386), specialised parts of the plant are set aside for different functions. The base sends out root-like haptera which form a firm holdfast, anchoring the plant to the substratum. Unlike the roots of land plants, these haptera play no part in the uptake of nutrients.

From the holdfast arises a stalk-like stipe, which ends in a crown of fronds. These fronds are the main photosynthetic organs, and many species have gas-filled bladders that buoy the plants up, thus exposing them to sunlight. The fronds are usually strap-shaped and flexible so that they flow with the water movement, or they are cylindrical, wiry and strong, capable of withstanding wave action. In the case of *Macrocystis*, the fronds are flat and broad in young plants, exposing a large surface for the absorption of sunlight. But as they enlarge and are more likely to be shredded by wave action they split into long strap-shaped segments, each with its own gas float to hold it up to the light. The fronds also develop a rippled surface and this, too, serves to reduce the drag of water currents on the fronds (Fig. 387).

In many of the advanced brown algae certain fronds are set aside for a reproductive function and are known as receptacles. These are particularly obvious in *Bifurcaria* and *Bifurcariopsis*, forming outgrowths like bean pods (Plate 169a, b) and in *Turbinaria*, where they resemble squat trumpets (Plate 169g). The kelp *Macrocystis* bears its asexual spores on special fronds (sporophylls) near the base of the plant. This fact is of practical importance, for when *Macrocystis* is harvested (as it is in America), the reproductive portion of the plant can be left undisturbed. By contrast, the southern African *Ecklonia maxima* produces patches of spores all over its blades, and it is impossible to harvest the plant without reaping the fertile blades as well.

Most of these higher brown algae have intercalary meristems – that is to say, their growth points are confined to particular zones near the middle of the plant and are not apical. For instance, in the kelps *Laminaria* and *Ecklonia*, the meristem is positioned at the base of the fronds, and from this point cells are added to both the stipe and the fronds. The development of intercalary meristems is largely responsible for the specialisation of different regions of the plant body, for it allows particular groups of cells to be set aside for specific functions.

Perhaps one of the more unusual of these functions is the

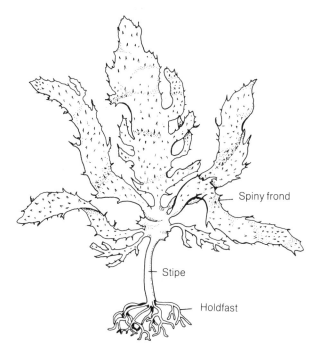

Fig. 386 *Ecklonia biruncinata* is the smallest of the southern African kelps. It demonstrates the specialised nature of many advanced brown algae. Other species of kelp are shown in Fig. 30.

Fig. 387 The young fronds of the kelp *Macrocystis* are broad and flat but soon split and form strap-shaped blades with gas floats and rippled surfaces (x ¼).

production of cells which secrete chemicals that deter herbivores. A striking example is *Desmarestia* (Plate 169d) which contains quantities of sulphuric acid in its tissues.

The larger brown algae have specially strengthened supportive cells in their stipes. These have thick cell walls and are inflated and turgid to give the stipe some rigidity. Also because of the size of these algae, special conductive tissues have been evolved to transport photosynthesised compounds from the blades to the lower parts of the algae which are shielded from the sun and unable to photosynthesise efficiently themselves. These conductive tissues consist of 'trumpet hyphae' – long cylindrical cells which meet end to end at expanded 'sieve-plates' through which materials pass from one cell to the next. The ability of conductive cells to translocate materials has only recently been proven: radioactive carbon (C^{14}) was introduced to the blade and was taken up during photosynthesis. Its incorporation into organic compounds and their passage through the trumpet hyphae to other parts of the plant could then be traced.

A section cut through the frond of a kelp gives some idea of the diversity and complexity of the cells found in these advanced brown algae, including their differentiation into reproductive, photosynthetic, supportive and conductive tissues (Fig. 388). When we remember that seaweeds are the most primitive of the multicellular plants, the specialisation achieved by some of the brown algae is remarkable.

The red algae

The prolific red algae cover a wide spectrum of body forms. Some of them parallel the structures already described for the brown algae. In the intertidal zone of wave-beaten shores most species are flattened to allow maximal uptake of light, but are fleshy and repeatedly branched to reduce the drag of waves. Two important genera that typify this type of structure are *Gigartina* and *Gymnogongrus* (shown on Plate 171a – h). Superficially similar, the two can be distinguished because *Gigartina* has a fleshy texture while *Gymnogongrus* is more springy and almost lacking in mucus. These intertidal species also tend to be reddish-brown in colour, for reasons that have been explained earlier in this chapter.

More finely-branched reds include *Chondrococcus* with its characteristically curled tips, and several species of *Plocamium* (Plate 175a – f).

Many of the red algae that grow low on the shore and in regions of very high wave-action have repeatedly divided cylindrical branches that are very wiry and tough, often supported internally by cells with thick walls (Fig. 33). *Hypnea spicifera*, *Gelidium amansii* and *Gelidium cartilagineum* are typical examples that form dense turfs low on Natal shores (Plates 175l & 176a – c). Incidentally, *Gelidium* species are a source of agar and are commercially harvested in southern Africa.

The deep-water red algae are quite different in both form and colour. They all suffer from a shortage of light and, as already mentioned, their red colour permits them to absorb the blue light that penetrates furthest into the water. Most

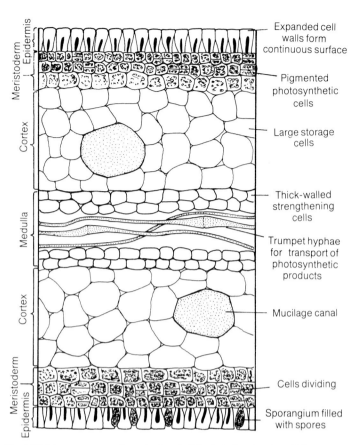

Fig. 388 A transverse section of a frond of the kelp *Laminaria pallida*, showing how the cells are specialised for different functions. (Much enlarged.)

of them are flat spreading plants, some species reaching half a metre in diameter, and this too is an adaptation to the low light-level they experience. This type of body structure is only possible in deep water where wave action is gentler. Typical examples of these flat reds include *Pachymenia* and *Kallymenia* (Plate 172c, d & g).

Understorey algae, living beneath a canopy of kelp plants, are also buffered from wave action by the kelp, but are in their shadow and therefore suffer from a shortage of light. Like deep-water species, these too are red in colour and broad and flat, although slightly more branched. Several examples are shown in Plate 173, and one particularly common species that must be singled out is *Epymenia obtusa* (Plate 173d).

There are of course exceptions to all these generalisations. Not all the broad flat reds occur in deep sheltered waters. *Aeodes* (Plate 172h) occurs intertidally, often in areas of strong wave action, but it has leathery tough blades and a large firm disc-like holdfast. It is also laden with mucus, which makes it instantly recognisable because of its slippery texture – and it is notorious as a veritable death trap for unwary rock-scramblers.

Many of the most graceful algae are epiphytic – growing attached to other plants. This habit has the advantage that the algae are held near the surface above most other algae, so that they are not short of light. But since this may also mean that they are more exposed to wave surge, most of the epiphytes are extremely fine and much branched so that they flex and sway with the current. Their small delicate structure also has the advantage that they do not pose a burden on their host. Notable examples are the dainty *Ceramium* species and *Aristothamnion* (Plate 174e – i).

Growing attached to kelp plants are much larger epiphytes, including *Carradoria* and *Suhria* (Plate 174a – c). These species are usually confined to the kelp *Ecklonia maxima*. *Carpoblepharis flaccida* not only attaches onto this particular kelp but parasitises it, sending out branches of its holdfast into the seaweed and drawing on its photosynthetic products to supplement its own. *Carpoblepharis minima* is a closely related species that parasitises a different kelp, *Laminaria pallida*.

The coralline algae are a distinctive group of red algae that deserve special mention. All of them load their tissues with calcium carbonate as a deterrent to herbivores, giving them an attractive porcelain-like appearance. Apart from this armature, the corallines must hold little appeal as a source of food, for their energy content is extremely low. Since calcium carbonate makes these algae brittle, most of them are broken into regular segments by joints that allow the plant to flex (Plate 170). These upright jointed species can usually be identified by the distinctive shape of their segments, but in some cases it is necessary to examine the position and structure of the tiny cysts that enclose the reproductive organs (and which are shown enlarged in Plate 170).

Some of the corallines form flat crusts on rocks, 'painting' them pink or white (see Plates 90 & 98). Two common genera of these encrusting corallines – *Lithothamnion* and *Lithophyllum* – are so similar that a microscopic examination of the cyst-like chambers which produce tetraspores is necessary to separate them. *Lithophyllum* has a single opening to each of these conceptacles, while *Lithothamnion* has many tiny pores. *Dermatolithon* has a similar encrusting form but is much smaller and forms tiny plates on other plants, particularly on the stems of sea grass.

Closely related to the coralline algae are two uncalcified species of *Hildenbrandia* which also encrust rocks, and the partly calcified *Peyssonnelia* which forms shelf-like outgrowths on the lower surfaces of rock, so that it resembles a bracket fungus (Plate 170m – o). Sharing this encrusting habit is a totally unrelated species – one of the brown algae – *Ralfsia expansa* (Plate 170p).

Encrusting algae are almost perfectly adapted for wave action for they are low-growing and firmly cemented to the rock face. At first sight, their low-growing habit would seem to expose them to attack from herbivores, such as limpets and chitons, which rasp the surface of the rock. But in fact, many species have entered into intimate associations with grazers. *Ralfsia expansa* is largely confined to the territorial 'gardens' of the long-spined limpet, *Patella longicosta*, which defends this alga against other herbivores (see Plates 100-102). *Ralfsia* shields its meristem well below its surface so that its growth points are not harmed by superficial grazing. Furthermore, the limpets cut paths through the alga without ever eliminating it, and this pattern of grazing actually stimulates the alga to grow faster.

This is not the only example of such an intimate relationship between a limpet and alga. *Patella compressa* only occurs on the kelp *Ecklonia* and also defends its plant against other limpets; while *Patella cochlear* cultivates a fringe of fast-growing red algae around its circumference (see Plate 98 and a more detailed description in Chapter 2, p. 47).

Encrusting algae face one major problem: their flat form makes it easy for other organisms such as barnacles, sponges and even algae to settle on them or to overgrow them. Some species of *Lithothamnion* actually depend on the activities of limpets and other herbivores to prevent this. While the tough calcareous *Lithothamnion* may lose its superficial cells to these grazers as they rasp over the plant, in the absence of grazers this alga is rapidly smothered by other faster-growing organisms. Far from suffering from the attentions of these herbivores, this coralline owes its very existence to them.

Ralfsia expansa has another solution to the problem: it produces antibiotic chemicals that kill settling organisms. Recent experiments on the colonisation of bare rocks show that once *Ralfsia* is established it inhibits barnacles and other algae from settling on it.

We begin to appreciate that algae are far more than static growths that cover rocky shores. Their morphology and physiology are finely tuned to the stresses of their habitats. They lie at the heart of inshore food webs and contribute to the balance of oxygen by their photosynthesis; their very presence alters the nature of the environment. While they may simply represent a source of food to some animals, there are other cases where they have entered into intricate relationships with animals, to their mutual benefit.

The fascination of their adaptations and their relationships with other organisms ensure that no longer can the seaweeds be relegated to a place of secondary interest in the world of marine biology.

REFERENCES

General books
Chapman, A. R. O. 1979. *Biology of Seaweeds.* University Park Press, Baltimore. 134 pp.
Chapman, V. J. & Chapman D. J. 1980. *Seaweeds and their Uses.* Chapman & Hall, New York. 334 pp.

Identification guides
Seagrief, S. C. 1967. *The Seaweeds of the Tsitsikama Coastal National Park: Die Seewiere van die Tsitsikama-Seekus Nasionale Park.* National Parks Board. 147 pp.

Seagrief, S. C. 1981. Seaweeds of Maputoland. In: '*Studies on the Ecology of Maputoland*'. (Edited by Bruton, M. N. & Cooper, K. H.). pp. 18-29.
Silva, P. C. 1959. The genus Codium (Chlorophyta) in South Africa. *Journal of S. Afr. Botany*, Vol. 25: 107-165.
Simons, R. H. 1976. Seaweeds of southern Africa: guidelines for their study and identification. *Fisheries Bulletin of S. Afr.*, Vol. 7: 1-113.

Scientific references
Branch, M. L. 1974. Limiting factors for the gametophytes of three South African Laminariales. *Investigational Report for Sea Fisheries Branch in S. Afr.*, Vol. 104: 1-38.

APPENDIX I: CLASSIFICATION OF THE MAJOR GROUPS OF ANIMALS

PHYLUM PORIFERA: Sponges. Body shapeless, spongy; lacking organs, but supported by a skeleton of spicules. 4 500 species.

PHYLUM CNIDARIA: Jellyfish, anemones, hydroids. Radially symmetrical (star-shaped) animals in which the gut is the only body cavity and lacks an anus; the body wall consists of two cellular layers. Tentacles armed with stinging cells. 11 000 species.

Class Hydrozoa: The hydroids. Small colonial organisms in which the polyp and medusa alternate during the life-cycle.

Class Scyphozoa: Large bell-shaped jellyfish.

Class Cubozoa: Box-shaped jellyfish with four tentacles.

Class Anthozoa: Anemones, corals. Complex polyps with mesenteries dividing the gut-cavity. No medusa in the life-cycle.

PHYLUM CTENOPHORA: The sea-gooseberries. Globular, transparent animals with 8 rows of cilia and usually a pair of tentacles. 80 species.

PHYLUM PLATYHELMINTHES: Flatworms, flukes and tapeworms. Body with three layers of cells. No body cavity. Gut (if present) lacking an anus. 15 000 species.

Class Turbellaria: Flatworms. Mostly free-living species with a flat body and a branching gut.

Class Trematoda: Liver flukes. Parasitic; gut two-branched & with anterior sucker.

Class Cestoda: Tapeworms. Parasitic; body lacking a gut & divided into 'segments' called proglottides.

PHYLUM NEMERTEA: Ribbon worms. Shaped like a shoe-lace. Gut with an anus. Proboscis lies in a separate body space called the rhynchocoel. 600 species.

PHYLUM NEMATODA: Roundworms. Elongate cylindrical worms with a body cavity known as a pseudocoel. Mouth anterior, anus posterior. 10 000 species.

PHYLUM SIPUNCULIDA: Peanut worms. Body unsegmented, peanut-shaped, with a long eversible proboscis. 275 species.

PHYLUM ECHIURIDA: Tongue worms. Unsegmented sac-like body with a single pair of hook-like chaetae and an extensible tongue-like hood on the head. 80 species.

PHYLUM ANNELIDA: Segmented worms in which the body cavity is a true coelom and is divided into segments. 9 000 species.

Class Oligochaeta: Earthworms with rounded bodies and few chaetae (bristles). Only a few marine species.

Class Hirudinea: Leeches. Body flat but flexible, and armed with anterior and posterior suckers.

Class Polychaeta: Marine worms. Body with lateral lobes (parapodia) & many chaetae.

PHYLUM ARTHROPODA: Insects, crustaceans, etc. Body segmented and covered by a hard chitinous exoskeleton. 1 000 000 species.

Class Crustacea: Sea lice, crabs, lobsters. Two pairs of antennae; at least some limbs biramous (two-branched). 60 000 species.

Class Insecta: Insects. Body divided into head, thorax (with three pairs of legs) and abdomen. 800 000 species, very few of which are marine.

Class Collembola: Springtails. Tiny animals (considered with the insects in this book), most of which have an abdominal springing organ.

Class Pycnogonida: Sea spiders. Tiny body with 4 pairs of spindly legs. Abdomen reduced to a stub. Head bears proboscis, palps and chelifers.

Class Arachnida: Spiders, scorpions, etc. Body divided into an anterior prosoma with a pair of nipper-like chelicerae on the head and 4 pairs of walking legs. Includes the spiders (order Araneae).

PHYLUM BRYOZOA: Lace or moss animals. Colonial animals forming a chitinous or calcareous skeleton, which may be coral-like, encrusting or bushy. 4 000 species.

PHYLUM BRACHIOPODA: Lamp shells. Body enclosed in a bivalved shell consisting of dorsal and ventral valves. Two curled 'arms' (the lophophore) used for feeding. 310 species.

PHYLUM MOLLUSCA: Mussels, snails, chitons, squids, etc. Unsegmented body divided into head, foot and visceral mass, and covered by a mantle, which in most species secretes a shell and shelters the gills. 110 000 species.

Class Polyplacophora: Chitons. Flat-footed, body covered by 8 shell plates.

Class Gastropoda: Snails. Body twisted (torted) and housed in a shell which is usually coiled. A few slug-like species lack a shell.

Class Bivalvia: Bivalves. Body compressed from side to side, enclosed in a bivalved shell.

Class Scaphopoda: Tusk shells. Shell tusk-like and open at both ends.

Class Cephalopoda: Squids, octopuses, nautilus. Head and foot fused, forming suckered tentacles. Shell reduced, usually internal.

PHYLUM ECHINODERMATA: Starfish, urchins, etc. Body radially symmetrical, often pentamerous (five-rayed). Skin tough and laden with platelets. Most species have suctorial tube-feet. 6 000 species.

Class Asteroidea: Starfish. Body flat and usually has five arms that merge into the central disc and bear rows of tube feet.

Class Ophiuroidea: Brittle stars. Body forms a distinct central disc from which slender brittle arms project. Arms lacking suctorial tube feet.

Class Echinoidea: Sea urchins. Body encased in a round or flat calcareous shell (test) and armed with spines.

Class Holothuroidea: Sea cucumbers. Body sausage-like with a tentacled head at one end and anus at the other. Five longitudinal rows of tube feet.

Class Crinoidea: Feather-stars. Body small, usually with a series of ventral cirri (hook-like grasping legs) that cling to the substratum, and 10 or more long feathery arms.

PHYLUM CHORDATA: Sea-squirts, lancelets and vertebrates. Nerve cord dorsal and tubular, supported by a rod-like notochord; gut swollen into a pharynx with gill-slits in it; tail extended beyond the anus. Not all these features are present in the adult but appear at least during embryonic or larval development. (Only class Ascidiacea is considered in this book.) 45 000 species.

SUBPHYLUM TUNICATA: Sea-squirts and salps. Larva tadpole-like and has a notochord, but adults barrel-like with a large pharynx that is used for filtering food. Adult attached to rocks or planktonic. 1 800 species.

Class Ascidiacea: Sea-squirts, red-bait. Adults attached to rocks, barrel-shaped and with two siphons.

Class Thaliacea: Salps. Barrel-like transparent planktonic forms with circular bands of muscles.

SUBPHYLUM CEPHALOCHORDATA: Lancelets. Eel-shaped but flattened from side to side. A notochord supports the hollow dorsal nerve cord but there is no vertebral column. All species marine, and burrow in sand although they can swim. *Amphioxus* is the only southern African representative.

SUBPHYLUM VERTEBRATA: The vertebrates. Nerve cord surrounded by a vertebral column that is bony or cartilaginous. Several classes including Cyclostomata (hagfish), Pisces (fish and sharks), Amphibia (frogs, newts), Reptilia (snakes, lizards, crocodiles), Aves (birds) and Mammalia (mammals).

APPENDIX 2 REGULATIONS ON BAIT AND FOOD ORGANISMS

In South Africa, marine life is protected by various parliamentary acts. No commercial trade is allowed except by licence or permit, and there are regulations governing the collection of organisms for personal use.

There are 11 coastal reserves in which the collection of animals or plants is prohibited or strictly controlled (see Fig. below). Some of these are controlled by the Sea Fisheries Institute, Natal Parks Board, National Parks Board or the Cape Provincial Administration. In addition there are three rock lobster sanctuaries. In other areas limits are placed on the number (or weight) and sometimes on the size of animals that may be collected for personal consumption.

Rock lobsters may not be caught during the closed season (from 1 July to 31 October for *Jasus lalandi* in the North Zone (Northwards of a mark 11 km North of Ysterfontein) and 1 July to 14 November in the South Zone (south of this mark), and from 1 November to 31 January in the case of *Panulirus homarus*). Scuba diving gear and gaffs or spears may not be used to hunt rock lobsters. Rock lobsters that are 'soft' – that are about to moult or have just moulted – may not be caught, nor may female rock lobsters or crabs that are 'in berry' – carrying eggs.

Oysters may not be collected between 1 December and the last day of February.

Restrictions are also placed on the type of implements that can be used to capture an animal. No spade, fork, plough or any other implement that has a blade broader than 3,8 cm may be used to dig an animal out of sand or to prise it off rocks. In the case of mud- or sand prawns it is illegal to use any digging implement, although 'prawn pumps' may be employed.

The table that follows summarises the minimum sizes and maximum numbers (or total weight) of various species that a single person may legally collect in a single day. Size is usually determined by testing whether the animal will fit through a wire hoop of a given diameter, although rock lobsters are measured along the length of the carapace (the 'shell' over the front of the body) from the tip of the central spine between the eyes to the posterior edge of the carapace.

There are additional controls on the numbers and sizes of fish that may be caught in particular areas and, since all the regulations are periodically updated, it is wise to check on local and current regulations.

Animal	Minimum size (cm)	Maximum number (or weight, kg)
Any polychaete worm	–	20
Bloodworm, Arenicola	–	5
Giant chiton, Dinoplax gigas	–	6
White mussels, Donax sp	3,5	50
Black, brown, ribbed mussels, Choromytilus, Perna, Aulacomya	–	25
Razor or pencil clams, Solen	–	20
Scallop, Pecten sulcicostata	–	10
Clams, Mactra glabrata	–	8
Oysters, Crassostrea, Ostrea, Pinctada, Saccostrea	5,08	25
Perlemoen (abalone), Haliotis midae	11,43	5
Siffie, Venus ear, Haliotis spadicea	3,17	11
Limpets, Patella, Cellana, Helcion	–	15
Alikreukel or giant periwinkle, Turbo sarmaticus	6,35	10
Periwinkles, Oxystele, other Turbo spp.	–	50
Octopus, Octopus	–	2
West coast rock lobster, Jasus lalandii	8,89	5
East coast rock lobster, Panulirus homarus	5,72	8
Mud- or sand prawn, Callianassa or Upogebia	–	50
'Sea crabs', Lupa pelagica, Plagusia chabrus	–	15
Other crabs, including Scylla serrata	11,43	2
Sea urchins	–	20
Sea cucumbers	–	20
Red-bait, Pyura stolonifera	–	1,8 kg

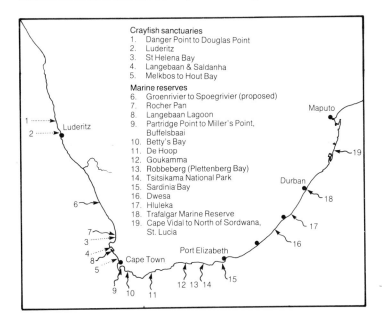

Crayfish sanctuaries
1. Danger Point to Douglas Point
2. Luderitz
3. St Helena Bay
4. Langebaan & Saldanha
5. Melkbos to Hout Bay

Marine reserves
6. Groenrivier to Spoegrivier (proposed)
7. Rocher Pan
8. Langebaan Lagoon
9. Partridge Point to Miller's Point, Buffelsbaai
10. Betty's Bay
11. De Hoop
12. Goukamma
13. Robbeberg (Plettenberg Bay)
14. Tsitsikama National Park
15. Sardinia Bay
16. Dwesa
17. Hluleka
18. Trafalgar Marine Reserve
19. Cape Vidal to North of Sordwana, St. Lucia

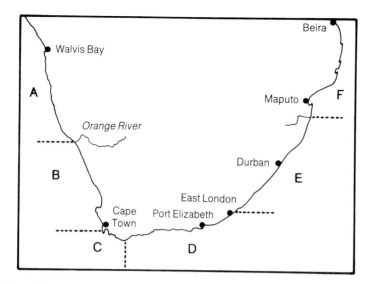

SCIENTIFIC INDEX

The scientific names of all species are indexed below. Numbers in **bold** type refer to plates, those in *italics* refer to the pages on which figures appear, and those in roman type refer to the text. Birds and mammals are not listed here but appear under their common names in the general index.
Geographic distribution is indicated by the letters A-F, as shown on the map, and 'for' indicates foreign species.

GENERAL INDEX

All numbers in **bold** type refer to Plates, those in italic refer to the pages on which figures appear, and the rest refer to the text.